Major Problems in American History Volume II Since 1865

Documents and Essays

THIRD EDITION

EDITED BY

ELIZABETH COBBS HOFFMAN

SAN DIEGO STATE UNIVERSITY

EDWARD J. BLUM

SAN DIEGO STATE UNIVERSITY

JON GJERDE

UNIVERSITY OF CALIFORNIA, BERKELEY

WADSWORTH
CENGAGE Learning™

Australia • Brazil • Japan • Korea • Mexico • Singapore • Spain • United Kingdom • United States

WADSWORTH
CENGAGE Learning

Major Problems in American History, Volume II: Since 1865, Documents and Essays, Third Edition
Elizabeth Cobbs Hoffman, Edward J. Blum, Jon Gjerde

Senior Publisher:
Suzanne Jeans

Senior Sponsoring Editor:
Ann West

Development Editor: Larry Goldberg

Assistant Editor: Megan Chrisman

Editorial Assistant: Patrick Roach

Media Editor: Robert St. Laurent

Senior Marketing Manager:
Katherine Bates

Marketing Coordinator: Lorreen Pelletier

Marketing Communications Manager: Caitlin Green

Content Project Management:
PreMediaGlobal

Senior Art Director: Cate Rickard Barr

Print Buyer: Karen Hunt

Rights Acquisition Specialist, Text: Jennifer Meyer Dare

Rights Acquisition Specialist, Image: Katie Huha

Production Service:
PreMediaGlobal

Cover Designer: Gary Ragaglia

Cover Image: The Jacob and Gwendolyn Lawrence Foundation/ Art Resource, NY. ©2010 Artists Rights Society (ARS), NY

Compositor: PreMediaGlobal

For product information and technology assistance, contact us at
Cengage Learning Customer & Sales Support, 1-800-354-9706

For permission to use material from this text or product, submit all requests online at **www.cengage.com/permissions**. Further permissions questions can be emailed to **permissionrequest@cengage.com**.

Library of Congress Control Number: 2010939469

ISBN-13: 978-1-111-34316-3

ISBN-10: 1-111-34316-0

Wadsworth
20 Channel Center Street
Boston, MA 02210
USA

Cengage Learning is a leading provider of customized learning solutions with office locations around the globe, including Singapore, the United Kingdom, Australia, Mexico, Brazil and Japan. Locate your local office at **international.cengage.com/ region**

Cengage Learning products are represented in Canada by Nelson Education, Ltd.

For your course and learning solutions, visit **www.cengage.com**.

Purchase any of our products at your local college store or at our preferred online store **www.cengagebrain.com**.

Instructors: Please visit **login.cengage.com** and log in to access instructor-specific resources.

Printed in the United States of America
1 2 3 4 5 6 7 14 13 12 11 10

For Jon Gjerde
Fine historian, fine editor,
fine friend—gone too soon

Contents

Chapter 4   Imperialism and World Power   105

Chapter 5   The Progressive Movement   133

Chapter 12 "We Can Do Better": The Civil Rights Revolution 361

Chapter 13 The Sixties: Left, Right, and the Culture Wars 396

Chapter 14   Vietnam and the Downfall of Presidents   427

Preface

History is a matter of interpretation. Individual scholars rescue particular stories from the flurry of human experience, organize them into patterns, and offer arguments to suggest how these phenomena reflected or reshaped human society at given moments. This means that other historians might select different stories, organize them into different patterns, and arrive at contrasting interpretations of the same period of time or even the same event. All scholars use evidence, but the choice and interpretation of evidence is to some extent inevitably an expression of personal judgment. History is not separate from historians.

The goal of *Major Problems in American History* is to place meat on this bare bones description of how the study of the past "works." Like most instructors, we want students to learn and remember the "important" facts, yet at the same time we want to make clear that historians often disagree on what is important. And, even when historians agree on what is worthy of commentary, they often disagree on what a certain piece of evidence signifies. For example, scholars agree fifty-six men signed the Declaration of Independence in 1776, but they debate why these colonists felt compelled to take this dramatic step.

The two volumes that comprise this book bring together primary documents and secondary sources on the major debates in American history. The primary sources give students evidence to work with. They represent a mix of the familiar and unfamiliar. Certain documents are a "must" in any compilation for a survey course because they had a powerful, widely noted impact on American history, such as Tom Paine's *Common Sense* (1776) or *Brown v. the Board of Education* (1954). We have also selected pieces that evoke the personal experiences of individuals who reflected their times. Included are letters, sermons, speeches, political cartoons, poems, and government reports. There are accounts from European explorers, pioneer women on the frontier, immigrant workers, soldiers, eyewitnesses to the terrors of World War I, and children in rebellion against their parents during the 1960s. These documents often show conflicting points of view, from the "bottom up," the "top down," and the various middles.

The secondary sources in these volumes fulfill a different goal. They expose students to the elemental historical debates for each broad period. We have chosen, therefore, to focus on classic debates, often combining very recent essays with more seasoned pieces by eminent historians who set the terms of discussion for an entire generation or more. Our purpose is to make the interpretive contrasts as clear as possible for students who are just learning to distinguish interpretation from fact, and to discern argument within description. In addition, the essays often make direct reference to the primary documents. This allows students to engage the historian on how she or he is using the primary documents. The students, therefore, can debate the use of the source and the differing historical arguments presented by the historians.

Volume II, prepared by Elizabeth Cobbs Hoffman in collaboration with Edward Blum, begins with Reconstruction and ends with the first decade of the twenty-first century. This volume examines some of the catastrophic and transformative events of the century, like World Wars One and Two, as well as the enduring themes of U.S. history, including the periodic waves of reform that have defined the nation since its inception and the impact of changing technologies on the lives of workers and families. The transformation of gender expectations and race relations are also highlighted throughout the volume.

This book follows the same general format as other volumes in the *Major Problems in American History* series. Each chapter begins with a short introduction that orients the student to the topic. Following this, we include a section called "Questions to Think About" to help students focus their reading of the subsequent material. Next come eight to eleven primary documents, followed by two essays that highlight contrasting interpretations. Headnotes at the start of the document and essay sections help readers identify key themes and debates. These headnotes also show how the documents relate to each other, and how the essays differ in perspective. Each chapter concludes with a brief "Further Reading" section to tempt readers into further research. In addition, at the start of the volume, we give suggestions on how to read sources and critically analyze their content, point of view, and inferences. This introduction encourages students to draw their own conclusions and use evidence to back up their reasoning.

New to the Third Edition

This new, third edition makes several changes to previous editions. First, there is a new focus on the visual and cultural. In several chapters there are now various images from the time period and a variety of songs and memoirs. We have retained many of the documents and essays that reviewers told us worked well in their survey courses, but each chapter has also been updated to reflect the latest scholarship and replace excerpts that instructors found difficult to use. Recognizing that the story of America is getting longer with time (and that some instructors devote minimal time to Reconstruction in the second half of the survey course), we have also added a sixteenth chapter. Chapter 16 brings American history through the cataclysmic events of September 11, 2001, and their aftermath, including the war in Iraq, while raising larger questions about the costs of globalization for American security and the American economy. This also gives us room to devote an entire new chapter (Chapter 15) to the rise of conservative movements in the last third of the twentieth century. Finally, heeding the advice of professors around the nation, the third edition incorporates more voices of everyday folk, including those of a draftee in the Vietnam War, a country-western singer, and young women seeking respite from constant childbirth, to name a few. More than ever, documents and essays in this volume highlight the connections between events in America and world trends, consistent with recent initiatives in our profession to internationalize the study of U.S. history.

Acknowledgments

Many friends and colleagues have contributed to these volumes. In the third edition we particularly wish to thank John Putman and Andrew Wiese from San Diego State University; Brian Balogh of the University of Virginia; Drew Cayton at Miami University of Ohio; Rebecca Goetz of Rice University; Paul Harvey of the University of Colorado, Colorado Springs; Eric Hinderaker at University of Utah; Anthony Kaye of Penn State University; Bruce Levine of the University of Illinois, Urbana-Champaign; Phil Morgan of Johns Hopkins; Daniel Rodgers of Princeton; Bruce Schulman of Boston University; Jason Scott Smith of the University of New Mexico; James Stewart of Macalaster College; and Matthew Avery Sutton of Washington State University.

For this edition, we also received detailed and extremely helpful reviews from Marc Abrams, Penn State University; Robert Bionaz, Chicago State University; David Brodnax, Trinity Christian College; Cara Converse, Moorpark College; Todd Estes, Oakland University; Peter Kuryla, Belmont University; Bernard Maegi, Normandale Community College; Todd Michney, Tulane University; Stephen Rockenbach, Virginia State University; and Robert Schultz, Illinois Wesleyan University. Thomas G. Paterson, the editor of the *Major Problems* series, provided sound advice. We are obliged to our editors at Cengage Learning/Wadsworth, Ann West and Larry Goldberg, for their kind encouragement and insightful recommendations.

The life of the mind is exceptionally fulfilling, but it is happiest when set within the life of the family. We wish to express our deep gratitude to our families, especially Jennifer Cherry Blum and Daniel Hoffman. We dedicate the book to Jon Gjerde, co-editor of the first two editions of *Major Problems in American History*. We miss him.

E. C. H.
E. J. B.

Introduction: How to Read Primary and Secondary Sources

College study encompasses a number of subjects. Some disciplines, such as mathematics, are aimed at problems and proofs. Students learn methods to discover the path to a correct answer. History is different. Unlike math, it is focused much more on interpretation and imagination. Historians study and analyze sources to construct arguments about the past. They generally understand that there is no "right" answer, even if there are some arguments that are more convincing than others. They search less for a proof than an interpretation, less for absolute truth than for understanding. A historical imagination is useful in creating these interpretations. People in the past thought and acted differently than we do today. Their views of science, of religion, of the place of women and men—to cite only a few examples—were not the same as our views. When we as historians create an argument about the past, we must imagine a world unlike the one we now inhabit. We must use empathy and suspend judgment to develop understanding.

The "problems" in U.S. history on which this text focuses, then, are different from math "problems." They are a series of issues in the American past that might be addressed, discussed, and debated, but not necessarily solved. This text provides readers with two types of tools to grapple with these problems. The first is the *primary source*, which is a piece of evidence that has survived from the period we are analyzing. Primary sources come in a variety of forms, including pictures, artifacts, and written texts. And they may have survived in a number of ways. Archaeologists uncover pieces of evidence when they undertake digs of lost civilizations; ethnologists transcribe stories told by people; economists take bits of evidence to create numerical measures of past behavior; and historians scrutinize surviving written sources. This volume by and large presents written texts, varying from political tracts to private letters. Some of the texts, however, are transcriptions, that is, texts written by someone who noted what another person said. Sometimes the texts are memoirs, in which a person recounts an event they personally experienced long before. On these occasions, you will see two dates: one that tells the year of the events, and a second in parentheses that tells the year in which the memoir was written.

As historians, we must be critical of primary sources for a number of reasons. First of all, we must consider whether a source is really from the historical period we are studying. You might have occasionally read stories in the newspaper about paintings that had been attributed to famous artists but were discovered to be frauds painted by an unknown copyist. When the fraud is discovered, the painting's value plummets. The same can be said for a primary source. If it is not valid, it is not as valuable. A letter alleged to have been written by George Washington clearly is not of much use for revealing his innermost thoughts if we discover the document was written in 1910. But we should also be aware of the opposite: not all pieces of evidence have survived to the present. We might ask if there is a bias in the likelihood of one point of view surviving and another being lost. The experiences of slaveholders, for example, were more commonly written and published than those of slaves. Because they were rarely given the opportunity to publish their thoughts, slaves (and others, such as Native Americans) have bequeathed us some sources that have survived as transcriptions. As essential as these sources are in reconstructing the past, as historians we must be critical of them as well. Did the people writing down the spoken words accurately set them to paper or did they inject their own thoughts? In the case of memoirs, how much might current events have affected memories of the past?

Once we consider the validity of sources and understand that some sources were more likely to survive than others, another reason to critique the sources is that they are not "objective" portrayals of the past. By nature, they are points of view. Like anyone in a society, the writer of each primary source provides us with his or her viewpoint and thus gives us a window through which to view his or her world, complete with its biases. When we read about the American Revolution, for example, we will see many different perspectives on the events leading up to the Declaration of Independence by the American colonies. Those who opposed independence saw the events in a very different light from those who supported the movement. We have often read about the advocates of independence who saw the British as threats to American freedom. They thought that the thirteen colonies would be better off as one independent nation. Americans for generations have viewed this as a truly heroic episode. But many contemporaries were not as sure that independence was the correct course of action. A substantial minority opposed independence because they felt they were more secure if they remained in the British Empire. Countless members of Indian nations were suspicious of the intentions of the American "patriots" and remained loyal to the king. African American slaves were often leery of the aims of their patriot owners. The fact that people had different viewpoints allows us to grapple with the multiple perspectives of the past.

When you are reading the documents in this volume, we urge you to look at each one critically. We are certain that these are valid sources, and so you should be especially critical of the point of view contained in each document.

Consider both the document and its author. Who wrote or spoke the words in the document? What was his or her reason for expressing the thoughts? Given the background and motivations of the authors, what were their perspectives and potential biases? How did they see the world differently from the way others did? And, why do *you* think these different perspectives existed? Whose viewpoint do you agree with most? Why? It is not too much to say that the student of history is similar to a detective who seeks out sources and clues that illuminate the lives and events of the past.

In addition to primary sources, each chapter in this volume contains two essays that represent what we call a *secondary source*. Secondary sources are the written work of historians who have conducted painstaking research in primary sources. Historians work with an array of primary sources that they uncover and use as evidence to construct an argument that addresses one of the major problems in American history. A secondary source is so named because it is one step removed from the primary source. As you will notice, the writers of the essays in each chapter do not necessarily reach similar conclusions. On the contrary, they illustrate differing opinions about why events occurred and what they mean for us today.

Hence secondary sources, like primary sources, do not provide us with the "truth," even to the extent that they are based on verifiable facts. Rather, historians' conclusions vary just as your ideas about the documents might differ from those of someone else in your class. And they differ for a number of reasons. First, interpretations are influenced by the sources on which they depend. Occasionally, a historian might uncover a cache of primary sources heretofore unknown to other scholars, and these new sources might shed new light on a topic. Here again historians are like detectives.

Second and more important, however, historians carry their own perspectives to the research. As they read secondary sources, analyze primary texts, and imagine the past, historians usually develop arguments that differ in emphasis from those developed by others. As they combine their analyses with their own perspectives, they create an argument to explain the past. Historians' individual points of view and even society's dominant point of view influence their thinking. If analyzing sources resembles working as a detective, writing history is similar to being a judge who attempts to construct the most consistent argument from the sources and information at hand. And historians can be sure that those who oppose their viewpoints will analyze their use of sources and the logic of their argument. Those who might disagree with them—and that might include you—will criticize them if they make errors of fact or logic.

The essays were selected for this text in part because they reflect differing conclusions with which you may or may not agree. For example, why did the United States intervene in World War I? For decades, historians have given us a number of answers. Some have said that Woodrow Wilson foolishly broke with a tradition of non-entanglement and isolationism dating back to George Washington. Others say that Wilson wisely recognized that a changed world required changes in America's international role. Or what are we to make of the 1950s? Some historians have celebrated this period as a flowering of American prosperity, unity, and democracy. Others have noted that the franchise applied only to whites and that McCarthyism suppressed freedom of conscience and personal non-conformity. Or how do we now make sense of the Vietnam War, nearly fifty years after the first American troops landed? Was it a terrible mistake that undermined confidence in the United States both at home and abroad, or was it, in President Ronald Reagan's words, a "noble cause"?

An important question left unanswered in all of these chapters is what do *you* think is the correct interpretation? In the end, maybe you don't agree completely with any of the essayists. In fact, you might wish to create your own argument that uses primary sources found here and elsewhere and that accepts parts of one essay and parts of another. When you do this, you have become a historian, a person who attempts to analyze texts critically, someone who is actively engaged in the topic. If that occurs, this volume is a success.

When we discuss the discipline of history with people, we typically get one of two responses. One group of people says something like "I hated history in school." The other group says something like "history was my favorite subject when I went to school." Invariably the people who hated history cite all the boring facts that they had to memorize. In contrast, those who loved history remember a teacher or professor who brought the subject alive by invoking the worlds of people in the past.

As we have tried to indicate in this short overview, history is not about memorizing boring facts but rather an active enterprise of thought and interpretation. Historians are not rote learners; studying history does not entail simply memorization. Instead, historians are detectives and judges, people who interpret and imagine what happened in history and why, individuals who study the past in order to understand the world in which they live in the present. Facts are important, but they are only building blocks in a larger enterprise of interpretation. In sum, our intent with this text is to show how primary and secondary sources can be utilized to aid you in understanding and interpreting major problems in the American past. It is also aimed at keeping that group of people who hates studying history as small as possible and enlarging that second group who considers history their passion. Frankly, it's more fun to talk to the latter.

CHAPTER 1

Reconstruction

Even before the Civil War was over, President Lincoln and congressional leaders began to puzzle over how best to reintegrate the people of the South into the Union. Before he was assassinated, President Lincoln proposed the "10 percent plan," which would have allowed a state government to reestablish itself once one-tenth of those who had voted in 1860 took an oath of loyalty to the United States. Radicals in Congress were appalled by the seemingly lenient plan and pushed through their own bill, which increased the proportion to one-half of the voters who were required to swear that they had never supported secession. Lincoln's assassination cut short this increasingly scathing debate and drastically altered the mood of Reconstruction. According to poet Herman Melville, the assassination shifted the northern mood. "They have killed him, The Forgiver," Melville versed, "The Avenger takes his place." What really took Lincoln's place was conflict and chaos for nearly fifteen years. Political disagreements over Reconstruction policy were vast, and the strategies advocated were so varied that Reconstruction took a crooked road. As approaches to rebuilding the South shifted, the hopes among some to transform southern society grew and then were dashed. Ultimately, despite important legal precedents that were made in the era, many of the social, political, and economic conventions that had characterized antebellum society endured after Reconstruction ended. Eventually, the racial system of segregation came to replace the system of slavery.

Although people differed on what was the best policy for Reconstruction, everyone agreed that the Confederate states were in dire straits and the primary goal of Reconstruction was to reincorporate those states politically and socially into the Union. The war had devastated the South: entire cities lay in ruins; two-thirds of southern railroads had been destroyed; and at least one-third of its livestock had disappeared. Likewise, the abolition of slavery unalterably transformed southern society at the same time that it gave hope to people freed from their bondage (known as freedmen). Following Lincoln's death, many believed that Andrew Johnson, who succeeded Lincoln as president, would advocate a severe Reconstruction of the South. Instead, Johnson engineered a plan that seemed to many Northerners as much too charitable. Ironically, Johnson's course of action, combined with the intransigence of unrepentant Southern leaders, was a major force in bringing about the era of Radical Reconstruction beginning in 1866. Because he was so impolitic, Johnson strengthened the resolve of Congress to enact a more radical policy. After the Republican

Party won a resounding victory in the elections of 1866, Congress reconvened in 1867 and set out to punish rebellious southern whites while offering more rights and freedoms to African Americans.

If Reconstruction was engineered in Washington, new social conventions were forged in the South that would be extremely important in the future. The lives of former slaves were dramatically changed and freedmen expressed their understanding of freedom in a variety of ways. Significantly, many African Americans played important roles in the new Republican Party of the South, and by 1868 black men were seated for the first time in southern state legislatures. These political gains, however, were short-lived. In spite of the electoral successes of African Americans, the Democratic Party enjoyed increasing political success in the South as former Confederates eventually had their political rights restored. Changes in the electorate in conjunction with intimidation shifted the trajectory of Reconstruction once again as radical transformation was replaced with a movement toward the white South's term for reclaiming the world they had known before the Civil War.

The end of Reconstruction was hastened by events in the North as well as the South. Ulysses S. Grant, elected president in 1868, was a better general than politician and his administration was already mired in scandal shortly after he took office. By 1873, the nation was rocked by a financial panic that led Americans into a depression lasting six years. Scandal and depression weakened the Republican Party. Meanwhile Congress and the Supreme Court were weakening in their resolve to continue a strict policy of Reconstruction. The death knell of Reconstruction was the national election of 1876, when it became clear that the North was no longer willing to pursue its earlier goals. The election of the Democratic candidate for president was avoided only by a compromise in 1877 wherein Rutherford B. Hayes would be declared president if he promised to withdraw federal troops from those states in the South where they still remained. The deal was made. Reconstruction was over—northern and southern whites agreed that national reunion was more important than the defense of civil rights for black men and women.

 # QUESTIONS TO THINK ABOUT

What were the failures of Reconstruction and what were its successes? Why did it collapse, to the extent that it did? How successful was the Union in reincorporating the southern states and people? Did Reconstruction come to an end primarily because the North abandoned it or because it was opposed by the South? How did African Americans feel about the possibilities and the terrors of Reconstruction?

DOCUMENTS

The first three documents represent the diversity of feelings at the end of the war regarding the federal government and rights for African Americans. Document 1 is an oration given by William Howard Day, an African American minister, in 1865. Notice how—unlike African Americans before the Civil War—he now celebrated the federal government. Day proclaimed the Fourth of July as "our day," the United States as "our nation," and Washington, D.C., as "our capital." In the South, though, many whites opposed the federal government and wanted to keep former slaves as second-class citizens. Document 2 is a song from the South where the white vocalist proclaims his hatred for the federal government. In law, many southern states enacted "black codes" immediately after the war, one of which is given in document 3. This example from Louisiana in 1865 illustrates the many ways in which the rights of "freedom" was abridged. The next two documents showcase conflict within the federal government over Reconstruction. In document 4, President Andrew Johnson argues against black suffrage. In contrast, Thaddeus Stevens, a Radical representative in Congress, argues for passage of the Reconstruction Act of 1867 in document 5 because he believes that only an unfaltering federal presence will prevent "traitors" from ruling the South. The bitterness that ensued resulted in the impeachment of President Andrew Johnson. Document 6, the opening argument in the impeachment trial, enumerates the accusations against President Johnson. The next two documents show frustrations with the civil rights agendas of Reconstruction. In document 7, Elizabeth Cady Stanton—an antebellum feminist and abolitionist—argues that the very radicals who are pushing for increased rights for freed slaves are deferring the issue of women's suffrage. Document 8 is the testimony of a freed woman about the violence of the Ku Klux Klan. The final two documents detail sectional feelings at the end of Reconstruction. Document 9 is a poem from Father Abram Ryan, a Catholic priest of the South. It illustrates the enduring notion of a "lost cause" and love for the Confederate States of America that was maintained by many white southerners well after reconstruction. "The Blue and the Gray," another Reconstruction poem, is document 10. It expresses the hopes for North-South reconciliation in the form of mutual love and respect for white Union and Confederate soldiers.

1. William Howard Day, an African American Minister, Salutes the Nation and a Monument to Abraham Lincoln, 1865

… We meet under new and ominous circumstances to-day. We come to the National Capital—our Capital—with new hopes, new prospects, new joys, in view of the future and past of the people; and yet with that joy fringed, tinged, permeated by a sorrow unlike any, nationally, we have ever known. A few weeks since all that was mortal of Abraham Lincoln was laid away to rest. And to-day, after the funeral cortege has passed, weeping thoughts march through our hearts—when the muffled drum has ceased to beat in a procession five hundred, aye, two thousand miles long, the chambers of your souls are still echoing the murmur—and though the coffin has been lowered into its place, "dust to dust," there ever falls across our way the coffin's shadow, and, standing in it, we come to-day to rear a monument to his blessed memory, and again to

---

Celebration by the Colored People's Educational Monument Association (1865).

pledge our untiring resistance to the tyranny by which he fell, whether it be in the iron manacles of the slave, or in the unjust written manacles for the free....

Up to now our nation,... [t]he shout of the freeman and the wail of the bondman have, I repeat, always been heard together, making "harsh discords." Hitherto a damning crime has run riot over the whole land. North and South alike were inoculated with its virus. It has lain like a gangrene upon the national life, until the nation, mortified, broke in twain. The hand of slavery ever moulded the Christianity of the nation, and wrote the national songs. What hand wrote the laws of the nation and marked this National District all over with scars? What hand went into the Capitol and half murdered Charles Sumner, nature's nobleman?...

All the heroes of all the ages, bond and free, have labored to secure for us the right we rejoice in to-day. To the white and colored soldiers of this war, led on as they were by our noble President and other officers, in the presence of some of whom I rejoice to-day, are we indebted, in the providence of God, for our present position. For want of time, I pass by any more detailed mention of the noble men and their noble deeds. Together they nobly labored—together they threw themselves into the breach which rebellion had made across the land, and thus closed up that breach forever. And now, in their presence, living and dead, as over the prostrate form of our leader, Abraham Lincoln—by the edge of blood-red waves, still surging, we pledge our resistance to tyranny, (I repeat,) whether in the iron manacles of the slave, or in the unjust written manacles of the free....

It is related in the diary of one of the writers of old that when the slave trade was at its height, a certain vessel loaded with its human freight started under the frown of God and came over the billows of the ocean. Defying God and man alike, in the open daylight, the slave was brought up from the hold and chained to the foot of the mast. The eye of the Omnipotent saw it, and bye and bye the thunders muttered and the lightnings played over the devoted vessel. At length the lightning leaped upon the mast and shivered it, and, as it did this, also melted the fetter which fastened the black slave to it; and he arising unhurt, for the first time walked the deck a free man.

Our ship of state, the Union, has for eighty years gone careering over the billows; our slave has been chained to our mast in the open daylight, and in the focal blaze of the eighteen centuries gone by, and we have hurried on in our crime regardless alike of the muttering of the thunder and the flashes of the lightning, until in one devoted hour the thunderbolt was sped from the hand of God. The mast was shivered; the ship was saved; but, thank God, the slave was free....

2. A Southern Song Opposes Reconstruction, c. 1860s

O, I'm a good old Rebel,

Now that's just what I am,

"O, I'm a Good Old Rebel," c. 1860s.

For this "Fair Land of Freedom"
I do not care at all;

I'm glad I fit against it–
I only wish we'd won,
And I don't want no pardon
For anything I done.

I hates the Constitution,
This Great Republic too,
I hates the Freedman's Buro,
In uniforms of blue;

I hates the nasty eagle,
With all his brags and fuss,
The lyin', thievin' Yankees,
I hates 'em wuss and wuss.

I hates the Yankee nation
And everything they do,
I hates the Declaration
Of Independence too;

I hates the glorious Union –
'Tis dripping with our blood –
I hates their striped banner,
I fit it all I could....

Three hundred thousand Yankees
Is stiff in Southern dust;
We got three hundred thousand
Before they conquered us;

They died of Southern fever
And Southern steel and shot,

I wish they was three million

Instead of what we got.

I can't take up my musket

And fight 'em now no more,

But I ain't going to love 'em,

Now that is sarten sure;

And I don't want no pardon

For what I was and am,

I won't be reconstructed

And I don't care a damn.

3. Louisiana Black Codes Reinstate Provisions of the Slave Era, 1865

Section 1. *Be it therefore ordained by the board of police of the town of Opelousas.* That no negro or freedman shall be allowed to come within the limits of the town of Opelousas without special permission from his employers, specifying the object of his visit and the time necessary for the accomplishment of the same....

Section 2. *Be it further ordained,* That every negro freedman who shall be found on the streets of Opelousas after 10 o'clock at night without a written pass or permit from his employer shall be imprisoned and compelled to work five days on the public streets, or pay a fine of five dollars.

Section 3. No negro or freedman shall be permitted to rent or keep a house within the limits of the town under any circumstances, and any one thus offending shall be ejected and compelled to find an employer or leave the town within twenty-four hours....

Section 4. No negro or freedman shall reside within the limits of the town of Opelousas who is not in the regular service of some white person or former owner, who shall be held responsible for the conduct of said freedman....

Section 5. No public meetings or congregations of negroes or freedmen shall be allowed within the limits of the town of Opelousas under any circumstances or for any purpose without the permission of the mayor or president of the board....

Section 6. No negro or freedman shall be permitted to preach, exhort, or otherwise declaim to congregations of colored people without a special permission from the mayor or president of the board of police....

Condition of the South, Senate Executive Document No. 2, 39 Cong., 1 Sess., pp. 92–93.

Section 7. No freedman who is not in the military service shall be allowed to carry firearms, or any kind of weapons, within the limits of the town of Opelousas without the special permission of his employer, in writing, and approved by the mayor or president of the board of police....

Section 8. No freedman shall sell, barter, or exchange any articles of merchandise or traffic within the limits of Opelousas without permission in writing from his employer or the mayor or president of the board....

Section 9. Any freedman found drunk within the limits of the town shall be imprisoned and made to labor five days on the public streets, or pay five dollars in lieu of said labor.

Section 10. Any freedman not residing in Opelousas who shall be found within the corporate limits after the hour of 3 p.m. on Sunday without a special permission from his employer or the mayor shall be arrested and imprisoned and made to work....

Section 11. All the foregoing provisions apply to freedmen and freedwomen....

E. D. ESTILLETTE,
President of the Board of Police.
JOS. D. RICHARDS, *Clerk.*

Official copy:

J. LOVELL,
Captain and Assistant Adjutant General.

4. President Andrew Johnson Denounces Changes in His Program of Reconstruction, 1867

It is manifestly and avowedly the object of these laws to confer upon negroes the privilege of voting and to disfranchise such a number of white citizens as will give the former a clear majority at all elections in the Southern States. This, to the minds of some persons, is so important that a violation of the Constitution is justified as a means of bringing it about. The morality is always false which excuses a wrong because it proposes to accomplish a desirable end. We are not permitted to do evil that good may come. But in this case the end itself is evil, as well as the means. The subjugation of the States to negro domination would be worse than the military despotism under which they are now suffering. It was believed beforehand that the people would endure any amount of military oppression for any length of time rather than degrade themselves by subjection to the negro race. Therefore they have been left without a choice. Negro suffrage was established by act of Congress, and the military officers were commanded to

Andrew Johnson, "Third Annual Message" (December 3, 1867), in *A Compilation of Messages and Papers of the Presidents, 1789–1897*, VI, ed. James D. Richardson (Washington, D.C.: Bureau of National Literature and Art, 1899), 564–565.

superintend the process of clothing the negro race with the political privileges torn from white men.

The blacks in the South are entitled to be well and humanely governed, and to have the protection of just laws for all their rights of person and property. If it were practicable at his time to give them a Government exclusively their own, under which they might manage their own affairs in their own way, it would become a grave question whether we ought to do so, or whether common humanity would not require us to save them from themselves. But under the circumstances this is only a speculative point. It is not proposed merely that they shall govern themselves, but that they shall rule the white race, make and administer State laws, elect Presidents and members of Congress, and shape to a greater or less extent the future destiny of the whole country. Would such a trust and power be safe in such hands?

The peculiar qualities which should characterize any people who are fit to decide upon the management of public affairs for a great state have seldom been combined. It is the glory of white men to know that they have had these qualities in sufficient measures to build upon this continent a great political fabric and to preserve its stability for more than ninety years, while in every other part of the world all similar experiments have failed. But if anything can be proved by known facts, if all reasoning upon evidence is not abandoned, it must be acknowledged that in the progress of nations negroes have shown less capacity for government than any other race of people. No independent government of any form has ever been successful in their hands. On the contrary, wherever they have been left to their own devices they have shown a constant tendency to relapse into barbarism. In the Southern States, however, Congress has undertaken to confer upon them the privilege of the ballot. Just released from slavery, it may be doubted whether as a class they know more than their ancestors how to organize and regulate civil society.

5. Congressman Thaddeus Stevens Demands a Radical Reconstruction, 1867

.... It is to be regretted that inconsiderate and incautious Republicans should ever have supposed that the slight amendments [embodied in the pending Fourteenth Amendment] already proposed to the Constitution, even when incorporated into that instrument, would satisfy the reforms necessary for the security of the Government. Unless the rebel States, before admission, should be made republican in spirit, and placed under the guardianship of loyal men, all our blood and treasure will have been spent in vain. I waive now the question of punishment which, if we are wise, will still be inflicted by moderate confiscations, both as a reproof and example. Having these States, as we all agree, entirely within the power of Congress, it is our duty to take care that no injustice shall remain in

Thaddeus Stevens, speech in the House (January 3, 1867), *Congressional Globe,* 39 Cong., 2 Sess., Vol. 37, pt. 1, pp. 251–253. This document can also be found in *Radical Republicans and Reconstruction,* ed. Harold M. Hyman (Indianapolis, Ind., and New York: Bobbs-Merrill, 1967), 373–375.

their organic laws. Holding them "like clay in the hands of the potter," we must see that no vessel is made for destruction. Having now no governments, they must have enabling acts. The law of last session with regard to Territories settled the principles of such acts. Impartial suffrage, both in electing the delegates and ratifying their proceedings, is now the fixed rule. There is more reason why colored voters should be admitted in the rebel States than in the Territories. In the States they form the great mass of the loyal men. Possibly with their aid loyal governments may be established in most of those States. Without it all are sure to be ruled by traitors; and loyal men, black and white, will be oppressed, exiled, or murdered. There are several good reasons for the passage of this bill. In the first place, it is just. I am now confining my argument to negro suffrage in the rebel States. Have not loyal blacks quite as good a right to choose rulers and make laws as rebel whites? In the second place, it is a necessity in order to protect the loyal white men in the seceded States. The white Union men are in a great minority in each of those States. With them the blacks would act in a body; and it is believed that in each of said States, except one, the two united would form a majority, control the States, and protect themselves. Now they are the victims of daily murder. They must suffer constant persecution or be exiled. The convention of southern loyalists, lately held in Philadelphia, almost unanimously agreed to such a bill as an absolute necessity.

Another good reason is, it would insure the ascendancy of the Union party. Do you avow the party purpose? exclaims some horror-stricken demagogue. I do. For I believe, on my conscience, that on the continued ascendancy of that party depends the safety of this great nation. If impartial suffrage is excluded in rebel States then every one of them is sure to send a solid rebel representative delegation to Congress, and cast a solid rebel electoral vote. They, with their kindred Copperheads of the North, would always elect the President and control Congress. While slavery sat upon her defiant throne, and insulted and intimidated the trembling North, the South frequently divided on questions of policy between Whigs and Democrats, and gave victory alternately to the sections. Now, you must divide them between loyalists, without regard to color, and disloyalists, or you will be the perpetual vassals of the free-trade, irritated, revengeful South. For these, among other reasons, I am for negro suffrage in every rebel State. If it be just, it should not be denied; if it be necessary, it should be adopted; if it be a punishment to traitors, they deserve it.

But it will be said, as it has been said, "This is negro equality!" What is negro equality, about which so much is said by knaves, and some of which is believed by men who are not fools? It means, as understood by honest Republicans, just this much, and no more: every man, no matter what his race or color; every earthly being who has an immortal soul, has an equal right to justice, honesty, and fair play with every other man; and the law should secure him those rights. The same law which condemns or acquits an African should condemn or acquit a white man. The same law which gives a verdict in a white man's favor should give a verdict in a black man's favor on the same state of facts. Such is the law of God and such ought to be the law of man. This doctrine does not mean that a negro shall sit on the same seat or eat at the same table with a white man. That is a matter of taste which every man must decide for himself. The law has nothing to do with it.

6. Representative Benjamin Butler Argues That President Andrew Johnson Be Impeached, 1868

This, then, is the plain and inevitable issue before the Senate and the American people:

Has the President, under the Constitution, the more than kingly prerogative at will to remove from office and suspend from office indefinitely, all executive officers of the United States, either civil, military, or naval, at any and all times, and fill the vacancies with creatures of his own appointment, for his own purposes, without any restraint whatever, or possibility of restraint by the Senate or by Congress through laws duly enacted?

The House of Representatives, in behalf of the people, join this issue by affirming that the exercise of such powers is a high misdemeanor in office....

Who does not know that Andrew Johnson initiated, of his own will, a course of reconstruction of the rebel States, which at the time be claimed was provisional only, and until the meeting of Congress and its action thereon? Who does not know that when Congress met and undertook to legislate upon the very subject of reconstruction, of which he had advised them in his message, which they alone had the constitutional power to do, Andrew Johnson last aforesaid again changed his course, and declared that Congress had no power to legislate upon that subject; that the two houses had only the power *separately* to judge of the qualifications of the members who might be sent to each by rebellious constituencies, acting under State organization which Andrew Johnson had called into existence by his late *fiat*, the electors of which were voting by his permission and under his limitations? Who does not know that when Congress, assuming its rightful power to propose amendments to the Constitution, had passed such an amendment, and had submitted it to the States as a measure of pacification, Andrew Johnson advised and counselled the legislatures of the States lately in rebellion, as well as others, to reject the amendment, so that it might not operate as a law, and thus establish equality of suffrage in all the States, and equality of right in the members of the electoral college, and in the number of the representatives to the Congress of the United States?...

Who does not know that from the hour he began these, his usurpations of power, he everywhere denounced Congress, the legality and constitutionality of its action, and defied its legitimate powers, and, for that purpose, announced his intentions and carried out his purpose, as far as he was able, of removing every true man from office who sustained the Congress of the United States? And it is to carry out this plan of action that he claims the unlimited power of removal, for

Trial of Andrew Johnson, President of the United States, on Impeachment by the House of Representatives for High Crimes and Misdemeanors (Washington, D.C.: Government Printing Office, 1868), 96, 121–123.

the illegal exercise of which he stands before you this day. Who does not know that, in pursuance of the same plan, he used his veto power indiscriminately to prevent the passage of wholesome laws, enacted for the pacification of the country and, when laws were passed by the constitutional majority over his vetoes, he made the most determined opposition, both open and convert, to them, and, for the purpose of making that opposition effectual, he endeavored to array and did array all the people lately in rebellion to set themselves against Congress and against the true and loyal men, their neighbors, so that murders, assassinations, and massacres were rife all over the southern States, which he encouraged by his refusal to consent that a single murderer be punished, though thousands of good men have been slain; and further, that he attempted by military orders to prevent the execution of acts of Congress by the military commanders who were charged therewith. These and his concurrent acts show conclusively that his attempt to get the control of the military force of the government, by the seizing of the Department of War, was done in pursuance of his general design, if it were possible, to overthrow the Congress of the United States; and he now claims by his answer the right to control at his own will, for the execution of this very design, every officer of the army, navy, civil, and diplomatic service of the United States. He asks you here, Senators, by your solemn adjudication to confirm him in that right, to invest him with that power, to be used with the intents and for the purposes which he has already shown.

The responsibility is with you; that safeguards of the Constitution against usurpation are in your hands; the interests and hopes of free institutions wait upon your verdict. The House of Representatives has done its duty. We have presented the facts in the constitutional manner; we have brought the criminal to your bar, and demand judgment at your hands for his so great crimes.

Never again, if Andrew Johnson go quit and free this day, can the people of this or any other country by constitutional checks or guards stay the usurpations of executive power.

I speak, therefore, not the language of exaggeration, but the words of truth and soberness, that the future political welfare and liberties of all men hang trembling on the decision of the hour.

7. Elizabeth Cady Stanton Questions Abolitionist Support for Female Enfranchisement, 1868

To what a depth of degradation must the women of this nation have fallen to be willing to stand aside, silent and indifferent spectators in the reconstruction of the nation, while all the lower stratas of manhood are to legislate in their interests, political, religious, educational, social and sanitary, moulding to their untutored will the institutions of a mighty continent....

Elizabeth Cady Stanton, "Who Are Our Friends?" *The Revolution*, 15 (January 1868).

While leading Democrats have been thus favorably disposed, what have our best friends said when, for the first time since the agitation of the question [the enfranchisement of women], they have had an opportunity to frame their ideas into statutes to amend the constitutions of two States in the Union.

Charles Sumner, Horace Greeley, Gerrit Smith and Wendell Phillips, with one consent, bid the women of the nation stand aside and behold the salvation of the negro. Wendell Phillips says, "one idea for a generation," to come up in the order of their importance. First negro suffrage, then temperance, then the eight hour movement, then woman's suffrage. In 1958, three generations hence, thirty years to a generation, Phillips and Providence permitting, woman's suffrage will be in order. What an insult to the women who have labored thirty years for the emancipation of the slave, now when he is their political equal, to propose to lift him above their heads. Gerrit Smith, forgetting that our great American idea is "individual rights," in which abolitionists have ever based their strongest arguments for emancipation, says, this is the time to settle the rights of races; unless we do justice to the negro we shall bring down on ourselves another bloody revolution, another four years' war, but we have nothing to fear from woman, she will not revenge herself!...

Horace Greeley has advocated this cause for the last twenty years, but to-day it is too new, revolutionary for practical consideration. The enfranchisement of woman, revolutionizing, as it will, our political, religious and social condition, is not a measure too radical and all-pervading to meet the moral necessities of this day and generation.

Why fear new things; all old things were once new.... We live to do new things! When Abraham Lincoln issued the proclamation of emancipation, it was a new thing. When the Republican party gave the ballot to the negro, it was a new thing, startling too, to the people of the South, very revolutionary to their institutions, but Mr. Greeley did not object to all this because it was new....

And now, while men like these have used all their influence for the last four years, to paralyze every effort we have put forth to rouse the women of the nation, to demand their true position in the reconstruction, they triumphantly turn to us, and say the greatest barrier in the way of your demand is that "the women themselves do not wish to vote." What a libel on the intelligence of the women of the nineteenth century. What means the 12,000 petitions presented by John Stuart Mill in the British Parliament from the first women in England, demanding household suffrage? What means the late action in Kansas, 10,000 women petitioned there for the right of suffrage, and 9,000 votes at the last election was the answer. What means the agitation in every State in the Union? In the very hour when Horace Greeley brought in his adverse report in the Constitutional Convention of New York, at least twenty members rose in their places and presented petitions from every part of the State, demanding woman's suffrage. What means that eloquent speech of George W. Curtis in the Convention, but to show that the ablest minds in the State are ready for this onward step?

8. Lucy McMillan, a Former Slave in South Carolina, Testifies About White Violence, 1871

SPARTANBURGH, SOUTH CAROLINA, July 10, 1871.

LUCY McMILLAN (colored) sworn and examined.

By the CHAIRMAN:

QUESTION. Where do you live?

ANSWER. Up in the country. I live on McMillan's place, right at the foot of the road.

QUESTION. How far is it?

ANSWER. Twelve miles.

QUESTION. Are you married?

ANSWER. I am not married. I am single now. I was married. My husband was taken away from me and carried off twelve years ago....

QUESTION. How old are you now?

ANSWER. I am called forty-six. I am forty-five or six.

QUESTION. Did the Ku-Klux come where you live at any time?

ANSWER. They came there once before they burned my house down. The way it was was this: John Hunter's wife came to my house on Saturday morning, and told they were going to whip me. I was afraid of them; there was so much talk of Ku-Klux drowning people, and whipping people, and killing them. My house was only a little piece from the river, so I laid out at night in the woods. The Sunday evening after Isham McCrary was whipped I went up, and a white man, John McMillan, came along and says to me, "Lucy, you had better stay at home, for they will whip you anyhow." I said if they have to, they might whip me in the woods, for I am afraid to stay there. Monday night they came in and burned my house down; I dodged out alongside of the road not far off, and saw them. I was sitting right not far off, and as they came along the river I know some of them. I know John McMillan, and Kennedy McMillan, and Billy Bush, and John Hunter. They were all together. I was not far off, and I saw them. They went right on to my house. When they passed me I run further up on the hill to get out of the way of them. They went there and knocked down and beat my house a right smart while. And then they all got still, and directly I saw the fire rise.

Excerpt from *Testimony Taken by the Joint Select Committee to Inquire into the Condition of Affairs in the Late Insurrectionary States* (Washington, 1872), printed in Dorothy Sterling. ed., *Trouble They Seen: The Story of Reconstruction in the Words of African Americans*. New York: Da Capo Press, 1994.

QUESTION. How many of these men were there?

ANSWER. A good many; I couldn't tell how many, but these I knew. The others I didn't.

QUESTION. Were these on foot or on horseback?

ANSWER. These were walking that I could call the names of, but the others were riding. I work with these boys everyday. One of them I raised from a child, and I knew them. I have lived with them twelve years.

QUESTION. How were they dressed?

ANSWER. They had just such cloth as this white cotton frock made into old gowns; and some had black faces, and some red, and some had horns on their heads before, and they came a-talking by me and I knew their voices.

QUESTION. How far were you from where they were?

ANSWER. Not very far. I was in the woods, squatted down, and staid still until they passed; but then I run further up the hill.

QUESTION. Have you any family with you there?

ANSWER. I had one little daughter with me. I had one grown daughter, but my grown daughter had been up the country to my mother's staying, and my little girl was staying there with me.

QUESTION. Had you your little girl out with you?

ANSWER. Yes, sir; I could not leave her there.

QUESTION. What was the reason given for burning your house?

ANSWER. There was speaking down there last year and I came to it. They all kept at me to go. I went home and they quizzed me to hear what was said, and I told them as far as my senses allowed me.

QUESTION. Where was the speaking?

ANSWER. Here in this town. I went on and told them, and then they all said I was making laws; or going to have the land, and the Ku-Klux were going to beat me for bragging that I would have land. John Hunter told them on me, I suppose, that I said I was going to have land....

9. Father Abram Ryan Proclaims Undying Love for the Confederate States of America, 1879

C. S. A.

Do we weep for the heroes who died for us?

Who living were true and tried for us,

And dying sleep side by side for us;—

Father Ryan's Poems (Mobile: John L. Rapier and Company Publishers, 1879).

The Martyr-band

That hallowed our land

With the blood they shed in a tide for us.

Ah! fearless on many a day for us

They stood in the front of the fray for us,

And held the foeman at bay for us,

And tears should fall

Fore'er o'er all

Who fell while wearing the gray for us.

How many a glorious name for us,

How many a story of fame for us,

They left,—would it not be a blame for us,

If their memories part

From our land and heart,

And a wrong to them, and shame for us?

No—no—no—they were brave for us,

And bright were the lives they gave for us,—

The land they struggled to save for us

Will not forget

Its warriors yet

Who sleep in so many a grave for us.

On many and many a plain for us

Their blood poured down all in vain for us,

Red, rich and pure,—like a rain for us;

They bleed,—we weep,

We live,—they sleep—

"All Lost"—the only refrain for us,

But their memories e'er shall remain for us,

And their names, bright names, without stain for us,—

The glory they won shall not wane for us,

In legend and lay

Our heroes in gray

Shall forever live over again for us.

10. Francis Miles Finch Mourns and Celebrates Civil War Soldiers from the South and North, 1867

The Blue and the Gray

By the flow of the inland river,

Whence the fleets of iron have fled,

Where the blades of the grave-grass quiver,

Asleep are the ranks of the dead:

Under the sod and the dew,

Waiting the judgment-day;

Under the one, the Blue,

Under the other, the Gray....

From the silence of sorrowful hours

The desolate mourners go,

Lovingly laden with flowers

Alike for the friend and the foe;

Under the sod and the dew,

Waiting the judgment-day;

Under the roses, the Blue,

Under the lilies, the Gray.

So with an equal splendor,

The morning sun-rays fall,

With a touch impartially tender,

On the blossoms blooming for all:

Frances M. Finch, "The Blue and the Gray: And Other Verses" (New York: Henry Holt and Company, 1909), 1–3.

Under the sod and the dew,

Waiting the judgment-day;

Broidered with gold, the Blue,

Mellowed with gold, the Gray.

So, when the summer calleth,

On forest and field of grain,

With an equal murmur falleth

The cooling drip of the rain:

Under the sod and the dew,

Waiting the judgment-day,

Wet with the rain, the Blue

Wet with the rain, the Gray.

Sadly, but not with upbraiding,

The generous deed was done,

In the storm of the years that are fading

No braver battle was won:

Under the sod and the dew,

Waiting the judgment-day;

Under the blossoms, the Blue,

Under the garlands, the Gray

No more shall the war cry sever,

Or the winding rivers be red;

They banish our anger forever

When they laurel the graves of our dead!

Under the sod and the dew,

Waiting the judgment-day,

Love and tears for the Blue,

Tears and love for the Gray.

ESSAYS

The collapse of Reconstruction had enormous costs for the African-American population of the South. Arguably, its failure also postponed the economic and social recovery of the entire region until well into the twentieth century. Historians have long debated the meaning of Reconstruction and particularly the reasons for its abandonment. In the first essay, Steven Hahn of the University of Pennsylvania shows that former slaves and Confederates were both prepared to mount an armed defense of their goals, reflecting a long tradition of Southern violence that had previously undergirded slavery. He argues that Reconstruction came to an end when freedmen lost the military support of the North, which had tired of the sixteen-year conflict (1861–1877). Essentially, the freedmen were outgunned. David W. Blight of Yale University takes a somewhat different tack. He depicts Reconstruction as a process in which two important but incompatible goals vied for attention: reconciliation and emancipation. The nation needed to heal the sectional divide in order to function as one country, yet it had also fought the war, at least in part, to bring justice to the former slaves. As it turned out, Southern resistance narrowed the terms on which reconciliation was possible. The emancipationist promise of the war was stunted as a result, and eventually forgotten in the attempt to minimize the differences between "the Blue and the Gray." Reconstruction became a contest over the memory and meaning of the war. Black southerners lost.

Continuing the War: White and Black Violence During Reconstruction

STEVEN HAHN

In March 1867, nearly two years after the Confederate armies had begun to surrender and more than a year after Congress had refused to seat representatives from the former Confederate states, the mark of Radicalism was indelibly inscribed into the cornerstone of the reconstructed American republic. It did not herald the draconian policies—imprisonments and executions, massive disfranchisement, or confiscation of landed estates—that some Republicans had advocated and many Rebels had initially feared. And it required a combination of white southern arrogance and vindictiveness, presidential intransigence, and mounting African American agitation before it could be set. But with the Military Reconstruction Acts, Congress gave the federal government unprecedented power to reorganize the ex-Confederate South politically, imposed political disabilities on leaders of the rebellion, and, most stunning of all, extended the elective franchise to southern black males, the great majority of whom had been

Reprinted by permission of the publisher from *A Nation Under Our Feet: Black Political Struggles in the Rural South* by Steven Hahn, pp. 165, 177, 178–181, 183, 184, 186, 189, 190, 219, 224–226, 265–269, 280, 281, 286, 288–292, 307, 308, 310–312, Cambridge, Mass.: The Belknap Press of Harvard University Press, Copyright © 2003 by the President and Fellows of Harvard College.

slaves. Never before in history, and nowhere during the Age of Revolution, had so large a group of legally dependent people been enfranchised....

By the summer of 1867, complaints of "armed organizations among the freedmen," of late-hour drilling, and of threatening "assemblages" had grown both in volume and geographical scope. The entire plantation South appeared to pulse with militant and quasi-military activity. But now, in the months after the passage of the Reconstruction Acts, investigation revealed a more formal process of politicization, and one tied directly to the extension of the elective franchise and the organizational initiatives of the Republican party. From Virginia to Georgia, from the Carolinas to the Mississippi Valley and Texas, the freed people showed "a remarkable interest in all political information," were "fast becoming thoroughly informed upon their civil and political rights," and, most consequentially, were avidly "organizing clubs and leagues throughout the counties." Of these, none was more important to the former slaves or more emblematic of the developing character of local politics in the postemancipation South than the often vilified and widely misunderstood body known as the Union League.

Emerging out of a network of organizations formed in the northern states in 1862 and 1863 to rally public support for the Lincoln administration and the war effort, the Union League embraced early the practices of both popular and patrician politics. Bound by secrecy, requiring oaths and rituals much in the manner of the Masons, and winning a mass base through local councils across the Midwest and Northeast, the league also took hold among loyalist elites meeting in stately clubs and townhomes in Philadelphia, New York, and Boston. In May 1863, a national convention defined goals, drew up a constitution, and elected officers, and councils were soon being established in Union-occupied areas of the Confederate South to advance the cause. Once the war ended, the league continued its educational and agitational projects and spread most rapidly among white Unionists in southern hill and mountain districts, where membership could climb into the thousands. But committed as the league was "to protect, strengthen, and defend all loyal men without regard to sect, condition, or race," it began as well to sponsor political events and open a few councils for the still unfranchised African Americans—chiefly in larger cities like Richmond, Norfolk, Petersburg, Wilmington, Raleigh, Savannah, Tallahassee, Macon, and Nashville.

With the provision for a black franchise and voter registration encoded in the Reconstruction Acts, league organizers quickly fanned out from these urban areas into the smaller towns and surrounding countryside, and particularly into the plantation belt....

It was arduous and extremely dangerous work, for as organizers trekked out to where the mass of freedpeople resided, they fell vulnerable to swift and deadly retaliation at the hands of white landowners and vigilantes. Having organized the Mount Olive Union League Council in Nottoway County, Virginia, in July of 1867, the Reverend John Givens reported that a "colored speaker was killed three weeks ago" in neighboring Lunenberg County. But Givens determined to "go there and speak where they have cowed the black man," hoping "by the help of God" to "give them a dose of my radical Republican pills and neutralize the corrosive acidity of their negro hate.".…

The formation of a Union League council officially required the presence of at least nine loyal men, each twenty-one years of age or older, who were, upon initiation, to elect a president and other officers from among those regarded as "prudent, vigilant, energetic, and loyal," and as "possess[ing] the confidence of their fellow citizens." They were expected to hold meetings weekly, to follow the ceremony, and to "enlist all loyal talent in their neighborhood.".…

The experience and operations of local councils depended to some extent on the training and ability of the organizer, but perhaps even more on the social and political conditions in the specific counties and precincts. In hilly Rutherford County, North Carolina, where only one in five inhabitants was black and where the Whig party had been dominant before the Civil War, the Union League seemed to function—at least initially—in an unusually open and relaxed manner. One Saturday a month at noon, the courthouse bell in the village of Rutherfordton would be rung to announce a meeting and summon "every citizen who wished to come." Membership in the league was not concealed and some men who had served in the Confederate army belonged.…

Yet where blacks made up between one-third and two-thirds of the population—and where, not incidentally, the great majority of Union League councils was to be found—the situation was rather different. Here, most league members were black and they encountered a substantial and largely antagonistic population of whites. Whether they met weekly, biweekly, or monthly (and there was considerable variation), they relied on word of mouth rather than bells, horns, or posters; they usually assembled at night; and they generally favored sites that would attract as little adverse attention as possible, often posting armed sentinels outside. Some league councils either organized their own drilling companies or linked with companies that already existed. One observer in the South Carolina piedmont district of Abbeville fretfully reported that local leagues with "their Captains, and other Officers," were meeting "with their Guns … in secret places, but do not meet twice in the same place." Recognizing the dangers, the freedman Caleb, who worked for a particularly hostile landowner in Maury County, Tennessee, where blacks formed just under half of the population, chose another course: he went to his employe in April 1867 "and whol[l]y den[i]ed having any thing to do with the Un[i]on League," insisting that he "has not joined it nor never will.".…

The Union League sprang to life through the plantation districts because its goal of mobilizing black support for the national government and the Republican party fed on and nourished the sensibilities and customs that organizers found in many African American communities. League councils served as crucial political schools, educating newly enfranchised blacks in the ways of the official political culture. New members not only were instructed in the league's history, in the "duties of American citizenship," and in the role of th[e] Republican party in advancing their freedom, but also learned about "parliamentary law and debating," about courts, juries, and militia service, about the conduct of elections and of various political offices, and about important events near and far. With meetings often devoted, in part, to the reading aloud of newspapers, pamphlets, and government decrees, freedmen gained a growing political literacy even if most could neither read nor write....

Indeed, league councils quickly constituted themselves as vehicles not only of Republican electoral mobilization, but also of community development, defense, and self-determination. In Harnett County, North Carolina, they formed a procession "with fife and drum and flag and banner" and demanded the return of "any colored children in the county bound to white men." In Oktibbeha County, Mississippi, they organized a cooperative store, accepting "corn and other products ... in lieu of money," and, when a local black man suffered arrest, "the whole League" armed and marched to the county seat. In Randolph County, Alabama, and San Jacinto County, Texas, they worked to establish local schools so that, as one activist put it, "every colored man [now] beleaves in the Leage."...

Among the diverse activities that Union League councils across the former Confederate South pursued in 1867, few commanded more immediate attention than those required to implement the provisions and goals of the Reconstruction Acts. Within months, the Republican party had to be organized in the states and counties, delegates had to be nominated and elected to serve in state constitutional conventions, new state constitutions enfranchising black men and investing state governments with new structures and responsibilities had to be written and ratified, and the general congressional expectations for readmission to the Union had to be fulfilled. First and foremost, the outlines of a new body politic had to be drawn and legitimated through a process of voter registration....

During Reconstruction, black men held political office in every state of the former Confederacy. More than one hundred won election or appointment to posts having jurisdiction over entire states, ranging from superintendent of education, assistant commissioner of agriculture, superintendent of the deaf and dumb asylum, and member of the state land commission to treasurer, secretary of state, state supreme court justice, and lieutenant governor. One African American even sat briefly as the governor of Louisiana. A great many more—almost eight hundred—served in the state legislatures. But by far the largest number of black officeholders were to be found at the local level: in counties, cities, smaller municipalities, and militia districts. Although a precise figure is almost impossible to obtain, blacks clearly filled over 1,100 elective or appointive local offices, and they may well have filled as many as 1,400 or 1,500, about 80 percent of which were in rural and small-town settings....

Union League and Republican party activists therefore had to prepare carefully for election day lest their other efforts be nullified. They had to petition military commanders and Republican governors to appoint favorable (and dismiss hostile) election officials and to designate suitable polling sites, particularly if Democrats still controlled county governing boards. They had to get their voters to the polls, at times over a distance of many miles, and make sure that those voters received the correct tickets. They had to minimize the opportunities for bribery, manipulation, and intimidation. And they had to oversee the counting of ballots. Voting required, in essence, a military operation. Activists often called a meeting of fellow leaguers or club members the night before an election to provide instructions and materials. The chairman of the Tunica County, Mississippi, Republican executive committee had men come to the town of Hernando from all over the county on the day before the election and distribute tickets to those political clubs meeting that night. At times groups of black voters might spend the night before an election on a safe plantation or in the woods, perhaps sending a small party ahead to check for possible traps or ambushes, and then move out at first light to arrive at the polls well before their opponents or "rebel spies" could gather. Henry Frazer, who organized for the Republican party in Barbour County, Alabama, claimed that he went out with as many as "450 men and camped at the side of the road" before going into the town of Eufaula at eight in the morning where they would "stand in a body until they got a chance to vote."…

Protecting black Republican voters from white intimidation was only the most obvious goal of such martial organization and display, however. There was also the need to prod the timid and punish the apathetic or disloyal within their own communities. Activists learned early that elections could only be carried by securing overwhelming allegiance to the Republican party and then by ensuring that the eligible voters overcame fear or inertia to cast ballots. Political parades and torchlight processions during election campaigns and on the eve of polling—often with black men dressed in their club uniforms, beating drums, "hallooing, hooping," and, on occasion, riding full gallop through the streets—thereby served several purposes: to inspire enthusiasm, advertise numbers and resolve, and coax the participation of those who might otherwise abstain. Where coaxing proved insufficient, more coercive tactics could be deployed. Union League members in a North Carolina county, upon learning of three or four black men who "didn't mean to vote," threatened to "whip them" and "made them go." In another county, "some few colored men who declined voting" were, in the words of a white conservative, "bitterly persecute[ed]." One suffered insults, the destruction of his fences and crops, and "other outrages."

Especially harsh reprisals could be brought against blacks who aligned with conservatives and Democrats, for they were generally regarded not merely as opponents but as "traitors." As black Mississippian Robert Gleed put it, "[W]e don't believe they have a right to acquiesce with a party who refuse to recognize their right to participate in public affairs." In the rural hinterlands of Portsmouth, Virginia, black Republicans attacked "colored conservatives" at a prayer meeting and beat two of them badly. In southside Virginia's Campbell County, a black man who betrayed the Union League was tied up by his heels and suspended from a tree for several hours until he agreed to take an oath of loyalty.…

When the U.S. Congress conducted an investigation of the Ku Klux Klan in the early 1870s, more than a few of the reputed leaders testified that the organization was a necessary response to the alarming activities and tactics of the Union League. They complained of secret oaths, clandestine meetings, accumulations of arms, nocturnal drilling, threatening mobilizations, and a general flaunting of civilities among former slaves across the plantation South. In so doing, they helped construct a discourse, later embraced by apologists for slavery and white supremacy, that not only justified vigilantism but also demonized Radical Reconstruction for its political illegitimacies. The enfranchisement of ignorant and dependent freedmen by vengeful outsiders, the Klansmen insisted, marked a basic corruption of the body politic and a challenge to order as it was widely understood....

Ku Klux Klan leaders and sympathizers who blamed the Union League for their resort to vigilantism were at least right about the chronology. Union League mobilizations generally preceded the appearance of the Klan. But the character and activities of the league itself reflected a well-established climate of paramilitarism that assumed both official and unofficial forms. Already during the summer and fall of 1865, despite the presence of a Union army of occupation, bands of white "regulators," "scouts," and cavalrymen rode the countryside disciplining and disarming freedpeople who looked to harvest their crops, make new labor and family arrangements, and perhaps await a federally sponsored land redistribution....

From the first, the Klan proved particularly attractive to young, white men who had served in the Confederate army. All of the founders in Pulaski, Tennessee, were youthful Confederate veterans, and most everywhere former Confederate officers, cavalrymen, and privates sparked organization and composed the bulk of membership. Klan dens and other vigilante outfits often became magnets for returning soldiers and, at times, they virtually mirrored the remainders of specific Confederate companies. Powell Clayton, the Republican governor of Arkansas who effectively combated the Klan, complained in retrospect about the Confederates being paroled or allowed to desert without surrendering their arms, ammunition, and horses. To this extent, the Klan not only came to embody the anger and displacement of a defeated soldiery and to capitalize on the intensely shared experiences of battlefields and prison camps; it also may be regarded as a guerilla movement bent on continuing the struggle or avenging the consequences of the official surrender.

But the very associations between the Klan and the Confederate army suggest a deeper historical and political context, for Confederate mobilization itself was enabled by longstanding and locally based paramilitary institutions. Militias were perhaps most important because state governments required the enrollment of all able-bodied white men while leaving much of the organizational initiative to counties and neighborhoods, where volunteer companies could elect their own officers, make their own by-laws, and then secure recognition by the legislature. The militias, in turn, were closely connected with slave patrols—for a time through formal control, and more generally by way of personnel and jurisdiction—which policed the African American population, instructed all white men in their responsibilities as citizens in a slave society, and could be enlisted as something of a posse by the state in the event of emergency. A martial spirit and military presence thus suffused the community life of the antebellum South....

The geography of Klan activity was, in essence, a map of political struggle in the Reconstruction South. Klan-style vigilantism surfaced at some point almost anywhere that a substantial Republican constituency—and especially a black

Republican constituency—was to be found: from Virginia to Florida, South Carolina to Texas, Arkansas to Kentucky. Reports of "outrages" and "depredations" emanated from areas that were heavily black (eastern North Carolina, west-central Alabama), heavily white (east Tennessee, northwest Georgia), and racially mixed (eastern Mississippi, northwest South Carolina, east-central Texas). But whether the eruptions were brief or prolonged and whether they achieved their objectives depended on the nature and effectiveness of black resistance and, by extension, the readiness of the state Republican governments to respond with necessary force....

Union Leagues and Republican party clubs had, in some places, already begun to mount a response to Klan violence, at times bringing pressure against suspected Klan leaders. Black members of a Pickens County, Alabama, Union League boycotted a white landowner thought to be "head of the Ku Klux." They were so effective that, in his words, he "could not hire a darkey at any price." In a number of locales scattered across the plantation districts, they appear to have taken even more direct and destructive action by torching the mills, barns, and houses of former slaveholders. But the leagues and clubs more likely moved to put themselves on a paramilitary footing, if they had not embraced rituals of armed self-defense from the outset. Black Union Leaguers in Darlington County, South Carolina, fearing Klan violence, gathered weapons, took control of a town, and threatened to burn it down in the event of attack. Near Macon, Mississippi, the combination of local outrages and the very bloody Meridian riot led blacks to organize "secretly" and ready themselves to "meet the mob." "There will be no more 'Meridians' in Mississippi," a white ally of theirs declared. "Next time an effort of this kind is made there will be killing on both sides." The tenor of conflict and mobilization in Granville County, North Carolina, in the fall of 1868 was such that a prominent Democrat offered Union League members a bargain: "If we would stop the leagues he would stop the Ku Klux."...

Like Tennessee, neighboring Arkansas had a white population majority, a solid base of Unionist sentiment in the mountains of the northwest, and a Republican party that looked to punish former Confederates. But Arkansas had been remanded to military rule by the Reconstruction Acts of 1867, and in the spring of 1868 eligible voters put Republicans in command of the general assembly and the carpetbagger Powell Clayton in the governor's chair. A native of Pennsylvania and a civil engineer by training, Clayton had been out in Kansas during the 1850s and commanded a Union cavalry regiment in Arkansas during the war, where he saw a good deal of action against Confederate guerrillas. After the surrender, he settled in Arkansas and bought a plantation, but run-ins with ex-Confederate neighbors led him into politics; he first helped to organize the state Republican party and then accepted the party's nomination for governor. By the time of Clayton's inauguration in July, Klan activity was sufficiently pronounced in the southern and eastern sections of the state that he wasted no time in responding: with the approval of the legislature, he began mobilizing a state militia and, as intimidation of Republican voters and local officials intensified and a Republican congressman fell victim to a Klan ambush, he declared marital law in ten counties. Armed skirmishes between militiamen and Klansmen, together with arrests, trials, and a few executions, followed. By early 1869, the Klan had pretty well "ceased to exist" in Arkansas....

The accession of Republican Ulysses S. Grant to the presidency in March of 1869 offered some welcome possibilities to those governors who stood ready to deploy state militia units. Previously, the Johnson administration had refused requests for arms, and governors were left scrambling to equip their troops. Arkansas's Powell Clayton first tried to borrow guns from various northern states and then, when this failed, sent an emissary to New York to purchase rifles and ammunition. Unfortunately, a contingent of well-prepared Klansmen intercepted the shipment between Memphis and Little Rock. Florida's carpetbag governor Harrison Reed chose to go personally to New York to procure arms soon after the legislature passed a militia law in August 1868, but the result was even more embarrassing. Under the nose of a federal detachment, Klansmen boarded the train carrying the armaments to Tallahassee and destroyed them. Grant, on the other hand, proved more receptive than Johnson and made substantial supplies of weapons available to Governors Holden and Scott in the Carolinas....

The Klan's effectiveness depended on a wider political climate that gave latitude to local vigilantes and allowed for explosions of very public violence. Louisiana and Georgia, which alone among the reconstructed states supported Democrat Horatio Seymour for the presidency in 1868, had at least seven bloody riots together with Klan raiding that summer and fall. The term "riot," which came into wide use at this time, quite accurately captures the course and ferocity of these eruptions, claiming as they did numerous lives, often over several days, in an expanding perimeter of activity. But "riot" suggests, as well, a disturbance that falls outside the ordinary course of political conduct, and so by invoking or embracing it we may miss what such disturbances can reveal about the changing dynamics and choreography of what was indeed ordinary politics in the postemancipation South....

Consider the Camilla riot in southwest Georgia, which captured the greatest attention but shared many features of the others. In late August 1868, Republicans in the state's Second Congressional District, most of whom were black, met in the town of Albany and nominated William P. Pierce, a former Union army officer, failed planter, and Freedmen's Bureau agent, for Congress. It would not be an easy campaign.... A "speaking" in the town of Americus on September 15 brought menacing harassment from local whites and Pierce barely escaped violence. But he did not interrupt plans for a similar event in Camilla on Saturday, September 19.

News of the rally—which would feature Pierce, several other white Republicans, and Philip Joiner, a former slave, local Loyal League president, and recently expelled state legislator—circulated through the neighboring counties. So, too, did rumors of a possible attack by armed whites who, it was said, proclaimed that "this is our country and we intend to protect it or die." Freedpeople did have ample cause for alarm. Camilla, the seat of relatively poor, white-majority Mitchell County in an otherwise black majority section of the state, crackled with tension. Gunfire had broken out there during the April 1868 elections, and many of the blacks had resolved that they would "not dare … go to town entirely unarmed as they did at that time." The white Republican leaders tried to quell these fears when the Dougherty County contingent gathered on their plantations on Friday night the 18th; and as the group moved out on Saturday morning for the twenty-odd mile trek to Camilla, most heeded the advice to leave their weapons behind and avoid a provocation.…

But to the whites of Camilla, such a procession could only constitute a "mob," with no civil or political standing, and mean "war, revolution, insurrection, or riot of some sort." Once spotted on Saturday morning, it thereby sparked another round of rumors, these warning of an "armed body of negroes" heading toward the town. Although evidence suggests that local Democrats had been busy for at least two days accumulating weapons and preparing to respond with force, the rumors clearly sped the mobilization of the town's "citizens," who appointed a committee to ride out with the sheriff and "meet the approaching crowd." A tense exchange followed, with the Republican leaders explaining that they only wished "to go peaceably into Camilla and hold a political meeting," and the sheriff warning them not to enter the town with arms.…

Suddenly, a local drunkard, waving a double-barreled shotgun, ran out to the wagon and, significantly, demanded that the drumming (associated both with a citizens' militia and slave communication) cease. A moment later he fired, and the "squads" of white townsmen immediately joined in. Freedmen who had guns briefly returned the volleys and then, with the others, commenced a desperate flight for safety. The sheriff and his "deputies" followed them into the woods and swamps with deadly purpose, some looking for "that d——d Phil Joiner." Joiner escaped, but eleven days later he reported that "the mobbing crowd is still going through Baker County and every Colored man that is farming to his self or supporting the nominee of Grant and Colfax he either have to leave his home or be killed."

Prospects for black retaliation briefly ran very high. As word of the shooting spread through Dougherty County that Saturday evening, agitated freedmen in Albany sought out the local Freedmen's Bureau agent. Some talked of going immediately to Camilla to rescue and protect those who remained at risk. A few hours later, African Methodist minister Robert Crumley heatedly reminded his congregants that he had advised those bound for Camilla the night before not to go with fewer than 150 well-armed men, and then suggested traveling there en masse the next day to "burn the earthy about the place." The Freedmen's Bureau agent managed to discourage such a course by promising a full investigation and urging his superiors in Atlanta to send federal troops. The investigation showed Camilla to be a massacre that had left at least nine African Americans dead and many more wounded. But all that came out of Atlanta was a proclamation by Republican governor Rufus Bullock urging civil authorities to keep the peace and safeguard the rights of the people. Election day proved to be remarkably quiet in southwest Georgia because the contest was over well before. Only two Republicans bothered to cast ballots in Camilla, and the turnout was so low elsewhere in the district that the Democrats, despite being greatly outnumbered among eligible votes, registered an official victory. There would be resurgences of local black power in the future, but this was the beginning of the end for Republican rule in Georgia.…

And yet we must not underestimate the extent and tenacity of black resistance. White toughs did, to their misfortune, in the village of Cainhoy, a short distance from Charleston. Attempting to intimidate a Republican speaker at a "joint discussion" in mid-October, they found themselves outgunned as well as outnumbered by a black crowd that included several militia companies. When the smoke cleared, five whites lay dead and as many as fifty had been wounded. Most in evidence among the coast, such militance was nonetheless to be found at various points in the interior. As rifle club activity intensified in Barnwell County, a "company of negroes," acting on their own authority, appropriated arms issued during Governor Scott's administration and threaten[ed] to destroy the town" of Blackville. In Darlington County, a "negro militia company consisting," according to a local Democrat, "of the worst elements in this section," continued to drill and cause "a great deal of trouble," coming in one instance to the aid of a favored trial justice. Sporadically, there were acts of arson and sabotage, ambushes and assaults....

The paramilitary politics of the Reconstruction South had previously produced dual state governments in Louisiana (1872), Texas (1873), and Arkansas (1874), but in 1876-1877 they also provoked a national crisis of governance. Not only were the state returns contested in both South Carolina and Louisiana, but there, as well as in Florida, the electoral college returns were contested too, leaving the outcome of the Presidential race—and control of the executive branch—in doubt. As Republicans and Democrats struggled to reach an accord before Grant's term expired in early March, tensions and threats that harked back to the winter of 1860–1861 seemed to abound. Yet through all of this, what appeared to be taking shape was less a "compromise" than a shared political sensibility in northern ruling circles that questioned the legitimacies of popular democracy. That sensibility had always been in evidence among conservatives and had spread during the 1850s, only to be pressed to the margins by the revolutionary mobilizations of the 1860s. It now expressed itself as weariness with the issues of Reconstruction, as skepticism about the capabilities of freedpeople, as concerns about the expansion of federal powers, as revulsion over political corruption, and, especially, as exasperation with the "annual autumnal outbreaks" in the Deep South and the consequent use of federal troops to maintain Republican regimes there.

It required elaborate fictions and willful ignorance for critics to argue, as some did, that the military had no business rejecting the popular will in the South. For if detachments of federal troops at the statehouses in Columbia, South Carolina, and New Orleans, Louisiana, alone enabled Republicans to hand onto the last threads of power, their Democratic rivals made no effort to conceal their own dependence on superior force of arms. In Louisiana, Democratic gubernatorial claimant and former Confederate brigadier general Francis T. Nicholls quickly demonstrated his understanding of political necessities. He designated local White League units as the legal state militia, commandeered the state arsenal, and took control of the New Orleans police. In South Carolina, Wade Hampton's allies succeeded in garrisoning the state capitol with as many as six thousand Red Shirts, while rifle clubs drove out Republican officeholders in upcountry counties....

The withdrawal of federal troops from the statehouses of South Carolina and Louisiana in April of 1877 did not therefore mark the end of their role in protecting the rights and property of American citizens; it only marked the end of their role, at least for nearly another century, in protecting the rights and property of African Americans and other working people....

Ending the War: The Push for National Reconciliation

DAVID W. BLIGHT

Americans faced an overwhelming task after the Civil War and emancipation: how to understand the tangled relationship between two profound ideas—*healing* and *justice*. On some level, both had to occur; but given the potency of racial assumptions and power in nineteenth-century America, these two aims never developed in historical balance. One might conclude that this imbalance between outcomes of sectional healing and racial justice was simply America's inevitable historical condition, and celebrate the remarkable swiftness of the reunion, as Paul Buck did in his influential book, *The Road to Reunion* (1937). But theories of inevitability—of irrepressible conflicts or irrepressible reconciliations—and rarely satisfying. Human reconciliations—when tragically divided people unify again around aspirations, ideas, and the positive bonds of nationalism—are to be cherished. But sometimes reconciliations have terrible costs, both intentional and unseen. The sectional reunion after so horrible a civil war was a political triumph by the late nineteenth century, but it could not have been achieved without the resubjugation of many of those people whom the war had freed from centuries of bondage. This is the tragedy lingering on the margins and infesting the heart of American history from Appomattox to World War I....

Reconstruction was one long referendum on the meaning and memory of the verdict at Appomattox. The great challenge of Reconstruction was to determine how a national blood feud could be reconciled at the same time a new nation emerged out of war and social revolution. The survivors on both sides, winners and losers in the fullest sense, would still inhabit the same land and eventually the same government. The task was harrowing: how to make the logic of sectional reconciliation compatible with the logic of emancipation, how to square black freedom and the stirrings of racial equality with a cause (the South's) that had lost almost everything except its unbroken belief in white supremacy. Such an effort required both remembering and forgetting. During Reconstruction, many Americans increasingly realized that remembering the war, even the hatreds and deaths on a hundred battlefields—facing all those graves on Memorial Day—became, with time, easier than struggling over the enduring ideas for which those battles had been fought....

Reprinted by permission of the publisher from *Race and Reunion: The Civil War in American Memory* by David W. Blight, pp. 3, 31, 44–47, 51, 64, 65, 69–71, 77–81, 83, 86, 87, 89, 91, 92, 97, Cambridge, Mass.: The Belknap Press of Harvard University Press, Copyright © 2001 by the President and Fellows of Harvard College.

In the immediate aftermath of the war, defeated and prostrate, it appeared to many that white Southerners would accept virtually any conditions or terms laid upon them. This was the initial conclusion of the northern journalist Whitelaw Reid, who believed that even black suffrage would be "promptly accepted"— that is, until he observed white Southern defiance revived by President Johnson's conciliatory Reconstruction measures. After his Southern tour, Reid left a mixed warning to policymakers about the disposition of white Southerners in 1866. "The simple truth is," Reid concluded, "they stand ready to claim everything, if permitted, and to accept anything, if required." Other Northern journalists observing the South reached similar conclusions. The initial war-bludgeoned compliance on the part of white Southerners gave way within a year to what Trowbridge called a "loyalty … of a negative sort: it is simply disloyalty subdued." A correspondent for the *New York Tribune* reported from Raleigh, North Carolina, that "the spirit of the Rebellion is not broken though its power is demolished." And a Northerner who had just returned from six months in South Carolina and Georgia informed Thaddeus Stevens in February 1866 that "the spirit which actuated the traitors … during the late rebellion is only sub- dued and *allows* itself to be *nourished* by *leniency*."

Against this backdrop, Andrew Johnson offered to the South his rapid Reconstruction policy. In late May 1865, Johnson announced his plan for the readmission of Southern states. It included a broad provision for amnesty and pardon for those participants in the rebellion who would take a loyalty oath to the Union. High-ranking ex-Confederate government officials were excluded from pardons for the time being, as were all Southerners who owned $20,000 or more worth of property. The latter group had to apply personally to the President for a pardon. Johnson's plan further required each former Confederate state to call a convention to revise its antebellum constitution, renounce seces- sion, and accept the Thirteenth Amendment abolishing slavery; they would then be promptly restored to the Union.

Johnson's plan put enormous authority back in the hands of white Souther- ners, but without any provisions for black civil or political rights. Indeed, Johnson himself was a thoroughgoing white supremacist and a doctrinaire state rightist. He openly encouraged the South to draft its notorious Black Codes, laws enacted across the South by the fall of 1865 that denied the freedmen political liberty and restricted their economic options and physical mobility. Designed as labor controls and a means for plantation discipline, such laws were part of the new constitutions produced by these "Johnson governments," and they expressed clearly white Southerners' refusal to face the deeper meanings of emancipation. Presidential Reconstruction, as it evolved in 1865, allowed Southerners to recreate governments of and for white men. Moreover, Johnson was openly hostile to the Freedmen's Bureau, the agency created by Congress in the last months of the war to provide food, medical care, schools, and labor contract adjudication for the freedpeople. The President overruled military and Freedmen's Bureau efforts to redistribute some land from masters to ex-slaves. By the fall of 1865, pardoned ex-Confederates were reclaiming their lands, and with such presidential encour- agement, reclaiming political power.…

Profoundly different memories and expectations collided in 1865-67, as presidential Reconstruction collapsed and the Republicans in Congress wrested control of the process away from Johnson. "These people [white Southerners] are not loyal; they are only conquered," wrote Union Brigadier General James S. Brisbin to Thaddeus Stevens in December 1865. "I tell you there is not as much loyalty in the South today as there was the day Lee surrendered to Grant. The moment they lost their cause in the field they set about to gain by politics what they had failed to obtain by force of arms." Brisbin thought the Black Codes would "reduce the blacks to a slavery worse than that from which they just escaped." Johnson's leniency seemed only to restore an old order and risk losing the very triumph that the Union forces had just won with so much sacrifice....

The radical Republicans had a genuine plan for Reconstruction. Their ideology was grounded in the notion of an activist federal government, a redefinition of American citizenship that guaranteed equal political rights for black men, and faith in free labor in a competitive capitalist system. The radicals greatly expanded federal authority, fixing their vision, as Sumner put it, on "the general principles" of "a national security and a national faith." Their cardinal principle was *equality before the law,* which in 1866 they enshrined in the Fourteen Amendment, expanding citizenship to all those born in the United States without regard to race. The same year Congress renewed the Freedmen's Bureau over Johnson's veto and passed the first civil rights act in American history.

Such legislation became reality because most Northerners were not ready to forget the results, and especially the sacrifices, of the war. The Southern states' rejection of the Fourteenth Amendment and Johnson's repeated vetoes of Reconstruction measures (as well as his repudiation at the polls in the Congressional elections of 1866) gave the radicals increased control over federal policy. In 1867 Congress divided the ex-Confederate states into five military districts and made black suffrage a condition of readmission to the Union. By 1870 all ex-Confederate states had rejoined the Union, and in most, the Republican Party—built as a coalition of "carpetbaggers" (Northerners who moved South), "scalawags" (native Southerners who gave allegiance to the new order), and thousands of black voters—held the reins of state government. Indeed black voters were the core constituency of Southern Republicanism and the means of power in 1867–68....

As Congress engaged in the fateful debates over national policy in 1866–67, the floors of the House and Senate became arenas of warring memories. Many Republicans were clearly driven by a combination of retribution against the South, a desire to remake the Constitution based on black equality, and a quest for long-term political hegemony. Stevens left no doubt of his personal attitude toward ex-slaveholders and ex-Confederates. "The murderers must answer to the suffering race," he said on May 8, 1866. "A load of misery must sit heavily upon their souls." The public debate in Congress was often sanguinary; it challenged everyone's ability to convert primal memory into public policy. "I know that there is a morbid sensibility, sometimes called mercy," declared Stevens, "which affects a few of all classes, from the priest to the clown, which has more sympathy for the murderer on the gallows than for his victim." Yankee retribution never had a more vehement voice than Stevens, and no one ever waved the "bloody shirt" with greater zeal. "I am willing they shall come in when they are ready," Stevens pronounced. "Do not, I pray you, admit those who have slaughtered half a million of our countrymen until their clothes are dried, and until they are reclad. I do not wish to sit side by side with men whose garments smell of the blood of my kindred."

"Bloody shirt" rhetoric lasted a long time in American politics; it was more than a slogan, and in these early years, it had many uses and diverse practitioners. As both raw personal memory and partisan raw material, the "bloody shirt" was a means to establish war guilt and a method through which to express war-induced hatreds....

Death and mourning were everywhere in America in 1865; hardly a family had escaped its pall. In the North, 6 percent of white males aged 13–43 had died in the war; in the South, 18 percent were dead. Of the 180,000 African Americans who served in the Union army and navy, 20 percent perished. Diseases such as typhoid, dysentery, and pneumonia claimed more than twice as many soldiers as did battle. The most immediate legacy of the war was its slaughter and how to remember it.

Death on such a scale demanded meaning. During the war, soldiers in countless remote arbors, or on awful battlefield landscapes, had gathered to mourn and bury their comrades, even while thousands remained unburied, their skeletons lying about on the killing fields of Virginia, Tennessee, or Georgia. Women had begun rituals of burial and remembrance in informal ways well before the war ended, both in towns on the homefront and sometimes at the battlefront. Americans carried flowers to graves or to makeshift monuments representing their dead, and so was born the ritual of "Decoration Day," known eventually also as Memorial Day.

In most places, the ritual was initially a spiritual practice. But very soon, remembering the dead and what they died for developed partisan fault lines. The evolution of Memorial Day during its first twenty years or so became a contest between three divergent, and sometimes overlapping, groups: blacks and their white former abolitionist allies, white Northerners, and white Southerners With time, in the North, the war's two great results—black freedom and the preservation of the Union—were rarely accorded equal space. In the South, a uniquely Confederate version of the war's meaning, rooted in resistance to Reconstruction, coalesced around Memorial Day practice. Decoration Day, and the ways in which it was observed, shaped Civil War memory as much as any other cultural ritual. The story of the origins of this important American day of remembrance is central to understanding how reconciliationist practices overtook the emancipationist legacies of the Civil War....

The "First Decoration Day," as this event came to be recognized in some circles in the North, involved an estimated ten thousand people, most of them black former slaves. During April, twenty-eight black men from one of the local churches built a suitable enclosure for the burial ground at the Race Course. In some ten days, they constructed a fence ten feet high, enclosing the burial ground, and landscaped the graves into neat rows. The wooden fence was whitewashed and an archway was built over the gate to the enclosure. On the arch, painted in black letters, the workmen inscribed "Martyrs of the Race Course." At nine o'clock in the morning on May 1, the procession to this special cemetery began as three thousand black schoolchildren (newly enrolled in free-men's schools) marched around the Race Course, each with an armload of roses and singing "John Brown's Body." The children were followed by three hun-dred black women representing the Patriotic Association, a group organized to distribute clothing and other goods among the freedpeople. The women carried baskets of flowers, wreaths, and crosses to the burial ground. The Mutual Aid Society, a benevolent association of black men, next marched in cadence around the track and into the cemetery, followed by large crowds of white and black citizens....

According to a reminiscence written long after the fact, "several slight dis-turbances" occurred during the ceremonies on the first Decoration Day, as well as "much harsh talk about the event locally afterward." But a measure of how white Charlestonians suppressed from memory this founding in favor of their own creation of the practice a year later came fifty-one years afterward, when the president of the Ladies Memorial Association of Charleston received an in-quiry for information about the May 1, 1865, parade. A United Daughters of the Confederacy official wanted to know if it was true that blacks and their white abolitionist friends had engaged in such a burial rite. Mrs. S. C. Beckwith responded tersely: "I regret that I was unable to gather any official information in answer to this." In Southern and national memory, the first Decoration Day was nearly lost in a grand evasion.

As a Northern ritual of commemoration, Memorial Day officially took hold in May 1868 and 1869, when General John A. Logan, commander-in-chief of the Grand Army of the Republic (GAR), called on all Union veterans to con-duct ceremonies and decorate the graves of their dead comrades. In general or-ders issued each of the two springs, Logan called for a national commemoration unlike anything in American experience save possibly the Fourth of July. In "almost every city, village, and hamlet church-yard in the land," charged Logan's circular, those who died to "suppress the late rebellion" were to be honored an-nually "while a survivor of the war remains." On May 30, 1868, when flowers were plentiful, funeral ceremonies were attended by thousands of people in 183 cemeteries in twenty-seven states. The following year, some 336 cities and towns in thirty-one states (including the South) arranged Decoration Day parades and orations. The observance grew manifold with time. In 1873, the New York leg-islature designated May 30 a legal holiday, and by 1890 every other Northern state had followed its lead....

For white Southerners, Memorial Day was born amidst the despair of defeat and the need for collective expressions of grief. By 1866, local memorial associa-tions had formed in many Southern communities, organized largely by women. Some new cemeteries were founded near battlefields, while existing ones in towns and cities were expanded enormously to accommodate the dead. In both sections, but especially in the South, the first monuments erected tended to be placed in cemeteries—the obvious sites of bereavement. By the 1890s,

hardly a city square, town green, or even some one-horse crossroads lacked a
Civil War memorial of some kind. But through most of the Reconstruction
years, the cemetery remained the public site of memorialization; obelisks and
stone pyramids appeared as markers of the recent past that so haunted every
community. Often directed by social elites who could fund monuments, the
Southern "memorial movement ... helped the South assimilate the fact of
defeat," as Gaines Foster writes, "without repudiating the defeated.".…

By the early 1870s, a group of ex-Confederate officers in Virginia had
forged a coalition of memorial groups that quickly took over the creation of
the Lost Cause tradition. They did so through print as much as through ritual
commemorations. In 1866, former Confederate general Daniel H. Hill founded
the magazine *The Land We Love*, a periodical devoted to demonstrating the skill
and prowess of Confederate armies against all odds. By 1869, Hill's journal had
become *Southern Magazine,* and most importantly, the Southern Historical Society (SHS) was founded as the vehicle for presenting the Confederate version of
the war to the world. By 1876, the SHS began publishing its regular *Southern
Historical Society Papers*, a series that ran for fourteen years under the editorship
of a former Confederate chaplain, John William Jones. The driving ideological
and emotional force behind the SHS was the former Confederate general Jubal
Early. Early had fled to Mexico at the end of the war and vowed never to return
to his native Virginia under the federal flag. Despite such bluster, and because of
threatening poverty, Early returned to his hometown of Lynchburg in 1869. He
made himself, as Gaines Foster observes, into the "prototypical unreconstructed
Rebel." His principle aim was not only to vindicate Southern secession and glorify the Confederate soldier, but also to launch a propaganda assault on popular
history and memory.…

In the South, monument unveiling days took on a significance equal to, if
not greater than, Memorial Day. In Richmond, Virginia, on October 26, 1875,
Confederate veterans by the thousands staged their first major coming-out as a
collective force. At the unveiling of the first significant monument to a Confederate hero, a standing statue of Stonewall Jackson sculpted by the British artist
T. H. Foley, nearly fifty thousand people gathered for an unprecedented parade
and a ceremony.…

At major intersections on the parade route, veterans, ladies memorial associations, and "the indefatigable K.K.K." (Ku Klux Klan) had assembled artisans to
construct arches and towers with elaborate decorations honoring Jackson. The
largest arch, at Grace and Eighth Streets, included huge letters that read: "Warrior,
Christian, Patriot." Above the inscription was a painting representing a stone wall,
"upon which was resting a bare saber, a Bible, and a Confederate cap.".…

One dispute among the planners of the Jackson statue unveiling nearly de-
railed the event. Governor Kemper was the grand marshal of the ceremonies and
had carefully planned the parade to the Capitol Square in Richmond. Kemper
was nervous that "nothing shall appear on the 26th to hurt the party" (Democrats). He feared that the "least excess" in the Confederate celebration would
give yet another "bloody shirt" to Northern Republicans, and he asked the leaders of the Confederate veterans to restrain their displays of battle flags. Only

days before the big event, Jubal Early wrote to Kemper complaining of rumors that black militia companies and civilians were to be "allowed in the procession." "I am inexpressibly shocked at the idea," said Early. He considered the involvement of blacks "an indignity to the memory of Jackson and an insult to the Confederates." Black Richmonders, the total of which Early judged to be between twenty thousand and thirty thousand, would swarm into the square, he believed, and whites would be forced to "struggle for place with buck negroes … anxious to show their consequence." Believing that blacks would wave "pictures of Lincoln and Fifteenth Amendment banners," Early threatened not to attend, and to take other veterans with him, if Kemper executed the plan.

In ferocious responses, Kemper told Early to mind his own business and begged him to "stay at home." Black militia officers and ministers in Richmond had petitioned Kemper to take part in the procession. For racial "peace" in the city, the governor accepted the petitioners' request. The small contingent of blacks were placed at the extreme rear of a parade several miles long, numbering many thousands of white marchers…. The position of blacks in this bitter argument between the ultimate irreconcilable [Jubal Early] and a redeemer-reconciliationist governor remained utterly subordinate. One would eliminate them altogether from Confederate memory; the other would declare them loyal and dispatch them to the rear of parades. In the long history of Lost Cause tradition, both got their wish.

As the immense crowd assembled at the state capital grounds where the Jackson monument was to be unveiled, Kemper welcomed them as the Democrat-redeemer governor of Virginia. He announced that Jackson was a national hero, not merely a Southern saint, whose memory was to be a "common heritage of glory" for both sections. The massive ceremony served as the South's reminder to the North of its insistence on "respect." The unveiling declared, in effect, that Reconstruction, as Northern Republicans had imagined it, was over….

In 1874–75, Union and Confederate veterans began to participate in Memorial Day exercises together in both North and South. In the wake of Memorial Day, 1875, in North Carolina, a black citizen in Raleigh, Osborne Hunter, anxiously observed in a letter to a newspaper "a noticeable spirit of reconciliation pervading the political atmosphere of both the Republican and Democratic parties of this state." In August 1874, the Democrats had regained power in North Carolina, and the highly racialized election had hinged, in part, on Southern resistance to federal enforcement of black civil rights. Until May 1875, blacks in Raleigh had always played a major role in Decoration Day ceremonies in that city. That year they were discouraged from participating, as the occasion was declared to be only a "soldier's turn-out." At the mark of a "decade in the history of freedom," concluded Hunter, Decoration Day seemed to be only an occasion for "ignoring the colored citizen and the colored voter."…

The disputed election of 1876 and the electoral crisis that culminated in the Compromise of 1877 brought the Republican Rutherford B. Hayes to the presidency, as well as the final three remaining Southern states not under Democratic control into that party's fold. Reconciliation seemed to sweep over the country's political spirit, as the Union survived another potential severing by sectional and partisan strife. Although it was hardly the first time that commentators in both sections had declared the final conclusion to the issues of the war, the political settlement of 1877 easily took its place as the traditional "end" of Reconstruction (a label it has carried ever since).

On Memorial Day, May 30, 1877, New York City experienced an array of parades and ceremonies unprecedented since the formal inception of the holiday nine years earlier. Virtually every orator and editorial writer declared the day one of forgetting, forgiveness, and equality of the Blue and the Gray veterans....

Decoration Day, 1877 in New York culminated with a special indoor event at the Brooklyn Academy of Music. The planning committee, dominated by democrats, had invited the prominent ex-Confederate general, lawyer, and then Brooklyn resident Roger A. Pryor to be orator of the evening. A committee member, Joseph Neilson, opened the proceedings with an explicit appeal for reconciliation. Neilson declared all the "causes" of the "late domestic contention" forgotten. As the voice of "healing," Pryor took the podium before an audience of nearly one thousand to deliver his extraordinary address, "The Soldier, the Friend of Peace and Union.",...

Unlike many Memorial Day orators, Pryor did not hide the issue of race behind a rhetoric of reunion. The war had nothing directly to do with slavery, he proclaimed, in what became an article of faith to Southern vindicationists and their Northern allies. Southerners were comfortably reconciled to the destruction of slavery because it had only been the "occasion not the cause of secession." Slavery was an impersonal force in history, a natural phenomenon subject only to divine control and beyond all human responsibility. It was good while it lasted, good once it was gone; no Southerner fought in its defense, and no Northerner died to end it. It just went away, like a change in the weather....

Following Pryor, former Union general Isaac S. Catlin delivered the final address of the evening. In full sympathy with the former Confederate's speech, Catlin spoke of military pathos and glory, of the victimhood and heroism of all soldiers on both sides. "I love the memory of a soldier," said Catlin. "I love the very dust that covers his mouldering body." Catlin called on all to be "exultant" that slavery was dead. "Is this not enough?" he asked. "Is it not enough that we are all American citizens, that our country is saved, that our country is one?" In this doctrine of "enough," the emancipationist legacy of the war had become bad taste among gentlemen soldiers. The "divine doctrine of forgiveness and conciliation" was the order of the day.

Dissent from this Blue–Gray reconciliationist version of the war's memory, while now on the margins, was by no means silenced in the larger culture or in New York. One year later, as though they had decided to invite a direct response to Pryor and his ilk, the integrated Abraham Lincoln Post of the GAR asked Frederick Douglass to address them in Madison Square on Decoration Day. As he did on so many occasions during the last quarter of his life, Douglass rose to the challenge with fire and indignation, offering an alternative, emancipationist memory of the war. "There was a right side and a wrong side in the late war," insisted Douglass "that no sentiment ought to cause us to forget.",... The reconciliationists were using memory to send the nation down the wrong road to reunion, he believed. Douglass had no patience for endless tales of Southern woes. "The South has suffered to be sure," he said, "but she has been the author of her own suffering.";...

The story of Civil War memory and the ritual of Decoration Days continued well beyond 1885 with the emancipationist legacy fighting endless rearguard actions against a Blue-Gray reconciliation that was to sweep through American culture. Those who remembered the war as the rebirth of the republic in the name of racial equality would continue to do battle with the growing number who would remember it as the nation's test of manhood and the South's struggle to sustain white supremacy.

FURTHER READING

Eric Anderson and Alfred Moss, eds., *The Facts of Reconstruction* (1991).

Michael Les Benedict, *A Compromise of Principle: Congressional Republicans and Reconstruction* (1974).

Edward J. Blum, *Reforging the White Republic: Race, Religion, and American Nationalism, 1865–1898* (2005).

Laura Edwards, *Gendered Strife and Confusion: The Political Culture of Reconstruction* (1997).

Eric Foner, *A Short History of Reconstruction, 1863–1877* (1990).

Tera Hunter, *To 'Joy My Freedom: Southern Black Women's Lives and Labors After the Civil War* (1997).

Charles Lane, *The Day Freedom Died: The Colfax Massacre, the Supreme Court, and the Betrayal of Reconstruction* (2008).

Leon Litwack, *Been in the Storm So Long: The Aftermath of Slavery* (1979).

Moon Ho-Jung, *Coolies and Cane: Race, Labor, and Sugar in the Age of Emancipation* (2008).

Michael Perman, *The Road to Redemption* (1984).

Heather Cox Richardson, *The Death of Reconstruction: Race, Labor, and Politics in the Post-Civil War North* (2001).

Heather Cox Richardson, *West from Appomattox: The Reconstruction of America after the Civil War* (2008).

Jonathan Wiener, *Social Origins of the New South* (1978).

CHAPTER 2

Western Settlement and the Frontier

Nineteenth-century historian Frederick Jackson Turner described the frontier as "an area of free land" that was continually receding as American settlers moved westward. The frontier closed, he said, when settlers reached the outer limit of the western wilds, which had "constituted the richest free gift that was ever spread out before civilized man." In Turner's portrayal, the West was an empty landscape that was gradually peopled. It was also the place where a uniquely American identity was forged: individualistic but cooperative, and deeply egalitarian. Today, historians view the frontier very differently. To them, a frontier is not a line marking the start of an empty place but a zone of interaction where two or more societies vie for the use of land. A frontier "opens" when one human group intrudes upon another, and "closes" when one of them establishes cultural or economic dominance. The process is often a brutal one.

The Civil War spurred the opening of the Far West by removing southern resistance to settlement of the territories by "free labor." In 1862, in the midst of the war, the Republican-dominated Congress passed the Homestead Act. This legislation offered 160 acres of western public land free of charge to any citizen who was over the age of twenty-one or who headed a family, so long as he or she stayed on the land for five continuous years. Congress also funded the first transcontinental railroad in 1862, the Union Pacific. These two events placed Indians, soldiers, freed slaves, migrants from the East, and immigrants from Europe and Asia in conflict for the following four decades.

The clash between these competing peoples led to murder and massacre during the last quarter of the nineteenth century. Military spending on the Indian wars amounted to 60 percent of the federal budget in 1880. The U.S.-Indian wars reached their climax and ended with the defeat of the Sioux under Sitting Bull in 1881 and the Apaches under Geronimo in 1886, at a cost of twenty-five white soldiers for every Indian warrior killed. But the frontier still remained open. "Whites" battled the Chinese, Mormons and "gentiles" vied for resources, and Indians struggled to hold onto their diminishing lands and rights well into the twentieth century. Native Americans, as well as Norwegians, Germans, Czechs, Mexicans, Chinese, African Americans, and numerous other peoples from around the globe struggled to sustain their cultures and establish safe homesteads. All vied for the territory "pacified" by the U.S. cavalry.

They also sometimes warred against the land itself. In the arid West, the water neces-
sary to sustain life was scarce. To the migrants, land was worth something only to the
extent it could be used for agriculture or mining. When they weren't fighting over territory,
natives and newcomers competed for resources. In the process, the romantic "West" of
Frederick Jackson Turner became part of the global, industrial economy.

 ## QUESTIONS TO THINK ABOUT

"Westerns" (both movies and novels) told generations of Americans "how the
West was won." Is frontier settlement best understood as the story of competing
ethnic, religious, and racial groups—or is it best understood as the place where
capitalism made its mark? Was the West truly the place where Americans were
most individualistic, democratic, and "free," as Turner argued, or was it actually
riddled with inequalities? And which had the greater effect on transforming the
West: individual or corporate enterprise?

DOCUMENTS

The following documents reveal a variety of perspectives on the western migration. Document 1 is Brigham Young's letter to the Mormon faithful he left behind to break ground at Salt Lake City in his absence. Among other things, he
urges them to work together to protect their water resources. Document 2 is a
popular song that expresses deep hostility towards "queer" Mormons in Utah
and an urge to tie Young "unto a stake." In document 3, Katie Bighead, a
Cheyenne woman who witnessed the massacre of U.S. troops under General
George Armstrong Custer, notes the superiority of arrows over guns in an ambush. The Commissioner of Indian Affairs expresses confidence in document 4
that the army will soon prevail over native warriors, but says that in the future
Indians should be given individual parcels of land to make them into farmers
(and release even more territory for whites). Chief Joseph of the Nez Percé,
the tribe that came to the aid of the Lewis and Clark expedition seventy years
earlier and that had welcomed teachers and missionaries, evokes the tragedy of
American expansionism in his famous surrender speech of 1877, document 5.
Document 6 shows that the struggle for land was not just between Indians and
settlers of European extraction. The North American frontier attracted peoples
from three continents. Miners in Wyoming responded violently to the perceived
threat of Chinese laborers, struggling to make new lives on the frontier. Document 7, an act of Congress, reveals that siphoning off the Indians' water resources went hand-in-hand with allotting them individual farming plots in
"severalty," as the practice was called. Historian Frederick Jackson Turner helped
to create the image of the romantic West, where (white) men were strong,
women virtuous, and democracy triumphant. In his 1893 statement (document 8),
Turner described the effects of the frontier both on democracy and on the

American personality. He also pronounced the frontier "closed." In document 9, a former slave, aged 97 years, recalls the primitive frontier as a place of opportunity. Settling it was the work of a lifetime.

1. Brigham Young Exhorts Mormon Pioneers to Plant and Irrigate, 1847

We have now fulfilled the mission on which we were sent, by selecting and pointing out to you a beautiful site for a city [Salt Lake City, Utah], which is destined to be a place of refuge for the oppressed, and one that is calculated to please the eye, to cheer the hearts and fill the hungry soul with food. At present … our duty calls us to return to our families, and the Saints who are far hence, who, like most of you, have been driven from their homes by a wicked mob; and who are now scattered on the Prairies and in the wilderness, yet desiring to learn your situation and longing to become once more one with you….

While with you we used the utmost diligence to erect a Fort, of sufficient size to contain houses for all who will be at the city the coming winter, and we hope the brethren will not relax their exertion until the fortification is completed, and the houses therein with all their necessary fixtures for health and convenience….

If all things remain quiet until spring as we anticipate, we recommend that the cattle yard within the fort be plowed and prepared in the best possible manner for gardens and a just portion thereof allotted to each family for a garden, so that your women and children may plant, and till, and water, and gather of the fruits thereof without being exposed abroad; for this and all domestic purposes, you will turn a portion of the City Creek within the walls of the fort, and pass it round at a convenient distance on every side….

A sun dried brick wall eight feet high is considered the best farming fence in our present situation. It is desirable that the brethren unite their labors so as to enclose their farming lands in large tracts, every one fencing in proportion to the land he agrees to occupy: thus much land may be enclosed with little labor…. Otherwise you may expect that your crops will be removed or trampled upon by the Indians and their horses; the last four feet may be built after planting, provided time would not admit previously….

We would remind the brethren that … you are located in a new country and untried climate, and as we know the drouth [drought] to be great in the latter part of summer, we recommend that you begin to plant and sow such seeds as soon as the snow is gone in the Spring, or even before Spring, so that we may know by experiments whether it is possible to ripen grain in the Valley before the summer's drouth shall demand the labor of irrigation….

Should irrigation be found necessary, the *City Creek* will yield an abundance of water for that purpose, and it is wisdom that you should provide for any such

Epistle to the Saints in the Great Salt Lake Valley from Brigham Young, September 9, 1847, Church History Library, Church of Jesus Christ of Latter Day Saints, Salt Lake City, Utah.

contingency. We would therefore recommend that you prepare pools, vats, tanks, reservoirs and ditches on the highest points of land in your field or fields that may be filled during the night, and be drawn off to any point you may find necessary, thro' a tight and permanent gate prepared for that purpose, when it shall have become sufficiently warm, so as not to check vegetation....

It is very important that the water of the *City Creek* should be preserved pure as possible, and that no mills be placed thereon, and the appropriation of all water privileges will be by the Council....

If the Saints will all hearken to counsel and work righteousness, they shall be blessed, and it is the duty of the council to break every yoke, to lighten every burden, to let the oppressed go free, to see that justice is administered to all, that righteousness may run down your streets like the overflowing stream....

Your present location is designed to you for a city of refuge, a place of rest, therefore see to it that ye pollute not your inheritance....

2. Irish Vocalist Sings of Slaying the Mormon "King," c. 1865

Oh hark kind friends while I do sing,
About Brigham Young the Mormon King,
Who swears that he'll do everything,
    Out in Salt Lake City.

He also says we'll rue the day,
That e'er we came into his way,
For all of us he'll surely slay,
    Out in Salt Lake City.

Poor Brigham's mind it can't be right,
Or else he's surely lost his sight,
To think he'd a Yankee 'fright,
    Away from Salt Lake City.

CHORUS. Old Brigham mind your P's and Q's,
    Or we will show you what to do,
    If we get our hands on you,
        Out in Salt Lake City.

Old Brigham he has somewhere's near,
About seventy wives and children dear,
Oh Lor' they must be very queer,
    Out in Salt Lake City.

Note: This song also found in Richard Lingenfelter, *Songs of the American West* (UC Berkeley, 1968), p. 214

"The Mormon King" by G. W. Anderson (New York: J. Andrews), c. 1865.

They say their children are quite tall,

And like their father loudly squall,

And often make old Brigham bawl,

> Out in Salt Lake City.

If that's the case some future day,

We'll make him bawl another way,

For his motley crew we'll surely slay,

> Out in Salt Lake City....

If any fuss he goes to make,

The whole of his city we will take,

And then fasten him unto a stake,

> Out in Salt Lake City.

3. Katie Bighead (Cheyenne) Remembers Custer and the Battle of Little Big Horn, 1876

I was with the Southern Cheyennes during most of my childhood and young womanhood. I was in the camp beside the Washita river, in the country the white people call Oklahoma, when Custer and his soldiers came there and fought the Indians (November, 1868). Our Chief Black Kettle and other Cheyennes, many of them women and children, were killed that day. It was early in the morning when the soldiers began the shooting. There had been a big storm, and there was snow on the ground. All of us jumped from our beds, and all of us started running to get away. I was barefooted, as were almost all of the others. Our tepees and all of our property we had to leave behind were burned by the white men.

The next spring Custer and his soldiers found us again (March, 1869). We then were far westward, on a branch of what the white people call Red river, I think. That time there was no fighting. Custer smoked the peace pipe with our chiefs. He promised never again to fight the Cheyennes, so all of us followed him to a soldier fort (Fort Sill). Our people gave him the name Hi-es-tzie, meaning Long Hair.

I saw Long Hair many times during those days. One time I was close to where he was mounting his horse to go somewhere, and I took a good look at him. He had a large nose, deep-set eyes, and light-red hair that was long and wavy. He was wearing a buckskin suit and a big white hat. I was then a young woman, 22 years old, and I admired him. All of the Indian women talked of him as being a fine-looking man.

My cousin, a young woman named Me-o-tzi, went often with him to help in finding the trails of Indians. She said he told her his soldier horses were given plenty of corn and oats to eat, so they could outrun and catch the Indians riding

As told to Thomas B. Marquis, reprinted in Thomas B. Marquis, *Custer on the Little Bighorn* (Algonac, Mich.: Reference Publications, 1986), 35–43.

ponies that had only grass to eat. All of the Cheyennes liked her, and all were glad she had so important a place in life. After Long Hair went away, different ones of the Cheyenne young men wanted to marry her. But she would not have any of them. She said that Long Hair was her husband, that he had promised to come back to her, and that she would wait for him. She waited seven years. Then he was killed....

I had seen other battles, in past times. I always liked to watch the men fighting. Not many women did that, and I often was teased on account of it. But this time [at the battle of Little Big Horn] I had a good excuse, for White Bull's son, my nephew, named Noisy Walking, had gone. I was but twenty-nine years old, so I had not any son to serve as a warrior, but I would sing strongheart songs for the nephew. He was eighteen years old. Some women told me he had expected me to be there, and he had wrapped a red scarf about his neck in order that I might know him from a distance....

The Indians were using bows and arrows more than they were using guns. Many of them had no guns, and not many who did have them had also plenty of bullets. But even if they had been well supplied with both guns and bullets, in that fight the bow was better. As the soldier ridge sloped on all sides, and as there were no trees on it nor around it, the smoke from each gun fired showed right where the shooter was hidden. The arrows made no smoke, so it could not be seen where they came from. Also, since a bullet has to go straight out from the end of a gun, any Indian who fired his gun had to put his head up so his eyes could see where to aim it. By doing this his head might be seen by a soldier and hit by a soldier bullet. The Indian could keep himself at all times out of sight when sending arrows. Each arrow was shot far upward and forward, not at any soldier in particular, but to curve down and fall where they were. Bullets would not do any harm if shot in that way. But a rain of arrows from thousands of Indian bows, and kept up for a long time, would hit many soldiers and their horses by falling and sticking into their heads or their backs...

I may have seen Custer at the time of the battle or after he was killed. I do not know, as I did [not] then know of his being there....

But I learned something more about him from our people in Oklahoma. Two of those Southern Cheyenne women who had been in our camp at the Little Bighorn told of having been on the battlefield soon after the fighting ended. They saw Custer lying dead there. They had known him in the South. While they were looking at him some Sioux men came and were about to cut up his body. The Cheyenne women, thinking of Me-o-tzi, made signs, "He is a relative of ours," but telling nothing more about him. So the Sioux men cut off only one joint of a finger. The women then pushed the point of a sewing awl into each of his ears, into his head. This was done to improve his hearing, as it seemed he had not heard what our chiefs in the South said when he smoked the pipe with them. They told him then that if ever afterward he should break that peace promise and should fight the Cheyennes the Everywhere Spirit surely would cause him to be killed.

Through almost sixty years, many a time I have thought of Hi-es-tzie as the handsome man I saw in the South. And I often have wondered if, when I was riding among the dead where he was lying, my pony may have kicked dirt upon his body.

4. Commissioner of Indian Affairs
Recommends Severalty and Discusses Custer, 1876

SIR: I have the honor to submit herewith, in accordance with law, the annual report of the Indian Office, accompanied by the reports of its superintendents and agents. These reports give detailed statements of the condition of the Indian tribes, and the progress which has been made during the past year, and indicate that the condition of this branch of the public service is steadily becoming more efficient and satisfactory.

The management of Indian affairs is always attended with much of difficulty and embarrassment. In every other department of the public service, the officers of the Government conduct business mainly with civilized and intelligent men. The Indian Office, in representing the Government, has to deal mainly with an uncivilized and unintelligent people, whose ignorance, superstition, and suspicion materially increase the difficulty both of controlling and assisting them....

From the first settlement of the country by white men until a comparatively recent period, the Indians have been constantly driven westward from the Atlantic. A zigzag, ever-varying line, more or less definitely marked, extending from Canada to the Gulf of Mexico, and always slowly moving west, has been known as the "frontier" or "border." Along this border has been an almost incessant struggle, the Indians to retain and the whites to get possession; the war being broken by periods of occasional and temporary peace, which usually followed treaties whereby the Indians agreed to surrender large tracts of their lands. This peace would continue until the lands surrendered had been occupied by whites, when the pressure of emigration would again break over the border, and the Indian, by force or treaty, be compelled to surrender another portion of his cherished hunting grounds....

No new hunting-grounds remain, and the civilization or the utter destruction of the Indians is inevitable. The next twenty-five years are to determine the fate of a race. If they cannot be taught, and taught very soon, to accept the necessities of their situation and begin in earnest to provide for their own wants by labor in civilized pursuits, they are destined to speedy extinction....

They can and do learn to labor; they can and do learn to read. Many thousands to-day are engaged in civilized occupations. But the road out of barbarism is a long and difficult one....

I have arrived at the conviction that the welfare and progress of the Indians require the adoption of three principles of policy:

First. Concentration of all Indians on a few reservations.
Second. Allotment to them of lands in severalty.
Third. Extension over them of United States law and the jurisdiction of United States courts....

J. Q. Smith, *Annual Report of the Commissioner of Indian Affairs to the Secretary of the Interior* (Washington: Government Printing office, 1876).

By the concentration of Indians on a few reservations, it is obvious that much of the difficulty now surrounding the Indian question will vanish.... The sale of liquors and arms could be more effectually prevented; bad white men could more easily be kept out of the Indian country; necessary supplies could be more cheaply furnished; a far smaller military force would be required to keep the peace; and generally, the Indians, being more compact, could be more efficiently aided and controlled by the officers of the Government. More-over, large bodies of land would be thrown open to [white] settlement, proceeds of whose sale would be ample to defray all expense of the removals.

Allotments in Severalty

It is doubtful whether any high degree of civilization is possible without individual ownership of land. The records of the past and the experience of the present testify that the soil should be made secure to the individual by all the guarantees which law can devise, and that nothing less will induce men to put forth their best exer-tions. No general law exists which provides that Indians shall select allotments in severalty, and it seems to me a matter of great moment that provision should be made not only permitting, but requiring, the head of each Indian family, to accept the allotment of a reasonable amount of land, to be the property of himself and his lawful heirs, in lieu of any interest in any common tribal possession....

By treaty the Government has ceded to the so-called civilized tribes, the Cherokees, Choctaws, Chickasaws, Creeks, and Seminoles, a section of country altogether disproportionate in amount to their needs.... The question is thus directly raised whether an extensive section of fertile country is to be allowed to remain for an indefinite period practically an uncultivated waste, or whether the Government shall determine to reduce the size of the reservations.

The question is plainly a difficult one, and should be considered with calm-ness, and a full purpose to do no injustice to the Indians.... Public necessity must ultimately become supreme law; and in my opinion their highest good will re-quire these people to take ample allotments of lands in severalty, (to be inalien-able for at least twenty years, and then only among Indians,) and to surrender the remainder of their lands to the United States Government....

The Sioux War

For several years past a camp of Sioux on the Yellowstone River have been known as the northern, or hostile, or non-treaty Sioux, or more commonly as Sitting Bull's band. They are in no sense a recognized band or branch of the great Sioux Nation, but consist of representatives from all the bands, who have rallied around one as their leader who claims never to have been party to any treaty with the United States....

Having their headquarters in the center of the buffalo-country, surrounded by abundance of game, independent of the aid of the Government, scorning its au-thority, defying its power, and deriding its Army, these desperadoes have skillfully and successfully evaded the frontier-garrisons and roamed at will over the plains of

Western Dakota and portions of Montana and Wyoming, not only plundering, robbing, and frequently taking the lives of settlers, but extending their hostilities to every tribe of Indians in their vicinity friendly to the United States.

That the Crows, the Shoshones, Bannacks, Arickarees, Mandans, Utes, and the Blackfeet Nation have braved all threats and resisted all inducements offered by these adventurers, and, in spite of repeated losses by depredation, have steadfastly adhered to their friendship to the Government, has sufficiently proved their loyalty; but their pathway to civilization has been seriously obstructed. An Indian cannot be taught to work with a hoe in one hand and gun in the other....

The increase in the number of Sitting Bull's retainers by accessions from the agency Sioux, already alluded to, and the terrible slaughter of our forces under General Custer, the details of which are familiar to the public, have extended throughout the year what was expected be a campaign of but few weeks' duration. It is hoped that the coming winter-campaign, for which extensive preparations are now in progress, will result in the unconditional surrender and entire submission of these Sioux, and that this will be known hereafter as the last Indian war.

5. Chief Joseph (Nez Percé) Surrenders, 1877

Tell General Howard I know what is in his heart. What he told me before, I have in my heart. I am tired of fighting. Our chiefs are killed. Looking Glass is dead. Tulhulhutsut is dead. The old men are all dead. It is the young men who say yes or no. He who led the young men is dead. It is cold and we have no blankets. The little children are freezing to death. My people, some of them, have run away to the hills and have no blankets, no food; no one knows where they are—perhaps freezing to death. I want to have time to look for my children and see how many of them I can find. Maybe I shall find them among the dead. Hear me, my chiefs. I am tired; my heart is sick and sad. From where the sun now stands I will fight no more, forever.

6. Wyoming Gunfight: An Attack on Chinatown, 1885

ROCK SPRINGS, WYO., September 18,1885.

HON. HUANG SIH CHUEN,
Chinese Consul:

YOUR HONOR: We, the undersigned, have been in Rock Springs, Wyoming Territory, for periods ranging from one to fifteen years, for the purpose of working on the railroads and in the coal mines.

As quoted in Allen P. Slickpoo, *Noon-Nee-Me-Poo: We, the Nez Perce* (Lapwi, Idaho: Nez Perce Tribe, 1973), 193–194.

House, *Providing Indemnity to Certain Chinese Subjects,* 49th Cong., 1st Sess., 1886, 26–29.

Up to the time of the recent troubles we had worked along with the white men, and had not had the least ill-feeling against them. The officers of the companies employing us treated us and the white men kindly, placing both races on the same footing and paying the same wages.

Several times we had been approached by the white men and requested to join them in asking the companies for an increase in the wages of all, both Chinese and white men. We inquired of them what we should do if the companies refused to grant an increase. They answered that if the companies would not increase our wages we should all strike, then the companies would be obliged to increase our wages. To this we dissented, wherefore we excited their animosity against us.

During the past two years there has been in existence in "Whitemen's Town," Rock Springs, an organization composed of white miners, whose object was to bring about the expulsion of all Chinese from the Territory. To them or to their object we have paid no attention. About the month of August of this year notices were posted up, all the way from Evanston to Rock Springs, demanding the expulsion of the Chinese, &c....

About 2 o'clock in the afternoon [of September 2] a mob, divided into two gangs, came toward "Chinatown," one gang coming by way of the plank bridge, and the other by way of the railroad bridge....

Whenever the mob met a Chinese they stopped him, and pointing a weapon at him, asked him if he had a revolver, and then approaching him they searched his person, robbing him of his watch or any gold or silver that he might have about him, before letting him go. Some of the rioters would let a Chinese go after depriving him of all his gold and silver, while another Chinese would be beaten with the butt ends of the weapons before being let go. Some of the rioters, when they could not stop a Chinese, would shoot him dead on the spot, and then search and rob him. Some would overtake a Chinese, throw him down and search and rob him before they would let him go. Some of the rioters would not fire their weapons, but would only use the butt ends to beat the Chinese with. Some would not beat a Chinese, but rob him of whatever he had and let him go, yelling to him to go quickly. Some, who took no part either in beating or robbing the Chinese, stood by, shouting loudly and laughing and clapping their hands.

There was a gang of women that stood at the "Chinatown" end of the plank bridge and cheered; among the women, two of them each fired successive shots...

Some of the Chinese were killed at the bank of Bitter Creek, some near the railroad bridge, and some in "Chinatown." After having been killed, the dead bodies of some were carried to the burning buildings and thrown into the flames. Some of the Chinese who had hid themselves in the houses were killed and their bodies burned; some, who on account of sickness could not run, were burned alive in the houses. One Chinese was killed in "Whitemen's Town" in a laundry house, and his house demolished. The whole number of Chinese killed was twenty-eight and those wounded fifteen.

7. Congress "Relieves" Mission Indians... of Their Water, 1891

Be it enacted by the Senate and House of Representatives of the United States of America in Congress assembled, that immediately after the passage of this act the Secretary of the Interior shall appoint three disinterested persons as commissioners to arrange a just and satisfactory settlement of the Mission Indians residing in the State of California, upon reservations which shall be secured to them as hereinafter provided.

SEC. 2. That it shall be the duty of said commissioners to select a reservation for each band or village of the Mission Indians residing within said State, which reservation shall include, as far as practicable, the lands and villages which have been in the actual occupation and possession of said Indians, and which shall be sufficient in extent to meet their just requirements,...

That whenever any of the Indians residing upon any reservation patented under the provisions of this act shall, in the opinion of the Secretary of the Interior, be so advanced in civilization as to be capable of owning and managing land in severalty, the Secretary of the Interior may cause allotments to be made to such Indians as follows: To each head of family not more than six hundred and forty acres nor less than one hundred and sixty acres....

That previous to the issuance of a patent for any reservation as provided in section three of this act the Secretary of the Interior may authorize any citizen of the United States, firm, or corporation to construct a flume, ditch, canal, pipe, or other appliances for the conveyance of water over, across, or through such reservation for agricultural, manufacturing, or other purposes, upon condition that the Indians owning or occupying such reservation or reservations shall, at all times during such ownership or occupation, be supplied with sufficient quantity of water for irrigating and domestic purposes....

8. Historian Frederick Jackson Turner Articulates the "Frontier Thesis," 1893

The American frontier is sharply distinguished from the European frontier—a fortified boundary line running through dense populations. The most significant thing about the American frontier is, that it lies at the hither edge of free land. In the census reports it is treated as the margin of that settlement which has a density of two or more to the square mile....

In the settlement of America we have to observe how European life entered the continent, and how America modified and developed that life and reacted on Europe. Our early history is the study of European germs developing in an American environment. Too exclusive attention has been paid by institutional students to the Germanic origins, too little to the American factors. The frontier is the line of most rapid and effective Americanization. The wilderness masters

An Act for the Relief of the Mission Indians in the State of California, Statutes at Large 26, 712-14, Native American Documents Project, California State University, San Marcos, Document A1891B. Located at http://www2.csusm.edu/nadp/

Reprinted in Ray Allen Billington. ed. *The Frontier Thesis: Valid Interpretation of American History?* (New York: Robert Krieger, 1977), 10–20.

the colonist. It finds him a European in dress, industries, tools, modes of travel, and thought. It takes him from the railroad car and puts him in the birch canoe. It strips off the garments of civilization and arrays him in the hunting shirt and the moccasin. It puts him in the log cabin of the Cherokee and Iroquois and runs an Indian palisade around him. Before long he has gone to planting Indian corn and plowing with a sharp stick; he shouts the war cry and takes the scalp in orthodox Indian fashion. In short, at the frontier the environment is at first too strong for the man. He must accept the conditions which it furnishes, or perish, and so he fits himself into the Indian clearings and follows the Indian trails. Little by little he transforms the wilderness, but the outcome is not the old Europe.... The fact is, that here is a new product that is American. At first, the frontier was the Atlantic coast. It was the frontier of Europe in a very real sense. Moving westward, the frontier became more and more American....

But the most important effect of the frontier has been in the promotion of democracy here and in Europe. As has been indicated, the frontier is productive of individualism. Complex society is precipitated by the wilderness into a kind of primitive organization based on the family. The tendency is anti-social. It produces antipathy to control, and particularly to any direct control.... The frontier individualism has from the beginning promoted democracy....

From the conditions of frontier life came intellectual traits of profound importance. The works of travelers along each frontier from colonial days onward describe certain common traits, and these traits have, while softening down, still persisted as survivals in the place of their origin, even when a higher social organization succeeded. The result is that to the frontier the American intellect owes its striking characteristics. That coarseness and strength combined with acuteness and inquisitiveness; that practical, inventive turn of mind, quick to find expedients; that masterful grasp of material things, lacking in the artistic but powerful to effect great ends; that restless, nervous energy; that dominant individualism, working for good and for evil, and withal that buoyancy and exuberance which comes with freedom—these are traits of the frontier, or traits called out elsewhere because of the existence of the frontier.... What the Mediterranean Sea was to the Greeks, breaking the bond of custom, offering new experiences, calling out new institutions and activities, that, and more, the ever retreating frontier has been to the United States directly, and to the nations of Europe more remotely. And now, four centuries from the discovery of America, at the end of a hundred years of life under the Constitution, the frontier has gone, and with its going has closed the first period of American history.

9. An Ex-Slave Recalls His Migration Across the Prairie, 1936

"My name is Bill Simms.

I was born in Osceola, Missouri, March 16, 1839.

Interview with Bill Simms, *Slave Narratives: A Folk History of Slavery in the United States from Interviews with Former Slaves*, works Project Administration (Project Gutenberg). Obtained from http://infomotions.com/etexts/gutenberg /dirs/1/1/ 4/8/11485.htm.

I lived on the farm with my mother, and my master, whose name was Simms. I had an older sister, about two years older than I was. Master needed some money so he sold her, and I have never seen her since, except just a time or two.

On the plantation we raised cows, sheep, cotton, tobacco, corn, which were our principal crops. There was plenty of wild hogs, turkey, and deer and other game. The deer used to come up and feed with the cattle in the feed yards, and we could get all the wild hogs we wanted by simply shooting them in the timber.

A man who owned ten slaves was considered wealthy, and if he got hard up for money, he would advertise and sell some slaves.... We never knew what boughten clothes were. I learned to make shoes when I was just a boy and I made the shoes for the whole family. I used to chop wood and make rails and do all kinds of farm work.

I had a good master, most of the masters were good to their slaves. When a slave got too old to work they would give him a small cabin on the plantation and have the other slaves to wait on him. They would furnish him with victuals, and clothes until he died....

Slaves were never allowed to talk to white people other than their masters or someone their master knew, as they were afraid the white man might have the slave run away. The masters aimed to keep their slaves in ignorance and the ignorant slaves were all in favor of the Robel army, only the more intelligent were in favor of the Union army.

When the war started, my master sent me to work for the Confederate army. I worked most of the time for three years off and on, hauling cannons, driving mules, hauling ammunition, and provisions. The Union army pressed in on us and the Rebel army moved back. I was sent home. When the Union army came close enough I ran away from home and joined the Union army... until the war ended. Then I returned home to my old master, who had stayed there with my mother. My master owned about four hundred acres of good land, and had had ten slaves. Most of the slaves stayed at home.... My master's wife had been dead for several years and they had no children. The nearest relative being a nephew. They wanted my master's land and was afraid he would give it all away to us slaves, so they killed him, and would have killed us if we had stayed at home. I took my mother and ran into the adjoining, Claire County. We settled there and stayed for sometime, but I wanted to see Kansas, the State I had heard so much about.

I couldn't get nobody to go with me, so I started out afoot across the prairies for Kansas. After I got some distance from home it was all prairie. I had to walk all day long following buffalo trail. At night I would go off a little ways from the trail and lay down and sleep. In the morning I'd wake up and could see nothing but the sun and prairie. Not a house, not a tree, no living thing, not even could I hear a bird. I had little to eat, I had a little bread in my pocket. I didn't even have a pocket knife, no weapon of any kind.... It was in the spring of the year in June. I came to Lawrence, Kansas, where I stayed two years working on the farm. In 1874 I went to work for a man by the month at $35 a month and I made more money than the owner did, because the grasshoppers ate up the crops....

My master's name was Simms and I was known as Simm's Bill, just like horses. When I came out here I just changed my name from Simm's Bill, to Bill Simms.

Ottawa was very small at the time I came here, and there were several Indians close by that used to come to town. The Indians held their war dance on what is now the courthouse grounds. I planted the trees that are now standing on the courthouse grounds....

The people lived pretty primitive. We didn't have kerosene. Our only lights were tallow candles, mostly grease lamps, they were just a pan with grease in it, and one end of the rag dragging out over the side which we would light. There were no sewers at that time.

I had no chance to go to school when a boy, but after I came to Kansas I was too old to go to school, and I had to work, but I attended night school, and learned to read and write and figure....

I was married when I was about thirty years old. I married a slave girl from Georgia. Back in Missouri, if a slave wanted to marry a woman on another plantation he had to ask the master, and if both masters agreed they were married. The man stayed at his owners, and the wife at her owners. He could go to see her on Saturday night and Sunday....

My wife died when we had three children. She had had to work hard all her life and she said she didn't want her children to have to work as hard as she had, and I promised her on her death bed, that I would educate our girls. So I worked and sent the girls to school. My two girls both graduated from Ottawa university, the oldest one being the first colored girl to ever graduate from that school. After graduation she went to teach school in Oklahoma, but only got twenty-five dollars a month, and I had to work and send her money to pay her expenses. The younger girl also graduated and went to teach school, but she did not teach school long, until she married a well-to-do farmer in Oklahoma. The older girl got her wages raised until she got one hundred and twenty-five dollars per month. I have worked at farm work and tree husbandry all my life. My oldest daughter bought me my first suit of clothes I ever had."

ESSAYS

The western frontier looms large in the history of the United States. Historians like Frederick Jackson Turner and Theodore Roosevelt helped to enshrine the frontier experience by portraying the West as the rough-and-tumble setting in which Americans forged their commitment to political democracy and social equality. Whether one agrees with this may depend on whether one sees the drama as featuring a multiethnic cast, or as being primarily a tale of Anglo-American expansion and the commercial exploitation of natural resources. Today, historians debate the largest meanings of the Frontier for the transformation of America. Patricia Nelson Limerick of the University of Colorado at Boulder speaks for a generation of "new western historians" when she argues that western settlement was continuously multiethnic and fundamentally antidemocratic. Donald Worster speaks for a growing school of scholars who look upon the West as the cutting edge of global capitalism, and mourn what it did to the natural environment.

The Frontier as a Place of Ethnic and Religious Conflict

PATRICIA NELSON LIMERICK

In 1871 an informal army of Arizona civilians descended on a peaceful camp and massacred over one hundred Apaches, mostly women and children. Who were the attackers at Camp Grant? The usual images of Western history would suggest one answer: white men. In fact, the attackers were a consortium of Hispanics, Anglo-Americans, and Papago Indians. However different the three groups might have been, they could agree on the matter of Apaches and join in interracial cooperation. Hostility between Apaches and Papagoes, and between Apaches and Hispanics, had in fact begun long before conflict between Apaches and Anglo-Americans.

In the popular imagination, the frontier froze as a biracial confrontation between "whites" and "Indians." More complex questions of race relations seemed to be the terrain of other regions' histories. The history of relations between blacks and whites centered in the South, while "ethnic conflict" suggested the crowded cities of the Northeast, coping with floods of immigrants in the late nineteenth and early twentieth centuries. As blacks moved north and European immigrants crossed the Atlantic, new populations put the adaptability of American society to the test. Could native Americans of northern European stock tolerate these "others"? Was it better to deal with them through assimilation or through exclusion? How could old-stock Americans defend their valued "purity" against these foreign threats?

These are familiar themes in the history of the Southern and Northeastern United States, but ethnic conflict was not exclusive to the East. Western America shared in the transplanted diversity of Europe. Expansion involved peoples of every background: English, Irish, Cornish, Scottish, French, German, Portuguese, Scandinavian, Greek, and Russian. To that diversity, the West added a persistent population of Indians, with a multitude of languages and cultures; an established Hispanic population, as well as one of later Mexican immigrants; Asians, to whom the American West was the East; black people, moving west in increasing numbers in the twentieth century; and Mormons, Americans who lived for a time in isolation, evolving a distinctive culture from the requirements of their new faith. Put the diverse humanity of Western America into one

Patricia Nelson Limerick, *The Legacy of Conquest: The Unbroken Past of the American West* (New York: Norton, 1987), 259–264, 277–291. Copyright © 1987 by Patricia Nelson Limerick. Used by Permission of W.W. Norton & Company, Inc.

picture, and the "melting pot" of the Eastern United States at the turn of the century begins to look more like a family reunion, a meeting of groups with an essential similarity—dominantly European, Judeo-Christian, accustomed to the existence of the modern state.

The diversity of the West put a strain on the simpler varieties of racism. In another setting, categories dividing humanity into superior white and inferior black were comparatively easy to steer by. The West, however, raised questions for which racists had no set answers. Were Indians better than blacks—more capable of civilization and assimilation—perhaps even suitable for miscegenation? Were Mexicans essentially Indians? Did their European heritage count for anything? Were "mongrel" races even worse than other "pure" races? Where did Asians fit in the racial ranking? Were they humble, menial workers—or representatives of a great center of civilization, art, and, best of all, trade? Were the Japanese different from, perhaps more tolerable than, the Chinese? What about southern and eastern Europeans? When Greek workers in the mines went on strike and violence followed, was this race war or class war? Western diversity forced racists to think—an unaccustomed activity.

Over the twentieth century, writers of Western history succumbed to the easy temptation, embracing a bipolar West composed of "whites" and "Indians." Relations between the two groups shrank, moreover, to a matter of whites meeting obstacles and conquering them. Fought and refought in books and film, those "colorful" Indian wars raged on. Meanwhile, the sophisticated questions, the true study of American race relations, quietly slipped into the province of historians who studied other parts of the country.

In 1854, in the case of *People v. Hall,* California Supreme Court Chief Justice J. Murray demonstrated the classic dilemma of an American racist wrestling with the questions raised by Western diversity. Ruling on the right of Chinese people to testify in court against white people, Murray took up the white man's burden of forcing an intractable reality back into a unified racist theory.

No statute explicitly addressed the question of Chinese testimony, but Murray found another route to certainty. State law, he argued, already prevented blacks, mulattoes, and Indians from testifying as witnesses "in any action or proceeding in which a white person is a party." Although state law did not refer explicitly to Asians, this was, Murray argued, an insignificant omission. Columbus, he said, had given the name "Indians" to North American natives while under the impression that he was in Asia and the people before him were Asians. "Ethnology," having recently reached a "high point of perfection," disclosed a hidden truth in Columbus's error. It now seemed likely that "this country was first peopled by Asiatics." From Columbus's time, then, "American Indians and the Mongolian, or Asiatic, were regarded as the same type of the human species." Therefore, it could be assumed, the exclusion of "Indians" from testifying applied to Asians as well.

Judge Murray found an even more compelling argument in the essential "degraded" similarity of nonwhite races. The laws excluding "Negroes, mulattoes, and Indians" from giving testimony had obviously been intended to "protect the white person from the influence of all testimony" from another caste.

"The use of these terms ["Negro," "mulatto," and "Indian"] must, by every sound rule of construction, exclude everyone who is not of white blood."

Concluding that Asians could not testify, Murray spelled out the "actual and present danger" he had defused. "The same rule which would admit them to testify, would admit them to all the equal rights of citizenship, and we might soon see them at the polls, in the jury box, upon the bench, and in our legislative halls." With a smoke screen of scientific racism, using anthropology, Murray thus declared the essential unity of darker mankind. He did his best to keep power, opportunity, and justice in California in the hands of God's chosen, lighter-skinned people. And he did a good job of it....

To white workingmen, post–gold rush California did not live up to its promise. Facing limited job opportunities and uncertain futures, white laborers looked both for solutions and for scapegoats. Men in California came with high hopes; jobs proved scarce and unrewarding; someone must be to blame. In California, capital had at its command a source of controllable, underpaid labor. White workers, the historian Alexander Saxton has said, "viewed the Chinese as tools of monopoly." The workers therefore "considered themselves under attack on two fronts, or more aptly from above and below." Resenting big business and resenting competition from Chinese labor, frustrated workers naturally chose to attack the more vulnerable target. The slogan "The Chinese must go" could make it through Congress and into federal law; "Big business must go" was not going to earn congressional approval.

The issue of the Chinese scapegoat became a pillar of California politics, a guaranteed vote getter. In 1879, a state referendum on the Chinese question brought out "a margin of 150,000 to 900 favoring total exclusion." Opposition to the Chinese offered unity to an otherwise diverse state; divisions between Protestants and Catholics temporarily healed; Irish immigrants could cross the barrier separating a stigmatized ethnic group from the stigmatizing majority. Popular democratic participation in the rewriting of the California constitution showed this majority at work. "[N]o native of China, no idiot, insane person, or person convicted of any infamous crime," the constitution asserted, "... shall ever exercise the privileges of an elector of this State." Moreover, in the notorious Article XIX, the framers went on to prohibit the employment "of any Chinese or Mongolian" in any public works projects below the federal level or by any corporation operating under state laws. These provisions, the historian Mary Roberts Coolidge wrote early in the twentieth century, "were not only unconstitutional but inhuman and silly." They were also directly expressive of the popular will.

"To an American death is preferable to a life on a par with a Chinaman," the manifesto of the California Workingmen's Party declared in 1876. "... Treason is better than to labor beside a Chinese slave." Extreme threat justified extreme actions; extralegal, violent harassment followed closely on violent declarations. In harassing the Chinese, white Californians did not seek to violate American ideals and values; they sought to defend them. "They call us a mob," a female organizer said, single-handedly demolishing the image of women as the "gentle tamers" of the West. "It was a mob that a fought the battle of Lexington, and a mob that threw the tea over-board in Boston harbor, but they backed their principles.... I want to see every Chinaman—white or yellow—thrown out of this state."

California may have "catalyzed and spearheaded the movement for exclusion," but, as Stuart Miller has shown, this was not a matter of a narrow sectional interest pushing the rest of the nation off its preferred course. Negative images gleaned from traders, missionaries, and diplomats in China predisposed the whole country to Sinophobia; the use of Chinese workers as strikebreakers in Eastern industries clinched the question. The 1882 Chinese Exclusion Act, a product of national consensus, met little opposition....

In their anti–Oriental crusading, white Westerners often referred to the South and its "problem." In a search for case studies of discrimination and conflict in black/white relations, they did not need to go so far afield. During the nineteenth century, black people were sparsely represented in the West. Their numerical insignificance, however, did not stop white people from being preoccupied with the issues of black migration. Despite visions of Western fresh starts and new beginnings, the South's "problem" had long ago moved West.

The extension of slavery into the Western territories had, of course, been a prime source of sectional tension before the Civil War. The struggles over the admission of new states, free or slave, had alarmed those concerned with the survival of the Union; "a firebell in the night," Thomas Jefferson called the conflicts preceding the 1820 Missouri Compromise. Fantasies of Western innocence aside, the Western territories were deeply implicated in the national struggle over slavery.

In 1850, California was admitted as a free state; in 1857, Oregon was admitted with a similar status. That fact alone can give the impressions that the Westerners were, in some principled way, opposed to slavery. That impression needs closer examination.

Most white settlers in Oregon opposed the intrusion of slavery into their territory. However, they also opposed the intrusion of free blacks. Following on earlier territorial laws, the 1857 Oregon state constitution included a provision excluding free blacks and received heavy voter support. "The object," one early Oregon leader explained, "is to *keep* clear of this most troublesome class of population. We are in a new world, under most favorable circumstances, and we wish to avoid most of these great evils that have so much afflicted the United States and other countries." To the white Oregonians, this was a principled position. The project was to create and preserve a better social order and to steer clear of the problems and mistakes that plagued other, less pure regions. Oregon's exclusion of blacks thus appeared to be "a clear victory for settlers who came to the Far West to escape the racial troubles of the East."

The particular conditions of Oregon added another reason for black exclusion. The question of the admission of free blacks, Oregon's delegate to Congress explained in 1850,

is a question of life and death to us in Oregon.... The negroes associate
with the Indians and intermarry, and, if their free ingress in encouraged

or allowed, there would a relationship spring up between them and the different tribes, and a mixed race would ensure inimical to the whites; and the Indians being led on by the negro who is better acquainted with the customs, language, and manners of the whites, than the Indian, these savages would become much formidable than they otherwise would, and long and bloody wars would be the fruits of the comingling of the races. It is the principle of self preservation that justifies the actions of the Oregon legislature.

Beyond actual armed conspiracy, white Westerners saw in black rights the first link in a chain reaction. Permit blacks a place in American political and social life, and Indians, Asians, and Hispanics would be next. Western diversity thus gave an edge of urgency to each form of prejudice; the line had to be held against each group; if the barrier was breached once, it would collapse before all the various "others." White Southerners could specialize, holding off one group; white Westerners fought in a multifront campaign.

Post–Civil War Reconstruction thus posed a challenge to the institutions of the West as well as to those of the South. Western members of Congress could often join in imposing black rights on the South; the South had rebelled, after all, and deserved punishment. One punishment was black suffrage. But imposing black suffrage on Western states that had not rebelled—that was another matter, and the occasion for another round in the westward-moving battle of states' rights.

Confronted with the Fifteenth Amendment, giving blacks the vote, both California and Oregon balked. "If we make the African a citizen," an Oregon newspaper argued in 1865, "we cannot deny the same right to the Indian or the Mongolian. Then how long would we have peace and prosperity when four races separate, distinct and antagonistic should be at the polls and contend for the control of government?" In California, opposition to the Fifteenth Amendment hinged on the prospect that suffrage without regard to "race, color or previous condition of servitude" might include the Chinese. The Fifteenth Amendment became law without ratification by California or Oregon. The Oregon legislature "in a gesture of perverse defiance rejected the amendment in October, 1870, fully six months after its incorporation into the federal Constitution." The amendment, the state senate declared, was "in violation of Oregon's sovereignty, an illegal interference by Congress in Oregon's right to establish voting qualifications, and a change in law forced on the nation by the bayonet." White Southerners might have been reduced to a state of temporary impotence, but they could take comfort in the fact that others had adopted their favored arguments.

In their ongoing preoccupation with purity, various Western State legislatures also moved to hold the line against racial mixing. California, Oregon, and— most extraordinary, in light of its current flexibility in matrimonial matters— Nevada all passed laws against miscegenation. Below the level of law, white Westerners practiced their own, more casual versions of discrimination. Labor unions excluded black workers; owners of restaurants, inns, and hotels limited their clientele; housing segregation was common. Scattered through historical records are incidents in which individual communities abruptly resolved to expel their black residents. "In 1893," Elizabeth McLagan has reported, "the citizens of Liberty, Oregon, requested that all black people leave town." In 1904, facing high unemployment, the town of Reno, Nevada, set out to reduce its problems by "arresting all unemployed blacks and forcing them to leave the city." "There are too many worthless negroes in the city," the Reno police chief explained.

In the twentieth century, as black migration from the South to the West accelerated, Western states' discriminatory laws stayed on the books. Although never consistently enforced, Oregon's prohibition on free blacks was not formally repealed until 1926. California's ban on miscegenation lasted until 1948; Nevada's remained until 1959. Oregon and California finally consented to a symbolic ratification of the Fifteenth Amendment—in 1959 and 1962, respectively....

Race, one begins to conclude, was the key factor in dividing the people of Western America. Its meanings and distinctions fluctuated, but racial feeling evidently guided white Americans in their choice of groups to persecute and exclude. Differences in culture, in language, in religion, meant something; but a physically distinctive appearance seems to have been the prerequisite for full status as a scapegoat. If this conclusion begins to sound persuasive, then the Haun's Mill Massacre restores one to a realistic confusion.

On an October day, the Missouri militia attacked a poorly defended settlement of the enemy, killed seventeen, and wounded fifteen more. One militiaman discovered a nine-year-old boy in hiding and prepared to shoot him. Another intervened. "Nits will make lice," the first man said, and killed the boy.

Is this the classic moment in an Indian massacre? The murdered boy, like the other victims at the 1838 Haun's Mill Massacre, was white—and Mormon.

In the 1830s, Missourians hated Mormons for a variety of reasons. They had unsettling religious, economic, and political practices; they were nonetheless prosperous, did not hold slaves, and could control elections by voting in a bloc. They were a peculiar people, seriously flawed to the Gentile point of view. Mormons were white, but the Missourians still played on most of the usual themes of race hatred. When the governor of Missouri suggested a war of extermination against the Mormons, he made one point clear: the absence of a racial difference could not keep white people from thoroughly hating each other.

Mormonism, moreover, was an American product. In the 1820s, in upstate New York the young Joseph Smith had brooded about American religious diversity. With so many sects making competing claims to certainty, how was the seeker to make the right choice? "I found," Smith said, "that there was a great clash in religious sentiment; if I went to one society they referred me to one plan, and another to another...." It was obvious that "all could not be right" and "that God could not be the author of so much confusion." Wrestling with this chaos, Smith began to experience revelations, he said, leading him to the acquisition of buried golden plates. Translated, the golden plates became the Book of Mormon, and the basis of a new American religion, offering the certainty of direct revelation in modern times. To its believers, Mormonism was not so much a new religion as an old one restored. Over the centuries, true Christianity had become corrupted and factionalized, broken into the competing sects that had once perplexed Smith. The Church of Latter-day Saints of Jesus Christ restored the lost unity.

Against that backdrop of sects and denominations, Mormonism offered its converts certainty and community. In Mormon doctrine, earthly labors carried a direct connection to spiritual progress; one's exertions in the material world directly reflected one's spiritual standing. With nearly every daily action "mormonized," as a later observer put it, Saints clearly had to cluster, constructing communities in which they could keep each other on track. In converting to Mormonism, one converted to a full way of life within a community of believers. In their first decade, Mormons were already on their way to becoming a new ethnic group, something new under the American sun.

As Mormon numbers grew, and the majority of the converts clustered in the Midwest, they came into increasing conflict with their Gentile neighbors. Their novel religion, their occasional experiments in communitarianism, their ability to vote in a bloc, their very separatism, made them targets for suspicion and hostility. When Joseph Smith summarized his people's experience, he could not be accused of much exaggeration: "the injustice, the wrongs, the murders, the bloodshed, the theft, misery and woe that has been caused by the barbarous, inhuman and lawless proceedings" of their enemies, especially in the state of Missouri....

When the "Indian problem" grew heated in the early nineteenth century, the remote and isolated West had presented itself as a geographical solution: place the Indians in locations white people would not want anyway, and end the friction by a strategy of segregation. Geography appeared to offer the same solution to "the Mormon problem." Relocated in the remote and arid Great Basin, the Mormons could escape persecution by a kind of spatial quarantine; the dimensions of the continent itself would guard them. Even when the gold rush broke the quarantine and when Gentiles—and even Missourians—were suddenly provoked into crossing the continent, the Mormons had had the chance to reverse the proportions and become an entrenched majority in the territory of Utah....

The aridity of Utah meant that prosperity depended on a cooperation that the Mormons, uniquely, could provide. Land might be privately held, but water and timber were held in common and allocated by church authorities. The church leadership ordained the founding of towns and farms; communally organized labor could then build the dams and ditches that made irrigation possible. In their prosperity and good order, the settlements of the Mormons impressed even those who could find nothing else to admire in this peculiar people's way of life.

That peculiarity had become suddenly more dramatic. Established in their own territory, far from disapproving neighbors, leaders had felt empowered to bring the church's peculiar domestic practice into the open. In 1852, the Mormons stood revealed as practitioners of polygamy.

For the rest of the nineteenth century, the idea of one man in possession of more than one woman would strike most non-Mormon Americans as deviant, licentious, and *very* interesting—a shocking matter of sexual excess. In fact, Mormon polygamy was a staid and solemn affair. If the patriarchal family was a good thing, if bringing children into the world to be responsibly raised in the right religion was a major goal of life, then it was a logical—and very American—conclusion that more of a good thing could only be better. The Mormon family, properly conducted through this world, would reassemble in the afterlife. Adding more personnel to this sanctified unit gave Mormon patriarchs even greater opportunity to perform their ordained function....

... For thirty years, Congress tried to make the Mormons behave. Antipolygamy laws added up to a sustained campaign to change personal behavior, a campaign without parallel except in Indian affairs....

Antipolygamy laws finally drove the Mormon leaders into hiding, concealed—in defiance of federal law—by their loyal followers. The church had been placed in receivership; cohabitation prosecutions went on apace; zealous federal agents pursued the concealed leaders. Then, on September 24, 1890, President Wilford Woodruff of the LDS issued an official manifesto, advising the Latter-day Saints "to refrain from contracting any marriage forbidden by the law of the land." The year was 1890, and one kind of frontier opportunity had indeed closed....

Whatever else it tells us, the Mormon example shows that race was not the only provocation for strong antipathies and prejudices. White people could also become aliens, targets for voyeuristic exploitation, for coercive legislation, even for the use of the U.S. Army. But, the Mormon example also shows that in the long run it paid to be white.

At the Utah statehood convention in 1895, Charles S. Varian gave a speech of reconciliation. Varian had earlier been U.S. district attorney for Utah Territory "and relentless in his prosecution of polygamy." He had, however, found the convention to be an occasion of harmony. Every member, he thought, had "been taught by his fellowmen that, after all, we are very much alike, and that the same passions, and the same motives, actuate us all."

"After all, we are very much alike"—it was a statement no one at the time made to the Chinese or the Japanese. Once polygamy had been formally settled, the "differentness" of Mormons could be subordinated and their essentially American qualities celebrated....

When it came to pitting Western people against each other, politics and economics could work as well as race or religion. When White people appeared to threaten order and prosperity, the lesson was once again clear: race was no protector from vicious conflict. Consider three examples:

- In May 1912, the middle-class citizens of San Diego, California, forcibly expelled the anarchist speakers Emma Goldman and Ben Reitman. San Diego was, in that year, "an established city of more than 40,000 people," "progressive Republican" in politics. In their radicalism and also in their association with the Wobblies, the Industrial Workers of the World, Goldman and Reitman represented a threat that the city's boosters would not tolerate. Goldman "escaped violence only by the narrowest margin," a San Diego newspaper reported. But "treatment that the vigilantes would not give the woman was accorded to the man. Reitman was mysteriously spirited away from the hotel some time near midnight … and, it is reported, tarred and feathered and branded on the back with the letters 'I.W.W.' He is furthermore said to have been forced to kneel and kiss the American flag. The branding was done with a lighted cigar, which was traced through the tar…." The concerned citizens and policemen of San Diego were not always so gentle. In other confrontations, "at least two radicals were killed."

- On April 20, 1914, the Colorado militia attacked a tent colony of strikers and their families. Both sides had guns and used them, but bullets were not the major source of injury. In the middle of the battle, the tents burst into flames. Two women and eleven children burned to death. The Ludlow massacre "climaxed a labor struggle in Colorado which erupted into a civil war all over the state."

- On November 5, 1916, two steamboats carrying Wobblies left Seattle for the town of Everett, to support a strike under way against the timber industry. Armed vigilantes and policemen tried to prevent them from landing; in the exchange of bullets, five workers and two vigilantes died, while over fifty were wounded and seven were reported missing. "The water turned crimson," one historian has written, "and corpses were washing ashore for days afterward."

The conventional approach of blaming Western violence on the "frontier environment" does not explain these incidents. Although most of the strikers at Ludlow were of southern or eastern European origin, racial or ethnic explanations of conflict are also of limited help. Judging by the written record alone, a historian blind to actual physical characteristics might think that there were at least eight oppressed races in the West: Indians, Hispanics, Chinese, Japanese, blacks, Mormons, strikers, and radicals.

Exploring the ways in which "Mexicans, Chinese and Indians were shamefully abused by the Yankee majority," [historian] Ray Allen Billington in 1956 placed the responsibility on the "corrosive effect of the environment" and "the absence of social pressures." The abuse, he said, represented "a completely undemocratic nativism."

This explanation has an innocent certainty now beyond our grasp. Nativism was only in an ideal sense "undemocratic." The California votes on Chinese exclusion and the Oregon votes on black exclusion made the voice of democracy in these matters clear. Second, blaming "the corrosive effect of the environment" for nativism involved doubtful logic; white Americans brought the raw material for these attitudes with them, with little help from the "environment." And finally, on close examination, over the duration of Western history, the very concept of "the Yankee majority" was a coherent entity only if one retreated to a great distance, from which the divisions simply could not be seen….

When the weight of Southern civilization fell too heavily on Huckleberry Finn, Mark Twain offered the preferred American alternative: "I reckon I got to light out for the Territory ahead of the rest, because Aunt Sally she's going to adopt me and sivilize me, and I can't stand it. I been there before." The West, the theory had gone, was the place where one escaped the trials and burdens of American civilization, especially in its Southern version. Those "trials and burdens" often came in human form. Repeatedly, Americans had used the West as a mechanism for evading these "problems." Much of what went under the rubric "Western optimism" was in fact this faith in postponement, in the deferring of problems to the distant future. Whether in Indian removal or Mormon migration, the theory was the same: the West is remote and vast; its isolation and distance will release us from conflict; this is where we can get away from each other. But the workings of history carried an opposite lesson. The West was not where we escaped each other, but where we all met.

The Frontier as the Forefront of Capitalism

DONALD WORSTER

In his 1862 essay "Walking," Henry David Thoreau described a daily ritual that was characteristically American in his time. Coming out of his house on Main Street in Concord, Massachusetts, he would pause for a moment to consult his instincts. Which way should he go for his ramble into the countryside? Generally the needle of his inner compass would settle west or southwest, and he would head off in that direction, just as thousands of pioneers were doing, had done, and would go on doing for a long time to come. "The future lies that way to me," he wrote, "and the earth seems more unexhausted and richer on that side." Going west, he anticipated finding a wilder America where the trees grew taller, the sun shone brighter, and the field of action was still open to fresh heroic deeds.... "Eastward I go only by force; but westward I go free."

Had Thoreau kept on walking toward the west, traveling well beyond the outskirts of Concord clear to the Pacific shore, had he walked on and on through time into the late twentieth century, what would he have discovered? Would he have come upon a West that had delivered on its promise to him and the nation? Would he have found there in fact a greater scope for individuality, for innovation, for the creative mind, than existed in the East? A people who put less emphasis on the accumulation of property, who practiced less stratification in their society? Would he have found a more perfect democracy? A flourishing of personal freedom? A vindication of the idea of progress?

Thoreau died in the year his essay appeared in print and thus he could not have seen, could not even have anticipated, the real West as it has evolved.... Even now, a century and more past Thoreau's age of romantic optimism, many westerners—not to mention millions living elsewhere—remain confused by idealizing myths and ritualistic incantations of the old slogans. The West is still supposed, in popular thinking, to be a land of untrammeled freedom, and

Donald Worster, *Rivers of Empire: Water, Aridity, and the Growth of the American West* (New York: Oxford UP, 1985), p. 3–11, 52–53, 63–64, 74–77, 83, 101, 104–107. Reprinted by permission of the Gerard McCauley Agency, Inc.

in some of its corners it may be just that. However, that is not all it is, is not even the more important part of what it is. The American West is also more consistently, and more decisively, a land of authority and restraint, of class and exploitation, and ultimately of imperial power. The time has come to brush away the obscuring mythologies and the old lost ideals and to concentrate on that achieved reality....

Perhaps the best place to begin that reexamination of the West is by sauntering along one of its irrigation ditches. In it are important, neglected clues to the meaning of freedom and autonomy, of democratic self-determination and openness, in the historical as opposed to the mythical West. One might choose, for example, the Friant-Kern Canal coming down from the Sierra foothills to the desert lands around Bakersfield in the Great Central Valley of California. It is a vastly different stream of water from the Sudbury and Concord rivers on which Thoreau paddled his boat.... Friant-Kern, in contrast, is a work of advanced artifice, a piece not of nature but of technology. It has no watershed of its own but rather draws off water from a reservoir and transports it briskly to deficient areas to raise a cash crop. It means business. For long sections it runs straight as an arrow over the land, cutting across the terrain with a devastating efficiency. Engineers report that it carries, at maximum, 5,000 cubic feet of water per second. In that method of precise calculation is hinted the determination on the part of engineers, farmers, and other modern westerners to wrest every possible return from the canal and its flow. The American West literally lives today by that determination. Though its importance has seldom been well understand, more than any other single element, it has been the shaping force in the region's history. In that determination to exploit to the uttermost, there is little of Thoreau's ideal of freedom sought or expressed or possible. There is no freedom for nature itself, for natural rivers as free-flowing entities with their own integrity and order, and there is very little of the social freedom Thoreau expected humans to enjoy in the West. Friant-Kern offers a study in ecological and social regimentation....

It is a techno-economic order imposed for the purpose of mastering a difficult environment. People here have been organized and induced to run, as the water in the canal does, in a straight line toward maximum yield, maximum profit. This American West can best be described as a modern *hydraulic society*, which is to say, a social order based on the intensive, large-scale manipulation of water and its products in an arid setting. That order is not at all what Thoreau had in mind for the region. What he desired was a society of free association, of self-defining and self-managing individuals and communities, more or less equal to one another in power and authority. The hydraulic society of the West, in contrast, is increasingly a coercive, monolithic, and hierarchical system, ruled by a power elite based on the ownership of capital and expertise. Its face is reflected in every mile of the irrigation canal. One might see in that reflection the qualities of concentrated wealth, technical virtuosity, discipline, hard work, popular acquiescence, a feeling of resignation and necessity—but one cannot find in it much of what Thoreau conceived as freedom.

Few parts of the American West, or for that matter of the world, have been changed so thoroughly as the Great Valley of California. Already at the time

Thoreau wrote of walking west, the valley was beginning to undergo an eco-logical revolution. In turn, that upheaval brought about a social transformation of extraordinary proportions. In both respects, the valley can be seen as represen-tative of an emerging West and its sudden transition, more sudden than in any other region, from wilderness to technological dominance....

When Thoreau was coming of age in Concord, a town already two hundred years old in his lifetime, the Great Valley was still an environment virtually untouched by the white man. It was the undisputed province of those wild creatures and of several Indian peoples. The latter were the Wintun, Patwin, Valley Maidu, Valley or Plains Miwok, and, most numerous, the Valley Yokut tribes, of which there were fifty, each with its own name, dialect, and territory. All of the native peoples were lumped together by the invading white Americans under the contemptuous term "Diggers."

The Spanish rarely ventured into the valley, and when they did, they were repelled by the prospect. It was too hot, dry, and bleak, or alternately too swampy, to attract them away from their coastal missions. The American fur trapper and explorer Jedediah Smith passed through in 1827, and then in 1849 came a voracious horde from the east, from all over the world, looking for gold. To protect the gold seekers from the Indians and make maps of the valley, the American government dispatched Lieutenant George Derby in 1849 and 1850. Derby was a twenty-six-year-old topographical engineer, about Thoreau's age and from his part of the country, but he had received an education in the sciences at West Point and become a wide-ranging traveler with a practical mis-sion. Derby made the first thorough, systematic survey of the valley's agricultural potential. Of the possibilities for white settlers where the San Joaquin and Merced rivers converge, he wrote this: "Exceedingly barren, and singularly des-titute of resources, except a narrow strip on the borders of the stream; it was without timber and grass, and can never, in my estimation, be brought into req-uisition for agricultural purposes."...

In the period from 1850 to 1910, writes ecologist Raymond Dasmann, the state of California experienced a series of massive environmental changes, and nowhere more so than in the Great Valley. During those few decades, the fauna and flora went through an upheaval comparable only to the cataclysmic postgla-cial extinctions. However, in this later case, the changes were not the work of blind forces of nature but rather of conscious, rational men. Those men, driven by a vision of the valley's potential wealth and by a passion to possess it, shot out the waterfowl. They trapped out the furbearers. They cut down large numbers of the great spreading oaks, burned away the saltbush, the chaparral, the black-berry and willow thickets, and drained the tule marshes. They decimated the large grazing herds, until only a tiny remnant of the elk remained in a wildlife preserve. As their food and habitat disappeared, so did the grizzly, the condor, and the wolf. And so did the aboriginal human settlers, the Yokut and the rest, who became the victims of disease, of superior force, of land hunger. In their place developed the wealthiest agricultural operation in the United States....The technological control of water was the basis of a new West. It made possible not only the evolution of a prosperous agriculture but also, to a great extent, the growth of coastal cities like Los Angeles and San Francisco. It eventually made California the leading state in America, and perhaps the single most influential and powerful area in the world for its size....

Many books and articles have been written about the arid West and its search for water, and they are good, scholarly books, but they remain on the periphery; they have not yet penetrated very far the thinking of most generalizers and theorists of the region's character. In those generalizers' hands the history of the West has tended to remain, against all evidence to the contrary, ... a saga of individual enterprise, of men and women going out from civilization to carve with their own hands a livelihood from nature, a tale of release (or attempted release) from eastern form, tradition, and control. To be sure, the West was all of that at times, but for most of its history and for most of its people the region has had a very different story to tell: one of people encountering difficult environments, of driving to overcome them through technological means, of creating the necessary social organization to do so, of leading on and on to indigenous bureaucracy and corporatism. It is time that this emergent technological West, the West of the hydraulic society, the West as seen in the Great Valley of California, be put beside the storybook West of fur trappers, cowboys, sodbusters, and intrepid adventurers....

[C]apitalism has created over the past hundred years a new, distinctive type of hydraulic society, one that demonstrates once more how the domination of nature can lead to the domination of some people over others. Recognizing this, certain important questions must be addressed.... In what ways has that ecological domination expressed in the new water systems shaped the social order of places like the American West, creating new structures of power there, reconcentrating wealth and authority?...

The most fundamental characteristic of the latest irrigation mode is its behavior toward nature and the underlying attitudes on which it is based. Water in the capitalist state has no intrinsic value, no integrity that must be respected. Water is no longer valued as a divinely appointed means for survival, for producing and reproducing human life, as it was in local subsistence communities....

The behavior that follows making water into a commodity is aggressively manipulative beyond any previous historical experience. Science and technology are given a place of honor in the capitalist state and put to work devising ways to extract from every river whatever cash it can produce. Where nature seemingly puts limits on human wealth, engineering presumes to bring unlimited plenty. Even in the desert, where men and women confront scarcity in its oldest form—not the deprivation of a particular industrial resource, which is always a cultural contrivance, but the lack of a basic biological necessity—every form of growth is considered possible. Undaunted by any deficiency, unwilling to concede any landscape as unprofitable, planners and schemers assure that there is water in the driest rocks, requiring only a few spoken commands to make it gush forth without end. That collective drive to make the bleakest, most sterile desert produce more and more of everything comes from aggregating individual drives to maximize personal acquisitiveness without stint or hindrance. It is an ideology shared wholeheartedly by agriculturists and water bureaucrats, providing the bond that unites their potentially rival centers of power into a formidable alliance....

"I'm pushing on when dawn's a-breaking, going 'cross the wide Missouri." The words of that song, the most beautiful ever written in America, tell of an experience, repeated again and again, that began with anonymous longings and ended in myth. They tell of a solitary man swimming his horse across a brown, surging river and through a sea of grass, the unbroken prairie. They tell of a woman driving a team of oxen and a covered wagon into the river, pulling up on the other bank, dripping and breathless yet eager to go on. They tell of a family on a flatboat loaded with their belongings, poling and warping their way upstream to Wyoming, Idaho, the Oregon country. Always in that endless migration there was one more river to cross. After the Missouri were the Sweetwater, the Gunnison, the Owyhee, the Dirty Devil, the Salmon, the Pecos, the Tuolumne, the Yellowstone, the Green, the Cimarron, the Escalante, the Columbia. Each was unique in character and challenge. And on the other shore, or up near the headwaters, or somewhere in the unbounded space lying beyond, there was a new life to make. There was an ancient story of exodus to reenact, a new promised land to occupy. There was a West to invent....

The pattern I want to describe begins as pioneers came into western valleys, made their homes there, plowed new fields, and started a process of river development. They had passed through the waters; now they turned them to their advantage. That process was one of ecological intensification—of extracting more and more economic yield from the rivers and their watersheds. It was not a steady progression, but a broken rhythm of fits and starts, of long periods of intensity, then long or short periods of consolidation or regress when development ran up against obstacles. Again and again, nature imposed limits on the settler, and often he did not have the capital, the technology, or the social organization needed to overcome them....

The Mormons, or Latter-day Saints, of Utah have sometimes claimed, in moments of high filiopietism, that they were the first Americans to practice irrigation on a wide scale. A more careful statement is that they were the first Americans of northern European ancestry to do so. More important, they were the first in the West to propagate assiduously, in deeds as well as words, the gospel of desert conquest sanctioned by God. And they were the first to encounter the fact that that gospel had no logical point of closure. Its fate was that it worked and worked, until it worked its own undoing. River valley after river valley came under Mormon command, testifying to their religious zeal and organization. Then one day they passed the point where it was God they were primarily serving. In the end, money and the American marketplace had become the dominant forces driving them on. Their religion had served admirably, it turned out, as an impetus toward, and a justification for, the accumulation of capital. It had helped the Mormon people become the first commercially successful irrigators in North America....

Before the Mormons founded their desert kingdom, there were the Indians and the Spanish. To understand the Mormons as irrigators, we first need to see them in relation to those peoples who came before them. The southwestern

Indians, as described in the preceding chapter, had achieved a measure of water control and political concentration many centuries before white men arrived on the scene. The Spanish, whose techniques were hardly more advanced, were the first Europeans to irrigate in what is now the United States. A hundred years after Columbus's discovery they were on the Rio Grande, directing local Indians in digging a ditch near present-day San Juan, New Mexico. By 1800 they had constructed 164 *acequias,* or irrigation canals, in the upper part of that river basin. All of them were essentially communal undertakings, drawing on the peasant culture of southern Spain, on Moorish influences, and on the native pueblo experience....

The Mormons, when they came West in 1847, bypassed those older settlements, though they sent traders there and observed their irrigated fields. For their refuge the Mormons chose an area that no one before them had tried to irrigate—the slope from the Wasatch Mountains to the Great Salt Lake. Despite their efforts to collect advance information, they were frightfully innocent of the first principles of water application, and they had no vernacular or folk tradition to guide them in the enterprise. Moreover, they had virtually no capital when they first arrived. What they did have was an irrepressible confidence that God had picked out a part of the desert for their homeland and would see that they thrived on it....

On 23 July 1847, a committee of Mormons broke their first ground for farming. They had just walked over eight hundred miles from Iowa to the future site of Salt Lake City. They had staked out a piece of ground near City Creek where they would plant potatoes, beans, and corn. Now they were ready to dam the creek and cut a trench from it through the hardbaked Utah ground to their new fields. Shortly thereafter, stream after stream flowing from the mountains was turned out of its bed. The means available for that work were at first primitive. Planks bolted together in the shape of the letter A formed a "go-devil," a wedgelike tool the Saints used to tear canals across the landscape. A pan filled with water served, in the absence of levels and surveying instruments, to lay out the waterways with enough decline to make the water run smoothly in them: not too fast, or the current would erode the ditch; not too slow, or the silt would settle out and clog the works. Dirt and rocks scraped together with brush made a dam. These were not much better than Indian ways, but they were only a beginning.

From that first point of ad hoc innovation, Mormon irrigation diffused north, south, east, and west, creating a ganglion of colonies tied to the Mother Church in the capital city. Led by their astute patriarch Brigham Young, inspired by their murdered founder and prophet Joseph Smith, the Mormons wrote their imperial ambitions on the face of the earth for all to see. They took the bee and its hive as a symbol of their industry, but a more appropriate one would have been the beaver, for control over water became the ecological basis of their society.

One of the most remarkable aspects of Mormon irrigation was the speed of its conquest over the desert. By 1850 there were 16,333 irrigated acres in what would become the state of Utah, and on them were grown 44,000 bushels of potatoes, 4,800 tons of hay, and 107,700 bushels of wheat, along with oats, corn, and rye. Within another forty years, the irrigated acreage amounted to 263,473, and it supported more than 200,000 people. Almost every one of the 10,000 farms in the state was irrigated, and their average size was 27 acres. In forty years the potato crop had jumped over 1,000 percent, the wheat yield over 1,500 percent.

The Spanish irrigation settlements, after two-and-a-half centuries of endeavor, could still not show such results. For a people who had come without even a fund of experience or capital, the Mormons had made an impressive showing....

Though they came to the arid West with empty pockets and a lack of training, the Mormons did have a system of hierarchy and group discipline, and that critical quality made possible their rapid success in water manipulation. Under their first leader, Joseph Smith, they had taken the form of a religious corporation—a theocracy (in intent if not in actuality) constructed along the lines of modern rationality. At the top of their chain of authority stood the First Presidency, the Quorum of the Twelve Apostles, and the Council of Seventy; at the bottom, the local ward bishop....It provided a unified scheme of development and—within the limits of the available technology—a maximization of resource exploitation, and it freed the communities from individuals squabbling over water rights. It allowed the amassing of capital to undertake new projects and provided a cushion of security when projects failed. And, most important, it claimed to speak with the voice of God....

Within the space of a few years the Mormons had broken the Hispanic-Indian monopoly on western irrigation. But then, beginning around 1870, their bold new wave was eclipsed in influence by even newer waves. About that date the center of innovation shifted to eastern Colorado, then to California....

[A]nother promoter of the irrigated colony was the Southern Pacific Railroad. Altogether that company had been given one-tenth of the state of California (11,588,000 acres) in federal land grants to encourage transportation development. Much of that land was sold to capitalists, the proceeds being put into track, bringing a direct connection with marketplace America to the entire central valley by 1876. For many wheat farmers, the railroad was "the Octopus," an enormous power squeezing life and profit out of them, "huge, terrible, flinging the echo of its thunder over all the reaches of the valley, leaving blood and destruction in its path." But the railroad also sold lots to small farmers and promoted the irrigated farmstead in the valley. William Mills, who worked as chief land agent for Southern Pacific from 1883 to 1907, strongly believed that it was in the economic interest of the company to encourage diversified agriculture in the state and the growth in population it would require. He sent salesmen all over the world to promote California, and through the Southern Pacific Colonization Agency attempted to help newcomers make a go of it raising fruits and vegetables along the company's tracks....

As the Visalia *Delta* paper said, "All that is desired is that these barren plains should be made to blossom as the rose. And all that is necessary to make them bloom is to give them away in chunks."

One river, the Kern, small and erratic, with no outlet to the sea. Two claimants, with large, insatiable appetites. In 1881 they met in court in the case

Lux v. *Haggin* (Lux was Miller's partner and stand-in) to settle which man would rule the desert, and until the state supreme court resolved their dispute five years later, the California law of water rights hung in the balance. [Henry] Miller claimed the river was his under the common law of riparian rights, which the state had implicitly adopted in its constitution of 1850. He owned land along the Kern's banks, making the stream his property (if one stretched the riparian doctrine of usufruct and natural use beyond all recognition). [James] Haggin, on the other hand, claimed the river through purchase of rights of prior appropriation, which, in California as in Colorado, had emerged out of the mining frenzy. The courts, he argued, had established those rights, beginning with the case of *Irwin* v. *Phillips* (1855), and so had the state legislature, in the Civil Code of 1872. Thus the battle was joined, not between an archaic, foreign riparian idea and a modern, indigenous appropriationist idea, as the historians sometimes describe it, but between two versions of capitalist grab.

As the battle of the Kern River barons commenced, California agriculturalists began organizing themselves into rival water camps—for Miller or for Haggin. The word "rival" comes from the Latin *rivalis*, "one using the same brook as another," usually referring to parties standing on opposite banks trying to monopolize the flow. In California of the 1880s the rivalry was not of one bank against the other. Instead, it pitted the riparian landowners, who as a rule were cattlemen, against those living at a remove but needing water if they were to grow grapes and oranges. The riparianists took Miller, of course, as their champion and were sure that he would vindicate their rights. The opposing appropriationists had the clear majority, for most people wanting access to water did not, and could not, live along a river's banks. Whether they had come early or late, whether they possessed twenty or twenty thousand acres, they claimed the rivers ought to be available to them too. James Haggin, they believed, was fighting their case in court.

The dispute quickly took on false ideological tones: a struggle of democracy versus elitism. At stake, the appropriationists argued, was whether a small, privileged group of men could achieve a monopoly on a resource, thereby denying economic opportunity to the masses. In 1883, a state irrigation convention assembled in Riverside to make that argument loudly and forcefully to state legislators....

The legislators, they demanded, should establish once and for all the doctrine of appropriation and free the state from the dead hand of the past—from a riparianism that was like a medieval suit of armor, imprisoning the youthful energies of California and preventing its natural growth. Making appropriation the sole basis of water law in the state would promote "natural justice," they asserted, and assure the triumph of democracy.

The convention's statement obscured the real issues confronting democratic land use in California. In the first place, irrigation was practiced to some extent by both sides in the dispute, though the riparianists typically relied on stock raising for their main source of income and used the water only for raising native grass or a little alfalfa in the bottomlands. Second, no one in the convention proposed to take Haggin's lands away from him, though they had been acquired by dubious means, and distribute them in twenty-acre irrigated homesteads to the world's poor. The appropriationists, though more numerous, could hardly be said to represent agrarian democracy when their number included some of the biggest land monopolizers around, when it included investors like Haggin who lived far off in San Francisco and bought up appropriation claims as readily as railroad or mining stock. Third, the doctrine of appropriation could create an elite as small as, or smaller than, the riparian principle did. Under appropriation, a single individual could acquire rights to an entire river and, conceivably, take its water a hundred or more miles away, leaving streamside dwellers with a dry bed. Water taken out and used immediately along the banks might find its way back into the stream, or most of it would, but appropriated water was commonly lost water for all who lived downstream.

The notion that appropriation was a more democratic approach to water rights rested on a single assumption, unexamined and unsubstantiated in the convention: that democracy was promoted by intensive reclamation of the desert. The more land that was irrigated, the more wealth it produced, the nearer the state would come to realizing democratic ideals. It is obvious, the convention's statement implies, that following the legal principle of appropriation must mean more irrigation development than is possible under riparianism. *Ipso facto*, democracy must flourish....

Given sentiments like those expressed by the irrigation conventions of 1883 and 1884 and by most of the newspapers in the central and southern parts of the state, it came as a shock and an outrage that Henry Miller won his case. In 1886 the California supreme court, in a split decision, upheld the riparian doctrine and gave Miller priority over the Kern. Immediately, there were charges that he had bought the justices. There were Jeremiahs who predicted that the state would be left behind in the western rush for development. And there was a move initiated to get the constitution changed, a move that would take forty years to accomplish. For his part, Henry Miller proved to be a magnanimous winner. Having established that he was indeed lord of the waters, he turned around and offered a partnership to Haggin. The two barons agreed to build an upstream reservoir on the Kern to provide enough water for both, with Miller to get one-third of the downstream current thereafter, Haggin two-thirds. After all, they were big men, and big men act big, even over a little water....

FURTHER READING

Thomas Andrews, *Killing for Coal: America's Deadliest Labor War* (2008).

William Cronon, George Miles, Jay Gitlin, eds., *Under an Open Sky: Rethinking America's Western Past* (1992).

Pekka Hämäläinen, *The Comanche Empire* (2008).

Kenneth M. Hamilton, *Black Towns and Profit: Promotion and Development in the Trans-Appalachian West, 1877–1915* (1991).

Andrew Isenberg, *The Destruction of the Bison: An Environmental History* (2000).

Peter Iverson, *When Indians Became Cowboys: Native Peoples and Cattle Ranching in the American West* (1994).

Joy Kasson, *Buffalo Bill's Wild West: Celebrity, Memory, and Popular History* (2000).

John Putman, *Class and Gender Politics in Progressive-Era Seattle* (2008).

Theodore Roosevelt, *The Winning of the West*, 4 volumes (1889–1896).

Richard Slotkin, *Gunfighter Nation: The Myth of the Frontier in Twentieth Century America* (1992).

Frederick Jackson Turner, *The Frontier in American History* (1920).

Louis Warren, *Buffalo Bill's America: William Cody and the Wild West Show* (2005).

Elliott West, *The Contested Plains: Indians, Goldseekers, and the Rush to Colorado* (1998).

Richard White, *It's Your Misfortune and None of My Own: A New History of the American West* (1991).

CHAPTER 3

Industrialization, Workers, and the New Immigration

The Industrial Revolution and the migration of Europeans to the Americas were well under way before the American Civil War, but in the years after the war these phenomena restructured the American landscape in ways that would have made it unrecognizable to previous generations. Improvements in steel production allowed architects to design buildings that shot into the sky out of the flat prairie. Railroads built by laborers from China and Ireland linked the East Coast to the West Coast with an iron ribbon 3,000 miles long. Huge processing centers took the products of farms and ranches and converted them into consumer goods with a rapidity that made country and city folk alike rub their eyes in disbelief. Industrialists amassed fortunes in a way never before seen in human history, while knowledgeable artisans found their training and judgment less and less called for in an age of mass production. Skilled and unskilled alike competed for jobs that often paid hardly enough to keep a family from starving.

In the midst of this industrial transformation, a second giant wave of immigration hit the United States. Sometimes called the "new immigration" to distinguish it from the influx of Germans and Irish earlier in the nineteenth century, this wave brought Poles, Italians, Scandinavians, and eastern European Jews, among others. Crowded together in tenements and jostled into factories and sweatshops, these immigrants struggled to adapt their old skills to new working conditions. They also sought to maintain their sense of themselves in the midst of change. At work, they organized labor unions to create decent working conditions. At home, they struggled over parental and gender roles, challenged by the new environment. During their leisure, they gathered in churches, saloons, and public parks, where they could escape the watchful eye of employers and enjoy the camaraderie of their "own kind." Sometimes they decided that America was not for them, and they returned home.

Across the economic spectrum, Americans struggled to define the meaning of industrial concentration for democracy and social justice. Unions like the American Federation of Labor focused on specific reforms for particular classes of skilled workers. Congressmen and journalists investigated social conditions for the poorest of immigrants. Industrialists may have occasionally worried about the downtrodden, but they obsessed about profits.

Competition to achieve ever more profitable advantages of scale led to a rush of corporate mergers between 1897 and 1900. Integrating vertically and horizontally, the largest companies formed "trusts" into which smaller companies disappeared. By 1900, seventy-three such trusts had swallowed up more than 3,000 companies, creating combinations like Standard Oil, U.S. Steel, and the American Tobacco Company. Industrialists defended their actions as the inevitable outcome of "progress" and industrial development. Although they violently resisted the demands of workers for a more equitable sharing of profits, a few also sought to express traditional American concerns for equality and "uplift" through the creation of a new set of institutions—philanthropic foundations and free libraries, such as those funded by steel magnate (and Scottish immigrant) Andrew Carnegie. Increased immigration, industrialization, and urbanization all contributed to making this a particularly turbulent transition in U.S. history.

QUESTIONS TO THINK ABOUT

How did immigrants cope with conditions as they found them in America's brimming cities? Did industry crush immigrants or provide them with new opportunities? In what ways did workers set the terms of their own experience? Lastly, how did men and women experience immigration differently, and how did it reshape family life?

DOCUMENTS

The documents in this chapter present different reactions to immigration and industrialization. In document 1 a laborer from China reflects upon his conflicts with immigrants from other parts of the world, and their prejudice towards the Chinese. Document 2 is a poem by Emma Lazarus, the daughter of a prosperous Jewish family in New York. She wrote it to help raise funds for a pedestal for the Statue of Liberty. The verse appears at the base of the statue, which was often the first thing that immigrants saw when they sailed into New York Harbor. Document 3 is an immigrant account drawn from congressional testimony on the replacement of skilled adult labor with unskilled child labor in factories. It shows the devastating poverty encountered by many working families. Document 4 is a photograph taken by Jacob Riis for his exposé of New York tenement slums, *How the Other Half Lives*. Riis hoped to shock the wealthy and middle class into taking action to improve conditions for the working poor. He assumed that only destitution and desperation would lead men to crowd together "like pigs." Document 5 reveals the practical emphasis of the American Federation of Labor, which focused its efforts on bettering conditions for skilled labor and giving them "eight hours for what we will." Document 6 is by the Pulitzer Prize–winning novelist and socialist Upton Sinclair. His masterpiece of muckraking, *The Jungle*, helped Progressive reformers (see Chapter 5) pass the Pure Food and Drug Act. But Sinclair also created one of the most disturbing descriptions of immigrant life ever written. In this selection, the defeated, depressed Polish immigrant Jurgis discovers the saloon. Document 7 is a European boy's perspective on the stories of the "Golden Country" told by returned immigrants. It gives insight into the forces beguiling immigrants to the New World, and it suggests that at least some returned to the old country as heroes. In document 8, the famous efficiency expert Frederick Winslow Taylor details how he persuaded men to work faster by selecting an "ideal worker" and training him to follow instructions slavishly— leaving no room for "unscientific" personal initiative. If immigrants were to find avenues for self-expression, they would have to look for them in places other than their work. Finally, document 9 suggests that men and women (and parents and children) experienced the new environment differently. A Jewish teenager observes that Old World tradition meant her father ate first and best. She and millions of others would seize the opportunity to live life in new ways.

1. Chinese Immigrant Lee Chew Denounces Prejudice in America, 1882

I worked on my father's farm till I was about sixteen years of age, when a man of our tribe came back from America and took ground as large as four city blocks and made a paradise of it. He put a large stone wall around and led some streams through and built a palace and summer house and about twenty other structures, with beautiful bridges over the streams and walks and roads. Trees and flowers, singing birds, waterfowl and curious animals were within the walls.

The man had gone away from our village a poor boy. Now he returned with unlimited wealth, which he had obtained in the country of the American wizards. After many amazing adventures he had become a merchant in a city called Mott Street, so it was said....

The wealth of this man filled my mind with the idea that I, too, would like to go to the country of the wizards and gain some of their wealth, and after a long time my father consented, and gave me his blessing, and my mother took leave of me with tears, while my grandfather laid his hand upon my head and told me to remember and live up to the admonitions of the Sages, to avoid gambling, bad women and men of evil minds, and so to govern my conduct that when I died my ancestors might rejoice to welcome me as a guest on high.

My father gave me $100, and I went to Hong Kong with five other boys from our place and we got steerage passage on a steamer, paying $50 each. Everything was new to me. All my life I had been used to sleeping on a board bed with a wooden pillow, and I found the steamer's bunk very uncomfortable, because it was so soft. The food was different from that which I had been used to, and I did not like it at all. I was afraid of the stews, for the thought of what they might be made of by wicked wizards of the ship made me ill. Of the great power of these people I saw many signs. The engines that moved the ship were wonderful monsters, strong enough to lift mountains. When I got to San Francisco,

As found in David M. Katzman and William M. Tuttle, Jr. (eds.) *Plain Folk: The Life Stories of Undistinguished Americans* (Chicago: University of Illinois Press, 1982). Reprinted in Jon Gjerde, ed. *Major Problems in American Immigration and Ethnic History* (Boston: Houghton Mifflin, 1988), 172–174.

which was before the passage of the Exclusion act, I was half starved, because I was afraid to eat the provisions of the barbarians, but a few days' living in the Chinese quarter made me happy again. A man got me work as a house servant in an American family, and my start was the same as that of almost all the Chinese in this country.

The Chinese laundryman does not learn his trade in China; there are no laundries in China. The women there do the washing in tubs and have no washboards or flat irons. All the Chinese laundrymen here were taught in the first place by American women just as I was taught.

When I went to work for that American family I could not speak a word of English, and I did not know anything about housework. The family consisted of husband, wife, and two children. They were very good to me and paid me $3.50 a week, of which I could save $3....

... Men of other nationalities who are jealous of the Chinese, because he is a more faithful worker than one of their people, have raised such a great outcry about Chinese cheap labor that they have shut him out of working on farms or in factories or building railroads or making streets or digging sewers. He cannot practice any trade, and his opportunities to do business are limited to his own countrymen. So he opens a laundry when he quits domestic service.

The treatment of the Chinese in this country is all wrong and mean. It is persisted in merely because China is not a fighting nation. The Americans would not dare to treat Germans, English, Italians or even Japanese as they treat the Chinese, because if they did there would be a war....

Irish fill the almshouses and prisons and orphan asylums, Italians are among the most dangerous of men, Jews are unclean and ignorant. Yet they are all let in, while Chinese, who are sober, or duly law abiding, clean, educated and industrious, are shut out. There are few Chinamen in jails and none in the poor houses. There are no Chinese tramps or drunkards. Many Chinese here have become sincere Christians, in spite of the persecution which they have to endure from their heathen countrymen. More than half the Chinese in this country would become citizens if allowed to do so, and would be patriotic Americans. But how can they make this country their home as matters now are! They are not allowed to bring wives here from China, and if they marry American women there is a great outcry.

2. Poet Emma Lazarus Praises the New Colossus, 1883

Not like the brazen giant of Greek fame,
With conquering limbs astride from land to land;
Here at our sea-washed, sunset gates shall stand
A mighty woman with a torch, whose flame

As appears in Eve Merriam, *Emma Lazarus: Woman with a Torch!* (New York: Citadel Press, 1956), p. 126.

Is the imprisoned lightning, and her name
Mother of Exiles. From her beacon-hand
Glows world-wide welcome; her mild eyes command
The air-bridged harbor that twin cities frame.
"Keep, ancient lands, your storied pomp!" cries she
With silent lips. "Give me your tired, your poor,
Your huddled masses yearning to breathe free,
The wretched refuse of your teeming shore.
Send these, the homeless, tempest-tost to me,
I lift my lamp beside the golden door!"

3. Immigrant Thomas O'Donnell Laments the Worker's Plight, 1883

BOSTON, MASS., *October 18, 1883*

THOMAS O'DONNELL examined.

By the CHAIRMAN:

QUESTION. Where do you live?

ANSWER. At Fall River.

Q. How long have you lived in this country?

A. Eleven years.

Q. Where were you born?

A. In Ramsbotham, England.

Q. Have you been naturalized here?

A. No, sir.

Life of a Mule-Spinner

Q. What is your business?

A. I am a mule-spinner by trade. I have worked at it since I have been in this country—eleven years.

Q. Are you a married man?

A. Yes, sir; I am a married man; have a wife and two children. I am not very well educated. I went to work when I was young, and have been working ever since in the cotton business; went to work when I was about eight or nine years old. I was going to state how I live. My children get along very

---

Testimony of Thomas O'Donnell, Fall River mule-spinner, *Report of Senate Committee upon the Relations Between Labor and Capital*, III (1883), 451–457.

well in summer time, on account of not having to buy fuel or shoes or one thing and another. I earn $1.50 a day and can't afford to pay a very big house rent. I pay $1.50 a week for rent, which comes to about $6 a month....

Q. Do you have work right along?

A. No, sir; since that strike we had down in Fall River about three years ago I have not worked much more than half the time, and that has brought my circumstances down very much.

Q. Why have you not worked more than half the time since then?

A. Well, at Fall River if a man has not got a boy to act as "back-boy" it is very hard for him to get along. In a great many cases they discharge men in that work and put in men who have boys.

Q. Men who have boys of their own?

A. Men who have boys of their own capable enough to work in a mill, to earn 30 or 40 cents a day.

Child Labor Necessary to the Employment of Parents

Q. Is the object of that to enable the boy to earn something for himself?

A. Well, no; the object is this: They are doing away with a great deal of mule-spinning there and putting in ring-spinning, and for that reason it takes a good deal of small help to run this ring work, and it throws the men out of work because they are doing away with the mules and putting these ring-frames in to take their places. For that reason they get all the small help they can to run these ring-frames. There are so many men in the city to work, and whoever has a boy can have work, and whoever has no boy stands no chance. Probably he may have a few months of work in the summer time, but will be discharged in the fall. That is what leaves me in poor circumstances. Our children, of course, are very often sickly from one cause or another, on account of not having sufficient clothes, or shoes, or food, or something. And also my woman; she never did work in a mill; she was a housekeeper, and for that reason she can't help me to anything at present, as many women do help their husbands down there, by working, like themselves. My wife never did work in a mill, and that leaves me to provide for the whole family. I have two children....

Supporting a Family on $133 a Year

...

Q. Taking a full year back can you tell how much you have had?

A. That would be about fifteen weeks' work. Last winter, as I told you, I got in, and I worked up to about somewhere around Fast Day, or maybe New Year's day; anyway, Mr. Howard has it down on his record, if you wish to have an exact answer to that question; he can answer it better than I can, because we have a sort of union there to keep ourselves together.

Q. Do you think you have had $150 within a year?

A. No, sir.

Q. Have you had $125?

A. Well, I could figure it up if I had time. The thirteen weeks is all I have had....

Q. That would be somewhere about $133, if you had not lost any time?

A. Yes, sir.

Q. That is all you have had?

A. Yes, sir.

Q. To support yourself and wife and two children?

A. Yes, sir.

Q. Have you had any help from outside?

A. No, sir.

Q. Do you mean that yourself and wife and two children have had nothing but that for all this time?

A. That is all. I got a couple dollars' worth of coal last winter, and the wood I picked up myself. I goes around with a shovel and picks up clams and wood....

Too Poor to Go West

Q. Well, I want to know why you do not go out West on a $2,000 farm, or take up a homestead and break it and work it up, and then have it for yourself and family?

A. I can't see how I could get out West. I have got nothing to go with.

Q. It would not cost you over $1,500.

A. Well, I never saw over a $20 bill, and that is when I have been getting a month's pay at once. If some one would give me $1,500 I will go....

Q. Has there been any day in the year that you have had to go without anything to eat?

A. Yes, sir, several days.

Q. More than one day at a time?

A. No.

Q. How about the children and your wife—did they go without anything to eat too?

The Children Crying for Food

A. My wife went out this morning and went to a neighbor's and got a loaf of bread and fetched it home, and when she got home the children were crying for something to eat.

Q. Have the children had anything to eat to-day except that, do you think?

A. They had that loaf of bread—I don't know what they have had since then, if they have had anything.

Q. Did you leave any money at home?

A. No, sir....

4. Immigrants Crowd Together—By Choice, or Not?

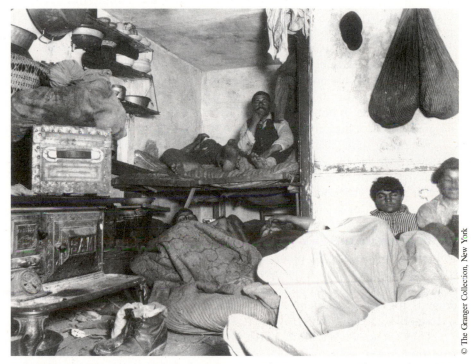

TENEMENT LIFE, NYC, c1889. Lodgers in a Bayard Street tenement. Photograph, c. 1889, by Jacob Riis.

5. Unionist Samuel Gompers Asks, "What Does the Working Man Want?" 1890

... My friends, we have met here today to celebrate the idea that has prompted thousands of working-people of Louisville and New Albany to parade the streets of y[our city]; that prompts the toilers of Chicago to turn out by their fifty or hundred thousand of men; that prompts the vast army of wage-workers in

"A News Account of an Address in Louisville," in *The Samuel Gompers Papers: The Early Years of the American Federation of Labor, 1887–90,* ed. Stuart Kaufman (Chicago: University of Illinois Press, 1987), 307–314.

New York to demonstrate their enthusiasm and appreciation of the importance of this idea; that prompts the toilers of England, Ireland, Germany, France, Italy, Spain, and Austria to defy the manifestos of the autocrats of the world and say that on May the first, 1890, the wage-workers of the world will lay down their tools in sympathy with the wage-workers of America, to establish a principle of limitations of hours of labor to eight hours for sleep [applause], eight hours for work, and eight hours for what we will. [Applause.]

It has been charged time and again that were we to have more hours of leisure we would merely devote it to debauchery, to the cultivation of vicious habits—in other words, that we would get drunk. I desire to say this in answer to that charge: As a rule, there are two classes in society who get drunk. One is the class who has no work to do in consequence of too much money; the other class, who also has no work to do, because it can't get any, and gets drunk on its face. [Laughter.] I maintain that that class in our social life that exhibits the greatest degree of sobriety is that class who are able, by a fair number of hours of day's work to earn fair wages—not overworked. The man who works twelve, fourteen, and sixteen hours a day requires some artificial stimulant to restore the life ground out of him in the drudgery of the day. [Applause.]...

We ought to be able to discuss this question on a higher ground, and I am pleased to say that the movement in which we are engaged will stimulate us to it. They tell us that the eight-hour movement cannot be enforced, for the reason that it must check industrial and commercial progress. I say that the history of this country, in its industrial and commercial relations, shows the reverse. I say that is the plane on which this question ought to be discussed—that is the social question. As long as they make this question an economic one, I am willing to discuss it with them. I would retrace every step I have taken to advance this movement did it mean industrial and commercial stagnation. But it does not mean that. It means greater prosperity; it means a greater degree of progress for the whole people; it means more advancement and intelligence, and a nobler race of people....

They say they can't afford it. Is that true? Let us see for one moment. If a reduction in the hours of labor causes industrial and commercial ruination, it would naturally follow increased hours of labor would increase the prosperity, commercial and industrial. If that were true, England and America ought to be at the tail end, and China at the head of civilization. [Applause.]

Is it not a fact that we find laborers in England and the United States, where the hours are eight, nine and ten hours a day—do we not find that the employers and laborers are more successful? Don't we find them selling articles cheaper? We do not need to trust the modern moralist to tell us those things. In all industries where the hours of labor are long, there you will find the least development of the power of invention. Where the hours of labor are long, men are cheap, and where men are cheap there is no necessity for invention. How can you expect a man to work ten or twelve or fourteen hours at his calling and then devote any time to the invention of a machine or discovery of a new principle or force? If he be so fortunate as to be able to read a paper he will fall asleep before he has read through the second or third line. [Laughter.]...

The man who works the long hours has no necessities except the barest to keep body and soul together, so he can work. He goes to sleep and dreams of work; he rises in the morning to go to work; he takes his frugal lunch to work; he comes home again to throw himself down on a miserable apology for a bed so that he can get that little rest that he may be able to go to work again. He is nothing but a veritable machine. He lives to work instead of working to live. [Loud applause.]

My friends, the only thing the working people need besides the necessities of life, is time. Time. Time with which our lives begin; time with which our lives close; time to cultivate the better nature within us; time to brighten our homes. Time, which brings us from the lowest condition up to the highest civilization; time, so that we can raise men to a higher plane....

We want eight hours and nothing less. We have been accused of being selfish, and it has been said that we will want more; that last year we got an advance of ten cents and now we want more. We do want more.... We live in the latter part of the Nineteenth century. In the age of electricity and steam that has produced wealth a hundred fold, we insist that it has been brought about by the intelligence and energy of the workingmen, and while we find that it is now easier to produce it is harder to live. We do want more, and when it becomes more, we shall still want more. [Applause.] And we shall never cease to demand more until we have received the results of our labor.

6. Jurgis Rudkus Discovers Drink in *The Jungle*, 1905

With one member trimming beef in a cannery, and another working in a sausage factory, the family had a first-hand knowledge of the great majority of Packingtown swindles. For it was the custom, as they found, whenever meat was so spoiled that it could not be used for anything else, either to can it or else to chop it up into sausage....

It was only when the whole ham was spoiled that it came into the department of Elzbieta. Cut up by the two-thousand-revolutions-a-minute flyers, and mixed with half a ton of other meat, no odor that ever was in a ham could make any difference. There was never the least attention paid to what was cut up for sausage; there would come all the way back from Europe old sausage that had been rejected, and that was mouldy and white—it would be dosed with borax and glycerine, and dumped into the hoppers and made over again for home consumption....

Such were the new surroundings in which Elzbieta was placed, and such was the work she was compelled to do. It was stupefying, brutalizing work; it left her no time to think, no strength for anything. She was part of the machine she tended, and every faculty that was not needed for the machine was doomed to be crushed out of existence. There was only one mercy about

Upton Sinclair, *The Jungle* (1905), 135–139.

the cruel grind—that it gave her the gift of insensibility. Little by little she sank into a torpor—she fell silent. She would meet Jurgis and Ona in the evening, and the three would walk home together, often without saying a word. Ona, too, was falling into a habit of silence—Ona, who had once gone about singing like a bird....

Yet the soul of Ona was not dead—the souls of none of them were dead, but only sleeping; and now and then they would waken, and these were cruel times. The gates of memory would roll open—old joys would stretch out their arms to them, old hopes and dreams would call to them, and they would stir beneath the burden that lay upon them, and feel its forever immeasurable weight. They could not even cry out beneath it; but anguish would seize them, more dreadful than the agony of death. It was a thing scarcely to be spoken—a thing never spoken by all the world, that will not know its own defeat.

They were beaten; they had lost the game, they were swept aside. It was not less tragic because it was so sordid, because that it had to do with wages and grocery bills and rents. They had dreamed of freedom; a chance to look about them and learn something; to be decent and clean, to see their child grow up to be strong. And now it was all gone—it would never be! They had played the game and they had lost. Six years more of toil they had to face before they could expect the least respite, the cessation of the payments upon the house; and how cruelly certain it was that they could never stand six years of such a life as they were living!...

Jurgis, being a man, had troubles of his own. There was another specter following him. He had never spoken of it, nor would he allow anyone else to speak of it—he had never acknowledged its existence to himself. Yet the battle with it took all the manhood that he had—and once or twice, alas, a little more. Jurgis had discovered drink.

He was working in the steaming pit of hell; day after day, week after week—until now there was not an organ of his body that did its work without pain, until the sound of ocean breakers echoes in his head day and night, and the buildings swayed and danced before him as he went down the street. And from all the unending horror of this there was a respite, a deliverance—he could drink! He could forget the pain, he could slip off the burden; he would see clearly again, he would be master of his brain, of his thoughts, of his will. His dead self would stir in him, and he would find himself laughing and cracking jokes with his companions—he would be a man again, and master of his life.

It was not an easy thing for Jurgis to take more than two or three drinks. With the first drink he could eat a meal, and he could persuade himself that that was economy; with the second he could eat another meal—but there would come a time when he could eat no more, and then to pay for a drink was an unthinkable extravagance, a defiance of the age-long instincts of his hunger-haunted class. One day, however, he took the plunge, and drank up all that he had in his pockets, and went home half "piped," as the men phrase it. He was happier than he had been in a year.

7. A Slovenian Boy Remembers
Tales of the Golden Country, 1909

As a boy of nine, and even younger, in my native village ... I experienced a thrill every time one of the men of the little community returned from America.

Five or six years before, as I heard people tell, the man had quietly left the village for the United States, a poor peasant clad in homespun, with a mustache under his nose and a bundle on his back; now, a clean-shaven *Amerikanec,* he sported a blue-serge suit, buttoned shoes very large in the toes and with india-rubber heels, a black derby, a shiny celluloid collar, and a loud necktie made even louder by a dazzling horseshoe pin, which, rumor had it, was made of gold, while his two suitcases of imitation leather, tied with straps, bulged with gifts from America for his relatives and friends in the village. In nine cases out of ten, he had left in economic desperation, on money borrowed from some relative in the United States; now there was talk in the village that he was worth anywhere from one to three thousand American dollars. And to my eyes he truly bore all the earmarks of affluence. Indeed, to say that he thrilled my boyish fancy is putting it mildly. With other boys in the village, I followed him around as he went visiting his relatives and friends and distributing presents, and hung onto his every word and gesture.

Then, on the first Sunday after his homecoming, if at all possible, I got within earshot of the nabob as he sat in the winehouse or under the linden in front of the winehouse in Blato, surrounded by village folk, ordering wine and *klobase*—Carniolan sausages—for all comers, paying for accordion-players, indulging in tall talk about America, its wealth and vastness, and his own experiences as a worker in the West Virginia or Kansas coal-mines or Pennsylvania rolling-mills, and comparing notes upon conditions in the United States with other local *Amerikanci* who had returned before him....

I remember that, listening to them, I played with the idea of going to America when I was but eight or nine....

In America everything was possible. There even the common people were "citizens," not "subjects," as they were in Austria and in most other European countries. A citizen, or even a non-citizen foreigner, could walk up to the President of the United States and pump his hand. Indeed, that seemed to be a custom in America. There was a man in Blato, a former steel-worker in Pittsburgh, who claimed that upon an occasion he had shaken hands and exchanged words with Theodore Roosevelt, to whom he familiarly referred as "Tedi"—which struck my mother very funny. To her it seemed as if someone had called the Pope of Rome or the Emperor of Austria by a nickname. But the man assured her, in my hearing, that in America everybody called the President merely "Tedi."

Mother laughed about this, off and on, for several days. And I laughed with her. She and I often laughed together.

---

8. Engineer Frederick Winslow Taylor
Manufactures the Ideal Worker, 1910

Our first step was the scientific selection of the workman. In dealing with work-men under this type of management, it is an inflexible rule to talk to and deal with only one man at a time, since each workman has his own special abilities and limitations, and since we are not dealing with men in masses, but are trying to develop each individual man to his highest state of efficiency and prosperity. Our first step was to find the proper workman to begin with. We therefore care-fully watched and studied these 75 men for three or four days, at the end of which time we had picked out four men who appeared to be physically able to handle pig iron at the rate of 47 tons [as opposed to the customary 12½ tons] per day. A careful study was then made of each of these men. We looked up their history as far back as practicable and thorough inquiries were made as to the character, habits, and the ambition of each of them. Finally we selected one from among the four as the most likely man to start with. He was a little Pennsylvania Dutchman who had been observed to trot back home for a mile or so after his work in the evening about as fresh as he was when he came trotting down to work in the morning. We found that upon wages of $1.15 a day he had succeeded in buying a small plot of ground, and that he was engaged in putting up the walls of a little house for himself in the morning before starting to work and at night after leaving. He also had the reputation of being exceedingly "close," that is, of placing a very high value on a dollar. As one man whom we talked to about him said, "A penny looks about the size of a cart-wheel to him." This man we will can Schmidt.

The task before us, then, narrowed itself down to getting Schmidt to handle 47 tons of pig iron per day and making him glad to do it. This was done as follows. Schmidt was called out from among the gang of pig-iron handlers and talked to somewhat in this way:

"Schmidt, are you a high-priced man?"

"Vell, I don't know vat you mean."

"Oh yes, you do. What I want to know is whether you are a high-priced man or not."

"Vell, I don't know vat you mean."

"Oh, come now, you answer my questions. What I want to find out is whether you are a high-priced man or one of these cheap fellows here. What I want to find out is whether you want to earn $1.85 a day or whether you are satisfied with $1.15, just the same as all those cheap fellows are getting."

"Did I vant $1.85 a day? Vas dot a high-priced man? Vell, yes, I vas a high-priced man."...

"Well, if you are a high-priced man, you will load that pig iron on that car to-morrow for $1.85. Now do wake up and answer my question. Tell me whether you are a high-priced man or not."

"Vell—did I got $1.85 for loading dot pig iron on dot car to-morrow?"

F. W. Taylor, *Scientific Management* (New York: Harper & Brothers, 1910), 5–8.

"Yes, of course you do, and you get $1.85 for loading a pile like that every day right through the year. That is what a high-priced man does, and you know it just as well as I do."

"Vell, dot's all right. I could load dot pig iron on the car to-morrow for $1.85, and I get it every day, don't I?"

"Certainly you do—certainly you do."

"Vell, den, I vas a high-priced man."

"Now, hold on, hold on. You know just as well as I do that a high-priced man has to do exactly as he's told from morning till night. You have seen this man here before, haven't you?"

"No, I never saw him."

"Well, if you are a high-priced man, you will do exactly as this man tells you to-morrow, from morning till night. When he tells you to pick up a pig and walk, you pick it up and you walk, and when he tells you to sit down and rest, you sit down. You do that right straight through the day. And what's more, no back talk. Now a high-priced man does just what he's told to do, and no back talk. Do you understand that? When this man tells you to walk, you walk; when he tells you to sit down, you sit down, and you don't talk back at him. Now you come on to work here to-morrow morning and I'll know before night whether you are really a high-priced man or not."…

Schmidt started to work, and all day long, and at regular intervals, was told by the man who stood over him with a watch, "Now pick up a pig and walk. Now sit down and rest. Now walk—now rest," etc. He worked when he was told to work, and rested when he was told to rest, and at half-past five in the afternoon had his 47½ tons loaded on the car. And he practically never failed to work at this pace and do the task that was set him during the three years that the writer was at Bethlehem. And throughout this time he averaged a little more than $1.85 per day, whereas before he had never received over $1.15 per day, which was the ruling rate of wages at that time in Bethlehem. That is, he received 60 percent higher wages than were paid to other men who were not working on task work. One man after another was picked out and trained to handle pig iron at the rate of 47½ tons per day until all of the pig iron was handled at this rate, and the men were receiving 60 percent more wages than other workmen around them.

The writer has given above a brief description of three of the four elements which constitute the essence of scientific management: first, the careful selection of the workman, and, second and third, the method of first inducing and then training and helping the workman to work according to the scientific method.

9. A Polish Immigrant Remembers Her Father Got the Best Food, 1920

… When we came to America, instead of taking along feather beds, and the samovar, and the brass pots and pans, like other people, Father made us carry

From *Bread Givers: A Novel*, by Anzia Yezierska (New York: Persea Books, 2003), p. 8–13. Copyright © 1970 by Louise Levitas Henriksen. Reprinted by permission of Persea Books, Inc., New York.

his books. When Mother begged only to take along her pot for *gefülte* fish, and the two feather beds that were handed down to her from her grandmother for her wedding presents, Father wouldn't let her.

"Woman!" Father said, laughing into her eyes. "What for will you need old feather beds? Don't you know it's always summer in America? And in the new golden country, where milk and honey flows free in the streets, you'll have new golden dishes to cook in, and not weigh yourself down with your old pots and pans. But my books, my holy books always were, and always will be, the light of the world. You'll see yet how all America will come to my feet to learn."

No one was allowed to put their things in Father's room, any more than they were allowed to use [my sister] Mashah's hanger.

Of course, we all knew that if God had given Mother a son, Father would have permitted a man child to share with him his best room in the house. A boy could say prayers after his father's death—that kept the father's soul alive forever. Always Father was throwing up to Mother that she had borne him no son to be an honour to his days and to say prayers for him when he died.

The prayers of his daughter didn't count because God didn't listen to women. Heaven and the next world were only for men. Women could get into Heaven because they were wives and daughters of men. Women had no brains for the study of God's Torah, but they could be the servants of men who studied the Torah. Only if they cooked for the men, and washed for the men, and didn't nag or curse the men out of their homes; only if they let the men study the Torah in peace, then, maybe, they could push themselves into Heaven with the men, to wait on them there.

And so, since men were the only people who counted with God, Father not only had the best room for himself, for his study and prayers, but also the best eating of the house. The fat from the soup and the top from the milk went always to him.

Mother had just put the soup pot and plates for dinner on the table, when Father came in.

At the first look on Mother's face he saw how she was boiling, ready to burst, so instead of waiting for her to begin her hollering, he started:

"Woman! when will you stop darkening the house with your worries?"

"When I'll have a man who does the worrying. Does it ever enter your head that the rent was not paid the second month? That to-day we're eating the last loaf of bread that the grocer trusted me?" Mother tried to squeeze the hard, stale loaf that nobody would buy for cash. "You're so busy working for Heaven that I have to suffer here such bitter hell."

We sat down to the table. With watering mouths and glistening eyes we watched Mother skimming off every bit of fat from the top soup into Father's big plate, leaving for us only the thin, watery part. We watched Father bite into the sour pickle which was special for him only; and waited, trembling with hunger, for our portion.

Father made his prayer, thanking God for the food. Then he said to Mother:

"What is there to worry about, as long as we have enough to keep the breath in our bodies? But the real food is God's Holy Torah." He shook her gently by the shoulder, and smiled down at her.

At Father's touch Mother's sad face turned into smiles. His kind look was like the sun shining on her....

"*Nu, Shenah?*" He wagged his head. "Do you want gold on earth, or wine of Heaven?"

"I'm only a sinful woman," Mother breathed, gazing up at him. Her fingers stole a touch of his hand, as if he were the king of the world. "God be praised for the little we have. I'm willing to give up all my earthly needs for the wine of Heaven with you. But, *Moisheh*"—she nudged him by the sleeve—"God gave us children. They have a life to live yet, here, on earth. Girls have to get married. People point their fingers on me—a daughters, twenty-five years already, and not married yet. And no dowry to help her get married."

"Woman! Stay in your place!" His strong hand pushed her away from him. "You're smart enough to bargain with the fish-peddler. But I'm the head of this family. I give my daughters brains enough to marry when their time comes, without the worries of a dowry."

"*Nu,* you're the head of the family." Mother's voice rose in anger. "But what will you do if your books are thrown in the street?"

At the mention of his books, Father looked up quickly.

"What do you want me to do?"...

ESSAYS

Immigration history is deeply intertwined with industrialization because workers from Europe provided much of the muscle for the new factories. For generations, historians have struggled to understand how immigrants adapted to the experience. In a manner of speaking, did they feel uprooted, or merely transplanted? Were they disempowered by immigrating to industrialized America, or was immigration a way of seizing power over their destinies? Mark Wyman of Illinois State University acknowledges the difficult conditions under which immigrants struggled, but he emphasizes the choices they made, rather than the ones made for them. Some of the conditions under which immigrants lived, such as the shocking scenes of overcrowding captured by photographer Jacob Riis, reflected the trade-offs made by men who hoped to save every penny they could, deferring immediate comfort so that they could send (or bring) money back to the Old Country. Wyman argues that immigrants calculated the risks and benefits associated with life in America, never gave up the fight for personal autonomy, and sometimes returned to their home countries as they had always planned—sadder and wiser, perhaps, but occasionally much richer. Victor Greene, emeritus professor at the University of Wisconsin at Milwaukee, paints a more ambivalent portrait, drawing for evidence upon the folk songs that immigrants wrote and sang. He portrays immigration as a painful, sorrowful disruption of family life and cultural identity. Many experienced a lessening of control over their lives, rather than a gain. Greene reminds us, however, to inquire into the differences between men and women, and parents and children.

Coming and Going: Round-Trip to America

MARK WYMAN

The Polish priest was surprised as he went over the parish census for 1894. He had known for some time that people were emigrating from the village of Miejsce, and so there was nothing startling in the total of 121 persons going to America in the ten years since the first traveler set out across the Atlantic.

What surprised him was the return flow: fifty-eight persons had come home to stay, just under half the overseas migration....

What surprised the Polish priest in 1894 continues to offer unexpected findings to those who look beneath the surface of American immigration. For the incoming tidal wave of peoples has always had an outflow, a reverse movement of immigrants turning their backs on the United States. Ignored by Fourth of July orators, over-looked by historians who concentrate on the newcomers' assimilation, return migration looms so large in world history, with critical implications for the homelands and the United States, that it cries out for attention....

The perils of ocean travel in these early periods, during the age of sail, helped keep return totals low. But by the middle of the nineteenth century a different picture emerged as railroads crisscrossed the continents and steamships began to ply the Atlantic. Not only were the European masses on the move for America, Canada, and elsewhere, but for large numbers it had become a round-trip. During this era of mass immigration, from approximately 1880 until 1930 when restriction laws and the Great Depression choked it off, from one-quarter to one-third of all European immigrants to the United States permanently returned home. The total may have reached four million persons.

European peasant villages that once seemed impenetrable in their backwardness, their isolation, now boasted residents who could describe the wonders of the New World—skyscrapers, elevated trains, deep tunnels. (Had not they themselves worked on these wonders?) Men and women who formerly quailed at the thought of a visit from the landlord now proudly described how they had seen the president of the United States in person, and one returned Slovenian even claimed to have shaken the hand of "Tedi." European politicians suddenly had to contend with subjects who knew different governmental systems, and clergymen confronted parishioners who had come into contact with other religious ideas. Life was not the same in Miejsce, nor in the Mezzogiorno, nor in thousands of peasant communities across the Continent....

The new migration was all built on the centuries-old European tradition of seasonal migration for work in nearby areas. This practice was so old, so extensive, that recent scholars have referred to it as "a way of life" among Russian and Galician Poles; as "the thing to do ... an accepted and socially supported form of behavior" in many areas of east-central Europe; as "a way of life for hundreds

Mark Wyman, *Round-Trip to America: The Immigrants Return to Europe, 1880–1930* (Ithaca: Cornell University Press, 1993), pp. 3–6, 17–19, 32, 39–40, 53, 60–62, 67–68, 76–77, 79, 83–87, 127, 129, 201–202. Used by permission of the publisher, Cornell University Press.

of thousands of Slovaks" and "as almost an ordinary routine of village life" in the Italian Apennines. It was known everywhere in Europe....

This movement within Europe was not new to the late nineteenth century, despite claims to the contrary by some writers. The modern world has struggled hard to maintain the comforting, nostalgic thought of a static peasant culture rooted to the soil, unchanging. Oscar Handlin wrote of "the enormous stability in peasant society.... From the westernmost reaches of Europe, in Ireland, to Russia in the east, the peasant masses had maintained an imperturbable sameness." He described a world where the village's self-sufficiency only rarely yielded to products or influences from outside, while cities were "regions of total strangeness into which the peasant never ventured, where not the people alone, but the very aspect of the earth, was unfamiliar."

But recent examinations into the past of European communities contradict the view of peasant life as stable and unchanging; this picture is inaccurate not only for the nineteenth century but for many centuries before. The Nordic countries' population "has been very mobile for centuries," one scholar found, and another showed that conditions in central Sweden's Dalarna province were driving people to seek work elsewhere perhaps as far back as the Middle Ages.... It was the same in Italy, where two scholars who examined the exodus from a northern community for 1865–1921 noted that this emigration really demonstrated "continuity in an apparently long-standing pattern of intense but short-distance migration." The inhabitants traditionally traveled for work away from home, but not overseas. Balkan men similarly trekked across much of southern Europe looking for jobs. An Irishman was therefore speaking for generations and an entire continent, not just for his 1881 peers, when he told the royal commissioners investigating the vast farm labor migration into England, "We are like wild geese, your honor."...

Frequently it was specific information from America that drew the emigrant. As an Italian politician put it, "the strongest emigration agent is the postage-stamp." Branko M. Colakovic's interviews with 500 Yugoslavs who had crossed the ocean before 1925 led him to conclude that the pull from America was more important than the push from even the harshest Yugoslav conditions. Higher wages were crucial, and pamphlets from American railroads and state immigration bureaus bombarded the would-be immigrant with statistics to support the agents' claims. "It was almost heaven," a Finn said in recalling tales of the wealth that allegedly awaited workers in the United States. "You could almost just grab the money!" And Swedish children in Småland called the distant land where their relatives were heading not America but *mer rika*—"more rich."...

As this emigration to America mushroomed, its makeup began to shift. It remained a heavily rural, peasant movement, but no longer did family groups dominate. Single women arrived, but their numbers were overwhelmed by those of men, especially young men. "They came in droves of males," a U.S. congressman remarked, and the change was dramatic enough to draw attention: the U.S. Census report for 1910 observed that with the increased immigration from southern and eastern Europe, the foreign-born showed "a very marked excess of males"—154.6 males to 100 females from Austria, 160.8 to 100 from Hungary, 190.6 to 100 from Italy, 137.3 to 100 from Russia....

The transformation in the makeup of this emigration was apparently not driven by racial or regional factors but by economic ones. In the decade ending in 1910, in fact, almost 70 percent of *all* immigrants into the United States were males, mainly young males. Women continued to arrive, but many found work not in the factories but as servants, or they remained within family groups. And for both men and women it was a migration of youth. Some of the Austro-Hungarian groups had more than 80 percent in the 14–44 age category after 1900; for U.S. immigration as a whole, persons in that age group accounted for 83.4 percent of the total in the exploding influx of 1906–10. This changing flow had a large impact on the emigration districts of Europe, too: the exodus of men from Slovak regions of Hungary was so heavy that by 1910 there only 532 men in Slovakia for every 1,000 women.

Part of the change in the exodus was that immigrants increasingly planned only a short stay in America—nothing to put down roots for, just enough to pile up some savings that could be used for better living or a specific project at home....

No one expected such work to be easy. "Everyone works like hell," a Finn wrote home from Michigan, and the experiences gave rise to a Polish saying: "America for the oxen, Europe for the peasant." A YMCA leader examining the immigrants' situation in Pittsburgh found that as a rule they earned the lowest wages and worked the "full stint" of hours, including twelve hours daily on a seven-day week at the blast furnaces. Long hours were common for immigrant workers; so was energy-sapping labor....

They agreed: you worked hard in America. One had to "sweat more during a day than during a whole week in Poland," a peasant immigrant wrote home. Returnees to Ireland said that they had worked like slaves, and some argued that "if people worked hard at home they would make as much money at home as anyone in America." Interviewers with Norwegian immigrants found general agreement that they had to work harder in America than in Norway. Similar comments appeared across the Continent as remigrants recounted their experiences....

Stories of the enormous sacrifices immigrants made to build up savings circulated in the industrial centers and even in the halls of Congress. Common laborers in Pittsburgh were reported to be putting away up to $15 a month; this is consistent with Ewa Morawska's conclusion that the savings by east-central European men in Johnstown averaged $100–200 annually. Italian laborers had the highest savings rate among European laborers, according to a 1907 Bureau of Labor report, putting away $25–27 monthly from railroad work. Floating immigrant workers in the western Midwest and Plains states were reported to have "clear saving" of $1 per day from wages of only $1.25–1.65. An American working in a steel mill found many employees who did not save, but he said that "practically all the 'Hunkies' of twenty-eight or thirty and over saved very successfully"—and these were expecting to return to Europe. One told him: "A good job, save money, work all time, go home, sleep, no spend."...

Closely related to the immigrants' desire to save and their willingness to put up with dismal job conditions was their acceptance of housing that was primitive and congested in the extreme. Some of this acquiescence stemmed from peasant backgrounds, but much arose also from "the desire of employees from the south and east of Europe to decrease expenses," as a government investigator put it. If they crowded together in sleeping rooms, their rent could be sharply reduced; if all went together in a communal cooking and eating plan, or hired a wife or "boss" to handle cooking—the Italian *bordo,* the Bulgarian *boort,* the "boarding boss" system—then costs could be cut even further....

In coal mining areas the immigrants sometimes lived in deserted pigpens and cowsheds: "You might call them outhouses," one critic said. A manufacturer told of seeing the homes of Italian and Hungarian miners at Honey Brook, Pennsylvania, where the huts were seven feet high, "built of slabs and rotten planks and poles, and I supposed when I saw them that they were places where these people, the miners around there, kept their pigs or something. I didn't really suppose, to look at them, that they were the habitations of human beings." Similarly, a Knights of Labor official encountered a settlement of Hungarian brick workers near Detroit: it had 127 persons living in a building ten feet by fifty feet, including five families cooped into a single room, "eating from one common kettle of food and sleeping in one common bed."...

Lacking a long-term commitment, these immigrants often rebuffed those seeking to enlist them in broader campaigns. They suffered their own maltreatment in silence rather than fight for justice. "These creatures are willing to take anything offered them, because they do not intend to remain, and will sacrifice anything to acquire a little fortune," the Brass-Workers national leader asserted contemptuously. Finns working in a Colorado mine drew a similar complaint from a coworker, who said that they were "ignorant of the language and ways of working in this country, and will take from the bosses any insult they may offer, and are willing to accept any usage in the company's boardinghouse." The central European peasant in America, it was said, "kissed the hand of the boss who sent him to work." Ultimately, then, the lower levels of America's booming industries were filling up with persons who willingly endured lower wages, coarse treatment, and poor conditions. They avoided friction with the boss so the paychecks would not stop coming. Because of this, they were widely regarded as a retarding influence in the drive for better conditions in the nation's workplaces....

It did not take long for reaction to build against such workers. A reporter covering Pennsylvania's mining strikes testified in 1888 that he saw Hungarians, Poles, and Italians "marched up to the shanties" from the train at the Highland mines in the Lehigh region; they were blamed with "breaking down the strike" there.

Recruitment of immigrants to break strikes was sometimes blatant, but often the onrushing tide made recruitment unnecessary: they arrived regardless. The *Chicagoer Arbeiter-Zeitung* was both pro-union and pro-immigrant and was therefore in a quandary as the influx began to affect the city's labor market: "We are not enemies of immigration and hence cannot choose to fight it; but we must still raise the question: What should be done to lessen, or eliminate, the decrease in wages resulting from the huge labor supply?" Given Chicago's scarcity of jobs, the newspaper asked, "What, then, can the new immigrants do save offer their labor below the established pay scale?" It feared the result: Chicago's established workers would be forced to give way to the cheaper immigrant labor....

Without a doubt, many immigrants returned because they had succeeded in America. The Finn who predicted that he would go home as soon as "the pockets [were] full of money" spoke for legions. And though a variety of explanations, including failure, appeared among those returning to Szamosszeg, Hungary, an investigator found that "more considered that they had fulfilled their purpose for going"—that is, they reached their saving target. Three to five years was the most frequent length of stay in America to reach the immigrant's goal, although many stayed longer and some, less. Slovaks reportedly set $1,000 as the "fortune" to be amassed before they would return, and among the workers in a 1919 steel mill pit was "a quiet-eyed Pole, who was saving up two hundred dollars to go to the old country." But interviews with other Poles who returned after World War I turned up many who were much more successful, including one who left the United States with $6,000 in his money belt—and on the ship discovered more: a vest with double lining sewed up with banknotes. Immediately he encountered a Croat running wildly and yelling, "Has anyone seen my vest?" It was returned to him. Such funds carried in belts, bags, clothing, and pockets formed an important portion of the transfer of American wealth across the ocean.

Interviews with returned Finns and questionnaire data disclosed the fact that, although these immigrants had performed some of the hardest drudgery in American capitalist enterprises during the 1880–1930 years—in such jobs as logging, mining, and steel mill work—they were still overwhelmingly positive about their achievements. A 1934 study found that 40.3 percent (255 persons) reported good results in America, 17.3 percent (109) had "quite good" results, and 16.4 percent (104) had a "fair results." Only 18.5 percent reported a bad result. Later studies uncovered similar findings....

If the journey to America was based heavily on the expectation of finding employment in American industry, it was therefore vulnerable to the vicissitudes of that industry. The label "migrant industrials" was fastened on these immigrants by an American scholar, but it was contemporary Italians who called the United States "the workshop." Italians flocked to this land of labor mainly in March, April, and May, and their heaviest returns were in October, November, and December, when layoffs were often most numerous. And the workshop could close, as it did at times, abruptly, sending throngs eastward across the Atlantic. One remigrant in late 1894 was a Pole who encountered many of his compatriots "running away from America. The stagnation existing there has now driven them out of their 'new homeland,'" he said. Remigration data revealed that a large proportion of those returning had been in factory work, mills, or mining, occupations especially vulnerable to the boom-and-bust nature of the American economy....

Many immigrants viewed the increasing returns not as a reason to celebrate the American economy but as grounds to condemn it. Some European observers charged that there would be even more returns if not for the shame that prevented some immigrants from going home; better to hang on and hope for improvement than return in disgrace. And many who went back were seemingly "worse than when they came, for many had failed and were broken in spirit," Edward Steiner observed after his steerage interviews.

Embitterment against America often followed, as with the Irishman who had arrived in Cleveland just in time for an economic depression. His brother was already there but had lost his savings when a bank failed, and only because a sister was married to a still-employed policeman was the Irishman able to remain alive—barely—until he could make his way back to Ireland. "He hates to talk about it, and he even hates the Yanks that come home," a friend later recalled; "he said America ruined his life." Another told of returning Irishmen who were so destitute when they landed that they had to walk all the way home to Kilkenny from the Dublin docks, some seventy miles. They were not proud of their time in America....

Other travelers on returning ships were repeatedly struck by the large numbers of injured, broken, or ill immigrants on board and the multiplicity of widows. One American was surprised that more than a fifth of those coming back on the steamship *Canopic* were sick. Steiner looked at returning Polish women who seemed crushed (their cheeks pale and pinched, their skin severely wrinkled) and asked himself how it could be otherwise: "They had lived for years by the coke ovens of Pennsylvania, breathing sulphur with every breath; their eyes had rarely seen the full daylight and their cheeks had not often felt the warm sunlight."...

Looming behind these health problems, the missing limbs and diseased lungs, were the conditions of labor in America. A leading Hungarian-American newspaper, *Szabadság* of Pittsburgh, featured in its yearly almanac a chapter titled "Fatal Accidents and Mine Disasters." It had plenty of material to chronicle—cave-ins, explosions, haulage accidents—and one recent estimate is that 25 percent of the New Immigrant workers in Carnegie Steel's South Works in Pittsburgh were killed or injured in the 1907–10 years. Immigrants struggled against such conditions mainly by quitting but also by forming their own mutual aid societies, often a carryover from home....

High on the list for condemnation, after unsafe working conditions, was the driving of workers in the American system—relentless, shoving, pushing, threatening. Peasants had been raised with different manners and a different pace of daily and yearly work. Gone now were the special holidays and festivals that dotted the work year in Europe; vanished as well were name days and wedding feasts when work was not allowed. And notably absent in the day-to-day handling of employment in large American concerns or labor gangs was consideration for individual problems: an illness, a need to visit a relative, a family problem that took someone away from work for a day.

Now there were supervisors who used fines or dismissal as weapons to enforce the speedup. Herbert Gutman stressed the personal costs of the peasant's transformation to wage laborer, and angry reactions by immigrants are not difficult to locate in the industrial records of the era. Many returned to Ireland to take up fishing again because, it was said, "they preferred that free life to bosses and clocks." One remigrant said that he was glad to be back where work was hard but free and easy, for "there is no clock or watch or boss to watch you here."…

New structures were going up all across Europe as the nineteenth century closed—houses with tile or slate roofs instead of thatch, a large window with a view to the road, walls of brick or plastered white, doorways sporting brass knobs and shiny varnish. Boards replaced logs, tile replaced thatch…. These "American" villages brought together many of the tangible, as well as intangible, results of return migration. The "American houses," which sprang up like mushrooms after a rain, were quickly noticed by visitors. When Carlo Levi was exiled to a tiny southern Italian town by Mussolini in the mid-1930s, his early walks through the poverty-stricken district brought him to some homes that were surprising, different. These had a second floor and balcony, even fancy varnish and doorknobs. They were exceptional among the drab huts of a peasant village. "Such houses belonged to the 'Americans,'" he noted.

The American houses were outward symbols of changes that affected not only the Continent's physical surfaces but also its inner life, customs, and traditions. For the remigrants were often different people when they returned, and their accomplishments soon reached beyond the Italian saying, "He who crosses the ocean can buy a house." Their determination, as well as the structures they built, could inspire their neighbors. It was said that "the people went wild from envy and desire" when a Pole returned and bought land on which he built two houses in his Galician community. He and his deeds were noted; his capacity for achievements and the source of his funds were obvious. All were explained by the fact of his round-trip journey abroad. Asked about the home he proudly showed, an Italian commented simply, "America bought this house."…

But, though negative experiences were abundant, travelers in Europe over the years encountered what seemed to be almost a single view among remigrants, a chorus that overwhelmed dissonant voices. This was a sentiment extolling the United States, an attitude that seemed surprising in view of the conditions they had known. It was surprising because most returners had seen firsthand the contradictions in American life; they could show missing fingers and arms and talk knowingly of the United States as "a challenging giant, both fair and unfair, ugly and beautiful." They accepted the view that life was cruel in America and that the nation's coarse citizenry did not appreciate beauty; as the Italian saying put it bluntly, "Had the peasant known all this, he wouldn't have gone to America." Critics at home feasted on such tales.

Still, despite their difficulties abroad, massive numbers of remigrants carried home attitudes toward America that were overwhelmingly positive. Some of this can be put down to the human tendency to remember happy times and submerge the difficult times. These contrasts did not survive in a simple relationship among remigrants, however: favorable memories involving the United States seem to have coexisted as an intricate part of some very bad experiences. Like a patent medicine that irritates the skin to produce a warm feeling, struggles in America's industrial cauldron were passed through the filter of memory and emerged as recollections of the proud role remigrants had played in creating the American industrial colossus. Their labors were essential. However small their part on the section gang or meat-packing line, they had helped build America....

In the final analysis, the story of the returned immigrants is a record of the endurance of home and family ties. It provides further evidence that, for many, immigration demonstrated the strength and unity of the family—both in going to America and in returning—rather than the family's weakening or destruction. For it was to rejoin their people, to walk again on their own land, to sit in the parish church once more, that the temporary immigrants repacked their America trunks and booked passage again, this time for home....

Permanently Lost: The Trauma of Immigration

VICTOR GREENE

... This book closely examines a part of the immigrants' expressive culture, namely the popular music and song of these groups, as an intimate reflection of their concerns about their migratory experience. The ballads in particular offer a sensitive evocation of the complex emotional feeling that individuals had about both their movement to America and their ties to their ethnic tradition. Knowing the lyrical content of those songs, their social and situational context, and the circumstances under which they were sung all lead to the conclusion that immigrants generally, though not uniformly, suffered personal discomfort from and disillusionment over their transfer. For most, such psychic unease was not total, however, for these newcomers also retained in America some of the optimistic sentiments that originally propelled them to the new land. They did recognize that it was in some ways a better place for them. But as aliens in an unfamiliar society, they soon came to understand better the sacrifice they made in moving. Most did stay while some returned. More significantly here, they developed a considerable ambivalence about their migration, rendered in both music and song....

Recent medical findings support the view that music is closely connected to the mind. They suggest that musical patterns have a special ability of enduring in listeners' consciousness. A familiar piece has such a profound retentive effect, both conscious and subconscious, that the affected individuals consider it a part of their identity. Psychological and musicological research refer to that property as "music on the brain."...

If individuals retain music as deeply affective, it follows that song added to melody also represents and even further contributes to a person's emotional state.

Victor Greene, *A Singing Ambivalence: American Immigrants Between Old World and New,* 1830–1930, Kent State University Press, 2004, p. xvii–xviii, 58, 60–64, 72–73, 76, 84–86, 95, 98, 104–105, 114, 116–117, 128–129, 132–137, 139, 154, 158. Copyright © 2004 by The Kent State University Press. Reprinted by permission.

One observer who has related the folksong to individual consciousness has cited one of its properties revealing ordinary people's *mentalité*....

Eastern European Jews

It is clear that the Jews are one of the most familiar minorities in the United States. Their conspicuous position is because they began coming to America as a group in colonial days and continued in much larger numbers into the nineteenth and early twentieth centuries. Also, they have achieved significant social mobility over the years and prominence in a number of fields. In addition, until recently outsiders knew them historically as a homeless people, spread around the world, peripatetic in the Diaspora. But not being Christian and traditionally regarded negatively as a marginal people, Jews have always been on the move. Ever since ancient times, when they were forced out of the Holy Land, they had to move elsewhere, first settling in lands around the Mediterranean Sea and later shifting farther into Europe and then overseas. Historically, as much as any other people, the Jews experienced migration and marginality. While some countries did offer them sanctuary even with privileges, they always lived as outsiders, everywhere a minority in a world dominated by Gentiles of differing religions, particularly Christianity and Islam....

Certainly, as previous writers have noted and as this work has already shown, Yiddish immigrant songs do express themes that were universal among all groups coming to America. These were feelings of discomfort and ambivalence over leaving familiar surroundings, fearing the dangers of the crossing, the difficulties at the arrival, and worry over not being accepted at the port of entry; despite their eternal wanderings, Jews even bemoaned nostalgic homesickness for the eastern European, Old World village from which they came. In their case, though, they romanticized their little Jewish village, the shtetl.

Admittedly, unhappiness over the weakening of family ties in the migration was universal among all groups going to America. But again, in the Jewish case the pressure and stress on the perceived parent–child relationship still appeared particularly heavy to bear. As a knowledgeable reviewer of a recent work on Jewish fathers and families puts it, "If the civilization of the Jews has one preoccupation, it is with the family."...

..., the marginal condition of Jews had traditionally meant that it was common for male breadwinners to have to leave home and look for work. This departure of men and husbands created a particular song genre known everywhere as *agune* ballads, forms of which date back to medieval times. Essentially, these musical works were the earnest cries of the deserted wife, the *agune*, whose spouse had gone off to work and had left her to shoulder the burdens of home and parenting. Her complaint of loss was additionally hurtful to those women who might seek another mate, for divorce in Jewish law was extremely difficult under such circumstances....

One of the best-known songs on both sides of the Atlantic dealing with departure and its effect on the family is the lullaby written by one of the Jews' best-known writer, Sholem Aleichem, probably in the 1880s. When it appeared as a published poem in 1892, it had already been set to music and became so hugely popular that it had many variants. "Shlof Mein Kind" ("Sleep My Child") is a mother's explanation to her child as to why she, the parent, is crying. The reason is largely from anxiety about being alone; the husband-father is thousands of miles away. Yet as the woman states, as unhappy as she is, she does anticipate that her situation will improve. She reminds her son that she expects the father to call for them soon and looks forward to the time when the family will all be reunited in America, where they will live in comfort:

Sleep my child.
By your cradle your mother sits
Sings a song and weeps....
In America is your father ...
In America there is for all ... real joy and a paradise
There on weekdays they eat Khale [Sabbath white bread]
[And there I will make broths ...]
God bidding he will send us ... letters ... [and] twenty dollars
And his picture, too ... he will take us ... over there
He will hug us then and kiss us ...
[So] Until the ticket comes ...
Sleep my little son.

... Nevertheless, while honoring America philosophically for the freedom it offered to a pariah people seeking a secure home, still on balance, as Slobin has stated, the Yiddish American song repertoire and especially its most popular pieces dwell on the unhappiness of the immigrant in his daily life, actually coming to and living in America....

Likely the most popular song among Jewish Americans when it appeared around World War I was "Di Grine Kusine" ("The Green Cousin"). Despite its extraordinary, widespread popularity, its origins and the true identity of its original composer are exceptionally complicated and uncertain. The song's creators were likely Abe Schwartz or Jacob Leiserowitz, who wrote the music, and Hyman Prizant, the lyricist. The most solid additional evidence is that "Di Grine Kusine" first appeared in a newspaper early in 1917 and was performed as a theater song at the Grand Theater in New York. It was such an instant sensation that in the next few years it spawned a rash of other ballads about the innocent female "greenhorn cousin."

Another certainty attested to by critics is the song's paramount significance, for it has been referred to as "the most famous of all Jewish immigrant songs," "one of the most popular songs of immigrant life of America," "the biggest song hit in the history of Jewish music," and "the most famous song of its time." As Leiserowitz was a satirist, some might place the piece in the comic tradition of a greenhorn's life like that of the Swedish Olle I Stkatthult group. But a reading of the lyrics certainly does not indicate such a lighthearted or humorous characterization. The song is a serious comment about the vulnerability, exploitation, and lost innocence of a newly arrived working girl in American capitalistic society. It was a "bitter song of defeat" that "provoked tears" and became "an enormous hit."...

> There came to me a cousin
> Pretty as gold was she, the green one
> Her cheeks were like red oranges
> Her little feet just begged for a dance....
> She walked not but she skipped
> She talked not but she sang
> Gay and cheerful was her manner
> This is how my cousin once was.

The narrator then gets her a job in millinery store, and in stating his gratitude to the "Golden Land" for providing employment, he expresses that ambivalence about America that affected so many other immigrants. In the end, though, her exhausting labor causes her ruination.

> Many years of collecting wages
> Till nothing was left of her
> Beneath her pretty blue eyes
> Black lines were drawn
> Her cheeks, once like red oranges
> Have turned completely green already
> Today, when I meet my cousin
> And I ask her: How are you green one?
> She'll reply with a grimace
> To blazes with Columbus's country!

The Italians

In numerous ways Italian immigrants to America had experiences and hence produced songs that spoke about themes similar to those of other newcomers. The Italians also produced a mix of optimistic and pessimistic songs, some of which glorified the attractions of the new land, such as several in thanking Columbus, their countryman, for finding the New World. They also lionized the Great Discoverer for his deed, for Italians, of course, had the greatest ethnic claim on the man. But recognizing him was not only done with praise; they referred to him in negative terms as well. Hence for this group as well, contradictory references blaming and lionizing their hero suggest a certain ambivalence about their emigration.

Once again, Italians echoed the concerns of other groups in their musical criticism of those emigrating, particularly stressing the perils of leaving. As in the case of northern Europeans and Germans, for example, some Italian lyrics commonly reject the whole idea of abandoning home and family. And as in the Irish case, much is made of the ominous threat of ship disasters. Generally with the others too was the pervasive theme of dissatisfaction and discomfort of arriving and settling in the new land. While these southern Europeans bemoaned the discriminatory treatment of the dominant Anglo-Americans, their accounts in song characteristically differ from the widespread unease by a particular unfamiliarity and confusion over a certain cultural norm of their hosts....

Sensitive accounts have dwelled on the difficult psychological state and conflict that immigrants felt when situated in America. Robert Orsi has identified a source of that mental struggle in his description of the popular religious manifestations in one of the ethnic group's major centers, Italian Harlem in New York City. That inner discomfort came to the fore, he asserts, when newcomers celebrated their patron-saint days. That pain was the result not only from the fond memory of "Calabria bella" but also of the heavy and constant pressure newcomers felt to assure themselves that their sacrifice in leaving home was worth the effort. As Orsi puts it, they suffered from "guilt that they were not doing enough, pressure to work harder and faster, and fear that they would be unsuccessful…, all this haunted the early arrivals."

Other evidence of the ambivalence of immigrants upon arrival is an autobiographical poem that a re-emigrant published in the early 1920s that reviews his overseas experience. The pain of marginality in the poem "A Hurried Man" has to do with the conflict of American vis-à-vis traditional values. In America there are fewer traditions for guidance than in the old country, and Americans are too absorbed with a spirited quest for progress. The new culture thus minimizes the warm old-country feelings of love and kindness. Thus ironically put, what is achieved in America causes an unhappy, permanent alienation from Italy. "America, you gather the *hungry* people and give them new hungers for the old ones."

Another song that indicates the conflict in the mind of the immigrant is "The Disillusioned Immigrant."…

Money, Money, Money!
Where is that money?
I dreamed a strange dream, I dreamed of finding it in trees
Money, Money, Money!
Stay right where you are
If this is what America is like,
I want to go back!

The Poles and Hungarians

… Both Polish and Hungarian immigrants came from the same regional and sociological origins, largely as peasants from the predominantly agrarian heartland of Eastern Europe, and with similar motives and goals. That was to supply the great and continual need in the burgeoning American heavy industry for unskilled labor in the mines, steel mills, meatpacking plants, oil refineries, and the like. This commonality of social class among the vast majority of Polish and Hungarian immigrants can also be applied to the other central and eastern Europeans, such as the Slovaks, Lithuanians, Rumanians, and other South Slavs, heading for the New World.

But while all these immigrant groups were much alike in the types of jobs they held and their economic goals, one must be careful not to describe each of the groups internally as sociologically homogeneous. Admittedly, the well-known depiction of Jurgis, the Lithuanian immigrant in Upton Sinclair's famous proletarian novel *The Jungle,* rightly indicates that getting work at a Chicago slaughter-house was apt for many, even perhaps most, Eastern Europeans. The muckraking author, in fact, based his novel on his experience living in the Yards section of the city. But his drawing such a figure undoubtedly contributed to the creation of the unflattering stereotype of the "Hunkie" in later years.

The generalized picture of that suffering, muscle-bound, unintelligent, naïve clod obscured an accurate picture of those peoples' communities....

Intimate evidence shows, like all the other European groups, the psychic strain on Poles of being connected to both Old and New Worlds, needing to go west for practical reasons but still reluctant to leave home and family. The decision-making process for these emigrants too was not an easy one.

Admittedly, many of those considering leaving did have sources of information that indicated the attractive potential for achieving success and prosperity. One source of the freer life and higher wage rates in America was the correspondence from earlier emigrants whom villagers knew, thus the importance of "chain" migration. Perhaps even more important as a prod to leave was the re-emigration and presence of returnees themselves. In her outstanding ethnographic study of the eastern Europeans in Johnstown, Pennsylvania, Ewa Morawska identifies in particular the dramatic and hence major stimulus for emigration as simply the personal appearance in the village of the prosperous, returned migrant. That personification of success was, more than any other evidence, proof of the possibility of achieving the ultimate and much desired status of the eastern European peasant, becoming *kmiec,* a yeoman farmer....

That Chicago Polish repertoire, then, is instructive, for it offers a complex of immigrant opinion, mainly dissatisfaction. "Chicago's Krakowiak" (a Polish dance form emanating from Galicia) condemns the law's arbitrary treatment of immigrants. Be careful, it says, for one will find deception in the smoky Chicago stockyards—if one gets into a quarrel with a neighbor, a policeman will put you in a patrol car, you will go to jail, and you will "not see the world for a long time." A more bitter piece, ironically titled "No Place Is Better than Chicago," says: "If you go out into the street from your miserable cell, then my brother [I am not lying], the policeman will shoot you straight in your head", with the refrain, "O let's dance, the policeman is always triumphant." Even when trying to romance a woman on the street by telling her she is lovely, "you can surely expect an arrest and immediately you will be in court." Politicians are no better than the police, for they punish simple people and, as city council members, "have glue on their palms."...

A notable exception to the dominant pessimism about life in the United States are a few songs about women, that is, songs that welcomed the freedom and independence for those who were single. The model of this genre is a cabaret song simply titled "Kuplet," in which a young woman characterizes her transition to America and her emancipation in the change of her name, from Kaszka to Katie. In Poland, Kaszka used "to tend geese, hungry, barefooted, and dirty all over." But in America, after being employed at several jobs where she earned money, Katie ultimately attains the status of "lady" as a saleswoman in a store. Not only did American employment help Katie's social mobility, but its laws were also an ally and protector. While men's songs criticize the police and the courts for mistreatment and corruption, the Katies welcome them as a defense against spousal abuse and violence, even forcing suitors into marriage when called for and assuring wives and divorcees of sufficient financial support.

That new female assertiveness also showed up at the workplace, if only on occasion. Since there is only one musical example of this, it is still not possible to know how widespread workforce assimilation was for females. But it certainly demonstrates a new spiritedness among immigrant working women. This *kuplet*, "Na Przyzbie" ("At the Home Conversation Bench"), which appeared in 1916, tells of a strike by women in a cigarette factory who then attack their boss after he has mistreated them and referred to them as "cattle."…

The Chinese

As one might readily imagine, the effect of the dominant Anglo-Americans society on the nonwhite immigrants from Asia and Latin America was clearly more devastating psychically than that on newly arriving Europeans. The basis of the difference was, of course, the racial one, a much greater hostility by whites toward others. That such prejudice and discrimination caused considerable pain and anguish among Chinese and Mexican immigrants hardly needs much debate. While the hope and dream of achieving financial success in the United States, or "Gold Mountain," as the Chinese referred to it, among Asian arrivals may have been undiminished down to recent times, certainly the mental and emotional distress in trying to earn income was well articulated in the songs and lyrics that both Chinese and Mexican immigrants sang.…

To be sure, again as elsewhere, the immigrant songs are not universal expressions of injury. Following the historical and sociological research of Madeline Hsu and Paul Siu among the Chinese, a few works (as I will suggest below) are positive about the Chinese prospects and even excited about the potential chances for material success. But overwhelmingly the songs consist of statements of dissatisfaction in America, directed at not only their Caucasian hosts but also on occasion at representatives of their own government for its failure to adequately protect its people. Overall then, Chinese American song does offer evidence of that "immigrant voice" that the newer historians, Wong and Chan, have asked for.…

The most obvious technical distinction in the Chinese immigrant repertoire, according to [Marlon] Hom, is the unusual way that the hopes and fears of women left behind are expressed by the *male* arrivals in America. Emigrant men would perform in gender reverse as wives or other females lamenting the loss of family members in works sung abroad. Overseas, males vocalized those female roles not only because few women had left home but also because cultural convention dictated that men could not speak openly about spousal affection. Thus they could do so only in disguise. This genre of song is important since by openly expressing themselves as women in song, men used the latter "as a vehicle of their own feelings."

Overall, more specific subjects covered by the immigrant songs in Hom's list are the standard ones of hoping to gain income abroad to buy land at home, the debate over whether one should marry a prospective male emigrant, and the difficulties of family separation. The particular concern among the Chinese was the inordinate length of time that husbands as sojourners were expected to be away. A work exemplifying these worries is one where the "wife" sings:

> Poverty leads to desperation:
> My husband took off to Gold Mountain
> You left home for Gold Mountain.
> Five years have since passed; I haven't seen him come home.
> Many times I write and ask geese to deliver my messages to him.

… Again, these songs are similar to the unhappiness of Europeans about the straining of family ties, but the conditions of departure and absence put a sharper edge on the disruption among the Chinese.

Besides the problems of separation, transportation to America was also exceptionally difficult for emigrants in particular. Unlike those coming from Europe, the greater length of the passage created more concern about personal security and even survival in the minds of the Asians….

As the first immigrant group to suffer legally racial discrimination and prejudice, Chinese immigrants found their reception both immediately and over time increasingly uncomfortable. Their songs reflect that change. While their experience in some ways was similar to European emigrants in their initial hopes to win wealth and return to a better life in the old country, along with much homesickness for family, loved ones, and their ancestral home, these Asian arrivals encountered a much more hostile reception. The longer distance from their village, both culturally and psychically, than those from Europe; the greater intensity of majority discrimination; and the more formidable legal barriers to their immigration all distinguished their settling here.

But the group did have a compensation: Their musical compositions provided not just an outlet for their emotional distress but also some insight into how they felt about their mistreatment. The songs not only bemoaned the discomfort of male loneliness and victimization but also offered a basis of action through united resistance. Thus, strangely enough, this music of pain and powerlessness also provided a sense of self-confidence, moral strength, and even ethnic identity.

The Mexicans

The last major immigrant group that appeared in the United States through the 1930s was the Mexicans. The proposition that song would indeed convey their mentality is perhaps least contentious in their case; many Americans have long recognized and admired Latino culture for its rich musical content. In fact, the assertion is widely accepted that the musical artistry of those groups, including dance, like African American jazz, has had an enduring influence on American popular music over the past century. The popularity of Latin American and especially Mexican music has been so obvious that Anglos would have to agree that it must be an important part of the lives of Mexicans and Latinos….

From 1850 to the end of the century, the discovery of gold in California, the demand for mineworkers in Arizona, and above all the agricultural expansion in Texas and the rest of the region pulled in a modest number of Mexicans from not only the northern provinces but also from those farther south. By 1890 about 75,000 immigrants were living the United States. Another cause for emigration was the harsh dictatorial regime of Porfirio Diaz, which lasted from 1877 until his deposition in the Mexican Revolution of 1910. The brutal internal conflicts during that era pushed out many ordinary Mexicans seeking a more stable existence in the freer political system of the north. This movement into south Texas occurred despite the ongoing deterioration of order and near anarchy along the border. There, as a result of discriminatory laws that weakened them politically, Texas–Mexican leaders clashed violently at times with local, state, and even federal authorities in the persons of sheriffs, Texas Rangers, and occasionally the U.S. Army. Vigilantes and guerilla bands from both sides roamed widely in the area with impunity during the 1880s, a condition that resulted in a virtual civil war along the border. These clashes would resonate in Mexican folk legend and song.

Still, in the midst of all this violence, Mexican immigration continued and enlarged in the early twentieth century, drawing workers north particularly after the enormous expansion of commercial agriculture as a result of the Federal Reclamation Act of 1902 and consequent labor needs in the region. The Mexicans generally increased not only as a result of the political chaos and the revolution in 1910 but also by other general "pull" factors, such as the growth of American heavy industry, particularly the steel mills, in the Midwest; the labor shortages caused by World War I; and the restrictive policies sharply limiting European immigration in the 1920s. Mexicans largely filled the vacuum of unskilled workers that resulted from the near barring of Europeans in that decade....

As with every other group, the emigrant psyche was one of ambivalence, wanting to leave but with some hesitation. Mexicans poured out that clash of impulses in song, especially the *corrido,* which developed during the mid–1800s. The essence of that form had actually appeared centuries earlier in a musical rendering known as the *romance,* a sixteen-syllable line work with no refrain, similar to an epic poem. The *conquistadores* had brought it over from Spain in the 1500s. By the time of Mexican independence in 1821, this musical genre had developed into another song form, the *decima,* an eight-syllable verse; a half century later it became in turn the *corrido....*

Musical performance became a widely practiced form of social expression for these immigrants from the nineteenth century to the present. For the purposes of this study, of most interest are those created to the end of the 1800s, during the large-scale immigration through the 1920s, and the era of the Great Depression, when hundreds of thousands of Mexican immigrants and Mexican Americans were repatriated back to Mexico in its early days. The character of these immigrant ballads, according to major published collections, suggests how this group felt about their lives, the conditions in their homeland, and their American destination. Of course, most significant in these musical messages in the opinion expressed about the two societies, Mexican and American, on both sides of the border....

One representative and early collection of the Mexican song repertoire about the decision to leave is that of labor economist Paul Taylor, who indicates that the dilemma of the emigrant was similar to the ambivalence of the other ethnic groups. Three works, likely dating from the major migration of the 1920s, typify the enduring clash of motives of necessity and reluctance. One, "Defensa de Los Norteños" ("Defense of the Emigrants"), is a plaintive plea of a Mexican in the United States who defensively responds to criticism from others for leaving home. He concludes:

> Many people have said that we are not patriotic
> Because we go to serve for the accursed *patotas* [Americans, derisively]
>
> But let them give us jobs and pay us decent wages;
> Not one Mexican then will go to foreign lands.
>
> We're anxious to return again to our adored country;
> but what can we do about it if the country is ruined?

... A related *corrido* is an unusually revealing dialogue between an emigrant returnee and one who never left. "A Conversation between Two Ranchers" again shows the rationalization that emigrants had to make to others for leaving as well as the importance of religious symbolism. The emigrant first brags about his success, his fine clothes, his "pockets always filled with plenty of silver," his winning "classy" women, and the higher standard of living in America, while

> Here [in Mexico] for twenty-five cents
> one works from sun to sun
> there is nothing else to eat
> but tortillas and beans.
> I grant that Mexico is very pretty,
> but it's down and out;
> one works day and night
> and never ceases to be a *pelado* [Indian].

... The conversation identifies and exposes a basic cultural difference between American and Mexican values, or better, a conflict *in the minds* of the emigrants themselves. Americans stress and uphold a forward-looking, acquisitive ethic that places money and material wealth in defining self-worth while Mexicans treasure their more humanistic culture based on tradition and the past. That difference may have festered *within* the mind of the immigrant....

But the most hostile criticism in the ballads over cultural decline is leveled at Mexican women in general, both immigrants and American born. The songs describe *Mexicanas* as particularly susceptible to adopting Yankee ways. In the Herrea-Sobek and Gamio lists of pre-1930 acculturation *corridos,* most of the ballads condemn the deleterious assimilative influence of modern, urbanized American fashion on Mexican females.

"Las Pollas de California" ("The [Anglo] Chicks from California"), for example, urges immigrant men in that state not to marry any women there, for they want only American clothes and food; "Los Mexicanos que Habla Inglés"

("The Mexicans Who Speak English") and "La Pochita" ("The Americanized Mexican Woman") refer derisively to those women who respond to Spanish questions only in English; and others like "El Rancho" ("The Ranch") and "Las Palonas" ("The Bobbed Heads") lament the destructive affects of the model American "flapper" among ethnic women. With her cosmetics and revealing dress, that gussied-up figure was hastening the demise of the old, noble feminine demeanor, a modest and restrained style of traditional attire and appearance.

More specifically, in another ballad, "Las Abolilladas" ("The Americanized Ones"), the up-to-date dresses make the woman in the song look like a "monkey" and the latest hairstyle makes her a "fool":

> You go out, showing your legs
> With your skirts up to your knees,
> God protect you because you have no modesty …
> [they] soon forget their native land
> And use skirts in place of pants.…
> They chew gum, try to speak English
> And are event ashamed of being Mexicans.

… The Mexicans, more aware of the obstacles to living in the United States, likely expressed the least enthusiasm for crossing the border and included anti-American heroes in their repertoire, but the prospect of these Latinos earning a better income in the land to the north still remained and was irresistible.

Admittedly, certain other groups produced popular songs that express a rather enthusiastic and positive optimism about leaving their Old World for the benefits of the New. German Forty-Eighters, liberal Europeans, Irish exiles, Italians and Jews who both commended Columbus for his great discovery, and young male and female emigrants were all eager to escape the oppression at home and the burdensome traditional family rules and obligations for a freer life in America. Even the greatest victims of racial prejudice, the Chinese, describing their destination as *Gam Saan* (Gold Mountain), and the Mexicans, both looked forward to gaining great wealth from more-lucrative employment and finding a more stable economic and political order too.

Yet that pervasive optimism about the future was dimmed by a number of hardships emigrants encountered on their journey and particularly after their arrival. These were the abuse and mistreatment of minorities, especially of non-whites, by both individuals and local authorities; the inequity, discrimination, and corruption of the U.S. judicial systems; and the excessive materialism and devastation inflicted on traditional cultural practices and gender roles.…

While appreciative of the greater personal freedom and economic opportunity one Greek elder found on this side of the Atlantic, he was still ambivalent about the crossing. He expressed his condition metaphorically, concluding that his heart was of two parts, each tied to the two countries. "You've got to love them both!" he concluded. But the response indicates a yet unresolved emotional condition.…

One unhappy woman, after six years in the United States, looked back on her coming as a mental dysfunction. It was like the attempted transplantation of "a flower that should live in black earth to sandy soil. It is still alive, but with each day it withers, and finally it stops blooming, and all that remains is a coarse stem." Yet while suffering all that spiritual erosion and being torn psychologically, she ultimately and painfully decided *not* to go back....

FURTHER READING

Richard Franklin Bensel, *The Political Economy of American Industrialization, 1877–1900* (2000).

Ron Chernow, *Titan: The Life of John D. Rockefeller, Sr.* (1998).

William Cronon, *Nature's Metropolis: Chicago and the Great West* (1991).

Hasia Diner, *Hungering for America: Italian, Irish and Jewish Foodways in the Age of Migration* (2002).

Ellen Eisenberg, Ava F. Kahn, and William Toll, *Jews of the Pacific Coast: Reinventing Community on America's Edge* (2010).

Wendy Gamber, *The Female Economy: The Millinery and Dressmaking Trades* (1997).

Elliot Gorn and Warren Goldstein, *A Brief History of American Sports* (1993).

Matthew Frye Jacobson, *Whiteness of a Different Color: European Immigrants and the Alchemy of Race* (1998).

Harold C. Livesay, *Andrew Carnegie and the Rise of Big Business* (2nd ed., 2000).

David Montgomery, *The Fall of the House of Labor* (1987).

Robert A. Orsi, *The Madonna of 115th Street: Faith and Community in Italian Harlem* (1985).

Kathy Peiss, *Cheap Amusements: Working Women and Leisure in Turn-of-the-Century New York* (1986).

Roy Rozenzweig, *Eight Hours for What We Will: Workers and Leisure in an Industrial City* (1983).

Philip Scranton, *Endless Novelty: Specialty Production and American Industrialization* (1997).

Stephen Thernstrom, *The Other Bostonians* (1973).

CHAPTER 4

Imperialism and World Power

In 1898 the United States embarked on its first war on behalf of the rights of people other than its own. Revolutionaries in Cuba had fought for thirty years (1868–1898) to break Spain's grasp on its last colony in the New World. With U.S. help, they finally did. Eighty years earlier, John Quincy Adams had warned at a similar moment that entanglement in foreign revolutions should be avoided because it would involve the United States "beyond the power of extrication in all the wars of interest and intrigue." No matter how righteous the initial cause, he stated, "the fundamental maxims of her policy would insensibly change from liberty to force.... She might become dictatress of the world. She would no longer be the ruler of her own spirit." The war against Spain to secure Cuba's independence, in line with Adams's prediction, in fact did not end there. The U.S. Congress passed the Platt Amendment in 1903, requiring Cuba to agree to unilateral American intervention indefinitely. More shockingly, in the course of the war the United States took the Philippine Islands, Guam, and Puerto Rico from Spain. The United States had initially collaborated with Filipino independence fighter Emilio Aguinaldo, but then, against his wishes, it transformed the islands into an American colony. When Aguinaldo detected this U.S. treachery, he launched a new rebellion, which the American army brutally suppressed. The U.S.-Philippine war lasted three years. Over four thousand U.S. troops died, along with nearly 200,000 Filipino rebels and civilians.

These first conflicts of the twentieth century contained in full measure the contradictions and danger that were to shape relations between the United States and the rest of the globe for the coming century. Presidents William McKinley, Theodore Roosevelt, and Woodrow Wilson, under whose direction the United States took up a leading role on the world stage, agreed that the time had come to exercise America's tremendous potential for international influence. They disagreed on the reasons for doing so. Should the United States be an imperial power, or should it fight to eradicate colonialism? Should the United States promote stability and the status quo, or should it promote decolonization and democracy? Should the United States "speak softly and carry a big stick," as Roosevelt argued, or should it exercise a moral diplomacy, as Woodrow Wilson believed?

Of course, even the existence of the debate reflected how far the United States had strayed from its traditional policy of "nonentanglement," dating back to George Washington. Any form of intervention involved the United States in disputes beyond its control and often beyond its understanding. Even the process of promoting democracy meant meddling in ways that undermined other people's self-determination. The United States did not have to exercise regional, and ultimately global, police power. But at the start of the twentieth century, it chose to do so. Why?

QUESTIONS TO THINK ABOUT

How could a nation with democratic values fight a colonial war? What rhetoric made this undertaking palatable—and what insecurities fueled it? Who opposed the war? Did democratic values stop at the water's edge?

DOCUMENTS

The documents in this chapter show the many sides to the debate over imperialism within the United States, and some of the ways in which people abroad perceived American actions and influence. In document 1, President William McKinley asks Congress to declare war against Spain "in the cause of humanity." Document 2 is a speech by New York Governor and former "Rough Rider" Theodore Roosevelt, given a year after the Spanish-American War. Roosevelt scorned anti-imperialists as weak. Only "the overcivilized man, who has lost the great fighting, masterful virtues," distrusted his country's motives, according to Roosevelt. The pugnacious New Yorker was elected vice president in 1898, and became president following the assassination of William McKinley in 1901. In document 3, the Filipino revolutionary Emilio Aguinaldo reveals what he thought of the United States in 1899: that it had sent an "army of occupation." The following two documents also condemn the policy of the McKinley administration. In document 4, the Anti-Imperialist League claims that the administration sought "to extinguish the spirit of 1776 in those islands." Mark Twain, author of *Tom Sawyer* and *Huckleberry Finn,* fiercely criticizes the racial and imperialist assumptions of the United States in document 5. In document 6, a soldier writes that American troops made more enemies than friends in the Philippines by calling the natives "Niggers" and by burning the houses of rebels and civilians alike. Document 7 reveals the world context: European powers often invaded countries that defaulted on their debts. Here, Argentine foreign minister Luis Drago reminds American leaders in 1902 of the equality of nations and their pledge under the Monroe Doctrine of 1823 to oppose European meddling in the Western Hemisphere. Would the U.S. help? Document 8 is the Platt Amendment, by which the U.S. government limited Cuban sovereignty following the war with Spain. In 1904, President Theodore Roosevelt expanded the meaning of the Monroe Doctrine, which had originally warned the great powers of Europe not to colonize or intervene in the affairs of the independent nations of Latin America. In the last reading, document 9, Roosevelt claimed a new role for the United States in his annual speech to

Congress as "an international police power" to prevent "chronic wrong-doing." In the following decade, the United States sent troops into the Dominican Republic, Haiti, Honduras, Mexico, and Nicaragua, all in the name of democracy and keeping the peace.

1. President William McKinley Asks for War to Liberate Cuba, 1898

...Our people have beheld a once prosperous community reduced to comparative want, its lucrative commerce virtually paralyzed, its exceptional productiveness diminished, its fields laid waste, its mills in ruins, and its people perishing by tens of thousands from hunger and destitution. We have found ourselves constrained, in the observance of that strict neutrality which our laws enjoin and which the law of nations commands, to police our own waters and watch our own seaports in prevention of any unlawful act in aid of the Cubans....

The war in Cuba is of such a nature that, short of subjugation or extermination, a final military victory for either side seems impracticable. The alternative lies in the physical exhaustion of the one or the other party, or perhaps of both—a condition which in effect ended the ten years' war by the truce of Zanjon. The prospect of such a protraction and conclusion of the present strife is a contingency hardly to be contemplated with equanimity by the civilized world, and least of all by the United States, affected and injured as we are, deeply and intimately, by its very existence....

The grounds for... intervention may be briefly summarized as follows:

First. In the cause of humanity and to put an end to the barbarities, bloodshed, starvation, and horrible miseries now existing there, and which the parties to the conflict are either unable or unwilling to stop or mitigate. It is no answer to say this is all in another country, belonging to another nation, and is therefore none of our business. It is specially our duty, for it is right at our door.

Second. We owe it to our citizens in Cuba to afford them that protection and indemnity for life and property which no government there can or will afford, and to that end to terminate the conditions that deprive them of legal protection.

Third. The right to intervene may be justified by the very serious injury to the commerce, trade, and business of our people and by the wanton destruction of property and devastation of the island.

Fourth, and which is of the utmost importance. The present condition of affairs in Cuba is a constant menace to our peace and entails upon this Government an enormous expense. With such a conflict waged for years in an island so near us and with which our people have such trade and business relations; when the lives and liberty of our citizens are in constant danger and their property destroyed and themselves ruined; where our trading vessels are liable to seizure and are seized at our very door by war ships of a foreign nation; the expeditions of filibustering that we are powerless to prevent altogether, and the irritating questions and

This document can be found in John Bassett Moore, *A Digest of International Law* (Washington, D.C.: Government Printing Office, 1906), VI, 211–223. Reprinted in Dennis Merrill and Thomas G. Paterson, eds., *Major Problems in American Foreign Relations*, Vol. I: to 1920, Sixth Ed. (Boston: Houghton Mifflin, 2005), 331–333.

entanglements thus arising—all these and others that I need not mention, with the resulting strained relations, are a constant menace to our peace and compel us to keep on a semi war footing with a nation with which we are at peace....

In view of these facts and of these considerations I ask the Congress to authorize and empower the President to take measures to secure a full and final termination of hostilities between the Government of Spain and the people of Cuba, and to secure in the island the establishment of a stable government, capable of maintaining order and observing its international obligations, insuring peace and tranquillity and the security of its citizens as well as our own, and to use the military and naval forces of the United States as may be necessary for these purposes....

2. Governor Theodore Roosevelt Praises the Manly Virtues of Imperialism, 1899

In speaking to you, men of the greatest city of the West, men of the state which gave to the country Lincoln and Grant, men who preeminently and distinctly embody all that is most American in the American character, I wish to preach not the doctrine of ignoble ease but the doctrine of the strenuous life; the life of toil and effort; of labor and strife; to preach that highest form of success which comes not to the man who desires mere easy peace but to the man who does not shrink from danger, from hardship, or from bitter toil, and who out of these wins the splendid ultimate triumph....

We of this generation do not have to face a task such as that our fathers faced, but we have our tasks, and woe to us if we fail to perform them! We cannot, if we would, play the part of China, and be content to rot by inches in ignoble ease within our borders, taking no interest in what goes on beyond them; sunk in a scrambling commercialism; heedless of the higher life, the life of aspiration, of toil and risk; busying ourselves only with the wants of our bodies for the day; until suddenly we should find, beyond a shadow of question, what China has already found, that in this world the nation that has trained itself to a career of unwarlike and isolated ease is bound in the end to go down before other nations which have not lost the manly and adventurous qualities. If we are to be a really great people, we must strive in good faith to play a great part in the world. We cannot avoid meeting great issues. All that we can determine for ourselves is whether we shall meet them well or ill. Last year we could not help being brought face to face with the problem of war with Spain. All we could decide was whether we should shrink like cowards from the contest or enter into it as beseemed a brave and high-spirited people; and, once in, whether failure or success should crown our banners. So it is now. We cannot avoid the responsibilities that confront us in Hawaii, Cuba, Puerto Rico, and the Philippines. All we can decide is whether we shall meet them in a way that will redound to the national credit, or whether we shall make of our dealings with these new problems a dark and shameful page in our history. To refuse to deal

---

Theodore Roosevelt, *The Strenuous Life and Other Essays* (New York, The Century Company, 1900), 4–10.

with them at all merely amounts to dealing with them badly. We have a given problem to solve. If we undertake the solution there is, of course, always danger that we may not solve it aright, but to refuse to undertake the solution simply renders it certain that we cannot possibly solve it aright.

The timid man, the lazy man, the man who distrusts his country, the over-civilized man, who has lost the great fighting, masterful virtues, the ignorant man and the man of dull mind, whose soul is incapable of feeling the mighty lift that thrills "stern men with empires in their brains"—all these, of course, shrink from seeing the nation undertake its new duties; shrink from seeing us build a navy and army adequate to our needs; shrink from seeing us do our share of the world's work by bringing order out of chaos in the great, fair tropic islands from which the valor of our soldiers and sailors has driven the Spanish flag. These are the men who fear the strenuous life, who fear the only national life which is really worth leading....

...I have scant patience with those who fear to undertake the tasks of governing the Philippines, and who openly avow that they do fear to undertake it, or that they shrink from it because of the expense and trouble; but I have even scanter patience with those who make a pretense of humanitarianism to hide and cover their timidity, and who cant about "liberty" and the "consent of the governed," in order to excuse themselves for their unwillingness to play the part of men. Their doctrines, if carried out, would make it incumbent upon us to leave the Apaches of Arizona to work out their own salvation, and to decline to interfere in a single Indian reservation. Their doctrines condemn your forefathers and mine for ever having settled in these United States....

I preach to you, then, my countrymen, that our country calls not for the life of ease, but for the life of strenuous endeavor. The twentieth century looms before us big with the fate of many nations. If we stand idly by, if we seek merely swollen, slothful ease, and ignoble peace, if we shrink from the hard contests where men must win at hazard of their lives and at the risk of all they hold dear, then the bolder and stronger peoples will pass us by and will win for themselves the domination of the world.

3. Filipino Leader Emilio Aguinaldo Rallies His People to Arms, 1899

By my proclamation of yesterday I have published the outbreak of hostilities between the Philippine forces and the American forces of occupation in Manila, unjustly and unexpectedly provoked by the latter.

In my manifest of January 8 [1899] last I published the grievances suffered by the Philippine forces at the hands of the army of occupation. The constant outrages and taunts, which have caused the misery of the people of Manila, and, finally the useless conferences and the contempt shown the Philippine government prove the premeditated transgression of justice and liberty.

Major-General E. S. Otis, *Report on Military Operations and Civil Affairs in the Philippine Islands, 1899* (Washington, D.C.: Government Printing Office, 1899), 95–96.

I know that war has always produced great losses; I know that the Philippine people have not yet recovered from past losses and are not in the condition to endure others. But I also know by experience how bitter is slavery, and by experience I know that we should sacrifice all on the altar of our honor and of the national integrity so unjustly attacked.

I have tried to avoid, as far as it has been possible for me to do so, armed conflict, in my endeavors to assure our independence by pacific means and to avoid more costly sacrifices. But all my efforts have been useless against the measureless pride of the American Government and of its representatives in these islands, who have treated me as a rebel because I defend the sacred interests of my country and do not make myself an instrument of their dastardly intentions....

Be not discouraged. Our independence has been watered by the generous blood of our martyrs. Blood which may be shed in the future will strengthen it. Nature has never despised generous sacrifices.

4. The American Anti-Imperialist League Denounces U.S. Policy, 1899

We hold that the policy known as imperialism is hostile to liberty and tends toward militarism, an evil from which it has been our glory to be free. We regret that it has become necessary in the land of Washington and Lincoln to reaffirm that all men, of whatever race or color, are entitled to life, liberty and the pursuit of happiness. We maintain that governments derive their just powers from the consent of the governed. We insist that the subjugation of any people is "criminal aggression" and open disloyalty to the distinctive principles of our Government.

We earnestly condemn the policy of the present National Administration in the Philippines. It seeks to extinguish the spirit of 1776 in those islands. We deplore the sacrifice of our soldiers and sailors, whose bravery deserves admiration even in an unjust war. We denounce the slaughter of the Filipinos as a needless horror. We protest against the extension of American sovereignty by Spanish methods.

We demand the immediate cessation of the war against liberty, begun by Spain and continued by us. We urge that Congress be promptly convened to announce to the Filipinos our purpose to concede to them the independence for which they have so long fought and which of right is theirs.

The United States have always protested against the doctrine of international law which permits the subjugation of the weak by the strong. A self-governing state cannot accept sovereignty over an unwilling people. The United States cannot act upon the ancient heresy that might makes right.

Imperialists assume that with the destruction of self-government in the Philippines by American hands, all opposition here will cease. This is a grievous error. Much as we abhor the war of "criminal aggression" in the Philippines, greatly as we regret that the blood of the Filipinos is on American hands, we

Frederic Bancroft, ed., *Speeches, Correspondence, and Political Papers of Carl Schurz* (New York: G. P. Putnam's Sons, 1913), VI, 77–79.

more deeply resent the betrayal of American institutions at home. The real firing line is not in the suburbs of Manila. The foe is of our own household. The attempt of 1861 was to divide the country. That of 1899 is to destroy its fundamental principles and noblest ideals....

We hold, with Abraham Lincoln, that "no man is good enough to govern another man without the other's consent. When the white man governs himself, that is self-government, but when he governs himself and also governs another man, that is more than self-government—that is despotism. Our reliance is in the love of liberty which God has planted in us. Our defense is in the spirit which prizes liberty as the heritage of all men in all lands. Those who deny freedom to others deserve it not for themselves, and under a just God cannot long retain it."

We cordially invite the cooperation of all men and women who remain loyal to the Declaration of Independence and the Constitution of the United States.

5. Mark Twain Satirizes "The Battle Hymn of the Republic," 1900

Mine eyes have seen the orgy of the launching of the Sword;
He is searching out the hoardings where the stranger's wealth is stored;
He hath loosed his fateful lightnings, and with woe and death has scored;
    His lust is marching on.

I have seen him in the watch-fires of a hundred circling camps,
They have builded him an altar in the Eastern dews and damps;
I have read his doomful mission by the dim and flaring lamps—
    His night is marching on.

I have read his bandit gospel writ in burnished rows of steel:
"As ye deal with my pretensions, so with you my wrath shall deal;
Let the faithless son of Freedom crush the patriot with his heel;
    Lo, Greed is marching on!"

We have legalized the strumpet and are guarding her retreat;
Greed is seeking out commercial souls before his judgment seat;
O, be swift, ye clods, to answer him! be jubilant my feet!
    Our god is marching on!

In a sordid slime harmonious, Greed was born in yonder ditch,
With a longing in his bosom—and for others' goods an itch—
As Christ died to make men holy, let men die to make us rich—
    Our god is marching on.

Frederick Anderson, ed., *A Pen Warmed Up in Hell: Mark Twain in Protest* (New York: Harper & Row, 1972).

6. A Soldier Criticizes American Racism in the Philippines, 1902

Almost without exception, soldiers and also many officers refer to natives in their presence as "Niggers," and natives are beginning to understand what the word "Nigger" means. The course now being pursued in this province and in the provinces of Batangas, Laguna, and Samar is in my opinion sowing the seeds for a perpetual revolution against us hereafter whenever a good opportunity offers. Under present conditions the political situation in this province is slowly retrograding, the American sentiment is decreasing, and we are daily making permanent enemies. In the course above referred to, troops make no distinction often between the property of those natives who are insurgent or insurgent sympathizers, and the property of those who heretofore have risked their lives by being loyal to the United States and giving us information against their countrymen in arms. Often every house in a barrio is burned. In my opinion the small number of irreconcilable insurgents still in arms, although admittedly difficult to catch, does not justify the means employed, and especially when taking into consideration the suffering that must be undergone by the innocent and its effects upon the relations with these people hereafter.

7. Argentina Condemns European Collection of Debts by Force, 1902

Among the fundamental principles of public international law which humanity has consecrated, one of the most precious is that which decrees that all states, whatever be the force at their disposal, are entities in law, perfectly equal one to another, and mutually entitled by virtue thereof to the same consideration and respect.

The acknowledgment of the debt, the payment of it in its entirety, can and must be made by the nation without diminution of its inherent rights as a sovereign entity, but the summary and immediate collection at a given moment, by means of force, would occasion nothing less than the ruin of the weakest nations, and the absorption of their governments, together with all the functions inherent in them, by the mighty of the earth. The principles proclaimed on this continent of America are otherwise. "Contracts between a nation and private individuals are obligatory according to the conscience of the sovereign, and may not be the object of compelling force," said the illustrious [Alexander] Hamilton....

As these are the sentiments of justice, loyalty, and honor which animate the Argentine people and have always inspired its policy, your excellency will understand that it has felt alarmed at the knowledge that the failure of Venezuela to meet the payments of its public debt is given as one of the

B. D. Flower, "Some Dead Sea Fruit of Our War Subjugation," *The Arena*, Vol. 27 (1902), 648–649.

A proclamation by Argentine Foreign Minister Luis Drago, this document can be found in U.S. Department of State, *Papers Relating to the Foreign Relations of the United States, 1903* (Washington, D.C.: Government Printing Office, 1904), pp. 1–5.

determining causes of the capture of its fleet, the bombardment of one of its ports [by Britain, Germany, and Italy], and the establishment of a rigorous blockade along its shores. If such proceedings were to be definitely adopted they would establish a precedent dangerous to the security and the peace of the nations of this part of America.

The collection of loans by military means implies territorial occupation to make them effective, and territorial occupation signifies the suppression or subordination of the governments of the countries on which it is imposed.

Such a situation seems obviously at variance with the principles many times proclaimed by the nations of America, and particularly with the Monroe doctrine, sustained and defended with so much zeal on all occasions by the United States, a doctrine to which the Argentine Republic has heretofore solemnly adhered.

Among the principles which the memorable message of December 2, 1823, enunciates, there are two great declarations which particularly refer to these republics, viz., "The American continents are henceforth not to be considered as subjects for colonization by any European powers," and "… with the governments… whose independence we have… acknowledged, we could not view any interposition for the purpose of oppressing them or controlling in any other manner their destiny by any European power in any other light than as the manifestation of an unfriendly disposition toward the United States.".…

And it will not be denied that the simplest way to the setting aside and easy ejectment of the rightful authorities by European governments is just this way of financial interventions—as might be shown by many examples. We in no wise pretend that the South American nations are, from any point of view, exempt from the responsibilities of all sorts which violations of international law impose on civilized peoples. We do not nor can we pretend that these countries occupy an exceptional position in their relations with European powers, which have the indubitable right to protect their subjects as completely as in any other part of the world against the persecutions and injustices of which they may be the victims. The only principle which the Argentine Republic maintains and which it would, with great satisfaction, see adopted, in view of the events in Venezuela, by a nation that enjoys such great authority and prestige as does the United States, is the principle, already accepted, that there can be no territorial expansion in America on the part of Europe, nor any oppression of the peoples of this continent, because an unfortunate financial situation may compel some one of them to postpone the fulfillment of its promises.…

8. The Platt Amendment Limits Cuban Independence, 1903

Article I. The Government of Cuba shall never enter into any treaty or other compact with any foreign power or powers which will impair or tend to impair the independence of Cuba, nor in any manner authorize or permit any foreign

Charles I. Bevans, comp., *Treaties and Other International Agreements of the United States of America, 1776–1949* (Washington, D.C.: Government Printing Office for Department of State, 1971), VI, 1116.

power or powers to obtain colonization or for military or naval purposes, or otherwise, lodgment in or control over any portion of said island.

Article II. The Government of Cuba shall not assume or contract any public debt to pay the interest upon which, and to make reasonable sinking-fund provision for the ultimate discharge of which, the ordinary revenues of the Island of Cuba, after defraying the current expenses of the Government, shall be inadequate....

Article VII. To enable the United States to maintain the independence of Cuba, and to protect the people thereof, as well as for its own defense, the Government of Cuba will sell or lease to the United States lands necessary for coaling or naval stations, at certain specified points [Guantanamo Bay], to be agreed upon with the President of the United States.

9. The Roosevelt Corollary Makes the United States the Police of Latin America, 1904

It is not true that the United States feels any land hunger or entertains any projects as regards the other nations of the Western Hemisphere save such as are for their welfare. All that this country desires is to see the neighboring countries stable, orderly, and prosperous. Any country whose people conduct themselves well can count upon our hearty friendship. If a nation shows that it knows how to act with reasonable efficiency and decency in social and political matters, if it keeps order and pays its obligations, it need fear no interference from the United States. Chronic wrongdoing, or an impotence which results in a general loosening of the ties of civilized society, may in America, as elsewhere, ultimately require intervention by some civilized nation, and in the Western Hemisphere the adherence of the United States to the Monroe Doctrine may force the United States, however reluctantly, in flagrant cases of such wrongdoing or impotence, to the exercise of an international police power. If every country washed by the Caribbean Sea would show the progress in stable and just civilization which with the aid of the Platt amendment Cuba has shown since our troops left the island, and which so many of the republics in both Americas are constantly and brilliantly showing, all question of interference by this Nation with their affairs would be at an end. Our interests and those of our southern neighbors are in reality identical. They have great natural riches, and if within their borders the reign of law and justice obtains, prosperity is sure to come to them. While they thus obey the primary laws of civilized society they may rest assured that they will be treated by us in a spirit of cordial and helpful sympathy. We would interfere with them only in the last resort, and then only if it became evident that their inability or unwillingness to do justice at home and abroad had violated the rights of the United States or had invited foreign aggression to the detriment of the entire body of American nations. It is a mere truism to say that

Congressional Record, XXXIX (December 6, 1904), Part I, 19.

every nation, whether in America or anywhere else, which desires to maintain its freedom, its independence, must ultimately realize that the right of such independence can not be separated from the responsibility of making good use of it.

ESSAYS

Historians have proposed many explanations for why the United States embarked on a war that spread far from its shores after having so long avoided what were called "foreign entanglements." Scholars have argued variously that it was for economic gain, that it grew out of concern for the Cuban people, that "yellow" journalists created a war hysteria to sell newspapers, and even that the war happened by accident. At base, most authors are troubled by a fundamental question: did the United States intend to exploit weaker nations by creating an empire, or did it intend to "spread the American dream" of self-determination? These essays show two possible explanations for the war. Both reflect a recent emphasis in historical scholarship on the ways that underlying values concerning race and gender may have influenced strategic decisions at the highest levels of government. Gail Bederman of Notre Dame University argues that Theodore Roosevelt, a leading proponent of the wars against Spain and the Philippines, was powerfully influenced by images of race and gender. These cultural concepts led him to see imperialism as the next stage in the healthy growth of the republic. As you read Bederman, think about how underlying psychological insecurities may have influenced the decisions of leaders. Paul A. Kramer of Vanderbilt University argues that racism was an intentional tool of empire-building. American leaders viewed much of the Filipino population as "savages" who needed to be conquered "for their own good." As you read Kramer, think about how underlying prejudices shaped strategic thinking. Also consider how foreign peoples sometimes utilized American precedents like the Monroe Doctrine and Declaration of Independence to resist or undermine U.S. and European dominance to the extent they could.

Gendering Imperialism: Theodore Roosevelt's Quest for Manhood and Empire

GAIL BEDERMAN

In 1882, a newly elected young state assemblyman arrived in Albany. Theodore Roosevelt, assuming his first elective office, was brimming with self-importance and ambition. He was only twenty-three—the youngest man in the legislature—and he looked forward to a promising career of wielding real political power. Yet Roosevelt was chagrined to discover that despite his intelligence, competence, and real legislative successes, no one took him seriously. The more strenuously he

Gail Bederman, *Manliness and Civilization: A Cultural History of Gender and Race in the U.S., 1880–1917.* © 1995 University of Chicago Press. Reprinted by permission of the University of Chicago Press.

labored to play "a man's part" in politics, the more his opponents derided his manhood.

Daily newspapers lampooned Roosevelt as the quintessence of effeminacy. They nicknamed him "weakling," "Jane-Dandy," "Punkin-Lily," and "the exquisite Mr. Roosevelt." They ridiculed his high voice, tight pants, and fancy clothing. Several began referring to him by the name of the well-known homosexual Oscar Wilde, and one actually alleged (in a less-than-veiled phallic allusion) that Roosevelt was "given to sucking the knob of an ivory cane." While TR might consider himself a manly man, it was becoming humiliatingly clear that others considered him effeminate.

Above all other things, Roosevelt desired power. An intuitive master of public relations, he knew that his effeminate image could destroy any chances for his political future. Nearly forty years before women got the vote, electoral politics was part of a male-only subculture, fraught with symbols of manhood. Besides, Roosevelt, who considered himself a man's man, detested having his virility impugned. Although normally restrained, when he discovered a Tammany legislator plotting to toss him in a blanket, TR marched up to him and swore, "By God! if you try anything like that, I'll kick you, I'll bite you, I'll kick you in the balls, I'll do anything to you—you'd better leave me alone!" Clearly, the effeminate "dude" image would have to go.

And go it did. Roosevelt soon came to embody powerful American manhood. Within five years, he was running for mayor of New York as the "Cowboy of the Dakotas" [in reference to his taking up residence on a South Dakota ranch in 1884]. Instead of ridiculing him as "Oscar Wilde," newspapers were praising his virile zest for fighting and his "blizzard-seasoned constitution." In 1898, after a brief but highly publicized stint as leader of a regiment of volunteers in the Spanish American War, he became known as Colonel Roosevelt, the manly advocate of a virile imperialism. Never again would Roosevelt's name be linked to effeminacy. Even today, historians invoke Roosevelt as the quintessential symbol of turn-of-the-century masculinity.

Roosevelt's great success in masculinizing his image was due, in large part, to his masterful use of the discourse of civilization. As a mature politician, he would build his claim to political power on his claim to manhood. Skillfully, Roosevelt constructed a virile political person for himself as a strong but civilized white man.

Yet Roosevelt's use of the discourse of civilization went beyond mere public relations: Roosevelt drew on "civilization" to help formulate his larger politics as an advocate of both nationalism and imperialism. As he saw it, the United States was engaged in a millennial drama of manly racial advancement, in which American men enacted their superior manhood by asserting imperialistic control over races of inferior manhood. To prove their virility, as a race and a nation, American men needed to take up the "strenuous life" and strive to advance civilization— through imperialistic warfare and racial violence if necessary....

...Beginning in 1894, unhappy with President Cleveland's reluctance to annex Hawaii, Roosevelt began to exhort the American race to embrace a manly, strenuous imperialism, in the cause of higher civilization. In Roosevelt's imperialistic pronouncements, as in *The Winning of the West* [a celebratory history of European American westward expansion published between 1889 and 1896], issues of racial dominance were inextricably conflated with issues of manhood. Indeed, when Roosevelt originally coined the term "the strenuous life," in an 1899 speech, he was explicitly discussing only foreign relations: calling on the United States to build up its army and to take imperialistic control of Cuba, Puerto Rico, and the Philippines. Ostensibly, the speech never mentions gender at all. Yet the phrase "the strenuous life" soon began to connote a virile, hard-driving manhood, which might or might not involve foreign relations, at all.

How did the title of an essay calling for American imperialism become a catchphrase to describe vigorous masculinity? To answer this question, we need to understand the logic behind Roosevelt's philosophies about American national-ism and imperialism. For Roosevelt, the purpose of American expansionism and national greatness was always the millennial purpose behind human evolution— human racial advancement toward a higher civilization. And the race that could best achieve this perfected civilization was, by definition, the one with the most superior manhood.

It was not coincidental that Roosevelt's advocacy of manly imperialism in the 1890s was contemporaneous with a widespread cultural concern about effeminacy, overcivilization, and racial decadence…. [T]hroughout Europe and Anglo-America intellectuals were worried about the emasculating tendencies of excessive civilization. Roosevelt shared many of his contemporaries' fears about the future of American manly power; and this gave his imperialistic writings an air of especial urgency….

…Roosevelt understood decadence in terms of the racial conflict through which he believed civilizations rose and fell. As he had shown in *The Winning of the West,* TR believed that manly racial competition determined which race was superior and deserved to control the earth's resources. A race which grew decadent, then, was a race which had lost the masculine strength necessary to prevail in this Darwinistic racial struggle. Civilized advancement required much more than mere masculine strength, of course; it also required advanced man-liness. Intelligence, altruism, and morality were essential traits, possessed by all civilized races and men. Yet, as important as these refined traits were, they were not enough, by themselves, to safeguard civilization's advance and prevent racial decadence. Without the "virile fighting virtues" which allowed a race to continue to expand into new territories, its more civilized racial traits would be useless. If American men lost their primal fighting virtues, a more manful race would strip them of their authority, land, and resources. This effem-inate loss of racial primacy and virility was what Roosevelt meant by overcivilized racial decadence….

This concept of overcivilized decadence let Roosevelt construct American imperialism as a conservative way to retain the race's frontier-forged manhood, instead of what it really was—a belligerent grab for a radically new type of nationalistic power. As Roosevelt described it, asserting the white man's racial power abroad was necessary to avoid losing the masculine strength Americans had already established through race war on the frontier. Currently the American race was one of the world's most advanced civilized races. They controlled a rich and mighty continent because their superior manhood had allowed them to annihilate the Indians on the Western frontier. If they retained their manhood, they could continue to look forward to an ever higher civilization, as they worked ever harder for racial improvement and expansion. But if American men ever lost their virile zest for Darwinistic racial contests, their civilization would soon decay. If they ignored the ongoing racial imperative of constant expansion and instead grew effeminate and luxury-loving, a manlier race would inherit their mantle of the highest civilization.

From 1894 until he became president in 1901, Roosevelt wrote and lectured widely on the importance of taking up what Rudyard Kipling, in 1899, would dub "the White Man's burden." Kipling coined this term in a poem written to exhort American men to conquer and rule the Philippines. "The white man"... simultaneously meant the white race, civilization itself, and white males as a group. In "The White Man's Burden," Kipling used the term in all these senses to urge white males to take up the racial burden of civilization's advancement. "Take up the White Man's burden," he wrote, capitalizing the essential term, and speaking to the manly civilized on behalf of civilization. "Send forth the best ye breed"—quality breeding was essential, because evolutionary development (breeding) was what gave "the White Man" the right and duty to conquer uncivilized races.

> Go bind your sons to exile
>   To serve your captives' need;
> To wait in heavy harness,
>   on fluttered folk and wild—
> Your new-caught, sullen peoples,
>   Half-devil and half-child....

Roosevelt called Kipling's poem "poor poetry but good sense from the expansionist standpoint." Although Roosevelt did not use the term "the white man's burden" in his writings on imperialism, he drew on the same sorts of race and gender linkages which Kipling deployed in his poem. TR's speeches of this period frequently conflate manhood and racial power, and draw extended analogies between the individual American man and the virile American race.

For example, "National Duties," one of TR's most famous speeches, represents both American men and the American race as civilized entities with strong virile characters—in popular parlance, both were "the white man." Roosevelt begins by outlining this racial manhood, which he calls "the essential manliness of the American character." Part of this manliness centered around individual and racial duties to the home. On the one hand, individual men must work to provide for the domestic needs of themselves and their families. On the other hand, the men of the race must work to provide for their collective racial home, their nation. Men who shirked these manly homemaking duties were despicably unsexed; or, as TR put it, "the willfully idle man" was as bad as "the willfully barren woman."

Yet laboring only for his own hearth and nation was not enough to satisfy a real man. Virile manhood also required the manly American nation to take up imperialistic labors outside its borders, just as manhood demanded individual men to labor outside the home: "Exactly as each man, while doing first his duty to his wife and the children within his home, must yet, if he hopes to amount to much, strive mightily in the world outside his home, so our nation, while first of all seeing to its own domestic well-being, must not shrink from playing its part among the great nations without." It would be as unmanly for the American race to refuse its imperialist destiny as it would be for a cowardly man to spend all his time loafing at home with his wife. Imperialist control over primitive races thus becomes a matter of manhood—part of a male-only public sphere, which TR sets in contradistinction to the home.

After setting up imperialism as a manly duty for both man and race, Roosevelt outlines the imperialist's appropriate masculine behavior—or, should we say, his appropriate masculine appendage? Roosevelt immediately brings up the "big stick." It may be a cheap shot to stress the phallic implications of TR's imagery, yet Roosevelt himself explained the meaning of the "big stick" in terms of manhood and the proper way to assert the power of a man: "A good many of you are probably acquainted with the old proverb: "Speak softly and carry a big stick— you will go far.' If a man continually blusters, if he lacks civility, a big stick will not save him from trouble; and neither will speaking softly avail, if back of the softness there does not lie strength, power." Just as a manly man avoided bluster, relying instead on his self-evident masculine strength and power, so virile American men should build a powerful navy and army, so that when they took up the white man's burden in primitive lands, they would receive the respect due to a master-ful, manly race….

Roosevelt was not content merely to make speeches about the need for violent, imperialistic manhood. He always needed to embody his philosophy. The sickly boy had remade himself into an adventure-book hunter–naturalist; the dude politician had remade himself into a heroic Western rancher. The 1898 outbreak of the Spanish-American war—for which he had agitated long and hard— let Roosevelt remake himself into Colonel Roosevelt, the fearless Rough Rider.

Reinventing himself as a charismatic war hero allowed Roosevelt to model the manful imperialism about which he had been writing for four years. TR became a walking advertisement for the imperialistic manhood he desired for the American race. Indeed, from the moment of his enlistment until his muster-ing out four months later, Roosevelt self-consciously publicized himself as a model of strenuous, imperialistic manhood. In late April 1898, against all advice, Roosevelt resigned as assistant secretary of the navy and enlisted to fight in the just-declared war on Spain. Aged thirty-nine, with an important subcabinet post, a sick wife, and six young children, no one but Roosevelt himself imagined he ought to see active service. Roosevelt's decision to enlist was avidly followed by newspapers all over the country….

The press, fascinated by the undertaking, christened [his] regiment "Roosevelt's Rough Riders." Roosevelt's heroic frontiersman identity thus came full circle, as he no doubt intended. As Richard Slotkin has pointed out, the term "Rough Riders" had long been used in adventure novels to describe Western horsemen. Thus, by nicknaming his regiment the "Rough Riders," the nation showed it understood the historical connections Roosevelt always drew between Indian wars in the American West and virile imperialism in Cuba and the Philippines....

After his mustering out, TR the politician continued to play the role of virile Rough Rider for all he was worth. In November, he was elected governor of New York, campaigning as a war hero and employing ex-Rough Riders to warm up the election crowds. By January 1899, his thrilling memoir, *The Rough Riders,* was appearing serially in *Scribner's Magazine*. And in 1900 his virile popularity convinced Republican party leaders that Roosevelt could counter [Democrat William Jennings] Bryan's populism better than any other vice-presidential candidate. Roosevelt had constructed himself and the Rough Riders as the epitome of civilized, imperialistic manhood, a model for the American race to follow. His success in modeling that imperialistic manhood exceeded even his own expectations and ultimately paved the way for his presidency.

On April 10, 1899, Colonel Roosevelt stood before the men of Chicago's elite, all-male, Hamilton Club and preached the doctrine of "The Strenuous Life." As governor of New York and a fabulously popular ex–Rough Rider, he knew the national press would be in attendance; and though he spoke *at* the Hamilton Club, he spoke *to* men across America. With the cooperation of the press and at the risk of his life, TR had made himself into a national hero—the embodiment of manly virtue, masculine violence, and white American racial supremacy—and the antithesis of over-civilized decadence. Now he urged the men of the American race to live the sort of life he had modeled for them: to be virile, vigorous, and manly, and to reject over-civilized decadence by supporting a strenuously imperialistic foreign policy. When contemporaries ultimately adopted his phrase "the strenuous life" as a synonym for the vigorous, vehement manhood Roosevelt modeled, they showed they correctly understood that his strenuous manhood was inextricably linked to his nationalism, imperialism, and racism.

Ostensibly, "The Strenuous Life" preached the virtues of military preparedness and imperialism, but contemporaries understood it as a speech about manhood. The practical import of the speech was to urge the nation to build up its army, to maintain its strong navy, and to take control of Puerto Rico, Cuba, and the Philippines. But underlying these immediate objectives lay the message that American manhood—both the manly race and individual white men—must retain the strength of their Indian-fighter ancestors, or another race would prove itself more manly and overtake America in the Darwinian struggle to be the world's most dominant race.

Roosevelt began by demanding manliness in both the American nation and American men. Slothful men who lacked the "desire and power" to strive in the world were despicable and unmanly. "We do not admire the man of timid peace. We admire the man who embodies victorious effort." If America and its men were not man enough to fight, they would not only lose their place among "the great nations of the world," they would become a decadent and effeminate race. Roosevelt held up the Chinese, whom he despised as the most decadent and unmanly of races, as a cautionary lesson: If we "play the part of China, and be content to rot by inches in ignoble ease within our borders," we will "go down before other nations which have not lost the manly and adventurous qualities." If American men lacked the manly fortitude to go bravely and willingly to a foreign war, the race would decay, preached TR, the virile war hero.

In stirring tones, the Rough Rider of San Juan Hill ridiculed the overcivilized anti-imperialists who had lost the "great fighting, masterful virtues." Lacking the masculine impulse toward racial aggression and unmoved by virile visions of empire, these men had been sapped of all manhood.

> The timid man, the lazy man, the man who distrusts his country, the over-civilized man, who has lost the great fighting, masterful virtues, the ignorant man, and the man of dull mind, whose soul is incapable of feeling the mighty lift that thrills stern men with empires in their brains— all these, of course shrink from seeing the nation undertake its new duties; shrink from seeing us build a navy and an army adequate to our needs; shrink from seeing us do our share of the world's work. These are the men who fear the strenuous life…. They believe in that cloistered life which saps the hardy virtues in a nation, as it saps them in the individual.

Like "cloistered" monkish celibates, these "over-civilized" men "shrink, shrink, shrink" from carrying the "big stick." Dishonorably, they refused to do their manly duty by the childish Fillipinos. Had the United States followed these anti-imperialists' counsel and refused to undertake "one of the great tasks set modern civilization," Americans would have shown themselves not only unmanly but also racially inferior. "Some stronger, manlier power would have to step in and do the work, and we would have shown ourselves weaklings, unable to carry to successful completion the labors that great and high-spirited nations are eager to undertake." As TR saw it, the man, the race, and the nation were one in their need to possess virile, imperialist manhood.

Then TR got down to brass tacks, dwelling at length on Congress' responsibility to build up the armed forces. After again raising the specter of Chinese decadence, which American men faced if they refused to strengthen their army and navy, Roosevelt stressed America's duty to take up the white man's burden in Cuba, Puerto Rico, and the Philippines. If the American race was "too weak, too selfish, or too foolish" to take on that task, it would be completed by "some stronger and more manful race." He ridiculed anti-imperialists as cowards who "make a pretense of humanitarianism to hide and cover their timidity" and to "excuse themselves for their unwillingness to play the part of men."

"The Strenuous Life" culminates with a Darwinian vision of strife between races for the "dominion of the world," which only the most manful race could win.

> I preach to you then, my countrymen, that our country calls not for the life of ease but for the life of strenuous endeavor…. If we stand idly by…then the bolder and stronger peoples will pass us by, and will win for themselves the domination of the world. Let us therefore boldly face the life of strife, resolute to do our duty well and manfully.

American men must embrace their manly mission to be the race which dominates the world. Struggle for racial supremacy was inevitable, but the most manful race—the American race—would triumph, if it made the attempt. Its masculine strength was proven by military victories over barbarous brown races. Its manly virtue was evident in its civilized superiority to the primitive childish races it uplifted. White American men must claim their place as the world's most perfect men, the fittest race for the evolutionary struggle toward a perfect civilization. This was the meaning of "The Strenuous Life."

We can now answer the question. "How did the title of an essay calling for American dominance over the brown races become a catchphrase to describe virile masculinity?" Roosevelt's desire for imperial dominance had been, from the first, intrinsically related to his views about male power. As he saw it, the manhood of the American race had been forged in the crucible of frontier race war; and to abandon the virile power of the violence would be to backslide toward effeminate racial mediocrity. Roosevelt wanted American men to be the ultimate in human evolution, the world's most powerful and civilized race. He believed that their victory over the Indians on the frontier proved that the American race possessed the racial superiority and masculine power to overcome any savage race; and he saw a glorious future for the race in the twentieth century, as it pressed on toward international dominance and the perfection of civilization. The only danger which Roosevelt saw menacing this millennial triumph of manly American civilization came from within. Only by surrendering to overcivilized decadence—by embracing unmanly racial sloth instead of virile imperialism—could American men fail. Thus, American men must work strenuously to uphold their civilization. They must refuse a life of ease, embrace their manly task, and take up the white man's burden. Only by living that "strenuous life" could American men prove themselves to be what Roosevelt had no doubt they were—the apex of civilization, evolution's most favored race, masterful men fit to command the barbarous races and the world's "waste spaces"—in short, the most virile and manly of men.

In later years, as Americans came to take international involvement for granted and as imperialism came to seem less controversial, the phrase "the strenuous life" underwent a subtle change of meaning. Always associated with Roosevelt, it came to connote the virile manhood which he modeled for the nation as the imperialistic Western hero and Rough Rider—the peculiar combination of moral manliness and aggressive masculinity which he was able to synthesize so well. As Roosevelt's presidency wore on, Americans grew accustomed to taking up the white man's burden, not only in the Philippines, but also in Cuba, Panama, and the Dominican Republic. The "strenuous life" came to be associated with any virile, manly effort to accomplish great work, whether imperialistic or not. Yet on a basic level, "the strenuous life" retained TR's original associations with the evolutionary struggle of the American race on behalf of civilization. "The strenuous life," as it came to be used, meant the opposite of "overcivilized effeminacy." Or, as Roosevelt summed it up himself in his *Autobiography*, the man who lives the strenuous life regards his life "as a pawn to be promptly hazarded whenever the hazard is warranted by the larger interests of the great game in which we are all engaged." That great game, for Roosevelt, was always the millennial struggle for Americans to perfect civilization by becoming the most manly, civilized, and powerful race in the world.

Racial Imperialism: America's Takeover of the Philippines

PAUL A. KRAMER

On January 9, 1900, Senator Albert Beveridge, Republican of Indiana, stood before the U.S. Senate, defending a war on the other side of the world that refused to end by American command. The previous November, Gen. Elwell Otis had declared victory and an end to major combat operations in the Philippines, where American troops were struggling to impose U.S. sovereignty on the forces of the Philippine Republic. Over the next months, however, much to the frustration of U.S. generals and the McKinley administration, resistance would both vanish and intensify as Filipinos adopted a guerrilla strategy to fight off the invaders. Beveridge was uniquely suited to justify the war before the Senate and "anti-imperialist" critics, having built his early reputation on thundering rhetoric in defense of American empire. Campaigning in Indianapolis on September 19, 1898, for example, he had turned the recent U.S. victory against Spain in the Caribbean into a mandate for global liberation. America's mission-field would be a world contracted by electricity and steam. "Distance and oceans are no arguments," he asserted. The seas did "not separate us from lands of our duty and desire" but bound Americans to them. A half century earlier, California had been "more inaccessible" from the eastern United States than was the present-day Philippines, where U.S. troops had captured the city of Manila from Spanish forces the previous month. For Beveridge, Americans had "world duties" as "a people imperial by virtue of their power, by right of their institutions, by authority of their Heaven-directed purposes." He urged his countrymen to "broaden [the] blessed reign" of freedom "until the empire of our principles is established over the hearts of all mankind." As for criticism that "we ought not to govern a people without their consent," Beveridge asked his audience, "Would not the people of the Philippines prefer the just, humane, civilizing government of this Republic to the savage, bloody rule of pillage and extortion from which we have rescued them?"

Filipinos had not, in fact, greeted the Americans as liberators. When Beveridge addressed the Senate in early 1900, nearly a year into the bloody conquest of the Philippine Islands, he did so as an expert who had himself beaten the oceans argument and traveled through the islands, guided by U.S. military commanders. In this second address, his sense of the Philippines' centrality to the United States' export trade to Asia was heightened, as was his rage at seeing "our mangled boys" on the battlefield, wounded indirectly by "anti-imperialism," or what he called "American assaults on our Government at home." As the war's terrors unfolded and its manifold costs were debated, Beveridge attempted to locate the invasion beyond dissent. Its true meaning, he stated, was "deeper than any question of party politics," than "any question of the isolated policy of our country," deeper even than "any question of constitutional power." "It is elemental," he

From Paul A Kramer, *The Blood of Government: Race, Empire, the United States, and the Philippines* (University of North Carolina Press, 2006), p. 1–3, 82–83, 91–95, 97–99, 102, 104, 109–110, 138, 145–146, 151–152. Copyright © 2006 by the University of North Carolina Press. Used by permission of the publisher. www.uncpress.unc.ed..

asserted. "It is racial." Sublimating conquest into liberation meant making race. The American cause was nothing less than that of the "English-speaking and Teutonic peoples" whom God had prepared for "a thousand years" to become "the master organizers of the world," possessors of what he had called, in the 1898 address, "the blood of government." The enemy had also become more focused in Beveridge's imagination as Filipino guerrillas disappeared into villages and forests. He urged his colleagues to "remember that we are not dealing with Americans or Europeans" but with "Malays" corrupted by "hundreds of years of savagery, other hundreds of years of Orientalism, and still other hundreds of years of Spanish character and custom." What "alchemy," he asked, "will change the oriental quality of their blood and set the self-governing currents of the American pouring through their Malay veins?" In a time of empire-building, blood and government were intimately connected. Newly drawn and challenged lines of race would separate and bind those who ruled and those who were ruled....

Among the formerly disparate regions of the world whose histories became permanently inseparable during this period were the Philippines and the United States. Contacts between these two societies had been sporadic before the end of the nineteenth century: with little trade or migration between them, each was virtually, if differently, unknown to the other. The force that ushered in their joint twentieth century pushed from the Caribbean, when U.S. intervention in Cuba against Spain in 1898 was accompanied by the launching of the United States' Asiatic Squadron to Spain's largest Asian colony. The U.S. defeat of the Spanish fleet at Manila Bay and the military occupation of Manila in the middle of that year placed the histories of U.S. empire and Philippine sovereignty on a collision course....

The arrival of that U.S. naval squadron was predicated on three decades of explosive American industrial and imperial growth. Since the end of the Civil War, the United States had expanded and consolidated into a continental empire of conquered subjects, migrant settlers, raw materials, and industrial products. At the center of its architecture were the railroads—linked transcontinentally after 1869, the same year in which the Suez Canal had been opened—which simultaneously pioneered modern corporate organization, made available new natural resources for extraction and development, opened up new consumer markets, and promoted dependent white colonization. By the mid-nineteenth century, white migrants had pushed west toward the Pacific in vast numbers; earlier treaties notwithstanding, the federal government forcibly removed eastern Native American peoples westward and established the reservation system to isolate them in arid and undesirable regions far from white settlements. Nomadic peoples in the West put up the greatest resistance to white encroachment and were conquered through genocidal wars by the U.S. Army in the 1870s and 1880s, a process aided by the telegraph, repeating rifle, and Gatling gun. By the end of the latter decade, Native Americans would find it difficult to maintain possession of the reservations themselves. The railroad, and the industries it gave birth to, in turn attracted diverse, novel working populations from around the globe. On the East Coast and in the Midwest, southern and eastern European migrants poured into the United States by the millions to labor in factories and mills. The West was still more dramatically altered, seeing the entry of Chinese and Japanese laborers in mines, lumber camps, farms, and on the railroad. Native American genocide and the wrenching social transformations of rapid industrialization were the preconditions of vast economic growth: U.S. resources in minerals, lumber, cattle, petroleum, and agriculture pushed the United States to the front ranks of the global economic powers by the end of the nineteenth century.

The U.S. empire had long burst over its continental limits by the time the U.S. census declared the land frontier closed in 1890....

Tensions of Recognition

The forces that pushed the Asiatic Squadron out to Manila Bay were complex and continue to be debated by historians. As early as late 1897, officers in the Navy Department and Naval War College anticipating war with Spain had drafted war plans that included the temporary occupation of Manila in order to deny Spain revenue, to provide a base of operations, and to gain leverage for a more favorable peace settlement. These war plans were compatible with, if they were apparently developed independently of, a political elite aggressively committed to overseas empire, advocates of a "large policy," such as Assistant Secretary of the Navy Theodore Roosevelt and Senator Henry Cabot Lodge, Republican of Massachusetts. In late 1897 and early 1898, both men pressured President William McKinley to see geopolitical opportunity in the war with Spain: by seizing Spain's largest Asian colony—in whole or in part—the United States would gain a strategic foothold from which to wedge open China's markets, a rationale for building up U.S. naval strength, and the recognition and respect of the world's imperial powers.

February 15, 1898, provided large-policy advocates the opening they had hoped for, when the uss *Maine* exploded mysteriously in Havana harbor, where it had been sent to hold American options open and to protect the property of U.S. citizens. An investigatory commission suspected Spanish weapons of mass destruction, and the *Maine* disaster was assumed to be the work of Spanish treachery by interventionists in the McKinley administration and in the imperialist press. While the advocates of intervention called for the "liberation" of Cuba, just ten days after the disaster, Roosevelt ordered Commodore George Dewey and the Asiatic Squadron to depart San Francisco for Hong Kong to await further instructions. Following a U.S. declaration of war, Dewey was to proceed to Manila Bay to engage Spanish naval forces there....

Exiled revolutionaries were divided and willing to play both sides. The end of April 1898 saw Miguel Malvar in Hong Kong negotiating with Spaniards for autonomy and Emilio Aguinaldo in Singapore negotiating with a U.S. consul for recognition of Philippine independence. From late March to early April, Aguinaldo had a number of meetings with Captain Wood, acting on behalf of Commodore Dewey, who had urged him to return and continue the revolution, assuring him that Americans would supply him with necessary arms. By Aguinaldo's account, Wood had stated that the United States was "a great and rich nation and neither needs nor desires colonies"; he would not put these commitments in writing without Dewey's approval....

On May 1, the U.S. Asiatic Squadron utterly destroyed the Spanish naval forces at Manila Bay, and the revolutionaries in Hong Kong debated strategy. Aguinaldo wanted a written promise of recognition from Dewey but also felt compelled to establish a revolutionary government quickly before his rivals could. The exiles were deeply suspicious of U.S. intentions, as reflected in a late-April circular sent to Manila with José Alejandrino, who had been allowed to travel with Dewey. The present situation, stated the circular, was "exceedingly dangerous for the Philippines." Having engaged in discussions with the consuls and Dewey, the exiles had "infer[red] that they are trying to make colonies of us, although they said they would give us independence." It was "advisable to simulate belief at the same time equipping ourselves with arms." A part of the revolutionary forces would "aid the Americans by fighting with them in order to conceal our real intentions," while "part will be held in reserve." If the United States "triumphs and proposes a colony we shall reject such offer and rise in arms."

The victorious dewey held Aguinaldo at arm's length until mid-May, sending a cruiser to bring him to Manila. The content of their meetings remains unclear, the controversy hinging on different understandings, and manipulations, of the symbolism of recognition. Aguinaldo claimed Dewey had honored him as a general, urged the lifting of a Philippine flag, and promised U.S. recognition of Philippine independence. Dewey had supplied arms to the revolutionaries upon their landing in Cavite on May 19. On the twenty-sixth, Secretary of the Navy John D. Long cabled Dewey warning him to avoid "political alliances with the insurgents or any faction in the Islands that would incur liability to maintain their cause in the future"; on June 3, Dewey answered that he had complied. At the same time, Dewey had "given [Aguinaldo] to understand that I consider insurgents as friends, being opposed to a common enemy."

Aguinaldo quickly mobilized forces throughout the region to resume the aborted revolution. In doing so, he was extremely aware of the tenuous diplomatic position in which the revolution found itself and urged a "civilized" war on Spanish land forces. The quest for recognition must continue in the context of war. "[I]n respect to our conduct," he wrote in a May 21 proclamation, he had informed Dewey and "other nations" that "we shall carry on a modern war." When a Spaniard surrendered, "he must be pardoned and treated well," so that subsequently "you will see that our reputation will be very good in the eyes of all Europe, which will declare for our independence." If "we do not conduct ourselves thus," he warned, "the Americans will decide to sell us or else divide up our territory, as they will hold us incapable of governing our land."...

Aguinaldo took advantage of his consolidation of revolutionary forces to declare the Philippine Islands independent at a ceremony held on June 12 in Cavite, three weeks after the first U.S. expedition's departure from San Francisco. Such a declaration might galvanize the Filipino populace behind Aguinaldo's leadership and simultaneously raise the stakes in negotiations with the United States and other powers, from the recognition of belligerency to the recognition of independent statehood. The "Act of the Proclamation of Independence of the Filipino People" was a bold statement of the "independence of our territory" and the "recovery of our sovereignty."...

The ceremony's success in gaining recognition was ambiguous. Commodore Dewey politely declined an invitation but sent a colonel of artillery, J. M. Johnson, who witnessed the ceremonies and signed the declaration as a witness, "the only foreigner" present. Statements of recognition flowed, however, freely from the consuls, Pratt and Wildman. Just days before the declaration, on June 8, a delegation of Filipinos had gone to Pratt's office—decorated simply with a U.S. flag and a portrait of Aguinaldo—and "serenaded" him. Dr. Isidoro de Santos expressed gratitude for Dewey's "moral and material support" through Pratt, "the genuine representative of the great and powerful American Republic." He hoped that "persevering in its humanitarian policy," the United States would "continue to support" Pratt's agreement with Aguinaldo, "that is to say, the independence of the Philippine Islands, under an American protectorate."...

As Aguinaldo and others feared, the arrival of U.S. Army expeditions from late June through late July turned the balance decisively against their recognition. With additional troop strength, U.S. commanders felt less need for Filipino allies against the Spanish and more concern for the question of how to keep the "insurgents" outside of Manila when it fell. This latter preoccupation emerged in secret dialogues between U.S. and Spanish officers who, understanding their desperately weakened position, agreed to surrender in a prearranged battle in mid-August with the assurance that Filipino troops would not be allowed to enter the city. U.S. officers alerted Filipino forces that the coming battle was to be entirely between Spaniards and Americans. On August 13, Anderson sent a telegram to Aguinaldo warning tersely, "Do not let your troops enter Manila. On this side of the Pasig River you will be under fire."...

The exclusion of Filipino troops from Manila was reflected in the first U.S. declaration of sovereignty over the Philippines: the instructions McKinley had given to General Merritt on May 12, which Merritt had translated into Tagalog and Spanish and circulated only on August 14. The instructions, which formally governed Filipino-American relations during the negotiations at Paris, preemptively claimed for the United States a wide degree of sovereignty in the islands. The Philippine Republic, its officers, and its army did not appear in them. In that manufactured vacuum, U.S. commanders were charged with guaranteeing the security of persons and property in the Philippines....

In the tense period between the U.S. occupation of Manila and early the following February, the Philippines found itself between two colliding declarations of sovereignty: Aguinaldo's declaration of June 12 and McKinley's, circulated after August 14. During that period, Manila and its outskirts were characterized by competitive state-building between Filipinos and Americans: both the Philippine Republic and U.S. Army forces in occupied Manila struggled to construct states to fill in the outlines of their respective declarations with political facts on the ground. Philippine state-building had a two-month lead on U.S. imperial state-building. Following the Declaration of Independence, Aguinaldo had moved quickly to build a viable state, formally renaming the "Dictatorial

Government" a "Revolutionary Government," issuing the terms for municipal and provincial governments and courts, establishing an executive cabinet, and providing for a future congress to be elected by an elite male suffrage....

The Philippine Republic took explicit steps to prevent U.S. advances in the game of competitive state-building. Officials passed a law requiring foreign travelers to carry passes signed and secured from high government officials; foreigners engaged in the shipping business would have to have permits to operate; laws prohibited Filipinos from contracting with foreigners without government consent; no laborers but Filipinos could unload cargoes. The new state also prohibited any foreign vessel from landing troops on Philippine soil. At the same time, Aguinaldo and other Filipino leaders strategically invoked American precedents in the interests of winning U.S. recognition. Speaking before the Malolos congress, Aguinaldo dispatched Spain by lamenting that it had once been "a kingdom well-known for goodness like the great North American nation," an "honorable friend" who showed "the greatness of her government to the world," by "aiding the enslaved countries to rise to their feet, and not colonizing them for her advantage." He then declared Philippine independence by borrowing and adapting the Monroe Doctrine against the United States itself. "[N]ow we witness the truth of what the famous President Monroe said, that the 'United States is for the Americans,'" he said. "[N]ow I answer that 'the Philippines is for the Filipinos.'" ...

On the ground, relations between Filipinos and American soldiers were as varied as the questions of recognition they raised. U.S. soldiers in occupied Manila found themselves in an enticing, disturbing, and illegible Filipino urban world; Filipinos unsure of the invading army's status were wary of the Americans in political terms but eager for their business. Most social contacts were commercial in nature, with Filipinos and Americans first meeting each other haggling over food, transport, liquor, and sex. Clashing interests, failed translations, mutual suspicions, and questions of jurisdiction sometimes erupted into animosity and conflict, especially where U.S. soldiers became drunk and disorderly or failed to pay their debts. Soldiers commonly characterized Filipinos on the whole as filthy, diseased, lazy, and treacherous in their business dealings, sometimes applying the term "nigger" to them. One anonymous black soldier, reflecting back on this period, stated that the subsequent war would not have broken out "if the army of occupation would have treated [Filipinos] as people." But shortly after the seizure of Manila, white troops had begun "to apply home treatment for colored peoples: cursed them as damned niggers, steal [from] them and ravish them, rob them on the street of their small change, take from the fruit vendors whatever suited their fancy, and kick the poor unfortunate if he complained."...

As U.S. troops' animosity intensified, Filipinos developed suspicions of the U.S. military presence in the islands in which circulating rumors of race played an important role. Where U.S. forces had deliberately left their ultimate intentions ambiguous, Filipinos filled this gap with their knowledge of the United States' domestic racial history. "One of the stories that received universal acceptance," reported General McReeve, "was that ever since the Americans had liberated their negro slaves they had been looking around for others and thought they had found them at last in the Philippines." Two naval officers reported that many Filipinos they encountered "have been prejudiced against us by the Spaniards," charges "so severe that what the natives have since learned has not sufficed to disillusion them." Two points in particular had stood out regarding "our policy toward a subject people": "that we have mercilessly slain and finally exterminated the race of Indians that were native to our soil and that we went to war in 1861 to suppress an insurrection of negro slaves, whom we also ended by exterminating. Intelligent and well-informed men have believed these charges. They were rehearsed to us in many towns in different provinces, beginning at Malolos. The Spanish version of our Indian problem in particularly well known."...

...U.S. and Spanish commissioners in France settled the disposition of the Philippine Islands, culminating in the signing of the Treaty of Paris on December 10, 1898. McKinley's intentions for the islands from May through October remain difficult to discern... The decisive month appears to have been October, when McKinley stumped for candidates in the Midwest and used the opportunity both to tutor and test political audiences on the Philippines. On October 28, McKinley had cabled the commissioners at Paris that they must press for the entire archipelago, as the cession of Luzon alone would leave the rest of the islands subject to Spanish authority and to potential great-power contention, neither of which could be "justified on political, commercial, or humanitarian grounds."

While the U.S. commissioners at Paris had differed on a proper course, they successfully pushed for what Spanish negotiators bitterly called the "immodest demands of a conqueror." With the United States occupying Manila and the Philippine Revolution spreading, Spanish representatives were left with few options and accepted a U.S. offer of $20 million for "Spanish improvements" to the islands, signing the treaty on December 10. While in Manila and its environs questions of recognition had been ambiguous over the previous months, they had been stark at Paris: no Filipino representatives were recognized in treaty negotiations, and the islands' inhabitants, their rights and aspirations, and the Philippine Republic that acted in their name had played a minimal role in Spanish and U.S. discussions.

McKinley effectively closed the first chapter in the recognition debate in his statement of December 21, with Wilcox and Sargent scarcely out of the woods. Authored by Elihu Root and later known as McKinley's "Benevolent Assimilation" proclamation, it narrated the American destruction of the Spanish fleet and the Treaty of Paris, laid a claim to U.S. sovereignty over the entire archipelago, and sketched a bare-bones military government with improvised ground rules for the maintenance of property rights, taxation, and tariffs....

Most significantly, the proclamation was a formal derecognition of the Philippine Republic and established the relationship between the United States and Filipinos as that of sovereign state to passive, individual subjects. The term "assimilation," by which the address would come to be known, held more than a hint of malice: the very fact that it required the adjective "benevolent" to soften it suggested more or less directly that there were kinds of assimilation that were not....

Race was at the core of the U.S. Army's effort to rethink and redefine the enemy in a context of guerrilla war.... Throughout the colonial world— including the republic's leadership—races were characterized in part by the way they made war. The General Orders No. 100 that [General Arthur] MacArthur had drawn upon had themselves relied on racial historical dichotomies between civilized and savage war. While "barbarous armies" and "uncivilized people," for example, offered no protection to civilians, the "inoffensive citizen" was protected in "modern regular wars of the Europeans, and their descendents in other portions of the globe." While the General Orders authorized retaliation by "civilized nations," when taken too far, this principle quickly devolved into "the internecine wars of savages."

By these lights, those who waged guerrilla war were, by definition, savage: Filipino warfare, therefore, did not take this form out of ignorance or strategy but because of race....

...If racialization encouraged U.S. soldiers to broaden the war toward exterminism, race also legitimated this process from above, undermining moral and legal claims against U.S. soldiers accused of wartime atrocities in the halls of American governance, in press debates, and in courts-martial. Race would not only justify the ends of the war—especially as the necessary response to Filipino savagery and tribal fragmentation—but would be used to justify many of the "marked severities" employed by U.S. soldiers to bring it to its desired conclusion.

Little if anything of the cruelties of the war became known to the U.S. public prior to early 1902, in part due to rigorous censorship of foreign correspondents by the U.S. Army. By mid-1902, however, the American press—particularly Democratic and independent papers—became more emboldened, particularly as editors learned of General Bell's "reconcentration" program in Batangas. Some critical press attention was due to the energetic efforts of anti-imperialists like Herbert Welsh, who resourcefully culled for republication references to the water cure and other atrocities in hometown newspapers and sent agents to interview returning soldiers firsthand. These efforts would culminate in the publication of the pamphlet *"Marked Severities" in Philippine Warfare,* a compilation by Moorfield Storey and Julian Codman of descriptions of U.S. atrocities attributed to U.S. soldier-witnesses, with attempts to connect atrocity to administration policy.

These propaganda efforts coincided with a Senate investigation between January and June 1902, initiated by Senator George Hoar, Republican of Massachusetts, to "examine and report into the conduct of the war in the Philippine Islands, the administration of the government there, and the condition and character of the inhabitants."... In both the press and the Senate hearings, the army's defenders repeatedly held that atrocities were rare; that where they occurred they were swiftly and thoroughly punished; and that testimony to the contrary was exaggerated, partisan, cowardly, and traitorous. But racial arguments, of at least four varieties, were crucial to defending the war's means, just as they had been to the justification of the war's ends. The first variant claimed that the Filipinos' guerrilla war, as "savage" war, was entirely outside the moral and legal standards and strictures of "civilized" war. Those who adopted guerrilla war, it was argued, surrendered all claims to bounded violence and mercy from their opponent. Capt. John H. Parker employed this line of argument in a November 1900 letter to Theodore Roosevelt complaining that the U.S. Army should not "attempt to meet a half civilized foe... with the same methods devised for civilized warfare against people of our own race, country and blood." The point was made plainly during the Senate hearings, when General Hughes described to Senator Rawlins the burning of entire towns by advancing U.S. troops as a means of "punishment," and Senator Joseph Rawlins inquired, "But is that within the ordinary rules of civilized warfare?" General Hughes replied succinctly, "These people are not civilized."...

The war's second end was declared in a public ceremony in front of the Ayuntamiento in Manila on July 4, 1901, with the formal transfer of all executive governmental functions from the military to the civil government under the Philippine Commission and William Howard Taft, who was inaugurated as the United States' first "civil governor" in the islands. The shift of authority had begun the previous September 1, when the military had handed over legislative and some executive powers to the commission. The capture of Aguinaldo the previous March [by U.S. forces] had been a serious blow to the revolution and led to the surrender of a number of key revolutionary generals. The July 4 transfer marked one of what Taft called the "successive stages in a clearly formulated plan" for making the islands "ripe for permanent civil government on a more or less popular basis." According to the *Manila Times,* the city had "never been decorated so much, and the profusion of flags, bunting, palms, lanterns and pictures in the house decorations was a marked difference from past Fourths." An editorial in the *Manila Times* cheered that "all races" could celebrate the event, which marked a "dividing line" between "the past of war and the future of peace." The choice of Independence Day had been felicitous, as the United States' own anti-imperial revolution had "made it possible to extend the liberties of her stable republicanism to these Eastern peoples in their day." Filipinos would one day recognize that "America's Fourth is their Fourth," once they came to "regard their conquest in a gratiful [*sic*] spirit, as an act necessary for their own good."...

FURTHER READING

César Ayala, *American Sugar Kingdom: The Plantation Economy of the Spanish Caribbean, 1898–1934* (1999).

H. W. Brands, *Bound to Empire: The United States and the Philippines* (1992).

Matthew Jacobson, *Barbarian Virtues: The United States Encounters Foreign Peoples at Home and Abroad, 1877–1900* (2000).

H. Paul Jeffers, *Colonel Roosevelt: Theodore Roosevelt Goes to War* (1996).

Stanley Karnow, *In Our Image: America's Empire in the Philippines* (1989).

Glenn May, *Social Engineering in the Philippines: The Aims, Execution, and Impact of American Colonial Policy* (1980).

Brian McAllister Linn, *The Philippine War, 1899–1902* (2000).

John L. Offner, *An Unwanted War: The Diplomacy of the United States and Spain Over Cuba, 1895–1898* (1992).

Louis Perez, Jr., *The War of 1898: The United States and Cuba in History and Historiography* (1998).

David Pletcher, *The Diplomacy of Trade and Investment: American Economic Expansion in the Hemisphere* (1998).

Robert Rydell, *All the World's a Fair: Visions of Empire at American International Expositions, 1876–1916* (1984).

Lars Schoultz, *Beneath the United States: A History of U.S. Policy Towards Latin America* (1999).

Edward Van Zile Scott, *The Unwept: Black American Soldiers and the Spanish-American War* (1996).

CHAPTER 5

The Progressive Movement

From the turn of the century up to the 1920s, Americans of all backgrounds wrestled with the notion of "progress." Giant cities peopled by impoverished immigrants, new technologies of mass production, political machines controlled by party bosses, and the spectacular concentration of wealth in the hands of the few left many people wondering, "Is this progress?" The nation had more money and technology, but it seemed to have more corruption, disease, and poverty as well.

A wide spectrum of middle- and upper-class activists throughout the nation called themselves Progressives. They sought to strengthen the moral fiber of American society and ameliorate the problems of modern life. They fought successfully for reforms such as woman suffrage, the prohibition of alcohol, antitrust legislation, laws curtailing child labor, the creation of a national income tax, conservation of natural resources, and the popular election of senators. But theirs was not the only definition of progress. Immigrants, politicians, businessmen, and experts in law, economics, engineering, and such newly invented fields as social work often disagreed over what constituted progress, and on whose terms it would take place. African Americans, meanwhile, saw the progress contained in the Fourteenth and Fifteenth Amendments undermined by federal law and local practice. In the 1890s, white mobs on average lynched more than one hundred blacks every year. In 1896, in Plessy vs. Ferguson, the Supreme Court legalized segregation by race. Left to work out their own solutions, African American leaders also debated the meaning of progress and the best methods for obtaining it.

Progressive reformers particularly prized efficient planning to promote the "public good," but they often failed to see that what was good for one public might be bad for another. Cleaning up city politics made sense to political reformers who hated to see party bosses buying votes. To immigrants, cleaning up city government meant losing those politicians who might look out for their specific interests. Regulating business helped consumers (as in the Pure Food and Drug Act), but it also gave big corporations an edge over less efficient small companies. Banning alcohol seemed an urgent reform to nondrinkers; banning cigarettes seemed an urgent reform to nonsmokers. Immigrants and the working class tended to favor both practices. Progressives in America looked abroad to other industrializing societies for ideas on how to solve the problems of modern life, but they also wrestled with some unique dilemmas, such as how to create a single nation out of the multilingual peoples suddenly inhabiting the land. They also struggled with how much power to give the state, considering America's particular tradition of hostility to centralized government.

Progressives attacked problems at the local level first. Both Woodrow Wilson and Theodore Roosevelt were reformist governors before they became president. Even before Congress passed Prohibition, nineteen states had banned alcohol. Sixteen states had outlawed cigarettes and passed the vote for women.

What followed was the greatest spate of Constitution-rewriting since the adoption of the Bill of Rights. Through women's suffrage and the direct election of senators, Progressives deepened America's commitment to democracy. By creating a federal income tax, they vastly amplified the resources and power of the national government. By prohibiting alcohol, they imposed their social values and medical advice on the nation. Reformers came from both political parties, and under former president Theodore Roosevelt some created a third party, the Progressive Party, in 1912. Politically, they may have been hard to categorize, but they were nothing if not bold.

 # QUESTIONS TO THINK ABOUT

What was Progressivism? Was it an inspirational movement to further the nation's democratic ideals, or was it an attempt at social control by self-important, moralistic busybodies? To what extent was Progressivism an expression of America's old utopian tendencies and the genuine challenges of the industrial age, and to what extent was it a reaction common to all industrializing nations, regardless of politics?

DOCUMENTS

The documents in this chapter display different perspectives on the problems and solutions of the Progressive era. In document 1, Frances E. Willard of the Women's Christian Temperance Union attacks the alcohol and tobacco interests. She makes an argument for women's suffrage by saying that women need more power to protect men and boys in their care, who are prey to such vices. Socialist Edward Bellamy wrote one of the nineteenth century's best-selling books, the novel *Looking Backward*. It inspired a spontaneous mass movement of "Bellamy Clubs" devoted to implementing the author's utopian ideas. Document 2 is the introduction to Bellamy's book, which scorns the indifference of the well-to-do towards the misery of the underclass. Bellamy argued that such misery did not have to be. Document 3 reflects the terrible predicament of African Americans in the Progressive era. Booker T. Washington, the founder of the Tuskegee Institute in Alabama and a former slave, promoted vocational training for blacks and accepted racial segregation as a temporary but necessary political compromise. This selection from his autobiography, *Up From Slavery,* explains why. In document 4, W. E. B. DuBois, a founder of the National Association for the Advancement of Colored People (NAACP), presents a counterargument and denounces Washington for giving up the birthright of any free people: the vote. In document 5, "muckraking" journalist Lincoln Steffens blames the American people for their descent into political corruption. In *The Shame of the Cities,* Steffens urged citizens to vote according to their consciences, not for the party "machines." In document 6, social worker Jane Addams underscores the WCTU argument that women need a political voice in order to do a better job of "civic housekeeping." In document 7, the reformer Frederic Howe compares American cities and governments with those of Germany. He concludes that the German system is less democratic, but more effective and fair. Americans have a lot to learn from Germany, he asserts. In document 8, Yale sociology professor William Graham Sumner vents the annoyance felt by some at Progressive zealotry. He criticizes the Progressives for their extravagant complaints, their attacks on business, and their overconfidence in the power of government legislation to right all wrongs. Document 9 is a cartoon that shows the sweep of Progressive concerns, and reformers' belief that they offered America a full meal of healthful reforms. The political "bosses" offered an empty plate and a leftover corncob.

1. W. C. T. U. Blasts Drinking and Smoking, and Demands Power to Protect, 1883

The W. C. T. U. stands as the exponent, not alone of that return to physical sanity which will follow the downfall of the drink habit, but of the reign of a religion of the body which for the first time in history shall correlate with Christ's wholesome, practical, yet blessedly spiritual religion of the soul. "The kingdom of heaven is within you"—shall have a new meaning to the clear-eyed, steady-limbed Christians of the future, from whose brain and blood the taint of alcohol and nicotine has been eliminated by ages of pure habits and noble heredity....

The saloon-keepers understand this new proverb,—"Through the eye to the heart." "King Gambrinus," in grab of green and red and purple, flourishing aloft his foaming mug of beer, and bestriding a huge cask of the same refining beverage, sits above the doors of all leading dram-shops. In Kansas, just after the [state] prohibition law went into force, I saw a picture displayed in the empty windows of the closed saloons, which was artfully contrived to arouse the dormant appetite of every drinking man who looked sorrowfully toward the scene of his former exploits. A generous glass of ale, brimming with beaded foam, was done in colors carefully laid on, and this tempting but now impossible draught was surrounded by separate hands, all the fingers of each one being represented in most ardent, expectant attitudes of grasping, clutching, and clawing all in vain, to reach the coveted but unattainable glass. The tobacconist, with similar wit and shrewdness, attracts attention to his demoralizing wares by placing before his door a statuesque Indian maiden, who offers a bunch

Frances E. Willard, *Woman and Temperance* (Chicago: J. S. Goodman and Company, 1883), pp. 42, 283–284, 326, 459. Found on Microfilm, Research Publication, New Haven, CT.

of artificial cigars, while to get the real ones, of which she sets the foolish young man thinking, he must go inside....

...[The] W. C. T. U., passing through the stages of petition work, local-option work, and constitutional-prohibition-amendment work, has come to the conviction that women must have the ballot as a "home protection" weapon....

The men of the liquor traffic have themselves contributed not a little to our schooling. In their official organs, secret circulars to political aspirants, and by the mightier eloquence of votes paid for with very hard cash, they have united in the declaration (here given in their own words): "Woman's ballot will be the death knell of the liquor traffic!"...

[It] is women who have given the costliest hostages to fortune. Out into the battle of life they have sent their best beloved, with fearful odds against them, with snares that men have legalized and set for them on every hand. Beyond the arms that held them along, their boys have gone forever. Oh! by the danger they have dared; by the hours of patient watching over beds where helpless children lay; by the incense of ten thousand prayers wafted from their gentle lips to Heaven, I charge you give them power to protect, along life's treacherous highway, those whom they have so loved. Let it no longer be that they must sit back among the shadows, hopelessly mourning over their strong staff broken, and their beautiful rod; but when the sons they love shall go forth to life's battle, still let their mothers walk beside them, sweet and serious, and clad in the garments of power.

2. Utopian Edward Bellamy Scorns the Callousness of the Rich, 1888

...By way of attempting to give the reader some general impression of the way people lived together in those days, and especially of the relations of the rich and poor to one another, perhaps I cannot do better than to compare society as it then was to a prodigious coach which the masses of humanity were harnessed to and dragged toilsomely along a very hilly and sandy road. The driver was hunger, and permitted no lagging, though the pace was necessarily very slow. Despite the difficulty of drawing the coach at all along so hard a road, the top was covered with passengers who never got down, even at the steepest ascents. These seats on top were very breezy and comfortable. Well up out of the dust, their occupants could enjoy the scenery at their leisure, or critically discuss the merits of the straining team. Naturally such places were in great demand and the competition for them was keen, every one seeking as the first end in life to secure a seat on the coach for himself and to leave it to his child after him. By the rule of the coach a man could leave his seat to whom he wished, but on the other hand there were many accidents by which it might at any time be wholly lost. For all that they were so easy, the seats were very insecure, and at every sudden jolt of the coach persons were slipping out of them and falling to the ground....

Edward Bellamy, *Looking Backward, 2000–1887* (New York: Modern Library, 1982), pp. 5–6.

But did they think only of themselves? you ask. Was not their very luxury rendered intolerable to them by comparison with the lot of their brothers and sisters in the harness, and the knowledge that their own weight added to their toil? Had they no compassion for fellow beings from whom fortune only distinguished them? Oh, yes; commiseration was frequently expressed by those who rode for those who had to pull the coach, especially when the vehicle came to a bad place in the road, as it was constantly doing, or to a particularly steep hill. At such times, the desperate straining of the team, their agonized leaping and plunging under the pitiless lashing of hunger, the many who fainted at the rope and were trampled in the mire, made a very distressing spectacle, which often called forth highly creditable displays of feeling on the top of the coach. At such times the passengers would call down encouragingly to the toilers of the rope, exhorting them to patience, and holding out hopes of possible compensation in another world for the hardness of their lot, while others contributed to buy salves and liniments for the crippled and injured. It was agreed that it was a great pity that the coach should be so hard to pull, and there was a sense of general relief when the specially bad piece of road was gotten over. This relief was not, indeed, wholly on account of the team, for there was always some danger at these bad places of a general overturn in which all would lose their seats.

It must in truth be admitted that the main effect of the spectacle of the misery of the toilers at the rope was to enhance the passengers' sense of the value of their seats upon the coach, and to cause them to hold on to them more desperately than before. If the passengers could only have felt assured that neither they nor their friends would ever fall from the top, it is probable that, beyond contributing to the funds for liniments and bandages, they would have troubled themselves extremely little about those who dragged the coach....

3. Black Educator Booker T. Washington Advocates Compromise and Self-Reliance, 1901

I was born a slave on a plantation in Franklin County, Virginia. I am not quite sure of the exact place or exact date of my birth, but at any rate I suspect I must have been born somewhere and at some time. As nearly as I have been able to learn, I was born near a cross-roads post-office called Hale's Ford, and the year was 1858 or 1859. I do not know the month or the day....

So far as I can now recall, the first knowledge that I got of the fact that we were slaves, and that freedom of the slaves was being discussed, was early one morning before day, when I was awakened by my mother kneeling over her children and fervently praying that Lincoln and his armies might be successful, and that one day she and her children might be free.... The night before the eventful day, word was sent to the slave quarters to the effect that something unusual was going to take place at the "big house" the next morning. There was little, if any, sleep that night. All was excitement and expectancy.

Up From Slavery by Booker T. Washington (Doubleday, 1901), pp. 1, 7, 20–22, 206, 210–211, 218–236.

The most distinct thing that I now recall in connection with the scene was that some man who seemed to be a stranger (a United states officer, I presume) made a little speech and then read a rather long paper—the Emancipation Proclamation, I think. After the reading we were told that we were all free, and could go when and where we pleased. My mother, who was standing by my side, leaned over and kissed her children, while tears of joy ran down her cheeks. She explained to us what it all meant, that this was the day for which she had been so long praying, but fearing that she would never live to see.

For some minutes there was great rejoicing, and thanksgiving, and wild scenes of ecstasy. But there was no feeling of bitterness. In fact, there was pity among the slaves for our former owners. The wild rejoicing on the part of the emancipated coloured people lasted but for a brief period, for I noticed that by the time they returned to their cabins there was a change in their feelings. The great responsibility of being free, of having charge of themselves, of having to think and plan for themselves and their children, seemed to take possession of them. It was very much like suddenly turning a youth of ten or twelve years out into the world to provide for himself. In a few hours the great questions with which the Anglo-Saxon race had been grappling for centuries had been thrown upon these people to be solved. These were the questions of a home, a living, the rearing of children, education, citizenship, and the establishment and support of churches....

I now come to that one of the incidents in my life which seems to have excited the greatest amount of interest, and which perhaps went further than anything else in giving me a reputation that in a sense might be called National. I refer to the address which I delivered at the opening of the Atlanta Cotton states and International Exposition, at Atlanta, Ga., September 18, 1895....

The receiving of this invitation brought to me a sense of responsibility that it would be hard for any one not placed in my position to appreciate. What were my feelings when this invitation came to me? I remembered that I had been a slave... It was only a few years before that time that any white man in the audience might have claimed me as his slave; and it was easily possible that some of my former owners might be present to hear me speak....

I was determined to say nothing that I did not feel from the bottom of my heart to be true and right.... The following is the address which I delivered:—...

A ship lost at sea for many days suddenly sighted a friendly vessel. From the mast of the unfortunate vessel was seen a signal, "Water, water; we die of thirst!" The answer from the friendly vessel at once came back, "Cast down your bucket where you are." A second time the signal, "Water, water; send us water!" ran up from the distressed vessel, and was answered, "Cast down your bucket where you are." And a third and fourth signal for water was answered, "Cast down your bucket where you are." The captain of the distressed vessel, at last heeding the injunction, cast down his bucket, and it came up full of fresh, sparkling water from the mouth of the Amazon River. To those of my race who depend on bettering their condition in a foreign land or who underestimate the importance of cultivating friendly relations with the Southern white man, who is their next-door neighbour, I would say: "Cast down your bucket where you are"—cast it down in making friends in every manly way of the people of all races by whom we are surrounded.

Cast it down in agriculture, mechanics, in commerce, in domestic service, and in the professions.... No race can prosper till it learns that there is as much dignity in tilling a field as in writing a poem. It is at the bottom of life we must begin, and not at the top. Nor should we permit our grievances to overshadow our opportunities.

To those of the white race who look to the incoming of those of foreign birth and strange tongue and habits for the prosperity of the South, were I permitted I would repeat what I say to my own race, "Cast down your bucket where you are." Cast it down among the eight millions of Negroes whose habits you know, whose fidelity and love you have tested in days when to have proved treacherous meant the ruin of your firesides.... While doing this, you can be sure in the future, as in the past, that you and your families will be surrounded by the most patient, faithful, law-abiding, and unresentful people that the world has seen. As we have proved our loyalty to you in the past, in nursing your children, watching by the sickbed of your mothers and fathers, and often following them with tear-dimmed eyes to their graves, so in the future, in our humble way, we shall stand by you with a devotion that no foreigner can approach.... In all things that are purely social we can be as separate as the fingers, yet one as the hand in all things essential to mutual progress....

The wisest among my race understand that the agitation of questions of social equality is the extremest folly, and that progress in the enjoyment of all the privileges that will come to us must be the result of severe and constant struggle rather than an artificial forcing. No race that has anything to contribute to the markets of the world is long in any degree ostracized. It is important and right that all privileges of the law be ours, but it is vastly more important that we be prepared for the exercises of these privileges. The opportunity to earn a dollar in a factory just now is worth infinitely more than the opportunity to spend a dollar in an opera-house....

The coloured people and the coloured newspapers at first seemed to be greatly pleased with the character of my Atlanta address, as well as with its reception. But after the first burst of enthusiasm began to die away, and the coloured people began reading the speech in cold type, some of them seemed to feel that they had been hypnotized. I think that for a year after the publication of this article every association and every conference or religious body of any kind, of my race, that met, did not fail before adjourning to pass a resolution condemning me, or calling upon me to retract or modify what I had said....

During the whole time of the excitement, and through all the criticism, I did not utter a word of explanation or retraction. I knew that I was right, and that time and the sober second thought of the people would vindicate me....

I believe it is the duty of the Negro—as the greater part of the race is already doing—to deport himself modestly in regard to political claims, depending upon the slow but sure influences that proceed from the possession of property, intelligence, and high character for the full recognition of his political rights. I think that the according of the full exercise of political rights is going to be a matter of natural, slow growth, not an over-night, gourd-vine affair....

4. NAACP Founder W. E. B. DuBois Denounces Compromise on Negro Education and Civil Rights, 1903

Mr. [Booker T.] Washington represents in Negro thought the old attitude of adjustment and submission; but adjustment at such a peculiar time as to make his programme unique. This is an age of unusual economic development, and Mr. Washington's programme naturally takes an economic cast, becoming a gospel of Work and Money to such an extent as apparently almost completely to over-shadow the higher aims of life. Moreover, this is an age when the more advanced races are coming in closer contact with the less developed races, and the race-feeling is therefore intensified; and Mr. Washington's programme practically accepts the alleged inferiority of the Negro races.... In other periods of intensified prejudice all the Negro's tendency to self-assertion has been called forth; at this period a policy of submission is advocated. In the history of nearly all other races and peoples the doctrine preached at such crises has been that manly self-respect is worth more than lands and houses, and that a people who voluntarily surrender such respect, or cease striving for it, are not worth civilizing.

In answer to this, it has been claimed that the Negro can survive only through submission. Mr. Washington distinctly asks that black people give up, at least for the present, three things,—

First, political power,
Second, insistence on civil rights,
Third, higher education of Negro youth,—

and concentrate all their energies on industrial education, and accumulation of wealth, and the conciliation of the South. This policy has been courageously and insistently advocated for over fifteen years, and has been triumphant for per-haps ten years. As a result of this tender of the palm-branch, what has been the return? In these years there have occurred:

1.   The disfranchisement of the Negro.
2.   The legal creation of a distinct status of civil inferiority for the Negro.
3.   The steady withdrawal of aid from institutions for the higher training of the Negro.

These movements are not, to be sure, direct results of Mr. Washington's teachings; but this propaganda has, without a shadow of doubt, helped their speedier accomplishment. The question then comes: Is it possible, and probable, that nine millions of men can make effective progress in economic lines if they are deprived of political rights, made a servile caste, and allowed only the most meager chance for developing their exceptional men? If history and reason give

W. E. B. DuBois, *The Souls of Black Folk* (New York: Signet, 1969), 87–89.

any distinct answer to these questions, it is an emphatic *No.* And Mr. Washington thus faces the triple paradox of his career:

1.   He is striving nobly to make Negro artisans business men and property-owners; but it is utterly impossible, under modern competitive methods, for working-men and property-owners to defend their rights and exist without the right of suffrage.
2.   He insists on thrift and self-respect, but at the same time counsels a silent submission to civic inferiority such as is bound to sap the manhood of any race in the long run.
3.   He advocates common-school and industrial training, and depreciates institutions of higher learning; but neither the Negro common-schools, nor Tuskegee itself, could remain open a day were it not for teachers trained in Negro colleges, or trained by their graduates....

...Such men feel in conscience bound to ask of this nation three things:

1.   The right to vote.
2.   Civic equality.
3.   The education of youth according to ability.

5. Journalist Lincoln Steffens Exposes the Shame of Corruption, 1904

...The misgovernment of the American people is misgovernment by the American people.

When I set out on my travels, an honest New Yorker told me honestly that I would find that the Irish, the Catholic Irish, were at the bottom of it all everywhere. The first city I went to was St. Louis, a German city. The next was Minneapolis, a Scandinavian city, with a leadership of New Englanders. Then came Pittsburg, Scotch Presbyterian, and that was what my New York friend was. "Ah, but they are all foreign populations," I heard. The next city was Philadelphia, the purest American community of all, and the most hopeless. And after that came Chicago and New York, both mongrel-bred, but the one a triumph of reform, the other the best example of good government that I had seen. The "foreign element" excuse is one of the hypocritical lies that save us from the clear sight of ourselves.

Another such conceit of our egotism is that which deplores our politics and lauds our business....

There is hardly an office from United States Senator down to Alderman in any part of the country to which the business man has not been elected; yet politics remains corrupt, government pretty bad, and the selfish citizen has to hold himself in readiness like the old volunteer firemen to rush forth at any hour, in any weather, to prevent the fire; and he goes out sometimes and he puts out the fire (after the damage is done) and he goes back to the shop sighing for the business man in politics. The business man has failed in politics as he has in citizenship....

Lincoln Steffens, *The Shame of the Cities* (New York: Hill and Wang, 1959), 2–7.

But there is hope, not alone despair, in the commercialism of our politics. If our political leaders are to be always a lot of political merchants, they will supply any demand we may create. All we have to do is to establish a steady demand for good government. The bosses have us split up into parties. To him parties are nothing but means to his corrupt ends. He "bolts" his party, but we must not; the bribe-giver changes his party, from one election to another, from one county to another, from one city to another, but the honest voter must not. Why? Because if the honest voter cared no more for his party than the politician and the grafter, then the honest vote would govern, and that would be bad—for graft. It is idiotic, this devotion to a machine that is used to take our sovereignty from us. If we would leave parties to the politicians, and would vote not for the party, not even for men, but for the city, and the State, and the nation, we should rule parties, and cities, and States, and nation. If we would vote in mass on the more promising ticket, or, if the two are equally bad, would throw out the party that is in, and wait till the next election and then throw out the other party that is in—then, I say, the commercial politician would feel a demand for good government and he would supply it....

6. Social Worker Jane Addams Advocates Civic Housekeeping, 1906

It has been well said that the modern city is a stronghold of industrialism quite as the feudal city was a stronghold of militarism, but the modern cities fear no enemies and rivals from without and their problems of government are solely internal. Affairs for the most part are going badly in these great new centres, in which the quickly-congregated population has not yet learned to arrange its affairs satisfactorily. Unsanitary housing, poisonous sewage, contaminated water, infant mortality, the spread of contagion, adulterated food, impure milk, smoke-laden air, ill-ventilated factories, dangerous occupations, juvenile crime, unwholesome crowding, prostitution and drunkenness are the enemies which the modern cities must face and overcome, would they survive. Logically their electorate should be made up of those who can bear a valiant part in this arduous contest, those who in the past have at least attempted to care for children, to clean houses, to prepare foods, to isolate the family from moral dangers; those who have traditionally taken care of that side of life which inevitably becomes the subject of municipal consideration and control as soon as the population is congested. To test the elector's fitness to deal with this situation by his ability to bear arms is absurd. These problems must be solved, if they are solved at all, not from the military point of view, not even from the industrial point of view, but from a third, which is rapidly developing in all the great cities of the world—the human-welfare point of view....

City housekeeping has failed partly because women, the traditional housekeepers, have not been consulted as to its multiform activities. The men have

Jane Addams, "The Modern City and the Municipal Franchise for Women" (speech at the NAWSA Convention, February 1906).

been carelessly indifferent to much of this civic housekeeping, as they have always been indifferent to the details of the household.... The very multifariousness and complexity of a city government demand the help of minds accustomed to detail and variety of work, to a sense of obligation for the health and welfare of young children and to a responsibility for the cleanliness and comfort of other people. Because all these things have traditionally been in the hands of women, if they take no part in them now they are not only missing the education which the natural participation in civic life would bring to them but they are losing what they have always had.

7. Reformer Frederic Howe Compares America and Germany, 1911

...The most obvious thing about the German city is its orderliness. The most obvious thing about the American city is its disorderliness. The American city is an accident, a railway, water, or industrial accident. It had its birth in the chance location of a body of settlers. It became a city because it could not help it. The German city, on the other hand, was either a fortress, a Hauptstadt, or an industrial community, like the cities of the lower Rhine in the neighborhood of Essen, Elberfeld, or Barmen. Berlin, Munich, Dresden, Cologne, Mannheim, Düsseldorf, Hanover, and Strassburg were the seats of kingdoms, principalities, or bishoprics. Frankfort, Hamburg, Bremen, and Lübeck were free Hanseatic towns, owing allegiance to no one—proud of their mediæval traditions and jealous of their freedom....

In America we have no such traditions or monuments. Our only memories are those of shops, mills, and factories ever repeating themselves like the concentric rings of a growing tree. Few men have any other idea of the city than this. In addition, all of the work of the American city had to be done at once. Streets and sewers had to be built. Gas, water, electric light, telegraph, and telephone wires, mains and conduits had to be laid, while schools, station-houses, and public structures had to be erected merely to keep pace with the inrush of people. Our officials were swamped with elemental needs. They had no traditions, no experience, to guide them. They had no time to dream dreams. They were driven, like the pioneer, by the fear of the coming winter....

But the foundations are now in. We are in a position to look about us. And everywhere there are signs that democracy is dissatisfied with its cyclone-proof cellar. Washington, New York, Cleveland, Chicago, Denver, Kansas City, San Francisco, Baltimore, St. Louis, and Pittsburg are planning to rebuild their cities and to relieve its disorderliness with parks, public structures, and open spaces, while democracy is seeking to find more efficient tools for the doing of its work. The next generation is bound to see tremendous advance in things municipal. And it is to Germany rather than to England or France that we must go for our models.

Excerpt from Frederic C. Howe, "The German and the American City," *Scribner's Magazine* 49 (1911), pp. 485–491.

I have said that the city was but a cross-section of the country in which it is found. It reflects the political, social, educational, and moral life of the people. Yet the German city, in spite of the autocratic personal government of the Kaiser, is free … free to dream big dreams, and when they are ready for realization, to achieve them and enjoy the fruits thereof.

The American city, on the other hand, is in chains. It has great power for evil and but limited power for good. Our cities are not permitted to become great if they can, from the fear that they may make mistakes in so doing. The German city, on the other hand, has almost complete autonomy. It can own, operate, lease, or regulate the franchise corporations which occupy its streets. And it very generally owns them. It can enter trade and industry….

The American city is bound, as was Gulliver by the Liliputians, with a thousand thongs. It has to secure the assent of suspicious farmers and hostile financial interests, before it can change the wages or salaries of its officials or alter the method of police administration. Its control over tenements, slums, and franchise corporations is generally such as the owners of these properties see fit to permit….

The German city has no mayor. It has an Oberbürgermeister, who corresponds roughly to our mayor. His legal authority is far less than that enjoyed by the patriarchal executives of New York, Baltimore, or Boston. In desperation over our inability to watch a hundred men we decided to watch but one….

The head of the German city is an expert….

Tenure of office is permanent. If a mayor is re-elected, after his first term of twelve years, he holds office for life. When a vacancy occurs, the town council sets about to fill it much as the British city finds a clerk, or the American railroad finds a president. From the candidates who present themselves from all Germany the council makes a choice, to which choice the Kaiser must assent. Approval, however, is rarely withheld….

The town council in Germany is the ultimate repository of power. It is chosen by the electors…. In the city, however, men vote as tax payers and not as individuals. The voters are divided into three classes. Those who pay one-third of the taxes elect one-third of the council; those who pay another third of the taxes elect another third, while the great mass of the people, who, under the income tax, pay the remaining third of the revenues elect the remaining third of the council. I heard of one city where a single man elected one-third of the council, and of another where one hundred and thirty persons did so. In consequence the German city is far from democratic, possibly less democratic than any of the cities of Europe….

Within the past decade the Rhine cities have developed a wonderful system of wharves and docks, together with the most scientific cranes, tracks, warehouses, and handling devices for the purpose of promoting trade….

All this pays. It pays handsomely, not only in health, in happiness, and in comfort; it pays in the language that the business man best understands. It pays in dividends. For the cities which do the most things and own the most enterprises have the lowest tax rate. They also have the most contented population….

But I have not yet touched on the thing that sets the German city apart and distinguishes it from all other cities in the world. The German official thinks in a different *milieu* than does the British or the American official. He starts with the presumption that the city should do anything it sees fit to do provided it will improve the city, reduce the tax rate, or make it a more comfortable, healthful, or better place in which to live. The Anglo-Saxon, on the other hand, starts with an ingrained conviction that the city should do just as little as possible, and that any concession from this principle is fraught with extreme danger. The German has no prejudice against government: he does not look upon it as *per se* evil and inefficient....

8. Sociologist William Graham Sumner Denounces Reformers' Fanaticism, 1913

As time runs on it becomes more and more obvious that this generation has raised up for itself social problems which it is not competent to solve, and that this inability may easily prove fatal to it. We have been boasting of the achievements of the nineteenth century, and viewing ourselves and our circumstances in an altogether rose-colored medium. We have not had a correct standard for comparing ourselves with our predecessors on earth, nor for judging soberly what we have done or what men can do.... We draw up pronunciamentos, every paragraph of which begins with: "we demand," without noticing the difference between the things which we can expect from the society in which we live, and those which we must get either from ourselves or from God and nature.

We believe that we can bring about a complete transformation in the economic organization of society, and not have any incidental social and political questions arise which will make us great difficulty, or that, if such questions arise, they can all be succinctly solved by saying: "Let the State attend to it"; "Make a bureau and appoint inspectors"; "Pass a law." But the plain fact is that the new time presents manifold and constantly varying facts and factors. It is complicated, heterogeneous, full of activity, so that its phases are constantly changing. Legislation and state action are stiff, rigid, inelastic, incapable of adaptation to cases; they are never adopted except under stress of the perception of some one phase which has, for some reason or other, arrested attention. Hence, the higher the organization of society, the more mischievous legislative regulation is sure to be....

We think that security and justice are simple and easy things which go without the saying, and need only be recognized to be had and enjoyed; we do not know that security is a thing which men have never yet succeeded in establishing. History is full of instruction for us if we will go to it for instruction....

We think that, if this world does not suit us, it ought to be corrected to our satisfaction, and that, if we see any social phenomenon which does not suit our notions, there should be a remedy found at once. A collection of these complaints and criticisms, however, assembled from the literature of the day, would show the most heterogeneous, contradictory, and fantastic notions.

William Graham Sumner, "Fantasies and Facts," in *Earth-Hunger and Other Essays* (New Brunswick, N.J.: Transaction, Inc., 1980), 207–210.

We think that this is a world in which we are limited by our wants, not by our powers; by our ideals, not by our antecedents.

We think that we are resisting oppression from other men, when we are railing against the hardships of life on this earth....

We think that capital comes of itself, and would all be here just the same, no matter what regulations we might make about the custody, use, and enjoyment of it....

We think that we can impair the rights of landlords, creditors, employers, and capitalists, and yet maintain all other rights intact.

We think that, although A has greatly improved his position in half a life-time, that is nothing, because B, in the same time, has become a millionaire.

We throw all our attention on the utterly idle question whether A has done as well as B, when the only question is whether A has done as well as he could.

We think that competition produces great inequalities, but that stealing or almsgiving does not.

9. Cartoon: The Women's Vote vs. Boss Rule, 1915

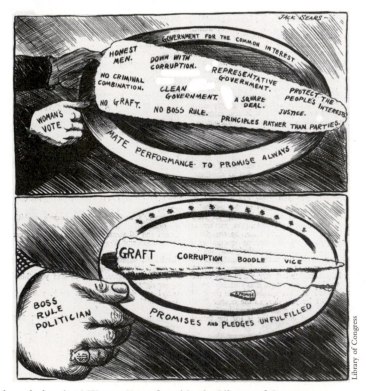

Corn or the cob drawing, *Woman Voter*, found in the Library of Congress.

ESSAYS

Progressivism was so multidimensional that it has provoked a wide variety of historical arguments about everything from its effect on business profits to its consequences for marriage. The following two essays stake out new territory in the debates over the character of Progressivism. Michael McGerr of Indiana University is critical of Progressivism, which he believes was an attempt by an insecure, fiercely discontented middle class to foist its values upon the working and upper classes. In doing so, busybody reformers passed a variety of intrusive laws, and gave too much power to the state. Tragically, they also acquiesced in the disfranchisement of the men and women freed by the Civil War. Daniel T. Rodgers of Princeton University argues that American Progressives learned their trade in Europe. They were part of a much larger transatlantic conversation over the best ways to provide for human welfare in the industrialized world. Fairly or not, Europeans of the era tended to see the Americans as latecomers and borrowers in the process of reform. Americans themselves wanted to catch up with European "good government," especially that of Germany and Britain.

Class, Gender, and Race at Home: The American Birthplace of Progressivism

MICHAEL McGERR

…The progressives developed a stunningly broad agenda that ranged well beyond the control of big business, the amelioration of poverty, and the purification of politics to embrace the transformation of gender relations, the regeneration of the home, the disciplining of leisure and pleasure, and the establishment of segregation. Progressives wanted not only to use the state to regulate the economy; strikingly, they intended nothing less than to transform other Americans, to remake the nation's feuding, polyglot population in their own middle-class image…

To make the world safe for themselves and their children, the progressive middle class sallied forth to reform the nation. In the face of spirited opposition from other groups, the progressives intended to build what William James sneeringly but accurately labeled the "middle-class paradise."

I believe progressivism was a radical movement, though not by the common measures of economic and political radicalism. More influenced by socialism than they liked to admit, progressives nevertheless shied away from a fundamental restructuring of the capitalist economy. They generally declined numerous opportunities to rethink the virtue of private property. Instead, progressives were radical in their conviction that other social classes must be transformed and in their boldness in going about the business of that transformation. As they themselves had been changed, so others should be changed, too. The sweep of

From Michael McGerr, *A Fierce Discontent: The Rise and Fall of the Progressive Movement in America,* 1870–1920 (Oxford University Press, 2007), p. xiv–xv, 7–11, 14–16, 19–20, 43–45, 48, 60–61, 64, 67, 81–83, 94, 182–183, 187, 317–318. Reprinted by permission of Oxford University Press, Inc.

progressivism was remarkable, but because the progressive agenda was so often carried out in settlement houses, churches, and schoolrooms, in rather unassuming day-to-day activities, the essential audacity of the enterprise can be missed. Progressivism demanded a social transformation that remains at once profoundly impressive and profoundly disturbing a century later....

The end of the nineteenth century saw more than just "signs of friction between the upper ten and the lower": wage workers, farmers, and the rich were alien to one another.... What would become the Progressive Era—an extraordinary explosion of middle-class activism—began as an unprecedented crisis of alienation amid the extremes of wealth and poverty in America.

In a land of some 76 million people, the "upper ten" were no more than a tiny minority, a mere sliver of the nation. Wealthy capitalists, manufacturers, merchants, landowners, executives, professionals, and their families made up not "ten," but only 1 or 2 percent of the population....

Concentrated in the Northeast and especially New York State, theirs were the famous names of American capitalism—Vanderbilt, Whitney, Carnegie, Harriman, and Morgan. Probably the greatest fortune of them all—a billion dollars by 1913—belonged to John D. Rockefeller, the leader of Standard Oil....

The upper ten attributed the hardships of the poor not to an unfair economic system but to individual shortcomings. The remedy was individual regeneration rather than government action. "[The] failures which a man makes in his life are due almost always to some defect in his personality, some weakness of body, or mind, or character, will, or temperament," wrote John D. Rockefeller. "The only way to overcome these failings is to build up his personality from within, so that he, by virtue of what is within him, may overcome the weakness which was the cause of the failure." Individualism, moreover, helped the wealthy resolutely deny the existence of social classes, despite all the signs of friction around them. "The American Commonwealth is built upon the individual," explained the renowned corporate lawyer and U.S. Senator Chauncey Depew of New York. "It recognizes neither classes nor masses.".…

The aristocratic and even regal bearing, with its assumption of individual prerogative, came easily for the men and women of the upper ten.... There was the financier E. H. Harriman, who "had the philosophy, the methods of an Oriental monarch." His niece, Daisy Harriman, recalled visiting him in his library one evening. "Daisy, I have a new plaything," he told her. "I have just bought the Erie [railroad] for five million dollars. I think I will call them up now.".…

Upper-class individualism was obviously self-serving and often self-deluding, but it was no sham. More than any other group, the upper ten carried individualism proudly into the organized and bureaucratized twentieth century....

Of course, the rich typically married and created homes. Cornelia Bradley Martin and other wealthy women, shunning careers in business or politics, seemingly devoted themselves to the domestic ideal as wives and mothers. But these women artfully turned their domestic duty as hostesses into quite public roles that earned them fame and notoriety. Cornelia Bradley Martin was more of a public figure than her husband. Meanwhile, in a notable departure from Victorian tradition, upper-class parents thrust their sons out of the protective cocoon of the home at an early age. Rather than bring in tutors to school their boys at home as in the past, many of the wealthy began sending their male heirs off to Groton, Choate, St. Paul's, and other exclusive boarding schools in New England.

The rich were also unusually willing to break up the home altogether. Before the Civil War, divorce had been as unthinkable for the wealthy as for middle-class Victorians. But with the rise of the industrial upper class after the war, May King Van Rensselaer of New York noted, society circles "began to sanction divorces.... All at once it became fashionable to divorce your helpmeet...." In a nation where, as late as 1920, less than one percent of adults had been divorced, the marriages of the rich collapsed with notable frequency. Ten percent of the Americans worth $20 million or more who were born between 1830 and 1865 were divorced; of those born between the end of the Civil War and the turn of the century, 20 percent were divorced....

The gulf between the upper ten and the working class was enormous. Of necessity, working men, women, and children lived by a different set of cultural rules.... The constraints and uncertainties of working-class life—low wages, lay-offs, accidents, limited opportunity, early death—made individualism at best a wasteful indulgence and at worst a mortal threat. Realizing that they had to depend on one another to survive, workers developed a culture of mutualism and reciprocity. At home and at work, they taught sometimes harsh lessons about the necessity of self-denial and collective action.

These were lessons that Rahel Golub learned painfully in the 1890s. Born in Russia, she came to America in 1892 at the age of eleven to help her father in a tailor shop in New York City....

Rahel and her father had to work and save to pay for the rest of the family's passage to the United States. Against that necessity, her needs and wishes, her chance for an education, did not matter at all. Rahel sometimes felt the tension between her family and her individuality. "One Saturday," she related, "while standing out on the stoop I saw one little girl show a cent to another and boasting that she was going to buy candy.... It occurred to me that I too would like to have a cent with which to do just as I pleased." So Rahel asked her father for the money. "He looked at me silently for a long moment," she recalled. "Then he rose slowly, took out his pocket book, took a cent from it, held it out to me, and said with a frown..., 'Here, and see that this never happens again.'" Rahel was stunned: "I felt as if the coin were burning my fingers. I handed it back quickly, left the room and walked about in the streets. I felt mortally hurt"....

Nevertheless, Rahel came to accept the self-denial at the heart of her life and her father's. "In the shop one morning I realised that he had been leaving out of his breakfast the tiny glass of brandy for two cents and was eating just the roll," she said. "So I too made my sacrifice. When as usual he gave me the apple and the roll, I took the roll but refused the apple. And he did not urge me." There were other sacrifices: Rahel avoided changing jobs because the loss of even one day's pay would slow her family's arrival....

In one way or another, the story of Rahel Golub was repeated over and over in the United States at the turn of the century. This was, at least numerically, a working-class nation. In 1900, more than half the country, perhaps

36 to 40 million men, women, and children, made up the laboring class that performed manual work for wages. They toiled with their hands on docks, roads, and farms, in factories, mines, and other people's houses. They practiced ancient crafts such as tailoring and carpentry, and newer arts such as iron molding and metal cutting. They were machine tenders in mills and factories, unskilled laborers in towns, farm hands in the countryside, cowboys on the range, and domestic servants in Victorian houses. All of them, even the best-paid skilled workers, lived circumscribed, vulnerable lives, constrained by low pay and limited opportunity, and menaced by unemployment, ill health, and premature death....

They worked hard, but their attitudes toward work were far from Victorian. Most workers labored out of compulsion, need, ambition, and pride. But given the dangers and indignities of wage labor, there was little chance that laboring men would mimic the Victorians and glorify hard work....

Despite the limits on their free time and income, many laboring men and women did share with the wealthy a powerful attraction to pleasures and objects. Countless immigrant workers were drawn to the United States because the country held out the promise of consumer pleasures. "My godfather was in Detroit and wrote me that he had paper on the walls, shoes, meat every day, fresh bread, milk, water in the house, beer on the corner, soup, and plenty of money," a Polish immigrant recalled. "From that time I was crazy to come." But industrializing America proved to be an expensive place. Rents in Pittsburgh were twice as high as in the English manufacturing city of Birmingham. In order to save money or even get by in this expensive country, many working-class Americans typically had to deny their appetites, just as Rahel gave up her apple at breakfast and her father skipped his brandy. Yet, other workers felt that lack of money and opportunity made self-restraint irrelevant. Many wage workers, notably single men and Southern plain folk, saw little point in trying to save their dollars and deny themselves.

As a result, a rich culture of release and expressiveness flourished. Some workers shared the upper-class obsession with fashion and display. Young laboring women spent precious dollars on flashy clothing intended to match or even outdo the upper ten....

Workers were known for their boisterous observance of the Fourth of July and their noisy, demonstrative behavior in theaters. Public drinking was a further element of this expressive life. Amid Victorian abstemiousness, the saloon had emerged as a vital working-class institution by the late nineteenth century. The barroom served many functions—meeting place, reading room, music hall, ethnic preserve, and male bastion. The saloon was also the place where workers dropped the discipline of the workplace and loosened self-control.

For many workers, sex offered a similar opportunity for expression and release. In towns and cities, working-class neighborhoods were associated with the public display of sexuality. Men and women made physical contact in the popular dance halls that featured such risqué steps as the hug me close, the shiver, the hump-back rag, and the lover's walk. "[C]ouples stand very close together," a middle-class observer noted, "the girl with her arms around the man's neck, the man with both his arms around the girl or on her hips; their cheeks are pressed close together, their bodies touch each other.".…

Like other classes, the middle class covered a wide range of circumstances at the turn of the twentieth century. It was defined most obviously by occupation. Victorian fathers and sons—and sometimes wives and daughters—were small proprietors and professionals, clerks and salespeople, managers and bureaucrats.… These men and women, along with their families, probably numbered between 12 and 16 million people in 1900. In all, about one American in five was middle-class at the turn of the century.

Their white-collar positions clearly set the Victorians apart from the working-class families who lived by manual labor. But it was money more than occupation that divided the middle class from the upper ten, whose fathers and sons also performed white-collar work. Though Victorian families lived fairly well, they had nothing like the fabulous resources of the upper class. The middle class lived always with a sense of constraint, a mixture of comforts and limits.

That was plainly true for the families of clerks and small shop owners, who with incomes of a thousand dollars or so a year might be little better off than the best-paid skilled workers. But it was also true for a prosperous bureaucrat such as Charles Spencer, an aide to the steel magnate Henry Clay Frick. Spencer and his family lived with their servants in a fine Queen Anne house on Amberson Avenue in Shadyside, an affluent neighborhood of Pittsburgh's East End. Yet, with seven children, the "roomy" house "nearly burst at the seams" and the Spencers had to scrimp and save. "We lived in a neighborhood where everyone had more money than we had…," Spencer's daughter, Ethel, recalled. "[T]here was never enough money in our house for unconsidered expenditure and every spare penny had to be put aside for the future use of the children." The eldest of them had started out "in aristocratic fashion" with a governess and private schools, but the others had to go off to public school despite "a little social sacrifice." At home, Ethel's mother, Mary Acheson Spencer, "was thrift personified.".… "When her seven children were at loose ends and demanded something to do," Ethel remembered, "she would set them down with some old patterns or torn sheets of tissue paper and a pair of blunt scissors to cut the paper into pieces of suitable size and shape for the toilet-paper box.".…

Middle-class children typically were not expected to contribute to family income; they needed to go to school in order to prepare for white-collar careers. Partly because nonworking children were so expensive to raise, the Victorians practiced family limitation more than workers and farmers did. Middle-class couples had fewer children—averaging between three and four to a household by the end of the nineteenth century. As a result, Victorian mothers lavished more attention on each child.…

From the outside, the world of the Spencers seemed safe, secure, and self-satisfied. But Victorianism was already a culture in crisis.

By the time reformer Jane Addams earned her degree from Rockford, domesticity was in trouble. Inside their Queen Anne houses, Victorian men and women, eyeing one another uneasily, postponed marriage. In the 1880s and 1890s, the marriage rate for white Americans decreased. Jane Addams's failure to marry was not unique: the generation of women arriving at maturity became the least likely to marry in American history. Once married, couples postponed having their first child. Judging by an apparently large increase in prostitution, those couples did not always find sexual satisfaction together. Perhaps not surprisingly, there was an increase in the divorce rate as well. On a typically more modest scale, the Victorians echoed the marital travails of the rich. As the breakup of middle-class unions helped push the national divorce rate from 1.5 per 1,000 marriages in 1870 up to 4.0 in 1900, Victorians began to worry about a "divorce crisis" in their ranks....

Marriage was unattractive, of course, because it meant intimacy with Victorian men. "The average young girl considers herself a finer product of human-ity than the average young man," Kate Gannett Wells reported. "The girl starts with the notion that her father, just because he was a man, has made life hard for her mother, and that all men are more or less explosive.... The feminine mind is preoccupied with the original sinfulness of man." Too many middle-class men seemed to spend too much time away from home in the evenings, enjoying the masculine camaraderie of clubs and fraternal lodges. The double standard, which allowed men pleasure outside the marriage bed and the home, seemed intolerable. "How can men bear to live double?" asked twenty-one-year-old Annie Winsor. "How can they be gentlemanly, of pure speech and right behavior at home and with ladies, and go to drink and swear and think foul thoughts, to see ugly sights... do ugly deeds and cover them over." Winsor knew the answer: "[T]here is a code of honour which will protect them from exposure."

Middle-class men had their own complaints about women. For Victorian males, life was a difficult balancing act. They had to be tough enough to succeed in the world of commerce, yet gentle enough to please at home. They could feel uncomfortable in the feminized parlor, where they had to keep their feet off the furniture, watch their tobacco, and generally mind their manners. They could feel uncomfortable, too, in the new office buildings, where more and more young women invaded the male preserve of white-collar work. A young man soon discovered that he could satisfy women only if he showed them he was not "like other men," that he did not live by the double standard....

As the Victorians reconsidered domesticity and individualism, they also had to reevaluate the place of work and pleasure in their lives. Industrial capitalism seemed to eat away at the ascetic discipline of Victorianism, especially its empha-sis on hard work, thrift, and self-denial. As the American economy grew, leisure, abundance, and pleasure beckoned seductively to the middle class.

In the Gilded Age, the work ethic lost its iron hold on the Victorian con-science. The middle class began to entertain the notion that one could work too hard. After all, it was hard work that had produced the upper ten and the con-sequent horrors of industrial America. And certainly the continued growth of the national economy appeared not to require quite as much labor—at least from middle-class white-collar workers. As in so many other areas, Bellamy's *Looking Backward* pointed hopefully toward change. Utopian Boston does not worship work: in fact, men and women labor short hours, take "regular" vacations, and look forward to an early retirement at forty-five....

Despite this greater emphasis on pleasure, the middle class was not ready to tighten its embrace of all forms of enjoyment. Rather than celebrate sexual pleasure, the Victorians tried to contain sexual desire. The single standard of sexual conduct that middle-class women had in mind was their own, not the looser standard of many men. The Gilded Age witnessed, as Charlotte Perkins Gilman put it, "a fine, earnest movement toward an equal standard of chastity for men and women an equalizing upward to the level of women." So the Victorians tried to rein in male sexuality by combating prostitution and encouraging voluntary motherhood, women's control of their own bodies....

The new identity of the middle class became plain as men and women considered how to end class conflict and create a safe society for themselves and their children. With individualism in disrepute, the middle class needed another doctrine to guide them in the world. Amid the poverty of Halstead Street and the social division of Chicago, Jane Addams felt that need acutely. When she and Ellen Starr moved into Hull-House in September 1889, they had no clear course of action. "I... longed," Addams wrote, "for the comfort of a definite social creed, which should afford at one and the same time an explanation of the social chaos and the logical steps towards its better ordering."...

Even as the middle class began to explore the implications of association and social solidarity with others, it also looked to a more coercive replacement for individualism—state power. Despite her interest in socialism, Jane Addams did not begin at Hull-House with any grand idea of the state. Instead, her experience in the settlement gradually moved her toward political action and regulatory government. To protect the interests of Hull-House and the neighborhood, Jane Addams participated in three campaigns "against a powerful alderman... notoriously corrupt." When she recognized the health problems caused by inadequate garbage collection, she tried to educate the neighborhood about waste disposal, setting up an incinerator at Hull-House and urging the city to enforce its sanitation laws....

Not all the contact across social boundary lines was as gentle as the touch of [women like Jane Addams]... On the morning of June 6, 1900, in the town of Medicine Lodge in southwestern Kansas, Carrie Nation gathered up brickbats and bottles of Schlitz-Malt. With these "smashers" loaded in her buggy, she drove, nervous and praying, to the nearby town of Kiowa. A respectable Christian woman in her sixties, known as Mother Nation for her compassion, Carrie Nation was angry nevertheless. Saloons had been outlawed in Kansas since the passage of an amendment to the state constitution in 1880. But the "joints" and "dives" still flourished with the connivance of police and local government. Carrie Nation was going to Kiowa to do something about that. The next morning, armed with the brickbats and bottles, she strode into Mr. Dobson's saloon. "I don't want to strike you," she told the proprietor, "but I am going to break up this den of vice." She hurled her "smashers" at Dobson's liquor bottles; she hurled some more at the mirror behind his bar. "Mr. Dobson...," she noted with satisfaction, "jumped into a corner, seemed very much terrified." Leaving Dobson behind, Carrie Nation attacked three more saloons that morning in Kiowa. Passersby, she observed, "seemed to look puzzled." Dive owners, the town marshal, and the mayor confronted her. But these men were puzzled, too. When they decided not to arrest Nation, she stood in her buggy and lifted her hands to the sky. "Peace on earth," she called to the people of Kiowa as she rode out of town, "good will to men.".…

An odd figure, Carry A. Nation was nevertheless quite representative. Her "smashings" laid bare much of the logic and passion that spurred the progressive crusades to reshape adult behavior. Nation's action may have been extreme, but the things that drove it were typically progressive: changing middle-class values and a profound sense of urgency. Like the scourge of the male-dominated saloon, the progressives wanted to regulate pleasure and alter masculine behavior. Like the traveling lecturer and professional reformer, the progressives accepted a new role for women outside traditional domesticity. Like the general of the Home Defenders, the progressives tended to wrap their worries about a host of problems in a consuming fear for the fate of the home.…

Progressives seldom suggested that middle-class status itself was problematic. Instead, the problems belonged to the other classes—wealthy, workers, and farmers. Progressives believed that the rich and workers led especially troubled domestic lives. "In the city," Josiah Strong observed, "the home is disappearing at both social extremes." "The American family is out of gear in two strata, in both of which pretty much everything else is out of gear," said sociologist Albion Small. "On the one hand is the stratum of the over-wealthed, over-leisured, over-stimulated, under-worked, under-controlled.… Only miracles could save this stratum from rot.".…

Reformers took a less fevered, more creative approach to the problems of the working class. From Jacob Riis's pioneering study of New York tenement life, *How the Other Half Lives,* published in 1890, to Robert Hunter's *Poverty,* published in 1904, to a host of surveys, studies, and magazine articles, the literature on the poor was far more compassionate than the writings about the upper ten. As in the vice crusades, the older emphasis on individuals' shortcomings had given way to a focus on the impact of environment. Reformers no longer quickly concluded that the poor were individually responsible for their plight.…

But when and where they could, many Americans pulled back from people who seemed different.… The early twentieth century became the great age of segregation in the United States, a time of enforced public separations. The word *segregation* itself took on its modern definition in the first years of the new century: *segregation* meant "Jim Crow," the laws and practices that separated white from black in the states of the old Confederacy.…

Superficially a deviation from progressivism, segregation actually drew on basic progressive values and aims. True to their mission to create a safe society for themselves and their children, the progressives turned to segregation as a way to halt dangerous social conflict that could not otherwise be stopped. True to their sense of compassion, the progressives turned to segregation as a way to preserve weaker groups, such as African-Americans and Native Americans, facing brutality and even annihilation. Unlike some other Americans, progressives did not support segregation out of anger, hatred, and a desire to unify whites; but they certainly displayed plenty of condescension and indifference, as well as compassion. Segregation was never the separation of equals; one party always ended up with less—less power, less wealth, less opportunity, less schooling, less health care, less respect. Progressives fairly readily accepted the inequitable arrangement of segregation. They did so because usually there were worse alternatives....

Nationwide, lynchings escalated in the 1880s and peaked at 230 in 1892. The numbers fell off somewhat because black men took pains to avoid trouble. Even so, there were 115 reported lynchings in America in 1900; 106 of the victims were black. Essentially unchecked by local, state, or national government, white Southerners usually invoked some imaginary assault on a white woman in order to murder a black man. There were hangings, shootings, burnings, castrations....

To more-moderate whites, including progressives and the wealthy, it seemed as if the South had gone out of control. These men and women were disgusted by the lynch mobs.... Obviously, there had to be some new means of stabilizing race relations.

As Jim Crow took hold with progressive support or acquiescence, the highest levels of the federal government did virtually nothing to help black Americans. Not surprisingly, the conservative United States Supreme Court gave segregation its imprimatur. In 1896, a majority of the justices ruled in *Plessy v. Ferguson* that segregation was legal on Louisiana trains as long as blacks were provided "separate but equal" accommodations....

Today, it is hard to believe that a majority of progressives actively opposed FDR presidential nominee Franklin Delans Roosevelt—but they did....

Tellingly, one of Roosevelt's first acts as President in 1933 was to support the repeal of prohibition, the ultimate symbol of the progressives' attempts to constrain individualism and pleasure. Explaining his position the year before, Roosevelt termed prohibition a "complete and tragic failure" caused by "this very good reason: we have depended too largely upon the power of governmental action...." Unlike many committed progressive activists, Roosevelt understood that liberalism needed to strike a new balance between the individual and the state.... For all the growth of federal regulatory power during the 1930s and 1940s, Roosevelt's New Deal was lees ambitious than the progressives' bold bid to create the middle-class paradise.... Roosevelt himself underscored the difference in ambition when he mentioned his old boss, Woodrow Wilson, during a campaign speech in 1932. "It is interesting, now, to read his speeches," Roosevelt observed. "What is called 'radical' today (and I have reason to know whereof I speak) is mild compared to the campaign of Mr. Wilson."...

American Progressivism in the Wider Atlantic World

DANIEL T. RODGERS

"Was there a world outside of America?" the muckraker Ray Stannard Baker tried to recollect his state of mind as an apprentice journalist in Chicago in the

Reprinted by permission of the publisher from *Atlantic Crossings: Social Politics in a Progressive Age* by Daniel T. Rodgers, pp. 12–13, 15–16, 52, 56, 58–59, 60, 64, 69–72, 74, 142–144, Cambridge, Mass.: The Belknap Press of Harvard University Press. Copyright © 1998 by the President and Fellows of Harvard College.

1890s. "If there was, I knew next to nothing at all about it—as a reality... I knew something of European history—the old tyranny of kings, the absurdity of aristocracy, the futility of feudal wars—out of which America, the wonderful, had stepped proudly into the enlightenment of the Bill of Rights and the Declaration of Independence. I was a true geocentric American."

In the face of a provincialism this profound, it is hard to resist a knowing smile. Every serious reader of the past instinctively knows what Baker had yet to learn: that nations lie enmeshed in each others' history. Even the most isolated of nation-states is a semipermeable container, washed over by forces originating far beyond its shores. Even the most powerful act their part within world systems beyond their full control.

If complicity in world historical forces marks all nations, it especially marks outpost nations, like the United States, which begin as other nations' imperial projects. From the earliest European settlements in North America forward, the Atlantic functioned for its newcomers less as a barrier than as a connective lifeline—a seaway for the movement of people, goods, ideas, and aspirations. A key outpost for European trade and a magnet for European capital, the eighteenth- and nineteenth-century United States cannot be understood outside the North Atlantic economy of which it was a part....

Social politics is a case in point. Of studies of progressive and New Deal politics there is no end. On the roots of the impulse to limit the social costs of aggressive, market capitalism, some of the very best American history writing has found its focus. As befits a large-order event, large-scale explanations have been employed to understand it. Thus the rise of the interventionist state in America has been traced to the shock of particularly rapid industrialization, the thin and distended nature of the mid-nineteenth-century American state and society, the status anxieties of a declining middle class, the scientistic ambitions of a new elite of experts and professionals, the social maternalism of middle-class women, the demands from below of farmers and wage workers, and the demands of industrial capitalists at the top for a more rationalized social order than capitalist competition, by itself, could create. But an unspoken "geocentrism," as Baker styled it, frames them all.

Familiar as these explanations are, they leave unstated what every contemporary who followed these issues knew: that the reconstruction of American social politics was of a part with movements of politics and ideas throughout the North Atlantic world that trade and capitalism had tied together....

Every age, even the most calculating and material, needs a symbol, and Gustave Eiffel, who knew a promotional opportunity when it came his way, was eager to provide one. A "factory chimney," critics called his tower at its birth in 1889, "gigantic and hideous." An upended illustration of the principles of railroad bridge design, it defied the scale of the city below it. The tile roofs of old Paris's neighborhoods, the mansards and boulevards of the Second Empire, even the great towers of Notre Dame (as the sketches by Eiffel's engineers pointedly showed) all shrank to Lilliputian dimensions beside this display of engineering hubris. The Eiffel Tower was an advertisement for the tradition-shattering, revolutionary possibilities of industrial technology. Little wonder that Paris's artists immediately petitioned to have it torn down.

Eiffel's tower had a second purpose as well. Built for the Paris exposition of 1889, it was designed as a giant billboard for a great, temporary market of the wares of nineteenth-century industrial capitalism. The exposition's official purpose was to celebrate the centenary of the French Revolution and, in its reflected glory, the still fragile political fortunes of the Third Republic. In fact, trade—not politics—had dominated every world exposition since the iron and glass Crystal Palace Exposition in London in 1851, and the Paris exhibition was no exception....

[I]n 1900, the French convened a still larger fair on the same site, this time to inventory the century itself. The Eiffel Tower was repainted a bright yellow for the occasion, its gas jets replaced by hundreds of new electric lights to keep it abreast of the onward rush of technological progress. On the fairground itself, a still larger stock of goods—the largest to be displayed in this fashion anywhere until the world's fairs of the 1930s—was crammed still more tightly into still more numerous galleries. The 1889 exposition, despite its planners' intentions, had been largely a French affair. This time both Germany, ostracized in 1889, and the United States were represented in force, elbowing Britain for exhibition space and prestige in their race for industrial primacy....

For the 1900 exposition, the Musée Social's organizers determined to lay on a much more elaborate and centrally placed social economy display. In the meeting hall of the social economy pavilion they convened a summer of international conferences on phases of the *question sociale*. For the pavilion's display rooms, they solicited the best examples of practical social amelioration the nations of the Atlantic economy could muster. If there were in the industrialized countries social designs to compensate for the privations and pains of the market revolution, here one might hope to find their outlines.

At first glance, the sheer confusion of issues assembled under the social economy umbrella was all but overwhelming. The French tried to make order out of the whole by carving it into subsections: apprenticeship and the protection of child workers, wages and profit sharing, workers' and employers' associations, farm credit, regulation of the conditions of work, workers' housing, cooperative stores, institutions for the intellectual and moral development of workers, savings and insurance institutions, hygiene (by which they meant not only public sanitation but the public battle against intemperance, slums, and the moral contamination of poverty), poor relief, and a residual category for whatever public or private initiatives for the well-being of the citizens were left over....

To move through the social economy exhibit hall, however, was to discover how far from unified the social economy experts were on solutions. From nation to nation, the shifts in theme were abrupt and arresting. The Russians brought a temperance exhibit. The Italians displayed the work of cooperative savings banks. The Belgians emphasized low-cost workers' housing. Great Britain, its government distracted by the escalating military hostilities in South Africa, barely mustered an exhibit at all. On one wall of the British alcove hung a chart illustrating the growth of the consumers' cooperative movement. On the other hung one of the maps created for Charles Booth's monumental survey of poverty in London—the class relations of the city outlined, street by street, in bright washes of wealth and dark masses of poverty.

In retrospect, Booth's poverty maps seem the most prescient exhibit of the display. It was the German exhibit, however, that stayed longest in visitors' minds. Even non-Germans in Paris were compelled to admit that Germany was the fair's overall victor in the contest of prestige. Germany's national pavilion boasted the exhibition's tallest tower, next to Eiffel's. The most impressive industrial exhibit was the Germans'. In deference to French sensibilities, the Germans had left their huge Krupp cannons and overt military displays at home, but their imperial ambitions were everywhere on exhibit.

In the social economy building, the Germans ignored the complex French categories. In the middle of their alcove they mounted instead a large, gilded obelisk representing the benefits the imperial social insurance funds had distributed to German workers since their inauguration sixteen years earlier. Compulsory, state-administered insurance against the risks of industrial accidents, sickness, and old age was Germany's great social-political invention of the 1880s. The second prong of Bismarck's campaign to crush the German socialists, state social insurance was Bismarck's device to win over the loyalty of the urban German masses through the preemptive, top-down "socialism" of the state. In a symbolic display of imperial largesse and power, surrounded by photos of the hospitals and sanitariums its agencies administered for the welfare of German workers, the state commanded the German exhibit, without a hint of competition.

The Germans spoke on the subject of the state with peculiar authority and zeal in 1900. From the imperial art collection in the German national pavilion to the gilded obelisk in the social economy palace, the German exhibits radiated the message of government's fostering and protective hand—over culture, art, labor, and the ravages of economic misfortune. What better alternative was there to the insecurities and predations of the market but the massive, countervailing, paternal power of the state?...

A visitor to the social economy building... would not have had an easy time locating the American exhibit. Despite its economic muscle in 1990, the United States was in many ways the exposition's stepchild. It had wrangled space in the front row of national pavilions only through vigorous effort. There, wedged between competitors, the American commissioners built a plaster building made up of the usual Greco-Roman architectural borrowings. The interior, however, they fitted out with American newspapers, typewriters, stenographers for hire, a telegraph, a money exchange, and a ticker tape—everything an American businessman on vacation might need. The Americans were the nouveau riche in Paris in 1990, scrambling hard for status, more eager than any others for the shoptalk of commerce. The German pavilion radiated learning, art, and empire. The French dwelt on politics and solidarity. The American pavilion, behind its classical false front, was about business.

In the social economy building, the same national themes recurred. There, too, the Americans scrambled for place. Squeezed into a tiny, twenty-seven-foot-square alcove, they crammed into their exhibition space a larger stock

of material than in any display but France's itself. On hinged boards and inge-
nious folding cases, they hung out the nation's social wares. For the center of the
room, the New York Tenement House Committee contributed a model of one
of the city's most notorious slum blocks, together with a model of how much
more fiercely crowded that block might become if built up to the density that
the city's building code allowed. Nearby, as proof that a sense of the state was
not wholly missing, was a handsome collection of the bound reports of the state
and national bureaus of labor statistics. In one corner was tucked an exhibit on
American Negro life, including examples of handwork made at the Tuskegee
Institute and W. E. B. Du Bois's statistical display of African Americans' progress
in Georgia since slavery.

Arrangements for the largest body of material in the American exhibit, however, fell to a fledgling social betterment clearinghouse, the League for Social
Service. Organized two years earlier, it styled itself a general clearinghouse for
information concerning "everything that tends to the social betterment of
humanity." Its moving spirit, William Tolman, was in many ways typical of those
now forgotten figures who shaped the early years of American social politics. From
the position of general agent of the New York Association for Improving the
Condition of the Poor, Tolman had been drawn into the Reverend Charles
Parkhurst's antivice crusade in the 1890s, and from there into Mayor William
Strong's reform administration in New York City, where he had made his particular concern the provision of public baths à la Berlin and London—no slight
matter to a city population jammed together, more than two thousand persons
to a city block, without benefit of bathrooms....

For the social economy display, however, Tolman hung the walls with
photos of the work of self-enlightened capitalism. The endeavors of the nation's
model industrial employers were represented there: the Heinz company's spotless
factory workrooms, the Cleveland Hardware company's employee restaurant, the
employee housing constructed by the Westinghouse Airbrake firm, and the elaborate employee morale work of the National Cash Register Company in
Dayton, Ohio. In the realm of *prévoyance* the welfare capitalist theme continued;
the biggest, most eye-catching displays were those of the Prudential, Metropolitan,
and Equitable life insurance companies. The normally acute reporter *L'Exposition
de Paris* never saw past the life insurance company advertisements; Charles Gide
thought the American exhibit formless. But the message of the American display
was clearer than Gide sensed: the most promising counterforce to the injuries of
industrial capitalism was the enlightened conscience of capitalism itself....

The new Atlantic economy of the late nineteenth century was to encourage a new
Atlantic-wide politics. From its first stirrings in the 1890s, the new social politics
was to emerge as a powerful political force by the 1910s, with representatives
in every capital in the North Atlantic world. Even the Americans, so distant
from the chief centers of policy and intellectual innovation, were to be drawn in.

Those who forged the new social politics in the generation before the First
World War never shared a common name. Some of them never found a consistent referential language even for themselves. William Beveridge referred to

himself variously as a "Tory democrat," a "Labour imperialist," "very nearly" a socialist, and a Liberal. Frederic C. Howe, the American municipal reformer, called himself a single-taxer, a "liberal," a "reformer," and a "radical.."...

One comes close to a common denominator, however, with "progressive." As a political designation it was English before it was American, born in the heated municipal politics of 1890s London before crossing to the United States in the first decade of the new century....

By the first decade of the twentieth century there was no party system within the North Atlantic economy that had not been profoundly shaken by the new social politics. In Britain, the Liberal government of 1906–1914 embarked on a flurry of legislation that, a quarter century later, still stuck in Franklin Roosevelt's mind for its daring. For the aged poor, it inaugurated an old-age pension system borrowed from New Zealand; for the crippling economic effects of sickness, a program of compulsory wage-earners' health insurance borrowed from Germany; for the most exploited of workers, a set of Australian-style wage boards empowered to establish legal minimum wages; for the sake of fiscal justice, progressive land and income taxes; for the unemployed, a German-style network of state-run employment offices; and, for workers in trades of particularly uneven labor demand, an untried experiment in pooling the risks of unemployment through state-administered insurance....

On both sides of the Atlantic, politicians rode the new issues to power and popularity: David Lloyd George and the young Winston Churchill in Britain, Georges Clemenceau in France, Theodore Roosevelt and Woodrow Wilson in the United States. Parties and pressure groups drew up sweeping social programs. For the rest of the twentieth century, although parties split and polarized over the new issues, no politics could be divorced from social politics....

Within Europe itself, one of the most striking signs of the new transnational social politics was the phenomenon of legislation passed from one nation to another, sometimes despite acute distrust and rivalry. An early example was British-modeled factory legislation, which began to turn up in France, Germany, and elsewhere in the 1870s. A generation later, borrowings of this sort formed a crazy quilt of transnational influences and appropriations. Danish old-age pensions were imported (via New Zealand) to Britain, British industrial liability codes to France, and French subsidarism to Denmark, Holland, and Scandinavia, even as more radical French progressives turned to German-style compulsory state insurance....

The settlement house movement was one of transatlantic social Protestantism's most striking productions. Here the innovators were English. From the opening of Toynbee Hall in Whitechapel at the edge of London's East End in 1884, Samuel Barnett's institution was a magnet for American visitors. Jane Addams made visits in 1887, 1888, and 1889....

Inevitably, American and English settlement house developments diverged. Rooted in a women's college network unknown in England, the American movement was much more quickly and deeply feminized than its English model. Sharing neither the Oxford cultural pretensions of Toynbee Hall (with its fine arts exhibits and reading rooms wreathed in pipe smoke) nor its residents' easy,

Oxbridge–greased access to government policy making, the American settlement houses were more alert to issues of family, immigrants, and neighborhoods. But the social investigations that from the outset kept the American settlements from becoming mere charity outposts were a direct offshoot of the London original. And the American settlement house residents worked extremely hard to sustain the English connection....

Weave as it did the interests and experiences of American and European progressives together, bind them as it did in a common understanding of the forces at work on both sides of the Atlantic, this evolving web of connections could not erase two enduring peculiarities of the transatlantic progressive relationship. The first was the asymmetry of the exchange. The second was the mediating effects of travel.

That American progressives should have found themselves drawing so much more heavily on the experience and ideas of their European counterparts than Europeans did on theirs was no historical given. In the transatlantic radical world of the 1880s, the biggest splash of all had been made by the American radical economist Henry George....

One of the painful signs of this imbalance was a marked contraction of European progressive interest in American politics. Where American attention to British progressive politics was "coherent and continuous," Kenneth Morgan writes of this period, the influences in the other direction were "intermittent and partial at best."...

Alfred Zimmern's seven-month pilgrimage in search of progressive America in 1911 and 1912 was more telling and more poignant. Fresh from studying civic republicanism in ancient Athens, Zimmern arrived in the United States fired with ideals of civic political culture, both ancient and modern. He worked hard to locate the centers of political vitality in the New World. In New York he looked in at the United Charities Building, hunted up the city's leading socialists, lunched with Theodore Roosevelt, and attended a mass meeting of protest and remembrance for the 146 garment workers who, locked in the Triangle Shirt–waist Company's loft, had been killed in a factory fire....

"Lots of new ideas," Zimmern wrote his sister, "which may be applied at home." But from there on, progressive America unraveled for him. The more he talked with Americans, the thinner his confidence wore. The raw, unmitigated capitalism of Chicago unnerved him. The U.S. Steel Corporation's model city, Gary, Indiana, seemed to him a monstrous "fortress." Six months after he began, he wrote home: "I have long ago given up looking at America as the land of progress. The only question left in my mind is how many years it's behind England. I think it's somewhere in the eighties and not going our pace at that."

By the time Zimmern picked it up, the metaphor of American behind-handedness was already a hardened trope among European progressives. Sometimes it was used as a general rhetoric of dismissal, as when E. R. Pease of the Fabian Society concluded, on reading John Graham Brook's latest account of labor relations in the United States, that "in the things that pertain to man as a social and intellectual being, America is decades, if not centuries, behind us."

Sometimes it was employed more precisely. Thus in labor legislation the British Labourite J. R. Clynes put the United States twenty years behind Britain in 1909; in trade union development, fifteen years....

The metaphor of laggards and leaders also helped to shield American progressives from the charges of political utopianism their antagonists were poised to hurl at them. It made their idealism hard-headed and practical. "Many persons think that the progressive movement proposes to usher in the millennium by legislation," Benjamin De Witt wrote in 1915. "Nothing could be farther from the minds of the men and women who call themselves progressive. What they propose to do is to bring the United States abreast of Germany and other European countries in the matter of remedial legislation." To catch up to the "civilized" nations of the world was a running progressive theme. Seconding Theodore Roosevelt's nomination at the Progressive Party convention of 1912, Jane Addams made the point official: "The new party has become the American exponent of a world-wide movement toward juster social conditions, a movement which the United States, lagging behind other great nations, has been unaccountably slow to embody in political action."...

What riveted the attention of most American admirers of European city life, however, were the absences: "No offensive bill boards; no heaps of offal and rubbish, no long stretches of untidy vacancy held for speculation in the midst of the city; no tumble-down tenements; no ragged, inebriate pedestrians," the National Municipal League's president William D. Foulke wrote of Frankfurt in 1911. No wretchedly paved streets and packed streetcars, no corrupt city bosses, no waste, no lawlessness, no anarchy. The "not"'s multiplied as the European cities took shape in reverse of the American cities to which the reformers could not avoid contrasting them. Everything played into these judgments, from the width and paving of the streets and the comparative hideousness of the advertisements to the political convictions of the observers. The reflections and mirrors, the inner eye always focused on America while the outer eye saw Europe: all of this affected judgments.

But admirers of European civic life like Howe were not politically naive. Howe knew the difference between the Junkers and the forces expanding, as he put it, like molten lava below the crust—even if, for his purposes, he chose to elide party divisions as unimportant. He was under no illusion that the European cities moving rapidly into new realms of provision and collective enterprise were democratic in the American understanding of the term. The word portraits of handsome city baths and well-run municipal streetcars in which writers like Howe invested so much were more than travelogue prose. They were part of a struggle to socialize the language of democracy—to balance its rhetoric of rights and privileges with a new rhetoric of services, outcomes, and results. In their stress on cities that *did* things, they tried to forge a language of democratic, civil action rather than mere democratic forms. The German city, Howe admitted, in almost the same words Boston's Josiah Quincy had used sixteen years earlier, was not democratic in its administrative structure; but it was "democratic, even socialistic, in its services."...

Among advanced urban progressives in the early-twentieth-century United States, it is hard to exaggerate the ambitions bound up in these half-imported visions of cities free of their swarms of contractors, grafters, entrepreneurs, and franchisers, of cities conscious of their own administration and directing their own fate. Or to exaggerate their sense of affinity with events across the Atlantic. That the American issue might be thought to turn, even for a moment, on the experience of Glasgow streetcars—this was the primary event. "You know that one of the best governed cities in the world is the great Scotch city of Glasgow," Woodrow Wilson casually told a crowd in Fall River, Massachusetts, in the campaign of 1912. "They are 'way ahead of us," Lincoln Steffens wrote of the European municipalizers. "Liberals and radicals all of them, they are in harness and down to the details."

FURTHER READING

John Milton Cooper, *Woodrow Wilson: A Biography* (2009).

Kathleen Dalton, *Theodore Roosevelt: A Strenuous Life* (2004).

Alan Dawley, *Struggles for Justice: Social Responsibility and the Liberal State* (1991).

Leon Fink, *Progressive Intellectuals and the Dilemmas of Democratic Government* (1997).

Maureen Flanagan, *America Reformed: Progressives and Progressivisms, 1890s–1920s* (2006).

Gayle Gullett, *Becoming Citizens: The Emergence and Development of the California Women's Movement, 1880–1911* (2000).

Alan Kraut, *Silent Travelers: Germs, Genes, and the "Immigrant Menace"* (1995).

Christopher Lasch, *The True and Only Heaven: Progress and its Critics* (1991).

William Link, *The Paradox of Southern Progressivism, 1880–1930* (1992).

Leon Litwack, *Trouble in Mind: Black Southerners in the Age of Jim Crow* (1998).

Peter McCaffery, *When Bosses Ruled Philadelphia: The Emergence of the Republican Machine* (1993).

Eric Rauchway, *Murdering McKinley: The Making of Theodore Roosevelt's America* (2003).

Kathryn Kish Sklar, *Florence Kelley and the Nation's Work* (1995).

Peter Stearns, *Schools and Students in Industrial Society: Japan and the West, 1870–1940* (1998).

Michael Willrich, *City of Courts: Socializing Justice in Progressive Era Chicago* (2003).

CHAPTER 6

America in World War I

In 1918, President Woodrow Wilson broke the precedent of more than one hundred years and sent American soldiers "over there," across the Atlantic. George Washington had declared the "Great Rule" of staying out of Europe's troubles in 1796, and James Monroe had underscored the principle in his famous Monroe Doctrine of 1823. Essentially, the Monroe Doctrine asserted that Europeans should stay out of political affairs in the Americas, and that Americans should stay out of political affairs in Europe. Following this venerable commitment, Wilson declared neutrality when the war first broke out on July 28, 1914. But the opportunity to sell food, arms, and other goods to the belligerents gradually led the United States deeper and deeper into the conflict. Britain declared a blockade of all German-occupied territory to prevent food and supplies from getting through to enemy soldiers and civilians on the continent. To enforce this blockade, Britain declared a war zone off the coast of Northern Europe and laced it with mines. Underwater bombs sent six U.S. merchant ships to the bottom along with their cargo and men. The British took no responsibility for these losses, claiming that all casualties resulted from mines that the Germans had sowed amongst theirs.

Germany retaliated against the blockade by declaring a war zone around the British Isles, enforced largely by the newly developed U-boats ("undersea boats"), which went after American ships heading for England, Ireland, and France. To Wilson, submarine warfare seemed particularly unfair and inhumane. When Kaiser Wilhelm of Germany resumed unrestricted submarine warfare in February 1917 in order to break Britain's starvation blockade, U-boats immediately sank two American merchant ships. By April 1, German submarines had sunk a total of ten American ships.

The difference in the number of ships sunk by anonymous mines (probably British) and by identifiably German U-boats is far too slight to explain why Wilson entered the so-named "Great War" on the side of the Allies, or even why he took the nation into a European conflict at all. Historians answer these questions in different ways. Some point to the German U-boat, which Wilson considered an especially heinous form of warfare, especially after one sunk the British passenger liner Lusitania in 1915—only three years after the disastrous, morbidly publicized but accidental sinking of the sister ship Titanic. Other historians point to Wilson's personality: his religious faith and predilection for moralizing, or his Progressive commitment to political reform and his messianic desire to "make the world safe for democracy." Scholars (and some Americans at the time) have also expressed the suspicion that the United States simply followed its economic interests in allying with the British and French. Although they disagree on why the U.S. went to war, historians concur that this decision set the nation on a course of continuing intervention in world affairs. During the war Wilson called for a "peace without victory" and a League of Nations to guarantee the right of all peoples to self-determination. After the war, the U.S. Senate refused to ratify the President's peace treaty. Ever since, historians and politicians have called the notion of an American democratic mission abroad by the name "Wilsonianism."

The consequences of America's new course were profound, both abroad and at home. The Wilson administration fostered hyper-patriotism through a Committee on Public Information, and repressed free speech through Espionage and Sedition Acts aimed at anyone who opposed the war. Americans rallied around the flag, and over 100,000 soldiers died under its colors. But afterward, disillusionment set in quickly: disillusionment with profiteers who had helped drag the United States into the conflict, with idealists who had sought to remake the Old World, and with war itself as a patriotic undertaking. World War I ultimately provided few lessons about when or how the United States should intervene in conflicts beyond its borders. George Washington's Great Rule against foreign entanglements had been broken, but the Senate's vote against the League of Nations showed that it could be restored.

QUESTIONS TO THINK ABOUT

Progressives such as Presidents Woodrow Wilson and Theodore Roosevelt supported American entry into the war. But other Progressives, such as Senator Robert La Follette and Secretary of State William Jennings Bryan, bitterly opposed it. How did the war further the Progressive agenda, and how did the war undermine it? And, what do you think of Woodrow Wilson's leadership? Was he a hopeless dreamer who bungled the attempt to restore peace, or was he the prescient architect of a new (and necessary) world order?

DOCUMENTS

The documents in this chapter illustrate a variety of attitudes about the decision to go to war and toward the war itself. In document 1, President Wilson asks Congress to declare war and pledge "our lives and our fortunes" to make the world free. Progressive Senator Robert La Follette of Wisconsin strenuously objected. In a speech to the U.S. Senate (document 2), he argues that America stands to lose its own freedom through conscription and other measures that take away free speech and free choice. Document 3 is a sworn statement by union organizers who were whipped, tarred, and feathered for not buying Liberty Bonds. This selection testifies to the domestic intolerance that grew out of the war, fulfilling La Follette's prophecy. Document 4 is the Espionage Act of 1918, designed to punish pacifists and quell dissent. In a speech on January 8, 1918, Wilson outlined the war aims of the United States, which included self-determination for all peoples. His so-called "Fourteen Points" (document 5) spoke to the historic ideals of the United States—ideals that would bedevil the nation's foreign policy for the ensuing century. Document 6 is an excerpt from the memoir of Harry Smith, an ambulance company surgeon on the front in France. The events he describes helped fuel a genre of memoirs and novels after the war (including the works of former ambulance driver Ernest Hemingway) that deplored the slaughter. In document 7, Emmett Scott, an attorney and former aid to Booker T. Washington, explains why African Americans considered the war their fight, too. In document 8, newspaperman George Creel recounts how the U.S. government used the newest propaganda techniques to "sell" the war and the international crusade for democracy. Document 9 shows cartoons that grappled with the essential choice faced by the United States once the guns went silent: to embrace "foreign entanglements" or turn its back on the problems confronting humanity.

1. President Woodrow Wilson Asks Congress to Declare War, 1917

On the third of February last I officially laid before you the extraordinary announcement of the Imperial German Government that on and after the first day of February it was its purpose to put aside all restraints of law of humanity and use its submarines to sink every vessel that sought to approach either the ports of Great Britain and Ireland or the western coasts of Europe or any of the ports controlled by the enemies of Germany within the Mediterranean. That had seemed to be the object of the German submarine warfare earlier in the war, but since April of last year the Imperial Government had somewhat restrained the commanders of its undersea craft in conformity with its promise then given to us that passenger boats should not be sunk and that due warning would be given to all other vessels which its submarines might seek to destroy, when no resistance was offered or escape attempted, and care taken that their crews were given at least a fair chance to save their lives in their open boats. The precautions taken were meagre and haphazard enough, as was proved in distressing instance after instance in the progress of the cruel and unmanly business, but a certain degree of restraint was observed. The new policy has swept every restriction aside. Vessels of every kind, whatever their flag, their character, their cargo, their destination, their errand, have been ruthlessly sent to the bottom without warning and without thought of help or mercy for those on board, the vessels of friendly neutrals along with those of belligerents. Even hospital ships and ships carrying relief to the sorely bereaved and stricken people of Belgium, though the latter were provided with safe conduct through the proscribed areas by the German Government itself and were distinguished by unmistakable marks of identity, have been sunk with the same reckless lack of compassion or of principle.

I was for a little while unable to believe that such things would in fact be done by any government that had hitherto subscribed to the humane practices of civilized nations. International law had its origin in the attempt to set up some law which would be respected and observed upon the seas, where no nation had

Congressional Record, LV (April 2, 1917), Part I, 102–104.

right of dominion where lay the free highways of the world. By painful stage after stage has that law been built up, with meagre enough results, indeed, after all was accomplished that could be accomplished, but always with a clear view, at least of what the heart and conscience of mankind demanded. This minimum of right the German Government has swept aside under the plea of retaliation and necessity and because it had no weapons which it could use at sea except these which it is impossible to employ as it is employing them without throwing to the winds all scruples of humanity or of respect for the understandings that were supposed to underlie the intercourse of the world. I am not now thinking of the loss of property involved, immense and serious as that is, but only of the wanton and wholesale destruction of the lives of noncombatants, men, women, and children, engaged in pursuits which have always, even in the darkest periods of modern history, been deemed innocent and legitimate. Property can be paid for; the lives of peaceful and innocent people cannot be. The present German submarine warfare against commerce is a warfare against mankind.

It is a war against all nations. American ships have been sunk, American lives taken, in ways which it has stirred us very deeply to learn of, but the ships and people of other neutral and friendly nations have been sunk and overwhelmed in the waters in the same way. There has been no discrimination. The challenge is to all mankind. Each nation must decide for itself how it will meet it. The choice we make for ourselves must be made with a moderation of counsel and a temperateness of judgment befitting our character and our motives as a nation. We must put excited feeling away. Our motive will not be revenge or the victorious assertion of the physical might of the nation, but only the vindication of right, of human right, of which we are only a single champion....

It is a distressing and oppressive duty, Gentlemen of the Congress, which I have performed in thus addressing you. There are, it may be, many months of fiery trial and sacrifice ahead of us. It is a fearful thing to lead this great peaceful people into war, into the most terrible and disastrous of all wars, civilization itself seeming to be in the balance. But the right is more precious than peace, and we shall fight for the things which we have always carried nearest our hearts—for democracy, for the right of those who submit to authority to have a voice in their own governments, for the rights and liberties of small nations, for a universal dominion of right by such a concert of free peoples as shall bring peace and safety to all nations and make the world itself at last free....

2. Senator Robert M. La Follette Passionately Dissents, 1917

The poor, sir, who are the ones called upon to rot in the trenches, have no organized power, have no press to voice their will upon this question of peace or war; but, oh, Mr. President, at some time they will be heard. I hope and I believe they will be heard in an orderly and a peaceful way. I think they may be heard from before long. I think, sir, if we take this step, when the people to-day who are staggering under the burden of supporting families at the present prices of the

Congressional Record, LV (April 4, 1917), Part I, 226, 228.

necessaries of the life find those prices multiplied, when they are raised a hundred percent, or 200 percent, as they will be quickly, aye, sir, when beyond that those who pay taxes come to have their taxes doubled and again doubled to pay the interest on the nontaxable bonds held by Morgan and his combinations, which have been issued to meet this war, there will come an awakening; they will have their day and they will be heard. It will be as certain and as inevitable as the return of the tides, and as resistless, too....

Just a word of comment more upon one of the points in the President's address. He says that this is a war "for the things which we have always carried nearest to our hearts—for democracy, for the right of those who submit to authority to have a voice in their own government." In many places throughout the address is this exalted sentiment given expression....

But the President proposes alliance with Great Britain, which, however liberty-loving its people, is a hereditary monarchy, with a hereditary ruler, with a hereditary House of Lords, with a hereditary landed system, with a limited and restricted suffrage for one class and a multiplied suffrage power for another, and with grinding industrial conditions for all the wageworkers. The President has not suggested that we make our support of Great Britain conditional to her granting home rule to Ireland, or Egypt, or India. We rejoice in the establishment of a democracy in Russia, but it will hardly be contended that if Russia was still an autocratic Government, we would not be asked to enter this alliance with her just the same. Italy and the lesser powers of Europe, Japan in the Orient; in fact all of the countries with whom we are to enter into alliance, except France and newly revolutionized Russia, are still of the old order—and it will be generally conceded that no one of them has done as much for its people in the solution of municipal problems and in securing social and industrial reforms as Germany....

Who has registered the knowledge or approval of the American people of the course this Congress is called upon in declaring war upon Germany? Submit the question to the people, you who support it. You who support it dare not do it, for you know that by a vote of more than ten to one the American people as a body would register their declaration against it....

The espionage bills, the conscription bills, and other forcible military measures which we understand are being ground out of the war machine in this country is the complete proof that those responsible for this war fear that it has no popular support and that armies sufficient to satisfy the demand of the entente allies can not be recruited by voluntary enlistments.

3. A Union Organizer Testifies to Vigilante Attack, 1917

"On the night of November 5, 1917, while sitting in the hall at No. 6 W. Brady Street, Tulsa, Okla. (the room leased and occupied by the Industrial Workers of the World, and used as a union meeting room), at about 8:45 P.M., five men entered the hall, to whom I at first paid no attention, as I was busy putting a monthly stamp in a member's union card book. After I had finished with the

Sworn testimony of the secretary of the Industrial Workers of the World local, Tulsa, Oklahoma, November 1917, from *Liberator*, April 1918.

member, I walked back to where these five men had congregated at the baggage-room at the back of the hall, and spoke to them, asking if there was anything I could do for them.

"One who appeared to be the leader, answered 'No, we're just looking the place over.' Two of them went into the baggage-room flashing an electric flash-light around the room. The other three walked toward the front end of the hall. I stayed at the baggage-room door, and one of the men came out and followed the other three up to the front end of the hall. The one who stayed in the baggage-room asked me if I was 'afraid he would steal something.' I told him we were paying rent for the hall, and I did not think anyone had a right to search this place without a warrant. He replied that he did not give a damn if we were paying rent for four places, they would search them whenever they felt like it. Presently he came out and walked toward the front end of the hall, and I followed a few steps behind him.

"In the meantime the other men, who proved to be police officers, appeared to be asking some of our members questions. Shortly after, the patrol–wagon came and all the members in the hall—10 men were ordered into the wagon. I turned out the light in the back end of the hall, closed the desk, put the key in the door and told the 'officer' to turn out the one light. We stepped out, and I locked the door, and at the request of the 'leader of the officers,' handed him the keys. He told me to get in the wagon, I being the 11th man taken from the hall, and we were taken to the police station….

"In about forty minutes, as near as we could judge about 11 P.M., the turn–key came and called 'Get ready to go out, you I.W.W. men.' We dressed as rapidly as possible, were taken out of the cells, and the officer gave us back our possessions, Ingersoll watches, pocketknives and money, with the exception of $3 in silver of mine which they kept, giving me back $27.87. I handed the re-ceipt for the $100 bond I had put up to the desk sergeant and he told me he did not know anything about it, and handed the receipt back to me, which I put in my trousers' pocket with the 87 cents. Twenty-seven dollars in bills was in my coat pocket. We were immediately ordered into automobiles waiting in the alley. Then we proceeded one block north to 1st Street, west one-half block to Boulder Street, north across the Frisco tracks and stopped.

"Then the masked mob came up and ordered everybody to throw up their hands. Just here I wish to state I never thought any man could reach so high as those policemen did. We were then bound, some with hands in front, some with hands behind, and others bound with arms hanging down their sides, the rope being wrapped around the body. Then the police were ordered to 'beat it,' which they did, running, and we started for the place of execution.

"When we arrived there, a company of gowned and masked gunmen were there to meet us standing at 'present arms.' We were ordered out of the autos, told to get in line in front of these gunmen and another bunch of men with automatics and pistols, lined up between us. Our hands were still held up, and those who were bound, in front. Then a masked man walked down the line and slashed the ropes that bound us, and we were ordered to strip to the waist, which we did, threw our clothes in front of us, in individual piles—coats, vests, hats, shirts, and undershirts. The boys not having had time to distribute their possessions that were given back to them at the police stations, everything was in the coats, everything we owned in the world.

"Then the whipping began, a double piece of new rope, ⅝ or ¾ hemp, being used. A man, 'the chief' of detectives, stopped the whipping of each man when he thought the victim had had enough. After each one was whipped another man applied the tar with a large brush, from the head to the seat. Then a brute smeared feathers over and rubbed them in.

"After they had satisfied themselves that our bodies were well abused, our clothing was thrown into a pile, gasoline poured on it and a match applied. By the light of our earthly possessions, we were ordered to leave Tulsa, and leave running and never come back."

4. The U.S. Government Punishes War Protesters: The Espionage Act, 1918

Be it enacted by the Senate and House of Representatives of the United States of America in Congress assembled, That section three of title one of the Act entitled, "An Act to punish acts of interference with the foreign relations, the neutrality, and the foreign commerce of the United States, to punish espionage, and better to enforce the criminal laws of the United States, and for other purposes," approved June fifteenth, nineteen hundred and seventeen, be, and the same is hereby, amended so as to read as follows:

"SEC. 3. Whoever, when the United States is at war, shall willfully make or convey false reports or false statements with intent to interfere with the operation or success of the military or naval forces of the United States, or to promote the success of its enemies, or shall willfully make or convey false reports or false statements, or say or do anything except by way of bona fide and not disloyal advice to an investor or investors, with intent to obstruct the sale by the United States of bonds or other securities of the United States or the making of loans by or to the United States, and whoever, when the United States is at war, shall willfully cause or attempt to cause, or incite or attempt to incite, insubordination, disloyalty, mutiny, or refusal of duty, in the military or naval forces of the United States, or shall willfully obstruct or attempt to obstruct the recruiting or enlistment service of the United States, and whoever, when the United States is at war, shall willfully utter, print, write, or publish any disloyal, profane, scurrilous, or abusive language about the form of government of the United States, or the Constitution of the United States, or the military or naval forces of the United States, or the flag of the United States, or the uniform of the Army or Navy of the United States, or any language intended to bring the form of government of the United States, or the Constitution of the United States, or the military or naval forces of the United States, or the flag of the United States, or the uniform of the Army or Navy of the United States into contempt, scorn, contumely, or disrepute, or shall willfully utter, print, write, or publish any language intended to incite, provoke, or

Espionage Act, U.S. Statutes at Large 40(1918), 553ff.

encourage resistance to the United States, or to promote the cause of its enemies, or shall willfully display the flag of any foreign enemy, or shall willfully by utterance, writing, printing, publication, or language spoken, urge, incite, or advocate any curtailment of production in this country of any thing or things, product or products, necessary or essential to the prosecution of the war in which the United States may be engaged, with intent by such curtailment to cripple or hinder the United States in the prosecution of the war, and whoever shall willfully advocate, teach, defend, or suggest the doing of any of the acts or things in this section enumerated, and whoever shall by word or act support or favor the cause of any country with which the United States is at war or by word or act oppose the cause of the United States therein, shall be punished by a fine of not more than $10,000 or imprisonment for not more than twenty years, or both...."

5. Wilson Proposes a New World Order in the "Fourteen Points," 1918

I. Open covenants of peace, openly arrived at, after which there shall be no private international understandings of any kind but diplomacy shall proceed always frankly and in the public view.

II. Absolute freedom of navigation upon the seas, outside territorial waters, alike in peace and in war, except as the seas may be closed in whole or in part by international action for the enforcement of international covenants.

III. The removal, so far as possible, of all economic barriers and the establishment of an equality of trade conditions among all the nations consenting to the peace and associating themselves for its maintenance.

IV. Adequate guarantees given and taken that national armaments will be reduced to the lowest point consistent with domestic safety.

V. A free, open-minded, and absolutely impartial adjustment of all colonial claims, based upon a strict observance of the principle that in determining all such questions of sovereignty the interests of the populations concerned must have equal weight with the equitable claims of the government whose title is to be determined.

VI. The evacuation of all Russian territory and such a settlement of all questions affecting Russia as will secure the best and freest cooperation of the other nations of the world in obtaining for her an unhampered and unembarrassed opportunity for the independent determination of her own political development and national policy and assure her of a sincere welcome into the society of free nations under institutions of her own choosing; and, more than a welcome, assistance also of every kind that she may need and may herself desire. The treatment accorded Russia by her sister nations in the months to come will be the acid test of their good will, of their comprehension of her needs as distinguished from their own interests, and of their intelligent and unselfish sympathy.

VII. Belgium, the whole world will agree, must be evacuated and restored, without any attempt to limit the sovereignty which she enjoys in common with

---

Congressional Record, LVI (January 8, 1918), Part I, 680–682.

all other free nations. No other single act will serve as this will serve to restore confidence among the nations in the laws which they have themselves set and determined for the government of their relations with one another. Without this healing act the whole structure and validity of international law is forever impaired.

VIII. All French territory should be freed and the invaded portions restored, and the wrong done to France by Prussia in 1871 in the matter of Alsace-Lorraine, which has unsettled the peace of the world for nearly fifty years, should be righted, in order that peace may once more be made secure in the interest of all.

IX. A readjustment of the frontiers of Italy should be effected along clearly recognizable lines of nationality.

X. The peoples of Austria–Hungary, whose place among the nations we wish to see safeguarded and assured, should be accorded the freest opportunity of autonomous development.

XI. Rumania, Serbia, and Montenegro should be evacuated; occupied territories restored; Serbia accorded free and secure access to the sea; and the relations of the several Balkan states to one another determined by friendly consul along historically established line of allegiance and nationality; and international guarantees of the political and economic independence and territorial integrity of the several Balkan states should be entered into.

XII. The Turkish portions of the present Ottoman Empire should be assured a secure sovereignty, but the other nationalities which are now under Turkish rule should be assured an undoubted security of life and an absolutely unmolested opportunity of autonomous development, and the Dardanelles should be permanently opened as a free passage to the ships and commerce of all nations under international guarantees.

XIII. An independent Polish state should be erected which should include the territories inhabited by indisputably Polish populations, which should be assured a free and secure access to the sea, and whose political and economic independence and territorial integrity should be guaranteed by international covenant.

XIV. A general association of nations must be formed under specific covenants for the purpose of affording mutual guarantees of political independence and territorial integrity to great and small states alike.

6. An Ambulance Surgeon Describes What It Was Like "Over There," 1918

We were in full view of the enemy and within easy reach of the shells the German gunners were sending toward the town with exceptional ferocity. Nothing happened to us on the first trip. On the second trip, however, as we approached the town at about dawn, we saw a strange sight in the valley below. A greenish-yellow cloud hovered thickly over the region in a dense, motionless pall. It was mustard gas, a violent irritant which would blister the skin at contact

---

Harry L. Smith, M.D., *Memories of an Ambulance Company Officer* (Rochester, Minn: Doomsday Press, 1940). Obtained from www.lib.byu.edu/~rdh/wwi/memoir/Ambco/officer3.html.

if the concentration were sufficient. Toward the end of the war this type of gas was used extensively in shells, being released when the projectiles exploded. Ville-Savoye had been bombarded mercilessly all the preceding night and the gas we saw had accumulated during the darkness.

Dressing stations had been set up in two very deep stone cellars in Ville-Savoye. A man probably was as safe there as he would have been anywhere else in the village. The walls were thick, and the ceiling, which was formed by what was left of the first floor of the old building, was supported by great timbers that no doubt had been hewn by hand and fitted with infinite care, after the manner of most building in rural France. The doors of the two cellars had been hung with Army blankets drenched with water to keep out poison gas. I lived through what must have been one of the most deathly barrages of the war. The Germans sent tons of steel and iron crashing into the town for hours on end, and detonations were so monstrous that the earth and walls about us shuddered and trembled, even though we were far below the surface of the ground. Our ears rang with the mighty tumult, and the very air in the damp cellar vibrated until it was painful. At times we could not hear the spoken voice, so we sat with our backs to the wall, wondering speechless on the floor when the infernal din would cease, or whether we would live to know quiet when it returned again.

7. A Negro Leader Explains Why Colored Men Fought for America, 1919

When the United States declared war against Germany and the Teutonic allies, there were internal conditions existing in America that were by no means ideal so far as the Negro was concerned, nor were they altogether conducive to *loyalty* and a healthy *morale* among this particular group of American citizens. Beset by a vicious and persistent propaganda on the one side, and by continued instances of lynching and mob violence of which he was the chief victim on the other, the Negro in America faced a real crisis at the beginning of the war. Temptation after temptation was presented to him to render lukewarm and half-hearted support to the Government in the prosecution of the war, without making himself criminally liable, but Negro leaders in all parts of the country recognized at once that the national crisis demanded, and the plain duty and best interests of the Negro racial group required that, without bargaining, there must be a pledge on the part of the Negro of his undiluted and unfaltering loyalty.

History records no parallel where, under similar conditions, any racial group has been more loyal to the Government.... A black skin during the war was a badge of patriotism.

The Negro was not unmindful of certain wrongs, injustices, and discriminations which were heaped upon his race in many sections of the country, but in the face of it all he remained adamant against all attempts to lower his morale, and realized that his first duty was *loyalty* to his country. America is indeed the

---

Emmett J. Scott, *Scott's Official History of the American Negro in the World War, 1919*, pp. 411–414. Obtained from Library of Congress, American Memory, African American Odyssey (on-line).

Negro's country, for he has been here three hundred years, which is about two hundred years longer than many of the white racial groups; he realized that ... the plain course before him was to perform all of the duties of citizenship and at the same time continue to press his demands for all of the rights and privileges which the Constitution has vouchsafed to him. He realized that he would not be in a position to demand his rights unless he fully performed his duties as an American citizen, and in thus lending his loyal allegiance he exemplified his belief in the doctrine expounded by Colonel Theodore Roosevelt to the effect that "rights and privileges" are contingent upon the faithful discharge of the "duties and responsibilities" of citizenship in any country....

The valiant, varied, and effective services rendered by four hundred thousand Negro soldiers who were called to the colors, both in camps and cantonments at home as well as upon the battlefields of Europe, canceled every possible doubt and furnished proof positive of the Negro's unfaltering loyalty....

[German] Propagandists emphasized racial discriminations of one kind or another and unfortunately were able to refer to the facts that the black American, supposedly a citizen, was in many states denied the ballot; that he was "Jim Crowed" on many of the railroads and public carriers, although charged first-class fare for transportation; that he was denied admission to most public places of amusement, hotels and the like. Using such arguments as a basis, the question was raised as to why the Negro was willing to jeopardize his life, his liberty, and his pursuit of happiness in coming to the rescue of America in her extremity and thus helping to defeat Germany—a country where, it was said, such racial discriminations did not exist.

None of these questions, however, disturbed the thoughtful leaders of the Negro people. They knew the designing motive back of such propaganda. They recognized, without question, that the moment the American Negro failed to perform all of the duties of citizenship, he immediately abdicated the right of claiming the full privileges of citizenship. The Negro leaders knew that the central thought in the German mind and the traditional policy of the Central Powers was *"might,"* and that *"compelling force"* was intended to be used, as a part of a world-wide conquest, to reduce to German domination the weaker and other peace-loving peoples of the earth. They remembered something of the history of Germany's African colonies....

8. Publicist George Creel Recalls Selling the War, 1920

Back of the firing-line, back of armies and navies, back of the great supply-depots, another struggle waged with the same intensity and with almost equal significance attaching to its victories and defeats. It was the fight for the *minds* of men, for the "conquest of their convictions," and the battle-line ran through every home in every country....

We strove for the maintenance of our own morale and the Allied morale by every process of stimulation; every possible expedient was employed to break through

George Creel, *How We Advertised America* (New York: Harper and Brothers, 1920), 3–8.

the barrage of lies that kept the people of the Central Powers in darkness and delusion; we sought the friendship and support of the neutral nations by continuous presentation of facts. We did not call it propaganda, for that word, in German hands, had come to be associated with deceit and corruption. Our effort was educational and informative throughout, for we had such confidence in our case as to feel that no other argument was needed than the simple, straightforward presentation of facts.

There was no part of the great war machinery that we did not touch, no medium of appeal that we did not employ. The printed word, the spoken word, the motion picture, the telegraph, the cable, the wireless, the poster, the sign-board—all these were used in our campaign to make our own people and all other peoples understand the causes that compelled America to take arms. All that was fine and ardent in the civilian population came at our call until more than one hundred and fifty thousand men and women were devoting highly specialized abilities to the work of the Committee, as faithful and devoted in their service as though they wore the khaki.

While America's summons was answered without question by the citizenship as a whole, it is to be remembered that during the three and a half years of our neutrality the land had been torn by a thousand divisive prejudices, stunned by the voices of anger and confusion, and muddled by the pull and haul of opposed interests. These were conditions that could not be permitted to endure. What we had to have was no mere surface unity, but a passionate belief in the justice of America's cause that should weld the people of the United States into one white-hot mass instinct with fraternity, devotion, courage, and deathless determination. The *war-will*, the will-to-win, of a democracy depends upon the degree to which each one of all the people of that democracy can concentrate and consecrate body and soul and spirit in the supreme effort of service and sacrifice. What had to be driven home was that all business was the nation's business, and every task a common task for a single purpose....

A speaking division toured great groups like the Blue Devils, Pershing's Veterans, and the Belgians, arranged mass-meetings in the communities, conducted forty-five war conferences from coast to coast, coordinated the entire speaking activities of the nation, assured consideration to the crossroads hamlet as well as to the city.

The Four Minute Men, an organization that will live in history by reason of its originality and effectiveness, commanded the volunteer services of 75,000 speakers, operating in 5,200 communities, and making a total of 755,190 speeches, every one having the carry of shrapnel.

With the aid of a volunteer staff of several hundred translators, the Committee kept in direct touch with the foreign-language press, supplying selected articles designed to combat ignorance and disaffection. It organized and directed twenty-three societies and leagues designed to appeal to certain classes and particular foreign-language groups, each body carrying a specific message of unity and enthusiasm to its section of America's adopted peoples.

It planned war exhibits for the state fairs of the United States, also a great series of interallied war expositions that brought home to our millions the exact nature of the struggle that was being waged in France. In Chicago alone two million people attended in two weeks, and in nineteen cities the receipts aggregated $1,432,261.36.

The Committee mobilized the advertising forces of the country—press, periodical, car, and outdoor—for the patriotic campaign that gave millions of dollars' worth of free space to the national service.

It assembled the artists of America on a volunteer basis for the production of posters, window-cards, and similar material of pictorial publicity for the use of various government departments and patriotic societies. A total of 1,438 drawings was used.

It issued an official daily newspaper, serving every department of government, with a circulation of one hundred thousand copies a day. For official use only, its value was such that private citizens ignored the supposedly prohibitive subscription price, subscribing to the amount of $77,622.58....

Through the medium of the motion picture, America's war progress, as well as the meanings and purposes of democracy, were carried to every community in the United States and to every corner of the world. "Pershing's Crusaders," "America's Answer," and "Under Four Flags" were types of feature films by which we drove home America's resources and determinations, while other pictures, showing our social and industrial life, made our free institutions vivid to foreign peoples.

9. Cartoons Against and For the League of Nations, 1920

INTERRUPTING THE CEREMONY

1918 Cartoon by McCutcheon, Public Domian

THE ACCUSER   *March 22, 1920*

ESSAYS

The stakes at the end of World War I turned out to be very high indeed, since in retrospect many historians have placed the blame for World War II on the faults of the Treaty of Versailles and the League of Nations. Walter McDougall of the University of Pennsylvania articulates the view that a messianic, egotistical Wilson ventured into matters far beyond his understanding. Wilson's idealistic but ill-considered crusade divided America and further unraveled the fabric of European stability. The president made terrible compromises in return for England and France's agreement to the Treaty of Versailles, while failing utterly to compromise with his rivals at home. Robert A. Pastor of American University in Washington, D.C., disputes the idea that Wilson was on a fool's errand, even though the president failed to get his treaty through Congress. Pastor points out that although the American model of a new world order was not fully implemented, the goals Wilson brought to the bargaining table at Versailles did become the basis for a more peaceable international system after 1945—*because* of the president's earlier efforts. Wilson lamented at the end of his career: "I had to negotiate with my back to the wall. Men thought I had all the power. Would to God I had had such power." Considering the powers that Wilson did have, do you think he employed them well? Was he wise, or not, in breaking George Washington's "Great Rule"?

Woodrow Wilson: Egocentric Crusader

WALTER McDOUGALL

"The only place in the world where nothing has to be explained to me is the South." An extraordinary admission by a man who would tell the whole world how to arrange its affairs, but that is what Wilson said. A Virginian descended from Presbyterian ministers on both sides of his family, he took the religion of his household for granted in the cerebral and sometimes smug way of the Calvinist elect. So certain was he of his spiritual correctness that a Catholic friend called him a "Presbyterian priest." And so deaf was Wilson to the aesthetics of other Christian liturgies that he pronounced the Episcopalian service "very stupid indeed … a ridiculous way of worshiping God, and one which must give very little pleasure to God." And yet this man who could parse a biblical text or dissect social ills with Presbyterian exactitude might also, of an evening, summon his family or friends to a naughty séance at the ouija board. He dabbled in numerology, too, his own lucky number being thirteen.

Wilson believed in predestination, not only in the hereafter but in time. He knew that God had chosen him to do great things, a faith that survived his indifferent schoolwork and utter failure while a student of law. As a Princeton undergraduate, "Tommy" Wilson drafted classmates into games and clubs so that he could play the leader and indulge his love of things British. In war games he fancied himself a British squadron commander, in political clubs a British minister swaying Parliament with his rhetoric. He kept a portrait of the crusading Christian prime minister William Ewart Gladstone on his desk, and he attributed the death of American oratory to the congressional system in which decisions were made through committee rather than debate on the floor....

Not surprisingly, Wilson embraced Progressive Imperialism. It suited his belief in the white man's calling and his notion of presidential government. So he cheered annexation of the Philippines and Puerto Rico—"They are children and we are men in these deep matters of government and justice"—and the fact that foreign policy again dominated U.S. politics. Now there would be "greatly increased power and opportunity for constructive statesmanship given the President." A strong executive, he wrote, "must utter every initial judgment, take every first step of action, supply the information upon which [the country] is to act, suggest and in large measure control its conduct."

In time, Wilson was named president of Princeton University—or "prime minister," as he liked to say—where he acquired a Cromwellian reputation for being a bold reformer and thorough authoritarian. Looking to Oxford and Cambridge for models, he placed junior faculty and graduate students (preceptors) in charge of the undergraduates, and tried to break up Princeton's exclusive fraternal clubs in favor of residential quadrangles. His purpose was "to attract more high school students of slender means to Princeton and to make the sons

Walter McDougall, *Promised Land, Crusader State* (Boston: Houghton Mifflin, 1997), 125–132, 134–135, 137–138, 140–146. Copyright © 1997 by Walter A. McDougall. Reprinted by permission of Houghton Mifflin Company. All rights reserved.

of the wealthy as unlike their fathers as possible." The expensive and radical project angered alumni and faculty, but Wilson refused to budge: "As long as I am president of Princeton, I propose to dictate the architectural policy of the university."

If any trait bubbles up in all one reads about Wilson, it is this: he loved, craved, and in a sense glorified power. That may seem anomalous in a pious Progressive and contemporary of Lord Acton, who warned, "Power tends to corrupt; absolute power corrupts absolutely." But Acton was a Catholic who believed in original sin; he was making a statement about the nature of man, not about the abstraction called power. Wilson, by contrast, leaned on "God's all-powerful arm," and defined power as the "capacity to make effective decisions" so as to nudge people and institutions along their appointed road toward perfection. In *Congressional Government* Wilson confessed, "I cannot imagine power as a thing negative and not positive." And in a 1911 address, "The Bible and progress," he said, "Let no man suppose that progress can be divorced from religion … the man whose faith is rooted in the Bible knows that reform cannot be stayed."

In the end, his one-crusader stance lost him the quad fight at Princeton but attracted the attention of New Jersey Democrats, who massaged Wilson's image into that of an incorruptible paladin of the common man. He was elected governor, then nominated for president in the year when Teddy Roosevelt's insurgency tore the Republican Party asunder. The campaign of 1912 thus became a three-way fight for the soul of industrial America. Taft represented stand-pat Republicanism in league with big business. Roosevelt praised corporations for their efficiency, but called for big government agencies to referee conflicts between capital and labor. Wilson blamed the ills of industrialism on simple greed, and promised a New Freedom based on competition and opportunity for all.

Everyone quotes Wilson's utterance that "it would be an irony of fate if my administration had to deal chiefly with foreign affairs." As it happened, he succeeded in introducing most of his domestic agenda, and won his fights for tariff reduction, the Federal Reserve Act, and the income tax. The real irony in his remark was that he had more latitude to exercise power and assert moral principles in foreign than in domestic policy—a fact that Wilson the political scientist had shrewdly observed. What is more, he did not shun foreign policy but jumped into it within days of his inauguration....

… Thus did Wilson reaffirm the Roosevelt Corollary, but strip from it any intimation that U.S. strategic or economic self-interest was involved. On the contrary, Wilson renounced all territorial ambition and, in a speech at Mobile in October 1913, called it "a very perilous thing to determine the foreign policy of a nation in terms of material interest. It not only is unfair to those with whom you are dealing, but it is degrading as regards your own actions."

Let us pause for a moment to let that sink in. According to Wilson, it was dangerous, unfair, and disgraceful to pursue a foreign policy based on material self-interest. Now, we may applaud the fact that he refused to commit the nation to conflict just to pull some bankers' bonds out of the fire. But what would John Quincy Adams have said of a policy that not only renounced but denounced the governments' obligation to protect American property and suggested instead that a policy was just and prudent only if it served platonic abstractions like justice?...

The British gave Wilson a blank check to do what he liked in Mexico, but otherwise were dumbfounded. Ambassador Sir Cecil Spring Rice wrote that Wilson talked to newspapermen or members of Congress "at length in excellent language, but when they leave him they say to each other, 'What on earth did he say?'" ... In 1914 British emissary Sir Edward Tyrrell told Wilson, "I shall be asked to explain your Mexican policy—can you tell me what it is?" Wilson replied, "I am going to teach the South American republics to elect good men."

A mystery indeed, because promising to make the Mexican revolution somehow turn out "right" only made Wilson a prisoner of events....

American diplomacy during World War I is usually described in terms of Wilson's struggle to uphold neutral rights at sea, as if it were a reprise of the situation during the Napoleonic Wars. There were parallels, for again Britain and her continental rival—France then, now Germany—blockaded each other and interfered with neutral commerce in systematic and arrogant ways. U.S. trade with German-occupied Europe shrank almost to nothing within eighteen months of the outbreak of war. By contrast, the German submarine blockade did not prevent U.S. exports to Britain and France from almost quadrupling by 1916 to $2.75 billion. But submarines necessarily took lives as well as property, and were for that reason more heinous than the Royal Navy's surface blockade. What is more, most U.S. diplomatic activity from 1914 to 1917 did concern neutral rights at sea, and the timing of Wilson's ultimate decision to fight derived in part from the German decision to sink without warning all ships of any nationality bound for Britain ("unrestricted submarine warfare").

Notwithstanding all that, the damage done to U.S. commerce seems to have interested Wilson little. Nor did he cling to neutrality because it was American tradition, or because he was a pacifist (he was not), or because the American people were almost unanimously in favor of staying out of the war. He did it because he believed that remaining above the battle was the only way that he, Wilson, could exert the moral authority needed to end the war on terms that would make for a lasting peace. Within a few weeks of the outbreak of war on August 1, 1914, Wilson told his brother-in-law that the principles guiding the future must be: no more territorial gains achieved by conquest; equality of rights for small nations; government control of arms manufacture; and an "association of nations wherein all shall guarantee the territorial integrity of each." Compared with this lofty quest, the material losses of American shippers were small beer indeed....

Buoyed by his [1916 electoral] victory, Wilson launched a final peace offensive. He had reason for optimism, since the German chancellor had quietly but urgently asked for a new U.S. initiative. (In truth, the German high command had given him a deadline to achieve a favorable peace or else it would resume unrestricted submarine warfare.) But the belligerents dared not trim their war aims sufficiently to interest their opponents, so Wilson aimed his Peace Without Victory speech of January 22, 1917, not at the governments but at "the peoples of the countries now at war." Any peace forced on the losers, he said, would be built on sand. Hence both alliances must renounce their ambitions and "with one accord adopt the doctrine of President Monroe as the doctrine of the whole world."

What sounded like reason and mercy to Wilson, however, was madness and cant in European ears. London and Paris took Wilson to mean that the United States had no intention of fighting Germany no matter what outrages the latter committed. Or, at best, the Americans might join the war but in opposition to Allied war aims as well as to Germany's. Bonar Law spoke for the British cabinet when he sighed, "What Mr. Wilson is longing for we are fighting for," and historian Sir George Trevelyan called Wilson "the quintessence of a prig. What a notion that the nations of Europe, after this terrible effort, will join him in putting down international encroachments by arms, at some future time, if he is afraid to denounce such encroachments even in words now!" Georges Clemenceau, soon to become French premier, said of Wilson's speech: "Never before has any political assembly heard so fine a sermon on what human beings might be capable of accomplishing if only they weren't human." But the bitterest critique of Peace Without Victory was Theodore Roosevelt's. Wilson's suggestion of a moral equivalence between the two sides was "wickedly false," talk of peacekeeping after the war "premature," and the reference to the Monroe Doctrine a contradiction in terms. "If his words mean anything, they would mean that hereafter we intended to embark on a policy of violent meddling in every European quarrel, and in return to invite Old World nations violently to meddle in everything American. Of course, as a matter of fact, the words mean nothing whatever." ...

Historians have rarely asked *whether* the United States should have gone to war in 1917, but rather what Wilson's motives were for doing so. In the 1930s critics charged that U.S. policy had become a hostage of munitions makers and Wall Street bankers, and that Wilson's unneutral acts had given the United States a stake in an Allied victory. The former contention was unfounded: as we know, Wilson rejected materialist policies and was contemptuous of big business. The latter contention seems to have been obvious, since the United States had solid security reasons for preferring an Allied victory. As U.S. diplomat Lewis Einstein had written in 1913, "The European balance of power is a political necessity which can alone sanction in the Western Hemisphere the continuance of an economic development unhandicapped by the burden of extensive armaments." Any European war would damage American interests, thought Einstein, but a German victory would be a calamity. He boldly suggested that the United States "extend the Monroe Doctrine to England" and deter Germany from launching a war. But few Americans were aware of their dependence on a balance of power and Anglo-American command of the seas, and however much Wilson might have appreciated that truth, he anathematized balance-of-power politics. Instead of telling the American people that they had to fight to defend the Atlantic Ocean from Germany, Wilson "managed to convert a successful national effort into a lost crusade."

And as always, Wilson stood alone. He was careful to describe the United States as an "associated" not an "allied" power, by which he meant that he did not recognize the Allies' war aims as codified in their secret treaties. So even as the United States lent military assistance to the Allies, it was implicitly a political rival of them. As of November 1917, it was also a rival of the de facto government of Russia. That was when Lenin and the Bolsheviks seized power in Petrograd and Moscow and called on the workers and soldiers of all nations to stop fighting and overthrow their imperialist governments. Echoing Wilson, Lenin called for a peace of "No Annexations, No Indemnities!" Echoing Lenin, Wilson announced his own war aims in the Fourteen Points speech of January 1918, to which he later added twenty-four principles, ends, particulars, and declarations. So it was that four, not two, contestants fought to control the world's future in 1918: the German militarists, the democratic but imperialist Allies, Wilson with his program of Liberal Internationalism, and Communists preaching social revolution....

Perhaps the greatest irony of the fight over the Treaty of Versailles, which contained the League Covenant, was that most Americans and members of the Senate were not especially hostile to its terms. Few Americans objected to the harsh conditions (disarmament, demilitarization and occupation of the Rhineland, loss of territories, seizure of Germany's fleet and overseas colonies) and open-ended reparations foisted on Germany (which Wilson himself called for in the Fourteen Points). Nor did most Americans care a fig for the fate of Fiume, which exercised the Italians, or the Chinese port of Kiao-Chow, which Japan had seized and would not give up. The Senate may even have been willing to ratify the guarantee against future German aggression that Wilson and Lloyd George promised to France even though it was entangling alliance. The harshest critics of the peace terms, in fact, were disheartened Democrats.

What did disturb senators was that the League of Nations Covenant—especially the collective security obligation in Article Ten—seemed incompatible with the existing traditions of U.S. policy....

Republican Herbert Hoover, for instance, did not like Article Ten because he thought the League's purpose should be "the pacific settlement of controversies among free nations," but he was willing to accept it with reservations. Roosevelt, too, wanted "to join the other civilized nations of the world in some scheme that in a time of great stress would offer a likelihood of obtaining settlements that will avert war." He insisted only that the League not be made a substitute for military preparedness and the national interest. Republicans Root and Hughes feared that Article Ten might prove to be "a trouble-breeder, and not a peace-maker." But they still viewed the League as a way to continue wartime cooperation, keep Germany down, and settle disputes so long as it complemented traditional deterrents. All were willing to follow Wilson's lead. They just wanted their doubts addressed before they were asked to endorse a new diplomatic tradition....

Upon his return to Paris, Wilson did obtain amendments to the Covenant including a right of withdrawal, removal of immigration and tariffs from the League's purview, and recognition of the Monroe Doctrine. So he came home confident that the revised Covenant he deposed on the Senate on July 10, 1919, would win swift ratification. "The stage is set, the destiny disclosed. It has come about by no plan of our conceiving, but by the hand of God, who led us into the way." Reporters asked if he would entertain reservations to the treaty. "I shall consent to nothing," said Wilson. "The Senate must take its medicine."

The Republican leadership refused the spoon. Lodge bought time by reading the entire Treaty of Versailles on the floor of the Senate, then called sixty witnesses to testify before the Foreign Relations Committee....

The Senate divided into four factions. Sixteen irreconcilables, led by Hiram Johnson (R., Calif.) and Borah, were opposed to the League in any form. As Borah said, "The proposition is force to destroy force, conflict to prevent conflict, militarism to destroy militarism, war to prevent war." It also meant the extinction of American nationality: "It is difficult to tell just how long the real Americans will sit still and permit the infamous propaganda to go on. I have just as much respect for the Bolshevist who would internationalize our whole system from below as I would for the broadcloth gentlemen who would internationalize it from above." The second and third factions were "hard" and "soft" reservationists, numbering twenty and twelve respectively. They were not "isolationists." As Root argued, "If it is necessary for the security of western Europe that we should agree to the support of France if attacked, then let us agree to do that particular thing plainly.... But let us not wrap up such a purpose in a vague universal obligation." All told, some fifty reservations and amendments were introduced, but Root and Lodge narrowed them down to fourteen and released them on November 19....

Clearly these reservations were designed not to gut the peace that Wilson had fashioned, but to ensure that his new order did not gut the sovereignty and Constitution of the United States and the Monroe Doctrine. Had Wilson been willing to swallow them, or an even milder package promoted by some Senate Democrats, the Treaty of Versailles would have been ratified. But he was convinced that the reservations would castrate the League, and in any case he hated Lodge. "Never, never! I'll never consent to adopt any policy with which that impossible man is so prominently identified." So he drafted a letter urging loyal Democrats, the fourth Senate faction, to oppose all reservations, with the perverse result that most Republicans voted *for* the League (with reservations) and almost all Democrats *against* it. The treaty with reservations failed 39 to 55, and the treaty without reservations 38 to 53....

Whether or not Wilsonianism was the message the world needed to hear after World War I, Woodrow Wilson was surely the wrong messenger—not because he was too religious, but because his religion was too personal, sanctimonious, gnostic. Senator Lawrence Y. Sherman (R., Ill.) put his finger on it when he called the League Covenant "a revolutionary document" inspired by the impossible dream of "a sinless world." Yet Wilson never doubted that he would be vindicated: "I would rather fail in a cause that will ultimately triumph than triumph in a cause that will ultimately fail."

Many historians would say that he was vindicated, since Wilson's Liberal Internationalist tenets informed the foreign policies of every administration after him. In 1920 the Republican platform endorsed an "agreement among the nations to preserve the peace of the world [but] without the compromise of national independence." ...

As a blueprint for world order, Wilsonianism has always been a chimera, but as an ideological weapon against "every arbitrary power anywhere," it has proved mighty indeed. And that, in the end, is how Wilson did truly imitate Jesus. He brought not peace but a sword....

Woodrow Wilson: Father of the Future

ROBERT A. PASTOR

The twentieth-century arrived two years early in American foreign policy. The Spanish-American War of 1898 constituted a watershed in America's relations with the world, separating an isolationist nineteenth century from a globally engaged twentieth century. Since its independence, America had viewed itself as special and different from Europe, but Americans were often divided as to how to translate this self-image into policy. Before 1898 the debates were largely resolved in favor of America standing aloof from the world as a "promised land." In the twentieth century, Americans gradually realized they had an important role to play in the world, but they still debated what that role should be—whether to be an example worthy of emulation or an activist shaping the world; whether or not to be imperialist; whether to define U.S. interests in a far-sighted or narrow way; and whether to act alone or with others.

The answers to those questions have not always been consistent, but a pattern became evident: U.S. policy was aimed not just to advance U.S. interests but to change the world. With deep roots in the country's unique heritage and favorable geography, an American idea of a new international system slowly began to crystallize. When it declared war against Spain, Washington shocked Europe by renouncing the war's main prize, Cuba. Theodore Roosevelt's goal of building a strong independent power that would open the world's door to trade and pledge not to take its neighbor's territory added two more elements to the developing vision, but it was Woodrow Wilson who gave fullest expression to a truly revolutionary worldview.

Wilson's goal went beyond winning World War I: He wanted to prevent all future wars and at the same time make the world safe for democracy. His proposal was quintessentially American: The European balance of power system must be dismantled in favor of a "community of power"—a League of Nations—that would guarantee the self-determination of all nations and therefore eliminate the cause of wars. The countries defeated in World War I must be given a stake and a place in the new systems; there must be "peace without victory"; there must be no indemnities and no colonies. These ideas were too radical to be accepted in 1918 but too compelling to be denied in 1945.

Robert A. Pastor, "The United States: Divided by a Revolutionary Vision" in Robert A. Pastor, ed., *A Century's Journey: How the Great Powers Shape the World* (New York: Basic Books, 1999), 191–193, 206–241, 233–235, 238. Reprinted by permission of Basic Books, a member of Perseus Books, L.L.C.

It was not just Europe that was unwilling to trade its sovereignty and self-defense for a new system based on collective security. The United States was never as committed to Wilsonianism in practice as it was in its rhetoric. Always watching the rearview mirror to make sure it wouldn't be rear-ended by the old order, the United States never allowed an international institution to replace its hands on the steering wheel or its foot on the brake pedal. America's idealism defined the world's mission, but its realism safeguarded its own security....

For a century following the Napoleonic Wars, the United States benefited from Europe's general peace and localized wars. When World War I began, the United States tried to avoid being drawn into it. Wilson declared U.S. neutrality and issued ten proclamations to define the rights of neutrals. Sensitive to their need for U.S. support but also wanting to prevent goods from reaching Germany, the British took care to respect U.S. rights. Germany's ability to compete against the British Navy depended on a new weapon, submarines, whose rules of engagement had not been defined. When German U-boats began to sink ocean liners, notably the *Lusitania,* whose passengers included 124 Americans, the United States protested vehemently. In an effort to keep the United States out of the war, Germany instructed its submarine commanders not to attack neutral merchant ships or any passenger ships. Nonetheless public opinion in the United States continued to turn against Germany, though Americans still did not want to fight.

Wilson had to walk a tightrope of neutrality. He was accused by Theodore Roosevelt of being too neutral in a war between democracy and autocracy, and by William Jennings Bryan, his secretary of state, of not being neutral enough. After Wilson sent a tough message to Germany condemning U-boat attacks, Bryan resigned on June 8, 1915. Wilson later healed the rift with Bryan, who endorsed him for a second term. Wilson won in a close election that included the slogan, "He kept us out of war."

Even before Wilson's second inaugural, the German government decided to try to bring the war to a quick end. On January 31, 1917, Germany informed the U.S. government that it would begin unrestricted submarine warfare in the war zone. The Germans believed that they could defeat England in five months and that even if the United States declared war, it could not mobilize quickly enough to affect the outcome. Wilson broke off relations with Germany. The British intercepted the "Zimmerman telegram" and three weeks later, turned over to Wilson this cable from the German foreign minister to his ambassador in Mexico City in which Germany proposed an alliance with Mexico against the United States. In the event of their victory, the Germans promised to help Mexico "reconquer the lost territory in Texas, New Mexico, and Arizona." The contents of the telegram were leaked to the press, and Americans were outraged.

The Zimmerman telegram and German attacks on three U.S. ships between March 12 and 18 were the events that finally convinced Wilson, his cabinet, and most Americans that they had to fight. On April 2, 1917, Wilson addressed Congress and asked for a declaration of war. He said that America must accept the "status of belligerent which thus has been thrust upon it" by German attacks on U.S. and other neutral ships. America must fight "for the rights of nations great and small and the privilege of men everywhere to choose their way of life. The world must be made safe for democracy."

Only five Senators spoke against the declaration. Senator George Norris said that he opposed entry into the war because the United States had not been completely neutral. Wall Street, in his judgment, was behind the war: "There is no doubt in my mind but the enormous amount of money loaned to the allies in this country has been instrumental in bringing about a public sentiment in favor of our country taking a course that would make every bond worth a hundred cents on the dollar." He urged his colleagues to recall George Washington's warning about entangling alliances: "Let Europe solve her problems as we have solved ours." Before the Germans sank U.S. ships, many Americans shared Norris's view. In April 1917, his was a lonely voice. The Senate voted for war 82 to 6, as did the House, 373 to 50.

By this time Wilson also wanted the United States to enter the war so that he could have a hand in constructing the peace. No other leader gave as much thought or solicited and synthesized more revolutionary ideas on how the world political system should be restructured to stop future wars. From the beginning of the war, Wilson's mind turned to the fundamental questions: How to mediate an end to the war? How to assure permanent peace? He sent his principal adviser, Colonel Edward House, to Europe several times in search of an answer to the first question, but the Europeans wanted to win, not settle. Wilson therefore spent most of his time on the longer-term issue. His first thought was to try to secure mutual guarantees of territorial integrity and political independence under republican forms of government, and he decided the power of this idea could be demonstrated in the Americas. He proposed to the ambassadors of Argentina, Brazil, and Chile a "Pan-American Pact" to "mutualize" the Monroe Doctrine and to be a model that Europe could follow to end the war. Argentina and Brazil approved the idea, but Chile had reservations. In the end, Wilson's interventions in Mexico and the Caribbean precluded hemispheric agreement, but the idea would be central in his subsequent peace proposals.

Beginning in May 1916 Wilson tried to awaken Americans to a new role as participants "in the life of the world" rather than as "disconnected lookers-on." In his "Peace Without Victory" address to a joint session of Congress on January 22, 1917, Wilson asked, "Is the present war a struggle for a just and secure peace, or only for a new balance of power?" He answered with a set of revolutionary principles that borrowed from James Monroe but reached all the way back to Immanuel Kant:

> There must be, not a balance of power, but a community of power; not organized rivalries, but an organized common peace … I am proposing, as it were, that the nations would with one accord adopt the doctrine of President Monroe as the doctrine of the world: that no nation should seek to extend its polity over any other nation or people, but that every people should be left free to determine its own polity.

If all sides would acknowledge the stalemate and accept "peace without victory," not only would the war end but there would be no defeated power

seeking revenge in a second war. Acceptance of self-determination would eliminate the causes of war (colonies and reparations), and a concert of powers, greater
than any nation, would be able to enforce the peace. Wilson was proposing nothing less than a complete change in the way states defined their interests and the
way the international system should work.

A year later, after the U.S. had entered the war, Wilson and House sat down
for two hours one morning and condensed their thoughts into a fourteen–point
peace plan, which Wilson delivered to Congress on January 8, 1918. The first
five points set out the basic elements of "progressive internationalism": no secret
treaties ("open covenants of peace, openly arrived at"); freedom of the seas; reduction of trade barriers and equality of trade conditions; reduction of national
armaments to the lowest possible level; and an impartial adjustment of colonial
claims based on the principle of self-determination. The next points called for
the withdrawal of foreign armies to their own lands, the welcoming of revolutionary Russia "into the society of free nations," the adjustment of boundaries
along clear lines of nationality, and the creation of a Polish state with access to
the sea. Wilson left the most important point, his proposal for a League of Nations, for last: "A general association of nations must be formed under specific
covenants for the purpose of affording mutual guarantees of political independence and territorial integrity to great and small states alike."

"These are American principles," Wilson proclaimed, and he added, "they are
the principles of mankind and must prevail." He also reached out to Germany:
"We have no jealousy of German greatness, and there is nothing in this program
that impairs it.… We wish her only to accept a place of equality among the peoples of the world."

The speech was praised widely, and it elicited some peace feelers. But the
Germans then imposed a punishing peace treaty on Russia and moved its forces
west. The United States raised an army of 5 million men within one year, but
they did not arrive in large enough numbers to make a difference until the autumn of 1918, when they helped blunt a German offensive. The Germans retreated to Belgium and appealed to Wilson for talks based on the Fourteen
Points, but the request came at a politically awkward time. Congressional elections were approaching, and the Republicans, more attuned to American anger
over 116,000 casualties, wanted Germany defeated, not accommodated. In order
to win the congressional elections, the Republican leadership united behind a
strategy of attacking Wilson's peace plan. Theodore Roosevelt demanded unconditional surrender and urged the Senate to reject the Fourteen points. Henry
Cabot Lodge accused Wilson of accepting "peace at any price" because his
advisers were "socialists and Bolsheviks." Wilson stiffened his demands to the
Germans. He then tried to bring the Germans and the Allies to the bargaining
table and to win the congressional elections. He succeeded only in gaining
German agreement to an armistice on November 11. Five days earlier, the
Republicans had won control of both houses of Congress. Henry Cabot Lodge
became chairman of the Senate Foreign Relations Committee. The election
campaign was so poisonous that Wilson refused to appoint Lodge or any senior
Republican to advise on the peace negotiations.

Europe's leaders dismissed Wilson's plan as naïve, but they could not ignore the vast and enthusiastic crowds that met Wilson in England, France, and Italy or the popular response to his speeches urging fundamental change in the international system. Still, when Wilson sat down to negotiate, he found himself alone, asking his European counterparts to discard the rules of a 400-years-old interstate system in exchange for a set of untried, idealistic principles. The first issue on the table was the disposal of Germany's colonies, and every country except the United States made claims based on the age-old principle "To the victor belongs the spoils." Wilson listened until his patience was exhausted. Then, like a professor who was frustrated with his students because they could not grasp the point of his lecture, he reminded the others of the purpose of their negotiations: "The world was against any further annexations. [If they occurred] the League of Nations would be discredited from the beginning." He explained his plan for ending colonialism and protecting the people "under the full view of the world, until they were able to take charge of their own affairs." The English were the most indignant, but all the Allied representatives responded as if they were from a different world, as indeed they were. All the major powers except the United States also opposed small power representation on the League's Executive Council. The Japanese requested a provision on racial equality, but the English blocked it, along with two American proposals, for freedom of religion and of the seas. Wilson nonetheless negotiated with great skill and perseverance and was able to preserve enough of his points that he could present a draft to the world on February 14, 1919, and return to the United States to consult and defend it.

Between February 23 and his return to France in early March, Wilson met with numerous groups and at least thirty-four senators for intensive discussions on the draft. There was great enthusiasm among the American public for the League of Nations Covenant, but on the day before Wilson's return to Pairs to continue the peace talks, Lodge offered a stiff critique that mixed vitriol with some searing substantive points. After accusing the president of abandoning George Washington in favor of "Trotsky, the champion of internationalism," Lodge displayed a round-robin letter, signed by thirty-seven senators, indicating that the treaty would not be approved in its current form. He then recommended four changes: an affirmation of the Monroe Doctrine, a provision for withdrawal from the League of Nations, explicit exclusion of domestic issues (such as immigration) from the League of Nations Covenant, and clarification of how the League would use force.

Former President William Howard Taft and the Senate Democratic leader Gilbert Hitchcock assured Wilson that if he could amend the treaty along the lines recommended by Lodge, "the ground will be completely cut from under the opposition." The Allies were aware of the round-robin letter, and they were ready to amend the League Covenant in exchange for Wilson's accepting harsh provisions in the Treaty of Versailles. France wanted to annex the Saar but accepted a fifteen-year Allied occupation of the Rhineland, a separate Anglo-American defense treaty, and an exorbitant increase in reparations from Germany. The Italians demanded parts of Austria; the Japanese threatened to bolt the conference unless they received German concessions in Shandong.

All insisted on a vengeful war-guilt clause against Germany. With a heavy heart, Wilson struck the compromises to accommodate Lodge. These changes diminished the enthusiasm of the progressive internationalists, the League's strongest supporters, which made selling the agreement that much harder. The Treaty of Versailles, which included the League Covenant, was signed on June 28, 1919, in the Hall of Mirrors, and Wilson turned to his next battle.

The Senate debate on the Treaty of Versailles has been described as having pitted internationalists against isolationists, but there were only twelve irreconcilably isolationist Republicans. The more interesting debate was not between them and the internationalists but between the "unilateral" and the "cooperative" internationalists. The unilateralists were thirty-seven Republican senators who supported Lodge; they wanted to constrain the League and ensure that the United States would retain the freedom to act unilaterally. The League's supporters, forty-seven Democratic senators, agreed with Wilson that international institutions should stop all wars.

Despite Wilson's success in amending the League Covenant and making it a part of the treaty, Lodge was still not reconciled to it because, in his words, it placed "the destiny of my country under the control of a politically selected tribunal of nine … sitting forever upon foreign soil…. The spirit of this plan to subordinate this great Republic into this international socialistic combine is absolutely in the face and teeth and eyes of our Constitution." His second point also had the ring of tradition: "Before I go into the stabilizing business abroad, I believe in making the foundations of a republican-democratic form of government safe and stable in my own county."

President Wilson met with groups of Republican senators and realized they supported Lodge, who was stalling the debate. On September 2, despite poor health, the president decided to build support for the League around the country, and he began a national tour that would take him to twenty-nine cities to give thirty-seven speeches to rebut his opponents' arguments: "I want to call you to witness that the peace of the world cannot be established without America … [and] the peace and goodwill of the world are necessary to America."

He returned to Washington exhausted, and on October 2 he suffered a stroke that paralyzed one side of his body. Wilson became inflexible both physically and temperamentally at the very moment compromises were desperately needed, although it is by no means clear that a compromise was possible. Lodge had crafted fourteen reservations that struck at the League's heart. For example, as a substitute for the League's collective security provision, Lodge proposed a provision stating, "The U.S. assumes no obligation to preserve the territorial integrity or political independence of any country … unless … Congress … by act or joint resolution [shall] so provide." Other reservations were aimed at releasing the United States from commitments agreed in the League Covenant and the treaty unless Congress specifically approved. The treaty came to the Senate floor for a vote three times, the first time with Lodge's reservations, the second without, and the third with some support by Democrats for Lodge's reservations. Each time, it failed.

The tragedy was that in order to secure the League of Nations, Wilson had to compromise on so many of his Fourteen Points that the Treaty of Versailles reflected the old order more than the new. The harsh reparations and the war-guilt clause imposed on Germany sowed seeds that were to bear bitter fruit for Europe. The decision to transfer Germany's concession in China to Japan not only alienated the Chinese from the United States but set the stage for the next war in Asia. Worse, Wilson could not deliver his own country. It was not at all clear that the League of Nations would have been able to deter or confront aggressors if the United States had been a member, but it was reasonably clear that it could not do so without the United States. Moreover, the U.S. failure to approve the agreement to defend France against German attack left France naked, with neither a new institution nor a balance of power that could prevent the next war.

Perhaps a stronger, more flexible Wilson could have won a weakened League. But it is also possible that he was just too far in front of the American people at that time. Beneath the debate among internationalists was a powerful postwar undercurrent tugging Americans home, back to "normalcy," fearful of Europe's wars and the Russian Revolution. The United States succumbed to a Red Scare in 1920 when A. Mitchell Palmer, Wilson's attorney general, launched anticommunist raids in thirty-three cities in one night. By the end of the year, Warren G. Harding won a landslide victory that reflected the nation's yearning to turn inward. Lodge interpreted Harding's victory as his as well: "So far as the United States is concerned, the League is dead."

Besides the rejection of the League and the World Court, other signs that America wanted to close the door on the world included congressional approval of the country's first laws limiting worldwide immigration. The nation's leaders, predominantly Anglo-Saxon Protestants, reacted to the heavy influx of immigrants form southern and eastern Europe. Nearly 20 million people had immigrated in the two decades before the war. Congress accepted as "scientific fact" that the new immigrants were of lower quality than those who had preceded them and that a successful America required more of the original and fewer of the newer immigrants. The quotas set by the laws reflected the ethnic composition of America in 1890, before the new wave of immigration. The immigration debate coincided with an ugly mood of intolerance, reflected in the rise of the Ku Klux Klan and other nativist groups....

The United States had the world's strongest economy at both the beginning and the end of the twentieth century, although over the course of the century it changed from a commodity producer and manufacturer to a nation that relied on information, technology, and services. Though it was still relatively autonomous economically as compared to most of the other powers, the United States was more than twice as dependent on trade in 1996 as it was in 1970, and that was roughly twice as dependent as in 1913. A century after emerging from its strategic cocoon, the United States stands alone, with a military capacity that dwarfs that of any plausible combination of rivals. The economic and military indicators, however, tell only a small part of the story of the U.S. impact on the international system in the twentieth century and its probable effect in the future. The real story is how unorthodox U.S. ideas changed the very character of the system.

In June 1914 Wilson posed the pivotal question for the United States:

What are we going to do with the influence and power of this great nation? Are we going to play the old role of using that power of our aggrandizement and material benefit only? You know what that may mean. It may upon occasion mean that we shall use it to make the peoples of other nations suffer in the way in which we said that it was intolerable to suffer when we uttered the Declaration of Independence.

Wilson's answer was evident from the way he posed the question: The United States would not play the "old role." Wilson defined new goals not just for the United States but for the world, and new instruments—international institutions and norms—to secure these goals of world peace and freedom. Tapping deep roots of U.S. idealism, Wilson offered answers to the fundamental questions of why wars occur and how they could be stopped, questions that challenged the foundations of the Westphalian interstate system. Balance of power, Wilson concluded, was not the solution; rather, it was part of the problem. Wilson's proposal, despite its utopian dress, was eminently practical: to reduce the benefits and increase the costs of war by gaining universal agreement on a powerful idea, self-determination, and an institution to enforce it, the League of Nations. This norm denies war's gains, and it increases its costs by giving a voice and legitimacy to those struggling for independence.

Wilson's ideas slowly grew legs and began to walk, uncertainly at first but within a few years after World War II territorial acquisition had virtually disappeared as a goal of states. Since 1945 only one state has tried to annex forcefully another UN member....

How can we explain the continuity and changes in U.S. foreign policy in the twentieth century? The continuity in U.S. foreign policy follows from both geography and political culture. Only a country sitting securely between two large oceans and weak or friendly neighbors could have afforded to devote so much time to its own affairs and so little time, relative to the other great powers, to the world. A country composed of middle-class citizens who distrust central authority and who fear that war would strengthen their government, reduce their democracy, and risk their children is a country that keeps its government out of war until a security threat compels it to act. Then it fights zealously to vanquish the foe and return home as quickly as possible. Only a county settled by refugees and blessed with distant threats and a puritan's heritage could imagine a world without war and would design institutions not just to defeat foes but to banish all war and injustice. And only a country whose reigning philosophy was pragmatism would preserve its own freedom of action even while proclaiming a new world order based on international institutions....

The twenty-first century will be very different from the twentieth. Testimony to the distance that the world has traveled toward America's vision is the grudging acknowledgment by Henry Kissinger, the classic realist, in his book, *Diplomacy*: "It is above all to the drumbeat of Wilsonian idealism that American foreign policy has marched since his watershed presidency and continues to march to this day." The United States changed the rules and the game of international politics in the twentieth century. The world today is different because the United States is different.

FURTHER READING

David Adelman, *A Shattered Peace: Versailles 1919 and the Price We Pay Today* (2007).

Nancy Bristow, *Making Men Moral: Social Engineering During the Great War* (1996).

Thomas Britten, *American Indians in World War I: At Home and at War* (1997).

John Milton Cooper, *Breaking the Heart of the World: Woodrow Wilson and the Fight for the League of Nations* (2001).

Leslie Midkiff DeBauche, *Reel Patriotism: The Movies and World War I* (1997).

Gerard DeGroot, *The First World War* (2001).

Milton and Susan Harries, *The Last Days of Innocence: America at War* (1997).

David M. Kennedy, *Over Here: The First World War and American Society* (1980).

Thomas J. Knock, *To End All Wars: Woodrow Wilson and the Quest for a New World Order* (1992).

Margaret MacMillan, *Paris 1919: Six Months That Changed the World* (2002).

Erez Manela, *The Wilsonian Moment: Self-Determination and the International Origins of Anticolonial Nationalism* (2007).

Ronald Schaffer, *America in the Great War: The Rise of the War Welfare State* (1991).

Susan Zeiger, *In Uncle Sam's Service: Women Workers with the American Expeditionary Force* (1999).

CHAPTER 7

Crossing a Cultural Divide:
The Twenties

The Nebraska-born novelist Willa Cather famously said of the 1920s: "the world broke in two in 1922 or thereabouts." In that decade, for the first time, more Americans lived in towns than on farms. Mass industrialization, higher wages, and the wide use of credit placed modern products like the car, the vacuum cleaner, and the washing machine at the disposal of millions. Science made new discoveries that appeared to challenge old truths. The vote for women became law in 1920, and though few women became politicians, millions became flappers. In six years, hemlines went from the ankle, where they had been for centuries, to the knee. Film, radio, and advertising came into the lives of everyday Americans, reshaping their desires and dreams, and reminding them constantly that they lived in a new era.

Cultural change provoked deep conflict over religion, sex, gender roles, and ethnicity. The decade that invented dating also coined the term fundamentalism. The rural vision of America seemed deeply at odds with the urban one. Myriad organizations formed to defend "white Anglo-Saxon Protestant" (WASP) traditions, including a revitalized Ku Klux Klan, which won legislative and executive elections throughout the Midwest and had nearly three million members by 1923. The most famous trial of the decade, the Scopes "monkey trial," epitomized the clash over modernism and the battle to hold the line against "Godless science." Ironically, Progressive icon William Jennings Bryan, leading the fight, appeared to stand against progress. Meanwhile, on a day-to-day level, the police struggled and failed to implement the crowning reform of the preceding decade, the prohibition of alcohol. The twenties became infamous for the willful flouting of Progressive-era moralizing. Men drank, women smoked, and, worst of all, they did these things in one another's company. Youth culture became distinct from adult culture in this decade, and many young people were discernibly amused by the puritanical streak of the older generation. Couples found it hard to support large families on limited wages. Women, especially, pleaded for relief from constant childbearing.

The decade also witnessed the culmination of xenophobic sentiment that had been building since the turn of the century. Many Americans concluded that the best way to keep out foreign ideas was to keep out foreigners. In 1924, Congress passed a National Origins Act that was specifically designed to limit Catholic and Jewish immigration and abolish Asian immigration altogether. Proponents gloried in the triumph of "Nordic" (north European) whites and the Protestant religion. But the gates swung closed on a population that was already enormously diverse in its religious beliefs and ethnic character, and whose face was turned to the future. The modern era was underway.

QUESTIONS TO THINK ABOUT

Why was there a great debate in the 1920s about the future? Who won it, the modernists or the fundamentalists? Would you characterize this period primarily as the Age of Jazz or as the Age of Prohibition?

DOCUMENTS

The documents in this chapter illustrate the cultural changes that took place in the 1920s. In document 1, the Governor of California decries the economic competition of the Japanese and their shockingly high fertility. He articulates a commitment to ending Asian immigration that went from the citizenry to the highest levels of government. Document 2 is a newspaper account of a radio sermon by the wildly popular fundamentalist preacher, Aimee Semple McPherson. McPherson organized the first super-sized congregation in Southern California, the Pentecostal Foursquare Church based in Los Angeles. She used modern media to get across "that old-timed religion." Here McPherson denounces modern sects that turn their back on revivals and have lost their faith in miracles. Document 3 is a cartoon from a religious tract that portrays modern preachers as bound and blinded by rationalism and science. Document 4 shows the famous clash between attorney Clarence Darrow and William Jennings Bryan in the Scopes "monkey trial." They spoke from opposite sides of the cultural divide noted by Willa Cather. Former Secretary of State Bryan defended a literal interpretation of the Bible, including the story of the Earth's origins as told in Genesis. Darrow, retained by the American Civil Liberties Union, spoke for modern science. Document 5 outlines the program of the Ku Klux Klan and reveals the extent to which religion, race, and patriotism were inseparably intertwined in the Klan definition of a "true" American. In document 6, reformer Margaret Sanger shares letters that mothers and fathers across America have sent her. They attest to the physical and financial ruin of parents for whom non-stop childbearing is a curse. A modern society ought to make modern methods of birth control legal, Sanger argued. Document 7 is from a famous sociological study of Muncie, Indiana (here called Middletown), in the 1920s that showed how new mass products like the automobile reshaped people's values. Document 8 expresses the literary power that brought Langston

Hughes to fame in the Harlem Renaissance and the sentiments that propelled some African Americans out of the South. The last selection reveals the onset of a sexual revolution in the turbulent twenties. In document 9, young women freely discuss something their mothers would never have condoned: "petting" and premarital sex.

1. The Governor of California Tells of the "Japanese Problem," 1920

The Japanese in our midst have indicated a strong trend to land ownership and land control, and by their unquestioned industry and application, and by standards and methods that are widely separated from our occidental standards and methods, both in connection with hours of labor and standards of living, have gradually developed to a control of many of our important agricultural industries. Indeed, at the present time they operate 458,056 acres of the very best lands in California. The increase in acreage control within the last decade, according to these official figures, has been 412.9 per cent. In productive values—that is to say, in the market value of crops produced by them—our figures show that as against $6,235,856 worth of produce marketed in 1909, the increase has been to $67,145,730, approximately tenfold.

More significant than these figures, however, is the demonstrated fact that within the last ten years Japanese agricultural labor has developed to such a degree that at the present time between 80 and 90 per cent of most of our vegetable and berry products are those of the Japanese farms. Approximately 80 per cent of the tomato crop of the state is produced by Japanese; from 80 to 100 per cent of the spinach crop; a greater part of our potato and asparagus crops, and so on. So that it is apparent without much more effective restrictions that in a very short time, historically speaking, the Japanese population within our midst will represent a considerable portion of our entire population, and the Japanese control over certain essential food products will be an absolute one....

These Japanese, by very reason of their use of economic standards impossible to our white ideals—that is to say, the employment of their wives and their very children in the arduous toil of the soil—are proving crushing competitors to our white rural populations. The fecundity of the Japanese race far exceeds that of any other people that we have in our midst. They send their children for short periods of time to our white schools, and in many of the country schools of our state the spectacle is presented of having a few white children acquiring their education in classrooms crowded with Japanese. The deep-seated and often outspoken resentment of our white mothers at this situation can only be appreciated by those people who have struggled with similar problems.

California State Board of Control, *California and the Oriental* (Sacramento: State Printing Office, June 1920), 8–13.

It is with great pride that I am able to state that the people of California have borne this situation and seen its developing menace with a patience and self-restraint beyond all praise. California is proud to proclaim to the nation that despite this social situation her people have been guilty of no excesses and no indignities upon the Japanese within our borders. No outrage, no violence, no insult and no ignominy have been offered to the Japanese people within California....

But with all this the people of California are determined to repress a developing Japanese community within our midst. They are determined to exhaust every power in keeping to maintain this state for its own people. This determination is based fundamentally upon the ethnological impossibility of assimilating the Japanese people and the consequential alternative of increasing a population whose very race isolation must be fraught with the gravest consequences.

2. Radio Broadcast: "Modern Church Is No Bridge to Heaven," 1923

Indictment of modern churches that would bridge the way to heaven with "chicken suppers and social psychology," instead of with the vital doctrines of the Son of God, featured a dramatic sermon preached from The Times Broadcasting Station yesterday morning by Mrs. Aimee Semple McPherson, pastor of the Angelus Temple [in Los Angeles].

Taking as her text the despairing cry of Mary, "They have taken away my Lord!" Mrs. McPherson spoke in part as follows:

"The Garden of Gethsemane was past. Golgotha with its agony of body and soul was over. The throbbing, rending rocks were still at last. The storm-swept heaven was clear, and the morning star shone down benignly. The day had not yet begun to dawn, and the Sacred City was wrapped in slumber. The frightened guards had taken their departure, and there was silence in the garden of Joseph of Arimanthaea.

Plaint is Heard

"Silence, did I say? No. What is that sound? 'Tis more than the whispering of the olive trees; more than the moan of the wind through the sycamores.' 'Tis a sound that strikes a chill through the heart of the listener—the sound of a woman weeping—heart-brokenly, inconsolably, and repeating over and over again in hopeless tones: 'They have taken away my Lord! They have taken away my Lord, and I know not where they have lain Him.'"

"There is a lump in our throat and a catch in our heart as we gaze upon that poor little disconsolate figure, rocking herself in her grief. 'Jesus,' I can hear her say. 'Jesus, who was born in Bethlehem, and whose birth the angels

"Evangelist Makes Plea for Lord of Scriptures," Los Angeles Times, August 6, 1923. Reprinted by permission.

did announce; Jesus, the light that did shine in the darkness though the darkness comprehended it not; Jesus, thou tender Shepherd of the sheep, who forgave the vilest sinner, who healed the sick and cooled the fevered brow; who cast out demons, raised the dead, set the captive free; Jesus, who did feed the hungry and calm the storm-swept billows of the sea—how—how am I ever going to live without you?'

Many at Empty Tomb

"Poor Mary! Dear Mary, forgiven much, loving much, her heart was well-nigh broken as she sat weeping at the empty tomb.

"Yet hundreds and thousands today sit at an empty tomb—a powerless revival-less church, devoid of the miraculous, prayer-answering Christ of the long-ago—... Jesus, the great I am, wrapped in the slumber of worldliness and unbelief, higher criticism and formality might well take up the cry of Mary: 'They have taken away my Lord; taken away the Lord of the Bible—taken away ... the Deity of my Lord and Master—taken away the inspiration of the Scriptures that declare atonement through the precious blood—taken away the preaching of the old-time born-again experience, and of the victorious life above the world and sin—taken away the old-time altar-calls—taken away the old all-night prayer meetings where saints of God were wont to lay upon their faces in prayer till a revival came down which swept the entire community—taken away the warmth, and fire, and faith, and fervor which they have now come to call emotionalism, and in its place they have left an empty tomb. My Lord they have taken away!'"

Tell of Changes

"Now men say that you have changed, Jesus dear, that you are far away beyond that dome of blue; that you are no longer the miracle-working, healing Christ of the Bible—and they have taken you away, and I know not where they have lain you. God only knows the number of Marys who today have been sitting before the empty tomb, mourning their departed Lord—mourning the need of a revival of the old-time power and the preaching of a Christ who is not dead, but risen. Oh, why have men limited the Holy One of Israel? Where have they taken away the Lord of the Bible? Weeping, yearning, longing for the return of the old-time glory of a Christ who lives and moves in the midst of His people, thousands have wept and prayed inconsolably. Motion pictures in the parish-house, chicken suppers, festivities, preaching of psychology, community uplift and social reform—none of these have been able to fill the empty void nor stilled the heart-broken cry. "'They have taken away my Lord....'"

3. Cartoon: Religious "Modernism" Offers Cold Comfort, 1924

FRIGID-AIR SEMINARY

DOCTRINE OF THE FRIGID SEMINARY

ACCOUNT OF CREATION IS A MYTH.

WE DENY THE VIRGIN BIRTH.

BIBLE IS FULL OF MISTAKES.

GRADUATION DAY

THE FIELDS ARE WHITE UNTO HARVEST.

Here is one real source of the trouble—the cold, revivalless, blood-less, back-slidden seminaries of the present age.

The Foursquare Church Archives

Frigid Air Seminary from Page 13 of the periodical The Bridal Call Foursquare published July 1928 in the book *Major Problems in American History: Documents and Essays, Volume II: Since 1865.*

4. Defense Attorney Clarence Darrow Interrogates Prosecutor William Jennings Bryan in the Monkey Trial, 1925

Examination of W. J. Bryan by Clarence Darrow, of counsel for the defense:

Q—You have given considerable study to the Bible, haven't you, Mr. Bryan?

The World's Most Famous Trial: Tennessee Evolution Case (Cincinnati: National Book Co.), 284–291.

A—Yes, sir, I have tried to....

Q—Do you claim that everything in the Bible should be literally interpreted?

A—I believe everything in the Bible should be accepted as it is given there; some of the Bible is given illustratively. For instance: "Ye are the salt of the earth." I would not insist that man was actually salt, or that he had flesh of salt, but it is used in the sense of salt as saving God's people.

Q—But when you read that Jonah swallowed the whale—or that the whale swallowed Jonah—excuse me please—how do you literally interpret that?

A—When I read that a big fish swallowed Jonah—it does not say whale.

Q—Doesn't it? Are you sure?

A—That is my recollection of it. A big fish, and I believe it, and I believe in a God who can make a whale and can make a man and make both do what He pleases....

Q—You believe the story of the flood [Noah] to be a literal interpretation?

A—Yes, sir.

Q—When was that flood?

A—I would not attempt to fix the date. The date is fixed, as suggested this morning.

Q—About 4004 B.C.?

A—That has been the estimate of a man that is accepted today. I would not say it is accurate.

Q—That estimate is printed in the Bible?

A—Everybody knows, at least, I think most of the people know, that was the estimate given.

Q—But what do you think that the Bible, itself, says? Don't you know how it was arrived at?

A—I never made a calculation.

Q—A calculation from what?

A—I could not say.

Q—From the generations of man?

A—I would not want to say that.

Q—What do you think?

A—I do not think about things I don't think about.

Q—Do you think about things you do think about?

A—Well, sometimes....

Mr. Darrow—How long ago was the flood, Mr. Bryan?...

The Witness—It is given here, as 2348 years B.C.

> Q—Well, 2348 years B.C. You believe that all the living things that were not contained in the ark were destroyed.
>
> A—I think the fish may have lived....
>
> Q—Don't you know there are any number of civilizations that are traced back to more than 5,000 years?
>
> A—I know we have people who trace things back according to the number of ciphers they have. But I am not satisfied they are accurate....

Mr. Darrow—You do know that there are thousands of people who profess to be Christians who believe the earth is much more ancient and that the human race is much more ancient?

> A—I think there may be.
>
> Q—And you never have investigated to find out how long man has been on the earth?
>
> A—I have never found it necessary....
>
> Q—Don't you know that the ancient civilizations of China are 6,000 or 7,000 years old, at the very least?
>
> A—No; but they would not run back beyond the creation, according to the Bible, 6,000 years.
>
> Q—You don't know how old they are, is that right?
>
> A—I don't know how old they are, but probably you do. (Laughter in the courtyard.) I think you would give the preference to anybody who opposed the Bible, and I give the preference to the Bible.

5. The Ku Klux Klan Defines Americanism, 1926

The Klan ... has now come to speak for the great mass of Americans of the old pioneer stock. We believe that it does fairly and faithfully represent them, and our proof lies in their support. To understand the Klan, then, it is necessary to understand the character and present mind of the mass of old-stock Americans. The mass, it must be remembered, as distinguished from the intellectually mongrelized "Liberals."

These are, in the first place, a blend of various peoples of the so-called Nordic race, the race which, with all its faults, has given the world almost the whole of modern civilization. The Klan does not try to represent any people but these....

From "The Ku Klux Klan's Fight for Americanism," by Hiram Wesley Evans from *North American Review* (March–May 1926), pp. 38–39, 52–54. Copyright 1926 by *North American Review*. Reproduced with permission.

... The Nordic American today is a stranger in large parts of the land his fathers gave him. Moreover, he is a most unwelcome stranger, one much spit upon, and one to whom even the right to have his own opinions and to work for his own interests is now denied with jeers and revilings. "We must Americanize the Americans," a distinguished immigrant said recently. Can anything more clearly show the state to which the real American has fallen in this country which was once his own?...

Thus the Klan goes back to the American racial instincts, and to the common sense which is their first product, as the basis of its beliefs and methods....

There are three of these great racial instincts, vital elements in both the historic and the present attempts to build an America which shall fulfill the aspirations and justify the heroism of the men who made the nation. These are the instincts of loyalty to the white race, to the traditions of America, and to the spirit of Protestantism, which has been an essential part of Americanism ever since the days of Roanoke and Plymouth Rock. They are condensed into the Klan slogan: "Native, white, Protestant supremacy."

First in the Klansman's mind is patriotism—America for Americans. He believes religiously that a betrayal of Americanism or the American race is treason to the most sacred of trusts, a trust from his fathers and a trust from God. He believes, too, that Americanism can only be achieved if the pioneer stock is kept pure. There is more than one race pride in this. Mongrelization has been proven bad. It is only between closely related stocks of the same race that interbreeding has improved men; the kind of interbreeding that went on in the early days of America between English, Dutch, German, Hugenot, Irish and Scotch....

The second word in the Klansman's trilogy is "white." The white race must be supreme, not only in America but in the world. This is equally undebatable, except on the ground that the races might live together, each with full regard for the rights and interests of others, and that those rights and interests would never conflict. Such an idea, of course, is absurd; the colored races today, such as Japan, are clamoring not for equality but for their supremacy. The whole history of the world, on its broader lines, has been one of race conflicts, wars, subjugation or extinction. This is not pretty, and certainly disagrees with the maudlin theories of cosmopolitanism, but it is truth. The world has been so made that each race must fight for its life, must conquer, accept slavery or die. The Klansman believes that the whites will not become slaves, and he does not intend to die before his time....

The third of the Klan principles is that Protestantism must be supreme; that Rome shall not rule America. The Klansman believes this not merely because he is a Protestant, nor even because the Colonies that are now our nation were settled for the purpose of wresting America from the control of Rome and establishing a land of free conscience. He believes it also because Protestantism is an essential part of Americanism; without it America could never have been created and without it she cannot go forward.

6. Margaret Sanger Seeks Pity for Teenage Mothers and Abstinent Couples, 1928

Thousands of letters are sent to me every year by mothers in all parts of the United States and Canada.

All of them voice desperate appeals for deliverance from the bondage of enforced maternity.

The present volume is made up of the confessions of these enslaved mothers....

It is my conviction that the publication of these profoundly human documents will do more toward the alleviation of the poignant miseries attested to than any other immediate step....

At times I have been discouraged and disheartened by the deliberate misrepresentation of the Birth Control movement by the opponents, and by the crude tactics used to combat it. But at such moments invariably comes back into my mind the vision of the enslaved and supplicant mothers of America. I hear the low moan of their cry for deliverance—a vision ever renewed in my imagination by the perusal of these letters. Painful as they are, they release fresh resources of energy and determination. They give me the courage to continue the battle....

One great student of the problem of reproduction has declared that mankind goes on bearing its young as it did in the Stone Age. Primitive man, alas, may have gone about this important racial business with crudity and brutality. But he was not confronted in addition with the problems of congenital defect, of weak bodies unfit to carry on the race. In a certain number of the records here presented, we discover women not only enslaved by poverty and instinct, but cruelly smitten by hereditary diseases and physiological defects—which they wish to avoid transmitting to their children....

... It is an easy gesture to point to the millions of dollars expended annually upon charities and philanthropies, to repeat the current platitudes concerning our national prosperity and the well-being of the working classes. The fact remains, as the testimony I herewith present proves, that here in our own country we are countenancing a type of slavery that is a disgrace to American ideals and that constitution which guarantees to every citizen the right to life, liberty and the pursuit of happiness....

One

I was married at the age of twelve years. One month before my thirteenth birthday I became the mother of my first child, and now at the age of thirty I am the mother of eleven children, ten of them living, the youngest now seven months old. My health has been poor the past two years now and I don't believe I could ever stand it to have any more. Please won't you send me information so I won't have to have more children, for we have more now than we can really take care of....

From Margaret Sanger, *Motherhood in Bondage* (Elmsford, NY, Maxwell Reprint Co., 1956, © 1928), p. xi, xiii, xvii, xviii, 5–6, 27, 328–330. Reprinted by permission of Alexander Sanger, Executor.

Two

The reason I send for information is because I think if any woman needs help I am the one. I am seventeen years old. I married when I was thirteen years old and I am the mother of six children. My first baby was thirteen months old when another one was born, then ten months after that I had twins and ten months later another set of twins. Now I am to have some more. My husband gets awful cross with me when I get this way, because, like you say in your book, he thinks we have got plenty. It is also wearing me down. I never feel well....

Three

I am a woman and I have eight children. I am twenty-nine years old. I feel as I am fifty-nine. My baby is eleven months and fourteen days. I never go over a year before I'm pregnant again, so please write me a letter at once. I can't attend these eight children that I have and they are not able to do anything for themselves. Lord, what am I to do with any more? I am a poor woman. I can't work far out for I have always got a young baby. My husband only makes $1.00 per day, some days nothing. How can we live—eight children, I and him on $1.00 per day? Please tell me what to do to prevent having any more children. What can I do with those poor miserable children?...

Four

My husband and I have been lovers from babyhood, but were married just before we were thirty. We have five children, beautiful gifted children—two sons, twenty-four years and twenty-two years, three daughters, twenty years, fifteen years and thirteen years old. We lived a normal sex life up to the birth of our fifth child as we had waited so long, living chaste lives up to our marriage and I did so appreciate his coming to me pure after twelve years of separation (he travelling with an invalid mother.) I felt nothing was too much to do for him.

When the babies came one after another and we were so very poor it did not seem right for intelligent people to live thus. The last birth nearly caused my death and my doctor said that "this must not happen again." Meantime I had contracted T.B. and nearly died with hemorrhages and heart trouble but begged to live to raise and educate my children. Finally when the baby was two weeks old and the nurse left, my husband and I agreed to try to forget our sex relation until my "change of life" was complete, for the children's sake. It was easy to adjust at first, as we were both very miserable and tired, poor and had to work so hard. Baby was frail after five months nursing poisonous milk from a T.B. mother.

So time went on (we occupying bedrooms in different parts of the house and trying to avoid anything that would stimulate passion). Meantime we have both gotten well. We have sent the two boys through school and both are university graduates, the oldest girl is attending university and the other two are in high school, so you see our self-denial has reacted beneficially for the children.

But the last two years and especially the last six months, my husband has been begging me to live in the sweet old way and I want to but I'm afraid.

The relations between myself and my husband became so strained a year ago I consulted our family physician but he said I would be more susceptible than ever now after this long separation. He said at this time in my life with my weak heart, another birth would certainly finish the story. I have had to tell the three older children what the trouble was, as they have noticed their father's apathy for me (for it has almost reached that) and I am afraid my own heart will turn if relief does not come soon, as I can hardly endure the indifferent ways he shows after all our loving life together from my earliest remembrance.

It is unthinkable that our lives should drift apart after all these years. My two fine sons have always confided in me and I hope may help in the next ten years to get some legislation that will sanction Birth Control without parents having to go on indefinitely bearing children whom they cannot educate or else living the strenuous, heart-breaking, nerve-racking prohibition of love-life that we have been through.

It was the only way we knew, and we have borne it through thirteen years but the end is not yet. There has absolutely been no sex relief in all those years for either of us. Can you please help us before our hearts drift too far apart?...

7. The Automobile Comes to Middletown, U.S.A., 1929

The first real automobile appeared in Middletown in 1900. About 1906 it was estimated that "there were probably 200 in the city and county." At the close of 1923 there were 6,221 passenger cars in the city, one for every 6.1 persons, or roughly two for every three families.... For some of the workers and some of the business class, use of the automobile is a seasonal matter, but the increase in surfaced roads and in closed cars is rapidly making the car a year-round tool for leisure-time as well as getting-a-living activities. As, at the turn of the century, business class people began to feel apologetic if they did not have a telephone, so ownership of an automobile has now reached the point of being an accepted essential of normal living....

Group-sanctioned values were disturbed by the inroads of the automobile upon the family budget. A case in point is the not uncommon practice of mortgaging a home to buy an automobile. Data on automobile ownership were secured from 123 working class families. Of these, sixty have cars. Forty-one of the sixty own their homes. Twenty-six of these forty-one families have mortgages on their homes....

Many families feel that an automobile is justified as an agency holding the family group together. "I never feel as close to my family as when we are all together in the car," said one business class mother, and one or two spoke of giving up Country Club membership or other recreations to get a car for this reason. "We don't spend anything on recreation except for the car. We save every place we can and put the money into the car. It keeps the family together," was an opinion voiced more than once. Sixty-one per cent of 337 boys and 60 per cent of 423 girls in the three upper years of the high school say that they motor more often with their parents than without them.

But this centralizing tendency of the automobile may be only a passing phase; sets in the other direction are almost equally prominent. "Our daughters [eighteen and fifteen] don't use our car much because they are always with somebody else in their car when we go out motoring," lamented one business class mother. And another said, "The two older children [eighteen and sixteen] never go out when the family motors. They always have something else on." "In the nineties we were all much more together," said another wife. "People brought chairs and cushions out of the house and sat on the lawn evenings. We rolled out a strip of carpet and put cushions on the porch step to take care of the unlimited overflow of neighbors that dropped by. We'd sit out so all evening. The younger couples perhaps would wander off for half an hour to get a soda but come back to join in the informal singing or listen while somebody strummed a mandolin or guitar." "What on earth *do* you want me to do? Just sit around home all evening!" retorted a popular high school girl of today when her father discouraged her going out motoring for the evening with a young blade in a rakish car waiting at the curb. The fact that 348 boys and 382 girls in the three upper years of the high school placed "use of automobile" fifth and fourth respectively in a list of twelve possible sources of disagreement between them and their parents suggests that this may be an increasing decentralizing agent.…

8. Langston Hughes: Poet of the 1920s Harlem Renaissance

ONE-WAY TICKET

I pick up my life
And take it with me
And I put it down in
Chicago, Detroit,
Buffalo, Scranton,
Any place that is
North and East—
And not Dixie.

I pick up my life
And take it on the train
To Los Angeles, Bakersfield,
Seattle, Oakland, Salt Lake,
Any place that is

"One Way Ticket" from *The Collected Poems of Langston Hughes.* Copyright © 1994 by the Estate of Langston Hughes. Used by permission of Alfred A. Knopf, a division of Random House, Inc.

North and West—
And not South.

I am fed up
With Jim Crow laws,
People who are cruel
And afraid,
Who lynch and run,
Who are scared of me
And me of them.

I pick up my life
And take it away
On a one-way ticket—
Gone up North,
Gone out West,
Gone!

9. Young Women Discuss Petting, 1930

The girl who has been brought up to believe that petting, smoking and drinking are wrong, but sees one or all of these things done by many of her friends, is doubtful as to what course she shall pursue. Shall she cleave to parental ideals or transfer her allegiance to her own age-group? The following letters from a newspaper advice column indicate how puzzling this question may become.

I've had a feeling that I never intended going out with everyone who cared to take me out, or I never wanted to be kissed by anyone except the one I would some day marry.... When I entered high school the rest of my girl friends went out with different boys, but I refused.... Now in the office the girls are the same as the ones I knew in high school. They do not think it is wrong to smoke and pet. I myself would never think of doing either, but I want you to understand that I would not look down on those girls, for all they do is their own personal affair.

Sometimes I get the blues so badly that if anyone were there I would do what the rest of my friends do, but, thank goodness, there is something that seems to hold me back.... Am I doing right, or have I been in a trance for twenty-one years?

My girl friend and I don't pet, smoke or drink. The fellows go out with me once. Is it because I don't pet? I hate to kiss any fellows. Why is it? My girl friends do.... My girl friends have boy friends, but not me. Where can I find

Phyllis Blanchard and Carlyn Manasses, *New Girls for Old* (New York: Macaulay Co., 1930), 62–66, 69–71.

one? ... I am only eighteen. Shall I wait, or shall I go out and pet every fellow I know? What shall I do?

I am not popular. Is it because I won't neck and pet? When the boys ask me for dates I very seldom go, but if I do it ends up by the person I am with being slapped. Then we don't speak for months at a time. I have told these boys again and again I don't care to be necked. Still they insist on having the same thing over every time we go out. The crowd I go with all say I am a "flat tire" because I won't neck.... Please tell me what to do....

That these girls should sufficiently need the help of another person to seek the impersonal advice of the newspaper columnist is an indication of how impossible they find it to settle the conflicts aroused by the clash between the old and new manners.... [W]e sent out questionnaires to a group of college and working girls, inquiring as to their attitudes on these various subject. Altogether we received 252 replies, from girls and young women between the ages of fifteen and twenty-six, nearly three-fourths being between eighteen and twenty-three years old. With the exception of a few young married women, the replies were about equally divided between the school and working groups.

Surprisingly enough, the replies indicated considerable disapproval of petting, for only twenty-three per cent of the girls accepted this as a routine part of their relationships with boys, and only eighteen per cent thought it necessary to insure popularity....

... [V]ery many girls draw a distinct line between the exploratory activities of the petting party and complete yielding of sexual favors to men. In the group of girls who answered our questionnaires, for instance, although twenty-three per cent placed no restrictions upon petting, only seven per cent were willing to permit themselves indulgence in extra-marital intercourse. Ninety-two per cent definitely classed extra-marital sex relations as immoral or unwise....

Nevertheless, many of the girls have advanced in their thinking so far beyond their early training as to draw a distinct line between promiscuity and premarital intercourse with the man they expect to marry. "Where one's love is deep and one's motives high, marriage is a mere form that does not deeply matter." "I have lost my virginity to the man I love and expect to marry." "I disapprove of promiscuous relations on moral grounds; not, however, between a man and woman in love." These are typical remarks. The code which the girls have worked out for themselves declares that sexual intercourse without marriage can safely be indulged in when it is a prelude to the more permanent arrangement of matrimony. Promiscuity is clearly differentiated, and largely condemned as "cheap" and "common."

ESSAYS

Like most periods characterized by rapid cultural change, the twenties are a bundle of contradictions. Paula S. Fass of the University of California, Berkeley, examines the social behavior of college youth in the 1920s, who, she asserts, changed gender roles and relationships between men and women. They invented "dating" (court-ship not tied to marriage), "petting" (erotic interactions not tied to intercourse), and provocative fashions not expected to provoke outrage (the short skirt). The author looks at the range of behaviors that young people redefined as socially acceptable, from petting to smoking to drinking. What gave college youth this much power and influence? In the second essay, Edward J. Larson of the University of Georgia places the Scopes trial—too easily caricatured as a clash between backward yokels and sophisticated city slickers—in the context of the struggle to reconcile science with faith. The term "fundamentalism" was coined in the 1920s to symbolize the fight against theological liberalism and the "updating" (or diluting) of the old-time religion in view of new scientific information. Both Fass and Larson look at phe-nomena linked to schools: textbook controversies and the attitudes of college under-graduates. Why did education emerge as a battleground? The State of Tennessee won its battle against teacher John Scopes, but who won the culture war?

Sex and Youth in the Jazz Age

PAULA S. FASS

"Most of 'em pet. I guess."
"All the pretty ones."
"Some do one night and don't the next—goddam funny."
"ALL of 'em pet. Good women. Poor women. All of 'em."
"If a girl doesn't pet, a man can figure he didn't rush 'er right."

Lynn Montross and Lois Montross, Town and Gown (1923)

Students of modern sexual behavior have quite correctly described the twenties as a turning point, a critical juncture between the strict double standard of the age of Victoria and the permissive sexuality of the age of Freud. Too often, however, the sexual revolution of the twenties has been described exclusively in terms of scat-tered data suggesting an increase in premarital sexual intercourse on the part of women. One is tempted to picture investigators hunting for that special morning between 1919 and 1929 when 51% of the young unmarried women in America awoke to find that they were no longer virgins. Instead, of course, investigators are forced to deduce revolutionary changes from small, though important, increases in what remained a minority pattern of behavior. This kind of thinking, not unlike the Victorian concept of all or nothing, overlooks the fact that changes in sexual habits, as in most other areas of social relations, are evolutionary....

College youth of the 1920's redefined the relationship between men and women. In good part this resulted from a simple rediscovery—love is erotic. The remainder drew on an old assumption—that the goal of relations between men and women was marriage. Together the new insight and the old tradition resulted

Paula S. Fass, *The Damned and the Beautiful: American Youth in the 1920s* (New York: Oxford University Press, 1977). Excerpts from Ch. 6, pp. 260–68, 271–72. Copyright © 1977 by Oxford University Press. Used by permission of Oxford University Press, Inc.

in a significant restructuring of premarital forms of sexual behavior as relationships were charged by a new sexual dynamism and a vigorous experimentalism. Sex for middle-class youths of the 1920's had become a significant premarital experience, but it continued to be distinctly marriage-oriented and confined by stringent etiquettes and sharply etched definitions. In the process of defining their future roles in the new society and within the context of already potent changes, the young helped to create the sexual manners of the twentieth century....

Dating was something definitely new in the ritual of sexual interaction. It was unlike the informal get-togethers that characterized youth socializing in the village or small town of the nineteenth century, for at such events there was no pairing early in an acquaintance. It was also unlike courting, which implied a commitment between two people. Dating permitted a paired relationship without implying a commitment to marriage and encouraged experimental relations with numerous partners. Dating emerged in response to a modern environment in which people met casually and irregularly, and in response to new kinds of recreations like movies, dance halls, and restaurants, where pairing was the most convenient form of boy-girl relation. Moreover, it developed as youths were increasingly freed from the direct supervision of family and community and allowed the freedom to develop private, intimate, and isolated associations. Dating opened the way for experimentation in mate compatibility. The lack of commitment permitted close and intimate associations and explorations of personality, and isolation and privacy laid the ground for sexual experimentation, both as a means for testing future compatibility and as an outlet for present sexual energies.

With the isolation of relations, the young were forced to rely on their own judgment in determining the degree and limits of permissible eroticism. It was this latitude for self-determination that produced the haunting fear of sexual promiscuity in the jeremiads of the twenties. The fear was unfounded. The young were thrown back on their own resources, but they were not free, either from the influence of childhood training or, more immediately, from the controls and sanctions of their peers. Basing their actions on an unyielding taboo against sexual intercourse and an elaborate network of peer norms and standards, they proceeded to open up the possibilities of sexual play without overstepping the bounds of family prohibition and peer propriety. After investigating female conduct in the late twenties, Phyllis Blanchard and Carlyn Manasses [above] concluded that "very many girls draw a distinct line between the exploratory activities of the petting party and complete yielding of sexual favors to men." In the behavior of young men and women in the twenties, this charting of distinctions was as important as the exploration. The two ran a parallel course, for the young experimented with eroticism within a clear sense of limits, thus tasting a little of the fruit and enjoying the naughtiness of their bravery without seriously endangering the crop.

"Petting" described a broad range of potentially erotic physical contacts, from a casual kiss to more intimate caresses and physical fondling. Even such limited eroticism would have automatically defined a woman as loose and disreputable in the nineteenth century. To the Victorians, who divided good women from bad, revered ideal purity, and were suspicious of female sexuality, all forms of eroticism on the part of women could be equated with total submission. Even in the twenties, it was not unknown for reformers to introduce legislation that would prohibit petting and define it along with fornication as illegal as well as immoral. But the young drew distinct boundaries between what was acceptable erotic behavior and what was not. Petting was the means to be safe and yet not sorry, and around this form of sexual activity they elaborated a code of permissible eroticism.... A casual first date might thus entail a good-night kiss, but greater intimacies and a certain amount of erotic play were permitted and expected of engaged couples. "Erotic play," as Ira Wile rightfully observed, had "become an end rather than a means," and the strong "distinctions made in petting recognize that erotic activity may or may not have coitus as a goal." The young first sanctioned eroticism and then imposed degrees and standards of acceptability....

Dating and petting were, moreover, distinctly marriage-oriented in the twenties. Since mating was one of the chief aims of both rituals, immediate sexual satisfactions had to be carefully weighed in view of long-term goals. And while virginity in a bride was no longer an absolute prerequisite for most men, it was still considered desirable. For men, female chastity appears to have taken a back seat to considerations of compatibility, but there was still some ambiguity on this point, and the devaluation of virginity in the bride was probably related to a growing acceptance of intercourse among engaged couples rather than to a tolerance of casual promiscuity. Women too continued to display considerable anxiety about the consequences of lost virginity. These multiple ambivalences reinforced the sense of acceptable limitations on sexual indulgence.

For most youths, this meant an acceptance of eroticism with very clear limits of permissible expression. Petting established a norm that deviated from that of the family but was still not antagonistic to its basic taboo. The majority could pet because it filled the need for response in a specific relationship, and in filling that need they believed they had the security of peer-group opinion. Of course, many ambivalences remained. But by the 1930's these sexual definitions had congealed into a dependable norm, a norm which, in the words of one investigation, provided ample room for "spontaneous demonstrations of affection." In their study of sexual behavior on the thirties campus, Dorothy Bromley and Florence Britten discovered that the fact "that a girl should feel she can give within limits or permit exploratory intimacies without compromising her essential virginity is one of the phenomena of the contemporary younger generation's mores." During the twenties, peer pressure to pet was still strong, and behavior patterns were, as a result, less stable, more inhibiting, altogether more full of anxieties. Probably many youths petted less to express personal needs than to conform to group standards and to demonstrate what Ernest Burgess called "the outstanding attitude of modern youth"—their "self-consciousness and sophistication about sex."...

Not surprisingly, the new attention to sexuality colored a whole range of related behavior. Language became more candid and conversations more frank as the fact of freer association between the sexes was accompanied by a basic commitment to freedom of expression. As women became companions to men in work and play, it was easier to see them as "pals" and partners, and the informal access between the sexes radically affected ideas of *de facto* equality and the manners that reflected that equality. At the same time, this access encouraged a pronounced attention to sexual attractiveness and to the cultivation of styles that operated on a purely sexual level.

What is at first glance enigmatic in the fashions and manners of young women in the twenties—the apparent conflict between those modes that emphasized her boyish characteristics, her gamin quality, and those that consciously heightened her sexual piquancy—must be understood in terms of the two distinct but related consequences of this new access between the sexes. They express not conflict but a well-poised tension between the informal boyish companion and the purposefully erotic vamp. They served at once a symbolic and a functional role in the new variety of relationships between the sexes. Bobbed hair, for example, which was the prevailing style for women on all campuses, was enthusiastically defended on the grounds that it was carefree and less troublesome to care for than the long ponderous mane, which was *de rigueur* in the prewar period. It facilitated indulgence in ad-hoc and informal activities like sports and made it easier for women to remain well-groomed during an increasingly busy campus or work day. It was indeed liberating, as it emphasized the woman's more informal existence and behavior. It allowed her to feel equal with men and unencumbered by a traditional symbol of her different role.

At the same time, the short hair was carefully marcelled, a process that occasioned no end of campus humor. The well-sculpted head was, in fact, in the context of the twenties, more self-consciously erotic than fluffy long hair that was girlish and young. Long hair was often inimical to real sexual allure because it was necessary to wear it carefully tied in a bun or chignon. Hair worn loose had for a long time been restricted to very young girls. Older girls, forced to compose it because it was improper to wear hair so informally and because it was unmanageable in an active day, often appeared staid and sedate. Short hair, on the other hand, could be worn freely and the possibility of prudish compactness averted. Bobbed hair was often attacked as a symbol of female promiscuity, of explicit sexuality, and of a self-conscious denial of respectability and the domestic ideal. Once we suspend absolute definitions of sexual attractiveness, we can begin to see the sexuality implicit in bobbed hair in the context of the period. It was not mannish but liberating, and that liberation implied a renunciation of sexual stereotypes....

Short skirts, which became increasingly abbreviated as the decade progressed, were defined on the same grounds of comfort and practicality. Again, women could feel less encumbered and freer to engage in all the purportedly male activities. But the provocation of bared calves and knees was not overlooked. One outraged observer, a divinity student at Duke University, was so repelled by the bared knees of coeds that he was provoked to write a disgusted letter to the school paper. What really offended him, more even than the fashion, was the women's manipulation of the fashions. The coed, he observed, "would look every now and then to assure herself that they [her knees] were exposed to the nth degree."...

... To accompany the trend in skirt lengths and form-revealing silhouettes, there was a keen calorie-consciousness among young women. Dieting became so popular that newspapers often cited the calorie value of foods and gave nutritional advice about the amount of food intake that would help to sustain or shed weight. Young women were conscious of the new vamp silhouette and sought to imitate the lean, honed-down proportions of the movie queens....

Cosmetics were used to increase attractiveness, but they were more than that—they were provocative. The use of cosmetics symbolized the woman's open acceptance of her own sexuality. Whatever the long history of cosmetics and their general use, the reference point for women in the twenties was not ancient Egypt or India but the America of the late nineteenth and early twentieth centuries. And by the mores of that period, cosmetics were immoral. They were associated with prostitutes. By appropriating the right to use such sexual aids, respectable women proclaimed that they too were endowed with a sexual personality. They had taken on themselves as potential wives all the characteristics of lovers. The two kinds of women were no longer separate and distinguishable at first glance but one and the same.

Young women did not generally abuse their new-found cosmetic allies. They used powder, rouge, and lip color in moderation with an eye to increasing allure without offending propriety. The moderate use was in conformity with the standards and expectations of their peers, who had incorporated cosmetics as a permissible part of fashion. That the peer group that encouraged the use of cosmetics also limited its over-indulgence was lost on adults. The adult world, its eyes still fixed on an older standard, stood aghast. But among the young the moderate use of cosmetics was encouraged and recognized for what it was, an attempt to increase physical attractiveness and to score points in the game of rating within the rules set by the peer group....

So too, the male "line" was a conscious extension of the cultivated attention to sexual manners. A line was a well-rehearsed and oft-repeated set of phrases used by men when introduced to women. The line was a mark of sophistication, a demonstration of worldliness, a touch of cynicism that made a man more attractive by making him more dangerous. "As for the co-eds," remarked a solicitous Trinity editor, "don't the young sweet things know that the senior law students have a line so long and slippery that it can't be caught?" But it was the very slipperiness that made the line effective. It was a staged ritual, a self-conscious and even a self-protective form of sexual aggression in the new and potentially dangerous sexual explorations in which the young were engaged. It was well known that the line was not spontaneous but used as a staged approach in meeting and cultivating female company. It identified a man as experienced, so the approval of the line reflected the desirability of "experience" in meeting respectable women. A man without a line was an innocent, basically not savvy in the ways of the world. Like a woman without her cosmetics, a man without his line went out naked into the frightening wilderness of a newly sexual world. With its barely veiled sexual naughtiness, the line pointed up the ways in which conscious sexuality had been incorporated into the rituals of attack and protection that governed male and female interaction....

Smoking was perhaps the one most potent symbol of young woman's testing of the elbow room provided by her new sense of freedom and equality. Prostitutes and women in liberated bohemian and intellectual sets had been known to flaunt their cigarettes publicly and privately before the twenties. But in respectable middle-class circles, and especially among young women, smoking, like rouging, was simply not done. Throughout the twenties, smoking could still provoke heated commentary, and for many young women, to smoke in public was a welcome form of notoriety. Although young women in college did not initiate the smoking habit, they increasingly took advantage of the cigarette as a symbol of liberation and as a means of proclaiming their equal rights with men. More importantly, within the college community they had the support of peer-group opinion. Among the young, smoking for women became widely accepted during the twenties, and while smoking remained an issue, as the decade wore on it became an acceptable and familiar habit among college women.

Smoking is not a sexual activity in itself. In the abstract, it is morally neutral. In the context of the specific values of American society, however, it was both morally value-laden and sexually related. Like cosmetics, smoking was sexually suggestive and associated with disreputable women or with bohemian types who self-consciously rejected traditional standards of propriety and morality. College administrators objected to smoking because it undermined an ideal of proper female behavior and decency. As the Dean of Women at Ohio State University noted, smoking was simply not "done in the best circles," and it was, in the words of the Dean of Rhode Island Slate College, "an unladylike act."...

Women and men on the campuses of the twenties proclaimed that women had a right to smoke if they pleased: "If a man can enjoy his coke more by smoking as he drinks it, why isn't it logical to assume that a woman can enjoy hers more when it is accompanied by a cigarette?" asked one woman correspondent at Illinois. "Why shouldn't a woman have a taste for cigarettes just as a man has? It is not the smoking that breaks down the bonds of convention between men and women ... a woman can command just as much respect with a cigarette in her mouth as without." At New York University women claimed their rights by announcing that they would hold a smoker rather than a traditional tea. The Dean was outraged and prohibited the event, but the women went ahead with their plans anyway. Blanchard and Manasses found that 80% of the young women they questioned approved of smoking for women. In marked contrast, only 26% of the parents approved....

In the twenties, young men and women danced whenever the opportunity presented itself. Unquestionably the most popular social pastime, dancing was, of all potentially questionable and morally related behaviors, the least disreputable in the view of the young. For most youths dancing was not even questionable but a thoroughly respectable and almost compulsory form of socializing. Even at denominational schools, where dancing continued to be regarded as morally risky by officials, students clamored for a relaxation of the older bans as they asked officials to give up outdated "prejudiced feelings" and respond to "the bending of current public opinion." A dance was an occasion. It was a meeting ground between young men and women. It was a pleasurable recreation. But above all it was a craze.

The dancers were close, the steps were fast, and the music was jazz. And because popular forms of dancing were intimate and contorting, and the music was rhythmic and throbbing, it called down upon itself all the venom of offended respectability. Administrative officials as well as women's clubs and city fathers found the dancing provocative and indecent and tried at least to stop the young from engaging in its most egregious forms, if not from the dances entirely. But the young kept on dancing.

They started during the war years, and they danced through the decade. Dancing would leave its stamp on the twenties forever, and jazz would become the lingering symbol for an era. But whatever its symbolic value during the twenties and thereafter, dancing and jazz were forms of recreation, even a means of peer-group communication, that youth appropriated to itself....

Drinking for youth in the twenties was unlike sex, smoking, or dancing, because the young labored under a specific legal ordinance forbidding alcoholic indulgence of any kind. Prohibition was an anomaly in an age of increasing freedoms. Students had been permitted to drink at least off-campus before the passage of the Eighteenth Amendment and the Volstead Act, and beer drinking had been a regular form of celebration and socializing among male students. Prohibition cut off a former freedom. Moreover, unlike the other moral issues of the twenties, drinking was a male-centered problem that secondarily involved women. Drinking had always been a male prerogative. Respectable women were effectively barred from indulgence by tradition. Drinking among youths during the twenties therefore involved a number of distinct issues: the attitude toward the moral code, the attitude toward the law, and the question of female roles....

It is difficult to determine how many students actually drank during the twenties and what the significance of their behavior was. By the end of the decade, the polls of the Congressional Hearing on the Repeal of the Prohibition Amendment presented overwhelming evidence that men and women students drank in a proportion close to two drinkers to every non-drinker. This was the case in all parts of the nation.... Of the total number of ballots cast in the nationwide congressional poll, 29,794 in all, only 34% of the students claimed not to be drinkers. By 1930, at least, drinking appears to have been very common among the majority of all students.

Coming to the end of the decade, the Congressional survey reflected the campus situation when anti-Prohibition sentiment had reached a peak. But the college newspapers suggest that there were changes over the course of the decade in the amount and style of drinking. Drinking among the young appears to have been greatest at the very beginning and again in the second half of the twenties. There was a short period between 1921 and 1924 when the amount of drinking was kept to a minimum, the result of initial attempts by the young spurred on by the administration to control drinking, especially at official university parties and at fraternity dances. At this time, the papers, after important events like proms and homecomings, were filled with self-congratulations on the commendable way in which the students were controlling the drinking problem and enforcing the national and school anti-drinking laws. In 1921, the

Cornell Sun, for example, which noted that the previous year had been especially wet, observed, "The low point has been passed in regard to the liquor situation, and the upward swing is beginning. All evidence, at least, points to a slowly growing public sentiment against drinking at dances—which is the crux of the whole matter. The parties in the last three or four weeks have had a different tone from those of a year ago." Even homecomings, usually the wettest weekends of the year because returning alumni brought liquor in abundance, were reported to be relatively dry. At Madison, Wisconsin, as at most schools, there was reported to be "a determined effort ... to stamp out drinking." In the second half of the decade, however, there was a marked increase in the agitation for repeal or modification of Prohibition and a general decrease in the commitment with which the now formal injunctions against drinking were issued. This happened first at the Eastern schools, which appear to have had a shorter dry spell, and gradually affected the Midwest.

In the early period, some editors observed that Prohibition needed time to prove its efficacy and that slowly the public would be educated toward a self-imposed abstinence. On this assumption, students were urged to give Prohibition a chance. But most arguments supporting Prohibition were based on the law rather than on the social or moral objection to drinking. The injunction that the law should be obeyed was a constant aspect of the formally expressed attitudes toward drinking. This remained true throughout the decade. At Cornell, where editorial comment was consistently hostile to Prohibition and to all attempts to impose morality, the editor of the *Sun* nevertheless maintained that in respect to the law, there was but one answer, "to enforce the law ... it is one thing for a citizen of the United States to be in doubt on the question of prohibition and it is another for him to be in doubt on the question of the dignity and power of the Constitution."...

At the same time, students were openly contemptuous of the kind of moral reformers who had succeeded in passing Prohibition. Self-righteous moralists trying to impose their own standards on everyone were the butt of derision. The *Daily Princetonian* struck just the right tone of contempt: "If the projects of the crusaders for virtue and purity are realized ... once more the tottering world and western civilization will be made safe for unsullied virgins and old ladies above sixty. The absurdity of such efforts is second only to the presumption with which they are undertaken by ... certain self-styled upholders of public morals.... To presume that one can define decency or legislate virtue is folly."...

These two very distinct and clearly articulated attitudes—the strong sentiment supporting the law and the hostility toward the idea of Prohibition—were accompanied by a less clearly enunciated ethic that made drinking an unofficially sanctioned peer activity. The editorials reflected this view. While always serious when denouncing law-breaking, editors were rarely serious about drinking. Usually drinking and Prohibition were fair game for humor and "smartness." The informal approval demonstrated by making Prohibition a joke cannot possibly have done other than undercut the effectiveness of the formal injunctions to obey the law contained in the very same papers. In this sense the spirit of Prohibition, if not the letter of the law, was officially denied. Drinking jokes were a staple of the humor columns and, more insidiously, of the side comments of the purportedly serious editorial columns. Even when intending to scold, editorials came off as shoulder-shrugging at the antics of college youths....

In the early twenties, there was a clear code of limitations on drinking that reflected traditional attitudes toward propriety in drinking. Thus, drinking at athletic events and with other men was permissible, but drinking at dances and in the presence of women was not. When editors denounced drinking with alumni or at athletic events, for example, they usually invoked the law rather than the moral code. But the same editors were disturbed by drinking at dances, where it was believed to be improper because it was public and in the presence of women. The *Cornell Sun* called such drinking "an offense to good manners and against decency," and the *Sun* noted that while there was never a time in Cornell history when students did not drink, "there are times, when it is considered bad manners." So too, at the University of Wisconsin 2000 women students signed a pledge to boycott any social function where men were under the influence of liquor. The action reflected the prevailing ethic that drinking in the presence of women was improper.

The code also drew a fundamental distinction between drinking and drunkenness. In 1921, the editor of the *Daily Illini* noted that "The number of persons who object to an individual taking a drink of intoxicating liquor is probably in the minority," but that the student public strenuously objected to drinking to the point of intoxication. The editor concluded his message by advising that drinking "must not become open or offensive to student society." When the young drank according to these self-limiting rules, they were, in effect, conforming to the traditional standard of adult society that operated in the days before the Prohibition law went into effect.

During the twenties, however, the young increasingly deviated from these unofficial codes of conduct. There was a subterranean ethic developing that worked counter to these self-limiting rules. In this ethic, one drank to become drunk or, failing that, to appear drunk. Thus the *Cornell Sun* noted that where once it had been the aim to see how much one could drink without appearing drunk, it had now become part of "the game" to get as drunk as possible on whatever drink was available and to see who "can get the Greatest Publicity while in a state of Pseudo Ginification." "Contrary to the rabid assertions of matronly sewing circles and pessimistic male reformers," the *Dartmouth* declared, "the college student of today is sober ninety-nine one hundredths of the time. When he does drink, it is usually to parade his drunkenness—at a football game, at a dance, during a vacation, at a social gathering—and it is on such occasions that a shocked older generation is most liable to see youth in action." In addition, one drank in the company and together with women. It was not until the middle of the decade when this new ethic began to jell that drinking among women became an issue. Before then it was considered a strictly male-centered problem. Drinking at dances, with women, and to excess had become, by the latter twenties, a new code of permissible behavior among college students because it was sanctioned by peer opinion.

"Terpsichordian tippling," as the *Cornell Sun* called it, had become commonplace on most campuses and the editor explained quite accurately why this was so. " 'Is it the smart thing to be drunk at a college function?' 'Yes,' reply the undergraduates by their indulgence in liquor consumption at dances, house parties and the like, and by their tolerance of it by others. Right there we believe lies the solution of the drinking problem at colleges in general.... Campus leaders set the style by drinking openly and laughingly approving the drunken actions of fellow students." A similar situation prevailed at Duke, where "a dance among the younger set can hardly be called a success nowadays unless most of the boys get 'high,' not to mention the occasional girl who cannot be outdone by her masculine companions."...

Did the young use sex and morals as a basis for conscious generational revolt? On the whole the answer would appear to be no, although their sexual attitudes and practices did distinguish them from their elders and made them appear rebellious. They welcomed the lingering naughtiness of which they were accused, but more in the spirit of play than with any serious display of anger. As eager capitalists, the young were anything but rebellious in social and political questions. They emphasized style in personal matters and severely demarcated the personal from the social sphere. In so doing they were in the advance guard of twentieth-century American culture.

Fundamentalists Battle Modernism in the Roaring Twenties

EDWARD J. LARSON

Fossil discoveries provided persuasive new evidence for human evolution and as such provoked a response from antievolutionists. Henry Fairfield Osborn threw down the gauntlet in his reply to [William Jennings] Bryan's 1922 plea in the *New York Times* for restrictions on teaching evolution. Bryan had argued that "neither Darwin nor his supporters have been able to find a fact in the universe to support their hypothesis," prompting Osborn to cite "the Piltdown man" and other recent hominid fossil finds. "All this evidence is today within reach of every schoolboy," Osborn wrote. "It will, we are convinced, satisfactorily answer in the negative [Bryan's] question, 'Is it not more rational to believe in the creation of man by separate act of God than to believe in evolution without a particle of evidence?' " Of course, the fact that all this evidence *was* within the reach of every public-school student constituted the nub of Bryan's concern, and Osborn further baited antievolutionists by stressing how it undermined belief in the special creation of humans.

During the years leading up to the Scopes trial, antievolutionists responded to such evidence in various ways....

The culprit, they all agreed, was a form of theological liberalism known as "modernism" that was gaining acceptance within most mainline Protestant

Excerpts from *Summer for the Gods: The Scopes Trial and America's Continuing Debate over Science and Religion* by Edward J. Larson, pp. 31, 33–41, 43, 45, 49–50, 56–58, 60–61, 63–65, 74–75, 83. Copyright © 1997 by Edward J. Larson. Reprinted by permission of Basic Books, a member of Perseus Books, L.L.C.

denominations. Modernists viewed their creed as a means to save Christianity from irrelevancy in the face of recent developments in literary higher criticism and evolutionary thinking in the social sciences. Higher criticism, especially as applied by German theologians, subjected the Bible to the same sort of literary analysis as any other religious text, interpreting its "truths" in light of its historical and cultural context. The new social sciences, particularly psychology and anthropology, assumed that Judaism and Christianity were natural developments in the social evolution of the Hebrew people. Modernists responded to these intellectual developments by viewing God as immanent in history. Conceding human (rather than divine) authorship for scripture and evolutionary development (rather than revelational truth) for Christianity, modernists nevertheless claimed that the Bible represented valid human perceptions of how God acted. Under this view, the precise historical and scientific accuracy of scripture did not matter. Judeo–Christian ethical teachings and individual religious sentiments could still be "true" in a realm beyond the "facts" of history and science. "In belief," the modernist leader Shailer Mathews of the University of Chicago divinity school wrote in 1924, "the use of scientific, historical, and social methods in understanding and applying evangelical Christianity to the needs of living persons, is Modernism."

Conservative Christians drew together across denominational lines to fight for the so-called fundamentals of their traditional faith against the perceived heresy of modernism, and in so doing gave birth to the fundamentalist movement and antievolution crusade. Certainly modernism had made significant inroads within divinity schools and among the clergy of mainline Protestant denominations in the North and West, and fundamentalism represented a legitimate theological effort to counter these advances. Biblical higher criticism and an evolutionary world view, as twin pillars of this opposing creed, stood as logical targets of a conservative counterattack. A purely theological effort, however, rarely incites a mass movement, at least in pluralistic America; much more stirred up fundamentalism—and turned its fury against teaching evolution in public schools.

The First World War played a pivotal role. American intervention, as part of a progressive effort to defeat German militarism and make the world "safe for democracy," was supported by many of the modernists, who revered the nation's wartime leader, Woodrow Wilson, himself a second-generation modernist academic. A passionate champion of peace, William Jennings Bryan opposed this position and in 1915 resigned his post as Wilson's secretary of state in protest over the drift toward war. He spent the next two years criss-crossing the country campaigning against American intervention....

When a horribly brutal war led to an unjust and uneasy peace, the rise of international communism, worldwide labor unrest, and an apparent breakdown of traditional values, the cultural crisis worsened for conservative Christians in the United States. "One indication that many premillennialists were shifting their emphasis—away from just evangelizing, praying, and waiting for the end time, toward more intense concern with retarding [social] degenerative trends—was the role they played in the formation of the first explicitly fundamentalist organization," [historian of religion George M.] Marsden noted. "In the summer of 1918, under the guidance of William B. Riley, a number of leaders in the Bible school and prophetic conference movement conceived of the idea of the World's Christian Fundamentals Association."

During the preceding two decades, Riley had attracted a 3,000-member congregation to his aging Baptist church in downtown Minneapolis through a distinctive combination of conservative dispensational-premillennialist theology and politicized social activism. "When the Church is regarded as the body of God-fearing, righteous-living men, then, it ought to be in politics, and as a powerful influence," he proclaimed in a 1906 book that urged Christians to promote social justice for the urban poor and workers. During the next decade, Riley focused his social activism on outlawing liquor, which he viewed as a key source of urban problems. By the twenties, he turned against teaching evolution in public schools. Later, he concentrated on attacking communism. Following the First World War and flushed with success upon ratification of the Eighteenth Amendment authorizing Prohibition, he was ideally suited to lead premillennialists into the cultural wars of the twenties.

In 1919, Riley welcomed some 6,000 conservative Christians to the World's Christian Fundamentals Association (WCFA) inaugural conference with the warning that their Protestant denominations were "rapidly coming under the leadership of the new infidelity, known as 'modernism.'" One by one, seventeen prominent ministers from across the country—the future high priests of fundamentalism—took the podium to denounce modernism as, in the words of one speakers, "the product of Satan's lie," and to call for a return to biblical fundamentals in church and culture. "It is ours to stand by our guns," Riley proclaimed in closing the conference. "God forbid that we should fail him in the hour when the battle is heavy." Participants then returned to their separate denominations, ready to battle the modernists.... Indeed, it was during the ensuing intradenominational strife within the Northern Baptist Convention that conservative leader Curtis Lee Laws coined the word *fundamentalist* to identify those willing "to do battle royal for the Fundamentals." Use of the term quickly spread to include all conservative Christians militantly opposed to modernism....

Bryan's crusade against teaching evolution capped a remarkable thirty-five-year-long career in the public eye. He entered Congress in 1890 as a 30-year-old populist Democratic politician committed to roll back the Republican tariff for the dirt farmers of his native Nebraska. His charismatic speaking ability and youthful enthusiasm quickly earned him the nickname The Boy Orator of the Platte. Bryan's greatest speech occurred at the 1896 Democratic National Convention, where he defied his party's conservative incumbent president, Grover Cleveland, and the eastern establishment that dominated both political parties by demanding an alternative silver-based currency to help debtors cope with the crippling deflation caused by exclusive reliance on limited gold-backed money. Using a potent mix of radical majoritarian arguments and traditional religious oratory, he demanded, "You shall not press down upon the brow of labor this crown of thorns, you shall not crucify mankind upon a cross of gold." The speech electrified the convention and secured the party's presidential nomination for Bryan. For many, he became known as the Great Commoner; for some, the Peerless Leader.

... After helping Woodrow Wilson secure the White House in 1912, Bryan became secretary of state and idealistically (some said naively) set about negotiating a series of international treaties designed to avert war by requiring the arbitration of disputes among nations. This became more of a religious mission than a political task for Bryan, who called on America to "exercise Christian forbearance" in the face of increasing German aggression and vowed, "There will be no war while I am Secretary of State." Of course, he had to resign from office to keep this promise....

Bryan's antievolutionism was compatible with his progressive politics because both supported reform, appealed to majoritarianism, and sprang from his Christian convictions. Bryan alluded to these issues in his first public address dealing with Darwinism, which he composed in 1904 at the height of his political career. From this earliest point, he described Darwinism as "dangerous" for both religious and social reasons. "I object to the Darwinian theory," Bryan said with respect to the religious implications of a naturalistic explanation for human development, "because I fear we shall lose the consciousness of God's presence in our daily life, if we must accept the theory that through all the ages no spiritual force has touched the life of man and shaped the destiny of nations." Turning to the social consequences of the theory, Bryan added, "But there is another objection. The Darwinian theory represents man as reaching his present perfection by the operation of the law of hate—the merciless law by which strong crowd out and kill off the weak."

The Great Commoner was no more willing to defer to ivy tower scientists on this issue than to Wall Street bankers on monetary matters. "I have a right to assume," he declared in this early speech, "a Designer back of the design [in nature]—a Creator back of the creation; and no matter how long you draw out the process of creation; so long as God stands back of it you can not shake my faith in Jehovah." This last comment allowed for an extended geologic history and even for limited theistic evolution; but Bryan dug in his heels regarding the supernatural creation of humans and described it as "one of the test questions with the Christian." Although Bryan regularly delivered this speech on the Chautauqua circuit during the early years of the century, he said little else against Darwinism until the twenties, when he began blaming it for the First World War and an apparent decline in religious faith among educated Americans.

As a devout believer in peace, Bryan could scarcely understand how supposedly Christian nations could engage in such a brutal war until two scholarly books attributed it to misguided Darwinian thinking. In *Headquarters Nights,* the renowned Stanford University zoologist Vernon Kellogg, who went to Europe as a peace worker, recounted his conversations with German military leaders. "Natural selection based on violent and fatal competitive struggle is the gospel of the German intellectuals," he reported, and served as their justification "why, for the good of the world, there should be this war." Whereas Kellogg used this evidence to promote his own non-Darwinian view of evolutionary development through mutual aid, Bryan saw it as a reason to suppress Darwinian teaching. The philosopher Benjamin Kidd's *The Science of Power* further explored the link between German militarism and Darwinian thinking by examining Darwin's influence on the German philosopher Friedrich Nietzsche. Bryan regularly referred to both books when speaking and writing against teaching evolution....

A third book had an even greater impact on Bryan and touched an even more sensitive nerve. In 1916, the Bryn Mawr University psychologist James H. Leuba published an extensive survey of religious belief among college students and professors. The result confirmed Bryan's worst fears. "The deepest impression left by these records," Leuba concluded, "is that ... Christianity, as a system of belief, has utterly broken down." Among students, Leuba reported, "the proportion of disbelievers in immortality increases considerably from the freshman to the senior year in college." Among scientists, he found disbelief higher among biologists than physicists, and higher among scientists of greater than lesser distinction, such that "the smallest percentage of believers is found among the greatest biologists; they count only 16.9 per cent of believers in God." Leuba did not identify teaching evolution as the cause for this rising tide of disbelief among educated Americans, but Bryan did. "Can Christians be indifferent to such statistics?" Bryan asked in one speech. "What shall it profit a man if he shall gain all the learning of the schools and lose his faith in God?" This became his ultimate justification for the Scopes trial....

The campaign for restrictive legislation spread quickly and all but commandeered the antievolution movement. Fundamentalist leader John Roach Straton began advocating antievolution legislation for his home state of New York in February 1922. J. Frank Norris, pastor of the largest church in the Dallas–Fort Worth area, soon took up the cause in Texas. The evangelist T.T. Martin carried the message throughout the South. By fall 1922, William Bell Riley was offering to debate evolutionists on the issue as he traveled around the nation battling modernism in the church. "The whole country is seething on the evolution question," he reported to Bryan in early 1923. Three years later, these same four ministers became the most prominent church figures to actively support the prosecution of John Scopes....

Individual rights lost out under this political philosophy. "If it is contended that an instructor has a right to teach anything he likes, I reply that the parents who pay the salary have a right to decide what shall be taught," Bryan maintained. "A scientific soviet is attempting to dictate what is taught in our schools," he warned. "It is the smallest, the most impudent, and the most tyrannical oligarchy that ever attempted to exercise arbitrary power." He gave a similarly facile response to charges that antievolution laws infringed on the rights of nonfundamentalist parents and students. Protestants, Catholics, and Jews shared a creationist viewpoint, Bryan believed, and he sought to enlist all of them into his crusade. As for nontheists, he asserted, "The Christians who want to teach religion in their schools furnish the money for denominational institutions. If atheists want to teach atheism, why do they not build their own schools and employ their own teachers?" Such a position assumed that the separation of church and state precluded teaching the Genesis account in public schools. "We do not ask that teachers paid by taxpayers shall teach the Christian religion to students," Bryan told West Virginia lawmakers, "but we do insist that they shall not, under the guise of either science or philosophy, teach evolution as a fact." He apparently expected them to skip the topic of organic origins altogether, or to teach evolution as a hypothesis....

"Fundamentalism drew first blood in Tennessee today," a January 20, 1925 article in the *Commercial Appeal* reported, "in the introduction of a bill in the Legislature by Senator [John A.] Shelton of Savannah to make it a felony to teach evolution in the public schools of the state." A day later, John W. Butler offered similar legislation in the House of Representatives. Both legislators had campaigned on the issue and their actions were predictable. Butler justified his proposal on Bryanesque grounds: "If we are to exist as a nation the principles upon which our Government is founded must not be destroyed, which they surely would be if ... we set the Bible aside as being untrue and put evolution in its place." Butler was a little-known Democratic farmer-legislator and Primitive Baptist lay leader. For him, public schools served to promote citizenship based on biblical concepts of morality. Evolutionary beliefs undermined those concepts. Driven by such reasoning, Butler proposed making it a misdemeanor, punishable by a maximum fine of $500, for a public school teacher "to teach any theory that denies the story of the Divine Creation of man as taught in the Bible, and to teach instead that man had descended from a lower order of animal." Most of Butler's colleagues apparently agreed with this proposal, because six days later the House passed it without any amendments. The vote was seventy-one to five. Although three of the dissenters came from Memphis and one from Nashville, the bill gained the support of both rural and urban representatives, including most delegates from every major city in the state....

Outnumbered Senate opponents of the legislation countered with pleas for individual rights. "It isn't a question of whether you believe in the Book of Genesis, but whether you think the church and state should be kept separate," one senator asserted. "No law can shackle human thought," another declared. A Republican lawmaker quoted passages on religious freedom from the state constitution, and blamed the entire controversy on "that greatest of all disturbers of the political and public life from the last twenty-eight or thirty years, I mean William Jennings Bryan." But a proponent countered, "This bill does not attempt to interfere with religious freedom or dictate the beliefs of any man, for it simply endeavors to carry out the wishes of the great majority of the people." Such sentiments easily carried the Senate.

State and national opponents of antievolution laws appealed to Governor Peay to veto the legislation. Owing to the governor's national reputation as a progressive who championed increased support for public education and a longer school year—efforts that later led to the naming of a college in his honor—those writing from out of state probably entertained some hope for success. Urged on by the California science writer Maynard Shipley and his Science League of America, a new organization formed to oppose antievolutionism, letters of protest poured in from across America. For example, taking the line of Draper and White, a New Yorker asked, "The Middle Ages gave us heretics, witches burnt at the stake, filth and ignorance. Do we want to return to the same?" From within Tennessee, some concerned citizens appealed for a veto. The dean of the state's premiere African-American college, Fisk University, wrote, "As a clergyman and educator, I hope that you will refuse to give your support to the Evolution Bill. It would seem most unfortunate to me should the State of Tennessee legislate against the beliefs of liberal Christianity." The Episcopal bishop of Tennessee added, "I consider such restrictive legislation not only unfortunate but calamitous."

Yet most letters to the governor from Tennesseans supported the measure, and two potentially significant opponents kept silent. The University of Tennessee's powerful president Harcourt A. Morgan, who privately opposed the antievolution bill, held his tongue so long as Peay's proposal for expanding the university still awaited action in the state legislature—and admonished his faculty to do likewise. In a confidential note, he assured the governor, "The subject of Evolution so intricately involves religious belief, which the University has no disposition to dictate, that the University declines to engage in controversy." Only after the legislature adjourned and the new law became the primary subject of ridicule at the annual student parade did the depth of university opposition to it become apparent....

The governor explained his decision to sign the bill in a curious message to the legislature. On one hand, Peay firmly asserted for proponents, "It is the belief of our people and they say in this bill that any theory of man's descent from lower animals,... because a denial of the Bible, shall not be taught in our public schools." On the other hand, he assured opponents that this law "will not put our teachers in any jeopardy." Indeed, even though the most cursory review of Tennessee high school biology textbooks should have shown him otherwise, Peay wrote, "I can find nothing of consequence in the books now being taught in our schools with which this bill will interfere in the slightest manner." Nevertheless, he went on to hail the measure as "a distinct protest against an irreligious tendency to exalt *so-called* science, and deny the Bible in some schools and quarters—a tendency fundamentally wrong and fatally mischievous in its effects on our children, our institutions and our country."

Peay, whose progressivism grew out of his traditional religious beliefs, simply could not accept a conflict between public education and popular religion.... Yet he could not totally ignore the tension between a fundamentalist's fear of modern education and a progressive's faith in it. In his message to the legislature on the antievolution bill, he fell back on Bryan's populist refrain: "The people have a right and must have the right to regulate what is taught in their schools." Trapped between fundamentalism and progressivism, Peay may have viewed majoritarianism as an excuse for the law. Caught in the same bind, Bryan saw it as the law's ultimate justification....

Activists with the American Civil Liberties Union did not dismiss the enactment of the Tennessee law against teaching evolution as an insignificant occurrence in some remote intellectual backwater. More critically, they did not view the antievolution crusade in isolation; if they had, they probably would have ignored it along with countless other laws and movements to advance Protestant culture then prevalent throughout the United States. Prior to the Scopes trial, the ACLU did not display any particular interest in challenging government efforts to protect or promote religious beliefs. To the contrary, Quakers played a major role in founding and financing the organization during the First World War as a vehicle to protect religiously motivated pacifists from compulsory military service. Yet ACLU leaders saw the new Tennessee statute in a different light, one that made it stand out as a threat to freedom and individual liberty in the broader American society.

A fashionable new book of the era, *The Mind in the Making* by James Harvey Robinson of the left-wing New School for Social Research in New York City, captured the reactionary mood of the times as perceived by many of the socially prominent, politically radical New Yorkers who led the ACLU during the early twenties. According to this book, which incorporated an evolutionary view of intellectual and social history, a systematic assault on personal liberty in the United States began during the First World War; various state and local authorities had limited freedom prior to this period, to be sure, but these earlier restrictions represented isolated incidents and could be dealt with accordingly. The war changed everything.

"It is a terrible thing to lead this great and peaceful people into war," President Wilson declared in his 1917 war message to Congress. He then added to the terror of some by warning that "a firm hand of stern repression" would curtail domestic disloyalty during wartime. At Wilson's request, Congress imposed a military draft, enacted an Espionage Act that outlawed both obstructing the recruitment of troops and causing military insubordination, and authorized the immigration service to denaturalize and deport foreign-born radicals. The federal Justice Department broadly construed the Espionage Act to cover statements critical of the war effort, while the postal service revoked mailing privileges for publications it considered to "embarrass or hamper the government in conducting the war."…

Proponents of civil liberties expected conditions to improve after the armistice in 1918, but to them the repression appeared only to intensify. "The war brought with it a burst of unwanted and varied animation…. It was common talk that when the foe, whose criminal lust for power had precipitated the mighty tragedy, should be vanquished, things would 'no longer be the same.'" Robinson wrote, "Never did bitter disappointment follow such high hopes. All the old habits of nationalistic policy reasserted themselves at Versailles…. Then there emerged from the autocracy of the Tsars the dictatorship of the proletariat, and in Hungary and Germany various startling attempts to revolutionize hastily and excessively." From these developments the so-called Red Scare ensued. "War had naturally produced its machinery for dealing with dissenters,… and it was the easiest thing in the world to extend the repression to those who held exceptional or unpopular views, like the Socialists and members of the I.W.W.," Robinson reasoned….

The government reacted swiftly. Most states outlawed the possession or display of either the red flag of communism or the black flag of anarchism. They also enacted the strictly enforced tough new "criminal syndicalism" laws against organized violent or unlawful activities designed to disrupt commercial or governmental activities....

"Well, of course, it was a time of tremendous labor unrest, highlighted by the two general strikes in the steel mills and coal mines. And it was also, and I guess above all, a time of intense radical agitation, brought on by the Russian Revolution," Roger Baldwin later recalled. "So by the time the World War was over we had a new war on our hands—a different one. Then, instead of arresting and persecuting opponents of the war, we were arresting and persecuting friends of Russia." Thus events stood when Baldwin ... reassumed leadership of the National Civil Liberties Bureau. He promptly concluded, as he stated in a memorandum to the executive committee, that the bureau should be "reorganized and enlarged to cope more adequately with the invasions of civil liberties incident to the industrial struggle which had followed the war." Direct action to protect labor unions would replace legal maneuvers on behalf of pacifists as the bureau's principal focus. The bureau assumed a new name to go with its new mission: the American Civil Liberties Union. "The cause we now serve is labor," Baldwin proclaimed at the time, and labor included public school teachers....

Academic freedom had been an ongoing concern of the ACLU from the organization's inception; naturally, it related to free speech, yet the interest ran even deeper. The pacifists who helped form the National Civil Liberties Bureau abhorred wartime efforts to promote patriotism and militarism in the schools. They defended teachers fired for opposing American involvement in the war and fought against efforts to purge the public school curriculum of German influences. After the war, when the ACLU turned its attention to defending unpopular speakers, its efforts widened to include fighting classroom restrictions on unpopular ideas. "The attempts to maintain a uniform orthodox opinion among teachers should be opposed," the ACLU's initial position statement declared. "The attempts of education authorities to inject into public schools and colleges instruction propaganda in the interest of any particular theory of society to the exclusion of others should be opposed."

This statement primarily reflected the ACLU's opposition to school patriotism programs. Building on wartime developments in New York, the Lusk Committee proposed legislation in 1920 to dismiss public school teachers who "advocated, either by word of mouth or in writing, a form of government other than the government of the United States." The ACLU helped persuade New York governor Al Smith to veto this bill in 1921, but Smith's successor signed similar legislation into law a year later. Dozens of other states required public school teachers and college professors to sign loyalty oaths. Powerful patriotic organizations, including the American Legion, lobbied for promoting "Americanism" in the public schools by mandatory patriotic exercises (typically a flag salute) and through classroom use of education materials that praised the military and disparaged all things "foreign" (often including the international labor movement). Publicity generated by the ACLU forestalled these programs in some places, but an ACLU lawsuit challenging compulsory military training for male students attending the state University of California at Los Angeles failed.

The rise of a militantly anti–Catholic Ku Klux Klan during the early 1920s led to ACLU efforts to protect both Catholic teachers from mass firings in Klan–dominated school districts and the free-speech rights of the Klan in Catholic communities. Repeatedly, the ACLU was drawn into courtrooms over education. Indeed, during the 1920s, it had to go to court to protect its own right to sponsor programs in New York City schools after the local board of education barred all ACLU representatives from "talking in school buildings" under a general regulation requiring classroom speakers to "be loyal to American institutions."…

This approach to education led to a de facto establishment of Christianity within American public schools. About the time of the Scopes trial, for example, the Georgia Supreme Court dismissed a Jewish taxpayer's complaint against Christian religious exercises in public schools with the observation, "The Jew may complain to the court as a taxpayer just exactly when and only when a Christian may complain to the court as taxpayer, *i.e.,* when the Legislature authorizes such reading of the Bible or such instruction in the Christian religion in the public schools as give one Christian sect a preference over others." The Tennessee legislature codified a similar practice in 1915 when it mandated the daily reading of ten Bible verses in public schools but prohibited any comment on the readings. This suggestion that constitutional limits on the establishment of religion simply forbade the government from giving preference to any one church denomination reflected a traditional view of religious freedom that dated at least as far back as the great federalist U.S. Supreme Court justice Joseph Story. By the 1920s, however, an increasing number of liberally educated Americans, including leaders of the ACLU, rejected the idea that public education should promote any particular political, economic, or religious viewpoint—even one broadly defined as democratic, capitalistic, or Christian.…

The ACLU press release offering to challenge the Tennessee law appeared in its entirety on May 4 in the *Chattanooga Times,* which had opposed enactment of the antievolution statute. "We are looking for a Tennessee teacher who is willing to accept our services in testing this law in the courts," the release stated. "Our lawyers think a friendly test case can be arranged without costing a teacher his or her job. Distinguished counsel have volunteered their services. All we need now is a willing client." Pursuing the story, a *Chattanooga Times* reporter inquired whether city schools taught evolution. "That depends on what is meant by evolution. If you have reference to the Darwinian theory, which, I suppose, was aimed at in the law passed by the Tennessee legislature, it is not," the city school superintendent assured the reporter. "It is recognized by all our teachers that this is a debatable theory and, as such, has no place in our curriculum." Earlier, in making similar assurances regarding his schools, the Knoxville superintendent had noted. "Our teachers have a hard enough time teaching the children how to distinguish between plant and animal life." These urban school officials clearly did not want to test the new law, but midway between these cities enterprising civic boosters in Dayton craved some attention for their struggling community, and accepted the ACLU offer. They got more than they bargained for. Powerful social forces converged on Dayton that summer: populist majoritarianism and traditional evangelical faith versus scientific secularism and modern concepts of individual liberty. America would never be the same again— or perhaps it had changed already from the country that had nurtured Bryan and Darrow in its heartland.

FURTHER READING

Paul Avrich, *Sacco and Vanzetti: The Anarchist Background* (1991).

Kathleen M. Blee, *Women of the Klan: Racism and Gender in the 1920s* (1991).

Lendol Calder, *Financing the American Dream: A Cultural History of Consumer Credit* (1995).

Stanley Coben, *Rebellion Against Victorianism: The Impetus for Cultural Change in 1920s America* (1991).

David Gutierrez, *Walls and Mirrors: Mexican Americans, Mexican Immigrants, and the Politics of Ethnicity* (1995).

John Higham, *Strangers in the Land: Patterns of American Nativism* (1963).

George Hutchinson, *The Harlem Renaissance in Black and White* (1995).

David Levering Lewis, *When Harlem Was in Vogue* (1989).

Alan Lichtman, *White Protestant Nation: The Rise of the American Conservative Movement* (2008).

Roland Marchand, *Advertising the American Dream: Making Way for Modernity* (1985).

Joan Shelley Rubin, *The Making of Middlebrow Culture* (1992).

Virginia Scharff, *Taking the Wheel: Women and the Coming of the Motor Age* (1991).

Mark Avery Sutton, *Aimee Semple McPherson and the Resurrection of Christian America* (2007).

Ronald Takaki, *Strangers from a Different Shore: A History of Asian Americans* (1989).

CHAPTER 8

The Depression, the New Deal, and Franklin D. Roosevelt

In the "Dirty Thirties," as sufferers of the Dust Bowl called the decade, it seemed that everything that could go wrong, did go wrong. The stock market crash of 1929, terrifying as it was to investors who saw their shares fall by 40 percent, was only a harbinger of the international economic collapse and natural calamities to come. The run on banks that began in 1930—when panicked depositors tried to withdraw their money—ultimately forced more than five thousand banks to shut their doors. With no government insurance on these deposits, families lost their life savings. Industrial production fell to 20 percent of capacity. Unemployment zoomed to nearly 25 percent in the worst year. The most heavily industrialized cities were the hardest hit. In Chicago, for example, 50 percent of workers in manufacturing lost their jobs. With no money to make mortgage payments, millions lost their homes. Local governments that tried to provide relief quickly exhausted their resources, and some went bankrupt. The federal government, which could have provided broad relief, largely refused to do so, as President Herbert Hoover feared creating a welfare-dependent class. Mismanagement by banks, corporations, and the titans of the stock market—combined with a lack of government oversight—created the fear that capitalism had rotted from within, and the nation with it.

Farmers were the first to feel the coming Depression. Economic stagnation had afflicted agriculture throughout the twenties. To feed the hungry of World War I, farmers had broken the sod of millions of acres of prairie in areas with unreliable rainfall. The end of the war and economic instability in Europe in the twenties lessened the demand for their bountiful crops. A persistent drought beginning in 1932, combined with poor farming practices, left soil exposed. Farmers everywhere saw prices for their products plummet as the Depression deepened, but few were more deeply afflicted than those who inhabited the five states making up the "Dust Bowl" (Oklahoma, Texas, Kansas, Colorado, and New Mexico). Winds caught at the dry, loosened dirt, blowing up storms of topsoil that blacked out the sky, asphyxiated animals, choked children and old people, and swept grit all the way to New York City. Foreclosures on desolated lands stimulated an exodus of desperate, starving families to more fertile areas, particularly California. And where crops still grew, they sometimes rotted on the ground for a lack of buyers. Angry farmers, angry workers, and angry veterans cried out for relief.

Franklin D. Roosevelt came into office prepared to experiment broadly with measures to "fix" some of the most egregious failings of the nation's economic system. The New Deal, as Roosevelt called his programs, aimed at all elements of the crisis, from the stock market on Wall Street to hog markets in Nebraska. The New Deal established the first federal minimum wage, the first government system of unemployment benefits, the first system of old-age pensions (Social Security), the first protections for labor unions, the first regulatory agency for stocks and bonds (the Securities and Exchange Commission), the first government insurance for individual bank deposits (FDIC), and a host of other institutions. Some of the Roosevelt administration's relief programs were fleeting, but many endure today. The New Deal did not end the Depression, which continued until World War II, nor did it eliminate all the social inequities; these had existed long before the thirties and continued after them. But the New Deal did dramatically recast the role of Washington by giving it a responsibility for the general social welfare. "Big government," like big business, was here to stay.

QUESTIONS TO THINK ABOUT

Who was Franklin D. Roosevelt? Was he a compassionate man of the people who salvaged and strengthened the American system, or a political opportunist who irresponsibly expanded the power of government to the detriment of society? What were the strengths and what were the shortcomings of the New Deal?

DOCUMENTS

The documents in this chapter illustrate the various ways in which people experienced the Depression and some of their responses to it. The first document is the song "Brother, Can You Spare a Dime?" Written in 1931, this became a number one radio hit shortly before the election of Franklin Delano Roosevelt. It appeals to fraternal obligations, and expresses disillusionment with industrialization and patriotism. In document 2, President Herbert Hoover warns the American people that too great a federal role in fighting the Depression might destroy the moral character of the nation's citizens and undermine their freedom. In document 3, a woman reporter chronicles the Depression background of the near lynching of the "Scottsboro Boys," nine young Black men falsely accused of raping two white women. Charges against some of the defendants were dropped after seven years of trial and imprisonment, but one was not pardoned until 1976, by Governor George Wallace of Alabama. In document 4, auto manufacturer Henry Ford agrees with President Hoover that "self-help" is the best remedy for unemployment, assuming that private Americans will volunteer to help one another out. In document 5 the editors of *The Nation* scathingly denounce the president's concern for citizens' moral character when many are near starvation. Document 6 is Roosevelt's first inaugural address, which he gave on March 3, 1933. In it he called for government action to put our "national house in order." Critics on both the left and the right criticized the president—some for doing too little, others for doing too much. As document 7 reveals, however, it was not always easy to peg where on the political spectrum some of these opponents fell. One of them was Father Charles Coughlin, an anti-Semitic Catholic priest who used the airwaves first to praise Roosevelt, and then denounce him. Coughlin proposed doing away with the Federal Reserve System, which he said enslaved Americans to bankers. One of Roosevelt's key reforms was the 1935 Social Security Act, designed to provide an old-age pension to all working Americans. But as document 8 shows, the benefits were not evenly distributed, reflecting the authors' belief that widows needed less money than widowers because women could live more easily on a tight budget than men. Document 9 is an excerpt from John Steinbeck's epic novel, *The Grapes of Wrath*. In it, the fictional Joad family is forced to migrate to California, where they learn a hard lesson about being unwelcome in their own country. Steinbeck's novel publicized the plight of the "Okies," landless refugees from Oklahoma and other parts of the Dust Bowl. This excerpt makes plain the limits of neighborly (or brotherly) compassion. It appears to counter the blithe optimism of industrial leaders like Henry Ford.

1. Song of the Depression: "Brother, Can You Spare a Dime?" 1931

They used to tell me I was building a dream, and so I followed the mob,

When there was earth to plow, or guns to bear, I was always there right on the job.

They used to tell me I was building a dream, with peace and glory ahead,

Why should I be standing in line, just waiting for bread?

Once I built a railroad, I made it run, made it race against time.

Once I built a railroad; now it's done. Brother, can you spare a dime?

Once I built a tower, up to the sun, brick, and rivet, and lime;

Once I built a tower, now it's done. Brother, can you spare a dime?

Once in khaki suits, gee we looked swell,

Full of that Yankee Doodly Dum,

Half a million boots went slogging through Hell,

And I was the kid with the drum!...

Say, don't you remember, they called me Al; it was Al all the time.

Say, don't you remember, I'm your pal? Buddy, can you spare a dime?

2. President Herbert Hoover
Applauds Limited Government, 1931

The Federal Government has assumed many new responsibilities since Lincoln's time, and will probably assume more in the future when the states and local communities can not alone cure abuse or bear the entire cost of national programs, but there is an essential principle that should be maintained in these matters. I am convinced that where Federal action is essential then in most cases it should limit its responsibilities to supplement the states and local communities, and that it should not assume the major role or the entire responsibility, in replacement of the states or local government. To do otherwise threatens the whole foundation of local government, which is the very basis of self-government.

The moment responsibilities of any community, particularly in economic and social questions, are shifted from any part of the Nation to Washington, then that community has subjected itself to a remote bureaucracy with its minimum of understanding and of sympathy. It has lost a large part of its voice and its control of its own destiny. Under Federal control the varied conditions of life in our country are forced into standard molds, with all their limitations upon life, either of the individual or the community. Where people divest themselves of local government responsibilities they at once lay the foundation for the destruction of their liberties.

And buried in this problem lies something even deeper. The whole of our governmental machinery was devised for the purpose that through ordered liberty we give incentive and equality of opportunity to every individual to rise to that highest achievement of which he is capable. At once when government is centralized there arises a limitation upon the liberty of the individual and a restriction of individual opportunity. The true growth of the Nation is the growth of character in its citizens. The spread of government destroys initiative and thus destroys character. Character is made in the community as well as in the individual by assuming responsibilities, not by escape from them. Carried to its logical extreme, all this shouldering of individual and community responsibility upon the Government can lead but to the superstate where every man becomes the servant of the State and real liberty is lost. Such was not the government that Lincoln sought to build.

There is an entirely different avenue by which we may both resist this drift to centralized government and at the same time meet a multitude of problems. That is to strengthen in the Nation a sense and an organization of self-help and cooperation to solve as many problems as possible outside of government. We are today passing through a critical test in such a problem arising from the economic depression.

Due to lack of caution in business and to the impact of forces from an outside world, one-half of which is involved in social and political revolution, the

---

Herbert Hoover, "Radio Address on Lincoln's Birthday" (February 12, 1931), in *The State Papers and Other Public Writings of Herbert Hoover*, collected and edited by William Starr Myers (Garden City, N.Y.: Doubleday, 1934), Vol. 1, 503–505.

march of our prosperity has been retarded. We are projected into temporary unemployment, losses, and hardships. In a Nation rich in resources, many people were faced with hunger and cold through no fault of their own. Our national resources are not only material supplies and material wealth but a spiritual and moral wealth in kindliness, in compassion, in a sense of obligation of neighbor to neighbor and a realization of responsibility by industry, by business, and the community for its social security and its social welfare.

The evidence of our ability to solve great problems outside of Government action and the degree of moral strength with which we emerge from this period will be determined by whether the individuals and the local communities continue to meet their responsibilities.

Throughout this depression I have insisted upon organization of these forces through industry, through local government and through charity, that they should meet this crisis by their own initiative, by the assumption of their own responsibilities. The Federal Government has sought to do its part by example in the expansion of employment, by affording credit to drought sufferers for rehabilitation, and by cooperation with the community, and thus to avoid the opiates of Government charity and stifling of our national spirit of mutual self-help....

We are going through a period when character and courage are on trial, and where the very faith that is within us is under test. Our people are meeting this test. And they are doing more than the immediate task of the day. They are maintaining the ideals of our American system. By their devotion to these ideals we shall come out of these times stronger in character, in courage, and in faith.

3. A Journalist Investigates the Charges Against the Scottsboro Boys, 1931

The International Labor Defense, which had representatives on the scene at the time of the trial in Scottsboro, and whose attorney, George Chamlee, of Chattanooga, later made investigations of various phases of the case not brought out at the trial, claims that when the two girls [Ruby Bates and Victoria Price] were taken from the train at Paint Rock, they made no charges against the Negroes, until after they were taken into custody; that their charges were made after they had found out the spirit of the armed men that came to meet the train and catch the Negroes, and that they were swept into making their wholesale accusation against the Negroes by the men who seized the nine Negroes.

There is no way of proving this conclusively, but from the interview I had with the two girls separately several weeks after the trial, I would say that there is a strong possibility of truth in this statement. The talk with Victoria Price, particularly, convinced me that she was the type who welcomes attention and publicity at any price. The price in this case meant little to her, as she has no

Hollace Ransdall, *Report on the Scottsboro, Alabama, Case*, pp. 3–10. Obtained from http://www.law.umkc.edu/faculty/projects/ftrials/scottsboro/sb_hrrep.html

notions of shame connected with sexual intercourse in any form and was quite unbothered in alleging that she went through such an experience as the charges against the nine Negro lads imply. Having been in direct contact from the cradle with the institution of prostitution as a side-line necessary to make the meager wages of a mill worker pay the rent and buy the groceries, she has no feeling of revulsion against promiscuous sexual intercourse such as women of easier lives might suffer. It is very much a matter of the ordinary routine of life to her, known in both Huntsville and Chattanooga as a prostitute herself....

About 5:45 in the morning on April 6, a picked detachment of the 167th infantry under Major Joe Stearnes, made up of 118 members of five national guard companies of Gadsden, Albertville and Guntersville, Alabama, brought the nine negroes from Gadsden and locked them in the county jail at Scottsboro until the hour of their trial. People from surrounding counties and states began arriving by car and train with the coming of dawn....

Officials and residents of Scottsboro maintained that the crowd was peaceful and showed no evidence of lynching spirit....

Chance conversation with residents of the town, however, did not tend to substantiate this view of the officials. A kind-faced, elderly woman selling tickets at the railroad station, for instance, said to me that if they re-tried the Negroes in Scottsboro, she hoped they would leave the soldiers home next time. When I asked why, she replied that the next time they would finish off the "black fiends" and save the bother of a second trial. Then she told me a lurid story of the mistreatment suffered by the two white girls at the hands of those "horrible black brutes" one of whom had had her breast chewed of[f] by one of the Negroes.

When I called to her attention that the doctor's testimony for the prosecution was to the effect that neither of the girls showed signs of any rough handling on their bodies, it made not impression upon her. Her faith in her atrocity story which had been told to her "by one who ought to know what he was talking about," remained unshaken....

Dr. M. H. Lynch, County Health Physician, and Dr. H. H. Bridges, of Scottsboro, testified at the trial that the medical examination of the girls made shortly after they were taken from the train, showed that both the girls had had recent sexual intercourse, but that there were no lacerations, tears, or other signs of rough handling; that they were not hysterical when brought to the doctor's office first, but became so later....

In three days' time, eight Negro boys all under 21, four of them under 18 and two of them sixteen or under, were hurried through trials which conformed only in outward appearance to the letter of the law. Given no chance even to communicate with their parents and without even as much as the sight of one friendly face, these eight boys, little more than children, surrounded entirely by white hatred and blind venomous prejudice, were sentenced to be killed in the electric chair at the earliest possible moment permitted by law. It is no exaggeration certainly to call this a legal lynching....

Huntsville, the town seat of Madison County in northern Alabama, has within its city limits, some 12,000 inhabitants. Taking in the four mill villages which surround it, the population is about 32,000. There are seven cotton mills in and around Huntsville, the largest being the Lincoln mill made up of four units.... Then there are two old fashioned plants under the same management and owned by local capitalists—the Helen knitting mill and the Margaret spinning mill. It is in this last place, the Margaret Mill, that both Victoria and Ruby Bates worked before the trial and afterward....

"These mill workers are as bad as the Niggers," said one social service worker with a mixture of contempt and understanding. "They haven't any sense of morality at all. Why, just lots of these women are nothing but prostitutes. They just about have to be, I reckon, for nobody could live on the wages they make, and that's the only other way of making money open to them.",...

Ruby [Bates] lives in a bare but clean unpainted shack at 24 Depot Street, in a Negro section of town, with her mother, Mrs. Emma Bates. They are the only white family in the block....

The house in which the Bateses lived when I visited them on May 12, several weeks after the trial, had been vacated recently by a colored family. The social service worker who accompanied me on the visit sniffed when she came in and said to Mrs. Bates: "Niggers lived here before you, I smell them. You can't get rid of that Nigger smell." Mrs. Bates looked apologetic and murmured that she had scrubbed the place down with soap and water. The house looked clean and orderly to me. I smelled nothing, but then I have only a northern nose....

4. Business Leader Henry Ford Advocates Self-Help, 1932

I have always had to work, whether any one hired me or not. For the first forty years of my life, I was an employe. When not employed by others, I employed myself. I found very early that being out of hire was not necessarily being out of work. The first means that your employer has not found something for you to do; the second means that you are waiting until he does.

We nowadays think of work as something that others find for us to do, call us to do, and pay us to do. No doubt our industrial growth is largely responsible for that. We have accustomed men to think of work that way....

But something entirely outside the workshops of the nation has affected this hired employment very seriously. The word "unemployment" has become one of the most dreadful words in the language. The condition itself has become the concern of every person in the country....

I do not believe in routine charity. I think it a shameful thing that any man should have to stoop to take it, or give it. I do not include human helpfulness under the name of charity. My quarrel with charity is that it is neither helpful nor human. The charity of our cities is the most barbarous thing in our system, with the possible exception of our prisons. What we call charity is a modern substitute for being personally kind, personally concerned and personally involved in the work of helping others in difficulty. True charity is a much more costly effort than money-giving....

Literary Digest, June 18, 1932. Reprinted courtesy of Ford Motor Company.

Methods of self-help are numerous and great numbers of people have made the stimulating discovery that they need not depend on employers to find work for them—they can find work for themselves. I have more definitely in mind those who have not yet made that discovery, and I should like to express certain convictions I have tested.

The land! That is where our roots are. There is the basis of our physical life. The farther we get away from the land, the greater our insecurity. From the land comes everything that supports life, everything we use for the service of physical life. The land has not collapsed or shrunk in either extent or productivity. It is there waiting to honor all the labor we are willing to invest in it, and able to tide us across any dislocation of economic conditions.

No unemployment insurance can be compared to an alliance between a man and a plot of land. With one foot in industry and another foot in the land, human society is firmly balanced against most economic uncertainties. With a job to supply him with cash, and a plot of land to guarantee him support, the individual is doubly secure. Stocks may fall, but seedtime and harvest do not fail.

I am not speaking of stop-gaps or temporary expedients. Let every man and every family at this season of the year cultivate a plot of land and raise a sufficient supply for themselves or others. Every city and village has vacant space whose use would be permitted. Groups of men could rent farms for small sums and operate them on the co-operative plan. Employed men, in groups of ten, twenty or fifty, could rent farms and operate them with several unemployed families. Or, they could engage a farmer with his farm to be their farmer this year, either as employe or on shares. There are farmers who would be glad to give a decent indigent family a corner of a field on which to live and provide against next winter. Industrial concerns everywhere would gladly make it possible for their men, employed and unemployed, to find and work the land. Public-spirited citizens and institutions would most willingly assist in these efforts at self-help.

I do not urge this solely or primarily on the ground of need. It is a definite step to the restoration of normal business activity. Families who adopt self-help have that amount of free money to use in the channels of trade. That in turn means a flow of goods, an increase in employment, a general benefit.

5. *The Nation* Asks, "Is It to Be Murder, Mr. Hoover?" 1932

Is it to be mass murder, Herbert Hoover? Murder by starvation, murder by disease, murder by killing all hope—and the soul? We ask, Mr. President, because this terrible fate is now staring multitudes in the face in the sight of plenty and because the responsibility now rests entirely upon you. Congress has adjourned after voting only $300,000,000 for direct relief—and that only for the States. No one can call it together again for five months except you. Day by day more cities approach the line of bankruptcy; day by day the plight of the

"Is It to Be Murder, Mr. Hoover?" by *The Nation's* editors, is reprinted with permission from the August 3, 1932 issue of *The Nation*. For subscription information, call 1-800-333-8536. Portions of each week's *Nation* magazine can be accessed at http://www.thenation.com. Cartoon by Edmund Duffy. Text and cartoon reproduced with permission.

individual States of the Union gets worse. In community after community the authorities and the leading citizens can see no hope whatever of heading off the starvation of innocents. And that is murder, Mr. President, cold-blooded and utterly unnecessary murder, far worse than if the victims were to be stood up against a wall and shot down by firing squads. Every death by starvation today—and there are men, women, and children perishing daily because of plain lack of food and undernourishment—must be charged up against the government of the United States, and in the last analysis against *you.* That is not merely because you are President, but because you as an individual have from the first set your face against direct federal relief to those who through no fault of their own are without work and food. You are deeply and sincerely convinced that if necessary it is better that some should starve than that multitudes should have their characters wrecked and their initiative killed by a dole.

But Mr. President, are you living in the United States? Do you know what is happening? Do you know that it is no longer starvation of a few which is at hand? We ask these questions because your statement to the press on July 17 indicates that you are living entirely detached from the actual situation, that you do not know what is happening under the flag of which you are the chief guardian. You stated on that day that you would sign the so-called relief bill granting $300,000,000 for temporary loans by the Reconstruction Finance Corporation "to such States as are absolutely unable to finance the relief of distress." You then went on to say that, through this provision, "We have a solid back log of assurance that there need be no hunger and cold in the United States." You added that these loans were to be based only upon "absolute need and evidence of financial exhaustion," and concluded with the statement: "I do not expect any State to resort to it except as a last extremity." ... Is it any wonder that we ask you if you know what is happening in the United States today?

... Have you not heard that city authorities in St. Louis and the charitable agencies have just turned adrift 13,000 families which they can no longer support, while the city of Detroit has dropped 18,000 who now have nowhere to turn, no assurance that even a single crust of bread will be forthcoming for their support? Have you not learned that the city of Bridgeport, and other cities and towns in Connecticut have let it be known that if the State does not come to their aid at once they have no hope whatever of caring further for their unemployed, their own resources being entirely exhausted? Did you read that eight hundred men marched into the Indiana State Capitol last week demanding food, declaring that if they were not given help they would return 300,000 strong? Have you learned that the police in St. Louis have already fired on a mob demanding bread? Have you not read of the town of Clinton, Mass., where on July 7 "more than three hundred men, women, and crying children crowded the corridors of the Town Hall appealing for food"—only to learn that the town treasury has been exhausted, that it is unable to borrow a cent from any bank, and that it has been, and still is, trying to support one out of every six residents of the town who are destitute? These are not exceptional cases; they can be multiplied a hundredfold and from almost every section of the country. Is it any

Cartoon of stooped man looking at a Hoovers sign, which reads—We have a solid backlog of assurance that there need be no hunger or cold in the United States.

wonder, Mr. President, that thirty States moved at once? And how long do you think the $300,000,000 is going to last in the face of this?

6. President Franklin D. Roosevelt Says Government Must Act, 1933

… This is preeminently the time to speak the truth, the whole truth, frankly and boldly. Nor need we shrink from honestly facing conditions in our country today. This great Nation will endure as it has endured, will revive and will prosper. So, first of all, let me assert my firm belief that the only thing we have to fear is fear itself—nameless, unreasoning, unjustified terror which paralyzes needed efforts to convert retreat into advance. In every dark hour of our national life a leadership of frankness and vigor has met with that understanding and support of the people

Franklin D. Roosevelt, Inaugural Address, March 4, 1933, as published in Samuel Rosenman, ed., *The Public Papers of Franklin D. Roosevelt, Volume Two: The Year of Crisis, 1933* (New York: Random House, 1938) 11–16.

themselves which is essential to victory. I am convinced that you will again give that support to leadership in these critical days.

In such a spirit on my part and on yours we face our common difficulties. They concern, thank God, only material things. Values have shrunken to fantastic levels; taxes have risen; our ability to pay has fallen; government of all kinds is faced by serious curtailment of income; the means of exchange are frozen in the currents of trade; the withered leaves of industrial enterprise lie on every side; farmers find no markets for their produce; the savings of many years in thousands of families are gone....

Yet our distress comes from no failure of substance. We are stricken by no plague of locusts. Compared with the perils which our forefathers conquered because they believed and were not afraid, we have still much to be thankful for. Nature still offers her bounty and human efforts have multiplied it. Plenty is at our doorstep, but a generous use of it languishes in the very sight of the supply. Primarily this is because the rulers of the exchange of mankind's goods have failed, through their own stubbornness and their own incompetence, have admitted their failure, and abdicated. Practices of the unscrupulous money changers stand indicted in the court of public opinion, rejected by the hearts and minds of men....

The money changers have fled from their high seats in the temple of our civilization. We may now restore that temple to the ancient truths. The measure of the restoration lies in the extent to which we apply social values more noble than mere monetary profit....

Restoration calls, however, not for changes in ethics alone. This Nation asks for action, and action now.

Our greatest primary task is to put people to work. This is no unsolvable problem if we face it wisely and courageously. It can be accomplished in part by direct recruiting by the Government itself, treating the task as we would treat the emergency of a war, but at the same time, through this employment, accomplishing greatly needed projects to stimulate and reorganize the use of our natural resources....

We must act and act quickly.

Finally, in our progress toward a resumption of work we require two safeguards against a return of the evils of the old order; there must be strict supervision of all banking and credits and investments; there must be an end to speculation with other people's money, and there must be provision for an adequate but sound currency....

Through this program of action we address ourselves to putting our own national house in order and making income balance outgo. Our international trade relations, though vastly important, are in point of time and necessity secondary to the establishment of a sound national economy. I favor as a practical policy the putting of first things first. I shall spare no effort to restore world trade by international economic readjustment, but the emergency at home cannot wait on that accomplishment....

In the field of world policy I would dedicate this Nation to the policy of the good neighbor—the neighbor who resolutely respects himself and, because he does so, respects the rights of others—the neighbor who respects his obligations and respects the sanctity of his agreements in and with a world of neighbors....

It is to be hoped that the normal balance of executive and legislative authority may be wholly adequate to meet the unprecedented task before us. But it may be that an unprecedented demand and need for undelayed action may call for temporary departure from that normal balance of public procedure.

I am prepared under my constitutional duty to recommend the measures that a stricken nation in the midst of a stricken world may require. These measures, or such other measures as the Congress may build out of its experience and wisdom, I shall seek, within my constitutional authority, to bring to speedy adoption.

But in the event that the Congress shall fail to take one of these two courses, and in the event that the national emergency is still critical, I shall not evade the clear course of duty that will then confront me. I shall ask the Congress for the one remaining instrument to meet the crisis—broad Executive power to wage a war against the emergency, as great as the power that would be given to me if we were in fact invaded by a foreign foe....

7. Father Charles Coughlin Denounces Roosevelt and Proposes a Third Party, 1936

Ladies and gentlemen, may I gratefully acknowledge that these broadcasting facilities have been extended to me by the Columbia Broadcasting System?

It is my purpose to engage your attention as I discuss, first, why I do not find it morally possible to support either the Republicans and their platform or the Democrats and their promises....

In the Autumn of 1932 it was my privilege to address the American people on the causes of the so-called depression and upon the obvious remedies required to bring about a permanent recovery.

Those were days which witnessed a complete breakdown of the financial system under which our Western civilization had been developed. It was also evident that under this financial system there resulted a concentration of wealth and a multiplication of impoverished families. Unjust wages and unreasonable idleness were universally recognized as contradictions in an age of plenty. To my mind it was inconceivable that irrational and needless want should exist in an age of plenty....

What was the basic cause which closed factories, which created idleness, which permitted weeds to overrun our golden fields and plowshares to rust? There was and is but one answer. Some call it lack of purchasing power. Others, viewing the problem in a more philosophic light, recognize that the financial system which was able to function in an age of scarcity was totally inadequate to operate successfully in an age of plenty....

Father Charles E. Coughlin, "A Third Party," speech given June 19, 1936. Reprinted by permission of the Charles E. Coughlin Collection, Special Collection Series XXV, at the Charles Deering McCormick Library of Special Collections, Northwestern University.

... it is inconceivable how such a thing as a so-called depression should blight the lives of an entire nation when there was a plentitude of everything surrounding us, only to be withheld from us because the so-called leaders of high finance persisted in clinging to an outworn theory of privately issued money, the medium through which wealth is distributed.

I challenged this private control and creation of money because it was alien to our Constitution....

Our governments, through a policy of perversion and subterfuge, established, step by step, the Federal Reserve Banking System. Power was given to a handful of our fellow-citizens to create and control more than 90 per cent of all our money mostly by a mere stroke of the fountain pen;...

At last, when the most brilliant minds amongst the industrialists, bankers and their kept politicians had failed to solve the cause of the needless depression, there appeared upon the scene of our national life a new champion of the people, Franklin Delano Roosevelt! He spoke golden words of hope. He intimated to the American people that the system of permitting a group of private citizens to create money, then to issue it to the government as if it were real money, then to exact payment from the entire nation through a system of taxation earned by real labor and service, was immoral. With the whip of his scorn he castigated these usurers who exploited the poor. With his eloquent tongue he lashed their financial system which devoured the homes of widows and orphans.

No man in modern times received such plaudits from the poor as did Franklin Roosevelt when he promised to drive the money changers from the temple— the money changers who had clipped the coins of wages, who had manufactured spurious money and who had brought proud America to her knees.

March 4, 1933! I shall never forget the inaugural address, which seemed to re-echo the very words employed by Christ Himself as He actually drove the money changers from the temple....

Such were our hopes in the springtime of 1933....

In 1936, when our disillusionment is complete, we pause to take inventory of our predicament. You citizens have shackled about your limbs a tax bill of $35,000,000,000, most of which, I repeat, was created by a flourish of a fountain pen. Your erstwhile saviour, whose golden promises ring upon the counter of performance with the cheapness of tin, bargained with the money changers that, with seventy billion laboring hours in the ditch, or in the factory, or behind the plow, you and your children shall repay the debt which was created with a drop of ink in less than ten seconds.

Is that driving the money changers out of the temple?

Every crumb you eat, every stitch of clothing you wear, every menial purchase which you make is weighted down with an unseen tax as you work and slave for the debt merchants of America. But the $55,000,000,000 of debt bonds, held mostly by the debt merchants and the well circumstanced of this country, have been ably safeguarded from taxation by this peerless leader who sham battles his way along the avenue of popularity with his smile for the poor and his blindness for their plight. Is that driving the money changers from the temple?...

It is not pleasant for me who coined the phrase "Roosevelt or ruin"—a phrase fashioned upon promises—to voice such passionate words. But I am constrained to admit that "Roosevelt and ruin" is the order of the day because the money changers have not been driven from the temple.

My friends, I come before you tonight not to ask you to return to the Landons, to the Hoovers, to the Old Deal exploiters who honestly defended the dishonest system of gold standardism and rugged individualism. Their sun has set never to rise again....

My friends, there is a way out, a way to freedom! There is an escape from the dole standard of Roosevelt, the gold standard of [Alf] Landon. No longer need you be targets in no-man's land for the financial crossfire of the sham-battlers!

Six hours ago the birth of "the Union party" was officially announced to the newspapers of the nation, thereby confirming information which hitherto was mine unofficially....

Behind it will rally agriculture, labor, the disappointed Republicans and the outraged Democrats, the independent merchant and industrialist and every lover of liberty who desires to eradicate the cancerous growths from decadent capitalism and avoid the treacherous pitfalls of red communism.

8. Social Security Advisers
Consider Male and Female Pensioners, 1938

Mr. Myers One very good solution would be to require that the woman must be married to an annuitant for at least five years before she receives any benefits. If a man who is 65 retires and he has been married for three years, he receives 110% for the next two years and following that they will be married five years and they will receive 150% thereafter. Under the plan as it is here they are supposed to be married five years and would receive 100%. Under the plan she would have to be married five years before he retired. He would receive nothing for two years and after that he would receive 150%. Under this plan he would receive 100% for the two-year period and then 150%....

Mr. Mowbray It seems to me that the restriction on the marital period and the period of waiting is only desirable to keep out the designing woman. That wouldn't affect things at all. I made the remark that I thought a two-year period was long enough in a life insurance policy, but I was not at all sure that a five-year period was long enough as a defense against a designing woman.

Mr. Brown How far should those in need be kept in need to protect the system against designing women and old fools? Do you think it ought to be longer than five years?...

Miss Dewson I am confused about one point. The single man or single person gets less than the married person. Supposing that the man who is married, say at 66, loses his wife and becomes a single man, would that change his annuity?

Federal Advisory Council Minutes (April 29, 1938), morning session, 18. File 025, Box 12, Chairman's Files, RG 47, Records of the Social Security Administration, National Archives.

Mr. Brown He would drop back. He drops back to the 100%. He no longer gets wife allowance, whereas if the wife survives him it would drop back to the 75%.

Miss Dewson That is what makes it more for the married man?

Mr. Brown Yes, on the principle that it is more costly for the single man to live than for the single woman if she is able to avail herself of the home of the child. A woman is able to fit herself into the economy of the home of the child much better than the single man; that is, the grandmother helps in the raising of the children and helps in home affairs, whereas the aged grandfather is the man who sits out on the front porch and can't help much in the home….

Mr. Brown Are there any other points? In regard to the widows' benefits at 75% of the base we could put in a corollary as to whether 75% of the base is proper.

Mr. Linton I wonder why we didn't make the widows' benefit the regular individual annuity without cutting it down 25%…. Why not cut it 50%? Why should you pay the widow less than the individual himself gets if unmarried?

Mr. Williamson She can look after herself better than he can.

Mr. Linton Is that a sociological fact?

Mr. Brown Can a single woman adjust herself to a lower budget on account of the fact that she is used to doing her own housework whereas the single man has to go out to a restaurant?

9. John Steinbeck Portrays the Outcast Poor in *The Grapes of Wrath*, 1939

Two men dressed in jeans and sweaty blue shirts came through the willows and looked toward the naked men. They called, "How's the swimmin'?"

"Dunno," said Tom. "We ain't tried none. Sure feels good to set here, though."

"Mind if we come in an' set?"

"She ain't our river. We'll len' you a little piece of her."

The men shucked off their pants, peeled their shirts, and waded out. The dust coated their legs to the knee; their feet were pale and soft with sweat. They settled lazily into the water and washed listlessly at their flanks. Sun-bitten, they were, a father and a boy. They grunted and groaned with the water.

Pa asked politely, "Goin' west?"

"Nope. We come from there. Goin' back home. We can't make no livin' out there."

"Where's home?" Tom asked.

"Panhandle, come from near Pampa."

Pa asked, "Can you make a livin' there?"

"Nope. But at leas' we can starve to death with folks we know. Won't have a bunch a fellas that hates us to starve with."

Pa said, "Ya know, you're the second fella talked like that. What makes 'em hate you?"

"Dunno," said the man. He cupped his hands full of water and rubbed his face, snorting and bubbling. Dusty water ran out of his hair and streaked his neck.

"I like to hear some more 'bout this," said Pa.

"Me too," Tom added. "Why these folks out west hate ya?"

The man looked sharply at Tom. "You jus' goin' wes'?"

"Jus' on our way."

"You ain't never been in California?"

"No, we ain't."

"Well, don' take my word. Go see for yourself."

"Yeah," Tom said, "but a fella kind a likes to know what he's gettin' into."

"Well, if you truly wanta know, I'm a fella that's asked questions an' give her some thought. She's a nice country. But she was stole a long time ago. You git acrost the desert an' come into the country aroun' Bakersfield. An' you never seen such purty country—all orchards an' grapes, purtiest country you ever seen. An' you'll pass lan' flat an' fine with water thirty feet down, and that lan's layin' fallow. But you can't have none of that lan'. That's a Lan' and Cattle Company. An' if they don't want ta work her, she ain't gonna git worked. You go in there an' plant you a little corn, an' you'll go to jail!"

"Good lan', you say? An' they ain't workin' her?"

"Yes, sir. Good lan' an' they ain't! Well, sir, that'll get you a little mad, but you ain't seen nothin'. People gonna have a look in their eye. They gonna look at you an' their face says, 'I don't like you, you son-of-a-bitch.' Gonna be deputy sheriffs, an' they'll push you aroun'. You camp on the roadside, an' they'll move you on. You gonna see in people's face how they hate you. An'—I'll tell you somepin. They hate you 'cause they're scairt. They know a hungry fella gonna get food even if he got to take it. They know that fallow lan's a sin an' somebody' gonna take it. What the hell! You never been called 'Okie' yet."

Tom said, "Okie? What's that?"

"Well, Okie use' ta mean you was from Oklahoma. Now it means you're a dirty son-of-a-bitch. Okie means you're scum. Don't mean nothing itself, it's the way they say it. But I can't tell you nothin'. You got to go there. I hear there's three hunderd thousan' of our people there—an' livin' like hogs, 'cause ever'thing in California is owned. They ain't nothin' left. An' them people that owns it is gonna hang on to it if they got ta kill ever'body in the worl' to do it. An' they're scairt, an' that makes 'em mad. You got to see it. You got to hear it. Purtiest goddamn country you ever seen, but they ain't nice to you, them folks. They're so scairt an' worried they ain't even nice to each other."

Tom looked down into the water, and he dug his heels into the sand. "S'pose a fella got work an' saved, couldn' he get a little lan'?"

The older man laughed and he looked at his boy, and his silent boy grinned almost in triumph. And the man said, "You ain't gonna get no steady work. Gonna scrabble for your dinner ever' day. An' you gonna do her with people lookin' mean at you."...

... Ma turned over on her back and crossed her hands under her head. She listened to Granma's breathing and to the girl's breathing. She moved a hand to start a fly from her forehead. The camp was quiet in the blinding heat, but the noises of hot grass—of crickets, the hum of flies—were a tone that was close to silence. Ma sighed deeply and then yawned and closed her eyes. In her half-sleep she heard footsteps approaching, but it was a man's voice that started her awake.

"Who's in here?"

Ma sat up quickly. A brown-faced man bent over and looked in. He wore boots and khaki pants and a khaki shirt with epaulets. On a Sam Browne belt a pistol holster hung, and a big silver star was pinned to his shirt at the left breast. A loose-crowned military cap was on the back of his head. He beat on the tarpaulin with his hand, and the tight canvas vibrated like a drum.

"Who's in here?" he demanded again.

Ma asked, "What is it you want, mister?"

"What you think I want? I want to know who's in here."

"Why, they's jus' us three in here. Me an' Granma an' my girl."

"Where's your men?"

"Why, they went down to clean up. We was drivin' all night."

"Where'd you come from?"

"Right near Sallisaw, Oklahoma."

"Well, you can't stay here."

"We aim to get out tonight an' cross the desert, mister."

"Well, you better. If you're here tomorra this time I'll run you in. We don't want none of you settlin' down here."

Ma's face blackened with anger. She got slowly to her feet. She stooped to the utensil box and picked out the iron skillet. "Mister," she said, "you got a tin button an' a gun. Where I come from, you keep your voice down." She advanced on him with the skillet. He loosened the gun in the holster. "Go ahead," said Ma. "Scarin' women. I'm thankful the men folks ain't here. They'd tear ya to pieces. In my country you watch your tongue."

The man took two steps backward. "Well, you ain't in your country now. You're in California, an' we don't want you god-damn Okies settlin' down."

Ma's advance stopped. She looked puzzled. "Okies?" she said softly. "Okies."

"Yeah, Okies! An' if you're here when I come tomorra, I'll run ya in."

ESSAYS

Franklin D. Roosevelt excited both admirers and critics in his own day, and still does. Herbert Hoover called him a "chameleon on plaid," implying that Roosevelt adjusted his temperament and policies as the situation dictated, without regard to any core values or personal vision. David M. Kennedy of Stanford University, whose book on this era won the Pulitzer Prize, describes a man of immense complexity, whose own experience of crippling disease gave him exceptional fortitude and empathy for others' plight. Roosevelt's leadership, Kennedy states, contrasted markedly with that of Hoover and made the New Deal what it was. Burton Folsom, a professor at Hillsdale College, sees Roosevelt very differently. He criticizes other historians for placing too much emphasis on Roosevelt's good intentions while soft-peddling the New Deal's ill effects. Folsom argues that the New Deal prolonged the Depression, gave too much power to unions, and created an intrusive federal bureaucracy. Which description of the president and his programs is most convincing? Did the New Deal rewrite government's contract with the people, or not?

FDR: Advocate for the American People

DAVID M. KENNEDY

Hoover brought a corporate executive's sensibility to the White House. Roosevelt brought a politician's. Hoover as president frequently dazzled visitors with his detailed knowledge and expert understanding of American business. "His was a mathematical brain," said his admiring secretary, Theodore Joslin. "Let banking officials, for instance, come into his office and he would rattle off the number of banks in the country, list their liabilities and assets, describe the trend of fiscal affairs, and go into the liquidity, or lack of it, of individual institutions, all from memory." Roosevelt, in contrast, impressed his visitors by asking them to draw a line across a map of the United States. He would then name, in order, every county through which the line passed, adding anecdotes about each locality's political particularities. Where Hoover had a Quaker's reserve about the perquisites of the presidency, Roosevelt savored them with gusto. By 1932 Hoover wore the mantle of office like a hair shirt that he could not wait to doff. Roosevelt confided to a journalist his conviction that "no man ever willingly gives up public life—no man who has ever tasted it." Almost preternaturally self-confident, he had no intimidating image of the presidential office to live up to, it was said, since his untroubled conception of the presidency consisted quite simply of the thought of himself in it.

Hoover's first elected office was the presidency. Roosevelt had been a professional politician all his life. He had spent years charting his course for the White House. To a remarkable degree, he had followed the career path blazed by his cousin Theodore Roosevelt—through the New York legislature and the office of assistant secretary of the navy to the governor's chair in Albany. In 1920 he had been the vice-presidential candidate on the losing Democratic ticket.

The following year, while vacationing at his family's summer estate on Campobello Island, in the Canadian province of New Brunswick, he had been stricken with poliomyelitis. He was thirty-nine years of age. He would never again be able to stand without heavy steel braces on his legs. Through grueling effort and sheer will power, he eventually trained himself to "walk" a few steps, an odd shuffle in which, leaning on the strong arm of a companion, he threw one hip, then the other, to move his steel-cased legs forward. His disability was

David M. Kennedy, *Freedom from Fear: The American People in Depression and War* (New York: Oxford University Press, 1999), 94–96, 115–117, 133–137, 144–146, 160–163, 168, 258, 261–263, 372, 377–379. Copyright © 1999 by David Kennedy. Used by permission of Oxford University Press, Inc.

no secret, but he took care to conceal its extent. He never allowed himself to be photographed in his wheelchair or being carried.

Roosevelt's long struggle with illness transformed him in spirit as well as body. Athletic and slim in his youth, he was now necessarily sedentary, and his upper body thickened. He developed, in the manner of many paraplegics, a wrestler's torso and big, beefy arms. His biceps, he delighted in telling visitors, were bigger than those of the celebrated prizefighter Jack Dempsey. Like many disabled persons, too, he developed a talent for denial, a kind of forcefully willed optimism that refused to dwell on life's difficulties. Sometimes this talent abetted his penchant for duplicity, as in the continuing love affair he carried on with Lucy Mercer, even after he told his wife in 1918 that the relationship was ended. At other times it endowed him with an aura of radiant indomitability, lending conviction and authority to what in other men's mouths might have been banal platitudes, such as "all we have to fear is fear itself." Many of Roosevelt's acquaintances also believed that his grim companionship with paralysis gave to this shallow, supercilious youth the precious gift of a purposeful manhood....

Though Roosevelt was never a systematic thinker, the period of lonely reflection imposed by his convalescence allowed him to shape a fairly coherent social philosophy. By the time he was elected governor, the distillate of his upbringing, education, and experience had crystallized into a few simple but powerful political principles. [Raymond] Moley summarized them this way: "He believed that government not only could, but should, achieve the subordination of private interests to collective interests, substitute co-operation for the mad scramble to selfish individualism. He had a profound feeling for the underdog, a real sense of the critical imbalance of economic life, a very keen awareness that political democracy could not exist side by side with economic plutocracy." As Roosevelt himself put it:

> [O]ur civilization cannot endure unless we, as individuals, realize our responsibility to and dependence on the rest of the world. For it is literally true that the "self-supporting" man or woman has become as extinct as the man of the stone age. Without the help of thousands of others, any one of us would die, naked and starved. Consider the bread upon our table, the clothes upon our backs, the luxuries that make life pleasant; how many men worked in sunlit fields, in dark mines, in the fierce heat of molten metal, and among the looms and wheels of countless factories, in order to create them for our use and enjoyment.... In the final analysis, the progress of our civilization will be retarded if any large body of citizens falls behind.

Perhaps deep within himself Roosevelt trembled occasionally with the common human palsies of melancholy or doubt or fear, but the world saw none of it. On February 15, 1933, he gave a memorable demonstration of his powers of self-control. Alighting in Miami from an eleven-day cruise aboard Vincent Astor's yacht *Nourmahal*, FDR motored to Bay Front Park, where he made a few remarks to a large crowd. At the end of the brief speech, Mayor Anton J. Cermak of Chicago stepped up to the side of Roosevelt's open touring car and said a few words to the president-elect. Suddenly a pistol barked from the crowd. Cermak doubled over. Roosevelt ordered the Secret Service agents, who were reflexively accelerating his car away from the scene, to stop. He motioned to have Cermak, pale and pulseless, put into the seat beside him. "Tony, keep quiet—don't move. It won't hurt you if you keep quiet," Roosevelt repeated as he cradled Cermak's limp body while the car sped to the hospital.

Cermak had been mortally wounded. He died within weeks, the victim of a deranged assassin who had been aiming for Roosevelt. On the evening of February 15, after Cermak had been entrusted to the doctors, Moley accompanied Roosevelt back to the *Nourmahal,* poured him a stiff drink, and prepared for the letdown now that Roosevelt was alone among his intimates. He had just been spared by inches from a killer's bullet and had held a dying man in his arms. But there was nothing—"not so much as the twitching of a muscle, the mopping of a brow, or even the hint of a false gaiety—to indicate that it wasn't any other evening in any other place. Roosevelt was simply himself—easy, confident, poised, to all appearances unmoved." The episode contributed to Moley's eventual conclusion "that Roosevelt had no nerves at all." He was, said Frances Perkins, "the most complicated human being I ever knew."…

Roosevelt began inaugural day by attending a brief service at St. John's Episcopal Church. His old Groton School headmaster, Endicott Peabody, prayed the Lord to "bless Thy servant, Franklin, chosen to be president of the United States." After a quick stop at the Mayflower Hotel to confer urgently with his advisers on the still-worsening banking crisis, Roosevelt donned his formal attire and motored to the White House. There he joined a haggard and cheerless Hoover for the ride down Pennsylvania Avenue to the inaugural platform on the east side of the Capitol.

Braced on his son's arm, Roosevelt walked his few lurching steps to the rostrum. Breaking precedent, he recited the entire oath of office, rather than merely repeating "I do" to the chief justice's interrogation. Then he began his inaugural address, speaking firmly in his rich tenor voice. Frankly acknowledging the crippled condition of the ship of state he was now to captain, he began by reassuring his countrymen that "this great nation will endure as it had endured, will revive and will prosper…. The only thing we have to fear," he intoned, "is fear itself." The nation's distress, he declared, owed to "no failure of substance." Rather, "rulers of the exchange of mankind's goods have failed through their own stubbornness and their own incompetence, have admitted their failure, and have abdicated…. The money changers have fled from their high seats in the temple of our civilization. We may now restore that temple to the ancient truths." The greatest task, he went on, "is to put people to work," and he hinted at "direct recruiting by the Government" on public works projects as the means to do it….

Just weeks before his inaugural, while on his way to board the *Nourmahal* in Florida, Roosevelt had spoken restlessly of the need for "action, action." President at last, he now proceeded to act with spectacular vigor.

The first and desperately urgent item of business was the banking crisis. Even as he left the Mayflower Hotel to deliver his inaugural condemnation of the "money changers," he approved a recommendation originating with the outgoing treasury secretary, Ogden Mills, to convene an emergency meeting of bankers from the leading financial centers. The next day, Sunday, March 5, Roosevelt issued two proclamations, one calling Congress into special session on March 9, the other invoking the Trading with the Enemy Act to halt all transactions in gold and declare a four-day national banking holiday—both of them measures that Hoover had vainly urged him to endorse in the preceding weeks. Hoover's men and Roosevelt's now began an intense eighty hours of collaboration to hammer out the details of an emergency banking measure that could be presented to the special session of Congress. Haunting the corridors of the Treasury Department day and night, private bankers and government officials both old and new toiled frantically to rescue the moribund corpse of American finance. In that hectic week, none led normal lives, Moley remembered. "Confusion, haste, the dread of making mistakes, the consciousness of responsibility for the economic well-being of millions of people, made mortal inroads on the health of some of us … and left the rest of us ready to snap at our images in the mirror…. Only Roosevelt," Moley observed, "preserved the air of a man who'd found a happy way of life."

Roosevelt's and Hoover's minions "had forgotten to be Republicans or Democrats," Moley commented. "We were just a bunch of men trying to save the banking system." William Woodin, the new treasury secretary, and Ogden Mills, his predecessor, simply shifted places on either side of the secretary's desk in the Treasury Building. Otherwise, nothing changed in the room. The kind of bipartisan collaboration for which Hoover had long pleaded was now happening, but under Roosevelt's aegis, not Hoover's—and not, all these men hoped, too late. When the special session of Congress convened at noon on March 9, they had a bill ready—barely.

The bill was read to the House at 1:00 P.M., while some new representatives were still trying to locate their seats. Printed copies were not ready for the members. A rolled-up newspaper symbolically served. After thirty-eight minutes of "debate," the chamber passed the bill, sight unseen, with a unanimous shout. The Senate approved the bill with only seven dissenting votes—all from agrarian states historically suspicious of Wall Street. The president signed the legislation into law at 8:36 in the evening. "Capitalism," concluded Moley, "was saved in eight days."…

On Monday the thirteenth the banks reopened, and the results of Roosevelt's magic with the Congress and the people were immediately apparent. Deposits and gold began to flow back into the banking system. The prolonged banking crisis, acute since at least 1930, with roots reaching back through the 1920s and even into the days of Andrew Jackson, was at last over. And Roosevelt, taking full credit, was a hero. William Randolph Hearst told him: "I guess at your next election we will make it unanimous." Even Henry Stimson, who so recently had thought FDR a "peanut," sent his "heartiest congratulations."

The common people of the country sent their congratulations as well—and their good wishes and suggestions and special requests. Some 450,000 Americans wrote to their new president in his first week in office. Thereafter mail routinely poured in at a rate of four to seven thousand letters per day. The White House mail-room, staffed by a single employee in Hoover's day, had to hire seventy people to handle the flood of correspondence. Roosevelt had touched the hearts and imaginations of his countrymen like no predecessor in memory....

Meanwhile, the steady legislative drumbeat of the Hundred Days continued. Relishing power and wielding it with gusto, Roosevelt next sent to Congress, on March 21, a request for legislation aimed at unemployment relief. Here he departed most dramatically from Hoover's pettifogging timidity, and here he harvested the greatest political rewards. He proposed a Civilian Conservation Corps (CCC) to employ a quarter of a million men on forestry, flood control, and beautification projects. Over the next decade, the CCC became one of the most popular of all the New Deal's innovations. By the time it expired in 1942, it had put more than three million idle youngsters to work at a wage of thirty dollars a month, twenty-five of which they were required to send home to their families. CCC workers built firebreaks and lookouts in the national forests and bridges, campgrounds, trails, and museums in the national parks. Roosevelt also called for a new agency, the Federal Emergency Relief Administration (FERA), to coordinate and eventually increase direct federal unemployment assistance to the states. And he served notice, a bit halfheartedly, that he would soon be making recommendations about a "broad public works labor-creating program."

The first two of these measures—CCC and FERA—constituted important steps along the road to direct federal involvement in unemployment relief, something that Hoover had consistently and self-punishingly resisted. Roosevelt showed no such squeamishness, just as he had not hesitated as governor of New York to embrace relief as a "social duty" of government in the face of evident human suffering. As yet, Roosevelt did not think of relief payments or public works employment as means of significantly increasing purchasing power. He proposed them for charitable reasons, and for political purposes as well, but not principally for economic ones....

These first modest steps at a direct federal role in welfare services also carried into prominence another of Roosevelt's associates from New York, Harry Hopkins, whom Roosevelt would soon name as federal relief administrator. A chain-smoking, hollow-eyed, pauper-thin social worker, a tough-talking, big-hearted blend of the sardonic and sentimental, Hopkins represented an important and durable component of what might be called the emerging political culture of the New Deal. In common with Brain Truster Adolf Berle, future treasury secretary Henry Morgenthau Jr., and Labor Secretary Frances Perkins, Hopkins was steeped in the Social Gospel tradition. Ernest, high-minded, and sometimes condescending, the Social Gospelers were middle-class missionaries to America's industrial proletariat. Inspired originally by late nineteenth-century Protestant clergymen like Walter Rauschenbusch and Washington Gladden, they were committed to the moral and material uplift of the poor, and they had both the courage and the prejudices of their convictions. Berle and Morgenthau had worked for a time at Lillian Wald's Henry Street settlement house in New York, Perkins at Jane Addams's Hull House in Chicago, and Hopkins himself at New York's Christadora House. Amid the din and squalor of thronged immigrant neighborhoods, they had all learned at first hand that poverty could be an exitless way of life, that the idea of "opportunity" was often a mockery in the precarious, threadbare existence of the working class. Together with Franklin Roosevelt, they meant to do something about it....

"What I want you to do," said Harry Hopkins to Lorena Hickok in July 1933, "is to go out around the country and look this thing over. I don't want statistics from you. I don't want the social-worker angle. I just want your own reaction, as an ordinary citizen.

"Go talk with preachers and teachers, businessmen, workers, farmers. Go talk with the unemployed, those who are on relief and those who aren't. And when you talk with them don't ever forget that but for the grace of God you, I, any of our friends might be in their shoes. Tell me what you see and hear. All of it. Don't ever pull your punches."

The Depression was now in its fourth year. In the neighborhoods and hamlets of a stricken nation millions of men and women languished in sullen gloom and looked to Washington with guarded hope. Still they struggled to comprehend the nature of the calamity that had engulfed them. Across Hopkins's desk at the newly created Federal Emergency Relief Administration flowed rivers of data that measured the Depression's impact in cool numbers. But Hopkins wanted more—to touch the human face of the catastrophe, taste in his mouth the metallic smack of the fear and hunger of the unemployed, as he had when he worked among the immigrant poor at New York's Christadora settlement house in 1912. Tied to his desk in Washington, he dispatched Lorena Hickok in his stead. In her he chose a uniquely gutsy and perceptive observer who could be counted on to see without illusion and to report with candor, insight, and moxie....

From the charts and tables accumulating on his desk even before Hickok's letters began to arrive, Hopkins could already sketch the grim outlines of that history. Stockholders, his figures confirmed, had watched as three-quarters of the value of their assets had simply evaporated since 1929, a colossal financial meltdown that blighted not only the notoriously idle rich but struggling neighborhood banks, hard-earned retirement nest eggs, and college and university endowments as well. The more than five thousand bank failures between the Crash and the New Deal's rescue operation in March 1933 wiped out some $7 billion in depositors' money. Accelerating foreclosures on defaulted home mortgages—150,000 homeowners lost their property in 1930, 200,000 in 1931, 250,000 in 1932—stripped millions of people of both shelter and life savings at a single stroke and menaced the balance sheets of thousands of surviving banks. Several states and some thirteen hundred municipalities, crushed by sinking real estate prices and consequently shrinking tax revenues, defaulted on their obligations to creditors, pinched their already scant social services, cut payrolls, and slashed paychecks. Chicago was reduced to paying its teachers in tax warrants and then, in the winter of 1932–33, to paying them nothing at all.

Gross national product had fallen by 1933 to half its 1929 level. Spending for new plants and equipment had ground to a virtual standstill. Businesses invested only $3 billion in 1933, compared with $24 billion in 1929.... Residential and industrial construction shriveled to less than one-fifth of its pre-Depression volume, a wrenching contraction that spread through lumber camps, steel mills, and appliance factories, disemploying thousands of loggers, mill hands, sheet-metal workers, engineers, architects, carpenters, plumbers, roofers, plasterers, painters, and electricians. Mute shoals of jobless men drifted through the streets of every American city in 1933.

Nowhere did the Depression strike more savagely than in the American countryside. On America's farms, income had plummeted from $6 billion in what for farmers was the already lean year of 1929 to $2 billion in 1932. The net receipts from the wheat harvest in one Oklahoma county went from $1.2 million in 1931 to just $7,000 in 1933. Mississippi's pathetic $239 per capita income in 1929 sank to $117 in 1933.

Unemployment and its close companion, reduced wages, were the most obvious and the most wounding of all the Depression's effects. The government's data showed that 25 percent of the work force, some thirteen million workers, including nearly four hundred thousand women, stood idle in 1933....

Hickok set out in quest of the human reality of the Depression. She found that and much more besides. In dingy working-class neighborhoods in Philadelphia and New York, in unpainted clapboard farmhouses in North Dakota, on the ravaged cotton farms of Georgia, on the dusty mesas of Colorado, Hickok uncovered not just the effects of the economic crisis that had begun in 1929. She found herself face to face as well with the human wreckage of a century of pell-mell, buccaneering, no-holds-barred, free-market industrial and agricultural capitalism. As her travels progressed, she gradually came to acknowledge the sobering reality that for many Americans the Great Depression brought times only a little harder than usual. She discovered, in short, what historian James Patterson has called the "old poverty" that was endemic in America well before the Depression hit. By his estimate, even in the midst of the storied prosperity of the 1920s some forty million Americans, including virtually all nonwhites, most of the elderly, and much of the rural population, were eking out unrelievedly precarious lives that were scarcely visible and practically unimaginable to their more financially secure countrymen. "The researches we have made into standards of living of the American family," Hopkins wrote, "have uncovered for the public gaze a volume of chronic poverty, unsuspected except by a few students and by those who have always experienced it." From this perspective, the Depression was not just a passing crisis but an episode that revealed deeply rooted structural inequities in American society.

The "old poor" were among the Depression's most ravaged victims, but it was not the Depression that had impoverished them. They were the "one-third of a nation" that Franklin Roosevelt would describe in 1937 as chronically "ill-housed, ill-clad, ill-nourished." By suddenly threatening to push millions of other Americans into their wretched condition, the Depression pried open a narrow window of political opportunity to do something at last on behalf of that long-suffering one-third, and in the process to redefine the very character of America....

... The Emergency Relief Appropriation Act addressed only the most immediate of his [FDR's] goals. Most of the agencies it spawned were destined to survive less than a decade. The longer-term features of Roosevelt's grand design—unemployment insurance and old-age pensions—were incorporated in a separate piece of legislation, a landmark measure whose legacy endured and reshaped the texture of American life: the Social Security Act.

No other New Deal measure proved more lastingly consequential or more emblematic of the very meaning of the New Deal. Nor did any other better reveal the tangled skein of human needs, economic calculations, idealistic visions, political pressures, partisan maneuverings, actuarial projections, and constitutional constraints out of which Roosevelt was obliged to weave his reform program. Tortuously threading each of those filaments through the needle of the legislative process, Roosevelt began with the Social Security Act to knit the fabric of the modern welfare state. It would in the end be a peculiar garment, one that could have been fashioned only in America and perhaps only in the circumstances of the Depression era.

No one knew better the singular possibilities of that place and time than Secretary of Labor Frances Perkins. To her the president in mid-1934 assigned the task of chairing a cabinet committee to prepare the social security legislation for submission to Congress. (Its other members were Treasury Secretary Henry Morgenthau, Attorney General Homer Cummings, Agriculture Secretary Henry Wallace, and Relief Administrator Harry Hopkins.) "[T]his was the time, above all times," Perkins wrote, "to be foresighted about future problems of unemployment and unprotected old age." The president shared this sense of urgency—and opportunity. Now is the time, he said to Perkins in 1934, when "we have to get it started, or it will never start."…

At the outset the president entertained extravagantly far-reaching ideas about the welfare system he envisioned. "[T]here is no reason why everybody in the United States should not be covered," he mused to Perkins on one occasion. "I see no reason why every child, from the day he is born, shouldn't be a member of the social security system. When he begins to grow up, he should know he will have old-age benefits direct from the insurance system to which he will belong all his life. If he is out of work, he gets a benefit. If he is sick or crippled, he gets a benefit…. And there is no reason why just the industrial workers should get the benefit of this," Roosevelt went on. "Everybody ought to be in on it—the farmer and his wife and his family. I don't see why not." Roosevelt persisted, as Perkins shook her head at this presidential woolgathering. "I don't see why not. Cradle to the grave—from the cradle to the grave they ought to be in a social insurance system."

That may have been the president's ideal outcome, but he knew as well as anyone that he would have to temper that vision in the forge of political and fiscal reality. Much of the country, not least the southern Democrats who were essential to his party's congressional majority, remained suspicious about all forms of social insurance. So Perkins, with dour Yankee prudence, went to work in a more practical vein. In the summer of 1934 she convened the Committee on Economic Security (CES), an advisory body of technical experts who would hammer out the precise terms of the social security legislation. She instructed the CES in words that spoke eloquently about her sensitivity to the novelties and difficulties of what they were about to undertake. "I recall emphasizing," she later wrote, "that the President was already in favor of a program of social insurance, but that it remained for them to make it practicable. We expected them," she recollected, in a passage that says volumes about her shrewd assessment of American political culture in the 1930s, "to remember that this was the United States in the years 1934–35. We hoped they would make recommendations based upon a practical knowledge of the needs of our country, the prejudices of our people, and our legislative habits."

The needs of the country were plain enough. But what of those prejudices and habits? What, in particular, of that phrase "under state laws" in the Democratic platform? Few items more deeply vexed the CES planners. Given the mobility of American workers and the manifest desirability of uniformity in national laws, most of the CES experts insisted that a centralized, federally administered system of social insurance would be the most equitable and the easiest to manage. They deemed a miscellany of state systems to be utterly impractical. Yet deeply ingrained traditions of states' rights challenged that commonsense approach, as did pervasive doubts about the federal government's constitutional power to act in this area.

Thomas Eliot, the young, Harvard-educated general counsel to the CES who played a major role in drafting the final bill, worried above all about "the omnipresent question of constitutionality." The lower federal courts, Eliot knew, had already handed down hundreds of injunctions against other New Deal measures. Constitutional tests of NRA and AAA were working their way to the Supreme Court. There, four justices—the "Battalion of Death" that included Justices McReynolds, Butler, VanDevanter, and Sutherland—were notoriously hostile to virtually any expansion of federal power over industry and commerce, not to mention the far bolder innovation of federal initiatives respecting employment and old age. Eliot brooded that "I could not honestly assure the committee that a national plan … would be upheld by the Supreme Court."…

Against their better judgment, the CES experts therefore resigned themselves to settling for a mixed federal-state system. Perkins took what comfort she could from the reflection that if the Supreme Court should declare the federal aspects of the law to be unconstitutional, at least the state laws would remain. Though they would not be uniform, they would be better than nothing.…

The pattern of economic reforms that the New Deal wove arose out of concrete historical circumstances. It also had a more coherent intellectual underpinning than is customarily recognized. Its cardinal aim was not to destroy capitalism but to devolatilize it, and at the same time to distribute its benefits more evenly.…

… And ever after, Americans assumed that the federal government had not merely a role, but a major responsibility, in ensuring the health of the economy and the welfare of citizens. That simple but momentous shift in perception was the newest thing in all the New Deal, and the most consequential too.

Humankind, of course, does not live by bread alone. Any assessment of what the New Deal did would be incomplete if it rested with an appraisal of New Deal economic policies and failed to acknowledge the remarkable array of social innovations nourished by Roosevelt's expansive temperament.…

For all his alleged inscrutability, Franklin Roosevelt's social vision was clear enough. "We are going to make a country," he once said to Frances Perkins, "in which no one is left out." In that unadorned sentence Roosevelt spoke volumes about the New Deal's lasting historical meaning. Like his rambling, comfortable, and unpretentious old home on the bluff above the Hudson River, Roosevelt's New Deal was a welcoming mansion of many rooms, a place where millions of his fellow citizens could find at last a measure of the security that the patrician Roosevelts enjoyed as their birthright.

Perhaps the New Deal's greatest achievement was its accommodation of the maturing immigrant communities that had milled uneasily on the margins of American society for a generation and more before the 1930s. In bringing them into the Democratic Party and closer to the mainstream of national life, the New Deal, even without fully intending to do so, also made room for an almost wholly new institution, the industrial union. To tens of millions of rural Americans, the New Deal offered the modern comforts of electricity, schools, and roads, as well as unaccustomed financial stability. To the elderly and the unemployed it extended the promise of income security, and the salvaged dignity that went with it.

To black Americans the New Deal offered jobs with CCC, WPA, and PWA and, perhaps as important, the compliment of respect from at least some federal officials. The time had not come for direct federal action to challenge Jim Crow and put right at last the crimes of slavery and discrimination, but more than a few New Dealers made clear where their sympathies lay and quietly prepared for a better future. Urged on by Eleanor Roosevelt, the president brought African-Americans into the government in small but unprecedented numbers. By the mid-1930s they gathered periodically as an informal "black cabinet," guided often by the redoubtable Mary McLeod Bethune. Roosevelt also appointed the first black federal judge, William Hastie. Several New Deal Departments and agencies, including especially Ickes's Interior Department and Aubrey Williams's National Youth Administration, placed advisers for "Negro affairs" on their staffs....

Above all, the New Deal gave to countless Americans who had never had much of it a sense of security, and with it a sense of having a stake in their country. And it did it all without shredding the American Constitution or sundering the American people. At a time when despair and alienation were prostrating other peoples under the heel of dictatorship, that was no small accomplishment.

FDR: Architect of Ineffectual Big Government

BURTON FOLSOM

On May 9, 1939, Henry Morgenthau, Jr., the secretary of the treasury and one of the most powerful men in America, had a startling confession to make....

> We have tried spending money. We are spending more than we have ever spent before and it does not work. And I have just one interest,

Burton Folsom, *New Deal or Raw Deal? How FDR's Economic Legacy Has Damaged America* (New York: Simon & Schuster, 2008), p. 1–4, 7–13, 15, 60–62, 119–121, 237–239, 245–246, 251, 254–256, 259–260. Reprinted by permission.

and if I am wrong … somebody else can have my job. I want to see this country prosperous. I want to see people get a job. I want to see people get enough to eat. We have never made good on our promises…. I say after eight years of this Administration we have just as much unemployment as when we started…. And an enormous debt to boot!

In these words, Morgenthau summarized a decade of disaster, especially during the years Roosevelt was in power. Indeed, average unemployment for the whole year in 1939 would be higher than that in 1931, the year before Roosevelt captured the presidency from Herbert Hoover. Fully 17.2 percent of Americans, or 9,480,000, remained unemployed in 1939, up from 16.3 percent, or 8,020,000 in 1931. On the positive side, 1939 was better than 1932 and 1933, when the Great Depression was at its nadir, but 1939 was still worse than 1931, which at that time was almost the worst unemployment year in U.S. history. No depression, or recession, had ever lasted even half this long….

High unemployment was just one of many tragic areas that made the 1930s a decade of disaster. The *Historical Statistics of the United States,* compiled by the Census Bureau, fills out the rest of the grim picture. The stock market, which picked up in the mid-1930s, had a collapse later in the decade. The value of all stocks dropped almost in half from 1937 to 1939. Car sales plummeted one-third in those same years, and were lower in 1939 than in any of the last seven years of the 1920s. Business failures jumped 50 percent from 1937 to 1939; patent applications for inventions were lower in 1939 than for any year of the 1920s. Real estate fore-closures, which did decrease steadily during the 1930s, were still higher in 1939 than in any year during the next two decades….

Did the New Deal, rather than helping to cure the Great Depression, actually help prolong it? That is an important question to ask and ponder. Almost all historians of the New Deal rank Roosevelt as a very good to great president and the New Deal programs as a step in the right direction. With only a few exceptions, historians lavish praise on Roosevelt as an effective innovator, and on the New Deal as a set of programs desperately needed and very helpful to the depressed nation.

An example of this adulation is the appraisal by Henry Steele Commager and Richard B. Morris, two of the most distinguished American historians of the twentieth century. Commager, during a remarkable career at Columbia University and Amherst College, wrote over forty books and became perhaps the bestselling historian of the century. From the first year of Roosevelt's presidency, Commager lectured and wrote articles in defense of the New Deal.

Richard Morris, his junior partner at Columbia, was a prolific author and president of the American Historical Association….

Commager and Morris's assessment highlights four main points of defense for Roosevelt and the New Deal that have been adopted by most historians for the last seventy years: first, the 1920s were an economic disaster; second, the New Deal programs were a corrective to the 1920s, and a step in the right direction; third, Roosevelt (and the New Deal) were very popular; and fourth, Roosevelt was a good administrator and moral leader.

These four points constitute what many historians call "the Roosevelt legend." Since the works of Arthur M. Schlesinger, Jr., and William Leuchtenburg have been essential in shaping and fleshing out this view of Roosevelt, I will quote from them liberally....

First, as Commager and Morris state, "The character of the Republican ascendancy of the twenties had been pervasively negative; the character of the New Deal was overwhelmingly positive." In other words, the 1920s was an economic disaster that helped lead to the Great Depression, from which Roosevelt with his New Deal provided useful tools of relief, partial recovery, and reform for the American economy.

To promote this view, both Schlesinger and Leuchtenburg support the underconsumption thesis, which states that the Great Depression was accelerated because workers did not have adequate purchasing power during the 1920s to buy the products of industrial America. According to Schlesinger, "Management's disposition [in the 1920s] to maintain prices ... meant that workers and farmers were denied the benefits of increased in their own productivity. The consequence was the relative decline of mass purchasing power." President Calvin Coolidge and his treasury secretary, Andrew Mellon, contributed to great income disparities by enacting tax cuts for the rich. "The Mellon tax policy," Schlesinger says, "placing its emphasis on relief for millionaires rather than for consumers, made the maldistribution of income and oversaving even worse." Along similar lines, Leuchtenburg argues, "Insofar as one accepts the theory that underconsumption explains the Depression, and I do, then one can say that the Presidents of the 1920's are to blame...."

Second, "the character of the New Deal was overwhelmingly positive." Its intentions were excellent, and its results tended to be positive. Historians cite statistics to support this point: unemployment was 25 percent in 1933, Roosevelt's first year in office, and dropped steadily to about 15 percent by the end of his term in early 1937. The New Deal, then, did not solve the Great Depression, but it was a move in the right direction. William Leuchtenburg writes, "The New Deal achieved a more just society by recognizing groups which had been largely unrepresented—staple farmers, industrial workers, particular ethnic groups, and the new intellectual-administrative class." Samuel Eliot Morison, longtime professor at Harvard University, echoed this view: "The New Deal was just what the term implied—a new deal of old cards, no longer stacked against the common man." Textbook writers often pick up this theme. Historian Joseph Conlin concludes, "The greatest positive accomplishment of the New Deal was to ease the economic hardships suffered by millions of Americans...."

Third, Roosevelt was a popular and beloved president. He received unprecedented amounts of fan mail and he won reelection by a smashing 523 to 8 landslide in the electoral college—and then won two more terms after that. His fireside chats on the radio uplifted Americans and mobilized them behind his New Deal. "He came through to people," Schlesinger wrote, "because they felt—correctly—that he liked them and cared about them."...

Fourth, Roosevelt was an admirable executive and a good moral leader. Schlesinger, like all historians, concedes that Roosevelt "made mistakes both in policy and in politics," but he was a great president nonetheless. "Roosevelt had superb qualities of leadership, superb instincts for the crucial problems of his age, superb ability to select and manage vigorous subordinates, enormous skill as a public educator, and enormous ability to lift the spirits of the republic and to mobilize national energies."…

These four parts of the Roosevelt legend have a strong cumulative effect and historians regularly place Roosevelt among the top three presidents in U.S. history. In fact, the most recent Schlesinger poll (1996) ranks Roosevelt and Lincoln as *the* greatest president in the U.S. history.…

Of course, historians are often nigglers and all students of Roosevelt and his presidency have some complaints. What's interesting is that most of these complaints are that Roosevelt should have done more than he did, not less. "The havoc that had been done before Roosevelt took office," Leuchtenburg argues, "was so great that even the unprecedented measures of the New Deal did not suffice to repair the damage."…

Some New Deal historians of the 1980s, 1990s, and 2000s—loosely called the "constraints school"—argue that the New Deal did promote many needed changes, but that Roosevelt was constrained in what he could accomplish and therefore he did as much reform as circumstances would permit.…

Two examples will help illustrate this point. David Kennedy and George McJimsey, both of whom loosely fit in the "constraints school," have written recent books on the Roosevelt presidency. Kennedy's book won the Pulitzer Prize in history and McJimsey's is part of the distinguished American Presidency Series. Kennedy praises "the remarkable generation of scholars" who did "pioneering work on the New Deal era." He cites Leuchtenburg, Schlesinger, and four other similar historians and writes, "Though I sometimes disagree with their emphases and evaluations, they laid the foundation on which all subsequent study of that period has built, including my own." Kennedy, like these predecessors, concludes, "Roosevelt's New Deal was a welcoming mansion of many rooms, a place where million of his fellow citizens could find at last a measure of … security.…" McJimsey, also like his predecessors, praises Roosevelt: "No president in our history has faced such critical problems with the courage, vision, and stamina that Roosevelt displayed." McJimsey concludes that "one of Roosevelt's major achievements was to create an institutional structure for the modern welfare state.… Subsequent presidents," McJimsey notes approvingly, "were freer than ever to use government in creative ways."…

As historian Ray Allen Billington noted, the New Deal "established for all time the principle of positive government action to rehabilitate and preserve the human resources of the nation." Yet, as we have seen, there is that nagging observation in 1939 by Henry Morgenthau, the secretary of the treasury, the friend of Roosevelt's and the man in the center of the storm.…

The Agricultural Adjustment Act (AAA), which was Roosevelt's plan for farmers, also passed Congress in 1933 with expectations almost as high as those for the NRA [National Recovery Act]. "I tell you frankly," Roosevelt said of the AAA, "that it is a new and untrod path.…" During the president's busy first hundred days in office in 1933, that was his opening salvo in restructuring the whole American farm program.

The AAA was very complicated, but in a nutshell here is how it worked. First, some farmers would be paid not to produce on part of their land; second, farm prices would be pegged to the purchasing power of farm prices in 1910; third, millers and processors would pay for much of the cost of the program. What's more, power would be centralized through the secretary of agriculture, who would set the processing taxes, target the price of many commodities, and tell farmers how much land to remove.

Why would congress pass such a strange law in the first place? The origin was in the severe farm crisis after World War I: over-production of crops and the low prices received for those crops. Of course, in a sense that was the perennial problem of the American farmer. In 1790, about 80 percent of Americans made their living as farmers. In the 1800s and 1900s, mechanization of crops (especially the major crops of wheat, corn, and cotton), improved seeds, and improved fertilizers meant that each farmer could feed more and more people. The economics of supply and demand typically worked against the farmer. The more he produced, the lower his price was, and, therefore, the more that farmers moved to the city and took up jobs there in the expanding factories and businesses.

By the 1930s, urbanization was well under way. Only 30 percent of Americans made their living as farmers in 1933. But selling the farm and moving to the city— the traditional response to low prices and overproduction—did not happen in the 1930s, and for three reasons. First, because the Great Depression was nationwide, few businesses were expanding and few jobs, therefore, were available in the city. Second, the Smoot-Hawley tariff, the highest tariff in U.S. history, created retaliatory tariffs. Few Europeans were buying American farm exports and thus foreign markets—the traditional outlet for overproduction—were shut off. Third, both Hoover and Roosevelt were more willing to experiment with government solutions to farm problems, even though the Constitution made no provision for direct farm relief.

The Federal Farm Board was Hoover's futile effort at intervention. He picked two major crops, wheat and cotton, both of which had strong political constituencies. He pegged the price of wheat at 80 cents/bushel and cotton at 20 cents/pound. Those were price floors, minimum prices. The government promised these prices for every bushel of wheat and every pound of cotton that American farmers produced. That way, two large groups of farmers would be protected from falling prices. Disaster quickly resulted. Wheat and cotton farmers, with prices guaranteed, expanded acreage and grew as much as possible. Farmers of other crops shifted to wheat and cotton, where their prices could then be guaranteed. Soon Hoover's Farm Board was building grain elevators to store wheat, and warehouses to store surplus cotton. After about two years of wild overproduction, the government had spent the $500 million allocated to the Farm Board. They stopped the programs and gave away or sold at huge losses about 250 million bushels of wheat and 10 million bales of cotton.

To many Americans, the Farm Board showed the damage created when government interfered with supply and demand. If more farmers would have moved to the city, which was an expanding job market before the 1930s, less would have been produced and prices would have risen for the more efficient farmers who remained on the farm. But few of the 30 percent of Americans who remained as farmers wanted to leave the land. The Farm Board gave them a precedent for government intervention and the high tariff gave them a reason to complain that others were getting help from the government. Why not farmers as well? Since farmers were a potentially strong political group in many states, politicians emerged to argue for more intervention. Hence Roosevelt and others made the case for the AAA, paying farmers not to produce....

Labor Relations

Employer-employee arrangements drastically changed during the New Deal. Before the Great Depression, "liberty of contract" tended to be the rule. "Whatever may be the advantages of 'collective bargaining,' it is not bargaining at all, in any just sense, unless it is voluntary on both sides," wrote Justice Mahlon Pitney of the Supreme Court in 1917. "The same liberty which enables men to form unions, and through the union to enter into agreements with employers willing to agree, entitles other men to remain independent of the union and other employers to employ no man who owes any allegiance or obligation to the union."

President Roosevelt wanted to tilt the balance of power more in favor of unions. The year he was elected president he had help from two of his friends, Senator George Norris of Nebraska and Representative Fiorello La Guardia of New York. Their Norris–La Guardia Anti-Injunction Act, passed in 1932, made it harder for employers to stop union organizing. Yellow-dog contracts, which required employees to agree not to join a union, were made unenforceable by law, and federal courts could issue no injunctions in labor disputes except in cases of fraud or violence.

When Roosevelt became president, his NRA gave further help to union organizing. According to the NRA, in the writing of industrial codes, workers had "the right to organize and bargain collectively through representatives of their own choosing, and shall be free from interference, restraint, or coercion of employers of labor." Workers were free to have a variety of unions, including company unions, represent them. The NRA did not require a "closed shop," that is, a single union mandated as the bargaining representative for all workers in an industry.

Even before the NRA was struck down by the Supreme Court, Senator Robert Wagner of New York, with Roosevelt's later tacit approval, began formulating a law that would strengthen the power of unions. The National Labor Relations Act, or the Wagner Act as it was sometimes called, proposed to sharply alter the industrial workforce. The key part of the bill had a list of "unfair labor practices." Employers were not allowed to stop any union from organizing. They could not fire anyone because he or she was a union member, and they had to agree to bargain collectively with union representatives. If 30 percent of employees in an industry wanted a union, they could have a vote and whichever union they might select would represent all workers....

The Wagner Act certainly weighted the scales toward labor. The United Stated had thousands of strikes and work stoppages as unionization proceeded rapidly in the 1930s and 1940s. Wages, of course, increased for many workers in the newly unionized industries. But from a standpoint of the Great Depression and overall employment, the new labor relations had problems as well. Since much higher wages were the cost of doing business for many corporations, they hired fewer workers and trimmed down their labor forces when possible—especially by mechanization, which occurred rapidly in the coal industry, for example. Unions often discriminated against blacks, so they rarely benefited from new labor laws. And American exports were sometimes less competitive on world markets. That also diminished sales and new hiring, which prolonged the Great Depression.…

If the evidence suggests that the New Deal failed, that raises a legitimate question: What should Roosevelt have done about the Great Depression? Put another way, what better path might Roosevelt have taken to achieve economic recovery?

Such a question is, of course, speculative and counterfactual. No one can be sure what alternatives would have produced a stronger economy and less unemployment. The Great Depression was a complicated, worldwide crisis and difficult to handle. It's easy many decades later to see errors in policy. Also, Roosevelt and other leaders were constrained politically and economically. They did not have the hindsight we have today. For example, few politicians of the 1920s and 1930s saw the damage done by the Federal Reserve, and not just in the higher interest rates, but in its demand that banks change their reserve ratios. Few saw at the time how the declining money supply, a by-product of Fed actions, damaged the economy and hindered recovery. In any case, however, because the Fed is independent, no one can really fault Hoover or Roosevelt for problems created by the new federal banking system.

Given the constraints on Roosevelt, then, and the confusion created by this unique depression, what could Roosevelt have done to achieve better recovery for the economy and more employment? Some comparisons might help. In the Panic of 1893, U.S. unemployment briefly hit what was then the all-time high of 18.4 percent, but the panic was over in a little more than five years. In the mini-recession of 1921, unemployment reached 11.7 percent, but hard times lasted less than two years. In both of these economic downturns, Presidents Cleveland and Harding cut federal expenses and, in the case of Harding, cut the income tax rate as well. Soon investments in business became attractive again, capital slowly flowed back into the American economy, and it bounced back. In recessions before 1893 and 1921, presidents followed roughly the same plan and the crises were short-lived.

In 1929, however, after the stock market crash, President Hoover did the opposite of Cleveland and Harding. Hoover increased federal spending—through the Federal Farm Board, the Reconstruction Finance Corporation, and public works. Then in 1932 he agreed to sharply increase both income and excise taxes to help pay for his costly programs. With the top income tax rate hiked to 63 percent, and with almost all Americans paying some excise taxes for the first time in U.S. history, private investment did not bounce back and unemployment reached 25 percent. Thus Roosevelt had an especially difficult task when he entered the White House. Some of his emergency measures—the banking holiday and taking the United States off the gold standard (to stop the outflow of gold)—may have been in order. His New Deal, however, is another story because there he applied ideas from underconsumption theory.

What if, instead of expanding Hoover's programs and starting many new ones of his own, Roosevelt had kept his campaign promises to cut spending, reduce taxes, and lower the Smoot-Hawley tariff immediately? In the Democrat Party platform, and in speech after speech during the campaign, Roosevelt promised these three things....

If Roosevelt's New Deal programs did not break the Great Depression, then what did? Most historians have argued that America's entry into World War II was the key event that ended it. Federal spending drastically increased as twelve million U.S. soldiers went to war, and millions more mobilized in the factories to make war materiel. As a result, unemployment plummeted and, so the argument goes, the Great Depression receded.

William Leuchtenburg, who has written the standard book on the New Deal, claims, "The real impetus to recovery was to come from rapid, large-scale spending." Roosevelt, according to Leuchtenburg, was reluctant to take this step. When, at last, Pearl Harbor was bombed, "The war proved that massive spending under the right conditions produced full employment."

Recently, David M. Kennedy, in his Pulitzer Prise–winning book on Roosevelt, echoed Leuchtenburg's argument. "Roosevelt," Kennedy insisted, "remained reluctant to the end of the 1930s to engage in the scale of compensatory spending adequate to restore the economy to pre-Depression levels, let alone expand it." At the end of his book, Kennedy concluded, "It was a war that had brought [Americans] as far as imagination could reach, and beyond, from the ordeal of the Great Depression...." More specifically, "The huge expenditures for weaponry clinched the Keynesian doctrine that government spending could underwrite prosperity...."

Economists, Keynes notwithstanding, have always been less willing to believe this theory than historians. F.A. Hayek, who won the Nobel Prize in economics, argued against this view in 1944 in *The Road to Serfdom*. Economist Henry Hazlitt, who wrote for the *New York Times* during the Roosevelt years, observed, "No man burns down his own house on the theory that the need to rebuild it will stimulate his energies." And yet, as historians and others viewed World War II, "they see almost endless benefits in enormous acts of destruction. They tell us how much better off economically we all are in war than in peace. They see 'miracles of production' which it requires a war to achieve." Thus, in Hazlitt's argument, the United States merely shifted capital from private markets, where it could have made consumer goods, to armament factories, where it made tanks, bombs, and planes for temporary use during war....

In retrospect, we can see that Roosevelt's special-interest spending created insatiable demands by almost all groups of voters for special subsidies. That, in itself, created regime uncertainty. Under the RFC [Reconstruction Finance

Corporation], for example, the federal government made special loans to banks and railroads; then the AAA had price supports for farmers; soon the operators of silver mines were demanding special high prices for their product. At one level, as we have seen, Roosevelt used these subsidies as political tools to reward friends and punish enemies. But beyond that, where would the line be drawn? Who would get special taxpayer subsidies and who would not? As Walter Waters, who led the veterans' march on Washington in 1932, observed, "I noticed, too, that the highly organized lobbies in Washington for special industries were producing results: loans were being granted to their special inter-ests and these lobbies seemed to justify their existence. Personal lobbying paid, regardless of the justice or injustice of their demand."...

Why would so many historians heap so much praise on Roosevelt? Most historians are, along with Roosevelt, influenced by the "progressive view of his-tory" that began to dominate American life during the presidency of Woodrow Wilson. Before the early 1900s, the constitutional views of the Founders domi-nated American political thought. In writing the Declaration of Independence and Constitution, the Founders emphasized natural rights—the process of ensur-ing God-given rights to life, liberty, and property to every American. "If men were angels, no government would be necessary," Madison wrote. But men were not angels, so to protect natural rights, the Constitution was written with power widely dispersed to prevent a strong president or legislature from increas-ing its authority and gradually turning the United States into a tyranny.

In crafting the Constitution, the Founders emphasized process, not results. If we follow the Constitution, we won't have a perfect society, which is unattain-able by imperfect humans. But we will provide opportunity for people to use their natural rights to pursue the acquisition of property and their personal happiness. The results may yield sharp inequalities of income, but the process will guarantee chances for almost everyone....

Woodrow Wilson—both as a Ph.D. in history and as a two-term president—represented a break with the Constitution and its constrained view of history. Government, in Wilson's progressive view, did not exist merely to protect rights. "We are not," Wilson insisted, "bound to adhere to the doctrines held by the signers of the Declaration of Independence." The limited government enshrined in both the Declaration and the Constitution may have been an advance for the Founders, Wilson conceded, but society had evolved since then. Separation of powers was inefficient and hindered modern government from promoting prog-ress. "The only fruit of dividing power," Wilson asserted, "was to make it irresponsible." A strong executive was needed, Wilson believed, to translate the interests of the people into public policy....

Roosevelt served in the Wilson administration and believed deeply in Wilson's progressive view of the Constitution. When Chief Justice Charles Evans Hughes was swearing in Rossevelt for his second term, he apparently read with great emphasis the words "promise to support the Constitution of the United States." Roosevelt met Hughes's challenge and repeated these words with force. Later the president said he wanted to shout, "Yes, but it's the Constitution as *I* understand it...." In a fireside chat on Court packing, Roosevelt dropped his argument for judicial efficiency and called the Constitution "a system of living law." He added, "We must have Judges who will bring to the courts a present-day sense of the Constitution."...

In the progressive view, intentions and sincerity are among the noblest virtues a president can possess. According to Schlesinger, "In the welter of confusion and ignorance [during the Great Depression], experiment corrected by compassion was the best answer." Experiment is valued by Schlesinger more than experience, and compassion, not results, is described as "the best answer." Leuchtenburg follows a similar line and notes, "many workingmen, poor farmers, and others who felt themselves to have been neglected in the past regarded Roosevelt as their friend. They sensed that his was a humane administration, that the President cared what happened to them." Historians seem to focus on "caring" and "compassion" more than on the unprecedented lack of recovery for the eleven years from 1929 to 1940....

The constitutional view of the Founders gives little weight to intentions. Good intentions assume that the leader, or leaders, know what is best for society. All they need is the authority to implement their ideas and reconstruct society. People with good intentions, however, can be busybodies who use the power of government to do more harm than good....

FURTHER READING

H. W. Brands, *Traitor to His Class: The Privileged Life and Radical Presidency of Franklin Delano Roosevelt* (2008).

Alan Brinkley, *Voices of Protest: Huey Long, Father Coughlin, and the Great Depression* (1982).

Lizabeth Cohen, *Making a New Deal: Industrial Workers in Chicago* (1990).

Blanche D. Coll, *Safety Net: Welfare and Social Security* (1995).

Lewis A. Erenberg, *Swingin' the Dream: Big Band Jazz and the Rebirth of American Culture* (1998).

Colin Gordon, *New Deals: Business, Labor, and Politics in America* (1994).

James N. Gregory, *American Exodus: The Dust Bowl Migration and Okie Culture in California* (1989).

Robert Higgs, *Against Leviathan: Government Power and a Free Society* (2004).

George T. McJimsey, *The Presidency of Franklin Delano Roosevelt* (2000).

Guiliana Muscio, *Hollywood's New Deal* (1997).

Harvard Sitkoff, *Fifty Years Later: The New Deal Evaluated* (1985).

Jason Scott Smith, *Building New Deal Liberalism: The Political Economy of Public Works, 1933–1956* (2006).

Patricia Sullivan, *Days of Hope: Race and Democracy in the New Deal Era* (1996).

Studs Terkel, *Hard Times: An Oral History of the Great Depression* (1970).

CHAPTER 9

The Ordeal of World War II

The Japanese bombing of American warships at Pearl Harbor, Hawaii, on December 7, 1941, brought the United States into a series of wars that had been underway in Asia and then in Europe for nearly a decade.

In 1931, the Japanese Imperial Army began a program of expansion and conquest that eventually reached from the cold far north of China down to the tropical jungles of Indochina. The United States consistently opposed Japan's military aggressiveness. Then, in 1933, Adolf Hitler seized dictatorial power in Germany, determined to rebuild his country. This would require, he decided, eliminating what he called the "parasites" within the nation (Jews), putting "inferior human material" (Poles, Russians, and other Slavs) to work for Germany, and obtaining the territory of other European nations for the enlargement of what he called the Third Reich (Third Empire of Germany).

England and France went to war against Germany when Hitler invaded and occupied Poland in September 1939, following his previous annexation of Austria and Czechoslovakia. The following spring, Hitler's massive army and air force attacked Norway, Denmark, Holland, Belgium, and France, all of which fell within a few weeks and remained occupied until the Allied invasion, four years later. The bombing of Pearl Harbor finally brought the United States into the war on the side of Britain and Russia, the last nations with any capacity to resist Hitler, who had allied himself with both Japan and the fascist government of Italy in a "Triple Axis." The United States, Britain, and Soviet Russia formed the nucleus of a worldwide, fifty-nation Grand Alliance, which eventually forced the Axis to surrender. The war culminated in the discovery of the Nazi death camps, where six million Jews and millions of Slavs had perished, and in the dropping of atomic bombs by the United States on the Japanese cities of Hiroshima and Nagasaki.

The war transformed America and the world. Great Britain and France witnessed the collapse of their overseas empires. The Soviet Union found itself in control of nations that had been traditionally hostile to it, and used the process of liberating central Europe from the Nazis to create a new security zone. The United States, which had entered both world wars late, emerged as the most powerful and wealthy nation on earth following the war, blessed with the opportunity and burdened with the responsibility of restructuring world politics, resurrecting the world economy, and preventing future wars. The Grand Alliance created a new organization called the United Nations designed to mediate all subsequent conflicts. The task was Herculean, but the effort to find rational alternatives to global self-destruction had begun.

Franklin D. Roosevelt and the Grand Alliance announced at the start of American participation in World War II that the war was being fought on behalf of elemental human rights—the "four freedoms." Hitler's deliberate slaughter of peoples who did not belong to the Aryan "race" helped to stir revulsion toward racism. Japan's horrific treatment of Allied prisoners of war (one out of three died) and Chinese civilians helped fuel a new definition of "war crimes." One of the unforeseen consequences of the conflict for the United States was to highlight the extent to which the "land of the free" itself violated the dignity of citizens who were not from European or Protestant backgrounds. The war reinforced American liberalism, strengthened the hand of advocates for civil rights, brought women into the workforce in greater numbers than ever before, ended the Great Depression, and heralded the onset of what the publisher of Time *and* Life *magazines called "the American Century."*

QUESTIONS TO THINK ABOUT

How did the war change Americans' expectations of their nation's role in the world? In what ways did participation in World War II differ from participation in World War I, and what were the consequences of these differences? Was the nation truly threatened? How did the war transform the nation internally?

DOCUMENTS

The documents in this chapter reflect the global character of the war. What people said and did thousands of miles away from the United States mattered deeply to the history of the nation. Japanese and German actions not only brought the United States into the war, but also cast new light on issues of human rights in the United States. Document 1 contains eyewitness accounts of the first large-scale massacre of captive civilians, for which World War II became infamous. American missionaries in China protested the genocidal warfare undertaken by Japanese soldiers during "the Rape of Nanking" and tried to alert their fellow Americans to the scope and consequences of unopposed Japanese aggression. Navy and army nurses on duty at Pearl Harbor were among the first Americans to experience the shock of warfare on December 7, 1941. Document 2 recounts their fears, but also the determination to resist that the surprise attack provoked. In document 3, British Prime Minister Winston Churchill recounts the moment at which he learned of the attack on Hawaii. American entry into the war marked the end of a lonely and desperate vigil for Great Britain, almost the only western European nation not yet conquered by, or allied with, Nazi Germany. The alliance with Britain proved crucial to Allied victory, as the final great assault was launched from its shores. Early in the war, Roosevelt declared that the United States was fighting on behalf of what he called the "four freedoms." His statements in document 4 helped raise expectations at home and abroad that the nation struggled to measure up to in following decades. Document 5 is a painting by Norman Rockwell, a popular American artist who volunteered to help alert the public to the stake it had in who won the war. "Freedom From Want" was one of four Rockwell illustrations for the cover of *Saturday Evening Post* that the Office of War Information subsequently used to sell war bonds. Document 6 reveals the ways in which the war also curtailed freedom, however, especially for Japanese Americans who found themselves the target of suspicion and discrimination. The U.S. government imprisoned most Japanese residing in the western states for the duration of the war, as did the government of Canada. In this selection, a girl recalls how dormitory life during internment gradually undermined the closeness of her nuclear family, though they had food and shelter adequate to physical survival. Document 7 shows the connection that African American citizens drew between Roosevelt's goals for the world and their own aspirations for greater freedom. Blacks stationed at segregated bases and consigned to non-fighting units complained there was a "lack of democracy" right at home. Document 8 shows another side of the Japanese-American experience. This article from the *Los Angeles Times* reveals that Nisei soldiers sometimes received decorations for bravery, and were defended by "average" Americans who opposed racism. One of these was Jackie Robinson, the soldier who integrated professional baseball three years later. In the final excerpt (document 9), General Dwight D. Eisenhower reports to General George C. Marshall about his discoveries at the German concentration camps, where more than six million Jews perished from execution or starvation. The Holocaust later contributed to American support for the creation of Israel, and came to symbolize the worst excesses of demagogic racism and unchecked aggression.

1. American Missionaries Speak Out About the Rape of Nanking, 1937

December 17: M. Searle Bates to the Japanese Embassy in Nanking

The reign of terror and brutality continues in the plain view of your buildings and among your own neighbors.

1. Last night soldiers repeatedly came to our Library buildings with its great crowd of refugees, demanding money, watches, and women at the point of the bayonet. When persons had no watches or money, usually because they had been looted several times in the two preceding days, the soldiers broke windows near them and roughly pushed them about. One of our own staff members was wounded by a bayonet in this manner.
2. At the Library building, as in many other places throughout this part of the city last night, soldiers raped several women.
3. Soldiers beat our own unarmed watchmen, because the watchmen did not have girls ready for the use of the soldiers.

American Missionary Eyewitnesses to the Nanking Massacre, 1937–1938 (Yale Divinity School Library Occasional Publication, No. 9, 1997, pp. 19, 21–24).

4. Last night several of our American-owned residences, with flags and Embassy proclamations on them, were entered irregularly by roving groups of soldiers, some of them several times. These residences included houses in which three American members of our staff are living.

We respectfully ask you to compare these acts, which are small samples of what is happening to large numbers of residents of Nanking, with your Government's official statements of its concern for the welfare of the people of China, likewise of its protection of foreign property....

December 19: James McCallum to His Family

It has been just one week now since the collapse of the Chinese Army in its Nanking defense. Japanese soldiers came marching down Chung Shan road past the hospital on Monday and Japanese flags began to appear here and there. We all breathed a sigh of relief thinking now order would be restored after the panic and stampede caused by the retreating Chinese army. Airplanes could fly over our head without causing apprehension or tension. But a week has passed and it has been hell on earth.

It is a horrible story to relate; I know not where to begin nor to end. Never have I heard or read of such brutality. Rape: Rape: Rape: We estimate at least 1,000 cases a night and many by day. In case of resistance or anything that seems like disapproval there is a bayonet stab or a bullet. We could write up hundreds of cases a day; people are hysterical; they get down on their knees and "Kotow" any time we foreigners appear; they beg for aid. Those who are suspected of being soldiers as well as others, have been led outside the city and shot down by hundreds, yes, thousands. Three times has the staff of our Hospital been robbed of fountain pens, watches and money. Even the poor refugees in certain centers have been robbed again and again until the last cent, almost the last garment and last piece of bedding only remains and this may go ere long. Women are being carried off every morning, afternoon and evening. The whole Japanese Army seems to be free to go and come anywhere it pleases and to do what it pleases. American flags have frequently been torn down from Ginling and the University and Hillcrest school....

December 19: John Magee to His Wife

The horror of the last week is beyond anything I have ever experienced. I never dreamed that the Japanese soldiers were such savages. It has been a week of murder and rape, worse, I imagine, than has happened for a very long time unless the massacre of the Armenians by the Turks was comparable. They not only killed every prisoner they could find but also a vast number of ordinary citizens of all ages. Many of them were shot down like the hunting of rabbits in the streets. There are dead bodies all over the city from the south city to Hsiakwan. Just day before yesterday we saw a poor wretch killed very near the house where we are living. So many of the Chinese are timid and when challenged foolishly start to run. This is what happened to that man. The actual killing we did not see as it took place just around the corner of a bamboo fence from where we could see. Cola went there later and said the man had been shot twice in the head. These two Jap. soldiers were no more concerned than if they had been killing a rat and never stopped smoking their cigarettes and talking and laughing....

But the most horrible thing now is the raping of the women which has been going on in the most shameless way that I have ever known. The streets are full of men searching for women.... Several days ago a Buddhist priest from a little temple across the street came in and said he had heard that Japanese had carried off two Buddhist nuns and begged me to take some nuns in, which I have done. The house is really packed like sardines. They sleep in the halls upstairs and down and for a while we had a mother and daughter in our bathroom....

2. Nurses Rush to Aid the Wounded on the U.S. Naval Base in Hawaii, 1941

Lenore Terrell Rickert, U.S. Navy

Everybody wants to know if we were afraid. Fear never entered into it. Most everyone who was there says the same thing. We never even gave it a thought, never worried about our personal safety.

I was making rounds with the Medical Officer of the Day at the Pearl Harbor naval hospital when we heard a plane right overhead. Because of the patients, our aircraft never flew over the hospital.... We ran to look and the plane was coming in between the two wards. We knew right away what was happening.

I ran to the nurses' quarters to sound the alert, and that's when the actual bombing started....

The ambulatory patients immediately left the hospital to get back to their ships. One patient, whose eyes were both bandaged, got out of bed, crawled underneath, and pulled a blanket down to lie on, so we could use the bed for the wounded. Everyone was worrying about the others and not themselves.

The hospital really surprised me, everything went so smoothly. Up until that time, if you sent your weekly supply request on Friday, you were lucky if you received fifty percent of it the next week. On that day you scribbled what you needed on a piece of paper and someone ran over to the supply room and brought it right back. It was unbelievable, the way the whole hospital was that day.

Helen Entrikin, U.S. Navy

My twin sister was a U.S. Army nurse stationed in Hawaii and urged me to transfer there because it was so nice. We were both on duty that morning.

When the planes dropped their bombs, then strafed as they came back, I ran inside the hospital and gathered up the narcotics and everything we would need.

No Time for Fear: Voices of American Military Nurses in World War II by Diane Burke Fessler (Ann Arbor: Michigan State University Press, 1996), pp. 14–16.

A little dressing room became a mini-operating theater, because the regular operating rooms were so backlogged. The patients were scared, and when they died we received others right away in their place. We put mattresses on the hall-way floor to rest a little at a time....

Sara Entrikin, U.S. Army

Hearing the explosions, I ran outside and saw the red sun on a plane that was coming in so close that I could see the faces of the pilots. One of them looked at us and smiled. I rushed to the hospital. Casualties were coming in fast and furious because the barracks were right along the runway and that's where the bombs hit first. Our hospital was close to the runway also, and we had a lot of noise and smoke from shells ricocheting over to it. There were only seven of us nurses, and we couldn't possibly begin to take care of all the wounded and dying men. The decision was made to treat patients with first-aid-type care and send them to Tripler General Hospital in ambulances. Soon there weren't enough ambulances, so the local people drove patients in their cars.

Not too far from the hospital there was an American flag flying, and after the Japs dropped their bombs, one plane came back and circled, shooting until the flag was torn to shreds. That night we put up blackout window covers; we were told that if captured, to only give our name, rank, and serial number....

Mildred Irene Clark Woodman, U.S. Army

Loud explosions awakened me and I heard planes overhead. I opened the door and saw planes coming through the pass in the mountains between Honolulu and Schofield. The large bright insignia of the rising sun was boldly on the side of each plane. They flew so close I could hear the radio communications between the pilots. In one minute I dressed and ran to the hospital.

The hospital was hit, even though the hospital building had a large red cross painted on the roof, according to the provisions of the Geneva Convention. Casualties were arriving on stretchers as I reported to the operating room, with ambulance sirens wailing in the background. In a short time, the nine operating rooms were extremely busy, while patients waited for care in the corridor. I kept hearing planes overhead, but we were too busy to be afraid or to ask what was happening.... [W]we had seen too much death and were involved with the most serious wounds and bravest of men. Patients had arms and legs amputated, severe chest and spinal wounds, abdominal and cranial wounds. Many wanted to go out and fight back....

Sometime near early morning following the attack, several of us had the opportunity for a quiet moment to talk to each other and exchange our limited knowledge of what happened. We talked quietly since there was a rumor that the Japanese had eighty transports off Diamond Head and were landing parachute troops in the nearby cane fields. The subject of being captured and becoming pris-oners of war came up and each voiced her plan. Two indicated they would walk into the sea, others would hide in caves, some would go with their friends to prison, while others of us would fight to the death and never be captured alive.

3. British Prime Minister Winston Churchill Reacts to Pearl Harbor, 1941

It was Sunday evening, December 7, 1941. Winant and Averell Harriman were alone with me at the table at Chequers. I turned on my small wireless set shortly after the nine o'clock news had started. There were a number of items about the fighting on the Russian front and on the British front in Libya, at the end of which some few sentences were spoken regarding an attack by the Japanese on American shipping at Hawaii, and also Japanese attacks on British vessels in the Dutch East Indies. There followed a statement that after the news Mr. Somebody would make a commentary, and that the Brains Trust programme would then begin, or something like this. I did not personally sustain any direct impression, but Averell said there was something about the Japanese attacking the Americans, and, in spite of being tired and resting, we all sat up. By now the butler, Sawyers, who had heard what had passed, came into the room, saying, "It's quite true. We heard it ourselves outside. The Japanese have attacked the Americans." There was a silence. At the Mansion House luncheon on November 11 I had said that if Japan attacked the United States a British declaration of war would follow "within the hour." I got up from the table and walked through the hall to the office, which was always at work. I asked for a call to the President. The Ambassador followed me out, and, imagining I was about to take some irrevocable step, said, "Don't you think you'd better get confirmation first?"

In two or three minutes Mr. Roosevelt came through. "Mr. President, what's this about Japan?" "It's quite true," he replied. "They have attacked us at Pearl Harbour. We are all in the same boat now." I put Winant onto the line and some interchanges took place, the Ambassador at first saying. "Good" "Good"—and then, apparently graver, "Ah!" I got on again and said, "This certainly simplifies things. God be with you," or words to that effect. We then went back into the hall and tried to adjust our thoughts to the supreme world event which had occurred, which was of so startling a nature as to make even those who were near the centre gasp. My two American friends took the shock with admirable fortitude. We had no idea that any serious losses had been inflicted on the United States Navy. They did not wail or lament that their country was at war. They wasted no words in reproach or sorrow. In fact, one might almost have thought they had been delivered from a long pain....

No American will think it wrong of me if I proclaim that to have the United States at our side was to me the greatest joy. I could not foretell the course of events. I do not pretend to have measured accurately the martial might of Japan, but now at this very moment I knew the United States was in the war, up to the neck and in to the death. So we had won after all! Yes, after Dunkirk; after the fall of France; after the horrible episode of Oran; after the threat of invasion, when, apart from the Air and the Navy, we were an almost unarmed people; after the deadly struggle of the U-boat war—the first Battle of the Atlantic, gained by a hand's-breadth; after seventeen months of lonely fighting and nineteen months of my responsibility in dire stress. We had won the war. England would live; Britain would live; the Commonwealth of Nations and the Empire would live. How long the war would last or in what fashion it would end no man could tell, nor did I at this moment care. Once again in our long island history we should emerge, however mauled or mutilated, safe and victorious. We should not be wiped out. Our history would not come to an end. We might not even have to die as individuals. Hitler's fate was sealed. Mussolini's fate was sealed. As for the Japanese, they would be ground to powder. All the rest was merely the proper application of overwhelming force. The British Empire, the Soviet Union, and now the United States, bound together with every scrap of their life and strength, were, according to my lights, twice or even thrice the force of their antagonists....

Silly people, and there were many, not only in enemy countries, might discount the force of the United States. Some said they were soft, others that they would never be united. They would fool around at a distance. They would never come to grips. They would never stand blood-letting. Their democracy and system of recurrent elections would paralyse their war effort. They would be just a vague blur on the horizon to friend or foe. Now we should see the weakness of this numerous but remote, wealthy, and talkative people. But I had studied the American Civil War, fought out to the last desperate inch. American blood flowed in my veins. I thought of a remark which Edward Grey had made to me more than thirty years before—that the United States is like "a gigantic boiler. Once the fire is lighted under it there is no limit to the power it can generate." Being saturated and satiated with emotion and sensation, I went to bed and slept the sleep of the saved and thankful.

4. Roosevelt Identifies the "Four Freedoms" at Stake in the War, 1941

... There is nothing mysterious about the foundations of a healthy and strong democracy. The basic things expected by our people of their political and economic systems are simple. They are:

Equality of opportunity for youth and for others.
Jobs for those who can work.
Security for those who need it.
The ending of special privilege for the few.
The preservation of civil liberties for all.
The enjoyment of the fruits of scientific progress in a wider and constantly rising standard of living.

These are the simple, basic things that must never be lost sight of in the turmoil and unbelievable complexity of our modern world. The inner and

The Public Papers and Addresses of Franklin D. Roosevelt (New York: Macmillan, 1941), Vol. 9, 671–672.

abiding strength of our economic and political systems is dependent upon the degree to which they fulfill these expectations.

Many subjects connected with our social economy call for immediate improvement.

As examples:

> We should bring more citizens under the coverage of old-age pensions and unemployment insurance.
> We should widen the opportunities for adequate medical care.
> We should plan a better system by which persons deserving or needing gainful employment may obtain it.

I have called for personal sacrifice. I am assured of the willingness of almost all Americans to respond to that call.

A part of the sacrifice means the payment of more money in taxes. In my Budget Message I shall recommend that a greater portion of this great defense program be paid for from taxation than we are paying today. No person should try, or be allowed, to get rich out of this program; and the principle of tax payments in accordance with ability to pay should be constantly before our eyes to guide our legislation.

If the Congress maintains these principles, the voters, putting patriotism ahead of pocketbooks, will give you their applause.

In the future days, which we seek to make secure, we look forward to a world founded upon four essential human freedoms.

> The first is freedom of speech and expression—everywhere in the world.
> The second is freedom of every person to worship God in his own way— everywhere in the world.
> The third is freedom from want—which, translated into world terms, means economic understandings which will secure to every nation a healthy peacetime life for its inhabitants—everywhere in the world.
> The fourth is freedom from fear—which, translated into world terms, means a world-wide reduction of armaments to such a point and in such a thorough fashion that no nation will be in a position to commit an act of physical aggression against any neighbor—anywhere in the world.

That is no vision of a distant millennium. It is a definite basis for a kind of world attainable in our own time and generation. That kind of world is the very antithesis of the so-called new order of tyranny which the dictators seek to create with the crash of a bomb.

To that new order we oppose the greater conception—the moral order. A good society is able to face schemes of world domination and foreign revolutions alike without fear.

Since the beginning of our American history, we have been engaged in change—in a perpetual peaceful revolution—a revolution which goes on steadily, quietly adjusting itself to changing conditions—without the concentration camp or the quicklime in the ditch. The world order which we seek is the cooperation of free countries, working together in a friendly, civilized society.

This nation has placed its destiny in the hands and heads and hearts of millions of free men and women; and its faith in freedom under the guidance of God. Freedom means the supremacy of human rights everywhere. Our support goes to those who struggle to gain those rights or keep them. Our strength is our unity of purpose.

To that high concept there can be no end save victory.

5. Norman Rockwell Depicts "Freedom From Want" for the Office of War Information, 1942

Ours to fight for ... freedom from want/Norman Rockwell. Washington, D.C. U.S. Government Printing Office AA 1943. 1 photomechanical printcol.

6. A Japanese American Recalls the Effect of Internment on Family Unity, 1942

… The War Department was in charge of all the camps at this point. They began to issue military surplus from the First World War—olive-drab knit caps, ear-muffs, peacoats, canvas leggings. Later on, sewing machines were shipped in, and one barracks was turned into a clothing factory. An old seamstress took a peacoat of mine, tore the lining out, opened and flattened the sleeves, added a collar, put arm holes in and handed me back a beautiful cape. By fall dozens of seamstresses were working full-time transforming thousands of these old army clothes into capes, slacks and stylish coats. But until that factory got going and packages from friends outside began to fill out our wardrobes, warmth was more important than style. I couldn't help laughing at Mama walking around in army earmuffs and a pair of wide-cuffed, khaki-colored wool trousers several sizes too big for her. Japanese are generally smaller than Caucasians, and almost all these clothes were oversize. They flopped, they dangled, they hung.

It seems comical, looking back: we were a band of Charlie Chaplins marooned in the California desert. But at the time, it was pure chaos. That's the only way to describe it. The evacuation had been so hurriedly planned, the camps so hastily thrown together, nothing was completed when we got there, and almost nothing worked.

I was sick continually, with stomach cramps and diarrhea. At first it was from the shots they gave us for typhoid, in very heavy doses and in assembly-line fashion; swab, jab, swab, *Move along now,* swab, jab, swab, *Keep it moving.* That knocked all of us younger kids down at once, with fevers and vomiting. Later, it was the food that made us sick, young and old alike. The kitchens were too small and badly ventilated….

"The Manzanar runs" became a condition of life, and you only hoped that when you rushed to the latrine, one would be in working order.

That first morning, on our way to the chow line, Mama and I tried to use the women's latrine in our block. The smell of it spoiled what little appetite we had. Outside, men were working in an open trench, up to their knees in muck—a common sight in the months to come. Inside, the floor was covered with excrement, and all twelve bowls were erupting like a row of tiny volcanoes.

Mama stopped a kimono-wrapped woman stepping past us with her sleeve pushed up against her nose and asked, "What do you do?"

"Try Block Twelve," the woman said, grimacing. "They have just finished repairing the pipes."

It was about two city blocks away. We followed her over there and found a line of women waiting in the wind outside the latrine. We had no choice but to join the line and wait with them.

From Jeanne Wakatsuki Houston and James D. Houston, Farewell to Manzanar: *A True Story of Japanese American Experience During and After the World War II Internment,* pp. 20-27. Copyright © 1973 by James D. Houston. Reprinted by permission of Houghton Mifflin Harcourt Publishing Company. All rights reserved.

Inside it was like all the other latrines. Each block was built to the same design, just as each of ten camps, from California to Arkansas, was built to a common master plan. It was an open room, over a concrete slab. The sink was a long metal trough against one wall, with a row of spigots for hot and cold water. Down the center of the room twelve toilet bowls were arranged in six pairs, back to back, with no partitions. My mother was a very modest person, and this was going to be agony for her, sitting down in public, among strangers.

One old woman had already solved the problem for herself by dragging in a large cardboard carton. She set it up around one of the bowls, like a three-sided screen. OXYDOL was printed in large black letters down the front. I remember this well, because that was the soap we were issued for laundry; later on, the smell of it would permeate these rooms. The upended carton was about four feet high. The old woman behind it wasn't much taller. When she stood, only her head showed over the top.

She was about Granny's age. With great effort she was trying to fold the sides of the screen together. Mama happened to be at the head of the line now. As she approached the vacant bowl, she and the old woman bowed to each other from the waist. Mama then moved to help her with the carton, and the old woman said very graciously, in Japanese, "Would you like to use it?"

Happily, gratefully, Mama bowed again and said, *"Arigato"* (Thank you). *"Arigato gozaimas"* (Thank you very much). "I will return it to your barracks."

"Oh, no. It is not necessary. I will be glad to wait."

The old woman unfolded one side of the cardboard, while Mama opened the other; then she bowed again and scurried out the door.

Those big cartons were a common sight in the spring of 1942. Eventually sturdier partitions appeared, one or two at a time. The first were built of scrap lumber. Word would get around that Block such and such had partitions now, and Mama and my older sisters would walk halfway across the camp to use them. Even after every latrine in camp was screened, this quest for privacy continued. Many would wait until late at night. Ironically, because of this, midnight was often the most crowded time of all.

Like so many of the women there, Mama never did get used to the latrines. It was a humiliation she just learned to endure: *shikata ga nai,* this cannot be helped....

At seven I was too young to be insulted. The camp worked on me in a much different way. I wasn't aware of this at the time, of course. No one was, except maybe Mama, and there was little she could have done to change what happened.

It began in the mess hall. Before Manzanar, mealtime had always been the center of our family scene. In camp, and afterward, I would often recall with deep yearning the old round wooden table in our dining room in Ocean Park, the biggest piece of furniture we owned, large enough to seat twelve or thirteen of us at once. A tall row of elegant, lathe-turned spindles separated this table from the kitchen, allowing talk to pass from one room to other. Dinners were always noisy, and they were always abundant with great pots of boiled rice, platters of home-grown vegetables, fish Papa caught.

He would sit at the head of this table, with Mama next to him serving and the rest of us arranged around the edges according to age, down to where Kiyo and I sat, so far away from our parents, it seemed at the time, we had our own enclosed nook inside this world. The grownups would be talking down at their end, while we two played our secret games, making eyes at each other when Papa gave the order to begin to eat, racing with chopsticks to scrape the last grain from our rice bowls, eyeing Papa to see if he had noticed who won.

Now, in the mess halls, after a few weeks had passed, we stopped eating as a family. Mama tried to hold us together for a while, but it was hopeless. Granny was too feeble to walk across the block three times a day, especially during heavy weather, so May brought food to her in the barracks. My older brothers and sisters, meanwhile, began eating with their friends, or eating somewhere blocks away, in the hope of finding better food. The word would get around that the cook over in Block 22, say, really knew his stuff, and they would eat a few meals over there, to test the rumor. Camp authorities frowned on mess hall hopping and tried to stop it, but the good cooks liked it. They liked to see long lines outside their kitchens and would work overtime to attract a crowd.

Younger boys, like Ray, would make a game of seeing how many mess halls they could hit in one meal period—be the first in line at Block 16, gobble down your food, run to 17 by the middle of the dinner hour, gulp another helping, and hurry to 18 to make the end of the chow line and stuff in the third meal of the evening. They didn't *need* to do that. No matter how bad the food might be, you could always eat till you were full.

Kiyo and I were too young to run around, but often we would eat in gangs with other kids, while the grownups sat at another table. I confess I enjoyed this part of it at the time. We all did. A couple of years after the camps opened, sociologists studying the life noticed what had happened to the families. They made some recommendations, and edicts went out that families *must* start eating together again. Most people resented this; they griped and grumbled. They were in the habit of eating with their friends. And until the mess hall system itself could be changed, not much could really be done. It was too late.

My own family, after three years of mess hall living, collapsed as an integrated unit. Whatever dignity or feeling of filial strength we may have known before December 1941 was lost, and we did not recover it until many years after the war, not until after Papa died and we began to come together, trying to fill the vacuum his passing left in all our lives....

7. An African American Soldier Notes the "Strange Paradox" of the War, 1944

33rd AAF Base Unit (CCTS(H))
Section C
DAVIS-MONTHAN FIELD
Tucson, Arizona
9 May 1944.

President Franklin Delano Roosevelt
White House
Washington, D.C.

Dear President Roosevelt:

It was with extreme pride that I, a soldier in the Armed Forces of our country, read the following affirmation of our war aims, pronounced by you at a recent press conference:

"The United Nations are fighting to make a world in which tyranny, and aggression cannot exist; a world based upon freedom, equality, and justice; a world in which all persons, regardless of race, color and creed, may live in peace, honor and dignity."...

But the picture in our country is marred by one of the strangest paradoxes in our whole fight against world fascism. The United States Armed Forces, to fight for World Democracy, is within itself undemocratic. The undemocratic policy of jim crow and segregation is practiced by our Armed Forces against its Negro members. Totally inadequate opportunities are given to the Negro members of our Armed Forces, nearly one tenth of the whole, to participate with "equality" ... "regardless of race and color" in the fight for our war aims. In fact it appears that the army intends to follow the very policy that the FEPC [Fair Employment Practices Commission] is battling against in civilian life, the pattern of assigning Negroes to the lowest types of work.

Let me give you an example of the lack of democracy in our Field, where I am now stationed. Negro soldiers are completely segregated from the white soldiers on the base. And to make doubly sure that no mistake is made about this, the barracks and other housing facilities (supply room, mess hall, etc.) of the Negro Section C are covered with black tar paper, while all other barracks and housing facilities on the base are painted white.

It is the stated policy of the Second Air Force that "every potential fighting man must be used as a fighting man. If you have such a man in a base job, you have no choice. His job must be eliminated or be filled by a limited service man, WAC, or civilian." And yet, leaving out the Negro soldiers working with the Medical Section, fully 50% of the Negro soldiers are working in base jobs, such as, for example, at the Resident Officers' Mess, Bachelor Officers' Quarters, and Officers' Club, as mess personnel, BOQ orderlies, and bar tenders. Leaving out the medical men again, based on the section C average only 4% of this 50% would not be "potential fighting men."...

Taps for a Jim Crow Army: Letters from Black Soldiers in World War II, ABC-CLIO, 1983, 134–139.

How can we convince nearly one tenth of the Armed Forces, the Negro members, that your pronouncement of the war aims of the United Nations means what it says, when their experience with one of the United Nations, the United States of America, is just the opposite?...

With your issuance of Executive Order 8802, and the setting up of the Fair Employment Practices Committee, you established the foundation for fighting for democracy in the industrial forces of our country, in the interest of victory for the United Nations. In the interest of victory for the United Nations, another Executive Order is now needed. An Executive Order which will lay the base for fighting for democracy in the Armed Forces of our country. An Executive Order which would bring about the result here at Davis-Monthan Field whereby the Negro soldiers would be integrated into all of the Sections on the base, as fighting men, instead of in the segregated Section C as housekeepers.

Then and only then can your pronouncement of the war aims of the United Nations mean to *all* that we "are fighting to make a world in which tyranny, and aggression cannot exist; a world based upon freedom, equality and justice; a world in which all persons, regardless of race, color and creed, may live in peace, honor and dignity."

Respectfully yours,

Charles F. Wilson, 36794590

Private, Air Corps.

8. Nisei Soldier Honored with the Gold Star— and by Jackie Robinson, 1944

"Even unto death, we'll show we're Americans in every way..."

So wrote Henry Kondo, Pasadena Nisei, from his Army station somewhere in Italy.

Yesterday a gold star appeared opposite Kondo's name on the roll of honor for Japanese Americans in the armed forces dedicated at the Pasadena Federated Mission. He was the first one of the 109 Pasadena Nisei to be killed in action.

Present at the ceremonies was 19-year-old Esther Takel, whose recent enrollment at Pasadena Junior College aroused controversy throughout California, and Dr. John W. Harbeson, Junior College principal, who declared the school would always be open to all American citizens regardless of race, color or religion.

Rev. Clare Blauvelt, pastor of Throop Memorial Church of Pasadena, conducted the dedication and the salute to the Flag was led by Lt. Jack Robinson, Negro football star of past years. Stephen Rayes spoke in behalf of the Pasadena Interracial Commission and the Mexican-American minority group. F. W. Parsons of the Federated Mission pleaded for proper recognition of Nisei servicemen.

"Gold Star Honors Nisei Killed in Action," *Los Angeles Times* Nov. 18, 1944, p.4. Reprinted by permission.

Other speakers were Herbert V. Nicholson and William C. Carr, chairman of the Friends of the American Way Society. Prayer was offered by Rev. Leonard Oechsll of the Pasadena Methodist Church.

9. General Dwight Eisenhower Testifies to the German Concentration Camps, 1945

To GEORGE CATLETT MARSHALL   *April 15, 1945*
Secret

Dear General:...

On a recent tour of the forward areas in First and Third Armies, I stopped momentarily at the salt mines to take a look at the German treasure. There is a lot of it. But the most interesting—although horrible—sight that I encountered during the trip was a visit to a German internment camp near Gotha. The things I saw beggar description. While I was touring the camp I encountered three men who had been inmates and by one ruse or another had made their escape. I interviewed them through an interpreter. The visual evidence and the verbal testimony of starvation, cruelty and bestiality were so overpowering as to leave me a bit sick. In one room, where they [there] were piled up twenty or thirty naked men, killed by starvation, George Patton would not even enter. He said he would get sick if he did so. I made the visit deliberately, in order to be in position to give *first-hand* evidence of these things if ever, in the future, there develops a tendency to charge these allegations merely to "propaganda."...

April 19, 1945

From Eisenhower to General Marshall for eyes only: We continue to uncover German concentration camps for political prisoners in which conditions of indescribable horror prevail. I have visited one of these myself and I assure you that whatever has been printed on them to date has been understatement. If you would see any advantage in asking about a dozen leaders of Congress and a dozen prominent editors to make a short visit to this theater in a couple of C-54's, I will arrange to have them conducted to one of these places where the evidence of bestiality and cruelty is so overpowering as to leave no doubt in their minds about the normal practices of the Germans in these camps. I am hopeful that some British individuals in similar categories will visit the northern area to witness similar evidence of atrocity.

ESSAYS

World War II is sometimes called "the good war"—even though it is widely recognized that all war is "hell." The bombing of Pearl Harbor created a broader consensus of support for this war than for any other war in the nation's

The Papers of Dwight D. Eisenhower, vol. 4, *The War Years*, ed. Alfred D. Changler, Jr. (Baltimore: Johns Hopkins Press, 1970), 2615–2617, 2623.

history, including the Revolution. Historians have thus tended to debate the consequences of the war more than its origins. The following two essays look at the experience of the war from different vantage points: that of the soldier fighting for his own elemental survival as well as for his country, and that of the society back home. John Morton Blum, retired from Yale University, depicts combat soldiers as largely disconnected from the geopolitical goals articulated by President Roosevelt. When they said they were fighting for America and apple pie, they were mostly thinking of the pie—in other words, about getting home. Place yourself in their boots: think about how might the war have affected that generation's view of life afterward, and of their nation's role in the world. In the second essay, Alan Brinkley of Columbia University discusses the effects of World War II on the domestic character of the United States. The war, he shows, not only brought the Great Depression to an end and established the nation as a superpower, but it helped to reshape race relations, gender roles, and the ideology of liberalism itself. Brinkley emphasizes that Americans fought, at least to some extent, to advance liberal values and social justice. Reading Blum and Brinkley together may lead you to wonder whom the war affected most: the soldiers who fought it, or the society they left behind at home.

G.I. Joe: Fighting for Home

JOHN MORTON BLUM

On September 21, 1943, War Bond Day for the Columbia Broadcasting System, Miss Kate Smith spoke over the radio at repeated intervals, in all, sixty-five times, from eight o'clock in the morning until two in the morning the next day. Her pleas to her listeners, some 20 million Americans, resulted in the sale of about $39 million worth of bonds. The content of her messages, according to a convincing analysis of her marathon, was less important than her person. [Smith was a popular singer best known for her rendition of "God Bless America."] Her listeners responded as they did in large part because for them she symbolized, in heroic proportions, values they honored: patriotism, sincerity, generosity. In that, of course, she was not alone. Edward L. Bernays, the premier public-relations counselor in the United States, accepted a commission during the war from the Franklin Institute "to give Benjamin Franklin greater fame and prestige in the hierarchy of American godhead symbols." As Bernays went about his business of persuading local communities to name streets, buildings, even firehouses after his subject, he found his task easy, for, as he put it, "our society craves heroes."

War accentuated that craving, especially for those at home who sought symbols on which to focus the sentiments they felt or were, they knew, supposed to feel—symbols that would assist the imagination in converting daily drabness into a sense of vicarious participation in danger. The battlefield provided a plenitude of such symbols, of genuine heroes who were then ordinarily clothed, whether

"The GI's: American Boys" and "In Foreign Foxholes" from *V Was For Victory: Politics and American Culture During World War II*. Copyright © 1976 by John Morton Blum, reprinted by permission of Harcourt, Inc.

justly or not, with characteristics long identified with national virtue. The profiles of the heroes of the war followed reassuring lines, some of them perhaps more precious than ever before because they had become less relevant, less attainable than they had been in a simpler, more bucolic past. Some others, less sentimental, were no less reassuring, for they displayed the hero as a man like other men, not least the man who wanted to admire someone whose place and ways might have been his own, had chance so ruled.

No leap of a reader's imagination, however, could easily find believable heroes in the Army's official communiqués. Though they sometimes mentioned names, those accounts supplied only summaries of action that generally obliterated both the brutality and the agony of warfare. Robert Sherrod, who landed with the marines at Tarawa and wrote a piercing description of that ghastly operation, deplored the inadequacy of American information services. "Early in the war," he commented, "one communiqué gave the impression that we were bowling over the enemy every time our handful of bombers dropped a few pitiful tons from 3,000 feet. The stories … gave the impression that any American could lick any twenty Japs.… The communiqués … were rewritten by press association reporters who waited for them back at rear headquarters. The stories almost invariably came out liberally sprinkled with 'mash' and 'pound' and other 'vivid' verbs.… It was not the correspondents' fault.… The stories which … deceived … people back home were … rewritten … by reporters who were nowhere near the battle." Bill Mauldin, the incomparable biographer of the GI, made a similar complaint about reporting from Italy. Newspapers, he recommended, should "clamp down … on their rewrite men who love to describe 'smashing armored columns,' the 'ground forces sweeping ahead,' 'victorious cheering armies,' and 'sullen supermen.'" W. L. White, who interviewed the five survivors of Motor Torpedo Boat Squadron 3, the group that evacuated MacArthur from Corregidor, quoted Lieutenant Robert B. Kelly to the same point: "The news commentators … had us all winning the war.… It made me very sore. We were out here where we could see these victories. There were plenty of them. They were all Japanese.… Yet if even at one point we are able to check … an attack, the silly headlines chatter of a victory."

The resulting deception was not inadvertent. While the Japanese early in 1942 were overpowering the small, ill-equipped American garrisons on Pacific islands, the armed services invented heroic situations, presumably to encourage the American people, who might better have been allowed to face depressing facts. So it was with the mythic request of the embattled survivors on Wake Island: "Send us more Japs." That phrase, which the motion pictures tried later to immortalize, had originated merely as padding to protect the cryptographic integrity of a message from Wake to Pearl Harbor describing the severity of the American plight. So, too, in the case of Colin Kelly, a brave pilot stationed in the Philippines, who died in action when the Japanese attacked. The Army exploited his valor by exaggerating his exploits, a ruse soon exposed to the desecration of Kelly's memory. His heroism, like that of the marines on Wake Island, deserved better treatment than it received. It deserved the truth.

The truth about American soldiers, heroic or not, centered in their experience in the Army, in training, in the field, under fire. In contrast to the official communiqués, the best independent reporting revealed that truth, which was often comic or poignant when it was not triumphant or glorious. It was harder to find out much about the men themselves, their lives before they had become soldiers, their homes and parents, rearing and calling, character and hopes. About those matters even the best reporters had ordinarily to work from partial evidence and had to write, given the wartime limits of time and space, selectively.

In the first instance, from among all the men in arms, the heroes selected themselves. Their bravery, self-sacrifice, and sheer physical endurance earned them a martial apotheosis. Usually that was the end of the story, except for a parenthesis identifying the hero's home town. But on occasion, moving to a next stage, correspondents at the front used what data they had to endow the soldiers they knew with recognizable qualities of person and purpose. In the process, truth became selective. Whether consciously or inadvertently, the reporters tended to find in the young men they described the traits that Americans generally esteemed. Those in uniform shared with their countrymen a common exposure to values dominant in the United States and to the special circumstances of the Great Depression, just ended. They had a sameness that in some degree set them apart from servicemen of other countries. But the necessarily selective reporting about them, governed as it was by the comfortable conventions of American culture, made the GI's and their officers more than merely representative Americans. It freed them from the sterile anonymity of official communiqués, but it also made them exemplars of national life, heroic symbols that satisfied the normal social preferences and the wartime psychological needs of American civilians....

"The range of their background was as broad as America." Robert Sherrod wrote of the marines at Tarawa, but his "hard-boiled colonel," he noted, was "born on a farm" and his bravest captain came from a small town. Ira Wolfert, in *Battle for the Solomons,* provided background information about only two of the dozens of men he mentioned. One was an accountant who loved the blues; the other "a farm boy out in Wisconsin." Of the relatively few heroes whom *Time* chose for special attention in 1944, one was a sharecropper, another "a big, silent farm hand."

The strains in American culture that related the virtuous to the rural or the outdoors or the gridiron recalled the images of the early twentieth century, of the Rough Riders and Theodore Roosevelt's "strenuous life." Similarly, *Life* and the *New York Times,* commenting upon the long odds against victorious GI's, evoked the cult of the underdog, the sentiments that in times of peace had often given an allure to the antitrust laws or, for the apolitical, to the Brooklyn Dodgers. The victory of character over hard work, over the long odds of the society or the economy, had provided, too, the stuff of the folklore of success, the scenario for the poor boy whose struggle to overcome the handicaps of his background won him fortune and fame. That kind of struggle, though rarely successful, had particularly marked American experience and consciousness during the 1930's. It was a part of the civilian past of most soldiers, and, naturally enough, a part frequently remarked by war correspondents.

The habit of joyful hard work, one ingredient of the cult of success, had always beguiled *The Saturday Evening Post,* which build its circulation not the least upon continual publication of updated Alger stories. The *Post* found an illustrious example of its favorite theme in Dwight David Eisenhower. As a boy in a household of modest means, he had "always had plenty to do. They had an orchard, a large garden, a cow, a horse, and always a dog. The boys did all the outdoor work, milked the cow and ... helped with the housework.... They also all found additional jobs...." Dwight pulled ice in the local ice plant, or helped near-by farmers. "It taught them a lot," their mother said. By implication, Sherrod and Hersey said as much about their young heroes on the Pacific islands who had faced the vicissitudes of the Depression as they faced the ordeals of the jungle. There was, for one, "Hawk," a marine captain, promoted from the ranks, killed at Tarawa. Before the war, "he ... was awarded a scholarship to the Texas College of Mines.... Like most sons of the poor, he worked.... He sold magazines and delivered newspapers.... He was a ranchhand, a railroadhand, and a bellhop."...

Aviators, when they won attention as heroes, shared many attributes of the foot soldiers but also represented uncommon qualities, those of a glamorous elite. The pilots and navigators, bombardiers and gunners were special men. They had to pass rigorous physical and mental tests. They received rapid promotion and high hazardous-duty pay. Instead of mud or jungle heat or desert cold, they enjoyed, at least part of the time, the amenities of an air base and always the romantic environment of the sky. There, exploring a vertical frontier, operating complex, powerful machinery, they flew into sudden and explosive danger. As Ernie Pyle observed: "A man approached death rather decently in the Air Force. He died well-fed and clean-shaven."...

Of all the war correspondents, Pyle, Hersey, and Mauldin wrote most intimately and extensively about the men they knew, about their hopes and dreams in the context of their fright and hardship. "In the magazines," Pyle wrote, "war seemed romantic and exciting, full of heroics and vitality ... yet I didn't seem capable of feeling it.... Certainly there were great tragedies, unbelievable heroism, even a constant undertone of comedy. But when I sat down to write, I saw instead men ... suffering and wishing they were somewhere else ... all of them desperately hungry for somebody to talk to besides themselves, no women to be heroes in front of, damned little wine to drink, precious little song, cold and fairly dirty, just toiling from day to day in a world full of insecurity, discomfort, homesickness and a dulled sense of danger. The drama and romance were ... like the famous falling tree in the forest—they were no good unless there was somebody around to hear. I knew of only twice that the war would be romantic to the men: once when they could see the Statue of Liberty and again on their first day back in the home town with the folks."

The GI's shared, in Pyle's words, "the one really profound goal that obsessed every ... American." That goal was home. Before the landing in Sicily they talked to Pyle about their plans: "These gravely yearned-for futures of men going into battle include so many things—things such as seeing the 'old lady' again, of going to college … of holding on your knee just once your own kid … of again becoming champion salesman of your territory, of driving a coal truck around the streets of Kansas City once more and, yes, of just sitting in the sun once more on the south side of a house in New Mexico…. It was these little hopes … that made up the sum total of our worry … rather than any visualization of physical agony to come."…

Soldiers in the armies of all nations in all wars have yearned to go home, but the GI's sense of home was especially an American sense. "Our men," Pyle wrote, "… are impatient with the strange peoples and customs of the countries they now inhabit. They say that if they ever get home they never want to see another foreign country." Home for the soldier, according to the *New York Times,* was "where the thermometer goes below 110° at night … where there are chocolate milk shakes, cokes, iced beer, and girls." The GI had had enough of crumpets and croissants: "Tea from the British and vin rouge from the French … have only confirmed his original convictions: that America is home, that home is better than Europe." Even the sophisticated missed homely American fare. Richard L. Tobin, a correspondent for the New York *Herald Tribune,* had arrived in London only a few days before he complained, like the GI's, about English food: "What wouldn't I give right now for a piece of bread spread with soft butter, heaped with American peanut butter, and accompanied by a big glass of ice-cold milk!"

Food, of course, was metaphor. Its full meaning was best expressed when John Hersey went into that Guadalcanal valley with a company of marines. "Many of them," Hersey wrote, "probably had brief thoughts, as I did, of home. But what I really wondered was whether any of them gave a single thought to what the hell this was all about. Did these men, who might be about to die, have any war aims? What were they fighting for, anyway?" Far along the trail into the jungle, "these men … not especially malcontents" gave Hersey his answer. "What would you say you were fighting for?" he asked. "Today, here in this valley, what are you fighting for?"

> … Their faces became pale. Their eyes wandered. They looked like men bothered by a memory. They did not answer for what seemed a very long lime.
>
> Then one of them spoke, but not to me. He spoke to the others, and for a second I thought he was changing the subject or making fun of me, but of course he was not. He was answering my question very specifically.
>
> He whispered: "Jesus, what I'd give for a piece of blueberry pie."
>
> … Fighting for pie. Of course that is not exactly what they meant… here pie was their symbol of home.
>
> In other places there are other symbols. For some men, in places where there is plenty of good food but no liquor, it is a good bottle of Scotch whiskey. In other places, where there's drink but no dames, they

say they'd give their left arm for a blonde. For certain men, books are the things; for others, music; for others, movies. But for all of them, these things are just badges of home. When they say they are fighting for these things, they mean they are fighting for home—"to get the goddam thing over and get home."

Perhaps this sounds selfish.... But home seems to most marines a pretty good thing to be fighting for. Home is where the good things are—the generosity, the good pay, the comforts, the democracy, the pie.

Hersey, a decent man, listed democracy, but soldiers usually talked about creature comforts, secure routines, even affluence. There were three sailors Ernie Pyle knew. One wanted to build a cabin on five acres of his own in Oregon. Another wanted to return to earning bonuses as a salesman for Pillsbury flour. As for a third, a photographer before the war: "His one great postwar ambition ... was to buy a cabin cruiser big enough for four, get another couple, and cruise down the Chattahoochee River to the Gulf of Mexico, then up the Suwannee, making color photos of the whole trip." A marine lieutenant colonel in the South Pacific had simpler fancies: "I'm going to start wearing pajamas again.... I'm going to polish off a few eggs and several quarts of milk.... A few hot baths are also in order.... But I'm saving the best for last—I'm going to spend a whole day flushing a toilet, just to hear the water run."

Home spurred the troops to fight. Even the self-consciously reflective soldiers, who linked the real and the ideal as Hersey did, stressed the palpable. *The Saturday Evening Post* ran a series by GI's on "What I am Fighting For." One characteristic article began: "I am fighting for that big house with the bright green roof and the big front lawn." The sergeant-author went on to include his "little sister," his gray-haired parents, his "big stone church" and "big brick schoolhouse," his "fine old college" and "nice little roadster," his piano, tennis court, black cocker spaniel, the two houses of Congress, the "magnificent Supreme Court," "that President who has led us," "everything America stands for." It was a jumble: he mentioned "freedom" one sentence after he wrote about "that girl with the large brown eyes and the reddish tinge in her hair, that girl who is away at college right now, preparing herself for her part in the future of America and Christianity." The jumble satisfied the *Post* and its readers, who would have liked less the findings of the Army Air Corps Redistribution Center at Atlantic City. Returnees there in 1944, a representative group of men, "surprisingly normal physically and psychologically," in the opinion of the physicians who examined them, felt contempt for civilians, distrusted "politicians," and resented labor unions. According to the Assistant Secretary of War for Air, "there is very little idealism. Most regard the war as a job to be done and there is not much willingness to discuss what we are fighting for."

The Assistant Secretary thought indoctrination lectures would help. On the basis of his own experience, Ernie Pyle would probably have disagreed:

Awhile back a friend of mine ... wrote me an enthusiastic letter telling of the ... Resolution in the Senate calling for the formation of a United

Nations organization to coordinate the prosecution of the war, administer reoccupied countries, feed and economically reestablish liberated nations, and to assemble a ... military force to suppress any future military aggression.

My friend ... ordered me ... to send back a report on what the men at the front thought of the bill.

I didn't send my report, because the men at the front thought very little about it one way or the other.... It sounded too much like another Atlantic Charter....

The run-of-the-mass soldiers didn't think twice about this bill if they heard of it at all....

We see from the worm's eye view, and our segment of the picture consists only of tired and dirty soldiers who are alive and don't want to die... of shocked men wandering back down the hill from battle ... of ... smelly bed rolls and C rations ... and blown bridges and dead mules ... and of graves and graves and graves....

The mood of the soldiers conformed in large measure to the mood of Washington. There was, as Henry Morgenthau had said, "little inspirational" for young men and women. The President, deliberately avoiding talk about grand postwar plans, concentrated on victory first and almost exclusively. So did the GI, for he knew that he had to win the war before he could get home, his ultimate objective. He felt, the *New York Times* judged, "that the war must be finished quickly so that he can return to take up his life where he left it." There was not "any theoretical proclamation that the enemy must be destroyed in the name of freedom," Pyle wrote after the Tunisian campaign; "it's just a vague but growing individual acceptance of the bitter fact that we must win the war or else.... The immediate goal used to be the Statue of Liberty; more and more it is becoming Unter den Linden."

Winning the war, his intermediate goal, turned the soldier to his direct task, combat. There impulses for friendship and generosity had to surrender to instincts for killing and hate. "It would be nice ... to get home," one pilot told Bob Hope, "... and stretch my legs under a table full of Mother's cooking.... But all I want to do is beat these Nazi sons-of-bitches so we can get at those little Jap bastards." The hardening process of training and danger, in Marion Hargrove's experience, made "a civilian into a soldier, a boy into a man." "Our men," Pyle concluded, "can't ... change from normal civilians into warriors and remain the same people.... If they didn't toughen up inside, they simply wouldn't be able to take it." The billboard overlooking Tulagi harbor carried the message: "Kill Japs; kill more Japs; you will be doing your part if you help to kill those yellow bastards."

Bill Mauldin was more reflective: "I read someplace that the American boy is not capable of hate ... but you can't have friends killed without hating the men who did it. It makes the dogfaces sick to read articles by people who say, 'It isn't the Germans, it's the Nazis.'... When our guys cringe under an 88 barrage, you don't hear them say 'Those dirty Nazis.' You hear them say, 'Those goddam Krauts.'" Mauldin understood hate and hated war:

> Some say the American soldier is the same clean-cut young man who left his home; others say morale is sky-high at the front because everybody's face is shining for the great Cause.
>
> They are wrong. The combat man isn't the same clean-cut lad because you don't fight a Kraut by Marquis of Queensberry rules. You shoot him in the back, you blow him apart with mines, you kill or maim him… with the least danger to yourself. He does the same to you … and if you don't beat him at his own game you don't live to appreciate your own nobleness.
>
> But you don't become a killer. No normal man who has smelled and associated with death ever wants to see any more of it.… The surest way to become a pacifist is to join the infantry.

War, Bob Hope thought, made "a lot of guys appreciate things they used to take for granted," and Pyle believed that "when you've lived with the unnatural mass cruelty that man is capable of … you find yourself dispossessed of the faculty for blaming one poor man for the triviality of his faults. I don't see how any survivor of war can ever again be cruel." Mauldin put it more bluntly: "The vast majority of combat men are going to be no problem at all. They are so damned sick and tired of having their noses rubbed in a stinking war that their only ambition will be to forget it." Consequently Mauldin was not much worried about the adaptability of the veteran:

> I've been asked if I have a postwar plan for Joe and Willie. I do.… Joe and Willie are very tired of war.… While their buddies are … trying to learn to be civilians again, Joe and Willie are going to do the same.… If their buddies find their girls have married somebody else, and if they have a hard time getting jobs back, and if they run into difficulties in the new, strange life of a free citizen, then Joe and Willie are going to do the same. And if they finally get settled and drop slowly into the happy obscurity of a humdrum job and a little wife and a household of kids, Joe and Willie will be happy to settle down too. They might even shave and become respectable.…

Indeed they might. The GI, a homely hero, naturally decent and generous, inured slowly to battle and danger, would be in the end still generous, still trusting, wiser but still young, dirtier but still more content in his office or factory or on his sunswept farm. He was as plain, as recognizable, as American as the militiamen of the past, he was the conscript citizen—competent enough but fundamentally an amateur, a transient, and an unhappy warrior. He was the essential republican, the common good man. He was the people's hero.

Like them, he had little visible purpose but winning the war so that he could return to a familiar, comfortable America, to what an earlier generation meant, more or less, by "normalcy."…

American Liberals: Fighting for a Better World

ALAN BRINKLEY

Few would disagree that World War II changed the world as profoundly as any event of this century, perhaps any century. What is less readily apparent, perhaps, is how profoundly the war changed America—its society, its politics, and … its image of itself. Except for the combatants themselves, Americans experienced the war at a remove of several thousand miles. They endured no bombing, no invasion, no massive dislocations, no serious material privations. Veterans returning home in 1945 and 1946 found a country that looked very much like the one they had left—something that clearly could not be said of veterans returning home to Britain, France, Germany, Russia, or Japan.

But World War II did transform America in profound, if not immediately visible, ways. Not the least important of those transformations was in the nature of American liberalism, a force that would play a central role in shaping the nation's postwar political and cultural life. Liberalism in America rests on several consistent and enduring philosophical assumptions: the high value liberals believe society should attribute to individual rights and freedoms and the importance of avoiding rigid and immutable norms and institutions. But in the half century since the New Deal, liberalism in America has also meant a prescription for public policy and political action; and in the 1940s this "New Deal liberalism" was in a state of considerable uncertainty and was undergoing significant changes. Several broad developments of the war years helped lay the foundations for the new liberal order that followed the war.

Among those developments was a series of important shifts in the size, distribution, and character of the American population. Not all the demographic changes of the 1940s were a result of the war, nor were their effects on liberal assumptions entirely apparent until well after 1945. But they were a crucial part of the process that would transform American society and the way liberals viewed their mission in that society.

Perhaps the most conspicuous demographic change was the single biggest ethnic migration in American history: the massive movement of African Americans from the rural South to the urban North, a migration much larger than the "great migration" at the time of World War I. Between 1910 (when the first great migration began) and 1940, approximately 1.5 million blacks moved from the South to the North. In the 1940s alone, 2 million African Americans left the South, and 3 million more moved in the twenty years after that. The migration brought substantial numbers of them closer to the center of the nation's economic, cultural, and institutional life. The number of blacks employed in manufacturing more than doubled during the war. There were major increases in the number of African Americans employed as skilled craftsmen or enrolled in unions. There was a massive movement of African American women out of

Excerpts from Brinkley, A., "World War II and American Liberalism" in *The War in American Culture*, Erenberg and Hirsch, eds., pp. 314–323, 326–327. Copyright © 1996 by The University of Chicago. Reprinted by permission of the University of Chicago.

domestic work and into the factory and the shop. Much of this would have occurred with or without World War II, but the war greatly accelerated the movement by expanding industrial activity and by creating a labor shortage that gave African American men and women an incentive to move into industrial cities.

This second great migration carried the question of race out of the South and into the North, out of the countryside and into the city, out of the field and into the factory. African American men and women encountered prejudice and discrimination in the urban, industrial world much as they had in the agrarian world; but in the city they were far better positioned to organize and protest their condition, as some were beginning to do even before the fighting ended. World War II therefore began the process by which race would increase its claim on American consciousness and, ultimately, transform American liberalism.

Just as the war helped lay the groundwork for challenges to racial orthodoxies, so it contributed to later challenges to gender norms. Three million women entered the paid workforce for the first time during the war, benefiting—like black workers—from the labor shortage military conscription had created. Many women performed jobs long considered the exclusive province of men. Women had been moving into the workforce in growing numbers before the war began, to be sure, and almost certainly they would have continued to do so even had the United States remained at peace. Many of their wartime gains, moreover, proved short lived. Female factory workers in particular were usually dismissed as soon as male workers returned to take their places, even though many wanted to remain in their jobs.

Still, most women who had begun working during the war continued working after 1945 (if not always in the same jobs). And while popular assumptions about women's roles (among both women and men) were slow to change, the economic realities of many women's lives were changing dramatically and permanently—in ways that would eventually help raise powerful challenges to ideas about gender. The war, in short, accelerated a critical long-term shift in the role of women in society that would produce, among other things, the feminist movements of the 1960s and beyond.

Similar, if less dramatic, changes were affecting other American communities during the war. Men and women who had long lived on the margins of American life—because of prejudice or geographical isolation or both—found their lives transformed by the pressures of war. Asian Americans, Latino Americans, Native Americans, and others served in the military, worked in factories, moved into diverse urban neighborhoods, and otherwise encountered the urban–industrial world of the midtwentieth century. Life was not, perhaps, much better for many such people in their new roles than it had been in traditional ones. For Japanese Americans on the West Coast, who spent much of the war in internment camps, victims of popular and official hysteria, it was considerably worse. But for many such communities the changes helped erode the isolation that had made it difficult to challenge discrimination and demand inclusion.

No one living in the era of multiculturalism will be inclined to argue with the proposition that the changing composition of the American population over the past fifty years—and the changing relations among different groups within the population—is one of the most important events in the nation's recent history. Those changes have reshaped America's economy, its culture, its politics, and its intellectual life. They have forced the nation to confront its increasing diversity in more direct and painful ways than at any time since the Civil War. They have challenged America's conception of itself as a nation and a society. And they have transformed American liberalism. In the 1930s, most liberals considered questions of racial, ethnic, or gender difference of distinctly secondary importance (or in the case of gender, virtually no importance at all). Liberal discourse centered much more on issues of class and the distribution of wealth and economic power. By 1945 that was beginning to change. One sign of that change was the remarkable reception among liberals of Gunnar Myrdal's *An American Dilemma,* published in 1944. Myrdal identified race as the one issue most likely to shape and perplex the American future. The great migration of the 1940s helped ensure that history would vindicate Myrdal's prediction and that American liberals would adjust their outlook and their goals in fundamental ways in the postwar years.

Perhaps the most common and important observation about the domestic impact of World War II is that it ended the Great Depression and launched an era of unprecedented prosperity. Between 1940 and 1945 the United States experienced the greatest expansion of industrial production in its history. After a decade of depression, a decade of growing doubts about capitalism, a decade of high unemployment and underproduction, suddenly, in a single stroke, the American economy restored itself and—equally important—seemed to redeem itself. Gross national product in the war years rose from $91 billion to $166 billion; 15 million new jobs were created, and the most enduring problem of the depression—massive unemployment—came to an end; industrial production doubled; personal incomes rose (depending on location) by as much as 200 percent. The revival of the economy is obviously important in its own right. But it also had implications for the future of American political economy, for how liberals in particular conceived of the role of the state in the postwar United States.

One of the mainstays of economic thought in the late 1930s was the belief that the United States had reached what many called "economic maturity": the belief that the nation was approaching, or perhaps had reached, the end of its capacity to grow, that America must now learn to live within limits. This assumption strengthened the belief among many reformers that in the future it would be necessary to regulate the economy much more closely and carefully for the benefit of society as a whole. America could not rely any more on a constantly expanding pie; it would have to worry about how the existing pie was to be divided.

The wartime economic experience—the booming expansion, the virtual elimination of unemployment, the creation of new industries, new "frontiers"—served as a rebuke to the "mature economy" idea and restored the concept of growth to the center of liberal hopes. The capitalist economy, liberals suddenly discovered, was not irretrievably stagnant. Economic expansion could achieve, in fact had achieved, dimensions beyond the wildest dreams of the 1930s. Social and economic advancement could proceed, therefore, without structural changes in capitalism, without continuing, intrusive state management of the economy. It could proceed by virtue of growth.

Assaults on the concept of economic maturity were emerging as early as 1940 and gathered force throughout the war. Alvin Hansen, one of the most prominent champions in the 1930s of what he called "secular stagnation," repudiated the idea in 1941. "All of us had our sights too low," he admitted. The *New Republic* and the *Nation,* both of which had embraced the idea of economic maturity in 1938 and 1939, openly rejected it in the 1940s—not only rejected it, but celebrated its demise. The country had achieved a "break," exulted the *Nation,* "from the defeatist thinking that held us in economic thraldom through the thirties, when it was assumed that we could not afford full employment or full production in this country."

But along with this celebration of economic growth came a new and urgent fear: that the growth might not continue once the war was over. What if the depression came back? What if there was a return to massive unemployment? What could be done to make sure that economic growth continued? That was the great liberal challenge of the war years—not to restructure the economy, not to control corporate behavior, not to search for new and more efficient forms of management, but to find a way to keep things going as they were.

And in response to that challenge, a growing number of liberal economists and policymakers became interested in a tool that had begun to attract their attention in the 1930s and that seemed to prove itself during the war: government spending. That was clearly how the economy had revived—in response to the massive increase in the federal budget in the war years, from $9 billion in 1939 to $100 billion in 1945. And that was how the revival could be sustained—by pumping more money into the economy in peacetime. What government needed to do, therefore, was to "plan" for postwar full employment.

Those who called themselves "planners" in the 1940s did not talk much anymore, as planners had talked in earlier years, about the need for an efficient, centrally planned economy in which the government would help direct the behavior of private institutions. They talked instead about fiscal planning— about public works projects, about social welfare programs, about the expansion of the Social Security system. The National Resource Planning Board, the central "planning" agency of the New Deal since 1933, issued a report in 1942 called *Security, Work, and Relief Policies.* In the past, the NRPB had been preoccupied largely with older ideas of planning—regional planning, resource management, government supervision of production and investment. Now, in their 1942 report, the members turned their attention to the new kind of planning. The government should create a "shelf" of public works projects, so that after the war—whenever the economy showed signs of stagnating—it could pull projects off the shelf and spend the money on them to stimulate more growth. The government should commit itself to more expansive Social Security measures so that after the war—if the economy should slow down— there would be welfare mechanisms in place that would immediately pick up the slack and start paying out benefits, which would increase purchasing power and stimulate growth.

All of this reflected, among other things, the increasing influence in American liberal circles of Keynesian economics. The most important liberal economist of the war years—Alvin Hansen of Harvard, who contributed to many NRPB reports—was also the leading American exponent of Keynesianism. Keynesianism provided those concerned about the future of the American economy with an escape from their fears of a new, postwar depression. Economic growth, it taught them, did not require constant involvement in the affairs of private institutions—which the 1930s (and the war itself) had shown to be logistically difficult and politically controversial. Growth could be sustained through the *indirect* manipulation of the economy by fiscal and monetary levers.

The wartime faith in economic growth led, in other words, to several developments of great importance to the future of American liberalism. It helped relegitimize capitalism among people who had, in the 1930s, developed serious doubts about its viability. It helped rob the "administrative" reform ideas of the late 1930s—the belief in ever greater regulation of private institutions—of their urgency. It helped elevate Keynesian ideas about indirect management of the economy to the center of reform hopes. And it made the idea of the welfare state—of Social Security and public works and other social welfare efforts—come to seem a part of the larger vision of sustaining economic growth by defining welfare as a way to distribute income and stimulate purchasing power. It helped channel American liberalism into a new, less confrontational direction—a direction that would produce fewer clashes with capitalist institutions; that tried to define the interests of capitalists and the interests of the larger public in identical terms; that emphasized problems of consumption over problems of production; that shaped the liberal agenda for more than a generation and helped shape the next great episode in liberal policy experiments: the Great Society of the 1960s.

World War II had other important and more purely ideological effects on American liberalism—some of them in apparent conflict with others, but all of them important in determining the permissible range of liberal aspirations for the postwar era. First, the war created, or at least greatly reinforced, a set of anxieties and fears that would become increasingly central to liberal thought in the late 1940s and 1950s. It inflamed two fears in particular: a fear of the state and a fear of the people. Both were a response, in large part, to the horror with which American liberals (and most other Americans as well) regarded the regimes the United States was fighting in World War II. Both would be sustained and strengthened by the similar horror with which most Americans came to view the regime the nation was beginning to mobilize against in peacetime even before the end of the war: the Soviet Union.

The fear of the state emerged directly out of the way American liberals (and the American people generally) defined the nature of their enemy in World War II. During World War I many Americans had believed the enemy was a race, a people: the Germans, the beastlike "Huns," and their presumably savage culture. In World War II racial stereotypes continued to play an important role in portrayals of the Japanese; but in defining the enemy in Europe—always the principal enemy in the 1940s to most Americans—the government and most of the media relied less on racial or cultural images than on political ones. Wartime propaganda in World War II did not personify the Germans and Italians as evil peoples. It focused instead on the Nazi and fascist states.

The war, in other words, pushed a fear of totalitarianism (and hence a general wariness about excessive state power) to the center of American liberal thought. In particular, it forced a reassessment of the kinds of associational and corporatist arrangements that many had found so attractive in the aftermath of World War I. Those, after all, were the kinds of arrangements Germany and Italy had claimed to be creating. But it also created a less specific fear of state power that made other kinds of direct planning and management of the economy of society seem unappealing as well. "The rise of totalitarianism," Reinhold Niebuhr noted somberly in 1945, "has prompted the democratic world to view all collectivist answers to our social problems with increased apprehension." Virtually all experiments in state supervision of private institutions, he warned, contained "some peril of compounding economic and political power." Hence "a wise community will walk warily and test the effect of each new adventure before further adventures." To others the lesson was even starker. *Any* steps in the direction of state control of economic institutions were (to use the title of Friedrich A. Hayek's celebrated antistatist book of 1944) steps along "the road to serfdom." This fear of the state was one of many things that lent strength to the emerging Keynesian-welfare state liberal vision of political economy, with its much more limited role for government as a manager of economic behavior.

Along with this fear of the state emerged a related fear: a fear of "mass politics" or "mass man"; a fear, in short, of the people. Nazi Germany, fascist Italy, even the Soviet Union, many liberals came to believe, illustrated the dangers inherent in trusting the people to control their political life. The people, the "mass," could too easily be swayed by demagogues and tyrants. They were too susceptible to appeals to their passions, to the dark, intolerant impulses that in a healthy society remained largely repressed and subdued. Fascism and communism were not simply the products of the state or of elite politics, many liberals believed; they were the products of mass movements, of the unleashing of the dangerous and irrational impulses within every individual and every society.

This fear of the mass lay at the heart of much liberal cultural and intellectual criticism in the first fifteen years after World War II. It found expression in the writings of Hannah Arendt, Theodor Adorno, Richard Hofstadter, Lionel Trilling, Daniel Bell, Dwight Macdonald, and many others. Like the fear of the state, with which it was so closely associated, it reinforced a sense of caution and restraint in liberal thinking; a suspicion of ideology, a commitment to pragmatism, a wariness about moving too quickly to encourage or embrace spontaneous popular movements; a conviction that one of the purposes of politics was to defend the state against popular movements and their potentially dangerous effects.

There were, in short, powerful voices within American liberalism during and immediately after World War II arguing that the experience of the war had introduced a dark cloud of doubt and even despair to human society. A world that could produce so terrible a war; a world that could produce Hiroshima, Nagasaki, the Katyn Forest, Auschwitz; a world capable of profound evil and inconceivable destruction: such a world, many American liberals argued, must be forever regarded skeptically and suspiciously. Humankind must move cautiously into its uncertain future, wary of unleashing the dark impulses that had produced such horror.

Some liberal intellectuals went further. Americans, they argued, must resist the temptation to think of themselves, in their hour of triumph, as a chosen people. No people, no nation, could afford to ignore its own capacity for evil. Reinhold Niebuhr spoke for many liberals when he wrote of the dangers of the "deep layer of Messianic consciousness in the mind of America" and warned of liberal culture's "inability to comprehend the depth of evil to which individuals and communities may sink, particularly when they try to play the role of God in history." Americans, he said, would do well to remember that "no nation is sacred and unique.... Providence has not set Americans apart from lesser breeds. We too are part of history's seamless web."

But Niebuhr's statements were obviously written to refute a competing assumption. And as it suggests, there was in the 1940s another, very different ideological force at work in America, another form of national self-definition that affected liberal thought and behavior, at home and in the world, at least as much as the somber assessments of Niebuhr and others. Indeed even many liberal intellectuals attracted to Niebuhr's pessimistic ideas about human nature and mass politics were simultaneously drawn to this different and, on the surface at least, contradictory assessment of the nation's potential. For in many ways the most powerful ideological force at work in postwar American liberalism, and in the postwar United States generally, was the view of America as an anointed nation; America as a special moral force in the world; America as a society with a unique mission, born of its righteousness. This is an ideological tradition that is often described as the tradition of American innocence. But innocence is perhaps too gentle a word for what has often been an aggressive and intrusive vision, a vision that rests on the belief that America is somehow insulated from the sins and failures and travails that affect other nations, that America stands somehow outside of history, protected from it by its own strength and virtue.

World War II did not create those beliefs. They are as old as the nation itself. But the American experience in the conflict, and the radically enhanced international stature and responsibility of the United States in the aftermath of the war, strengthened such ideas and gave them a crusading quality that made them as active and powerful as they had been at any moment in the nation's history....

The war left other ideological legacies for American liberalism as well. In the glow of the nation's victory, in the sense of old orders shattered and a new world being born, came an era of exuberant innovation, an era in which, for a time, nothing seemed more appealing than the new. The allure of the new was visible in the brave new world of architectural modernism, whose controversial legacy is so much a part of the postwar American landscape. It was visible in the explosive growth of the innovative and iconoclastic American art world, which made New York in the 1940s and 1950s something of what Paris had been in the nineteenth century. It was visible in the increased stature and boldness of the American scientific community, and in the almost religious faith in technological progress that came to characterize so much of American life.

Above all, perhaps, it was visible in the way it excited, and then frustrated, a generation of American liberals as they imagined new possibilities for progress and social justice. That is what Archibald MacLeish meant in 1943 when he spoke about the America of the imagination, the society that the war was encouraging Americans to create:

> We have, and we know we have, the abundant means to bring our boldest dreams to pass—to create for ourselves whatever world we have the courage to desire.... We have the tools and the skill and the intelligence to take our cities apart and put them together, to lead our roads and rivers where we please to lead them, to build our houses where we want our houses, to brighten the air, to clean the wind, to live as men in this Republic, free men, should be living. We have the power and the courage and the resources of good-will and decency and common understanding ... to create a nation such as men have never seen.... We stand at the moment of the building of great lives, for the war's end and our victory in the war will throw that moment and the means before us.

There was, of course, considerable naïveté, and even arrogance, in such visions. But there was also an appealing sense of hope and commitment—a belief in the possibility of sweeping away old problems and failures, of creating "great lives." Out of such visions came some of the postwar crusades of American liberals—the battle for racial justice, the effort to combat poverty, the expansion of individual rights. And although all of those battles had some ambiguous and even unhappy consequences, they all reflected a confidence in the character and commitment of American society—and the possibility of creating social justice within it—that few people would express so blithely today. Postwar liberalism had suffered many failures and travails in the half century since 1945. But surely its postwar faith in the capacity of America to rebuild—and perhaps even redeem—itself remains one of its most appealing legacies.

FURTHER READING

Michael C. C. Adams, *The Best War Ever: America and World War II* (1994).

Elizabeth Borgwardt, *A New Deal for the World: America's Vision for Human Rights* (2005).

Joanna Bourke, *The Second World War: A People's History* (2002).

Richard Breitman, et al. *U.S. Intelligence and the Nazis* (2005).

Steven Casey, *Cautious Crusade: Franklin D. Roosevelt, American Public Opinion, and the War Against Nazi Germany* (2001).

Iris Chang, *The Rape of Nanking: The Forgotten Holocaust of World War II* (1997).

Robert Dallek, *Franklin D. Roosevelt and American Foreign Policy, 1932–1945* (1979).

Michael Doubler, *Closing with the Enemy: How GIs Fought the War in Europe* (1994).

John W. Dower, *War Without Mercy: Race and Power in the Pacific War* (1986).

Ellen Eisenberg, *The First to Cry Down Injustice? Western Jews and Japanese Removal During World War II* (2008).

Marilyn S. Johnson, *The Second Gold Rush: Oakland and the East Bay in World War II* (1993).

Tetsuden Kashima, *Judgment Without Trial: Japanese American Internment During World War II* (2003).

David M. Kennedy, *Freedom from Fear: The American People in Depression and War* (1999).

Greg Robinson, *A Tragedy of Democracy: Japanese Confinement in North America* (2009).

Andrew Rotter, *Hiroshima: The World's Bomb* (2008).

CHAPTER 10

The Cold War
and the Nuclear Age

Winning the peace can be more difficult than winning the war, as both the United States and the Soviet Union learned in the decade following V-E Day (Victory-Europe). "We may not get 100 percent of what we want in the postwar world, but I think we can get 85 percent," President Harry Truman optimistically told his advisers.

Yet the United States was not the only victor, and more importantly not the only superpower, to arise from the ashes. The Soviet Union had lost more than 20 million of its people, compared with American losses of less than half a million. The Soviet resolve to maintain a security zone in Eastern Europe after the war clashed with American expectations, as well as with the wishes of most Eastern and Western Europeans. Some historians contend that the cold war began with the initial American decision to keep the atomic bomb a secret from its Soviet ally, stirring Stalin's suspicions. Others cite the influence of people like diplomat George Kennan, who saw no end to Soviet ambition and gave advice that helped to crystallize the policy called containment. Still other historians cite the actions of the Russian army, which made the Soviet Union thoroughly unpopular in the zones where the USSR hoped to maintain a sphere of influence.

Whatever its causes, discord between the two most powerful members of the former Grand Alliance created a cold war that lasted more than forty years. With the Truman Doctrine of 1947, the United States adopted the role of "global policeman." With the Marshall Plan of 1948, the United States adopted the role of economic caretaker of Europe. Both actions originated as attempts to stop the perceived communist threat to world peace and stability. When the Korean War broke out in 1950, the Truman administration approved a policy drafted by the National Security Council (NSC), NSC-68. This policy drastically expanded American defense expenditures, placed the nation on a permanent war footing, and created what President Eisenhower later dubbed "the military-industrial complex."

Two of the most important effects of the cold war for the United States were the "Red Scare" at home and the nuclear arms race. Unable to understand why the United States could not better control the outcomes of World War II, many Americans readily believed critics who charged that traitors in government were responsible. Senator Joseph McCarthy was not the first to make these claims, but he became the most famous. McCarthy's subcommittee in the Senate publicly interrogated citizens on their loyalty, as did the Un-American Activities Committee of the House of Representatives. These congressional initiatives coincided with the prosecution of suspected Communists under a new federal loyalty program created by Truman in 1947. Between 1947 and 1952, 6.6 million federal employees were investigated for disloyalty. As a consequence of the Red Scare, thousands of people lost their jobs and sometimes their freedom as a result of tenuous connections to leftist causes or ideas.

The nuclear buildup went into full swing when the Soviet Union tested its first nuclear weapon in 1949. The United States immediately began construction of the more powerful hydrogen bomb. Some scientists who opposed the arms race, including J. Robert Oppenheimer, the "father" of the atom bomb, were run out of government on grounds of disloyalty. Under President Dwight D. Eisenhower, the U.S. government gradually developed a policy of nuclear deterrence—backed up by immense lethal arsenals—which later developed into MAD, or Mutual Assured Destruction. The potential for nuclear annihilation contrasted bizarrely with a booming economy and with the happy families portrayed on television in the 1950s. Some Americans wondered what to believe: that life was wonderful, or that the world might be destroyed the next day. Ironically, both things could be true.

QUESTIONS TO THINK ABOUT

Why was there a cold war? Did Russian aggression make conflict inevitable, or did the United States overreact to the battered Soviet Union's quest for security? What was the effect of the cold war on the worldview and psychology of American citizens?

DOCUMENTS

The documents in this chapter provide various perspectives on the cold war. At the end of World War II, the United States was the only nation with atomic bombs. Document 1 is American diplomat George F. Kennan's famous 1946 telegram from Moscow to Washington, in which he states that the Russians cannot be trusted and must be met with force before they destroy "our traditional way of life." In document 2, Henry A. Wallace, secretary of commerce and former vice president, states that Americans should try to understand how their attempts to reshape the world order and their monopoly on nuclear weaponry might appear to the Soviets. Soon thereafter, Wallace, the last of the New Dealers in Truman's cabinet, was forced to resign. Document 3 gives a Soviet perspective: that of Ambassador Nikolai Novikov, who tells his superiors that the United States seems bent on world dominance.

Document 4 shows contrasting images of nuclear weaponry and how they changed over time. In the first photograph, from 1946, American naval officials smile happily while cutting a cake to celebrate the successful detonation of a nuclear bomb in the South Pacific, one in a series of atmospheric tests designed to improve the nation's nuclear arsenal. The second photograph is from the Japanese film *Godzilla*, a science fiction series about a sea monster accidentally created by nuclear testing. The mutated, fire-breathing monster shoots atomic rays from its mouth. In document 5, the president outlines to Congress what came to be known as the Truman Doctrine: a U.S. commitment to police the world to ensure that free peoples are able to "work out their own destinies in their own way." Although his bill initially authorized the government to aid only Greece and Turkey, the commitment soon spread to all areas of the globe. The next three documents show some of the domestic consequences of Truman's campaign. In his famous Wheeling, West Virginia, speech (document 6), Senator Joseph McCarthy claimed that the international Communist threat was actually the result of treason at home, especially within the U.S. Department of State. The Truman administration's own campaign against subversion lent credence to McCarthy's claims, having stirred up doubts about numerous federal employees, often on the basis of flimsy evidence. In document 7, a temporary postal clerk loses his job because, among other things, a college professor once required him to read *Das Kapital* by Karl Marx. Document 8 illustrates the fear of nuclear war that gradually permeated the popular psyche as the arms race escalated. *Life* magazine praises Republican Governor Nelson Rockefeller for urging the development of fallout shelters for those living outside "the blast area" of targets like New York City. After all, not everyone need die in World War III. In the last excerpt (document 9), President Dwight D. Eisenhower warns against a "military-industrial complex" that he feared would increasingly dominate American life. For the first time in its long history, the nation had a permanent standing army. The implications for democracy, Eisenhower believed, were potentially grave.

1. Diplomat George F. Kennan Advocates Containment, 1946

At bottom of Kremlin's neurotic view of world affairs is traditional and instinctive Russian sense of insecurity. Originally, this was insecurity of a peaceful agricultural people trying to live on vast exposed plain in neighborhood of fierce nomadic peoples. To this was added, as Russia came into contact with economically advanced West, fear of more competent, more powerful, more highly organized societies in that area…. For this reason they have always feared foreign penetration, feared direct contact between Western world and their own, feared

U.S. Department of State, *Foreign Relations of the United States, 1946, Eastern Europe: The Soviet Union* (Washington, D.C.: U.S. Government Printing Office, 1969), VI, 699–701, 706–707.

what would happen if Russians learned truth about world without or if foreigners learned truth about world within. And they had learned to seek security only in patient but deadly struggle for total destruction of rival power, never in compacts and compromises with it.

It was no coincidence that Marxism, which had smouldered ineffectively for half a century in Western Europe, caught hold and blazed for first time in Russia. Only in this land which had never known a friendly neighbor or indeed any tolerant equilibrium of separate powers, either internal or international, could a doctrine thrive which viewed economic conflicts of society as insoluble by peaceful means. After establishment of Bolshevist regime, Marxist dogma, rendered even more truculent and intolerant by Lenin's interpretation, became a perfect vehicle for sense of insecurity with which Bolsheviks, even more than previous Russian rulers, were afflicted. In this dogma, with its basic altruism of purpose, they found justification for their instinctive fear of outside world, for the dictatorship without which they did not know how to rule, for cruelties they did not dare not to inflict, for sacrifices they felt bound to demand. In the name of Marxism they sacrificed every single ethical value in their methods and tactics. Today they cannot dispense with it. It is fig leaf of their moral and intellectual respectability....

In summary, we have here a political force committed fanatically to the belief that with US there can be no permanent *modus vivendi,* that it is desirable and necessary that the internal harmony of our society be disrupted, our traditional way of life be destroyed, the international authority of our state be broken, if Soviet power is to be secure. This political force has complete power of disposition over energies of one of world's greatest peoples and resources of world's richest national territory, and is borne along by deep and powerful currents of Russian nationalism. In addition, it has an elaborate and far flung apparatus for exertion of its influence in other countries, an apparatus of amazing flexibility and versatility, managed by people whose experience and skill in underground methods are presumably without parallel in history.... Problem of how to cope with this force [is] undoubtedly greatest task our diplomacy has ever faced and probably greatest it will ever have to face. It should be point of departure from which our political general staff work at present juncture should proceed. It should be approached with same thoroughness and care as solution of major strategic problem in war, and if necessary, with no smaller outlay in planning effort. I cannot attempt to suggest all answers here. But I would like to record my conviction that problem is within our power to solve—and that without recourse to any general military conflict. And in support of this conviction there are certain observations of a more encouraging nature I should like to make:

1. Soviet power, unlike that of Hitlerite Germany, is neither schematic nor adventuristic. It does not work by fixed plans. It does not take unnecessary risks. Impervious to logic of reason, and it is highly sensitive to logic of force. For this reason it can easily withdraw—and usually does—when strong resistance is encountered at any point. Thus, if the adversary has sufficient force and makes clear his readiness to use it, he rarely has to

do so. If situations are properly handled there need be no prestige-engaging showdowns.

2. Gauged against Western World as a whole. Soviets are still by far the weaker force. Thus, their success will really depend on degree of cohesion, firmness and vigor which Western World can muster. And this is factor which it is within our power to influence.

3. Success of Soviet system, as form of internal power, is not yet finally proven. It has yet to be demonstrated that it can survive supreme test of successive transfer of power from one individual group to another.

2. Secretary of Commerce Henry A. Wallace Questions the "Get Tough" Policy, 1946

How do American actions since V-J Day appear to other nations? I mean by actions the concrete things like $13 million for the War and Navy Departments, the Bikini tests of the atomic bomb and continued production of bombs, the plan to arm Latin America with our weapons, production of B-29s and planned production of B-36s, and the effort to secure air bases spread over half the globe from which the other half of the globe can be bombed. I cannot but feel that these actions must make it look to the rest of the world as if we were only paying lip service to peace at the conference table. These facts rather make it appear either (1) that we are preparing ourselves to win the war which we regard as inevitable or (2) that we are trying to build up a predominance of force to intimidate the rest of mankind. How would it look to us if Russia had the atomic bomb and we did not, if Russia had ten thousand-mile bombers and air bases within a thousand miles of our coast lines and we did not?

Some of the military men and self-styled "realists" are saying: "What's wrong with trying to build up a predominance of force? The only way to preserve peace is for this country to be so well armed that no one will dare attack us. We know that America will never start a war."

The flaw in this policy is simply that it will not work. In a world of atomic bombs and other revolutionary new weapons, such as radioactive poison gases and biological warfare, a peace maintained by a predominance of force is no longer possible....

Insistence on our part that the game must be played our way will only lead to a deadlock. The Russians will redouble their efforts to manufacture bombs, and they may also decide to expand their "security zone" in a serious way. Up to now, despite all our outcries against it, their efforts to develop a security zone in Eastern Europe and in the Middle East are small change from the point of view of military power as compared with our air bases in Greenland, Okinawa and many other places thousands of miles from our shores. We may feel very

Henry A. Wallace, "The Path to Peace with Russia," *New Republic*, 115 (1946), 401–406.

self-righteous if we refuse to budge on our plan and the Russians refuse to accept it, but that means only one thing—the atomic armament race is on in deadly earnest....

I should list the factors which make for Russian distrust of the United States and of the Western world as follows: The first is Russian history, which we must take into account because it is the setting in which Russians see all actions and policies of the rest of the world. Russian history for over a thousand years has been a succession of attempts, often unsuccessful, to resist invasion and conquest—by the Mongols, the Turks, the Swedes, the Germans and the Poles. The scant thirty years of the existence of the Soviet government has in Russian eyes been a continuation of their historical struggle for national existence....

Second, it follows that to the Russians all of the defense and security measures of the Western powers seem to have an aggressive intent. Our actions to expand our military security system—such steps as extending the Monroe Doctrine to include the arming of the Western Hemisphere nations, our present monopoly of the atomic bomb, our interest in outlying bases and our general support of the British Empire—appear to them as going far beyond the requirements of defense....

Finally, our resistance to her attempts to obtain warm water ports and her own security system in the form of "friendly" neighboring states seems, from the Russian point of view, to clinch the case. After twenty-five years of isolation and after having achieved the status of a major power, Russia believes that she is entitled to recognition of her new status. Our interest in establishing democracy in Eastern Europe, where democracy by and large has never existed, seems to her an attempt to reestablish the encirclement of unfriendly neighbors which was created after the last war and which might serve as a springboard of still another effort to destroy her.

If this analysis is correct, and there is ample evidence to support it, the action to improve the situation is clearly indicated. The fundamental objective of such action should be to allay any reasonable Russian grounds for fear, suspicions and distrust. We must recognize that the world has changed and that today there can be no "one world" unless the United States and Russia can find some way of living together.

3. Soviet Ambassador Nikolai Novikov Sees a U.S. Bid for World Supremacy, 1946

The foreign policy of the United States, which reflects the imperialist tendencies of American monopolistic capital, is characterized in the postwar period by a striving for world supremacy. This is the real meaning of the many statements by President Truman and other representatives of American ruling circles: that

Origins of the Cold War: The Novikov, Kennan, and Roberts 'Long Telegram' of 1946. Kenneth M. Jensen, editor. Copyright © 1991 by the Endowment of the United States Institute of Peace. Used with permission by the United States Institute of Peace. Washington, D.C.

the United States has the right to lead the world. All the forces of American diplomacy—the army, the air force, the navy, industry and science—are enlisted in the service of this foreign policy....

The foreign policy of the United States is not determined at present by the circles in the Democratic party that (as was the case during Roosevelt's lifetime) strive to strengthen the cooperation of the three great powers that constituted the basis of the anti–Hitler coalition during the war. The ascendance to power of President Truman, a politically unstable person but with certain conservative tendencies, and the subsequent appointment of [James F.] Byrnes as Secretary of State meant a strengthening of the influence on U.S. foreign policy of the most reactionary circles of the Democratic party....

At the same time, there has been a decline in the influence on foreign policy of those who follow Roosevelt's course for cooperation among peace-loving countries. Such persons in the government, in Congress, and in the leadership of the Democratic party are being pushed farther and farther into the background. The contradictions in the field of foreign policy existing between the followers of [Henry] Wallace and [Claude] Pepper, on the one hand, and the adherents of the reactionary "bi-partisan" policy, on the other, were manifested with great clarity recently in the speech by Wallace that led to his resignation from the post of Secretary of Commerce....

In the summer of 1946, for the first time in the history of the country, Congress passed a law on the establishment of a peacetime army, not on a volunteer basis but on the basis of universal military service. The size of the army, which is supposed to amount to about one million persons as of July 1, 1947, was also increased significantly. The size of the navy at the conclusion of the war decreased quite insignificantly in comparison with wartime. At the present time, the American navy occupies first place in the world, leaving England's navy far behind, to say nothing of those of other countries.

Expenditures on the army and navy have risen colossally, amounting to 13 billion dollars according to the budget for 1946–47 (about 40 percent of the total budget of 36 billion dollars). This is more than ten times greater than corresponding expenditures in the budget for 1938, which did not amount to even one billion dollars....

The "hard-line" policy with regard to the USSR announced by [Secretary of State James F.] Byrnes after the rapprochement of the reactionary Democrats with the Republicans is at present the main obstacle on the road to cooperation of the Great Powers. It consists mainly of the fact that in the postwar period the United States no longer follows a policy of strengthening cooperation among the Big Three (or Four) but rather has striven to undermine the unity of these countries. The objective has been to impose the will of other countries on the Soviet Union.

4. Images of Nuclear Destruction:
Atomic Cake vs. Godzilla, 1946 and 1954

US Navy officials slice into the Atomic Cake to celebrate the Bikini Islands bombs tests in 1946.

Movie, "Godzilla" (Gojira), JPN 1954, director: Inoshiro Honda, scene with Godzilla, fantasy, spitting fire, dinosaur.

5. The Truman Doctrine Calls for the United States to Become the World's Police, 1947

The gravity of the situation which confronts the world today necessitates my appearance before a joint session of the Congress.

The foreign policy and the national security of this country are involved.

One aspect of the present situation, which I present to you at this time for your consideration and decision, concerns Greece and Turkey.

The United States has received from the Greek Government an urgent appeal for financial and economic assistance. Preliminary reports from the American Economic Mission now in Greece and reports from the American Ambassador in Greece corroborate the statement of the Greek Government that assistance is imperative if Greece is to survive as a free nation....

The British Government has informed us that, owing to its own difficulties, it can no longer extend financial or economic aid to Turkey.

As in the case of Greece, if Turkey is to have the assistance it needs, the United States must supply it. We are the only country able to provide that help.

I am fully aware of the broad implications involved if the United States extends assistance to Greece and Turkey, and I shall discuss these implications with you at this time.

One of the primary objectives of the foreign policy of the United States is the creation of conditions in which we and other nations will be able to work out a way of life free from coercion. This was a fundamental issue in the war with Germany and Japan. Our victory was won over countries which sought to impose their will, and their way of life, upon other nations....

The peoples of a number of countries of the world have recently had totalitarian regimes forced upon them against their will. The Government of the United States has made frequent protests against coercion and intimidation, in violation of the Yalta agreement, in Poland, Rumania, and Bulgaria. I must also state that in a number of other countries there have been similar developments....

I believe that it must be the policy of the United States to support free peoples who are resisting attempted subjugation by armed minorities or by outside pressures.

I believe that we must assist free peoples to work out their own destinies in their own way.

I believe that our help should be primarily through economic and financial aid which is essential to economic stability and orderly political processes....

I therefore ask the Congress to provide authority for assistance to Greece and Turkey in the amount of $400,000,000 for the period ending June 30, 1948....

In addition to funds, I ask the Congress to authorize the detail of American civilian and military personnel to Greece and Turkey, at the request of those

Public Papers of the Presidents of the United States: Harry S. Truman, 1947 (Washington, D.C: U.S. Government Printing Office, 1963), 176–180.

countries, to assist in the tasks of reconstruction, and for the purpose of supervising the use of such financial and material assistance as may be furnished. I recommend that authority also be provided for the instruction and training of selected Greek and Turkish personnel....

This is a serious course upon which we embark.

I would not recommend it except that the alternative is much more serious. The United States contributed $341,000,000,000 toward winning World War II. This is an investment in world freedom and world peace.

The assistance that I am recommending for Greece and Turkey amounts to little more than 1/10 of 1 percent of this investment. It is only common sense that we should safeguard this investment and make sure that it was not in vain.

6. Senator Joseph McCarthy Describes the Internal Communist Menace, 1950

Five years after a world war has been won, men's hearts should anticipate a long peace, and men's minds should be free from the heavy weight that comes with war. But this is not such a period—for this is not a period of peace. This is a time of the "cold war." This is a time when all the world is split into two vast, increasingly hostile armed camps—a time of a great armaments race....

Six years ago, at the time of the first conference to map out the peace—Dumbarton Oaks—there was within the Soviet orbit 180,000,000 people. Lined up on the antitotalitarian side there were in the world at that time roughly 1,625,000,000 people. Today, only 6 years later, there are 800,000,000 people under the absolute domination of Soviet Russia—an increase of over 400 percent. On our side, the figure has shrunk to around 500,000,000. In other words, in less than 6 years the odds have changed from 9 to 1 in our favor to 8 to 5 against us. This indicates the swiftness of the tempo of Communist victories and American defeats in the cold war. As one of our outstanding historical figures once said, "When a great democracy is destroyed, it will not be because of enemies from without, but rather because of enemies from within."...

The reason why we find ourselves in a position of impotency is not because our only powerful potential enemy has sent men to invade our shores, but rather because of the traitorous actions of those who have been treated so well by this Nation. It has not been the less fortunate or members of minority groups who have been selling this Nation out, but rather those who have had all the benefits that the wealthiest nation on earth has had to offer—the finest homes, the finest college education, and the finest jobs in Government we can give.

This is glaringly true in the State Department. There the bright young men who are born with silver spoons in their mouths are the ones who have been the worst.... In my opinion the State Department, which is one of the most important government departments, is thoroughly infested with Communists.

Congressional Record, 81 Cong., 2d Sess., pp. 1954–1957.

I have in my hand 57 cases of individuals who would appear to be either card carrying members or certainly loyal to the Communist Party, but who nevertheless are still helping to shape our foreign policy....

As you know, very recently the Secretary of State proclaimed his loyalty to a man guilty of what has always been considered as the most abominable of all crimes—of being a traitor to the people who gave him a position of great trust. The Secretary of State in attempting to justify his continued devotion to the man who sold out the Christian world to the atheistic world, referred to Christ's Sermon on the Mount as a justification and reason therefore, and the reaction of the American people to this would have made the heart of Abraham Lincoln happy.

When this pompous diplomat in striped pants, with a phony British accent, proclaimed to the American people that Christ on the Mount endorsed communism, high treason, and betrayal of a sacred trust, the blasphemy was so great that it awakened the dormant indignation of the American people.

He has lighted the spark which is resulting in a moral uprising and will end only when the whole sorry mess of twisted, warped thinkers are swept from the national scene so that we may have a new birth of national honesty and decency in government.

7. The Federal Loyalty–Security Program Expels a Postal Clerk, 1954

In late February 1954, the employee was working in a clerical capacity as a substitute postal employee. He performed no supervisory duties. His tasks were routine in nature.

One year prior to the initiation of proceedings, the employee had resigned from his position as an executive officer of a local union whose parent union had been expelled from the CIO in 1949 as Communist dominated. The employee had served as an officer for one year prior to the expulsion, had helped to lead his local out of the expelled parent and back into the CIO, and had thereafter remained in an executive capacity until his resignation in 1953. He resigned from that position upon being appointed a substitute clerk with the United States Post Office in early 1953....

In the last week of February 1954, the employee received notice, by mail, that he was under investigation by the Regional Office of the United States Civil Service Commission....

[The employee immediately answered the first set of charges against him only to be suspended without pay at the end of March on the following charges.——Ed.]

> "3. In January 1948, your name appeared on a general mailing list of the Spanish Refugee Appeal of the Joint Anti-Fascist Refugee Committee....

Case Studies in Personnel Security, ed. Adam Yarmolinsky (Washington, D.C.: Bureau of National Affairs, 1955), 142–149.

"5. Your wife … was a member of the … Club of the Young Communist League.
"6. In 1950, Communist literature was observed in the bookshelves and Communist art was seen on the walls of your residence in ————.
"7. Your signature appeared on a Communist Party nominating petition in the November 1941 Municipal Elections in ————." …

The employee had a hearing four months later, in July 1954. The members of the Board were three (3) civilian employees of military installations. None of them were attorneys. The Post Office establishment was represented by an Inspector, who administered the oath to the employee and his witnesses, but did not otherwise participate in the proceedings. There was no attorney-advisor to the Board. There was no testimony by witnesses hostile to the employee, nor was any evidence introduced against him.…

… Before the employee testified, he submitted a nine-page autobiography to the Hearing Board.…

… The autobiography set forth in some detail the employee's activities as an Officer of his local union, and discussed particularly his role therein as an anti-Communist, and his opposition to the pro-Communist policies of the National Organization with which his local was affiliated. The autobiography recited that when his National Union was expelled from the CIO, he and his supporters successfully won a struggle within his local and as a direct result thereof, caused the said local to disaffiliate from the expelled parent, and affiliate with a new organization established within the CIO. The employee's autobiography recited that the aforesaid struggle directly involved the question of Communist domination of the local's parent union, that the victory of the employee and his supporters represented a victory over Communist adherents in the local, and that the employee was the frequent target of threats and slander by the pro-Communist faction of his local.…

With respect to the third charge against the employee (that his name had been on a general mailing list of the Spanish Refugee Appeal of the Joint Anti-Fascist Refugee Committee), the employee reiterated his denial of any knowledge concerning it, and his counsel reminded the Board that no Attorney General's list existed in January 1948—the date contained in the charge. The employee testified, further, that he had no recollection of ever having received any mail from the organization involved.…

With respect to charge No. 5 against the employee (that his wife had been a member of the Young Communist League), the Chairman of the Hearing Board advised the employee that the date involved was March 1944. The employee testified that he and his wife were married in February 1944, and that the charge was ridiculous. He testified, further, that he had no independent recollection that his wife was ever a member of the said organization. In addition, the employee testified that he had never lived in the neighborhood in which the organization was alleged to have existed, and that he had never heard of said organization.…

The Chairman then read charge No. 6 in which it was alleged that Communist literature was observed in the employee's bookshelves at home....

Counsel for the employee then questioned him concerning his courses in college, and the books which he was there required to read for those courses. In this connection, counsel for the employee asked whether books had been recommended as part of study courses by instructors, and whether one of these books had been *Das Kapital* by Karl Marx, and whether the employee had bought *Das Kapital*, following such a recommendation. The employee responded that certain books had been recommended by his instructors, that *Das Kapital* was one, and that he had bought the Modern Library Giant Edition of *Das Kapital*....

Thereafter, in response to counsel's question, the employee testified that he had not read *Das Kapital* in its entirety, that he had been required to read "a chapter or two for classwork," and that "he had found it a little dull and tedious."....

... In early September, 1954, and without notices as to whether the Board had reached a decision in his case, the employee received notice from the Post Office Department that the Postmaster General had ordered the employee's removal.... The employee [also] received a letter from the Regional Office of the United States Civil Service Commission. This letter advised the employee that he had been rated ineligible for Civil Service appointment, and that he was barred from competing in Federal Civil Service Examinations for a period of three years.

8. *Life* Magazine Reassures Americans "We Won't All Be Dead" After Nuclear War, 1959

The governor of New York last week became the first important elected official to espouse a mandatory fallout shelter program, one which may become law for the people of his state. Nelson Rockefeller has thus identified himself with the least popular issue in the U.S. today. He has done the whole country a political service. For if his example succeeds and is coped by other states, it could be the means of saving any where from 20 to 100 million American lives.

Why do most Americans go deaf or change the subject when asked to think about defending themselves against a possible nuclear attack? There has been a federal civilian defense office since 1951, but it has neither carried conviction nor made itself heard. It has spent $500 million on studies, pamphlets, volunteers, over-head, etc., yet our population is almost totally ignorant of how to behave in case Khrushchev should carry out his repeated threat. We don't even recognize the alarm signals. It is U.S. government policy that every surviving American family should be prepared to feed and protect itself without help for two weeks after a nuclear attack. How many Americans have even heard that—let alone made any preparations?

Most of us evidently either hope to die quickly or expect some authority or other to keep us alive. One New York paper greeted Rocky's program with the scornful determination to "die gaily but not daily." That is nonsense. It is as if we had adopted a couple of new national vices from our later enemies—the shrug from Italy and the kamikaze spirit (through of a strangely passive variety) from Japan. Our military policy is based on the possibility of a nuclear war in which we expect to receive—not to strike—the first blow. Yet the defensive preparedness this strategy obviously calls for is zero. Its lack saps the deterrent power of SAC and our bargaining power with Russia.

Helplessness is not a sound reason for the general apathy. The fact is that nuclear war, though a catastrophe, would he a catastrophe with limits which can be narrowed in advance. A full shelter program against blast and heat, as described by Willard Bascom in LIFE (March 18, 1957), would cost at least $20 billion and for that reason alone arouses little interest. But according to the latest government studies, blast and heat would account for only a quarter of the total deaths (even in a fat-target state like New York) if we were attacked tomorrow. The other three quarters would die more slowly from "the silent killer," called radioactive fallout. This would threaten the remotest farm, but anyone outside the blast area could, by *taking the right precautions,* expect to survive.

These precautions need not cost much. You probably would have some protection now if you knew how to use it. According to a committee of Governor Rockefeller's, present houses with cellars can be made fallout-proof for the critical two weeks for $150 to $200. In addition each member of the family needs a "survival kit" (dehydrated food, water container) costing about $7. Above all you need instruction on how to wash, measure radiation, etc. The place to get that is from your local CD director. He may be the least popular man in town, but he is in business for your health.

Yours and the nation's. The number of individual survivors and their morale will determine whether or not the U.S.A. can survive a nuclear war. All we can assume about Russian military planning, target dispersion and CD instructions to the people indicates that they are much better prepared for D+1 and D+14 *et seq.* than we are. Russia has survived a high order of casualties before. Our national preoccupation with an eight-hour war, which we also think of as the end of the world, could easily condemn us to lose the negotiations that would prevent such a war, or once it has started, cause us to succumb to "post-attack blackmail" on a day we had wrongly expected to be dead.

We won't all be dead, that's sure. It is also sure that we can ourselves limit the casualties by taking thought now about this dreadful subject. Since when has survival been too dreadful to think about? It's a complex subject, but not an unmanageable one. Governor Rockefeller has done quite right to open it up. Let it stay open until all of us—Washington, the states and the people—have faced up to what needs to be done.

9. President Eisenhower Warns of the Military-Industrial Complex, 1961

A vital element in keeping the peace is our military establishment. Our arms must be mighty, ready for instant action, so that no potential aggressor may be tempted to risk his own destruction.

Our military organization today bears little relation to that known by any of my predecessors in peacetime, or indeed by the fighting men of World War II or Korea.

Until the latest of our world conflicts, the United States had no armaments industry. American makers of plowshares could, with time and as required, make swords as well. But now we can no longer risk emergency improvisation of national defense: we have been compelled to create a permanent armaments industry of vast proportions. Added to this, three and a half million men and women are directly engaged in the defense establishment. We annually spend on military security more than the net income of all United States corporations.

This conjunction of an immense military establishment and a large arms industry is new in the American experience. The total influence—economic, political, even spiritual—is felt in every city, even State house, every office of the Federal government. We recognize the imperative need for this development. Yet we must not fail to comprehend its grave implications. Our toil, resources and livelihood are all involved; so is the very structure of our society.

In the councils of government, we must guard against the acquisition of unwarranted influence, whether sought or unsought, by the military-industrial complex. The potential for the disastrous rise of misplaced power exists and will persist.

We must never let the weight of this combination endanger our liberties or democratic processes. We should take nothing for granted....

Today the solitary inventor, tinkering in his shop, has been overshadowed by task forces of scientists in laboratories and testing fields. In the same fashion, the free university, historically the fountainhead of free ideas and scientific discovery, has experienced a revolution in the conduct of research. Partly because of the huge costs involved, a government contract becomes virtually a substitute for intellectual curiosity. For every old blackboard there are now hundreds of new electronic computers.

The prospect of domination of the nation's scholars by Federal employment, project allocations, and the power of money is ever present—and is gravely to be regarded.

Yet, in holding scientific research and discovery in respect, as we should, we must also be alert to the equal and opposite danger that public policy could itself become the captive of a scientific-technological elite.

Public Papers of the Presidents of the United States: Dwight D. Eisenhower. 1961 (Washington, D.C.: U.S. Government Printing Office, 1961). 1037–1040.

It is the task of statesmanship to mold, to balance, and to integrate these and other forces, new and old, within the principles of our democratic system—ever aiming toward the supreme goals of our free society.

ESSAYS

The cold war had tremendous costs for both the United States and the Soviet Union. It helped justify domestic repression in both nations, led to enormous expenditures on weapons that could destroy the earth many times over, and involved both countries in costly "proxy" wars at the margins of their spheres of influence. (For the United States, Korea and Vietnam are the best examples.) Thus, for many scholars, the question of who started the cold war prompts passionate debate about which nation should bear primary responsibility.

Walter LaFeber of Cornell University makes the argument that the United States unintentionally, but quite clearly, provoked the conflict. President Harry Truman came into office an insecure and uninformed man who was determined not to appear soft and therefore took the advice of hard-liners in his administration. Strategists who held opposite views and who had earlier advised President Roosevelt were largely shunted aside. John Lewis Gaddis of Yale University takes a different tack. Gaddis acknowledges that both superpowers sought to mold the world in their own images, but that the system advocated by the United States was inherently more benign. In this essay he contrasts the ways in which Soviets and Americans acted abroad. He argues that the American "empire" was more enduring and attractive because it consulted its allies and promised security. The Soviets provoked the cold war by treating their neighbors in Eastern Europe so harshly that they could be kept "friendly" only through coercion, and by scaring Western Europeans into a military alliance with the United States. Soviet behavior, far more than American, gradually led to the creation of two hostile blocs.

Truman's Hard Line Prompted the Cold War

WALTER LAFEBER

… Truman entered the White House a highly insecure man. ("I felt like the moon, the stars, and all the planets had fallen on me," he told reporters.) And he held the world's most responsible job in a world that was changing radically. Truman tried to compensate for his insecurity in several ways. First, he was extremely jealous of his presidential powers and deeply suspicious of anyone who challenged those powers. Truman made decisions rapidly not only because that was his character but also because he determined "the buck stopped" at his

Walter LaFeber, *America, Russia, and the Cold War, 1945–2000* (New York: McGraw-Hill, 2001) pp. 17–20, 22–26, 29–30, 42–43, 48, 55, 62–65, 67–68, 74, 76–77, 81, 88, 91, 101–103. Reproduced with permission of The McGraw-Hill Companies.

desk. There would be no more sloppy administration or strong, freewheeling bureaucrats as in FDR's later years.

Second, and more dangerously, Truman was determined that these decisions would not be tagged as "appeasement." He would be as tough as the toughest. After only twenty-four hours in the White House, the new President confidently informed his secretary of state, "We must stand up to the Russians," and he implied "We had been too easy with them." In foreign-policy discussions during the next two weeks, Truman interrupted his advisers to assure them he would certainly be "tough."

His determination was reinforced when he listened most closely to such advisers as Harriman, Leahy, and Secretary of the Navy James Forrestal, who urged him to take a hard line. Warning of a "barbarian invasion of Europe," Harriman declared that postwar cooperation with the Soviets, especially economically, must depend on their agreement to open Poland and Eastern Europe. In a decisive meeting on April 23, Secretary of War Henry Stimson argued with Harriman. Stimson declared that peace must never be threatened by an issue such as Poland, for free elections there were impossible, Russia held total control, and Stalin was "not likely to yield ... in substance." Stimson was not an amateur; he had been a respected Wall Street lawyer and distinguished public servant for forty years, including a term as Herbert Hoover's secretary of state.

But Truman dismissed Stimson's advice, accepted Harriman's, and later that day berated Soviet Foreign Minister Molotov "in words of one syllable" for breaking the Yalta agreements on Poland. Truman demanded that the Soviets agree to a "new" (not merely "reorganized") Polish government. An astonished Molotov replied, "I have never been talked to like that in my life." "Carry out your agreements," Truman supposedly retorted, "and you won't get talked to like that."

The next day Stalin rejected Truman's demand by observing that it was contrary to the Yalta agreement. The dictator noted that "Poland borders with the Soviet Union, what [sic] cannot be said of Great Britain and the United States." After all, Stalin continued, the Soviets do not "lay claim to interference" in Belgium and Greece where the Americans and British made decisions without consulting the Russians.... Stimson had been correct. Truman's toughness had only stiffened Russian determination to control Poland.

An "iron fence" was falling around Eastern Europe, Churchill blurted out to Stalin in mid-1945. "All fairy-tales," the Soviet leader blandly replied. But it was partly true. The crises over Rumania and Poland only raised higher the fence around those two nations. In other areas, however, the Soviet approach varied. A Russian-sponsored election in Hungary produced a noncommunist government. In Bulgaria the Soviet-conducted elections satisfied British observers, if not Americans. Stalin agreed to an independent, noncommunist regime in Finland if the Finns would follow a foreign policy friendly to Russia. An "iron fence" by no means encircled all of Eastern Europe. There was still room to bargain if each side wished to avoid a confrontation over the remaining areas.

But the bargaining room was limited. Stalin's doctrine and his determination that Russia would not again be invaded from the west greatly narrowed his diplomatic options. So too did the tremendous devastation of the war. Rapid rebuilding under communism required security, required access to resources in Eastern and Central Europe, and continued tight control over the Russian people. The experience of war was indelible. Russians viewed almost everything in their lives through their "searing experience of World War II," as one psychologist has phrased it. The conflict had destroyed 1700 towns, 70,000 villages and left 25 million homeless. Twenty million died; 600,000 starved to death at the single siege of Leningrad....

Some scholars have examined Stalin's acts of 1928–1945, pronounced them the work of a "paranoid," and concluded that the United States had no chance to avoid a cold war since it was dealing with a man who was mentally ill. That interpretation neatly avoids confronting the complex causes of the Cold War but is wholly insufficient to explain those causes. However Stalin acted inside Russia, where he had total control, in his foreign policy during 1941–1946 he displayed a realism, a careful calculation of forces, and a diplomatic finesse that undercut any attempt to explain away his actions as paranoid. If he and other Soviets were suspicious of the West, they were realistic, not paranoid: the West had poured thousands of troops into Russia between 1917 and 1920, refused to cooperate with the Soviets during the 1930s, tried to turn Hitler against Stalin in 1938, reneged on promises about the second front, and in 1945 tried to penetrate areas Stalin deemed crucial to Soviet security.

American diplomats who frequently saw Stalin understood this background. In January 1945 Harriman told the State Department, "The overriding consideration in Soviet foreign policy is the preoccupation with 'security,' as Moscow sees it." The problem was that Americans did not see "security" the same way. They believed their security required an open world, including an open Eastern Europe....

By mid-1945 Stalin's policies were brutally consistent, while Truman's were confused. The confusion became obvious when the United States, opposed to a sphere of interest in Europe, strengthened its own sphere in the Western Hemisphere. Unlike its policies elsewhere, however, the State Department did not use economic weapons. The economic relationship with Latin America and Canada could simply be assumed....

But Latin America was not neglected politically. A young assistant secretary of state for Latin American affairs, Nelson Rockefeller, and Senator Arthur Vandenberg (Republican from Michigan) devised the political means to keep the Americas solidly within Washington's sphere. Their instrument was Article 51 of the U.N. Charter. This provision was largely formulated by Rockefeller and Vandenberg at the San Francisco conference that founded the United Nations in the spring of 1945. The article allowed for collective self-defense through special regional organizations to be created outside the United Nations but within the principles of the charter. In this way, regional organizations would escape Russian vetoes in the Security Council. The United States could control its own sphere without Soviet interference....

The obvious confusion in that approach was pinpointed by Secretary of War Stimson when he condemned Americans who were "anxious to hang on to exaggerated views of the Monroe Doctrine [in the Western Hemisphere] and at the same time butt into every question that comes up in Central Europe." Almost alone, Stimson argued for an alternative policy. Through bilateral U.S.-U.S.S.R. negotiations (and not negotiations within the United Nations, where the Russians would be defensive and disagreeable because the Americans controlled a majority), Stimson hoped each side could agree that the other should have its own security spheres. But as he had lost the argument over Poland, so Stimson lost this argument. Truman was prepared to bargain very little. He might not get 100 percent, the President told advisers, but he would get 85 percent. Even in Rumania, where the Russians were particularly sensitive, the State Department secretly determined in August 1945, "It is our intention to attain a position of equality with the Russians." When, however, the Americans pressed, the Soviets only tightened their control of Rumania....

Although Truman did not obtain his "85 percent" at Potsdam, en route home he received the news that a weapon of unimaginable power, the atomic bomb, had obliterated Hiroshima, Japan, on August 6. Eighty thousand had died. This was some 20,000 fewer than had been killed by a massive American fire bombing of Tokyo earlier in the year, but it was the newly opened secret of nature embodied in a single bomb that was overwhelming. Roosevelt had initiated the atomic project in 1941. He had decided at least by 1944 not to share information about the bomb with the Soviets, even though he knew Stalin had learned about the project. By the summer of 1945 this approach, and the growing Soviet-American confrontation in Eastern Europe, led Truman and Byrnes to discuss securing "further *quid pro quos*" in Rumania, Poland, and Asia from Stalin before the Russians could share the secret of atomic energy....

... Stimson, about to retire from the War Department, made one final attempt to stop an East-West confrontation. In a September 11 memorandum to Truman, Stimson prophesied "that it would not be possible to use our possession of the atomic bomb as a direct lever to produce the change" desired inside Eastern Europe. If Soviet-American negotiations continue with "this weapon rather ostentatiously on our hip, their suspicions and their distrust of our purposes and motives will increase." He again urged direct, bilateral talks with Stalin to formulate control of the bomb and to write a general peace settlement. Stimson's advice was especially notable because several months before he himself had hoped to use the bomb to pry the Soviets out of Eastern Europe. Now he had changed his mind.

Truman again turned Stimson's advice aside. A month later the President delivered a speech larded with references to America's monopoly of atomic power, then attacked Russia's grip on Eastern Europe. Molotov quickly replied that peace could not be reconciled with an armaments race advocated by "zealous partisans of the imperialist policy." In this connection, he added. "We should mention the discovery of ... the atomic bomb."

With every utterance and every act, the wartime alliance further disintegrated....

During early 1946 Stalin and Churchill issued their declarations of Cold War. In an election speech of February 9, the Soviet dictator announced that Marxist-Leninist dogma remained valid, for "the unevenness of development of the capitalist countries" could lead to "violent disturbance" and the consequent splitting of the "capitalist world into two hostile camps and war between them." War was inevitable as long as capitalism existed. The Soviet people must prepare themselves for a replay of the 1930s by developing basic industry instead of consumer goods and, in all, making enormous sacrifices demanded in "three more Five-Year Plans, I should think, if not more." There would be no peace, internally or externally. These words profoundly affected Washington. Supreme Court Justice William Douglas, one of the reigning American liberals, believed that Stalin's speech meant "The Declaration of World War III." The *New York Times* front-page story of the speech began by declaring that Stalin believed "the stage is set" for war.

Winston Churchill delivered his views at Fulton, Missouri, on March 5. The former prime minister exalted American power with the plea that his listeners recognize that "God has willed" the United States, not "some Communist or neo-Fascist state" to have atomic bombs. To utilize the "breathing space" provided by these weapons, Churchill asked for "a fraternal association of the English-speaking peoples" operating under the principles of the United Nations, but not inside that organization, to reorder the world. This unilateral policy must be undertaken because "from Stettin in the Baltic to Trieste in the Adriatic, an iron curtain has descended across the Continent" allowing "police government" to rule Eastern Europe. The Soviets, he emphasized, did not want war: "What they desire is the fruits of war and the indefinite expansion of their power and doctrines."

The "iron curtain" phrase made the speech famous. But, as Churchill himself observed, the "crux" of the message lay in the proposal that the Anglo-Americans, outside the United Nations and with the support of atomic weaponry (the title of the address was "The Sinews of Peace"), create "a unity in Europe from which no nation should be permanently outcast." The Soviets perceived this as a direct challenge to their power in Eastern Europe. Within a week Stalin attacked Churchill and his "friends" in America, whom he claimed resembled Hitler by holding a "racial theory" that those who spoke the English language "should rule over the remaining nations of the world." This, Stalin warned, is "a set-up for war, a call to war with the Soviet Union."

Within a short period after the Churchill speech, Stalin launched a series of policies which, in retrospect, marks the spring and summer of 1946 as a milestone in the Cold War. During these weeks the Soviets, after having worked for a loan during the previous fifteen months, finally concluded that Washington had no interest in loaning them $1 billion, or any other amount. They refused to become a member of the World Bank and the International Monetary Fund. These rejections ended the American hope to use the lure of the dollar to make the Soviets retreat in Eastern Europe and join the capitalist-controlled bank and IMF.

Actually there had never been reason to hope. Control of their border areas was worth more to the Russians than $1 billion, or even $10 billion....

... Truman's difficulties came into the open during the autumn of 1946, when he was attacked by liberals for being too militaristic and by conservatives for his economic policies.

The liberal attack was led by Henry Agard Wallace, a great secretary of agriculture during the early New Deal, Vice President from 1941–1945, maneuvered out of the vice-presidential nomination in 1944 so that Harry Truman could be FDR's running mate, and finally secretary of commerce in 1945. Here he devoted himself to the cause of what he liked to call the "Common Man," by extending increased loans to small businessmen and, above all, enlarging the economic pie by increasing foreign trade. Wallace soon discovered that Truman threatened to clog the trade channels to Russia, Eastern Europe, perhaps even China, with his militant attitude toward the Soviets.

At a political rally in New York on September 12, 1946, Wallace delivered a speech, cleared personally, and too rapidly, by Truman. The address focused on the necessity of a political understanding with Russia. This, Wallace declared, would require guaranteeing Soviet security in Eastern Europe.... At that moment Byrnes and Vandenberg were in Paris, painfully and unsuccessfully trying to negotiate peace treaties with Molotov. They immediately demanded Wallace's resignation. On September 20, Truman complied....

On March 12, 1947, President Truman finally issued his own declaration of Cold War. Dramatically presenting the Truman Doctrine to Congress, he asked Americans to join in a global commitment against communism. The nation responded. A quarter of a century later, Senator J. William Fulbright declared, "More by far than any other factor the anti-communism of the Truman Doctrine has been the guiding spirit of American foreign policy since World War II." ...

The Truman Doctrine was a milestone in American history for at least four reasons. First, it marked the point at which Truman used the American fear of communism both at home and abroad to convince Americans they must embark upon a Cold War foreign policy. This consensus would not break apart for a quarter of a century. Second..., Congress was giving the President great powers to wage this Cold War as he saw fit. Truman's personal popularity began spiraling upward after his speech. Third, for the first time in the postwar era, Americans massively intervened in another nation's civil war. Intervention was justified on the basis of anticommunism. In the future, Americans would intervene in similar wars for supposedly the same reason and with less happy results....

Finally, and perhaps most important, Truman used the doctrine to justify a gigantic aid program to prevent a collapse of the European and American economies. Later such programs were expanded globally. The President's arguments about the need to fight communism now became confusing, for the Western economies would have been in grave difficulties whether or not communism existed. The complicated problems of reconstruction and U.S. dependence on world trade were not well understood by Americans, but they easily comprehended anticommunism. So Americans embarked upon the Cold War for the good reasons given in the Truman Doctrine, which they understood, and for real reasons, which they did not understand....

The President's program evolved naturally into the Marshall Plan. Although the speech did not limit American effort, Secretary of State Marshall did by concentrating the administration's attention on Europe. Returning badly shaken from a Foreign Ministers conference in Moscow, the secretary of state insisted in a nationwide broadcast that Western Europe required immediate help. "The patient is sinking," he declared, "while the doctors deliberate." Personal conversations with Stalin had convinced Marshall that the Russians believed Europe would collapse. Assuming that the United States must lead in restoring Europe, Marshall appointed a policy-planning staff under the direction of George Kennan to draw up guidelines....

Building on this premise, round-the-clock conferences in May 1947 began to fashion the main features of the Marshall Plan. The all-important question became how to handle the Russians. Ostensibly, Marshall accepted Kennan's advice to "play it straight" by inviting the Soviet bloc. In reality the State Department made Russian participation improbable by demanding that economic records of each nation be open for scrutiny. For good measure Kennan also suggested that the Soviets' devastated economy, weakened by the war and at that moment suffering from drought and famine, participate in the plan by shipping Soviet goods to Europe. Apparently no one in the State Department wanted the Soviets included. Russian participation would vastly multiply the costs of the program and eliminate any hope of its acceptance by a purse-watching Republican Congress, now increasingly convinced by Truman that communists had to be fought, not fed....

The European request for a four-year program of $17 billion of American aid now had to run the gauntlet of a Republican Congress, which was dividing its attention between slashing the budget and attacking Truman, both in anticipation of the presidential election only a year away. In committee hearings in late 1947 and early 1948, the executive presented its case. Only large amounts of government money which could restore basic facilities, provide convertibility of local currency into dollars, and end the dollar shortage would stimulate private investors to rebuild Europe, administration witnesses argued....

The Marshall Plan now appears to have signaled not the beginning but the end of an era. It marked the last phase in the administration's use of economic tactics as the primary means of tying together the Western world. The plan's approach ... soon evolved into military alliances. Truman proved to be correct in saying that the Truman Doctrine and the Marshall Plan "are two halves of the same walnut." Americans willingly acquiesced as the military aspects of the doctrine developed into quite the larger part....

The military and personal costs of the Truman Doctrine ... were higher than expected. And the cost became more apparent as Truman and J. Edgar Hoover (director of the Federal Bureau of Investigation) carried out the President's Security Loyalty program. Their search for subversives accelerated after Canadians uncovered a Soviet spy ring.

The House Un-American Activities Committee began to intimate that Truman was certainly correct in his assessment of communism's evil nature but lax in destroying it. In March 1948 the committee demanded the loyalty records gathered by the FBI. Truman handled the situation badly. Unable to exploit the committee's distorted view of the internal communist threat, he accused it of trying to cover up the bad record of the Republican Congress. He refused to surrender the records, ostensibly because they were in the exclusive domain of the executive, more probably because of his fear that if the Republicans saw the FBI reports, which accused some federal employees of disloyalty on the basis of hearsay, unproven allegations, and personal vendettas, November might be an unfortunate month for Truman's political aspirations. Unable to discredit the loyalty program he had set in motion, trapped by his own indiscriminating anti-communist rhetoric designed to "scare hell" out of the country, Truman stood paralyzed as the ground was carefully plowed around him for the weeds of McCarthyism....

And then came the fall of Czechoslovakia. The Czechs had uneasily coexisted with Russia by trying not to offend the Soviets while keeping doors open to the West. This policy had started in late 1943, when Czech leaders signed a treaty with Stalin that, in the view of most observers, obligated Czechoslovakia to become a part of the Russian bloc. President Edvard Beneš and Foreign Minister Jan Masaryk, one of the foremost diplomatic figures in Europe, had nevertheless successfully resisted complete communist control. Nor had Stalin moved to consolidate his power in 1946 after the Czech Communist party emerged from the parliamentary elections with 38 percent of the vote, the largest total of any party. By late 1947 the lure of Western aid and internal political changes began to pull the Czech government away from the Soviets. At this point Stalin, who like Truman recalled the pivotal role of Czechoslovakia in 1938, decided to put the 1943 treaty into effect. Klement Gottwald, the Czech Communist party leader, demanded the elimination of independent parties. In mid–February 1948 Soviet armies camped on the border as Gottwald ordered the formation of a wholly new government. A Soviet mission of top officials flew to Prague to demand Beneš's surrender. The communists assumed full control on February 25. Two weeks later Masaryk either committed suicide, or, as Truman believed, was the victim of "foul play."

Truman correctly observed that the coup "sent a shock throughout the civilized world." He privately believed "We are faced with exactly the same situation with which Britain and France were faced in 1938–9 with Hitler."... Two days before, on March 14, the Senate had endorsed the Marshall Plan by a vote of 69 to 17. As it went to the House for consideration, Truman, fearing the "grave events in Europe [which] were moving so swiftly," decided to appear before Congress.

In a speech remarkable for its repeated emphasis on the "increasing threat" to the very "survival of freedom," the President proclaimed the Marshall Plan "not enough." Europe must have "some measure of protection against internal and external aggression." He asked for Universal Training, the resumption of Selective Service (which he had allowed to lapse a year earlier), and speedy passage of the Marshall Plan. Within twelve days the House approved authorization of the plan's money....

During the spring of 1948 a united administration, enjoying strong support on foreign policy from a Republican Congress, set off with exemplary single-mindedness to destroy the communist threat that loomed over Europe. Within two years this threat had been scotched. But the officials who created the policy had split, the Congress that ratified the policy had turned against the executive, the administration had fought off charges that it had been infiltrated by communists, and the United States found itself fighting a bloody war not in Europe but in Asia. These embarrassments did not suddenly emerge in 1950 but developed gradually from the policies of 1948–1949....

The world in which NATO was to be born was undergoing rapid change....

The Senate ratified the [NATO] treaty 82 to 13. On the day he added his signature in mid-July 1949, Truman sent Congress a one-year Mutual Defense Assistance (MDA) bill providing for $1.5 billion for European military aid. This was the immediate financial price for the NATO commitment. A memorandum circulating through the executive outlined the purpose of MDA: "to build up our own military industry," to "create a common defense frontier in Western Europe" by having the Allies pool "their industrial and manpower resources," and particularly, to subordinate "nationalistic tendencies." In the House, however, the bill encountered tough opposition from budget-cutting congressmen. On September 22, President Truman announced that Russia had exploded an atomic bomb. Within six days the NATO appropriations raced through the House and went to the President for approval.

Although publicly playing down the significance of the Russian bomb, the administration painfully realized that, in Vandenberg's words, "This is now a different world." Few American officials had expected the Soviet test this early. Because it was simultaneous with the fall of China, the American diplomatic attitude further stiffened....

... A grim President, pressed by domestic critics and the new Soviet bomb, demanded a wide-ranging reevaluation of American Cold War policies. In early 1950 the National Security Council began work on a highly secret document (declassified only a quarter of a century later, and then through an accident) that would soon be known as NSC-68. Truman examined the study in April, and it was ready for implementation when Korea burst into war.

NSC-68 proved to be the American blueprint for waging the Cold War. It began with two assumptions that governed the rest of the document. First, the global balance of power had been "fundamentally altered" since the nineteenth century so that the Americans and Russians now dominated the world: "What is new, what makes the continuing crisis, is the polarization of power which inescapably confronts the slave society with the free." It was us against them. Second, "the Soviet Union, unlike previous aspirants to hegemony, is animated by a new fanatic faith, antithetical to our own, and seeks to impose its absolute authority," initially in "the Soviet Union and second in the area now under [its] control." Then the crucial sentence: "In the minds of the Soviet leaders, however, achievement of this design requires the dynamic extension of their authority and the ultimate elimination of any effective opposition to their authority.... To that end Soviet efforts are now directed toward the domination of the Eurasian land mass."...

In conclusion, therefore, NSC–68 recommended (1) against negotiations with Russia since conditions were not yet sufficient to force the Kremlin to "change its policies drastically"; (2) development of hydrogen bombs to offset possible Soviet possession of an effective atomic arsenal by 1954; (3) rapid building of conventional military forces to preserve American interests without having to wage atomic war; (4) a large increase in taxes to pay for this new, highly expensive military establishment; (5) mobilization of American society, including a government-created "consensus" on the necessity of "sacrifice" and "unity" by Americans; (6) a strong alliance system directed by the United States; (7) and—as the topper—undermining the "Soviet totalitariat" from within by making "the Russian people our allies in this enterprise." How this was to be done was necessarily vague. But no matter. Truman and Acheson were no longer satisfied with containment. They wanted Soviet withdrawal and an absolute victory....

Stalin's Hard Line Prompted a Defensive Response in the United States and Europe

JOHN LEWIS GADDIS

Leaders of both the United States and the Soviet Union would have bristled at having the appellation "imperial" affixed to what they were doing after 1945. But one need not send out ships, seize territories, and hoist flags to construct an empire: "informal" empires are considerably older than, and continued to exist alongside, the more "formal" ones Europeans imposed on so much of the rest of the world from the fifteenth through the nineteenth centuries. During the Cold War years Washington and Moscow took on much of the character, if never quite the charm, of old imperial capitals like London, Paris, and Vienna. And surely American and Soviet influence, throughout most of the second half of the twentieth century, was at least as ubiquitous as that of any earlier empire the world had ever seen....

Let us begin with the structure of the Soviet empire, for the simple reason that it was, much more than the American, deliberately designed. It has long been clear that, in addition to having had an authoritarian vision, [Joseph] Stalin also had an imperial one, which he proceeded to implement in at least as single-minded a way. No comparably influential builder of empire came close to wielding power for so long, or with such striking results, on the Western side.

It was, of course, a matter of some awkwardness that Stalin came out of a revolutionary movement that had vowed to smash, not just tsarist imperialism, but all forms of imperialism throughout the world. The Soviet leader constructed his own logic, though, and throughout his career he devoted a surprising amount

John Lewis Gaddis, *We Now Know: Rethinking Cold War History* (New York: Oxford University Press, 1997). Reprinted by permission of Oxford University Press.

of attention to showing how a revolution and an empire might coexist. Bolsheviks could never be imperialists, Stalin acknowledged in one of his earliest public pronouncements on this subject, made in April 1917. But surely in a *revolutionary* Russia nine-tenths of the non-Russian nationalities would not *want* their independence. Few among those minorities found Stalin's reasoning persuasive after the Bolsheviks did seize power later that year, however, and one of the first problems [Vladimir] Lenin's new government faced was a disintegration of the old Russian empire not unlike what happened to the Soviet Union after communist authority finally collapsed in 1991.

Whether because of Lenin's own opposition to imperialism or, just as plausibly, because of Soviet Russia's weakness at the time, Finns, Estonians, Latvians, Lithuanians, Poles, and Moldavians were allowed to depart. Others who tried to do so—Ukrainians, Belorussians, Caucasians, Central Asians—were not so fortunate, and in 1922 Stalin proposed incorporating these remaining (and reacquired) nationalities into the Russian republic, only to have Lenin as one of his last acts override this recommendation and establish the multi-ethnic Union of Soviet Socialist Republics. After Lenin died and Stalin took his place it quickly became clear, though, that whatever its founding principles the USSR was to be no federation of equals. Rather, it would function as an updated form of empire even more tightly centralized than that of the Russian tsars....

Stalin's fusion of Marxist internationalism with tsarist imperialism could only reinforce his tendency, in place well before World War II, to equate the advance of world revolution with the expanding influence of the Soviet state....

Stalin had been very precise [after World War II] about where he wanted Soviet boundaries changed; he was much less so on how far Moscow's sphere of influence was to extend. He insisted on having "friendly" countries around the periphery of the USSR, but he failed to specify how many would have to meet this standard. He called during the war for dismembering Germany, but by the end of it was denying that he had ever done so: that country would be temporarily divided, he told leading German communists in June 1945, and they themselves would eventually bring about its reunification. He never gave up on the idea of an eventual world revolution, but he expected this to result—as his comments to the Germans suggested—from an expansion of influence emanating from the Soviet Union itself. "[F]or the Kremlin," a well-placed spymaster recalled, "the mission of communism was primarily to consolidate the might of the Soviet state. Only military strength and domination of the countries on our borders could ensure us a superpower role."

But Stalin provided no indication—surely because he himself did not know— of how rapidly, or under what circumstances, this process would take place. He was certainly prepared to stop in the face of resistance from the West: at no point was he willing to challenge the Americans or even the British where they made their interests clear....

What all of this suggests, though, is not that Stalin had limited ambitions, only that he had no timetable for achieving them. [Foreign minister Vyacheslav] Molotov retrospectively confirmed this: "Our ideology stands for offensive operations when possible, and if not, we wait." Given this combination of appetite with aversion to risk, one cannot help but wonder what would have happened had the West tried containment earlier. To the extent that it bears partial responsibility for the coming of the Cold War, the historian Vojtech Mastny has argued, that responsibility lies in its failure to do just that....

... The fact that Stalin was able to *expand* his empire when others were contracting and while the Soviet Union was as weak as it was required explanation. Why did opposition to this process, within and outside Europe, take so long to develop?

One reason was that the colossal sacrifices the Soviet Union had made during the war against the Axis had, in effect, "purified" its reputation: the USSR and its leader had "earned" the right to throw their weight around, or so it seemed. Western governments found it difficult to switch quickly from viewing the Soviet Union as a glorious wartime ally to portraying it as a new and dangerous adversary. President Harry S. Truman and his future Secretary of State Dean Acheson—neither of them sympathetic in the slightest to communism—nonetheless tended to give the Soviet Union the benefit of the doubt well into the early postwar era....

Resistance to Stalin's imperialism also developed slowly because Marxism-Leninism at the time had such widespread appeal. It is difficult now to recapture the admiration revolutionaries outside the Soviet Union felt for that country before they came to know it well. "[Communism] was the most rational and most intoxicating, all-embracing ideology for me and for those in my disunited and desperate land who so desired to skip over centuries of slavery and backwardness and to bypass reality itself," [Milovan] Djilas recalled, in a comment that could have been echoed throughout much of what came to be called the "third world." Because the Bolsheviks themselves had overcome one empire and had made a career of condemning others, it would take decades for people who were struggling to overthrow British, French, Dutch, or Portuguese colonialism to see that there could also be such a thing as Soviet imperialism. European communists—notably the Yugoslavs—saw this much earlier, but even to most of them it had not been apparent at the end of the war....

One has the impression that Stalin and the Eastern Europeans got to know one another only gradually. The Kremlin leader was slow to recognize that Soviet authority would not be welcomed everywhere beyond Soviet borders; but as he did come to see this he became all the more determined to impose it everywhere. The Eastern Europeans were slow to recognize how confining incorporation within a Soviet sphere was going to be; but as they did come to see this they became all the more determined to resist it, even if only by withholding, in a passive but sullen manner, the consent any regime needs to establish itself by means other than coercion. Stalin's efforts to consolidate his empire therefore made it at once more repressive and less secure. Meanwhile, an alternative vision of postwar Europe was emerging from the other great empire that established itself in the wake of World War II, that of the United States, and this too gave Stalin grounds for concern.

The first point worth noting, when comparing the American empire to its Soviet counterpart, is a striking reversal in the sequence of events. Stalin's determination to create his empire preceded by some years the conditions that made it possible: he had first to consolidate power at home and then defeat Nazi Germany, while at the same time seeing to it that his allies in that enterprise did not thwart his long-term objectives. With the United States, it was the other way around: the conditions for establishing an empire were in place long before there was any clear intention on the part of its leaders to do so. Even then, they required the support of a skeptical electorate, something that could never quite be taken for granted.

The United States had been poised for global hegemony at the end of World War I. Its military forces played a decisive role in bringing that conflict to an end. Its economic predominance was such that it could control both the manner and the rate of European recovery. Its ideology commanded enormous respect, as Woodrow Wilson found when he arrived on the Continent late in 1918 to a series of rapturous public receptions. The Versailles Treaty fell well short of Wilson's principles, to be sure, but the League of Nations followed closely his own design, providing an explicit legal basis for an international order that was to have drawn, as much as anything else, upon the example of the American constitution itself. If there was ever a point at which the world seemed receptive to an expansion of United States influence, this was it.

Americans themselves, however, were not receptive. The Senate's rejection of membership in the League reflected the public's distinct lack of enthusiasm for international peace-keeping responsibilities. Despite the interests certain business, labor, and agricultural groups had in seeking overseas markets and investment opportunities, most Americans saw few benefits to be derived from integrating their economy with that of the rest of the world....

This isolationist consensus broke down only as Americans began to realize that a potentially hostile power was once again threatening Europe: even their own hemisphere, it appeared, might not escape the consequences this time around. After September 1939, the Roosevelt administration moved as quickly as public Congressional opinion would allow to aid Great Britain and France by means short of war; it also chose to challenge the Japanese over their occupation of China and later French Indochina, thereby setting in motion a sequence of events that would lead to the attack on Pearl Harbor....

It did not automatically follow, though, that the Soviet Union would inherit the title of "first enemy" once Germany and Japan had been defeated. A sense of vulnerability preceded the identification of a source of threat in the thinking of American strategists: innovations in military technology—long-range bombers, the prospect of even longer-range missiles—created visions of future Pearl Harbors before it had become clear from where such an attack might come. Neither in the military nor the political-economic planning that went on in Washington during the war was there consistent concern with the USSR as a potential future adversary. The threat, rather, appeared to arise from war itself, whoever might cause it, and the most likely candidates were thought to be resurgent enemies from World War II.

The preferred solution was to maintain preponderant power for the United States, which meant a substantial peacetime military establishment and a string of bases around the world from which to resist aggression if it should ever occur. But equally important, a revived international community would seek to remove the fundamental causes of war through the United Nations, a less ambitious version of Wilson's League, and through new economic institutions like the International Monetary Fund and the World Bank, whose task it would be to prevent another global depression and thereby ensure prosperity. The Americans and the British assumed that the Soviet Union would want to participate in these multilateral efforts to achieve military and economic security. The Cold War developed when it became clear that Stalin either could not or would not accept this framework.

Did the Americans attempt to impose their vision of the postwar world upon the USSR? No doubt it looked that way from Moscow: both the Roosevelt and Truman administrations stressed political self-determination and economic integration with sufficient persistence to arouse Stalin's suspicions—easily aroused, in any event—as to their ultimate intentions. But what the Soviet leader saw as a challenge to his hegemony the Americans meant as an effort to salvage multilateralism. At no point prior to 1947 did the United States and its Western European allies abandon the hope that the Russians might eventually come around; and indeed negotiations aimed at bringing them around would continue at the foreign minister's level, without much hope of success, through the end of that year. The American attitude was less that of expecting to impose a system than one of puzzlement as to why its merits were not universally self-evident. It differed significantly, therefore, from Stalin's point of view, which allowed for the possibility that socialists in other countries might come to see the advantages of Marxism-Leninism as practiced in the Soviet Union, but never capitalists. They were there, in the end, to be overthrown, not convinced....

At the same time, though, it is difficult to see how a strategy of containment could have developed—with the Marshall Plan as its centerpiece—had there been nothing to contain.... The American empire arose *primarily,* therefore, not from internal causes, as had the Soviet empire, but from a perceived external danger powerful enough to overcome American isolationism.

Washington's wartime vision of a postwar international order had been premised on the concepts of political self-determination and economic integration. It was intended to work by assuming a set of *common* interests that would cause other countries to *want* to be affiliated with it rather than to resist it. The Marshall Plan, to a considerable extent, met those criteria....

The test of any empire comes in administering it, for even the most repressive tyranny requires a certain amount of acquiescence among its subjects. Coercion and terror cannot everywhere and indefinitely prop up authority: sooner or later the social, economic, and psychological costs of such measures begin to outweigh the benefits....

It is apparent now, even if it was not always at the time, that the Soviet Union did not manage its empire particularly well. Because of his personality and the structure of government he built around it, Stalin was—shall we say—less than receptive to the wishes of those nations that fell within the Soviet sphere. He viewed departures from his instructions with deep suspicion, but he also objected to manifestations of independent behavior where instructions had not yet been given. As a result, he put his European followers in an impossible position: they could satisfy him only by seeking his approval for whatever he had decided they should do—even, at times, before he had decided that they should do it.

An example occurred late in 1944 when the Yugoslavs—then the most powerful but also the most loyal of Stalin's East European allies—complained politely to Soviet commanders that their troops had been raping local women in the northern corner of the country through which they were passing. Stalin himself took note of this matter, accusing the Yugoslavs—at one point tearfully— of showing insufficient respect for Soviet military sacrifices and for failing to sympathize when "a soldier who has crossed thousands of kilometers through blood and fire and death has fun with a woman or takes some trifle." The issue was not an insignificant one: the Red Army's behavior was a problem throughout the territories it occupied, and did much to alienate those who lived there....

The United States, in contrast, proved surprisingly adept at managing an empire. Having attained their authority through democratic processes, its leaders were experienced—as their counterparts in Moscow were not—in the arts of persuasion, negotiation and compromise. Applying domestic political insights to foreign policy could produce embarrassing results, as when President Truman likened Stalin to his old Kansas City political mentor, Tom Pendergast, or when Secretary of State James F. Byrnes compared the Russians to the US Senate: "You build a post office in their state, and they'll build a post office in our state." But the habits of democracy had served the nation well during World War II: its strategists had assumed that their ideas would have to reflect the interests and capabilities of allies; it was also possible for allies to advance proposals of their own and have them taken seriously. That same pattern of mutual accommodation persisted after the war, despite the fact that all sides acknowledged—as they had during most of the war itself—the disproportionate power of the United States could ultimately bring to bear.

Americans so often deferred to the wishes of allies during the early Cold War that some historians have seen the Europeans—especially the British—as having managed *them*. The new Labour government in London did encourage the Truman administration to toughen its policy toward the Soviet Union; Churchill—by then out of office—was only reinforcing these efforts with his March 1946 "Iron Curtain" speech. The British were ahead of the Americans in pressing for a consolidation of Western occupation zones in Germany, even if this jeopardized prospects for an overall settlement with the Russians. Foreign Secretary Ernest Bevin determined the timing of the February 1947 crisis over Greece and Turkey when he ended British military and economic assistance to those countries....

But one can easily make too much of this argument. Truman and his advisers were not babes in the woods. They knew what they were doing at each stage, and did it only because they were convinced their actions would advance American interests. They never left initiatives entirely up to the Europeans: they insisted on an integrated plan for economic recovery and quite forcefully reined in prospective recipients when it appeared that their requests would exceed what Congress would approve. "[I]n the end we would not *ask* them," Kennan noted, "we would just *tell* them, what they would get." The Americans were flexible enough, though, to accept and build upon ideas that came from allies; they also frequently let allies determine the timing of actions taken....

The Americans simply did not find it necessary, in building a sphere of influence, to impose unrepresentative governments or brutal treatment upon the peoples that fell within it.... It was as if the Americans were projecting abroad a tradition they had long taken for granted at home: that civility made sense; that spontaneity, within a framework of minimal constraint, was the path to political and economic robustness; that to intimidate or to overmanage was to stifle. The contrast to Stalin's methods of imperial administration could hardly have been sharper.

Stalin saw the need, after learning of the Marshall Plan, to improve his methods of imperial management. He therefore called a meeting of the Soviet and East European communist parties, as well as the French and the Italian communists, to be held in Poland in September 1947, ostensibly for the purpose of exchanging ideas on fraternal cooperation. Only after the delegations had assembled did he reveal his real objective, which was to organize a new coordinating agency for the international communist movement....

Even with the Cominform in place, the momentary independence Czechoslovakia demonstrated must have continued to weigh on Stalin's mind. That country, more than any other in Eastern Europe, had sought to accommodate itself to Soviet hegemony. Embittered by how easily the British and French had betrayed Czech interests at the Munich conference in 1938, President Eduard Beneš welcomed the expansion of Soviet influence while reassuring Marxist-Leninists that they had nothing to fear from the democratic system the Czechs hoped to rebuild after the war. "If you play it well," he told Czech Communist Party leaders in 1943, "you'll win."

But Beneš meant "win" by democratic means. Although the Communists had indeed done well in the May 1946 parliamentary elections, their popularity began to drop sharply after Stalin forbade Czech participation in the Marshall Plan the following year. Convinced by intelligence reports that the West would not intervene, they therefore took advantage of a February 1948 government crisis to stage a *coup d'état*—presumably with Stalin's approval—that left them in complete control, with no further need to resort to the unpredictabilities of the ballot box....

Because of its dramatic impact, the Czech coup had consequences Stalin could hardly have anticipated. It set off a momentary—and partially manufactured—war scare in Washington. It removed the last Congressional objections to the Marshall Plan, resulting in the final approval of that initiative in April 1948. It accelerated plans by the Americans, the British, and the French to consolidate their occupation zones in Germany and to proceed toward the formation of an independent West German state. And it caused American officials to begin to consider, much more seriously than they had until this point, two ideas Bevin had begun to advance several months earlier: that economic assistance alone would not restore European self-confidence, and that the United States would have to take on direct military responsibilities for defending that portion of the Continent that remained outside Soviet control.

Stalin then chose the late spring of 1948 to attempt a yet further consolidation of the Soviet empire, with even more disastrous results....

West Europeans were meanwhile convincing themselves that they had little to lose from living within an American sphere of influence. The idea of a European "third force" soon disappeared, not because Washington officials lost interest in it, but because the Europeans themselves rejected it. The North Atlantic Treaty Organization, which came into existence in April 1949, had been a European initiative from the beginning: it was as explicit an invitation as has ever been extended from smaller powers to a great power to construct an empire and include them within it. When Kennan, worried that NATO would divide Europe permanently, put forward a plan later that spring looking toward an eventual reunification and neutralization of Germany as a way of ending both the Soviet and American presence on the continent, British and French opposition quickly shot it down....

... Why were allies of the United States willing to give up so much autonomy in order to enhance their own safety? How did the ideas of sovereignty and security, which historically have been difficult to separate, come to be so widely seen as divisible in this situation?

The answer would appear to be that despite a postwar polarization of authority quite at odds, in its stark bilateralism, from what wartime planners had expected, Americans managed to retain the multilateral conception of security they had developed during World War II. They were able to do this because Truman's foreign policy—like Roosevelt's military strategy—reflected the habits of domestic democratic politics. Negotiation, compromise, and consensus building abroad came naturally to statesmen steeped in the uses of such practices at home: in this sense, the American political tradition served the country better than its realist critics—Kennan definitely among them—believed it did....

It would become fashionable to argue, in the wake of American military intervention in Vietnam, the Soviet invasions of Czechoslovakia and Afghanistan, and growing fears of nuclear confrontation that developed during the early 1980s, that there were no significant differences in the spheres of influence Washington and Moscow had constructed in Europe after World War II: these had been, it was claimed, "morally equivalent," denying autonomy quite impartially to all who lived under them. Students of history must make their own judgments about morality, but even a cursory examination of the historical record will show that these imperial structures could hardly have been more different in their origins, their composition, their tolerance of diversity, and as it turned out their durability. It is important to specify just what these differences were....

One empire arose ... by invitation, the other by imposition. *Europeans* made this distinction, very much as they had done during the war when they welcomed armies liberating them from the west but feared those that came from the east. They did so because they saw clearly at the time—even if a subsequent generation would not always see—how different American and Soviet empires were likely to be. It is true that the *extent* of the American empire quickly exceeded that of its Soviet counterpart, but this was because *resistance* to expanding American influence was never as great. The American empire may well have become larger, paradoxically, because the American *appetite* for empire was less that of the USSR. The United States had shown, throughout most of its history, that it could survive and even prosper without extending its domination as far as the eye could see. The logic of Lenin's ideological internationalism, as modified by Stalin's Great Russian nationalism and personal paranoia, was that the Soviet Union could not.

FURTHER READING

Paul S. Boyer, *By the Bomb's Early Light: American Thought and Culture at the Dawn of the Atomic Age* (1985).

Richard M. Fried, *The Russians Are Coming! The Russians Are Coming! Pageantry and Patriotism in the Cold War* (1998).

John Earl Haynes and Harvey Klehr, *Venona: Decoding Soviet Espionage in the United States* (1999).

Margot Henriksen, *Dr. Strangelove's America: Society and Culture in the Atomic Age* (1997).

Michael J. Hogan, *A Cross of Iron: Harry S. Truman and the Origins of the National Security State* (1998).

Melvyn Leffler, *For the Soul of Mankind: The United States, the Soviet Union, and the Cold War* (2007).

Robbie Lieberman, *The Strangest Dream: Communism, Anticommunism, and the U.S. Peace Movement, 1945–1963* (2000).

Vojtech Mastny, *The Cold War and Soviet Insecurity* (1996).

Laura McEnany, *Civil Defense Begins at Home: Militarization Meets Everyday Life in the Fifties* (2000).

Thomas G. Paterson, *On Every Front: The Making and Unmaking of the Cold War* (1992).

Stanley Sandler, *The Korean War: No Victors, No Vanquished* (1999).

Ellen Schrecker, *Many Are the Crimes: McCarthyism in America* (1998).

Vladislav Zubok and Constantine Pleshakov, *Inside the Kremlin's Cold War* (1996).

CHAPTER 11

The Postwar "Boom":
Affluence and Anxiety

After World War II, everything about America seemed to get bigger: families, towns, highways, shopping centers, corporations, and government. Americans' wealth grew along with the domestic economy, and American power expanded with the Cold War. After the trials of the Great Depression and the war, Americans appeared to revel in stability and normalcy. The G.I. Bill, passed by Congress in 1944, paid millions of former soldiers to go to college, lent them money to buy homes, and helped finance their new careers. Although some people thought President Eisenhower bland, many more embraced the cheerful Republican slogan "I Like Ike." Patriotism soared, along with belief in the superiority of the so-called American Way. With political and economic confidence high, well-off consumers fueled a spectacular economic expansion. Middle-class families could afford to, and did, purchase most of the conveniences offered by mass production—including mass-produced homes in sprawling new suburbs. They had more babies than their parents' generation to fill these homes, and affluence enabled women to stay home in droves to take care of this special "baby boom" generation. Parents sought to give their children all the things they had not had growing up in the Depression and during the war.

Affluence sparked anxiety, however. Some critics asserted that the United States was becoming too complacent, and its citizens too coddled. Parents especially worried about the effect of abundance on their children's character development. Novelists and social commentators harped on the emergence of a new phenomenon that some called "juvenile delinquency." Blockbuster films such as Rebel Without a Cause, West Side Story, Splendor in the Grass, *and* Blackboard Jungle *told of a generation run wild: sophisticated, perhaps, but lost. Adult roles also occasioned commentary. The fifties witnessed an ongoing preoccupation with the lack of creative or "manly" jobs for men in mass society, and with women's place in the family. Some social critics asserted that, as Sigmund Freud put it, "anatomy is destiny." They believed that women who sought fulfillment in anything other than procreation or housekeeping were "abnormal" and neurotic—especially feminists. The prominent psychologist Marynia Farnham called modern women "the lost sex."*

Television contributed to the social ferment. At the start of the decade, only a small fraction of the population (roughly three million Americans) owned the new technology. By 1960, 50 million households had TV sets. More Americans had TVs than had running water and indoor toilets. Television helped to create a more uniform culture than had ever before existed in the United States. Coal miners in rural Appalachia could hear the bubbling Cuban accent of Desi Arnaz on I Love Lucy. *Schoolchildren in southern California could identify the nasal twang of the Boston Irish in the 1960 TV appearances of John Kennedy. Overtaking all of these regional speech patterns was the uniform, "accentless" cadence of a new generation of television performers and news announcers, whose dialect and appearance set the norm for "middle America." The new television shows also brought regions, classes, and ethnic groups together by giving them a common subject: 50 million households could laugh at the same jokes and pratfalls. Because the content of many shows focused on optimistic, happy portrayals of suburban life, these shows also helped to set a standard—rarely attainable—of the ideal postwar family. And, by establishing an ideal, television offered viewers a chance to compare their own lives with those of others, creating an anxiety about why they might not match the model.*

Although "traditional" by reputation, the fifties were a time of great flux. Pervasive television imagery, booming suburbs, and growing incomes dramatically changed how Americans lived and what they thought about it.

QUESTIONS TO THINK ABOUT

Were the fifties really *Happy Days*, as a television show once characterized the era, or is the period more accurately described as an era of psychological, social, and political tensions? Why do the fifties prompt (as they have) such nostalgia for poodle skirts, sock hops, hula hoops, stay-at-home moms, and Fourth of July parades?

DOCUMENTS

The documents in this chapter reveal many aspects of the postwar boom in population and prosperity. Document 1 is from Ron Kovic's memoir, *Born on the Fourth of July*. The author later lost the use of his legs (and his trust of government) in Vietnam, but his fifties childhood helps to explain the boundless admiration he and many other young people felt for America growing up. Document 2 shows that expectations for females were quite different from those for males. In this selection, Governor Adlai Stevenson addresses a graduating class at Smith, an elite Massachusetts women's college. He suggests that there is nothing more fulfilling for a woman than reminding her husband of the values of Western civilization as he goes to a specialized job each day—one that, in effect, diminishes his individuality and understanding of life's broader purpose. Document 3 is an article from *Good Housekeeping* that is typical of women's magazines during this era. The author disparages wives who are "nags," and encourages readers to stay at home and support their husbands' careers. As we see in document 4 from *Life* magazine, business grew along with the baby boom—though some people complained that "teenagers are spoiled to death these days" and fretted about the long-range consequences. Whereas social critics complained that America had become a "nation of sheep," in the words of one writer, others worried about a rise in delinquency. Document 5 is a newspaper survey that asks readers to evaluate their own tendencies towards conformism or rebellion. Document 6 is an example of the social science literature that proliferated in this era, and that depicted American culture as increasingly shallow and materialistic. Even religion, this author argues, had become a kind of status symbol. In document 7, sociologist David Riesman argues that suburban Americans had lost their frontier hardiness and self-sufficiency, and were becoming increasingly "other-directed." Document 8 contradicts the assumption that all Americans had climbed into the middle class. Instead, socialist reformer Michael Harrington argues, there is an "Other America" that is poorer and more isolated than ever. Lastly, document 9 reveals the first inklings of a rebellion against the gender roles of the 1950s. Here, feminist author Betty Friedan reports that millions of women wonder, "Is this all?"

1. A Young American Is "Born on the Fourth of July," 1946

For me it began in 1946 when I was born on the Fourth of July. The whole sky lit up in a tremendous fireworks display and my mother told me the doctor said I was a real firecracker. Every birthday after that was something the whole country celebrated. It was proud day to be born on....

The whole block grew up watching television. There was Howdy Doody and Rootie Kazootie, Cisco Kid and Gabby Hayes, Roy Rogers and Dale Evans. The Lone Ranger was on Channel 7. We watched cartoons for hours on Saturdays—Beanie and Cecil, Crusader Rabbit, Woody Woodpecker—and a show with puppets called Kukla, Fran, and Ollie. I sat on the rug in the living room watching Captain Video take off in his spaceship and saw thousands of savages killed by Ramar of the Jungle.

I remember Elvis Presley on the Ed Sullivan Show and my sister Sue going crazy in the living room jumping up and down. He kept twanging this big guitar and wiggling his hips, but for some reason they were mostly showing just the top of him. My mother was sitting on the couch with her hands folded in her lap like she was praying, and my dad was in the other room talking about how the Church had advised us all that Sunday that watching Elvis Presley could lead to sin.

I loved God more than anything else in the world back then and I prayed to Him and the Virgin Mary and Jesus and all the saints to be a good boy and a good American. Every night before I went to sleep I knelt down in front of my bed, making the sign of the cross and cupping my hands over my face,

Excerpt from R. Kovic, *Born on the Fourth of July*. © 1976, 2005 by Ron Kovic. Used by permission of Akashic Books.

sometimes praying so hard I would cry. I asked every night to be good enough to make the major leagues someday. With God anything was possible. I made my first Holy Communion with a cowboy hat on my head and two six-shooters in my hands....

Every Saturday afternoon we'd all go down to the movies in the shopping center and watch gigantic prehistoric birds breathe fire, and war movies with John Wayne and Audie Murphy. Bobbie's mother always packed us a bagful of candy. I'll never forget Audie Murphy in *To Hell and Back*. At the end he jumps on top of a flaming tank that's just about to explode and grabs the machine gun blasting it into the German lines. He was so brave I had chills running up and down my back, wishing it were me up there. There were gasoline flames roaring around his legs, but he just kept firing that machine gun. It was the greatest movie I ever saw in my life....

We'd go home and make up movies like the ones we'd just seen or the ones that were on TV night after night. We'd use our Christmas toys—the Matty Mattel machine guns and grenades, the little green plastic soldiers with guns and flamethrowers in their hands. My favorites were the green plastic men with bazookas. They blasted holes through the enemy. They wiped them out at thirty feet just above the coffee table. They dug in on the front lawn and survived countless artillery attacks....

The Communists were all over the place back then. And if they weren't trying to beat us into outer space, Castiglia and I were certain they were infiltrating our schools, trying to take over our classes and control our minds. We were both certain that one of our teachers was a secret Communist agent and in our next secret club meeting we promised to report anything new he said during our next history class. We watched him very carefully that year. One afternoon he told us that China was going to have a billion people someday. "One billion!" he said, tightly clenching his fist. "Do you know what that means?" he said, staring out the classroom window. "Do you know what that's going to mean?" he said in almost a whisper. He never finished what he was saying and after that Castiglia and I were convinced he was definitely a Communist.

About that time I started doing push-ups in my room and squeezing rubber balls until my arms began to ache, trying to make my body stronger and stronger....

I wanted to be a hero.

2. Governor Adlai Stevenson Tells College Women About Their Place in Life, 1955

I think there is much you can do about our crisis in the humble role of housewife.

The peoples of the West are still struggling with the problems of a free society and just now are in dire trouble. For to create a free society is at all times a

Adlai Stevenson, "A Purpose for Modern Woman," excerpted from Commencement Address, Smith College, 1955, in *Women's Home Companion* (September 1955).

precarious and audacious experiment. Its bedrock is the concept of man as an end in himself. But violent pressures are constantly battering away at this concept, reducing man once again to subordinate status, limiting his range of choice, abrogating his responsibility and returning him to his primitive status of anonymity in the social group. I think you can be more helpful in identifying, isolating and combatting these pressures, this virus, than you perhaps realize.

Let me put it this way: individualism has promoted technological advance, technology promoted increased specialization, and specialization promoted an ever closer economic interdependence between specialties....

Thus this typical Western man, or typical Western husband, operates well in the realm of means, as the Romans did before him. But outside his specialty, in the realm of ends, he is apt to operate poorly or not at all. And this neglect of the cultivation of more mature values can only mean that his life, and the life of the society he determines, will lack valid purpose, however busy and even profitable it may be.

And here's where you come in: to restore valid, meaningful purpose to life in your home; to beware of instinctive group reaction to the forces which play upon you and yours, to watch for and arrest the constant gravitational pulls to which we are all exposed—your workaday husband especially—in our specialized, fragmented society, that tend to widen the breach between reason and emotion, between means and ends....

Women, especially educated women, have a unique opportunity to influence us, man and boy, and to play a direct part in the unfolding drama of our free society. But I am told that nowadays the young wife or mother is short of time for such subtle arts, that things are not what they used to be; that once immersed in the very pressing and particular problems of domesticity, many women feel frustrated and far apart from the great issues and stirring debates for which their education has given them understanding and relish. Once they read Baudelaire. Now it is the Consumer's Guide. Once they wrote poetry. Now it's the laundry list. Once they discussed art and philosophy until late in the night. Now they are so tired they fall asleep as soon as the dishes are finished. There is, often, a sense of contraction, of closing horizons and lost opportunities. They had hoped to play their part in the crisis of the age....

The point is that whether we talk of Africa, Islam or Asia, women "never had it so good" as you do. And in spite of the difficulties of domesticity, you have a way to participate actively in the crisis in addition to keeping yourself and those about you straight on the difference between means and ends, mind and spirit, reason and emotion—not to mention keeping your man straight on the differences between Botticelli and Chianti.

3. *Good Housekeeping*: Every Executive Needs a Perfect Wife, 1956

Tomorrow your husband gets his big break. He's going to be interviewed for a key position that will be the turning point in his career—if he gets the job.

R.E. Dumas Milner, "Before I Hire Your Husband, I Want to Meet You!" *Good Housekeeping*, January 1956, p. 52.

To be sure, the decision will be based primarily on your husband's personality and qualifications. But more and more these days the decision also hinges on what the boss-to-be thinks of you, the man's wife.

We employers realize how often the wrong wife can break the right man. This doesn't mean that the wife is necessarily wrong for the man but that she is wrong for the job. On the other hand, more often than is realized the wife is the chief factor in the husband's success in his career. In the first place, she has a very definite effect on a man's spirit....

If a man has a peevish, nagging wife, if she is jealous and possessive, if she is lazy or overambitious or extravagant, that man is going to be unhappy. And his unhappiness will interfere with his concentration on his job. In the case of an important executive, this lack of concentration can affect the outcome of a business conference. It may even kill a profitable deal....

What do we look for in a wife? Here are six qualities that impress us most. And how a wife rates on these goes a long way in determining whether her husband gets that job or that next promotion.

1. **A good wife is friendly**. She smiles easily and she is pleasant to be with. She has many friends, whom she entertains within her means, but she is careful to prevent social activities from interfering with her husband's rest, health, and efficiency....

4. **A good wife is part of her community**. She is interested in town planning, local government, school conditions, church activities. In her community, she is a good-will ambassador for her husband....

6. **A good wife's primary interest is her husband, her home, and her children**. There may be many successful and happily married women doctors, lawyers, artists, musicians, writers, and the like, but I believe that being the wife of an executive is a full-time job in itself. A good wife is there when her husband needs her. She must be his sounding board. She must be able to listen patiently without giving advice, she must have the knack of commenting without interfering. Sometimes it may be necessary for her to make sacrifices for the sake of her husband and his business career; she cannot be free to do this if she is dedicated to a career of her own.

Of course it isn't possible to discover whether or not a woman has all these plus qualities in just one meeting. If we must make an immediate decision, we do the best we can. Our safeguard is that even more important than what a good wife *is*, is what she *is not*. And here it is surprisingly easy to form a judgment on short notice. Real troublemakers are fairly easy to spot. Here are the main types:

1. **The complaining woman**. The weather's bad, the child was cranky tonight, the waiter is sloppy, the food is cold: I know immediately that she is a nag. Sometimes she doesn't actually complain much, but she doesn't smile much either, and her sour expression gives her away. A nagging wife is a millstone around the neck of any man. She's a nuisance at home, and she consumes time on the telephone every day,

nagging her husband while he is at work. The complaining woman can toss a cloud over the brightest of days—and the brightest of men.

2. **The dominating woman**. She knows it all—from what a man should eat to how he should run his business. Her unwanted advice is offered free of charge for everything and anything. She shows up at her husband's office regularly, ready to revise staff and procedure. She can ruin her husband's career in just one evening. When I hire a man, I want to know that *he* will do his job, not his wife. It's *his* judgment I rely on, not others. The dominating woman is easiest to spot and hardest to control. She's anathema to me.…

3. **The wife-in-a-rut**. This pathetic little creature is just out of her element. She is self-conscious, nervous, and awkward. Her taste in clothes is usually pretty bad; her conversation centers on babies and how to wash the kitchen floor. Ten or 15 years ago she may have been the pretty little girl on Maple Street. Her husband has become a man of the world, but she is still on Maple Street.…

It hurts to discover that a good man has married the wrong woman, but he still deserves a chance. I might be more cautious about the position I give him, watch him more closely, advance him more slowly, give him more help than he needs, but if he can keep his wife successfully under control, he can keep his job.…

4. *Life* Magazine Identifies the New Teenage Market, 1959

To some people the vision of a leggy adolescent happily squealing over the latest fancy present from Daddy is just another example of the way teen-agers are spoiled to death these days. But to a growing number of businessmen the picture spells out the profitable fact that the American teen-agers have emerged as a big-time consumer in the U.S. economy. They are multiplying in numbers. They spend more and have more spent on them. And they have minds of their own about what they want.

The time is past when a boy's chief possession was his bike and a girl's party wardrobe consisted of a fancy dress worn with a string of dime-store pearls. What Depression-bred parents may still think of as luxuries are looked on as necessities by their offspring. Today teen-agers surround themselves with a fantastic array of garish and often expensive baubles and amusements. They own 10 million phonographs, over a million TV sets, 13 million cameras. Nobody knows how much parents spend on them for actual necessities nor to what extent teen-agers act as hidden persuaders on their parents' other buying habits. Counting only what is spent to satisfy their special teen-age demands, the youngsters and their parents will shell out about $10 billion this year, a billion more than the total sales of GM.…

At 17 Suzie Slattery of Van Nuys, Calif., fits any businessman's dream of the ideal teen-age consumer. The daughter of a reasonably well-to-do TV announcer, Suzie costs her parents close to $4,000 a year, far more than average for the country but not much more than many of the upper middle income families of her town. In an expanding economy more and more teen-agers will be moving up into Suzie's bracket or be influenced as consumers by her example.

Last year $1,500 was spent on Suzie's clothes and $550 for her entertainment. Her annual food bill comes to $900. She pays $4 every two weeks at the beauty parlor. She has her own telephone and even has her own soda fountain in the house. On summer vacation days she loves to wander with her mother through fashionable department stores, picking out frocks or furnishings for her room or silver and expensive crockery for the hope chest she has already started.

As a high school graduation present, Suzie was given a holiday cruise to Hawaii and is now in the midst of a new clothes–buying spree for college. Her parents' constant indulgence has not spoiled Suzie. She takes for granted all the luxuries that surround her because she has had them all her life. But she also has a good mind and some serious interests. A top student in her school, she is entering Occidental College this fall and will major in political science....

5. Newspaper Survey: Are You a Conformist or a Rebel?, 1959

"CONFORMITY" has become a bad word lately. Many people are concerned that they're "running with the crowd" too much and losing their individuality. Actually, every well-adjusted person should conform to our accepted customs. There's no point in being a rebel unless you have a cause.

The intelligent conformist observes the rules of society yet maintains his individuality. The "bad" type of conformist may conform too much.

Which kind of conformist are you? Here is a quiz that will show you. It was drawn up after interviews with a number of leading sociologists and psychiatrists. Just answer "yes" or "no" to each of the following. Before you start, though, here's a hint: the questions sound harmless but they may be booby trapped!

1. Every matchbook cover tells you to "close cover before striking." Do you?
   YES ☐   NO ☐
2. Do you use the best-seller lists as sole guide when you choose a book to read?   YES ☐   NO ☐
3. A sign in the lobby of a museum says "No Smoking," but the place is deserted and you're aching for a cigarette. Do you obey the sign?
   YES ☐   NO ☐

Lester David, "Are You a Conformist or a Rebel?" *Los Angeles Times*, Oct. 11, 1959. Reprinted by permission.

4. Everyone is talking about a new popular TV program. You watched it once but honestly don't think much of it. Do you keep watching it anyway?

    YES ☐   NO ☐

5. Do you write a "bread and butter" or thank-you note to your hostess after spending a weekend at her home?   YES ☐   NO ☐

6. A young man asks your help with a problem. He has a chance to strike out for himself in a field where he must risk failure but also has an opportunity for big success. Or, he can accept a steady job with a limited future. Would you advise him to play it safe and take the steady job?

    YES ☐   NO ☐

7. Do you avoid conspicuous extremes in dress?   YES ☐   NO ☐

8. Would you permit an 11-year-old girl to wear lipstick if she pleads that "all the kids in my set are doing it"?   YES ☐   NO ☐

9. When walking on the street, do you usually keep to the right?

    YES ☐   NO ☐

10. You have always wanted to live in a bright red house. Finally, you move to the suburbs but find that all the homes on your block are painted in subdued shades and yours—if painted red—will stand our sharply. Would you give up the idea and use a quieter color?   YES ☐   NO ☐

Everyone is either a *wise* conformist or an *unwise* one. Dr. Else B. Kris, professor of social psychiatry at Adelphi College, explains the difference between the two kinds:

"In many instances," she asserts, "doing what other people do can make your own life happier, more interesting and certainly safer."

"On the other hand, conforming is unwise when it means slavishly doing or thinking what everyone else does or thinks *even though you are rebelling inside*. In these cases, following your own judgment and convictions is the best choice despite the fact that it means bucking the main stream."

So, if you answered *Yes* to the odd-numbered questions, and *No* to the others, you are being an intelligent conformist....

Scoring

Count the *Yes* answers you gave to the *odd-numbered* questions. Here's what your rating means: 4 to 5—you're an intelligent conformist; 2 to 3—you have some maverick tendencies of an unwise kind; none to 2—you're a rebel without a cause!

6. Vance Packard Criticizes Religion as a Status Symbol, 1959

America, we keep reading, is undergoing a tremendous religious renaissance. Membership is growing by a million a year, and is now up to more than 104,000,000. Per member contributions are up. Nearly a billion dollars' worth of new structures are going up in the United States each year....

Vance Packard, *The Status Seekers* (Pocket Books/Simon & Schuster, 1959), p. 115–120. Reprinted by permission.

Going to church is a deeply felt, soul-searching experience for many millions of Americans. And religious faith still dominates and guides the lives of millions of people, some of whom may not be regular churchgoers. Many still kneel in fervent prayer at night. For the majority of American Christians, however, going to church is the nice thing that proper people do on Sundays. It advertises their respectability, gives them a warm feeling that they are behaving in a way their God-fearing ancestors would approve, and adds (they hope) a few cubits to their social stature by throwing them with a social group with which they wish to be identified. And even those who take their worshiping seriously often prefer to do it while surrounded by their own kind of people.

The status implications of attending a particular church are especially perceivable among the Protestant churchgoers....

The upper class in most United States communities is drawn more powerfully to the Episcopal church than to any other. The upper-class fascination with the Episcopalian church seems to stem, at least in part, from its close kinship ties with the Church of England.

Three other denominations strongly favored by the two top social classes of America are the Presbyterian, Congregationalist, and Unitarian. As you go north into New England, the Presbyterians tend to become Congregationalists. The Congregational churches can be found in mill towns. And in many New England villages they have congregations that represent the entire church-going population. But, in larger cities and growing suburbs, these churches tend to be especially appealing to people from the higher socioeconomic and educational levels. The Unitarian church, tiny in total number, outranks all denominations in the number of eminent Americans who have claimed it as their church....

Sociologist E. Franklin Frazier reports finding that some Negroes in professional occupations maintain two church memberships. They will maintain their colored Baptist or Methodist membership as they themselves move up the social ladder because most of their clients are still in those churches. This, Frazier points out, has financial advantages. At the same time, they may affiliate with Episcopal, Congregational, or Presbyterian churches, usually colored, "because of their social status."

As we drop down the social scale, we come to the denominations that have the largest (and usually the most enthusiastically active) followings. Methodism probably comes closer to being the choice of the average American than any other....

A shade below the Methodists, in the Federal Council analysis, are the Lutherans. The Lutheran church is particularly strong with farmers and skilled workers of Scandinavian or German backgrounds.

And somewhat below the Lutherans come the Baptists. In many communities, and especially in the South, the local Baptist church is the highest-prestige church in town; but, nationally, it is predominantly a workingman's church....

Jewry, too, has its denominations: Orthodox, Conservative, and Reform. And they are differentiated somewhat by social class. Lower-class Jews tend to remain in Orthodox synagogues. The upper-class Jews, especially those with higher educations, tend to move on to the Conservative and Reform denominations.

The Roman Catholic church, of course, does not have denominations, and so has escaped the trend to stratification by social classes that is becoming so conspicuous in the Protestant churches. Catholic parishes are organized on a geo-graphic basis, and each parish is expected to minister to all Catholics in its area....

To date, the proportion of Negro church members who are Catholic is small, about 1 in 25. At least one-third of them are affiliated with mixed parishes. The rest are in segregated churches. But even that record of integration is far higher than that of the Protestant churches. Until a few years ago, barely 1 per-cent of the Protestant congregations with white members had any Negro mem-bers. By a variety of techniques, about as gracious as that of the white waitress who spills soup in their laps, the white members have succeeded in making those Negroes who have ventured to approach white churches feel unwelcome. When a Negro persisted in coming to a church in one Kansas town, the minister took him aside and said that, of course, he was welcome but wouldn't he be happier in his "own" colored church of the same denomination on the other side of town, a mile's walk from his home?...

All of the foregoing indicates, I believe, that Christianity in mid-century America shows a sizable gulf between practice and preaching.

7. Sociologist David Riesman Describes "Other-Directed Men and Manipulative Children," 1961

The type of character I shall describe as other-directed seems to be emerging in very recent years in the upper middle class of our larger cities: more prominently in New York than in Boston, in Los Angeles than in Spokane, in Cincinnati than in Chillicothe. Yet in some respects this type is strikingly similar to the American, whom Tocqueville and other curious and astonished visitors from Europe, even before the Revolution, thought to be a new kind of man. Indeed, travelers' reports on America impress us with their unanimity. The American is said to be shallower, freer with his money, friendlier, more uncertain of himself and his values, more demanding of approval than the European....

Connected with such changes are changes in the family and in child-rearing practices. In the smaller families of urban life, and with the spread of "permis-sive" child care to ever wider strata of the population, there is a relaxation of older patterns of discipline. Under these newer patterns the peer-group (the group of one's associates of the same age and class) becomes much more impor-tant to the child, while the parents make him feel guilty not so much about violation of inner standards as about failure to be popular or otherwise to manage his relations with these other children. Moreover, the pressures of the school and the peer-group are reinforced and continued—in a manner whose inner para-doxes I shall discuss later—by the mass media: movies, radio, comics, and popular culture media generally. Under these conditions types of character emerge that we shall here term other-directed. To them much of the discussion in the ensu-ing chapters is devoted. *What is common to all the other-directed people is that their*

David Reisman, *The Lonely Crowd: A Study of the Changing American Character* (Yale UP, 1965), p. 19, 21, 50–52. Reprinted by permission of Yale University Press.

contemporaries are the source of direction for the individual—either those known to him or those with whom he is indirectly acquainted, through friends and through the mass media. This source is of course "internalized" in the sense that dependence on it for guidance in life is implanted early. The goals toward which the other-directed person strives shift with that guidance: it is only the process of striving itself and the process of paying close attention to the signals from others that remain unaltered throughout life. This mode of keeping in touch with others permits a close behavioral conformity, not through drill in behavior itself, as in the tradition-directed character, but rather through an exceptional sensitivity to the actions and wishes of others....

In this change of parental attitude the mass media of communication play a dual role. From the mass media—radio, movies, comics—as well as from their own peers, children can easily learn what the norm of parental behavior is, and hold it over their parents' heads....

Despite the diminution of their authority, the parents still try to control matters; but with the loss of self-assurance their techniques change. They can neither hold themselves up as a exemplars—when both they and the child know better—nor resort, in good conscience, to severe corporal punishment and deprivations. At most there are token spankings, with open physical warfare confined to the lower classes.

The parents' recourse, especially in the upper middle class, is to "personnel" methods—to manipulation in the form of reasoning, or, more accurately, of rationalizing. The child responds in the same manner. One might summarize the historical sequence by saying that the tradition-directed child propitiates his parents; the inner-directed child fights or succumbs to them; the other-directed child manipulates them and is in turn manipulated....

8. Michael Harrington Unveils "The Other America" Outside Suburbia, 1961

There is a familiar America. It is celebrated in speeches and advertised on television and in the magazines. It has the highest mass standard of living the world has ever known.

In the 1950's this America worried about itself, yet even its anxieties were products of abundance. The title of a brilliant book was widely misinterpreted, and the familiar America began to call itself "the affluent society." There was introspection about Madison Avenue and tail fins; there was discussion of the emotional suffering taking place in the suburbs. In all this, there was an implicit assumption that the basic grinding economic problems had been solved in the United States. In this theory the nation's problems were no longer a matter of basic human needs, of food, shelter, and clothing. Now they were seen as qualitative, a question of learning to live decently amid luxury.

While this discussion was carried on, there existed another America. In it dwelt somewhere between 40,000,000 and 50,000,000 citizens of this land. They were poor. They still are.

Michael Harrington, *The Other America: Poverty in the United States* (Scribner/Simon & Schuster, 1997), p. 1–7. Reprinted by permission.

To be sure, the other America is not impoverished in the same sense as those poor nations where millions cling to hunger as a defense against starvation. This country has escaped such extremes. That does not change the fact that tens of millions of Americans are, at this very moment, maimed in body and spirit, existing at levels beneath those necessary for human decency. If these people are not starving, they are hungry, and sometimes fat with hunger, for that is what cheap foods do. They are without adequate housing and education and medical care.

The Government has documented what this means to the bodies of the poor, and the figures will be cited throughout this book. But even more basic, this poverty twists and deforms the spirit. The American poor are pessimistic and defeated, and they are victimized by mental suffering to a degree unknown in Suburbia....

The millions who are poor in the United States tend to become increasingly invisible. Here is a great mass of people, yet it takes an effort of the intellect and will even to see them....

There are perennial reasons that make the other America an invisible land.

Poverty is often off the beaten track. It always has been. The ordinary tourist never left the main highway, and today he rides interstate turnpikes. He does not go into the valleys of Pennsylvania where the towns look like movie sets of Wales in the thirties. He does not see the company houses in rows, the rutted roads (the poor always have bad roads whether they live in the city, in towns, or on farms), and everything is black and dirty....

Now the American city has been transformed. The poor still inhabit the miserable housing in the central area, but they are increasingly isolated from contact with, or sight of, anybody else. Middle-class women coming in from Suburbia on a rare trip may catch the merest glimpse of the other America on the way to an evening at the theater, but their children are segregated in suburban schools. The business or professional man may drive along the fringes of slums in a car or bus, but it is not an important experience to him. The failures, the unskilled, the disabled, the aged, and the minorities are right there, across the tracks, where they have always been. But hardly anyone else is....

Clothes make the poor invisible too: America has the best-dressed poverty the world has ever known. For a variety of reasons, the benefits of mass production have been spread much more evenly in this area than in many others. It is much easier in the United States to be decently dressed than it is to be decently housed, fed, or doctored. Even people with terribly depressed incomes can look prosperous....

Then, many of the poor are the wrong age to be seen. A good number of them (over 8,000,000) are sixty-five years of age or better; an even larger number are under eighteen. The aged members of the other America are often sick, and they cannot move. Another group of them live out their lives in loneliness and frustration: they sit in rented rooms, or else they stay close to a house in a neighborhood that has completely changed from the old days.

And finally, the poor are politically invisible. It is one of the cruelest ironies of social life in advanced countries that the dispossessed at the bottom of society are unable to speak for themselves. The people of the other America do not, by far and large, belong to unions, to fraternal organizations, or to political parties. They are without lobbies of their own; they put forward no legislative program. As a group, they are atomized. They have no face; they have no voice....

9. Feminist Betty Friedan Describes the Problem That Has No Name, 1963

The problem lay buried, unspoken, for many years in the minds of American women. It was a strange stirring, a sense of dissatisfaction, a yearning that women suffered in the middle of the twentieth century in the United States. Each suburban wife struggled with it alone. As she made the beds, shopped for groceries, matched slipcover material, ate peanut butter sandwiches with her children, chauffeured Cub Scouts and Brownies, lay beside her husband at night—she was afraid to ask even of herself the silent question— "Is this all?"

For over fifteen years there was no word of this yearning in the millions of words written about women, for women, in all the columns, books and articles by experts telling women their role was to seek fulfillment as wives and mothers. Over and over women heard in voices of tradition and of Freudian sophistication that they could desire no greater destiny than to glory in their own femininity. Experts told them how to catch a man and keep him, how to breastfeed children and handle their toilet training, how to cope with sibling rivalry and adolescent rebellion; how to buy a dishwasher, bake bread, cook gourmet snails, and build a swimming pool with their own hands; how to dress, look, and act more feminine and make marriage more exciting; how to keep their husbands from dying young and their sons from growing into delinquents. They were taught to pity the neurotic, unfeminine, unhappy women who wanted to be poets or physicists or presidents. They learned that truly feminine women do not want careers, higher education, political rights—the independence and the opportunities that the old-fashioned feminists fought for. Some women, in their forties and fifties, still remembered painfully giving up those dreams, but most of the younger women no longer even thought about them. A thousand expert voices applauded their femininity, their adjustment, their new maturity. All they had to do was devote their lives from earliest girlhood to finding a husband and bearing children.

By the end of the nineteen-fifties, the average marriage age of women in America dropped to 20, and was still dropping, into the teens. Fourteen million girls were engaged by 17. The proportion of women attending college in comparison with men dropped from 47 per cent in 1920 to 35 per cent in 1958. A century earlier, women had fought for higher education; now girls went to college to get a husband. By the mid–fifties, 60 per cent dropped out of college to marry, or because they were afraid too much education would be a marriage bar. Colleges built dormitories for "married students," but the students were almost

Betty Friedan, *The Feminine Mystique* (New York: Norton, 1963), 15–17, 19–20. Copyright © 1983, 1974, 1973, 1963 by Betty Friedan. Used by permission of W. W. Norton & Company, Inc.

always husbands. A new degree was instituted for the wives—"Ph.T." (Putting Husband Through)....

If a woman had a problem in the 1950's and 1960's, she knew that something must be wrong with her marriage, or with herself. Other women were satisfied with their lives, she thought. What kind of a woman was she if she did not feel this mysterious fulfillment waxing the kitchen floor? She was so ashamed to admit her dissatisfaction that she never knew how many other women shared it. If she tried to tell her husband, he didn't understand what she was talking about. She did not really understand it herself. For over fifteen years women in America found it harder to talk about this problem than about sex. Even the psychoanalysts had no name for it....

But on an April morning in 1959, I heard a mother of four, having coffee with four other mothers in a suburban development fifteen miles from New York, say in a tone of quiet desperation, "the problem." And the others knew, without words, that she was not talking about a problem with her husband, or her children, or her home. Suddenly they realized they all shared the same problem, the problem that has no name. They began, hesitantly, to talk about it. Later, after they had picked up their children at nursery school and taken them home to nap, two of the women cried, in sheer relief, just to know they were not alone.

ESSAYS

Was America at its best in the fifties, or is that an illusion created by hindsight? In the first reading, John Patrick Diggins of the University of California, Irvine, charts social and economic change in the fifties. He characterizes the era as one of bountiful lifestyles, traditional values, and remarkable stability for families. Diggins further argues that the fifties were not an aberration, but represent "the steady norm of America's political temper." Stephanie Coontz, a professor at Evergreen State College, articulates almost the reverse argument: the fifties remade the nuclear family, trapped men and women in roles they came to loathe, and created a stereotype of the "perfect fifties family" that clouds political debate to the present. This stereotype, she insists, is "the way we never were."

A Decade to Make One Proud

JOHN PATRICK DIGGINS

Although McCarthyism, the cold war, Korea and politics dominated front pages in the fifties, opinion polls profiled the American people as preoccupied with their own lives and largely nonpolitical. To most white, middle-class Americans the fifties meant television; bobby sox and the bunny hop; bermuda shorts and

Reprinted from *The Proud Decades, America in War and Peace, 1941–1960*, by John Patrick Diggins, 177–178, 194–199, 204–207, 219, 348–350. Copyright © 1988 by John Patrick Diggins. Used by permission of W. W. Norton & Company, Inc.

gray flannel suits; "I Love Lucy"; Marlon Brando astride a motorcycle and Elvis belting out "Hound Dog"; Lolita the nymphet; crew cut and duck's ass hairstyles; Marilyn Monroe; James Dean; cruising and panty raids; preppies and their cashmeres and two-toned saddle shoes; Willie Mays; Rocky Graziano; drive-in movies and restaurants; diners with chrome-leg tables and backless stools; suburbia; barbecued steaks; Billy Graham and the way to God without sacrifice; the Kinsey Report and the way to sex without sin. Few items in this list would strike one as serious, but many of them have proved durable. Indeed, such subjects fascinate even members of the post-fifties generation. In the seventies and eighties mass magazines like *Newsweek* and *Life* devoted special issues to the fifties as "The Good Old Days" and Hollywood produced *The Last Picture Show, American Graffiti*, and *The Way We Were*. Nostalgia even succeeded in trivializing the Korean War, as with the immensely popular "M∗A∗S∗H."

Nostalgia is one way to ease the pain of the present. Those who survived the sixties, a decade that witnessed the turmoils of the Vietnam War and the tragedies of political assassination, looked back wistfully on the fifties as a period of peace and prosperity. Many of those who survived the fifties, however, particularly writers and professors, passed a different verdict. "Good-by to the fifties— and good riddance," wrote the historian Eric Goldman, "the dullest and dreariest in all our history." "The Eisenhower years," judged columnist William Shannon, "have been years of flabbiness and self-satisfaction and gross materialism.... The loudest sound in the land has been the oink-and-grunt of private hoggishness.... It has been the age of the slob." The socialist Michael Harrington called the decade "a moral disaster, an amusing waste of time," and the novelist Norman Mailer derided it as "one of the worst decades in the history of man." The poet Robert Lowell summed up his impatience in two lines: "These are the tranquil Fifties, and I am forty./Ought I to regret my seedtime?"

On the other side of the political spectrum, conservative writers tended to praise the fifties as "the happiest, most stable, most rational period the western world has ever known since 1914." They point to the seemingly pleasant fact that in the fifties, in contrast to the sixties, many nations like India and Burma achieved independence without resorting to armed force. The same era enjoyed a postwar prosperity and overcame a massive unemployment that had haunted the depression generation, and did it without raising inflation. Yet even conservatives conceded that the fifties were not a "creative time" in the realm of high culture. This was all right for many of them since "creative periods have too often a way of coinciding with periods of death and destruction."

Whatever the retrospective of writers and intellectuals, those who lived through the fifties looked upon them as a period of unbounded possibility. This was especially true of the beginning of the decade when the lure and novelty of material comforts seemed irresistible. Toward the end of the decade a barely noticeable under-current of dissatisfaction emerged and by the early sixties a minority of women and men would rebel against the conditions of the fifties and wonder what had gone wrong with their lives. A sweet decade for the many, it became a sour experience for the few who would go on to question not only the feminine mystique but the masculine as well. In dealing with the fifties one must deal with its contented and its discontents....

The economic context is crucial. Between 1950 and 1958, the economy expanded enormously. A steady high growth rate of 4.7 percent heralded remarkable increases in living standards and other conditions of life. This prosperity derived from a combination of factors: (a) the lingering postwar back-up demand for consumer goods together with increased purchasing power as a result of savings; (b) the expansion of plant and machine tool capacity, and other technological advances left by the war and revived by the cold war and Korean conflict; (c) the appearance of new and modernized industries ranging from electronics to plastics; (d) population growth and the expansion of large cities; (e) increases in the productivity, or output per man-hour, of the working force; and (f) the commitment to foreign aid, which made possible overseas credits and American exports.

America experienced three mild recessions in the fifties, but through them all the rate of personal income grew and reached a record high of a 3.9 percent rise in 1960. If few became rich, the great majority lived more comfortably than ever before and enjoyed shorter hours on the job, as America moved to the five-day work week. Prior to the Second World War only 25 percent of the farming population had electricity. By the end of the fifties more than 80 percent had not only lighting but telephones, refrigerators, and televisions.

The generation that had borne the depression and the war was now eager to put politics behind and move into a bountiful new world. One strong indicator of confidence in the future was a sudden baby boom. Demographers had been predicting a postwar relative decline in fertility rates and no expansion of immigration quotas. Instead, population leaped from 130 million in 1940 to 165 million by the mid-fifties, the biggest increase in the history of the Republic. Population migrated as well as grew, spreading into the region that came to be called "the sun belt," states like Florida, Texas, Arizona, and California. Farms and small towns lost population. Many big cities, while still growing with lower-class and minority inhabitants, witnessed the flight of the middle class to the periphery. The massive phenomenon of suburbia would rip apart and remake the texture of social life in America.

Suburbia met a need and fulfilled a dream. During the depression and the war most Americans lived in apartments, flats, or small houses within an inner city. After the war, with GIs returning and the marriage rate doubling, as many as two million young couples had to share a dwelling with their relatives. Some settled for a cot in the living room, while married college students often had to live in off-campus quonset huts. Their immediate need for space in which to raise a family was answered by the almost overnight appearance of tracts, subdivisions, and other developments that sprawled across the landscape. Ironically, while suburban growth cut into the natural environment, felling trees and turning fields into asphalt streets, the emotional appeal of suburbia lay in a desire to recapture the greenness and calm of rural life. Thus eastern tracts featured such names as "Crystal Stream," "Robin Meadows," and "Stonybrook," while in the West the Spanish motif of "Villa Serena" and "Tierra Vista" conveyed the ambience of old, preindustrial California. In California the tracts were developed by Henry J. Kaiser and Henry Doelger, who drew on their war-time skills for mass production to provide ranch-style homes complete with backyards and front lawns.... For young members of the aspiring middle class, suburbia was a paradise of comfort and convenience.

Others were not so sure. "Is this the American dream, or is it a nightmare?" asked *House Beautiful*. Architectural and cultural critics complained of the monotony of house after house with the same façade, paint, and lawn inhabited by people willing to sign an agreement to keep them the same. One song writer would call them "little boxes made of ticky-tacky." Some children who grew up in them would agree, rebelling in the following decade against all that was sterile and standardized. The most angry critic was the cultural historian Lewis Mumford, author of *The City in History*. Mumford feared that Levitt was doing more to destroy the modern city than did the World War II aerial bombings. He also feared that suburbia was transforming the American character, rendering it dreary and conformist when it should be daring and courageous. "In the mass movement into suburban areas a new kind of community was produced, which caricatured both the historic city and the archetypal suburban refuge, a multitude of uniform, unidentifiable houses, lined up inflexibly at uniform distances, on uniform roads, in a treeless communal waste, inhabited by people in the same class, the same income, the same age group, witnessing the same television performances, eating the same tasteless pre-fabricated foods from the same freezers, conforming in every outward and inward respect to a common mold."

Admonishments aside, Americans were falling in love with suburbia—at least at first; some would have second thoughts and later wonder what they had bought, the theme of the cheerless film *No Down Payment* (1957). By the end of the fifties one-fourth of the population had moved to such areas. If not beautiful, suburbia was affordable, and thousands of homeless veterans were grateful to have their place in the sun for $65 per month on a full purchase price of $6,990 that included separate bedrooms for the children and a kitchen full of glittering gadgets. Such amenities also enabled housewives to be free of some domestic chores as they became involved in community affairs while their husbands commuted to work in the cities....

In the fifties, car was king. Freeways, multilevel parking lots, shopping centers, motels, and drive-in restaurants and theaters all catered to the person behind the wheel. By 1956 an estimated seventy-five million cars and trucks were on American roads. One out of every seven workers held a job connected to the automobile industry. In suburbia the station wagon became a common sight. But really to fulfill the American dream one needed a Cadillac, or so advertisers informed the arriviste of new wealth with such effectiveness that one had to wait a year for delivery. Almost all American automobiles grew longer and wider. Their supersize and horsepower, together with more chrome and bigger tailfins, served no useful transportation purpose but were powerful enhancers of self-esteem. At the end of the decade, when many rich Texans, some country-western singers, salesmen, and even gangsters and pimps owned a Cadillac, it became what it always was, gauche, and its image declined from the sublime to the ridiculous.

In the fifties the spectacle of waste, once regarded by the older morality as a sign of sin, had become a sign of status. It was no coincidence that Americans junked almost as many cars as Detroit manufactured, thereby fulfilling Thorstein Veblen's earlier prediction that modern man would be more interested in displaying and destroying goods than in producing them. Veblen's insight into "conspicuous consumption" also took on real meaning in this era as Americans rushed out to buy the latest novelty, whether it was a convertible, TV set, deep-freeze, electric carving knife, or the "New Look" Christian Dior evening dress. The postwar splurge of consumption had been made possible by the $100 billion of savings Americans had banked during the war. Immediately after the war, household appliances were in demand, then luxuries like fashionable clothes and imported wines. For those who bought homes for $8,000 or more, luxuries were seen as necessities. The middle-class suburbanite looked out his window and "needed" what his neighbor had—a white Corvette or a swimming pool. Travel to Europe, once regarded as the "Grand Tour" only for the rich and famous, became accessible to millions of Americans in the fifties. For the masses who remained at home and took to the road, new tourist attractions sprang up, like Disneyland. Mass recreational mobility changed the nation's eating habits. In 1954 in San Bernardino, California, Ray Kroc, a high-school dropout, devised a precision stand for turning out French fries, beverages, and fifteen-cent hamburgers that grew rapidly into a fast-food empire: McDonald's.

Spending less time cooking and eating, Americans had more time for shopping. Discount houses such as Korvette's and Grant's opened up for the lower-middle class while the prestigious Neiman-Marcus catered to the needs of oil-rich Texans. Parents raised in the depression naturally felt that more was better, not only for themselves but particularly for their children. Teenagers splurged on phonograph records, bedroom decorations, cashmere sweaters, trips to Hawaii, motor scooters, and hot rods. The seemingly infinite indulgence of the young worried many parents even as they contributed to it. In a survey 94 percent of the mothers interviewed reported that their children had asked them to buy various goods they had seen on television.

Television in America, unlike in England and much of Western Europe, was supported by the advertising industry, which did more than any other institution to fill the viewer's eyes with images of abundance. Advertisers spent $10 billion a year to persuade, not to say manipulate, the people into buying products that promised to improve their lives, whether frozen peas or French perfume. Professional football, the prime target for beer ads, invented the "two-minute warning" in the last quarter to accommodate commercials. Confronted by a medical report linking smoking to lung cancer, tobacco companies increased their ad campaigns with jingles like "Be Happy Go Lucky!" Television bloomed with romantic scenes of a dashing young man offering a cigarette to a seductively beautiful woman under a full moon. As violins rose, the match was lit, and her face turned into that of a goddess—young, eager, divine. Partial takeoffs from the Bogart-Bacall films of the early forties, Madison Avenue could readily exploit such scenes, perhaps realizing that desire can always be tempted precisely because it can never be completely fulfilled.

What facilitated the illusion of fulfillment was a little rectangle of plastic dubbed the credit card. In 1950 Diner's Club distributed credit cards to select wealthy New Yorkers to give them the privilege of eating at swank restaurants without fumbling for money. By the end of the decade Sears Roebuck alone had more than ten million accounts for those who chose to live on credit or, more bluntly, to be in debt.…

During the forties and fifties music became widely accessible to the masses of people. Elaborate hi-fi sets replaced the simple victrola and the jukebox lifted the spirits of the lonely, the tense, and the bored. Light operas like "Oklahoma," "South Pacific," and "My Fair Lady" played to packed theaters, and Americans listened to Mary Martin and Ethel Merman belt out popular songs.

One of the most curious shifts in popular musical tastes that separated the forties and the fifties involved the careers of Frank Sinatra and Elvis Presley. During World War II Sinatra suddenly became the idol of hordes of bobby soxers who were mysteriously mesmerized by his crooning serenades, some shrieking and swooning, others fainting or possibly pretending to.… Yet the hysteria ended almost as suddenly as it began, and by the early fifties Sinatra could not land even a Hollywood film contract. Then another singer captured the youth's imagination and another mode of music determined the nation's sound and rhythm for years to come—Elvis and rock 'n' roll.

… Unlike Sinatra, who appeared so emaciated as to be starving, Presley exuded raw strength and sensuality. Parents brought up on the mawkish music of Bing Crosby tried in vain to shield their children from contamination by the new phenomenon sweeping the country. They were aghast watching "Elvis the Pelvis" with his tight pants, full, pouting lips, and shoulder–length black hair, grip the microphone and buck his hips in gestures so lewd that some TV producers would only film him from the waist up. Magnetic but aloof, self-possessed yet sad, Presley stood before screaming crowds as the icon of the fifties, charging teenagers with energy and emotion in scores like "I Want You, I Need You, I Love You," "Don't Be Cruel," and "Love Me Tender."

Commentators in the fifties often compared Presley to Marlon Brando, James Dean, and Montgomery Clift, three new film stars who revolutionized acting methods and left audiences emotionally drained and confused.… All were actors who conveyed complex emotions more felt than understand in an attempt to express what could not be voiced. In On the Waterfront, East of Eden, and From Here to Eternity, Brando, Dean, and Clift displayed a sensitivity and depth of pure feeling that rendered them almost defenseless against the world. Indeed the film Rebel Without a Cause is haunted by tragedy. All of its four stars—Dean, Natalie Wood, Sal Mineo, and Vic Morrow—would suffer tragic deaths.…

"Live fast, die young, and have a good-looking corpse." The lines by the novelist Willard Motley haunted sensitive youths of the fifties generation, many of whom experienced the era with more unease than did their parents. As children they had come to know the horrors of the bomb from the media; in school they were taught "duck-and-cover" exercises in case of attack; at home some of the affluent heard their parents speak of building bomb shelters in the backyards. Teenagers often knew someone who had been killed in an auto accident or drag race. A best-selling novel, Irving Shulman's The Amboy Dukes, intended to expose the brutality of urban street gangs; for young males it had the opposite effect of glorifying courage in the face of violence. A similar response could be felt after watching such films as *Rebel Without a Cause, The Wild One*, and *Black-board Jungle*, where the opening scene thunders with the theme song, "Rock-Around-the-Clock," a shrill of seething rebellion. Asked what he was rebelling against, Brando replied: "What've ya got?" Perhaps the quest for security on the part of the parents drove their children to desire risk and adventure all the more. Boys cruising in hot rods and quaffing six-packs of beer knew they were flirting with danger, as did those girls who risked pregnancy to discover the secret plea-sures of the body. Why not? The fifties was the first generation in modern his-tory to know that the world could end tomorrow....

The amount of attention the media devoted to sex in the fifties may be misleading since there is reason to doubt significant changes in behavior actually occurred. Sex was then an emotion more felt than fulfilled. It was also a fantasy, and if fantasies reflect what people desire and not necessarily what they do, de-sires nonetheless are a large part of the human secrets of life.

During the decade, while teachers and professors were lamenting the decline in educational standards and ministers and priests the decline of morality, teen-agers and college students were awakening to something stirring in their own bodies, something at once new, at least to them, and exciting and confusing, a subject more seen and felt than heard and understood. It could be seen in *Play-boy*, which started publishing in 1955, exposing more naked angles to the female body than male students could ever imagine, fleshy images that aroused erotic fantasies and made one forget Somerset Maugham's witty warning about sex: the pleasure is momentary, the price damnable, and the position ridiculous....

Their curiosities were met by two postwar publications, *Sexual Behavior in the Human Male* (1948) and *Sexual Behavior in the Human Female* (1953), both by Alfred Kinsey and his colleagues of the Institute for Sexual Research at Indiana University....

Fifty percent of American husbands had committed adultery and 85 percent had sexual intercourse before marriage. Ninety-five percent of males had been sexually active before the age of fifteen and by the ages sixteen and seventeen the activity was at a peak. The average unmarried male had three or four orgasms a week. Nearly 90 percent of men had relationships with prostitutes by their thirty-fifth birthday, and one out of six American farm boys had copulated with farm animals. As to females, two out of three had engaged in premarital petting. Fifty percent were non-virgins before marriage. One out of every six girls had ex-perienced orgasm prior to adolescence, and one in four by the age of fifteen....

The striking thing about the fifties was not the coming crisis of the modern family but its enduring stability. True, the rising divorce rate alarmed Americans in the immediate postwar years. But it soon leveled off and then decreased so that at the end of the fifties the rate was near that of the forties—1.4 percent versus 2.5 percent. Neither marriage nor the family had been threatened by the Kinsey report. Monogamy may have been strained by the freeing effect of carnal knowledge, but most Americans remained inhibited and feared their sexual feel-ings as soon as they felt them. "Sex is Fun—or Hell," was how J. D. Salinger put it in one of his short stories. In the words of one memoirist, women in particular vacillated between "titillation and terror." Ultimately most married men and women accepted their situation, for better or for worse. Society said they should, and in the fifties the pressures of society, not the risqué pleasures of the body, dictated the conduct of life....

The mixed messages were only part of the many paradoxes of the fifties. It was an age of stable nuclear families and marital tension, of student conformity on the campus and youth rebellion on the screen and phonograph, of erotic arousal before the visual and sexual hesitancy before the actual, of suburban contentment with lawns and station wagons and middle-class worry about money and status, of high expectations of upward mobility and later some doubts about the meaning and value of the age's own achievements. Members of the fifties generation were unique. They had more education and aspirations. They married younger and produced more babies. They possessed more buying power and enjoyed more material pleasure than any generation of men and women in American history. And it is a measure of the complexity of the fifties that its members could reach no consensus about the meaning of their accomplishments and disappointments. Looking back from the eighties, one male member, a building contractor and multimillionaire, put it this way:

> If you had a college diploma, a dark suit, and anything between the ears,
> it was like an escalator; you just stood there and you moved up....

The Truman and Eisenhower years gave Americans a sense of pride in themselves and confidence in the future. It is questionable whether either sentiment survived the fifties intact....

By 1960, all confidence that America could simply be accepted as a process of continual growth and change came to be questioned and in many instances rejected. "What is wrong with America?" queried the *U.S. News and World Report*. "What shall we do with our greatness?" asked the editors of *Life*.... "Something has gone wrong in America," complained the novelist John Steinbeck of his fellow people. "Having too many things, they spend their hours and money on the couch searching for a soul." Everywhere Americans were engaged in the "great debate" about "the national purpose." Americans have become worried, journalists concluded, because they feel they lack inspiring ideals and because they have been led to believe that they do not need them. "The case of the missing purpose," wrote a philosopher in *The Nation*, "is a case of human beings missing the purpose of life." The proud decades were over.

Or were they? Several months before Eisenhower's farewell and Kennedy's inauguration, things were changing. Within a few years America would be addressing problems it never knew existed and some people would be singing "We Shall Overcome!" Yet even before the sixties ended America would be more divided than ever, the two Kennedys and King dead, and the Republicans back in office. Now it was Nixon who promised to bring Americans "back together again." Henceforth, the period of the fifties, once regarded as a dreadful aberration standing between the more compassionate thirties and activist sixties, would seem more and more the steady norm of America's political temper. The generation of the sixties experienced the previous decade as a burden that had to be

radically transformed, and some of its worst aspects were confronted and eradi-
cated. But as the radical sixties petered out, it became all the more clear that the
two decades beginning with the Second World War shaped the nation's environment and consciousness in more enduring ways than had once been expected. The forties and perhaps especially the fifties are still living in the
present, and the assumptions and values of the two decades have become ingrained in our habits and institutions. "What is the national purpose?" asked
Dean Acheson in response to the great debate of the late fifties. "To survive
and, perchance, to prosper." In doing both well, America still had good reason
to be proud of itself.

Families in the Fifties: The Way We Never Were

STEPHANIE COONTZ

Our most powerful visions of traditional families derive from images that are still
delivered to our homes in countless reruns of 1950s television sit-coms. When
liberals and conservatives debate family policy, for example, the issue is often
framed in terms of how many "Ozzie and Harriet" families are left in America.
Liberals compute the percentage of total households that contain a breadwinner
father, a full-time homemaker mother, and dependant children, proclaiming that
fewer than 10 percent of American families meet the "Ozzie and Harriet" or
"Leave It to Beaver" model. Conservatives counter that more than half of all
mothers with preschool children either are not employed or are employed only
part-time. They cite polls showing that most working mothers would like to
spend more time with their children and periodically announce that the Nelsons
are "making a comeback," in popular opinion if not in real numbers.

Since everyone admits that nontraditional families are now a majority, why
this obsessive concern to establish a higher or a lower figure? Liberals seem to
think that unless they can prove the "Leave It to Beaver" family is on an irreversible slide toward extinction, they cannot justify introducing new family definitions and social policies. Conservatives believe that if they can demonstrate
the traditional family is alive and well, although endangered by policies that reward two-earner families and single parents, they can pass measures to revive the
seeming placidity and prosperity of the 1950s, associated in many people's minds
with the relative stability of marriage, gender roles, and family life in that decade.
If the 1950s family existed today, both sides seem to assume, we would not have
the contemporary social dilemmas that cause such debate.

At first glance, the figures seem to justify this assumption. The 1950s was a
profamily period if there ever was one. Rates of divorce and illegitimacy were
half what they are today; marriage was almost universally praised; the family was
everywhere hailed as the most basic institution in society; and a massive baby

boom, among all classes and ethnic groups, made America a "child-centered" society. Births rose from a low of 18.4 per 1,000 women during the Depression to a high of 25.3 per 1,000 in 1957. "The birth rate for third children doubled between 1940 and 1960, and that for fourth children tripled."

In retrospect, the 1950s also seem a time of innocence and consensus: Gang warfare among youths did not lead to drive-by shootings; the crack epidemic had not yet hit; discipline problems in the schools were minor; no "secular humanist" movement opposed the 1954 addition of the words *under God* to the Pledge of Allegiance; and 90 percent of all school levies were approved by voters. Introduction of the polio vaccine in 1954 was the most dramatic of many medical advances that improved the quality of life for children.

The profamily features of this decade were bolstered by impressive economic improvements for vast numbers of Americans. Between 1945 and 1960, the gross national product grew by almost 250 percent and per capita income by 35 percent. Housing starts exploded after the war, peaking at 1.65 million in 1955 and remaining above 1.5 million a year for the rest of the decade; the increase in single-family homeownership between 1946 and 1956 outstripped the increase during the entire preceding century and a half. By 1960, 62 percent of American families owned their own homes, in contrast to 43 percent in 1940. Eighty-five percent of the new homes were built in the suburbs, where the nuclear family found new possibilities for privacy and togetherness. While middle-class Americans were the prime beneficiaries of the building boom, substantial numbers of white working-class Americans moved out of the cities into affordable developments, such as Levittown.

Many working-class families also moved into the middle class. The number of salaried workers increased by 61 percent between 1947 and 1957. By the mid-1950s, nearly 60 percent of the population had what was labeled a middle-class income level (between $3,000 and $10,000 in constant dollars), compared to only 31 percent in the "prosperous twenties," before the Great Depression. By 1960, thirty-one million of the nation's forty-four million families owned their own home, 87 percent had a television, and 75 percent possessed a car. The number of people with discretionary income doubled during the 1950s.

For most Americans, the most salient symbol and immediate beneficiary of their newfound prosperity was the nuclear family. The biggest boom in consumer spending, for example, was in household goods. Food spending rose by only 33 percent in the five years following the Second World War, and clothing expenditures rose by 20 percent, but purchases of household furnishings and appliances climbed 240 percent. "Nearly the entire increase in the gross national product in the mid-1950s was due to increased spending on consumer durables and residential construction," most of it oriented toward the nuclear family.

Putting their mouths where their money was, Americans consistently told pollsters that home and family were the wellsprings of their happiness and self-esteem. Cultural historian David Marc argues that prewar fantasies of sophisticated urban "elegance," epitomized by the high-rise penthouse apartment, gave way in the 1950s to a more modest vision of utopia: a single-family house and a car. The emotional dimensions of utopia, however, were unbounded. When respondents to a 1955 marriage study "were asked what they thought they had sacrificed by marrying and raising a family, an overwhelming majority of them replied, 'Nothing.'" Less than 10 percent of Americans believed that an unmarried person could be happy. As one popular advice book intoned: "The family is the center of your living. If it isn't, you've gone far astray."

In fact, the "traditional" family of the 1950s was a qualitatively new phenomenon. At the end of the 1940s, all the trends characterizing the rest of the twentieth century suddenly reversed themselves: For the first time in more than one hundred years, the age for marriage and motherhood fell, fertility increased, divorce rates declined, and women's degree of educational parity with men dropped sharply. In a period of less than ten years, the proportion of never-married persons declined by as much as it had during the entire previous half century.

At the time, most people understood the 1950s family to be a new invention. The Great Depression and the Second World War had reinforced extended family ties, but in ways that were experienced by most people as stultifying and oppressive. As one child of the Depression later put it, "The Waltons" television series of the 1970s did not show what family life in the 1930s was really like: "It wasn't a big family sitting around a table radio and everybody saying goodnight while Bing Crosby crooned 'Pennies from Heaven.'" On top of Depression-era family tensions had come the painful family separations and housing shortages of the war years: By 1947, six million American families were sharing housing, and postwar family counselors warned of a widespread marital crisis caused by conflicts between the generations. A 1948 *March of Time* film, "Marriage and Divorce," declared: "No home is big enough to house two families, particularly two of different generations, with opposite theories on child training."

During the 1950s, films and television plays, such as "Marty," showed people working through conflicts between marital loyalties and older kin, peer group, or community ties; regretfully but decisively, these conflicts were almost invariably "resolved in favor of the heterosexual couple rather than the claims of extended kinship networks,… homosociability and friendship." Talcott Parsons and other sociologists argued that modern industrial society required the family to jettison traditional productive functions and wider kin ties in order to specialize in emotional nurturance, childrearing, and production of a modern personality. Social workers "endorsed nuclear family separateness and looked suspiciously on active extended-family networks."

Popular commentators urged young families to adopt a "modern" stance and strike out on their own, and with the return of prosperity, most did. By the early 1950s, newlyweds not only were establishing single-family homes at an earlier age and a more rapid rate than ever before but also were increasingly moving to the suburbs, away from the close scrutiny of the elder generation.

For the first time in American history, moreover, such average trends did not disguise sharp variations by class, race, and ethnic group. People married at a younger age, bore their children earlier and closer together, completed their families by the time they were in their late twenties, and experienced a longer period living together as a couple after their children left home. The traditional range of acceptable family behaviors—even the range in the acceptable number and timing of children—narrowed substantially.

The values of 1950s families also were new. The emphasis on producing a whole world of satisfaction, amusement, and inventiveness within the nuclear family had no precedents. Historian Elaine Tyler May comments: "The legendary family of the 1950s ... was not, as common wisdom tells us, the last gasp of 'traditional' family life with deep roots in the past. Rather, it was the first wholehearted effort to create a home that would fulfill virtually all its members' personal needs through an energized and expressive personal life."

Beneath a superficial revival of Victorian domesticity and gender distinctions, a novel rearrangement of family ideals and male-female relations was accomplished. For women, this involved a reduction in the moral aspect of domesticity and an expansion of its orientation toward personal service. Nineteenth-century middle-class women had cheerfully left housework to servants, yet 1950s women of all classes created makework in their homes and felt guilty when they did not do everything for themselves. The amount of time women spent doing housework actually *increased* during the 1950s, despite the advent of convenience foods and new, labor-saving appliances; child care absorbed more than twice as much time as it had in the 1920s. By the mid-1950s, advertisers' surveys reported on a growing tendency among women to find "housework a medium of expression for ... [their] femininity and individuality."...

On television, David Marc comments, all the "normal" families moved to the suburbs during the 1950s. Popular culture turned such suburban families into capitalism's answer to the Communist threat. In his famous "kitchen debate" with Nikita Khrushchev in 1959, Richard Nixon asserted that the superiority of capitalism over communism was embodied not in ideology or military might but in the comforts of the suburban home, "designed to make things easier for our women."

Acceptance of domesticity was the mark of middle-class status and upward mobility. In sit-com families, a middle-class man's work was totally irrelevant to his identity; by the same token, the problems of working-class families did not lie in their economic situation but in their failure to create harmonious gender roles. Working-class and ethnic men on television had one defining characteristic: They were unable to control their wives. The families of middle-class men, by contrast, were generally well behaved.

Not only was the 1950s family a new invention; it was also a historical fluke, based on a unique and temporary conjuncture of economic, social, and political factors. During the war, Americans had saved at a rate more than three times higher than that in the decades before or since. Their buying power was further enhanced by America's extraordinary competitive advantage at the end of the war, when every other industrial power was devastated by the experience. This privileged economic position sustained both a tremendous expansion of middle-class management occupations and a new honeymoon between management and organized labor: During the 1950s, real wages increased by more than they had in the entire previous half century.

The impact of such prosperity on family formation and stability was magnified by the role of government, which could afford to be generous with education benefits, housing loans, highway and sewer construction, and job training. All this allowed most middle-class Americans, and a large number of working-class ones, to adopt family values and strategies that assumed the availability of cheap energy, low-interest home loans, expanding educational and occupational opportunities, and steady employment....

Even aside from the exceptional and ephemeral nature of the conditions that supported them, 1950s family strategies and values offer no solution to the discontents that underlie contemporary romanticization of the "good old days." The reality of these families was far more painful and complex than the situation-comedy reruns or the expurgated memories of the nostalgic would suggest. Contrary to popular opinion, "Leave It to Beaver" was not a documentary.

In the first place, not all American families shared in the consumer expansion that provided Hotpoint appliances for June Cleaver's kitchen and a vacuum cleaner for Donna Stone. A full 25 percent of Americans, forty to fifty million people, were poor in the mid-1950s, and in the absence of food stamps and housing programs, this poverty was searing. Even at the end of the 1950s, a third of American children were poor. Sixty percent of Americans over sixty-five had incomes below $1,000 in 1958, considerably below the $3,000 to $10,000 level considered to represent middle-class status. A majority of elders also lacked medical insurance. Only half the population had savings in 1959; one-quarter of the population had no liquid assets at all. Even when we consider only native-born, white families, one-third could not get by on the income of the household head.

In the second place, real life was not so white as it was on television. Television, comments historian Ella Taylor, increasingly ignored cultural diversity, adopting "the motto 'least objectionable programming,'" which gave rise to those least objectionable families, the Cleavers, the Nelsons and the Andersons." Such families were so completely white and Anglo-Saxon that even the Hispanic gardener in "Father Knows Best" went by the name of Frank Smith. But contrary to the all-white lineup on the television networks and the streets of suburbia, the 1950s saw a major transformation in the ethnic composition of America. More Mexican immigrants entered the United States in the two decades after the Second World War than in the entire previous one hundred years. Prior to the war, most blacks and Mexican-Americans lived in rural areas, and three-fourths of blacks lived in the South. By 1960, a majority of blacks resided in the North, and 80 percent of both blacks and Mexican-Americans lived in cities. Postwar Puerto Rican immigration was so massive that by 1960 more Puerto Ricans lived in New York than in San Juan....

The happy, homogeneous families that we "remember" from the 1950s were thus partly a result of the media's denial of diversity. But even among sectors of the population where the "least objectionable" families did prevail, their values and behaviors were not entirely a spontaneous, joyful reaction to prosperity. If suburban ranch houses and family barbecues were the carrots offered to white middle-class families that adopted the new norms, there was also a stick....

Vehement attacks were launched against women who did not accept [the prevailing] self-definitions. In the 1947 bestseller, *The Modern Woman: The Lost*

Sex, Marynia Farnham and Ferdinand Lundberg described feminism as a "deep illness," called the notion of an independent woman a "contradiction in terms," and accused women who sought educational or employment equality of engaging in symbolic "castration" of men. As sociologist David Riesman noted, a woman's failure to bear children went from being "a social disadvantage and sometimes a personal tragedy" in the nineteenth century to being a "quasi-perversion" in the 1950s. The conflicting messages aimed at women seemed almost calculated to demoralize: At the same time as they labeled women "unnatural" if they did not seek fulfillment in motherhood, psychologists and popular writers insisted that most modern social ills could be traced to domineering mothers who invested too much energy and emotion in their children. Women were told that "no other experience in life … will provide the same sense of fulfillment, of happiness, of complete pervading contentment" as motherhood. But soon after delivery they were asked, "Which are you first of all, Wife or Mother?" and warned against the tendency to be "too much mother, too little wife."…

Men were also pressured into acceptable family roles, since lack of a suitable wife could mean the loss of a job or promotion for a middle-class man. Bachelors were categorized as "immature," "infantile," "narcissistic," "deviant," or even "pathological." Family advice expert Paul Landis argued: "Except for the sick, the badly crippled, the deformed, the emotionally warped and the mentally defective, almost everyone has an opportunity [and, by clear implication, a duty] to marry."

Families in the 1950s were products of even more direct repression. Cold war anxieties merged with concerns about the expanded sexuality of family life and the commercial world to create what one authority calls the domestic version of George F. Kennan's containment policy toward the Soviet Union: A "normal" family and vigilant mother became the "front line" of defense against treason; anticommunists linked deviant family or sexual behavior to sedition. The FBI and other government agencies instituted unprecedented state intrusion into private life under the guise of investigating subversives. Gay baiting was almost as widespread and every bit as vicious as red baiting.

The Civil Service Commission fired 2,611 persons as "security risks" and reported that 4,315 others resigned under the pressure of investigations that asked leading questions of their neighbors and inquired into the books they read or the music to which they listened. In this atmosphere, movie producer Joel Schumacher recalls, "No one told the truth.… People pretended they weren't unfaithful. They pretended that they weren't homosexual. They pretended that they weren't horrible."

Even for people not directly coerced into conformity by racial, political, or personal repression, the turn toward families was in many cases more a defensive move than a purely affirmative act. Some men and women entered loveless marriages in order to forestall attacks about real or suspected homosexuality or lesbianism. Growing numbers of people saw the family, in the words of one husband, as the one "group that in spite of many disagreements internally always will face its external enemies together." Conservative families warned children to beware of communists who might masquerade as friendly neighbors; liberal children learned to confine their opinions to the family for fear that their father's job or reputation might be threatened....

Although Betty Friedan's bestseller *The Feminine Mystique* did not appear until 1963, it was a product of the 1950s, originating in the discontented responses Friedan received in 1957 when she surveyed fellow college classmates from the class of 1942. The heartfelt identification of other 1950s women with "the problem that has no name" is preserved in the letters Friedan received after her book was published, letters now at the Schlesinger Library at Radcliffe.

Men tended to be more satisfied with marriage than were women, especially over time, but they, too, had their discontents. Even the most successful strivers after the American dream sometimes muttered about "mindless conformity." The titles of books such as *The Organization Man*, by William Whyte (1956), and *The Lonely Crowd*, by David Riesman (1958), summarized a widespread critique of 1950s culture. Male resentments against women were expressed in the only partly humorous diatribes of *Playboy* magazine (founded in 1953) against "money-hungry" gold diggers or lazy "parasites" trying to trap men into commitment.

Happy memories of 1950s family life are not all illusion, of course—there were good times for many families. But even the most positive aspects had another side. One reason that the 1950s family model was so fleeting was that it contained the seeds of its own destruction.... It was during the 1950s, not the 1960s, that the youth market was first produced, then institutionalized into the youth culture. It was through such innocuous shows as "Howdy Doody" and "The Disney Hour" that advertisers first discovered the riches to be gained by bypassing parents and appealing directly to youth. It was also during this period that advertising and consumerism became saturated with sex....

Whatever its other unexpected features, the 1950s family does appear, at least when compared to families in the last two decades, to be a bastion of "traditional" sexual morality. Many modern observers, accordingly, look back to the sexual values of this decade as a possible solution to what they see as the peculiarly modern "epidemic" of teen pregnancy. On closer examination, however, the issue of teen pregnancy is a classic example of both the novelty and the contradictions of the 1950s family.

Those who advocate that today's youth should be taught abstinence or deferred gratification rather than sex education will find no 1950s model for such restraint. "Heavy petting" became a norm of dating in this period, while the proportion of white brides who were pregnant at marriage more than doubled. Teen birth rates soared, reaching highs that have not been equaled since. In 1957, 97 out of every 1,000 girls aged fifteen to nineteen gave birth, compared to only 52 of every 1,000 in 1983. A surprising number of these births were illegitimate, although 1950s census codes made it impossible to identify an unmarried mother if she lived at home with her parents. The incidence of illegitimacy was also disguised by the new emphasis on "rehabilitating" the white mother (though not the black) by putting her baby up for adoption and encouraging her to "start over"; there was an 80 percent increase in the number of out-of-wedlock babies placed for adoption between 1944 and 1955.

The main reason that teenage sexual behavior did not result in many more illegitimate births during this period was that the age of marriage dropped sharply. Young people were not taught how to "say no"—they were simply handed wedding rings. In fact, the growing willingness of parents to subsidize young married couples and the new prevalence of government educational stipends and home ownership loans for veterans undermined the former assumption that a man should be able to support a family before embarking on marriage....

Contemporary teenage motherhood ... in some ways represents a *continuation* of 1950s values in a new economic situation that makes early marriage less viable. Of course, modern teen pregnancy also reflects the rejection of some of those earlier values. The values that have broken down, however, have little to do with sexual restraint. What we now think of as 1950s sexual morality depended not so much on stricter sexual control as on intensification of the sexual double standard. Elaine Tyler May argues that sexual "repression" gave way to sexual "containment." The new practice of going steady "widened the boundaries of permissible sexual activity," creating a "sexual brinksmanship" in which women bore the burden of "drawing the line," but that line was constantly changing. Popular opinion admitted, as the *Ladies' Home Journal* put it in 1956, that "sex suggestiveness" was here to stay, but insisted that it was up to women to "put the brakes on."...

People who romanticize the 1950s, or any model of the traditional family, are usually put in an uncomfortable position when they attempt to gain popular support. The legitimacy of women's rights is so widely accepted today that only a tiny minority of Americans seriously propose that women should go back to being full-time housewives or should be denied educational and job opportunities because of their family responsibilities. Yet when commentators lament the collapse of traditional family commitments and values, they almost invariably mean the uniquely female duties associated with the doctrine of separate spheres for men and women.

Karl Zinsmeister of the American Enterprise Institute, for example, bemoans the fact that "workaholism and family dereliction have become equal-opportunity diseases, striking mothers as much as fathers." David Blankenhorn of the Institute for American Values expresses sympathy for the needs of working women but warns that "employed women do not a family make. The goals of women (and of men, too) in the workplace are primarily individualistic: social recognition, wages, opportunities for advancement, and self-fulfillment. But the family is about collective goals...., building life's most important bonds of affection, nurturance, mutual support, and long-term commitment."

In both statements, a seemingly gender-neutral indictment of family irresponsibility ends up being directed most forcefully against women. For Blankenhorn, it is not surprising that *men's* goals should be individualistic; this is a parenthetical aside. For Zinsmeister, the problem with the disease of family dereliction is that it has spread to women. So long as it was confined to men, evidently, there was no urgency about finding a cure.

FURTHER READING

Joel A. Carpenter, *Revive Us Again: The Reawakening of American Fundamentalism* (1997).

Lizabeth Cohen, *A Consumer's Republic: The Politics of Mass Consumption in Postwar America* (2003).

Michael Coyne, *The Crowded Prairie: American National Identity in the Hollywood Western* (1997).

Henry Louis Gates, Jr., *Colored People: A Memoir* (1994).

William Graebner, *Coming of Age in Buffalo: Youth and Authority in the Postwar Era* (1990).

Julia Grant, *Raising Baby by the Book: The Education of American Mothers* (1998).

Andrew Hurley, *Diners, Bowling Alleys, and Trailer Parks: Chasing the American Dream in the Postwar Consumer Culture* (2001).

Kenneth T. Jackson, *Crabgrass Frontier: The Suburbanization of America* (1985).

Elaine Tyler May, *Homeward Bound: American Families in the Cold War Era* (1988).

Richard H. Pells, *The Liberal Mind in a Conservative Age: American Intellectuals in the 1940s and 1950s* (1985).

Lisle Rose, *The Cold War Comes to Main Street: America in 1950* (1999).

Robert Self, *American Babylon: Race and the Struggle for Postwar Oakland* (2003).

Jessica Weiss, *To Have and to Hold: Marriage, the Baby Boom, and Social Change* (2000).

Andrew Wiese, *Places of Their Own: African American Suburbanization in the Twentieth Century* (2004).

CHAPTER 12

"We Can Do Better":
The Civil Rights Revolution

The "American Way" meant something very different to blacks in the 1950s from what it meant to people like Ron Kovic (Born on the Fourth of July). For blacks in the South, the American Way was "Jim Crow," a system of segregation that included separate schools, separate drinking fountains, separate beaches, separate neighborhoods, and separate public accommodations. Most African Americans in the South could not vote, marry whites, sit in the front of buses, attend state colleges, or even try on clothes and hats in major department stores. Beyond the inconvenience and embarrassment lurked the potential for violence. Women and men who "stepped out of line" could expect the full force of the law—and perhaps even brutal vigilantes like the Ku Klux Klan or White Citizens Council—to turn upon them. It took incalculable bravery to confront this system, and in the 1950s a grassroots movement of men, women, and children did just this.

People like Rosa Parks, Martin Luther King, Jr., and Robert Williams helped to start the southern Civil Rights Movement, which led finally to the implementation of the Fourteenth and Fifteenth Amendments to the Constitution, placed on the books almost one hundred years earlier. The Civil Rights Act of 1964 outlawed segregation in public establishments and discrimination in employment. It extended equal protection under the law to all citizens, which had been the intent of the Fourteenth Amendment. The Civil Rights Act of 1965 guaranteed the right to vote, and the Civil Rights Act of 1968 prohibited discrimination in housing.

But the movement did not stop at legal reforms, nor did it pertain only to African Americans. Racial prejudice itself came under attack, and other groups whose rights had been abridged grabbed hold of the new, empowering rhetoric to proclaim their inalienable right to "life, liberty, and the pursuit of happiness." Women, American Indians, Chicanos, Asian Americans, gays, the elderly, and eventually the disabled all sought remedies for discrimination and inequality. They echoed one another's statements and demands, each asserting in turn that freedoms guaranteed to one group of people could not be denied to another.

Although none of these groups achieved their ultimate goal of creating a perfectly just society—what President Lyndon Baines Johnson called the Great Society—they changed many laws and practices within the United States. Legal segregation came to an end. No ethnic or racial group could be paid less than another, and women could no longer legally be paid less than men (or be beaten by their husbands). The very words that people spoke, and the jokes that they told, changed as the legacy of racism, sexism, ageism, and all the other "isms" came under attack.

Of course, the problem was as old as slavery, the solution as old as the American Revolution. Almost two hundred years before the modern Civil Rights Movement, Thomas Jefferson had penned the immortal words, "We hold these truths to be self-evident, that all men are created equal." In the 1950s and 1960s, for arguably the first time, the nation sought to put these words into practice across the board. Why then? There are many places to look for the answer to this question, including beyond the United States. The holocaust of World War II and the role of the United States as world leader during the cold war helped to reshape thinking about the place of discrimination in the "land of the free, home of the brave." Abundance, power, and the eyes of the world led leaders like John F. Kennedy to proclaim, "We can do better." This new thinking about civil rights was the most important reformist legacy of the post-war era.

QUESTIONS TO THINK ABOUT

Why were Jefferson's "self-evident" truths finally adopted in practice at this time? What was more important in bringing about these fundamental changes: black leadership at the grassroots, or the new world role of the United States? In the lingo of the Civil Rights era, how did the "white establishment" advance or hinder the cause of democracy? Also, how did grassroots tactics change over time, and with what effect?

DOCUMENTS

The documents in this chapter illustrate the various dimensions of the Civil Rights Movement. Document 1 is the Universal Declaration of Human Rights passed by the United Nations in 1948. Arising out of the genocide of World War II, this was the first global concord in human history that articulated the premise "All human beings are born free and equal in dignity and rights." Eleanor Roosevelt, a champion of civil rights in the United States, chaired the tumultuous U.N. committee that drafted the declaration. Document 2 is the Supreme Court's famous reversal of *Plessy v. Ferguson* (1896). Separate is not equal, the Court ruled in *Brown v. Board of Education*. Document 3 is from Martin Luther King, Jr.'s first speech on behalf of Rosa Parks at the Holt Street Baptist Church in Montgomery, Alabama. Returning home from work, Parks refused to give up her seat on a bus so that a white person would not have to occupy the same row as she. This 1955 sermon following Rosa Parks's arrest helped to launch the Montgomery bus boycott, as well as King's career as a civil rights leader. In document 4, Henry Louis Gates, Jr., now a professor at Harvard University, remembers growing up in the segregated South and learning about civil rights on TV. This selection shows the ways in which different generations perceived the movement. Older people tended to be more skeptical than the young. Document 5 is taken from Robert Williams's 1962 book, *Negroes With Guns*. A veteran of both the army and marines, Williams argued that "negroes" had as much right to self-defense as all other Americans. His ideas and actions later fueled the Black Power Movement. Document 6 is the founding statement of the National Organization for Women. The women's rights movement gathered force quickly in the 1960s, spurred by the Civil Rights Movement and by female activists. Document 7 shows the long reach of new ideas on racial equality. The television show *Star Trek* boasted prime-time TV's first multiracial cast— living together amicably sometime far in the future. Even Russians were invited. As you look at this photograph, examine the positioning of the characters, including the spaceship captain, James Kirk. Document 8 describes La Raza Unida, a third party started by Mexican Americans. It highlights the leadership of César Chávez and the inspiration that Chicanos drew from "Negro civil rights" as well as from the Cuban Revolution. Document 9 is a satirical manifesto sent to "the Great White Father" by the founders of the American Indian Movement after their occupation of Alcatraz Island in San Francisco Bay. The Indians offered to pay $24 in glass beads for the sixteen acres. Document 10 is an excerpt from journalist Tom Wolfe's biting depiction of white liberals in the late sixties, when anti-racism had become chic, rather than controversial, and of those Black activists (especially on the West Coast) who had broken altogether with the pacifist, non-violent rhetoric of the early movement. The last document, describing the rights of the developmentally disabled, is a clear outcome of the commitment made back in 1948 to respect the rights, dignity, and abilities of all humans regardless of condition. It shows how far the "minority rights revolution" ultimately spread.

1. The United Nations Approves a Universal Declaration of Human Rights, 1948

Preamble

Whereas recognition of the inherent dignity and of the equal and inalienable rights of all members of the human family is the foundation of freedom, justice and peace in the world,

Whereas disregard and contempt for human rights have resulted in barbarous acts which have outraged the conscience of mankind, and the advent of a world in which human beings shall enjoy freedom of speech and belief and freedom

---

United Nations web site, www.un.org/Overview/rights.html.

from fear and want has been proclaimed as the highest aspiration of the common people,

Whereas it is essential, if man is not to be compelled to have recourse, as a last resort, to rebellion against tyranny and oppression, that human rights should be protected by the rule of law,

Whereas it is essential to promote the development of friendly relations between nations,

Whereas the peoples of the United Nations have in the Charter reaffirmed their faith in fundamental human rights, in the dignity and worth of the human person and in the equal rights of men and women and have determined to promote social progress and better standards of life in larger freedom,

Whereas Member States have pledged themselves to achieve, in cooperation with the United Nations, the promotion of universal respect for and observance of human rights and fundamental freedoms,

Whereas a common understanding of these rights and freedoms is of the greatest importance for the full realization of this pledge,

Now, Therefore THE GENERAL ASSEMBLY proclaims THIS UNIVERSAL DECLARATION OF HUMAN RIGHTS as a common standard of achievement for all peoples and all nations, to the end that every individual and every organ of society, keeping this Declaration constantly in mind, shall strive by teaching and education to promote respect for these rights and freedoms and by progressive measures, national and international, to secure their universal and effective recognition and observance, both among the peoples of Member States themselves and among the peoples of territories under their jurisdiction.

Article 1.

All human beings are born free and equal in dignity and rights. They are endowed with reason and conscience and should act towards one another in a spirit of brotherhood.

Article 2.

Everyone is entitled to all the rights and freedoms set forth in this Declaration, without distinction of any kind, such as race, colour, sex, language, religion, political or other opinion, national or social origin, property, birth or other status....

Article 3.

Everyone has the right to life, liberty and security of person.

Article 4.

No one shall be held in slavery or servitude; slavery and the slave trade shall be prohibited in all their forms.

Article 5.

No one shall be subjected to torture or to cruel, inhuman or degrading treatment or punishment.

Article 6.

Everyone has the right to recognition everywhere as a person before the law.

2. The Supreme Court Rules on
Brown v. Board of Education, 1954

These cases come to us from the States of Kansas, South Carolina, Virginia, and Delaware. They are premised on different facts and different local conditions, but a common legal question justifies their consideration together in this consolidated opinion.

In each of the cases, minors of the Negro race, through their legal representatives, seek the aid of the courts in obtaining admission to the public schools of their community on a nonsegregated basis. In each instance, they had been denied admission to schools attended by white children under laws requiring or permitting segregation according to race. This segregation was alleged to deprive the plaintiffs of the equal protection of the laws under the Fourteenth Amendment. In each of the cases other than the Delaware case, a three-judge federal district court denied relief to the plaintiffs on the so-called "separate but equal" doctrine announced by this Court in *Plessy v. Ferguson*, 163 U.S. 537. Under that doctrine, equality of treatment is accorded when the races are provided substantially equal facilities, even though these facilities be separate....

The plaintiffs contend that segregated public schools are not "equal" and cannot be made "equal," and that hence they are deprived of the equal protection of the laws....

In approaching this problem, we cannot turn the clock back to 1868 when the Amendment was adopted, or even to 1896 when *Plessy v. Ferguson* was written. We must consider public education in the light of its full development and its present place in American life throughout the Nation. Only in this way can it be determined if segregation in public schools deprives these plaintiffs of the equal protection of the laws.

Today, education is perhaps the most important function of state and local governments. Compulsory school attendance laws and the great expenditures for education both demonstrate our recognition of the importance of education to

---

Brown v. Board of Education, 324, U.S. 483–496 (1954).

our democratic society. It is required in the performance of our most basic public responsibilities, even service in the armed forces. It is the very foundation of good citizenship. Today it is a principal instrument in awakening the child to cultural values, in preparing him for later professional training, and in helping him to adjust normally to his environment. In these days, it is doubtful that any child may reasonably be expected to succeed in life if he is denied the opportunity of an education. Such an opportunity, when the state has undertaken to provide it, is a right which must be made available to all on equal terms.

We come then to the question presented: Does segregation of children in public schools solely on the basis of race, even though the physical facilities and other "tangible" factors may be equal, deprive the children of the minority group of equal educational opportunities? We believe that it does.

... To separate them from others of similar age and qualifications solely because of their race generates a feeling of inferiority as to their status in the community that may affect their hearts and minds in a way unlikely ever to be undone....

We conclude that in the field of public education the doctrine of "separate but equal" has no place. Separate educational facilities are inherently unequal. Therefore, we hold that the plaintiffs and others similarly situated for whom the actions have been brought are, by reason of the segregation complained of, deprived of the equal protection of the laws guaranteed by the Fourteenth Amendment.

3. Reverend Martin Luther King, Jr., Defends Seamstress Rosa Parks, 1955

We are here this evening for serious business. We are here in a general sense because first and foremost we are American citizens, and we are determined to apply our citizenship to the fullness of its means. We are here because of our love for democracy, because of our deep-seated belief that democracy transformed from thin paper to thick action is the greatest form of government on earth. But we are here in a specific sense, because of the bus situation in Montgomery. We are here because we are determined to get the situation corrected.

This situation is not at all new. The problem has existed over endless years. For many years now Negroes in Montgomery and so many other areas have been inflicted with the paralysis of crippling fear on buses in our community. On so many occasions, Negroes have been intimidated and humiliated and oppressed because of the sheer fact that they were Negroes. I don't have time this evening to go into the history of these numerous cases.... But at least one stands before us now with glaring dimensions. Just the other day, just last Thursday to be exact, one of the finest citizens in Montgomery—not one of the finest

Excerpt front speech delivered by Martin Luther King, Jr., at Holt Street Baptist Church, Montgomery, Alabama, December 5, 1955, as reprinted in *The Eyes on the Price Civil Rights Reader* (New York: Viking, 1991), 48–51. Reprinted by arrangement with the Estate of Martin Luther King, Jr., c/o Writers House as agent for the proprietor. Copyright 1967 Martin Luther King, Jr., copyright renewed 1991 Coretta Scott King.

Negro citizens but one of the finest citizens in Montgomery—was taken from a bus and carried to jail and arrested because she refused to get up to give her seat to a white person…. Mrs. Rosa Parks is a fine person. And since it had to happen I'm happy it happened to a person like Mrs. Parks, for nobody can doubt the boundless outreach of her integrity. Nobody can doubt the height of her character, nobody can doubt the depth of her Christian commitment and devotion to the teachings of Jesus….

And just because she refused to get up, she was arrested…. You know my friends there comes a time when people get tired of being trampled over by the iron feet of oppression. There comes a time my friends when people get tired of being flung across the abyss of humiliation where they experience the bleakness of nagging despair. There comes a time when people get tired of being pushed out of the glittering sunlight of life's July and left standing amidst the piercing chill of an Alpine November.

We are here, we are here this evening because we're tired now. Now let us say that we are not here advocating violence. We have overcome that. I want it to be known throughout Montgomery and throughout this nation that we are Christian people. We believe in the Christian religion. We believe in the teachings of Jesus. The only weapon that we have in our hands this evening is the weapon of protest. And secondly, this is the glory of America, with all its faults. This is the glory of our democracy. If we were incarcerated behind the iron curtains of a Communistic nation we couldn't do this. If we were trapped in the dungeon of a totalitarian regime we couldn't do this. But the great glory of American democracy is the right to protest for right….

And as we stand and sit here this evening, and as we prepare ourselves for what lies ahead, let us go out with a grim and bold determination that we are going to stick together. We are going to work together. Right here in Montgomery when the history books are written in the future, somebody will have to say "There lived a race of people, black people, fleecy locks and black complexion, of people who had the moral courage to stand up for their rights." And thereby they injected a new meaning into the veins of history and of civilization. And we're gonna do that. God grant that we will do it before it's too late.

4. Author Henry Louis Gates, Jr., Remembers Civil Rights on TV, 1957, (1994)

Civil rights took us all by surprise. Every night we'd wait until the news to see what "Dr. King and dem" were doing. It was like watching the Olympics or the World Series when somebody colored was on. The murder of Emmett Till was one of my first memories. He whistled at some white girl, they said; that's all he did. He was beat so bad they didn't even want to open the casket, but his

mama made them. She wanted the world to see what they had done to her
baby.

In 1957, when I was in second grade, black children integrated Central High
School in Little Rock, Arkansas. We watched it on TV. All of us watched it.
I don't mean Mama and Daddy and Rocky. I mean *all* the colored people in
America watched it, together, with one set of eyes. We'd watch it in the morn-
ing, on the *Today* show on NBC, before we'd go to school; we'd watch it in
the evening, on the news, with Edward R. Murrow on CBS. We'd watch the
Special Bulletins at night, interrupting our TV shows.

The children were all well scrubbed and greased down, as we'd say. Hair
short and closely cropped, parted, and oiled (the boys); "done" in a "permanent"
and straightened, with turned-up bangs and curls (the girls). Starched shirts,
white and creased pants, shoes shining like a buck private's spit shine. Those
Negroes were *clean*. The fact was, those children trying to get the right to enter
that school in Little Rock looked like black versions of models out of *Jack & Jill*
magazine, to which my mama had subscribed for me so that I could see what
children outside the Valley were up to. "They hand-picked those children,"
Daddy would say. "No dummies, no nappy hair, heads not too kinky, lips not
too thick, no disses and no dats." At seven, I was dismayed by his cynicism. It
bothered me somehow that those children would have been chosen, rather than
just having shown up or volunteered or been nearby in the neighborhood.

Daddy was jaundiced about the civil rights movement, and especially about
the Reverend Dr. Martin Luther King, Jr. He'd say all of his names, to drag out
his scorn. By the mid-sixties, we'd argue about King from sunup to sundown.
Sometimes he'd just mention King to get a rise from me, to make a sagging
evening more interesting, to see if I had *learned* anything real yet, to see how
long I could think up counter arguments before getting so mad that my face
would turn purple. I think he just liked the color purple on my face, liked producing it there. But he was not of two minds about those children in Little
Rock....

The TV was the ritual arena for the drama of race. In our family, it was
located in the living room, where it functioned like a fireplace in the proverbial
New England winter. I'd sit in the water in the galvanized tub in the middle
of our kitchen, watching the TV in the next room while Mama did the laundry
or some other chore as she waited for Daddy to come home from his second
job. We watched people getting hosed and cracked over their heads, people
being spat upon and arrested, rednecks siccing fierce dogs on women and children, our people responding by singing and marching and staying strong. Eyes
on the prize. Eyes on the prize. George Wallace at the gate of the University of
Alabama, blocking Autherine Lucy's way. Charlayne Hunter at the University
of Georgia. President Kennedy interrupting our scheduled program with a
special address, saying that James Meredith will *definitely* enter the University of
Mississippi; and saying it like he believed it (unlike Ike), saying it like the big kids
said "It's our turn to play" on the basketball court and walking all through us as
if we weren't there.

5. Army Veteran Robert Williams Argues "Self-Defense Prevents Bloodshed," 1962

In June of 1961 the NAACP Chapter of Monroe, North Carolina, decided to picket the town's swimming pool. This pool, built by WPA money, was forbidden to Negroes although we formed one third the population of the town. In 1957 we had asked not for integration but for the use of the pool one day a week. This was denied and for four years we were put off with vague suggestions that someday another pool would be built. Two small Negro children had meantime drowned swimming in creeks....

There were about two or three thousand people lined along the highway. Two or three policemen were standing at the intersection directing traffic and there were two policemen who had been following us from my home. An old stock car without windows was parked by a restaurant at the intersection. As soon as we drew near, this car started backing out as fast as possible. The driver hoped to hit us in the side and flip us over. But I turned my wheel sharply and the junk car struck the front of my car and both cars went into a ditch.

Then the crowd started screaming. They said that a nigger had hit a white man. They were referring to me. They were screaming, "Kill the niggers! Kill the niggers! Pour gasoline on the niggers! Burn the niggers!"

We were still sitting in the car. The man who was driving the stock car got out of the car with a baseball bat and started walking toward us and he was saying, "Nigger, what did you hit me for?" I didn't say anything to him. We just sat there looking at him. He came up close to our car, within arm's length with the baseball bat, but I still hadn't said anything and we didn't move in the car. What they didn't know was that we were armed. Under North Carolina state law it is legal to carry firearms in your automobile so long as these firearms are not concealed.

I had two pistols and a rifle in the car. When this fellow started to draw back his baseball bat, I put an Army .45 up in the window of the car and pointed it right into his face and I didn't say a word. He looked at the pistol and he didn't say anything. He started backing away from the car.

Somebody in the crowd fired a pistol and the people again started to scream hysterically, "Kill the niggers! Kill the niggers! Pour gasoline on the niggers!" The mob started to throw stones on top of my car. So I opened the door of the car and I put one foot on the ground and stood up in the door holding an Italian carbine.

All this time three policemen had been standing about fifty feet away from us while we kept waiting in the car for them to come and rescue us. Then when they saw that we were armed and the mob couldn't take us, two of the policemen started running. One ran straight to me and he grabbed me on the shoulder and said, "Surrender your weapon! Surrender your weapon!" I struck him in the face and knocked him back away from the car and put my carbine in his face and I told him we were not going to surrender to a mob. I told him that we didn't intend to be lynched....

From Robert F. Williams, *Negroes With Guns*, (Wayne State UP, 1988), Excerpt from Ch. 1 - p. 42, 45–46. Copyright © 1988 Wayne State University Press. Reprinted by permission of Wayne State University Press.

There was a very old man, an old white man out in the crowd, and he started screaming and crying like a baby and he kept crying, and he said, "God damn, God damn, what is this God damn country coming to that the niggers have got guns, the niggers are armed and the police can't even arrest them!" He kept crying and somebody led him away through the crowd....

6. The National Organization for Women Calls for Equality, 1966

We, men and women who hereby constitute ourselves as the National Organization for Women, believe that the time has come for a new movement toward true equality for all women in America, and toward a fully equal partnership of the sexes, as part of the world-wide revolution of human rights now taking place within and beyond our national borders.

The purpose of NOW is to take action to bring women into full participation in the mainstream of American society now, exercising all the privileges and responsibilities thereof in truly equal partnership with men....

NOW is dedicated to the proposition that women first and foremost are human beings, who, like all other people in our society, must have the chance to develop their fullest human potential. We believe that women can achieve such equality only by accepting to the full the challenges and responsibilities they share with all other people in our society, as part of the decision-making mainstream of American political, economic and social life....

There is no civil rights movement to speak for women, as there has been for Negroes and other victims of discrimination. The National Organization for Women must therefore begin to speak.

WE BELIEVE that the power of American law, and the protection guaranteed by the U.S. Constitution to the civil rights of all individuals, must be effectively applied and enforced to isolate and remove patterns of sex discrimination, to ensure equality of opportunity in employment and education, and equality of civil and political rights and responsibilities on behalf of women, as well as for Negroes and other deprived groups....

WE BELIEVE that it is as essential for every girl to be educated to her full potential of human ability as it is for every boy—with the knowledge that such education is the key to effective participation in today's economy and that, for a girl as for a boy, education can only be serious where there is expectation that it will be used in society. We believe that American educators are capable of devising means of imparting such expectations to girl students. Moreover, we consider the decline in the proportion of women receiving higher and professional education to be evidence of discrimination.... We believe that the same serious attention must be given to high school dropouts who are girls as to boys.

NOW Statement of Purpose, October 1966. Excerpt reprinted by permission of the National Organization for Women. This is a historical document and may not reflect the current language or priorities of the organization.

WE REJECT the current assumptions that a man must carry the sole burden of supporting himself, his wife, and family, and that a woman is automatically entitled to lifelong support by a man upon her marriage, or that marriage, home and family are primarily woman's world and responsibility—hers, to dominate, his to support. We believe that a true partnership between the sexes demands a different concept of marriage, an equitable sharing of the responsibilities of home and children and of the economic burdens of their support. We believe that proper recognition should be given to the economic and social value of homemaking and child care. To these ends, we will seek to open a reexamination of laws and mores governing marriage and divorce, for we believe that the current state of "half-equality" between the sexes discriminates against both men and women, and is the cause of much unnecessary hostility between the sexes....

WE BELIEVE THAT women will do most to create a new image of women by *acting* now, and by speaking out in behalf of their own equality, freedom, and human dignity—not in pleas for special privilege, nor in enmity toward men, who are also victims of the current half-equality between the sexes—but in an active, self-respecting partnership with men. By so doing, women will develop confidence in their own ability to determine actively, in partnership with men, the conditions of their life, their choices, their future and their society.

7. Multiracialism (and Détente) on TV: *Star Trek*, 1967

The Crew of the Starship *Enterprise* reflected the show's attempt to "boldly go where no man has gone before": into a universe of ethnic diversity and inter-species harmony. From left: James Doohan as Scotty (a Scotsman), DeForest Kelley as Dr. McCoy (a Southernor), Walter Koenig as Chekov (a Russian), Majel Barrett as Nurse Chapel and William Shatner as Captain Kirk (regionally-unidentifiable, "white" Americans), Nichelle Nichols as Uhura (an African-American), Leonard Nimoy as Mr. Spock (a Vulcan), and George Takei as Sulu (an Asian-American). THE ORIGINAL SERIES/FIRST SERIES/SERIES 1/ SERIES ONE

PARAMOUNT TELEVISION / THE KOBAL COLLECTION

8. Mexican Americans Form La Raza Unida, 1968

1. What is LA RAZA UNIDA? It is a ground swell movement of Mexican-American solidarity throughout the Southwest comprising a loose fellowship of some two or three hundred civic, social, cultural, religious, and political groups.

2. What has brought it about? The need deeply felt among Mexican-Americans to dramatize their plight as a disadvantaged minority, to assert their rights as first-rate citizens, and to assume their rightful share of the social, economic, educational, and political opportunities guaranteed by the American democratic system.

3. Are Mexican-Americans a disadvantaged minority? The most recent study, the Mexican-American Study Project conducted at UCLA and funded by the Ford Foundation, has disclosed that in the Southwest, as compared to the Negro, the Mexican-American is on generally the same level economically, but substantially below educationally. As for dilapidated housing and unemployment, the Mexican-American is not too much better off than the Negro.

4. Why this sudden awakening? Actually, it is not as sudden as it looks. Its first manifestations begin in the period following the Second World War. Mexican-Americans emerged from that conflict with a new determination to make their sacrifice count. No ethnic group has received a larger proportion of decorations, and few had sustained as large a share of casualties. These veterans challenged in and out of court the blatant legacy of discrimination still prevailing in the Southwest, often displayed by the glaring signs or the brutal words "No Mexicans allowed." The G.I. Bill made it possible for quite a few to obtain college degrees, better jobs, and positions of leadership....

Since then Latin America has been rediscovered south and north of the Rio Grande, following the tremors set off by the Cuban revolution. Spanish is once again a prestige language, and being bilingual somehow is no longer un-American. Then came the radiation fall-out of the Negro civil rights struggle which made even the most disillusioned Mexican-American begin to dream large dreams again. But if anyone thought the new vision borrowed from this struggle would give way to violence, there emerged in 1965 the most inspirational of all, Cesar Chavez. It is he, more than anyone else, who has contributed to LA RAZA UNIDA the mystique of the pursuit of justice through nonviolent means. His recent 24-day penitential fast was undertaken to signify the Christian determination of himself and his followers not to be driven into acts of violence by the obdurate grape-growing firms near Delano, California, which refuse to enter into contract negotiations with his fledgling union, while using every conceivable means to discredit it.

5. Are all members of LA RAZA UNIDA non-violent? The vast majority abhor violence. Indeed, one of their most persistent criticisms is that they have been the victims of too much violence, and they are sick of it.... An unbiased look at this vigorous awakening of the Mexican-American will make us realize it

"What Is La Raza?" by Jorge Lara Braud, in *La Raza Yearbook*, Sept. 1968. This document can also be found in Luis Valdez and Stan Steiner (eds.), *Aztlan: An Anthology of Mexican-American Literature* (New York: Vintage, 1972), pp. 222–224.

is a tremendous affirmation of faith in the American dream. They actually believe, unlike many other sectors, that this society is still capable of undergoing a reformation of "freedom and justice for all."

9. A Proclamation from the Indians of All Tribes, Alcatraz Island, 1969

To the Great White Father and All His People—

We, the native Americans, re-claim the land known as Alcatraz Island in the name of all American Indians by right of discovery.

We wish to be fair and honorable in our dealings with the Caucasian inhabitants of this land, and hereby offer the following treaty:

We will purchase said Alcatraz Island for twenty-four dollars (24) in glass beads and red cloth, a precedent set by the white man's purchase of a similar island about 300 years ago. We know that $24 in trade goods for these 16 acres is more than was paid when Manhattan Island was sold, but we know that land values have risen over the years. Our offer of $1.24 per acre is greater than the 47 cents per acre the white men are now paying the California Indians for their land.

We will give to the inhabitants of this island a portion of the land for their own to be held in trust by the American Indian Affairs and by the bureau of Caucasian Affairs to hold in perpetuity—for as long as the sun shall rise and the rivers go down to the sea. We will further guide the inhabitants in the proper way of living. We will offer them our religion, our education, our life-ways, in order to help them achieve our level of civilization and thus raise them and all their white brothers up from their savage and unhappy state. We offer this treaty in good faith and wish to be fair and honorable in our dealings with all white men.

We feel that this so-called Alcatraz Island is more than suitable for an Indian reservation, as determined by the white man's own standards. By this we mean that this place resembles most Indian reservations in that:

1. It is isolated from modern facilities, and without adequate means of transportation.
2. It has no fresh running water.
3. It has inadequate sanitation facilities.
4. There are no oil or mineral rights.
5. There is no industry and so unemployment is very great.
6. There are no health care facilities.
7. The soil is rocky and non-productive, and the land does not support game.
8. There are no educational facilities.
9. The population has always exceeded the land base.
10. The population has always been held as prisoners and kept dependent upon others.

Peter Blue Cloud, ed., *Alcatraz Is Not an Island*, by Indians of All Tribes (Berkeley, CA: Wingbow Press, 1972), pp. 40–42.

Further, it would be fitting and symbolic that ships from all over the world, entering the Golden Gate, would first see Indian land, and thus be reminded of the true history of this nation. This tiny island would be a symbol of the great lands once ruled by free and noble Indians....

In the name of all Indians, therefore, we re-claim this island for our Indian nations.

Signed,
Indians of All Tribes
November 1969
San Francisco, California

10. Journalist Tom Wolfe Describes the New Politics of Confrontation, 1970

When black people first started using the confrontation tactic, they made a secret discovery. There was an extra dividend to this tactic. There was a creamy dessert. It wasn't just that you registered your protest and showed the white man that you meant business and weakened his resolve to keep up the walls of oppression. It wasn't just that you got poverty money and influence. There was something sweet that happened right there on the spot. You made the white man quake. You brought *fear* into his face.

Black people began to realize for the first time that the white man, particularly the educated white man, the leadership, had a deep dark Tarzan mumbo jungle voodoo fear of the black man's masculinity. This was a revelation. For two hundred years, wherever black people lived, north or south, mothers had been raising their sons to be meek, to be mild, to check their manhood at the front door in all things that had to do with white people, for fear of incurring the wrath of the Man. The *Man* was the white man. He was the only *man*. And now, when you got him up close and growled, this all-powerful superior animal turned out to be terrified. You could read it in his face....

This was the difference between a confrontation and a demonstration. A demonstration, like the civil rights march on Washington in 1963, could frighten the white leadership, but it was a general fear, an external fear, like being afraid of a hurricane. But in a confrontation, in mau-mauing, the idea was to frighten white men personally, face to face. The idea was to separate the man from all the power and props of his office. Either he had enough heart to deal with the situation or he didn't. It was like saying, "You—yes, you right there on the platform— we're not talking about the *government*, we're not talking about the *Office of Economic Opportunity*—we're talking about *you*, you up there with your hands shaking in your pile of papers...."

That may sound like a simple case of black people being good at terrifying whites and whites being quick to run scared. But it was more than that. The

Tom Wolfe, *Radical Chic & Mau-Mauing the Flak Catchers* (Farrar, Straus and Giroux, 1970), p. 119–125. Reprinted by permission.

strange thing was that the confrontation ritual was built into the poverty program from the beginning. The poverty bureaucrats depended on confrontations in order to know what to do.

Whites were still in the dark about the ghettos. They had been studying the "urban Negro" in every way they could think of for fifteen years, but they found out they didn't know any more about the ghettos than when they started. Every time there was a riot, whites would call on "Negro leaders" to try to cool it, only to find out that the Negro leaders didn't have any followers. They sent Martin Luther King into Chicago and the people ignored him. They sent Dick Gregory into Watts and the people hooted at him and threw beer cans....

But the idea that the real leadership in the ghetto might be the *gangs* hung on with the poverty-youth-welfare establishment. It was considered a very sophisticated insight. The youth gangs weren't petty criminals ... they were "social bandits," primitive revolutionaries.... Of course, they were hidden from public view. That was why the true nature of ghetto leadership had eluded everyone for so long.... So the poverty professionals were always on the lookout for the bad-acting dudes who were the "real leaders," the "natural leaders," the "charismatic figures" in the ghetto jungle.... From the beginning the poverty program was aimed at helping ghetto people rise up against their oppressors. It was a scene in which the federal government came into the ghetto and said, "Here is some money and field advisors. Now you organize your own pressure groups." It was no accident that Huey Newton and Bobby Seale drew up the ten-point program of the Black Panther Party one night in the offices of the North Oakland Poverty Center....

By 1968 it was standard operating procedure. To get a job in the post office, you filled out forms and took the civil-service exam. To get into the poverty scene, you did some mau-mauing. If you could make the flak catchers [mid-level bureaucrats] lose control of the muscles around their mouths, if you could bring fear into their faces, your application was approved.

Ninety-nine percent of the time whites were in no physical danger whatsoever during mau-mauing. The brothers understood through and through that it was a tactic, a procedure, a game. If you actually hurt or endangered somebody at one of these sessions, you were only cutting yourself off from whatever was being handed out, the jobs, the money, the influence. The idea was to terrify but don't touch. The term *mau-mauing* itself expressed this game-like quality. It expressed the put-on side of it. In public you used the same term the whites used, namely, "confrontation." The term *mau-mauing* was a source of amusement in private. The term *mau-mauing* said, "The white man has a voodoo fear of us, because deep down he still thinks we're savages. Right? So we're going to do that Savage number for him." It was like a practical joke at the expense of the white man's superstitiousness....

11. Federal Court Defends Rights of the Retarded

PHILADELPHIA, Oct. 8—A special three-judge Federal panel ordered Pennsylvania today to provide a free public education to all retarded children in the state.

Mrs. Patricia Clapp, president of the Pennsylvania Association for Retarded Children, hailed the ruling as a "landmark" that would lead to "similar civil action in other states across the nation."

The association sued the state in a class action last January, charging that Pennsylvania unconstitutionally discriminated against retarded children by permitting school psychologists to determine whether each child was educable.

The court ruled that all are capable of benefiting from an education and have a right to one.

The panel ordered that the state identify within 90 days every retarded child not now in school and begin teaching them no later than next Sept. 1.

Dr. Gunnar Dybwad, professor of human development at the Florence Heller Graduate School of Brandeis University, who is an internationally known authority on mental retardation, applauded the decision as making Pennsylvania "the first state in the Union to guarantee education and training to all of its retarded children now and in the future."

Last May, Dr. Sidney P. Marland Jr., United States Commissioner of Education, set a goal of 1980 for providing all retarded children in the country with education.

Expert testimony in the Pennsylvania case showed that most retarded persons could achieve self-sufficiency through education and the rest could attain some degree of self-care.

About 3 percent of the school-age population in the country is retarded. Thomas Gilhool, attorney for the K. Gilhool, Pennsylvania Association for Retarded Children, estimated that about half of the retarded children in the state and 62 per cent in the country were not now receiving a public education.

The ruling overturned several sections of the state's Public School Code, including provisions that a school psychologist could relieve a school of its obligation to educate a child by finding him "uneducable and untrainable" or finding a beginner had not reached "the mental age of 5."

'Cease and Desist'

The panel ordered Pennsylvania to "cease and desist" using such provisions to deny access to a free public education for the retarded.

Terms typically used for categorizing retarded children in most states include "educable," usually for children with intelligence quotients of about 50 to 80; "trainable," 25 to 50, and 'uneducable and untrainable.'"...

Court Bids Pennsylvania Provide School for All Retarded Children, By DONALD JANSON Special to The New York Times *New York Times (1923-Current file)*; Oct 9, 1971; ProQuest Historical Newspapers The New York Times (1851–2006) pg. 1.

The Governor said it would save the taxpayers money in the long run because it would reduce the need for long-term institutionalization and in the short run because many children now would live at home and go to public schools....

The decree makes retarded children eligible for schooling from the ages of 6 to 21, and earlier in districts where others begin earlier. It prohibits any school from postponing entry, from excluding a child after the usual graduating age of 17, or from changing a child's educational assignment without notice to parents and an opportunity for a hearing.

ESSAYS

One might well ponder how and why Americans "woke up" when they did to the full implications of their nation's founding principles. Historians have examined conditions external to the South, as well as the vision and dedication of charismatic African Americans like Martin Luther King, Jr., and Malcolm X, who persevered despite the constant threat of violent death. Timothy B. Tyson of Duke University looks at the career of Robert F. Williams, who first advocated the strategy of militant resistance to white violence. Williams's viewpoint was shocking to many at the time, but Tyson argues that Williams enjoyed more support among average black southerners than is commonly assumed. Self-defense had a longer tradition in American history than the tactics of Christian pacifism advocated by Martin Luther King. Tyson's article makes readers aware of how important the role of black leadership was in breaking the logjam over civil rights. John D. Skrentny of the University of California, San Diego, takes a somewhat different tack. He argues that world events made the triumph of the American Civil Rights Movement possible. The cause that had languished since the failure of Reconstruction blossomed again as a consequence of World War II, when the United States sought, once more, to construct a new international order in the midst of calamity. Skrentny's analysis encourages readers to look at the process of historical change from the top down, as well as the bottom up.

Robert F. Williams: Change from the Bottom Up

TIMOTHY B. TYSON

"The childhood of Southerners, white and colored," Lillian Smith wrote in 1949, "has been lived on trembling earth." For one black boy in Monroe, North Carolina, the earth first shook on a Saturday morning in 1936. Standing on the sidewalk on Main Street, Robert Franklin Williams witnessed the battering of an African American woman by a white policeman. The policeman, Jesse Alexander Helms, an admirer recalled, "had the sharpest shoe in town and he didn't mind

From Timothy B. Tyson, "Robert F. Williams: 'Black Power' and the Roots of the African American Freedom Struggle," *Journal of American History*, Sept. 1998, p. 540–541, 545–546, 549–551, 556–558, 562–565, 566–570. Reprinted by permission.

using it." The police officer's son, Sen. Jesse Helms, remembered "Big Jesse" as "a six-foot, two-hundred pound gorilla. When he said, 'Smile,' I smiled." Eleven-year-old Robert Williams watched in terror as Big Jesse flattened the black woman with his fist and then arrested her. Years later, Williams described the scene: Helms "dragged her off to the nearby jailhouse, her dress up over her head, the same way that a cave man would club and drag his sexual prey." He recalled "her tortured screams as her flesh was ground away from the friction of the concrete." The memory of this violent spectacle and of the laughter of white bystanders haunted Williams. Perhaps the deferential way that African American men on the street responded was even more deeply troubling. "The emasculated black men hung their heads in shame and hurried silently from the cruelly bizarre sight," Williams recalled.

Knowledge of such scenes was as commonplace as coffee cups in the South that had recently helped to elect Franklin D. Roosevelt. For the rest of his life, Robert Williams, destined to become one of the most influential African American radicals of his time, repeated this searing story to friends, readers, listeners, reporters, and historians. He preached it from street corner ladders to eager crowds on Seventh Avenue and 125th Street in Harlem and to congregants in Malcolm X's Temple Number 7. He bore witness to its brutality in labor halls and college auditoriums across the United States. It contributed to the fervor of his widely published debate with Martin Luther King Jr. in 1960 and fueled his hesitant bids for leadership in the black freedom struggle. Its merciless truths must have tightened in his fingers on the night in 1961 when he fled a Federal Bureau of Investigation (FBI) dragnet with his wife and two small children, a machine gun slung over one shoulder....

The life of Robert F. Williams illustrates that "the civil rights movement" and "the Black Power movement," often portrayed in very different terms, grew out of the same soil, confronted the same predicaments, and reflected the same quest for African American freedom. In fact, virtually all of the elements that we associate with "Black Power" were already present in the small towns and rural communities of the South where "the civil rights movement" was born. The story of Robert F. Williams reveals that independent black political action, black cultural pride, and what Williams called "armed self-reliance" operated in the South in tension and in tandem with legal efforts and nonviolent protest....

Student Nonviolent Coordinating Committee (SNCC) organizers knew better than to push nonviolence on reluctant black southerners. In 1955 a black women's newsletter published in Jackson, Mississippi, announced that since "no law enforcement body in ignorant Miss. will protect any Negro who has membership in the NAACP," "the Negro must protect himself." The editors warned "the white hoodlums who are now parading around the premises" that the editors were "protected by armed guard." SNCC's Charles Cobb observed, "In terms of the organizing ... you didn't go to the plantations, you didn't go to these towns and somehow enter into a discussion of violence and nonviolence." When white terrorists attacked the home of Hartman Turnbow, a local black farmer and SNCC stalwart in Holmes County, Mississippi, Cobb recalled, Turnbow "pushed his family out the back door and grabbed the rifle off the wall and started shooting. And his explanation was simply that, 'I was not being,' as he said, 'non-nonviolent, I was protecting my wife and family.'" Even Bob Moses, who was as deeply identified with philosophical nonviolence as anyone in the freedom movement, acknowledged how much his convictions violated the mores among those SNCC sought to organize. "Self-defense is so deeply engrained in rural southern America," Moses told SNCC volunteers in 1964, "that we as a small group can't effect it."

The tradition, rooted in the unforgettable experiences of slave resistance and Reconstruction militancy, had survived what Rayford Whittingham Logan called "the nadir" of African American life. After an 1892 triple lynching in Memphis, for example, the black editor Ida B. Wells "determined to sell my life as dearly as possible," she wrote; she urged other black southerners to do the same. "When the white man … knows he runs as great a risk of biting the dust every time his Afro-American victim does," Wells insisted, "he would have a greater respect for Afro-American life." When white mobs raged through the streets of Atlanta in 1906, W. E. B. Du Bois hastened home to defend his wife and family. "I bought a Winchester double-barreled shotgun and two dozen rounds of shells filled with buckshot," he wrote later….

This sensibility was not foreign to Martin Luther King Jr. nor to other members of his generation of black southerners. Glenn Smiley, who visited King's home on behalf of the Fellowship of Reconciliation in 1956, wrote back that "the place is an arsenal" and that King had armed guards. Probably the most crucial local ally of SNCC's campaigns in Mississippi, Amzie Moore, "like most politically active Blacks in Mississippi," Charles Payne writes, "often carried a gun. His home was well armed, and at night the area around his house may have been the best-lit spot in Cleveland."… Among the few historians who have explored his story, only John Dittmer summons the clarity to note that Williams's military service, his NAACP affiliation, and his willingness to defend home, family, and community by force if necessary made him "*typical* of the generation of southern blacks who launched the civil rights movement in the 1950s."

Upon his return to Monroe in 1955 [following service in both the army and marines], Williams joined both the local branch of the NAACP and a mostly white Unitarian fellowship. In a Sunday sermon delivered to his fellow Unitarians in 1956, Williams hailed the Montgomery, Alabama, bus boycott and celebrated what he called "the patriots of passive revolution."… Invoking "the spirit of Concord, Lexington and Valley Forge," Williams declared from the pulpit that, as he put it, "the liberty bell peals once more and the Stars and Stripes shall wave forever."

The atmosphere at the Monroe NAACP was less exuberant. In the wake of the *Brown v. Board of Education* decision and the triumph at Montgomery, Ku Klux Klan rallies near Monroe began to draw crowds as big as fifteen thousand. Dynamite attacks on black activists in the area were common and lesser acts of terror routine. "The echo of shots and dynamite blasts," the editors of the freedom movement journal the *Southern Patriot* wrote in 1957, "has been almost continuous throughout the South." The Monroe NAACP dwindled to six members, who then contemplated disbanding. When the newest member objected to dissolution, the departing membership chose him to lead the chapter. "They elected me president," Robert Williams recalled, "and then they all left."

Finding himself virtually a one-man NAACP chapter, Williams turned first to the black veterans with whom he had stood against the Klan…. Another veteran, the physician Dr. Albert E. Perry Jr., became vice-president. Finding it "necessary to visit homes and appeal directly to individuals," Williams informed the national office, he painstakingly recruited from the beauty parlors, pool halls, and street corners, building a cadre of some two hundred members by 1959. The largest group of new recruits were African American women who worked as domestics. The Monroe branch of the NAACP became "the only one of its kind in existence," the novelist Julian Mayfield, a key supporter of Williams in Harlem's black Left, wrote in *Commentary* in 1961. "Its members and supporters, who are mostly workers and displaced farmers, constitute a well-armed and disciplined fighting unit." The branch became "unique in the whole NAACP because of a working class composition and a leadership that was not middle class," Williams later wrote. "Most important, we had a strong representation of black veterans who didn't scare easily."

In response to the drownings of several local African American children whom segregation had forced to swim in isolated farm ponds, the Monroe NAACP launched a campaign to desegregate the local tax-supported swimming pool in 1957. Harry Golden, a prominent Jewish liberal from nearby Charlotte, observed that the specter of interracial sexuality "haunts every mention of the race question" and thought it "naive" of Williams to "experiment with the crude emotions of a small Southern agricultural community." Not surprisingly, the Ku Klux Klan blamed the affluent Dr. Perry for the resurgent black activism and a large, heavily armed Klan motorcade attacked Dr. Perry's house one night that summer. Black veterans greeted the night riders with sandbag fortifications and a hail of disciplined gunfire. The Monroe Board of Aldermen immediately passed an ordinance banning Ku Klux Klan motorcades, a measure they had refused to consider before the gun battle.

When Williams and the other black veterans organized self-defense networks, black women insisted that the men teach them to shoot. But for black men as well as white men, the rhetoric of protecting women was fraught with the politics of controlling women. Williams recalled that the women "had volunteered, and they wanted to fight. But we kept them out of most of it." Nevertheless, African American women who labored as domestics played crucial roles as gatherers of intelligence. They also worked the telephones and delivered the weekly newsletter, Williams acknowledged. But it was not easy to confine women to these roles. When police arrested Dr. Perry on trumped-up charges of "criminal abortion on a white woman," dozens of black citizens, most of them women, armed themselves and crowded into the police station. *Jet* magazine reported that the women "surged against the doors, fingering their guns and knives until Perry was produced." In short, black women both deployed and defied gender stereotypes–demanding of black men, in effect. "Why aren't you protecting us?"—even though they overturned such stereotypes in their daily lives.…

In 1959, two pressing local matters brought Robert Williams and a crowd of black women to the Union County courthouse. B. F. Shaw, a white railroad engineer, was charged with attacking an African American maid at the Hotel Monroe. Another inflammatory case was slated for trial the same day. Lewis Medlin, a white mechanic, was accused of having beaten and sexually assaulted Mary Ruth Reid, a pregnant black woman, in the presence of her five children. According to Williams, Reid's brothers and several of the black women of the Monroe NAACP had urged that the new machine guns be tried out on Medlin before his trial. "I told them that this matter would be handled through the law and the NAACP would help," Williams recalled, "that we would be as bad as the white people if we resorted to violence."

The proceedings against the two white men compelled Williams to reconsider his assessment. The judge dropped the charges against Shaw although he had failed even to appear in court. During the brief trial of Medlin, his attorney argued that he had been "drunk and having a little fun" at the time of the assault. Further, Medlin was married, his lawyer told the jury, "to a lovely white woman ... the pure flower of life ... do you think he would have left this pure flower for *that?*" He gestured toward Mary Ruth Reid, who began to cry uncontrollably. Lewis Medlin was acquitted in minutes. Robert Williams recalled that "the [black] women in the courtroom made such an outcry, the judge had to send Medlin out the rear door." The women then turned on Williams and bitterly shamed him for failing to see to their protection.

At this burning moment of anger and humiliation, Williams turned to wire service reporters and declared that it was time to "meet violence with violence." Black citizens unable to enlist the support of the courts must defend themselves. "Since the federal government will not stop lynching, and since the so-called courts lynch our people legally," he declared, "if it's necessary to stop lynching with lynching, then we must resort to that method." The next day, however, Williams disavowed the reference to lynching. "I do not mean that Negroes should go out and attempt to get revenge for mistreatments or injustice," he said, "but it is clear that there is no Fourteenth or Fifteenth Amendment nor court protection of Negroes' rights here, and Negroes have to defend themselves on the spot when they are attacked by whites."

Banner headlines flagged these words as symbols of "a new militancy among young Negroes of the South." Enemies of the NAACP blamed this "bloodthirsty remark" squarely on the national office. "High officials of the organization may speak in cultivated accents and dress like Wall Street lawyers," Thomas Waring of the *Charleston News and Courier* charged, "but they are engaged in a revolutionary enterprise." That very morning, when he read the words "meet violence with violence" in a United Press International (UPI) dispatch, Roy Wilkins telephoned Robert Williams to inform him that he had been removed from his post as president of the Monroe NAACP.

That summer of 1959, the fiftieth anniversary convention of the NAACP presented a highly public show trial whose central issue was whether the national organization would ratify Wilkins's suspension of Robert Williams. The national office printed a pamphlet, *The Single Issue in the Robert Williams Case,* and distributed it to all delegates. As part of the coordinated effort to crush Williams, Thurgood Marshall visited the New York offices of the FBI on June 4, 1959, and urged agents to investigate Williams "in connection with [Marshall's] efforts to combat communist attempts to infiltrate the NAACP," an FBI memorandum stated. Wilkins twisted every available arm. Gov. Nelson Rockefeller, in an unmistakable reference to the whisper campaign to discredit Williams, took the podium to congratulate the NAACP for "rejecting retaliation against terror" and "repulsing the threat of communism to invade your ranks." Daisy Bates, the pistol-packing heroine of Little Rock, agreed to denounce Williams for advocating self-defense—after the national office consented to buy six hundred dollars a month in "advertising" from her newspaper. "The national office not only controlled the platform," Louis Lomax wrote, but "they subjected the Williams forces to a heavy bombardment from the NAACP's big guns." Forty speakers, including Bates, King, Jackie Robinson, and dozens of distinguished lawyers, rose one after the other to denounce Williams. But when the burly ex-Marine from Monroe finally strode down the aisle to speak, he was neither intimidated nor penitent.

"There is no Fourteenth Amendment in this social jungle called Dixie," Williams declared. "There is no equal protection under the law." He had been angry, they all knew, trials had beset him, but never had he intended to advocate acts of war. Surely no one believed that. But if the black men of Poplarville, Mississippi, had banded together to guard the jail the night that Mack Parker was lynched, he said, that would not have hurt the cause of justice. If the young black men who escorted the co-ed who was raped in Tallahassee had been able to defend her, Williams reminded them, such action would have been legal and justified "even if it meant that they themselves or the white rapists were killed." "Please," he besought the assembly, "I ask you not to come crawling to these whites on your hands and knees and make me a sacrificial lamb."

And there the pleading stopped. Perhaps the spirit of his grandfather, Sikes Williams, the former slave who had fought for interracial democracy and wielded a rifle against white terrorists, rose up within him. Perhaps he heard within himself the voice of his grandmother, who had entrusted that rifle to young Robert. "We as men should stand up as men and protect our women and children," Williams declared. "I am a man and I will walk upright as a man should. I WILL NOT CRAWL." In a controversy that the *Durham Carolina Times* called "the biggest civil rights story of the year," the NAACP convention voted to uphold the suspension of Robert Williams....

"The great debate in the integration movement in recent months," Anne Braden of the Southern Conference Educational Fund wrote in late 1959, "has been the question of violence vs. nonviolence as instruments of change."...

More than the persuasive skills of their elders, the bold actions of African American college students set these philosophical debates aside and gave the battalions of nonviolence their brief but compelling historical moment. On February 1, 1960, four students from North Carolina Agricultural and Technical College walked into Woolworth's in Greensboro, sat down at a segregated lunch counter, and asked to be served. Within two months, the sit-ins had spread to fifty-four communities across nine states of the old Confederacy, infusing the freedom movement with fresh troops and new tactics. "Only in 1960, when black students entered the fray in large numbers, did a broad assault on segregation become possible," Adam Fairclough points out. "Young people made up the initial phalanx, the entering wedge." King flew to Durham, North Carolina, on February 16 to encourage the students with a speech, telling them that their protest was "destined to be one of the glowing epics of our time." He returned to Atlanta the following day. "While others were pioneering innovative methods of nonviolent direct action," Fairclough observes, "King seemed strangely ambivalent about embracing the new tactics by personal example. Although fulsome in his praise of the lunch counter protests, for example, he showed little interest to lead a sit-in himself."

On March 1, by contrast, Robert Williams followed a dozen black youths into Gamble's Drug Store in downtown Monroe and was the only person arrested. Marched down the street in handcuffs, a shotgun-toting guard on either side of him, Williams spoofed himself as "the dangerous stool-sitter bandit" and vowed that he had "never felt prouder in my life." Young insurgents in Monroe mounted an aggressive campaign of sit-ins that displayed its own unique style. "The Negroes remained in each store only a short time," the *Charlotte Observer* reported, "usually until management closed the counters." Under court orders to abide by the law or face imprisonment, Williams defied the judge and marched with his young troops. "We're using hit-and-run tactics," Williams told reporters. "They never know when we're coming or when we're going to leave. That way we hope to wear them down," he said, managing to sound like a platoon leader even while participating in a passive resistance campaign. "They were always doing something," the manager of Jones Drug Store recalled. "It's a wonder somebody didn't kill him." It was no mystery to Williams; the main difference between sit-ins in Monroe and elsewhere was that "not a single demonstrator was even spat upon during our sit-ins," Williams claimed.

The uneasy peace in Monroe would soon be broken, in large measure by followers of Dr. King. In 1961, Rev. Paul Brooks, an activist in the Nashville student movement investigating for SCLC, and James Forman, soon to become president of SNCC, came to Monroe in the company of seventeen Freedom Riders fresh out of jail in Jackson, Mississippi....

Two weeks of picketing at the Union County Courthouse grew progressively more perilous for the Freedom Riders. Crowds of hostile white onlookers grew larger and larger. Finally, on Sunday afternoon, August 28, a mob of several thousand furious white people attacked the approximately thirty demonstrators, badly injuring many of them; local police arrested the bleeding protesters. In his classic memoir, *The Making of Black Revolutionaries*, James Forman later called this riot his "moment of death," "a nightmare I shall never forget." To the consternation of SCLC, the nonviolent crusade swiftly deteriorated into mob violence; throughout the community, white vigilantes attacked black citizens and even fired fifteen shots into the home of the former mayor J. Ray Shute, a white moderate who had befriended Williams.

At the height of this violent chaos, a white married couple, for reasons that are unclear, entered the black community and drove straight into an angry black mob milling near Robert Williams's house. "There was hundreds of niggers there," the white woman stated, "and they were armed, they were ready for war." Black residents, under the impression that the demonstrators downtown were being beaten and perhaps slaughtered, threatened to kill the white couple. Williams, though busy preparing to defend his home, rescued the two whites from the mob and led them into his house, where they remained for about two hours. White authorities later charged Williams and several other people with kidnapping, although the white couple met two police officers on their way home and did not report their alleged abduction. The woman later conceded that "at the time, I wasn't even thinking about being kidnapped ... the papers, the publicity and all that stuff was what brought in that kidnapping mess." During a long night of racial terror, Williams slung a machine gun over his shoulder and walked several miles with his wife and two small sons to where Julian Mayfield waited with a car. "I didn't want those racist dogs to have the satisfaction of legally lynching me," he explained to Dr. Perry.

The Williams family fled first to New York City, then Canada, then on to Cuba to escape the hordes of FBI agents who combed the countryside in search of them. Supporters of Williams gloried in the escape. Some black residents of Monroe still maintain that Fidel Castro sent helicopters for Williams. Others tell of how he got away in a hearse owned by a black funeral director from Charlotte. An agent assigned to search for Williams locally reported his frustrations to FBI director Hoover: "Subject has become something of a 'John Brown' to Negroes around Monroe and they will do anything for him."

The FBI dragnet never snared Williams, but it did not take [FBI Director J. Edgar] Hoover long to hear from him. Every Friday night from eleven to midnight on Radio Havana, Williams hosted *Radio Free Dixie*, a program that from 1961 to 1964 could be heard as far away as New York and Los Angeles. KPFA Radio in Berkeley and WBAI in New York City occasionally rebroadcast the show, and bootleg tapes of the program circulated in Watts and Harlem....

As black activists began to reject even the tactical pretense of nonviolence, the influence of Robert Williams continued to spread. By spring 1962 "the example of the North Carolina militant," August Meier and Elliott Rudwick observe, had "had a profound effect" within the Congress of Racial Equality (CORE). "Armed self-defense is a fact of life in black communities—north and south—despite the pronouncements of the 'leadership,'" a North Carolina activist wrote to Williams. Long before Stokely Carmichael and Willie Ricks led the chants of "Black Power" that riveted national media attention in the summer of 1966, most elements invoked by that ambiguous slogan were already in place. "Your doctrine of self-defense set the stage for the acceptance of the Deacons For Defense and Justice," Lawrence Henry told Williams in the spring of 1966. "As quiet as it is being kept, the Black man is swinging away from King and adopting your tit-for-tat philosophy."

Williams's influence was not limited to the South. "As I am certain you realize," Richard Gibson, editor of *Now!* magazine in New York, wrote to

Williams in 1965, "Malcolm's removal from the scene [by assassination] makes you the senior spokesman for Afro-American militants." *Life* magazine reported in 1966 that Williams's "picture is prominently displayed in extremist haunts in the big city ghettos." Clayborne Carson names Williams as one of two central influences–the other being Malcolm X–on the 1966 formation of the Black Panther Party for Self-Defense in Oakland, "the most widely known black militant political organization of the late 1960s."

Even though he became friends with Che Guevara and Fidel Castro himself, Williams grew uneasy in Cuba; he yearned to return home. As the Soviet strings on the Cuban revolution shortened, Williams resisted pressure to make his own politics conform to the Soviet line. As early as 1962, when Williams had been in Cuba for less than a year, an FBI informant stated that Williams had "stubbed his toes" with Cuban Communists through his "criticism of [the] Communist Party for barring Negroes from leadership" and that he "may not be able to regain his footing."... Williams persuaded Castro to let him travel to North Vietnam in 1964, where he swapped Harlem stories with Ho Chi Minh and wrote antiwar propaganda aimed at African American soldiers. In 1965 the Williams family relocated to Beijing, where Williams was "lionized and feted by top Peking leaders," according to CIA intelligence reports. The Williams family dined with Mao Zedong and moved in the highest circles of the Chinese government for three years....

In the late 1960s, when the Nixon administration moved toward opening diplomatic relations with China, Williams bartered his almost exclusive knowledge of the Chinese government for safe passage home and a Ford Foundation–sponsored post at the Center for Chinese Studies at the University of Michigan....

The life of Robert Williams underlines many aspects of the ongoing black freedom struggle–the decisive racial significance of World War II, the impact of the Cold War on the black freedom struggle, the centrality of questions of sexuality and gender in racial politics, and the historical presence of a revolutionary Caribbean. But foremost it testifies to the extent to which, throughout World War II and the postwar years, there existed among African Americans a current of militancy—a current that included the willingness to defend home and community by force.

The Minority Rights Revolution: Top Down and Bottom Up

JOHN D. SKRENTNY

On January 6, 1969, Senator Barry Goldwater, Republican of Arizona, sent a letter to the new presidential administration of Richard M. Nixon. Goldwater personified the right wing of the Republican Party, argued passionately for limited government, and had previously written a book entitled *The Conscience of a*

Reprinted by permission of the publisher from *The Minority Rights Revolution* by John D. Skrentny. pp. 1–5, 7–9, 11–12, 19–21, 25–26, 31, 33, 35–37, 39–40, 49, 51–52, 57, Cambridge, MA: The Belknap Press of Harvard University Press. Copyright © 2002 by the President and Fellows of Harvard College.

Conservative. He had also famously stuck to his principles and voted against the Civil Rights Act of 1964, the landmark law that ended racial segregation. On this day, however, Goldwater offered a lesson in political savvy for dealing with a disadvantaged group. The senator reminded the new administration that Nixon had promised a White House conference on Mexican American issues during his campaign, and that Nixon wanted to have "Mexicans" serve in his administration. Goldwater explained that this group preferred to be called "Mexican-Americans" and that the administration should avoid referring to them as Latin American—save that term for South America, coached Goldwater. The White House conference should occur "at the earliest possible time because these people are watching us to see if we will treat them the way the Democrats have." He reminded them that New York was the largest Spanish-speaking city in the United States and that nationwide there were 6 million in this category. "You will hear a lot on this subject from me," the strident states' rights conservative warned, "so the faster you move, the less bother I will be."

A few years later, Robert H. Bork, who would become a famously right-leaning federal judge and author of the 1996 book *Slouching towards Gomorrah: Modern Liberalism and American Decline*, also promoted the cause of federal recognition of disadvantaged groups. In 1974, Bork was Nixon's solicitor general, and in that year co-authored a brief to the Supreme Court arguing that the failure to provide special language education for immigrant children was racial discrimination, according to both the Constitution and the Civil Rights Act of 1964. The Supreme Court agreed with the statutory argument, though it did not wish to go as far as Bork and create constitutional language rights in schools.

Goldwater and Bork were not alone in promoting rights for minorities. The 1965–75 period was a minority rights revolution. After the mass mobilization and watershed events of the black civil rights movement, this later revolution was led by the Establishment. It was a bipartisan project, including from both parties liberals and conservatives—though it was hard to tell the difference. Presidents, the Congress, bureaucracies, and the courts all played important roles. In the signature minority rights policy, affirmative action, the federal government went beyond African Americans and declared that certain groups were indeed "minorities"—an undefined term embraced by policymakers, advocates, and activists alike—and needed new rights and programs for equal opportunity and full citizenship. In the parlance of the period, minorities were groups seen as "disadvantaged" but not defined by income or education. African Americans were the paradigmatic minority, but there were three other ethnoracial minorities: Latinos, Asian Americans, and American Indians. Immigrants, women, and the disabled of all ethnic groups were also included and won new rights during this revolutionary period.

Bipartisanship was not the only notable aspect of the minority rights revolution. Consider also the *speed* of the development of its laws and regulations. While they appeared to have global momentum on their side, it still took two decades from the first proposition in 1941 that blacks be ensured nondiscrimination in employment to the law (Title VII of the Civil Rights Act of 1964) guaranteeing that right. Similarly, it took about twenty years between the first efforts to allow expanded immigration from outside northern and western Europe and the Immigration Act of 1965, ending all national origin discrimination in immigration. Following these landmarks, however, the government passed other laws and regulations almost immediately after first proposal. In most cases, it took only a few years to have a new law passed and there was little lobbying pressure. Bilingual education for Latinos, equal rights for women in education, and equal rights for the disabled all became law within two years of first proposal. Affirmative action expanded beyond blacks almost immediately. Such rapid success in American politics is rare. It is especially rare when achieved by groups that were defined precisely by their powerlessness and disadvantage in American society.

The rapidity and ease of the minority rights revolution brings up another puzzle. If minority rights were so easy to establish, why were not more groups included? For example, government officials perceived eastern and southern European Americans (Italians, Poles, Jews, Greeks, etc.) to be discriminated against, economically disadvantaged, or both. These "white ethnics" also had strong advocates. Yet they were never made the subjects of special policies for aid, protection, or preference. Despite widespread perceptions of their oppression, gays and lesbians similarly failed to gain a federal foothold in the minority rights revolution. Some members of Congress first submitted a bill to protect Americans from discrimination on the basis of sexual orientation in 1974. There still is no law ensuring this protection.

Another curious aspect of this minority rights revolution is that the 1960s recognition of the right to be free from discrimination was not just an American phenomenon. Nondiscrimination was quite suddenly a *world* right, a *human* right. That is, the United States was anything but alone in its recognition of minority rights. Consider the dates of major American minority-rights developments and United Nations conventions and covenants guaranteeing human-rights protections. Though usually (and notoriously) unperturbed by world trends, Americans were guaranteeing nondiscrimination and other rights at the same time that much of the world was coming to a formal consensus on these same issues. Was it just a coincidence that America and many other nations traveled on parallel paths? Moreover, was it happenstance that Africans and Asians simultaneously threw off the yoke of colonialism and their new nations joined the UN while American citizens of third-world ancestry also gained more control of their destinies?

The minority rights revolution is not only an intellectual puzzle. It was an event of enormous significance. It shaped our current understanding of American citizenship, which is more inclusive than ever before, while also drawing lines of difference between Americans. It was a major part of the development of the American regulatory state, later decried by those same conservatives who joined with liberals in building it up. And it offers a unique look at American democracy. When the stars and planets line up in just the right way, politicians, bureaucrats, and judges can offer a range of efforts to help disadvantaged Americans— even if those Americans did not ask for them....

Readers will almost certainly expect a book on the spread of minority rights in the 1960s and 1970s to be a study of social movements. The image that comes to most Americans' minds when they think of the period is angry protest—radical blacks, feminists, and Latinos shouting slogans, a white ethnic "backlash," newly assertive disabled and gay people, all joining Vietnam War protesters in creating a climate of upheaval. These images exist because there was, of course, a very large amount of social-movement activity. One account of the minority rights revolution might therefore emphasize the role of grassroots mobilizing....

Much of what I describe does not contradict this model. But a social-movement approach also leaves many questions unanswered. Most important, because social-movement theories are mostly about the emergence of social movements, they offer little guidance on the outcomes of social movements or the *content* of reforms. Second, they cannot explain why some groups during the same time period had to exert more pressure than others, some did not have to lobby at all, and still others failed completely despite lobbying and pressure. Why are "opportunistic politicians" so selective? Groups representing white ethnics and gays and lesbians found little and no success, respectively, during the revolution. Latinos succeeded marvelously despite small numbers, weak organization, and inconsistent demands. Women, who had better organization than Latino groups and ostensibly promised greater votes to opportunistic politicians, struggled for some of their new rights. A movement seeking rights for the disabled did not exist when the first disabled-rights law was passed....

The minority rights revolution could not have occurred without the prior world battle against the Nazis and Japanese and the Cold War struggle with the Soviet Union. World War II and especially the Cold War's broadly defined "national security" policy had important legacies in domestic politics. In some ways this was direct and obvious: the perceived need for national security led to great investment in the means of warfare, driving a large part of the economy and building up firms that created weapons and other equipment. But there were other, more far-reaching effects.

During this dynamic period, war threats were staggering and horrifying, and national security prompted policies that included everything from education to highways to racial and ethnic equality. The latter became part of national security because American strategy in World War II set in motion the creation of global human-rights norms that gave a cause for the Allies and a structure to the later Cold War struggle with the Soviet Union. World War II marked the beginning of an unprecedented global cultural integration and the establishment of a global public sphere, held together by the UN and a few basic premises. The sanctity of human rights was one. At the top of the rights list was nondiscrimination. Race or ethnic discrimination, especially when practiced by those of European ancestry, was wrong. In short, geopolitical developments set into motion a dynamic where policies defined as furthering the goal of national security by fighting Nazism or global communism—including equal rights policies—found bipartisan support and rapid change in political fortunes.

The legacies of black civil rights policy were complex and varied. One important legacy was the creation of new "institutional homes" (to borrow Chris Bonastia's term) for rights advocates to have positions of real policymaking power. Most important here were the Equal Employment Opportunity Commission (EEOC), the Department of Health, Education and Welfare's Office for Civil Rights, and the Department of Labor's Office of Federal Contract Compliance. All were created to enforce rights laws for blacks, and all attracted employees who supported equal-opportunity rights....

Other policy legacies of the black civil rights movement were more cultural in character, though equally important. The Civil Rights Act of 1964, as well as other efforts to help blacks, created a tool kit or repertoire of policy models that could be extended again and again and adapted to deal with the problems of groups other than black Americans. Through their own initiative, or when pressured by nonblack minority advocates, civil-rights bureaucrats responded with affirmative action—regardless of the specific demands of the minority advocates. Policymakers sometimes simply anticipated what minority constituents wanted. They created an "anticipatory politics" based on these policy tools and the new legitimacy of minority targeting. Activist members of Congress used the Civil Rights Act's Title VI, barring federal funds for any program that discriminated on the basis race, national origin, or religion, as part of a policy repertoire when seeking votes or social movement goals. Congress thus created Title IX of the Education Amendments of 1972, barring sex discrimination on the part of educational institutions receiving federal funds, and Section 504 of the Rehabilitation Act of 1973, which addressed discrimination on the basis of disability also by using the Civil Rights Act model....

... To attract support for the Allied side during World War II, President Franklin Delano Roosevelt strongly promoted the United States as a symbol of human rights and race equality. These efforts then invited first the Axis and then the Soviet Union's propaganda strategies highlighting American racism and ethnic inequality. Especially with the parts of government aware of this propaganda and engaged with foreign audiences, specifically presidents and State Department officials, there was a rapid recategorization of domestic nondiscrimination as part of foreign policy and national security. This is apparent in both Democratic and Republican administrations. Comprehensive policy change, however, required convincing Congress and the American public, and both government leaders and rights groups actively promoted the meaning of nondiscrimination as national security. Change was incremental and needed mass mobilization for black civil rights and lobbying campaigns for immigration reform before breakthrough victories finally came in the mid-1960s.

Other rights could not be categorized as easily as national security. Women, for example, made few gains because gender was not a dividing principle in geopolitics as was race. Gender equality was not a part of Nazi, Japanese, or Communist propaganda and therefore served no national security interest. Social rights and welfare state development similarly did not become part of national security policy, even during the Cold War when America confronted an ideology based on economic egalitarianism. This was in part because many business and professional interest groups and Republican party leaders could quite plausibly argue that excessive interference with the market economy and market-based wealth distributions would push America *toward* socialism, rather than save it from this threat.

This was not only a matter of simple voting power, lobbying, or protest strength. Success and the speed at which it was achieved in the minority rights revolution depended greatly on the meaning of the group in question. After advocates for black Americans helped break the taboo on targeting policy at disadvantaged groups, government officials quickly categorized some groups as "minorities"—a never-defined term that basically meant "analogous to blacks." These classifications were *not* based on study, but on simple, unexamined proto-types of groups. Most obviously, government officials saw the complex category of Latinos (then usually called "Spanish-surnamed" or "Spanish-speaking") in terms of a simple racial prototype, obscuring the fact that many Latinos consider themselves white. Racialized in this way, Latinos needed little lobbying to win minority rights. Women, who faced ridicule like no other group, needed signif-icant meaning entrepreneurship. Their advocates pushed hard to make the black analogy. Though Asian Americans presumably possessed a clearer group racial definition that did Latinos, the analogy between Asians and blacks was weaker than that between Latinos and blacks. Policymakers sometimes dropped Asian Americans from their lists. This was apparently just a cognitive forgetting—it required only small reminders for them to be included in minority policy, at least formally....

Two cases of the failure of the minority rights revolution highlight the importance of group meanings in shaping its limits. First, white ethnics, or the immigrants from eastern and southern Europe and their descendants, organized for action and were recognized as a disadvantaged and important political con-stituency. They nevertheless did not gain policy recognition and remained cate-gorized outside the minority rights revolution. Ethnic rights failed primarily because the meaning perceived in white ethnics as a group. On the one hand, government officials did not see ethnics as being within a threshold of oppression or victimhood that while unspoken, undebated, and unlegislated, nevertheless powerfully shaped policy. Additionally, politicians saw ethnics in multifaceted ways—as ethnic minorities, but also as Catholics, union members, and anti-Communists. These different perceived identities sent policy appeals off in direc-tions other than those derived from black rights. Second, gays and lesbians, though undeniably discriminated against, victimized, oppressed, and newly or-ganized for power, also were left out of the rights revolution during the 1965 to 1975 because of the meaning of homosexuality. The analogy with blacks again hit a wall: this group was different—too different. The basis of group difference—same-gender sexual attractions—remained taboo as a target of pro-tective policy recognition, and gay rights bills in Congress went nowhere....

Shortly before the passage of the Civil Rights Act of 1964, the Republican Senate minority leader, Everett Dirksen of Illinois, said he finally supported equal rights for blacks. He explained, "No army is stronger than an idea whose time has come." Dirksen was right. Any resistance to federally guaranteed black civil rights by a national political leader was anachronistic. The following year, Congress passed the Voting Rights Act, giving African Americans in the southern states the right to vote, and the Immigration Act, ending decades of discrimination against Asians and eastern and southern Europeans in their ability to come to the United States.

But why were federally guaranteed nondiscrimination rights such a powerful idea? The brilliant strategies and sacrifices of the black civil rights movement were certainly part of the story, as was their growing political strength in conventional electoral politics. These factors cannot explain, however, the establishment of immigration and naturalization rights for Asians, who had little political clout and no major lobbying or protest activities. Moreover, racial supremacy and blatant racial discrimination were anachronisms the world over, not just in the United States. This was not a coincidence. The development of minority rights in the United States was connected to their development elsewhere in the world....

Roosevelt died in 1944 but his vision of human rights lived on in the Truman administration. Various nongovernmental organizations—notably, black civil-rights groups—played a crucial role in keeping the commitment to equal rights part of the world order. At the founding UN meeting in San Francisco, black leaders such as the NAACP's W. E. B. Du Bois and Walter White lobbied for the inclusion of a bill of human rights, as they "huddled constantly" with officials from such diverse countries as the United States, France, the Philippines, Haiti, and Liberia. They sought to equally benefit both non-American nonwhite people and their fellow citizens. Du Bois and White saw these fates as linked. For example, Du Bois told the *San Francisco Chronicle* that the world's colonies were similar to "slums," and explained that a world bill of rights would hold all nations accountable for their discriminatory treatment of human beings. The historian Brenda Gayle Plummer credits these efforts with getting "human rights" mentioned in the official UN charter....

Another result was a commitment to produce a universal declaration of human rights. In 1946, President Harry Truman appointed Eleanor Roosevelt to represent the United States and chair a new UN Commission on Human Rights charged with creating the declaration. Despite conflicts (the Soviet Union was concerned by the inclusion of French- and Anglo-American-style liberties, and the State Department opposed the inclusion of socialist-style social or economic rights, such as a right to employment and health care), the UN ratified the declaration of December 10, 1948. Though unenforceable, this was a grand statement of world wide moral principles....

Government advocates for civil rights used links between world opinion and national security in propaganda aimed at American citizens. The strategy was to get Americans to think of the global audience and the different policies that could help in the fight against Communism. Truman's President's Committee on Civil Rights used this strategy prominently in its high-profile report, *To Secure These Rights*. After detailing the various rights being denied to blacks, the report concluded with justifications for federal action, including the "moral reason," the "economic reason," and the "international reason." Here the report explained that "our position in the postwar world is so vital to the future that our smallest actions have far-reaching effects." The report concluded, "The United States is not so strong, the final triumph of the democratic ideal is not so inevitable that we can ignore what the world thinks of us or our record."

National-security meanings also shaped campaign strategy and political speeches at home that discussed civil rights. Nongovernmental groups representing business and religious faiths argued for the same recategorization. The Advertising Council had embarked on a publicity campaign entitled "'United America' (Group Prejudice is a Post-War Menace)" designed to encourage Americans to respect human rights. The Institute for Religious and Social Studies—a graduate school created at the Jewish Theological Seminary of America, but which united Jewish, Catholic, and Protestant scholars—published lectures in a 1949 series called *Discrimination and National Welfare*. Leading scholars such as the sociologist Robert K. Merton as well as political activists such as Roger Baldwin of the ACLU and Adolph A. Berle, a leading member of the Roosevelt administration's "brains trust," contributed to the collected lectures. Readers encountered reasoned arguments that mostly stressed the cost of discrimination in terms of business, foreign policy, and national security....

More so than during the Truman presidency, the Eisenhower years and those following saw violent civil-rights conflicts that would provide the USSR with its most powerful propaganda—photographic evidence of American racial injustice. Especially worrisome were photos of southern repression of civil-rights demonstrations that filled the pages of the world's newspapers. [Mary] Dudziak has written, for example, of Eisenhower's great distress regarding the international consequences of his order to send troops into Little Rock, Arkansas, when disorder and violence threatened to engulf efforts at school desegregation. In recounting the incident in his memoirs and in private communications, Eisenhower revealed how he construed the crises in terms of national security and the moral boundaries then taken for granted in the UN....

Throughout the early 1960s, civil-rights leaders continued their effective strategy of directing world attention to black inequality and linking black civil rights to national security. They traveled to Africa and seized opportunities in the UN. Martin Luther King Jr. encouraged the nation to think globally, often stressing the links between the struggles of black people in the United States to those in Africa. And any time civil-rights leaders met white repression, the story made international headlines....

In this domestic and international context, and with domestic public opinion supporting civil rights at an all-time high, Kennedy sent legislation (later to become the Civil Rights Act of 1964) to Congress. Fearing more racial violence, he worked behind the scenes meeting with business leaders and other elites in an attempt to gain control of the racial situation. In a July 11, 1963 meeting with approximately seventy members of the Business Council, Kennedy, Vice President Lyndon Johnson, Attorney General Robert Kennedy, and Secretary of State Dean Rusk all urged these business leaders to help by employing more black Americans....

Lyndon Johnson presided over great propaganda triumphs for the global image of the United States. His time in office saw the Civil Rights Act of 1964, the Voting Rights Act of 1965, and the Civil Rights Act of 1968 (for equal rights in housing)—all crowning jewels of the black civil rights movement....

One difficulty with assessing the impact of war and geopolitics on minority rights is that in the case most often studied, that of black Americans, the impact of war coincided with growing organized black protest and increasing black voting power gained through migration to the northern states. Did national-security meanings really have any independent prorights impact? Evidence that it did comes from an examination of rights reform in the area of immigration and naturalization, a case where, at least in the early stages, there was no mass mobilization pressure and few electoral benefits for reform-minded lawmakers.

American immigration and naturalization policy used race and ethnic discrimination from the nation's founding. In 1790, Congress limited the right of naturalization to free whites. Blacks gained naturalization rights during Reconstruction, but Asians remained excluded....

In 1942, the new effort at allowing Asian immigration began, led by a small but elite group of sympathetic, non-Chinese New Yorkers. Magazines such as the *Christian Century*, the *New Republic*, and Richard Walsh's *Asia and the Americas* tried to raise awareness of the issue by publishing such articles as "Our Great Wall against the Chinese," "Repeal Exclusion Laws Now," "Are We Afraid to Do Justice?" and "Justice for the Chinese." Walsh was the husband of author Pearl Buck, whose novel of China, *The Good Earth*, won a Pulitzer prize in 1932. He formed a Citizen's Committee to Repeal Chinese Exclusion, which first met on May 25, 1943....

By the early 1960s, ending discrimination on the basis of national origin was a way to appeal to the ethnic groups that were disadvantaged by the current system. The success of the black civil rights movement further eroded the legitimacy of national origin discrimination in immigration. During the 1960 election, both parties supported immigration reform in their national party platforms....

Like the two presidents before him, President Kennedy lent the prestige of his office to the cause of immigration reform. He was a supporter of immigration (he even published a book on the subject in 1958), and was almost certainly aware of the electoral benefits of immigration reform. The State Department pressed for change as it did with black civil rights. By 1961, various nationality groups, especially Chinese, Polish, and Italian groups, were regularly sending letters in support of immigration reform....

Kennedy would not live to see reform, but his successor Lyndon Johnson maintained the pattern of past presidents in supporting reform, as did Secretary of State Dean Rusk in 1964 congressional hearings. Rusk pointed out that the national origins system "results in discrimination in our hospitality to different nationalities in a world situation which is quite different from that which existed at the time the national origins system was originally adopted"....

Eliminating that national-origins system, and especially the racist program for Asia, would therefore eliminate a millstone and fight enemy propaganda while only technically changing policy. Rusk explained, "We deprive ourselves of a powerful weapon in our fight against misinformation if we do not reconcile here, too, the letter of the law with the facts of immigration and thus erase the unfavorable impression made by our old quota limitation for Asian persons."...

The Immigration Act of 1965 is strangely neglected in studies of American politics and minority rights. Even major figures instrumental to its passage appear to think little of it. Momentous and hard fought, it is not discussed at all in Johnson's memoirs of his presidency—not a single mention. Dean Rusk, a star player in its passage, gave the topic only one paragraph in his memoirs, saying, "We at State helped promote it."

Still, it was a major policy development—much more so than was intended.... The point here, however, is that reform happened at about the same time as other major nondiscrimination laws and declarations in America and in the UN. By mostly benefiting Asians, it benefited a group that, in the initial stages at least, were unlike African Americans in that they were tiny parts of the population, promised few electoral benefits, and did not mass mobilize. But regardless of party, presidents and State Department officials were active players in the reform of immigration; mindful of foreign propaganda, they therefore saw nondiscrimination in immigration as they did black civil rights—as national-security policy.

FURTHER READING

Taylor Branch, *Parting the Waters* (1988), *Pillar of Fire* (1998), and *At Canaan's Edge* (2006).

Clayborne Carson, *In Struggle: SNCC and the Black Awakening of the 1960s* (1981).

George Pierre Castile, *To Show Heart: Native American Self-Determination and Federal Indian Policy* (1998).

John D'Emilio, *Sexual Politics, Sexual Communities: The Making of a Homosexual Minority in the United States, 1940–1970* (1983).

Mary L. Dudziak, *Cold War Civil Rights: Race and the Image of American Democracy* (2000).

Michael B. Friedland, *Lift Up Your Voice Like a Trumpet: White Clergy and the Civil Rights and Anti-War Movements* (1998).

Ignacio M. Garcia, *Viva Kennedy: Mexican Americans in Search of Camelot* (2000).

David Garrow, *Bearing the Cross: Martin Luther King, Jr., and the Southern Christian Leadership Conference* (1986).

Paul Harvey, *Freedom's Coming: Religious Culture and the Shaping of the South From the Civil War Through the Civil Rights Era* (2005).

G. Galvin Mackenzie and Robert Weisbrot, *The Liberal Hour: Washington and the Politics of Change in the 1960s* (2008).

Manning Marable, *Race, Reform, and Rebellion: The Second Reconstruction in Black America, 1945–1990* (1991).

Ruth Rosen, *The World Split Open: How the Modern Women's Movement Changed America* (2000).

Kenneth Stern, *Loud Hawk: The United States Versus the American Indian Movement* (1994).

CHAPTER 13

The Sixties: Left, Right, and the Culture Wars

Like the psychedelic music and drugs that were popular during the decade, the history of the sixties can be a mind-altering experience. Colorful reform movements shift, reshape, and overlap as in a kaleidoscope. Consumer advocacy, environmental reform, organic foods, communal living, the sexual revolution, personal growth groups, feminism, civil rights, the antiwar crusade, and dozens of other "issues" clamored for attention (and some of them still do). In fact, it was this bewildering hubbub that defined the sixties as a captivating and, for some, maddening period of time. Everything seemed open to question: politics, manners, sexual relations, and even the meaning of America.

Of course the sixties did not begin on New Year's Day 1960 and end on New Year's Eve 1969. As we have seen, the sources of unrest reached back into the 1950s for both liberals and conservatives. Liberals looked out on the political landscape and optimistically asked themselves, how can we enable the greatest nation on earth to live up to its full potential for social justice? They did not have to look far beyond the Mason-Dixon line to see one set of answers. As noted in Chapter 12, John Kennedy said explicitly in the debates that led to his election, "I think we can do better." The president consistently emphasized the theme of citizen responsibility, exhorting Americans: "Ask not what your country can do for you—ask what you can do for your country." Conservatives posed a different question to their constituencies: where did we go wrong? Brash new leaders like Barry Goldwater, George Wallace, and Ronald Reagan repudiated moderate "Eisenhower Republicanism," seeing it as an unholy compromise with disturbing trends unleashed by Roosevelt during the New Deal. They wanted "big government" out, "states' rights" in, and a return to so-called traditional values at all levels. As the decade wore on, activists on both the Right and the Left became more strident in their rhetoric and more radical in their demands.

But many of the social forces at work in the period were beyond the control of any political group, liberal or conservative. The invention of the birth control pill at Stanford University in 1960, for example, fundamentally altered the behavior of millions of women and men, regardless of religion, politics, or economic privilege. The so-called Sexual

Revolution had begun. The shame previously associated with psychotherapy ("head-shrinking") also fell away and millions of people from all political persuasions joined a "Human Potential" movement to search for happiness and fulfillment. Centered in California, the Human Potential Movement asked Americans not what they could do for their country, but what they should do for themselves. Gestalt therapy, encounter groups, and Transactional Analysis were so far outside the ken of official Washington that California was ridiculed as "Lala land." California was also a leader in a new physical fitness and health food craze, which got people on their feet in the search for personal fulfillment—and perhaps even perfection. For the first time, many Americans experimented openly with "lifestyle" choices, questioning monogamy, marriage, heterosexuality, and the nuclear family. Of course, the vast majority never considered living in a commune, but divorce, premarital sex, "bastardy," and homosexuality lost much of their dark stigma.

The period continues to excite debate in part because we are still not entirely sure of its legacies. By the end of the sixties, the liberal administrations of John F. Kennedy and Lyndon Johnson had implemented a number of reforms, but the Democratic Party had lost the presidency. Four of the greatest reformers ended their lives in pools of blood: John Kennedy, Robert Kennedy, Martin Luther King, Jr., and Malcolm X. The search for "enlightenment" also sometimes ended in death, when the route taken was paved with illegal, mind-altering drugs. Social mores associated with race and gender changed radically, and along with them many older forms of civility and prudence. Americans emerged from the decade on a much different footing with one another in their personal and social relationships—but that footing felt far from secure.

QUESTIONS TO THINK ABOUT

Were the sixties a decade of hedonism, or heightened social responsibility? How and why did both the Left and Right become radical by the end of the decade? Which changes initiated in the sixties are still with us today, and who "won" the culture wars?

DOCUMENTS

The documents in this chapter reflect the political polarization and social experimentation characteristic of the sixties. Document 1 articulates the goals of the Young Americans for Freedom, a group then on the "right-wing fringe" of the moderate Republican Party. The sixties are correctly remembered as a decade of liberal youth activism, but it's equally true that young conservatives struggled to make their voices heard. They believed in strictly limited government. Document 2 is from John F. Kennedy's inaugural speech, given January 20, 1961. As journalist Bill Moyers recalls in document 3, the president galvanized hopeful young Americans around an ideal of public service. Shortly after the inaugural, Moyers became deputy director of the Peace Corps, an organization started by Kennedy to send volunteers to the Third World. In document 4, Students for a

Democratic Society (also known as SDS) proclaim goals opposite those of Young Americans for Freedom. They express support for government activism to achieve a better world. Document 5 is a folk song by Malvina Reynolds that encourages young people to break out of a mass society that encourages conformism and puts people in "little boxes." Document 6 reveals what was sometimes called "the generation gap." Young people were at the forefront of activism in this decade, and they often derided "straight" (meaning traditional) values. In this excerpt, a nineteen-year-old participant in "sit-ins" at Columbia University in 1968 recalls conversations with his father about long hair and the meaning of student protest. In document 7, Vice President Spiro Agnew attacks student protestors as "impudent snobs" whose notion of popular democracy is "government by street carnival." In document 8, California psychologist Carl Rogers describes an alternative to the phoniness of mass society: focusing inward to find the "real" you. Encounter groups like those pioneered by Rogers probably had more participants than protest organizations. Their popularity reflects the transition from President Kennedy's "we" generation to the "me" generation, as Americans came to value "getting in touch with their feelings." Document 9 showcases a movement that grafted sexual freedom onto civil rights and came into its own in the 1970s: Gay Liberation.

1. Young Americans for Freedom Draft a Conservative Manifesto, 1960

In this time of moral and political crisis, it is the responsibility of the youth of America to affirm certain eternal truths.

We, as young conservatives, believe:

That foremost among the transcendent values is the individual's use of his God-given free will, whence derives his right to be free from the restrictions of arbitrary force;

That liberty is indivisible, and that political freedom cannot long exist without economic freedom;

That the purposes of government are to protect these freedoms through the preservation of internal order, the provision of national defense, and the administration of justice;

That when government ventures beyond these rightful functions, it accumulates power which tends to diminish order and liberty;

That the Constitution of the United States is the best arrangement yet devised for empowering government to fulfill its proper role, while restraining it from the concentration and abuse of power;

That the genius of the Constitution—the division of powers—is summed up in the clause which reserves primacy to the several states, or to the people, in those spheres not specifically delegated to the Federal Government;

John A. Andrew III. *The Other Side of the Sixties: Young Americans for Freedom and the Rise of Conservative Politics* (New Brunswick, N.J.: Rutgers University Press, 1997), pp. 221–222. Copyright © 1997, 1967 by John A. Andrew III. Reprinted by permission of Rutgers University Press.

That the market economy, allocating resources by the free play of supply and demand, is the single economic system compatible with the requirements of personal freedom and constitutional government, and that it is at the same time the most productive supplier of human needs;

That when government interferes with the work of the market economy, it tends to reduce the moral and physical strength of the nation; that when it takes from one man to bestow on another, it diminishes the incentive of the first, the integrity of the second, and the moral autonomy of both;

That we will be free only so long as the national sovereignty of the United States is secure: that history shows periods of freedom are rare, and can exist only when free citizens concertedly defend their rights against all enemies;

That the forces of international Communism are, at present, the greatest single threat to these liberties;

That the United States should stress victory over, rather than coexistence with, this menace; and

That American foreign policy must be judged by this criterion: does it serve the just interests of the United States?

2. President John Kennedy Tells Americans to Ask "What You Can Do," 1961

We observe today not a victory of party but a celebration of freedom—symbolizing an end as well as a beginning—signifying renewal as well as change. For I have sworn before you and Almighty God the same solemn oath our forebears prescribed nearly a century and three-quarters ago.

The world is very different now. For man holds in his mortal hands the power to abolish all forms of human poverty and all forms of human life. And yet the same revolutionary beliefs for which our forebears fought are still at issue around the globe—the belief that the rights of man come not from the generosity of the state but from the hand of God.

We dare not forget today that we are the heirs of that first revolution. Let the word go forth from this time and place, to friend and foe alike, that the torch has been passed to a new generation of Americans—born in this century, tempered by war, disciplined by a hard and bitter peace, proud of our ancient heritage—and unwilling to witness or permit the slow undoing of those human rights to which this nation has always been committed, and to which we are committed today at home and around the world.

Let every nation know, whether it wishes us well or ill, that we shall pay any price, bear any burden, meet any hardship, support any friend, oppose any foe to assure the survival and the success of liberty.

This much we pledge—and more....

Public Papers of the Presidents of the United States: John F. Kennedy, 1961 (Washington. D.C.: U.S. Government Printing Office, 1962), p. 1.

In your hands, my fellow citizens, more than mine, will rest the final success or failure of our course. Since this country was founded, each generation of Americans has been summoned to give testimony to its national loyalty. The graves of young Americans who answered the call to service surround the globe.

Now the trumpet summons us again—not as a call to bear arms, though arms we need,—not as a call to battle, though embattled we are—but a call to bear the burden of a long twilight struggle, year in and year out, "rejoicing in hope, patient in tribulation"—a struggle against the common enemies of man: tyranny, poverty, disease, and war itself.

Can we forge against these enemies a grand and global alliance, North and South, East and West, that can assure a more fruitful life for all mankind? Will you join in that historic effort?

In the long history of the world, only a few generations have been granted the role of defending freedom in its hour of maximum danger. I do not shrink from this responsibility—I welcome it. I do not believe that any of us would exchange places with any other people or any other generation. The energy, the faith, the devotion which we bring to this endeavor will light our country and all who serve it—and the glow from that fire can truly light the world.

And so, my fellow Americans: ask not what your country can do for you— ask what you can do for your country.

My fellow citizens of the world: ask not what America will do for you, but what together we can do for the freedom of man.

Finally, whether you are citizens of America or citizens of the world, ask of us here the same high standards of strength and sacrifice which we ask of you. With a good conscience our only sure reward, with history the final judge of our deeds, let us go forth to lead the land we love, asking His blessing and His help, but knowing that here on earth God's work must truly be our own.

3. Bill Moyers Remembers Kennedy's Effect on His Generation, 1988 (1961)

Of the private man John Kennedy I knew little. I saw him rarely. Once, when the 1960 campaign was over and he was ending a post-election visit to the LBJ Ranch, he pulled me over into a corner to urge me to abandon my plans for graduate work at the University of Texas and to come to Washington as part of the New Frontier. I told him that I had already signed up to teach at a Baptist school in Texas while pursuing my doctorate. Anyway, I said, "You're going to have to call on the whole faculty at Harvard. You don't need a graduate of Southwestern Baptist Theological Seminary." In mock surprise he said, "Didn't you know that the first president of Harvard was a Baptist? You'll be right at home."

And so I was.

Bill Moyers, *To Touch the World: The Peace Corps Experience* (Washington. D.C.: Peace Corps, 1995), pp. 152–153.

So I remember John Kennedy not so much for what he was or what he wasn't but for what he empowered in me. We all edit history to give some form to the puzzle of our lives, and I cherish the memory of him for awakening me to a different story for myself. He placed my life in a larger narrative than I could ever have written. One test of a leader is knowing, as John Stuart Mill put it, that "the worth of the state, in the long run, is the worth of the individuals composing it." Preserving civilization is the work not of some miracle-working, superhuman personality but of each one of us. The best leaders don't expect us just to pay our taxes and abdicate, they sign us up for civic duty and insist we sharpen our skills as citizens....

Public figures either make us feel virtuous about retreating into the snuggeries of self or they challenge us to act beyond our obvious capacities. America is always up for grabs, can always go either way. The same culture that produced the Ku Klux Klan, Lee Harvey Oswald, and the Jonestown massacre also produced Martin Luther King, Archibald MacLeish, and the Marshall Plan.

A desperate and alienated young man told me in 1970, after riots had torn his campus and town: "I'm just as good as I am bad. I think all of us are. But nobody's speaking to the good in me." In his public voice John Kennedy spoke to my generation of service and sharing; he called us to careers of discovery through lives open to others....

... It was for us not a trumpet but a bell, sounding in countless individual hearts that one clear note that said: "You matter. You can signify. You can make a difference." Romantic? Yes, there was romance to it. But we were not then so callous toward romance.

4. Students for a Democratic Society Advance a Reform Agenda, 1962

We are people of this generation, bred in at least modest comfort, housed now in universities, looking uncomfortably to the world we inherit.

When we were kids the United States was the wealthiest and strongest country in the world; the only one with the atom bomb, the least scarred by modern war, an initiator of the United Nations that we thought would distribute Western influence throughout the world. Freedom and equality for each individual, government of, by, and for the people—these American values we found good, principles by which we could live as men. Many of us began maturing in complacency.

As we grew, however, our comfort was penetrated by events too troubling to dismiss. First, the permeating and victimizing fact of human degradation, symbolized by the Southern struggle against racial bigotry, compelled most of us from silence to activism. Second, the enclosing fact of the Cold War, symbolized by the presence of the Bomb, brought awareness that we ourselves, and our friends, and millions of abstract "others" we knew more directly because of our

Excerpt from The Port Huron Statement, 1962. State Historical Society of Wisconsin.

common peril, might die at any time. We might deliberately ignore, or avoid, or fail to feel all other human problems, but not these two, for these were too immediate and crushing in their impact, too challenging in the demand that we as individuals take the responsibility for encounter and resolution.

While these and other problems either directly oppressed us or rankled our consciences and became our own subjective concerns, we began to see complicated and disturbing paradoxes in our surrounding America. The declaration "all men are created equal…" rang hollow before the facts of Negro life in the South and the big cities of the North. The proclaimed peaceful intentions of the United States contradicted its economic and military investments in the Cold War status quo….

Our work is guided by the sense that we may be the last generation in the experiment with living….

Some would have us believe that Americans feel contentment amidst prosperity—but might it not be better called a glaze above deeply-felt anxieties about their role in the new world? And if these anxieties produce a developed indifference to human affairs, do they not as well produce a yearning to believe there *is* an alternative to the present, that something *can* be done to change circumstances in the school, the workplaces, the bureaucracies, the government? It is to this latter yearning, at once the spark and engine of change, that we direct our present appeal. The search for truly democratic alternatives to the present, and a commitment to social experimentation with them, is a worthy and fulfilling human enterprise, one which moves us and, we hope, others today.

5. Folk Singer Malvina Reynolds Sees Young People in "Little Boxes," 1963

Little boxes on the hillside, little boxes made of ticky tacky
Little boxes on the hillside, little boxes all the same
There's a green one and a pink one and a blue one and a yellow one
And they're all made out of ticky tacky and they all look just the same.

And the people in the houses
All went to the university,
Where they were put in boxes
And they came out all the same,
And there's doctors and there's lawyers,
And business executives,
And they're all made out of ticky tacky
And they all look just the same.

And they all play on the golf course

And drink their martinis dry,

And they all have pretty children

And the children go to school,

And the children go to summer camp

And then to the university,

Where they are put in boxes and they come out all the same.

And the boys go into business

and marry and raise a family

In boxes made of ticky tacky

And they all look just the same.

6. A Protester at Columbia University Defends Long Hair and Revolution, 1969

Columbia used to be called King's College. They changed the name in 1784 because they wanted to be patriotic and *Columbia* means *America*. This week we've been finding out what America means.

Every morning now when I wake up I have to run through the whole thing in my mind. I have to do that because I wake up in a familiar place that isn't what it was. I wake up and I see blue coats and brass buttons all over the campus. ("Brass buttons, blue coat, can't catch a nanny goat" goes the Harlem nursery rhyme.) I start to go off the campus but then remember to turn and walk two blocks uptown to get to the only open gate. There I squeeze through the three-foot "out" opening in the police barricade, and I feel for my wallet to be sure I've got the two I.D.'s necessary to get back into my college. I stare at the cops. They stare back and see a red armband and long hair and they perhaps tap their night sticks on the barricade. They're looking at a radical leftist....

At the sundial are 500 people ready to follow Mark Rudd (whom they don't particularly like because he always refers to President Kirk as "that shithead") into the Low Library administration building to demand severance from IDA [Institute for Defense Analysis], an end to gym construction, and to defy Kirk's recent edict prohibiting indoor demonstrations....

I go upstairs to reconnoiter and there is none other than Peter Behr of Linda LeClair fame* chalking on the wall, "'Up against the wall, motherfucker,...' from a poem by LeRoi Jones." I get some chalk and write "I am sorry about defacing the walls, but babies are being burned and men are dying, and this University is at fault quite directly."

Excerpt from *The Strawberry Statement* by James S. Kunen, published by Brandywine Press. Reprinted by permission of Sll/Sterling Lord Literistic, Inc. Copyright by James S. Kunen.

*Peter Behr and Linda LeClair were students from Columbia and Barnard—both single-sex schools—who flouted university rules by living together off campus while unmarried.

... Medical science has yet to discover any positive correlation between hair length and anything—intelligence, virility, morality, cavities, cancer—anything.

Long hair on men, however, has been known to make some people sick.

My father, for instance. On July 8, 1968, he alleged that long hair on his sons made him sick. "You look like a woman," he said. "I'll get a haircut," I said. That threw him off, but only for a moment. "If I were a girl," he continued, "I wouldn't like the way you look." "You are not a girl," I said, "and anyway, I said I'd get a haircut." "I don't see how your hair could possibly get any longer," he added. "Would you agree," I asked, "that if I let it grow for another two months, it would get longer?" "Maybe," he conceded, "but it just couldn't possibly be any longer."

My father talks about the bad associations people make when they see someone with hair. I come back with the bad associations people make when they see someone replete with a shiny new Cadillac that looks like it should have a silk—raimented coachman standing at each fender. But as for bad vibrations emanating from my follicles, I say great. I want the cops to sneer and the old ladies swear and the businessmen worry. I want everyone to see me and say "There goes an enemy of the state," because that's where I'm at, as we say in the Revolution biz.

Also, I like to have peace people wave me victory signs and I like to return them, and for that we've got to be able to recognize each other. And hair is an appropriate badge. Long hair should be associated with peace, because the first time American men wore short hair was after World War I, the first time great numbers of American men had been through the military....

7. Vice President Spiro Agnew Warns of the Threat to America, 1969

A little over a week ago, I took a rather unusual step for a Vice President. I said something. Particularly, I said something that was predictably unpopular with the people who would like to run the country without the inconvenience of seeking public office. I said I did not like some of the things I saw happening in this country. I criticized those who encouraged government by street carnival and suggested it was time to stop the carousel....

Think about it. Small bands of students are allowed to shut down great universities. Small groups of dissidents are allowed to shout down political candidates. Small cadres of professional protestors are allowed to jeopardize the peace efforts of the President of the United States.

It is time to question the credentials of their leaders. And, if in questioning we disturb a few people, I say it is time for them to be disturbed. If, in challenging, we polarize the American people, I say it is time for a positive polarization.

It is time for a healthy in-depth examination of policies and constructive realignment in this country. It is time to rip away the rhetoric and to divide on

Alexander Bloom and Wini Breines, eds., *Takin' It to the Streets: A Sixties Reader* (New York: Oxford University Press, 1995), pp. 355–358.

authentic lines. It is time to discard the fiction that in a country of 200 million people, everyone is qualified to quarterback the government....

Now, we have among us a glib, activist element who would tell us our values are lies, and I call them impudent. Because anyone who impugns a legacy of liberty and dignity that reaches back to Moses, is impudent.

I call them snobs for most of them disdain to mingle with the masses who work for a living. They mock the common man's pride in his work, his family and his country....

Abetting the merchants of hate are the parasites of passion. These are the men who value a cause purely for its political mileage. These are the politicians who temporize with the truth by playing both sides to their own advantage. They ooze sympathy for "the cause" but balance each sentence with equally reasoned reservations. Their interest is personal, not moral. They are ideological eunuchs whose most comfortable position is straddling the philosophical fence, soliciting votes from both sides....

This is what is happening in this nation. We *are* an effete society if we let it happen here....

Because on the eve of our nation's 200th birthday, we have reached the crossroads. Because at this moment totalitarianism's threat does not necessarily have a foreign accent. Because we have a home-grown menace, made and manufactured in the U.S.A. Because if we are lazy or foolish, this nation could forfeit its integrity, never to be free again.

8. Psychologist Carl Rogers Emphasizes Being "Real" in Encounter Groups, 1970

I think of one government executive, a man with high responsibility and excellent technical training as an engineer. At the first meeting of the group he impressed me, and I think others, as being cold, aloof, somewhat bitter, resentful, cynical. When he spoke of how he ran his office he appeared to administer it "by the book" without warmth or human feeling entering in. In one of the early sessions, when he spoke of his wife a group member asked him, "Do you love your wife?" He paused for a long time, and the questioner said, "OK, that's answer enough." The executive said, "No, wait a minute! The reason I didn't respond was that I was wondering if I ever loved anyone. I don't think I have *ever* really *loved* anyone." It seemed quite dramatically clear to those of us in the group that he had come to accept himself as an unloving person.

A few days later he listened with great intensity as one member of the group expressed profound personal feelings of isolation, loneliness, pain, and the extent to which he had been living behind a mask, a façade. The next morning the engineer said, "Last night I thought and thought about what Bill told us.

Carl R. Rogers, *Carl Rogers on Encounter Groups* (New York: Harper & Row, 1970), 25–28. Copyright © 1970 by Carl Rogers. Reprinted by permission of HarperCollins Publishers, Inc.

I even wept quite a bit by myself. I can't remember how long it has been since I've cried and I really *felt* something. I think perhaps what I felt was love."...

Still another person reporting shortly after his workshop experience says, "I came away from the workshop feeling much more deeply that 'It's all right to be me with all my strengths and weaknesses.' My wife told me that I seem more authentic, more real, more genuine."

This feeling of greater realness and authenticity is a very common experience. It would appear that the individual is learning to accept and to *be* himself and is thus laying the foundation for change. He is closer to his own feelings, hence they are no longer so rigidly organized and are more open to change....

... As the sessions continue, so many things tend to occur together that it is hard to know which to describe first. It should again be stressed that these different threads and stages interweave and overlap. One of the threads is the increasing impatience with defenses. As time goes on the group finds it unbearable that any member should live behind a mask or front. The polite words, the intellectual understanding of each other and of relationships, the smooth coin of tact and cover-up—amply satisfactory for interactions outside—are just not good enough. The expression of self by some members of the group has made it very clear that a deeper and more basic encounter is *possible*, and the group appears to strive intuitively and unconsciously, toward this goal. Gently at times, almost savagely at others, the group *demands* that the individual be himself, that his current feelings not be hidden, that he remove the mask of ordinary social intercourse. In one group there was a highly intelligent and quite academic man who had been rather perceptive in his understanding of others but revealed himself not at all. The attitude of the group was finally expressed sharply by one member when he said, "Come out from behind that lectern, Doc. Stop giving us speeches. Take off your dark glasses. We want to know *you*."

9. Carl Wittman Issues a Gay Manifesto, 1969–1970

San Francisco is a refugee camp for homosexuals. We have fled here from every part of the nation, and like refugees elsewhere, we came not because it is so great here, but because it was so bad there. By the tens of thousands, we fled small towns where to be ourselves would endanger our jobs and any hope of a decent life; we have fled from blackmailing cops, from families who disowned or "tolerated" us; we have been drummed out of the armed services, thrown out of schools, fired from jobs, beaten by punks and policemen.

And we have formed a ghetto, out of self-protection. It is a ghetto rather than a free territory because it is still theirs. Straight cops patrol us, straight legislators govern us. Straight employers keep us in line, straight money exploits us. We have pretended everything is OK, because we haven't been able to see how to change it—we've been afraid.

Carl Wittman, "A Gay Manifesto,"from *Out of the Closets: Voices of Gay Liberation.* Copyright © 1992 NYU Press. Reprinted by permission of the editors.

In the past year there has been an awakening of gay liberation ideas and energy. How it began we don't know; maybe we were inspired by black people and their freedom movement; we learned how to stop pretending from the hip revolution. Amerika in all its ugliness has surfaced with the war and our national leaders. And we are revulsed by the quality of our ghetto life....

Homosexuality is *not* a lot of things. It is not a makeshift in the absence of the opposite sex; it is not hatred or rejection of the opposite sex; it is not genetic; it is not the result of broken homes except inasmuch as we could see the sham of American marriage. *Homosexuality is the capacity to love someone of the same sex....*

1. *Mimicry of straight society:* We are children of straight society. We still think straight: that is part of our oppression. One of the worst of straight concepts is inequality. Straight (also white, English, male, capitalist) thinking views things in terms of order and comparison. A is before B, B is after A; one is below two is below three; there is no room for equality. This idea gets extended to male/ female, on top/on bottom, spouse/not spouse, heterosexual/homosexual; boss/ worker, white/black and rich/poor. Our social institutions cause and reflect this verbal hierarchy. This is Amerika....

2. *Marriage:* Marriage is a prime example of a straight institution fraught with role playing. Traditional marriage is a rotten, oppressive institution. Those of us who have been in heterosexual marriages too often have blamed our gayness on the breakup of the marriage. No. They broke up because marriage is a contract which smothers both people, denies needs, and places impossible demands on both people. And we had the strength, again, to refuse to capitulate to the roles which were demanded of us....

If we are liberated we are open with our sexuality. Closet queenery must end. *Come out....*

ESSAYS

How one assesses the legacy of the sixties depends partly on which events or people one looks at. In the first essay, the late Kenneth Cmiel of the University of Iowa shows how the sixties reshaped popular notions of civility—what it meant to be "nice." How could one be polite, for instance, when being polite to white people meant yielding one's seat on a bus or quietly absorbing deliberate insults? Cmiel traces the effects of civil rights, the counterculture, the New Left, feminism, and the rulings of the Supreme Court on how Americans treated one another in the sixties and how they treat one another today. The essay by Gerard J. DeGroot, professor of history at the University of St. Andrews in Scotland, is sharply critical of "the sixties," which he portrays as a misbegotten decade in which civil society nearly collapsed—or at least did so in places like the Haight-Ashbury neighborhood of San Francisco. This decade was akin to a "bad trip" on LSD, in which Americans (and others) indulged in the worst forms of narcissistic, anti-social behavior. The best thing about the sixties, DeGroot implies, is that they finally came to an end.

Sixties Liberalism and the Revolution in Manners

KENNETH CMIEL

As the 1960s opened, civility was, quite literally, the law of the land. In 1942 the U.S. Supreme Court had declared that certain words were not protected by the First Amendment. Not only fighting words, but also the "lewd," "obscene," and "profane" were all excluded from protection. A statute declaring that "no person shall address any offensive, derisive or annoying word to any other person who is lawfully in any street" was upheld by the Court as perfectly legal. This decision, although modified in later years, was still law in 1960, and statutes like the one mentioned above continued to be on the books and enforced. They implied that free speech was possible only in what eighteenth-century writers had called "civil society." Civility, in other words, had to precede civil rights.

One part of the contentious politics of the sixties, however, was a fight over this notion. From a number of perspectives, prevailing attitudes toward social etiquette were attacked. African Americans argued that civil society as constructed by whites helped structure racial inequality. Counterculturalists insisted that civil politeness suppressed more authentic social relations. Some student radicals infused the strategic disruption of civility with political meaning. And finally, there was a moderate loosening of civil control at the center of society. Under this onslaught, the nation's courts struggled to redefine the relationship between law and civil behavior.

... This essay charts the shift within the United States from one sense of order to another. In reaction to various social changes and pressures, federal courts, most importantly the Supreme Court, altered the law of decorum. From the belief that civility took precedence over civil rights, the Supreme Court decided that in public forums, incivility was protected by the First Amendment. But this major change was qualified. No incivility, the Court argued, could disrupt the normal workings of a school, workplace, or courtroom....

The civil rights movement's nonviolent efforts to alter the social order marked the first powerful sortie into the politics of civility during the 1960s. As the sixties opened, nonviolent direct action was the tactic of choice for organizations like the Congress of Racial Equality (CORE), the Southern Christian Leadership Conference (SCLC), and the Student Nonviolent Coordinating Committee (SNCC)....

Nonviolent resistance asked demonstrators to peaceably and lovingly call attention to the inequities of the social system. For those believing in direct nonviolent action, the path of protest was a complicated and patient one, moving through four distinct stages—the investigation of a problem, efforts to negotiate a solution, public protest, and then further negotiation. One never proceeded to the next stage without warrant. Henry David Thoreau's "Civil Disobedience" was often cited as a precursor to direct action. Another important source was

Mahatma Gandhi. Indeed, Gandhi's 1906 campaign in South Africa was seen as the first example of a mass direct nonviolent action.

But while Gandhi and Thoreau were sources, for both black and white activists committed to direct nonviolent action there was something far more important—the Gospel's injunction to love one's enemies. All the early leaders of CORE, SCLC, and SNCC were deeply influenced by the Christian message of hope and redemption. SNCC's statement of purpose on its founding in May 1960 called attention to those "Judaic-Christian traditions" that seek "a social order permeated by love."…

Civil rights protest took a number of characteristic forms—the boycott, the sit-in, the freedom ride, and the mass march. At all, efforts were made to keep the protest civil. In 1960, when four neatly dressed black college students sat down at a white-only lunch counter in a downtown Woolworth's in Greensboro, North Carolina, one began the protest by turning to a waitress and saying, "I'd like a cup of coffee, please." Although the students were not served, they continued to be well mannered, sitting "politely" at the counter for days on end. This first effort set off a wave of sit-ins to desegregate southern restaurants. Typical were the instructions given in Nashville: "Do show yourself friendly on the counter at all times. Do sit straight and always face the counter. Don't strike back or curse back if attacked." Candie Anderson, one of the students at the Nashville sit-in, recalled: "My friends were determined to be courteous and well-behaved…. Most of them read or studied while they sat at the counters, for three or four hours. I heard them remind each other not to leave cigarette ashes on the counter, to take off their hats, etc."…

The meaning of the polite protests was complicated. Rosa Parks, who refused to move to the back of the bus in Montgomery, Alabama, the students integrating lunch counters in Greensboro, and the marchers at Selma were all not only acting with decorum, they were also all breaking the law, calling attention to the inadequacy of the present system, and violating long-standing white/black custom of the South. The southern caste system was reinforced through an elaborate etiquette. Blacks stepped aside on the street to let whites pass, they averted their eyes from whites, and even adult African Americans were called by a diminutive first name ("Charlie" or "Missie") while addressing all whites with the formal titles of "Sir," "Ma'am," "Mr.," or "Mrs." No distinctions in economic status changed this. Black ministers tipped their hats to white tradesmen. To the overwhelming majority of white southerners, the assertion of civil equality by civil rights protesters was in fact a radical *break* in decorum.

The protest, indeed, highlights some of the complexities of civility itself. On the one hand, politeness is a means of avoiding violence and discord. It is a way of *being nice*. One of sociologist Norbert Elias's great insights was to see that the introduction of civil etiquette in the early modern West was part of an effort to reduce the amount of interpersonal violence prevalent during the Middle Ages. At some time or other, all of us are polite to people we do not like simply because we do not want to live in an overly contentious world. On the other hand, however, civility *also* reaffirms established social boundaries. And when there are huge inequities in the social order, polite custom ratifies them in everyday life.

Direct nonviolent action attempted to undermine southern etiquette. It did so not by attacking civility pure and simple but by using polite behavior to challenge social inequality. More precisely, the first function of politeness (being nice) attacked the second (the caste system). The determined civility of the protesters dramatized the inequities of the South and at the same time signaled to the nation and world the "worthiness" (that is, civility) of African Americans.

Most southern whites did not see it this way. Even those who were called moderates in the early sixties often viewed the polite protests as an attack on civility. Sit-ins, boycotts, and marches openly challenged the caste system and, moderates argued, too easily slipped into violence. To the *Nashville Banner*, the sit-ins were an "incitation to anarchy."…

In Greensboro, it was *white* children who were the first to be arrested for disorderly conduct, who harassed blacks at the lunch counter, who got angry. At Selma, it was the white police who waded into crowds of protesters and began clubbing them. Black activists, in fact, had expected this to happen. Martin Luther King was typical, noting that nonviolent resistance forced "the oppressor to commit his brutality openly—in the light of day—with the rest of the world looking on."…

This style of protest was under assault almost as the sixties started. As early as 1961, and certainly by 1964, those partisans of "civil" protest were faced with a growing mass movement that was more assertive, less polite, and more willing to defend itself. A host of reasons explain this shift. The fiercely violent reaction of so many whites made nonviolent decorum extremely hard and dangerous to maintain. Black nationalism, grass roots activism, a growing sense of frustration, and burgeoning antiestablishment sentiment in the culture at large all helped throw bourgeois misrule on the defensive. It would be just a few more steps to the Black Panther party or the calls to violence by people like Stokely Carmichael and H. Rap Brown.…

One place we can spot the erosion of polite protest is in the Freedom Summer of 1964. Among an important group of young SNCC activists there was a certain skepticism about Martin Luther King. For these civil rights workers, nonviolent resistance was understood to be a strategic tactic rather than a principled commitment. And there was a change in style. As sociologist Robert McAdam has noted, there was a feeling among these civil rights activists that they had to free themselves as much as the southern blacks they worked for. And that meant abandoning middle-class norms. Consequently, more rural dress (blue jeans and work shirt) became the mode.…

Another sign was the filthy speech movement at Berkeley. In the fall of 1964, the University of California at Berkeley was rocked by the free speech movement, an effort by students to retain their right to distribute political material on campus. Many of the leaders of the free speech movement had worked for SNCC in the South the summer before and a number of Freedom Summer tactics were adopted at Berkeley. Students used mass civil disobedience and sit-ins to pressure campus officials in November and December. They were generally successful. But the next spring, after the campus had quieted, a new twist came. A nonstudent who hung around in New York beat circles drifted to

Berkeley to (in his words) "make the scene." On 3 March he stood on Bancroft and Telegraph and held up a sign that just said "FUCK." When asked to clarify his meaning, he added an exclamation point. His arrest threw the campus into another controversy. Other "dirty speech" protests were held, with other students arrested for obscenity.

The counterculture of the 1960s can be traced back to the beats of the 1950s, earlier still to artistic modernism, and even before that to Rousseau's mid-eighteenth-century attack on politeness. But if there is a long subterranean history, a very visible counterculture began to surface in 1964. The first underground newspapers appeared; they were dominated by countercultural themes. By 1966 the counterculture was a mass media phenomenon. Perhaps its height of popularity were the years 1967 and 1968. And while no precise date marks its end, by the early 1970s it was fading fast at least in its most utopian projections.

From Rousseau through the 1960s, advocates of a counterculture valued authenticity over civility. The command to be polite (that is, to *be nice*) does not encourage personal expression. It suppresses impulsive behavior, relying on established social forms to guarantee comity. As Norbert Elias has put it, the civilizing process is about affect control. Counterculture advocates challenged these presumptions, arguing for the liberation of the self. In the name of personal freedom they attacked the restraints and compromises of civil society. In a phrase introduced to American life by sixties freaks, they were dedicated to "doing their own thing."

This translated into an extraordinarily colorful form of life. Shoulder-length hair on men, Victorian dresses on women, day-glo painted bodies, elaborate slang, and more open sexuality—it was all far removed from "straight" (that is, civil) society. Hippies looked different, acted different, were different. At its best, there was a glorious joy in the freedom of hippie life-styles. The "be-ins" of 1967 celebrated the love that would replace the stilted conformity of the established world....

Drugs too were often defended as a liberating experience. (I myself did so ingenuously in the late sixties.) "It's like seeing the world again through a child's eye," one user noted in 1967. Drugs were "a transcendental glory." "When I first turned on," the owner of a San Francisco head shop reported in 1968, "it pulled the rug out from under me. Suddenly I saw all the bullshit in the whole educational and social system.... The problem with our schools is that they are turning out robots to keep the social system going." So "turning on, tuning in, and dropping out means to conduct a revolution against the system."...

To those with no respect for the counterculture, the alternative decorum was gross. There was just too much dirt. Hippies did not have the discipline to hold a job. The sex was too loose. The drugs were destructive. Some critics completely missed the claims to liberation and denounced hippies as simply negative....

Yet while the distance from straight culture was deep, the counterculture might best be seen not so much an attack on politeness as an alternative politeness, one not based on the emotional self-restraint of traditional civility but on the expressive individualism of liberated human beings. It is no surprise that "love" was an important theme running throughout the counterculture....

The counterculture, at its most utopian, tried to invent a new civility. It attacked the social roles of straight society and the implied social order contained within it. But it held firm to the other dimension of civility—that of being nice. But in the end, it could not be yoked together as easily as one thought. To some degree, the roles involved in civil etiquette are connected with the avoidance of discord....

By 1965, as the counterculture was coming to national consciousness, there was another debate going on about the civil society. At least some radical activists had moved beyond the talking stage. Violent behavior became a considered option.

This happened first among black activists, later among whites. African American radicals like H. Rap Brown and Stokely Carmichael decisively split with the earlier civil rights movement. Carmichael's 1966 call to let the cities burn, the stream of urban riots after 1965, and the growing militancy in general frightened numerous Americans....

Some white student and antiwar activists were making their own transition. The move from dissent to resistance was accompanied by a shift in rhetoric. "We're now in the business of wholesale disruption and widespread resistance and dislocation of the American society," Jerry Rubin reported in 1967. To be sure, not all white radicals accepted this, but some did, and the thought of disruption scared Middle America, whose more conservative press responded with almost breathless reports about imminent revolution. The heightened rhetoric, on both sides, contributed to the sense that the center might not hold. A string of burned buildings on university campuses as well as a handful of bombings over the next few years contributed as well.

Real violence, against property or person, however, was actually rare. Far more important was the *talk* about violence. The escalation of rhetoric, the easy use of hard words made more centrists very nervous. It reflected, in their eyes, a lack of faith in civil politics.

For these radicals, the hard words were part of their sense that polite society had its priorities backward. There was something grotesquely misguided about a middle-class decorum that masked the profound inequalities of America. The true obscenities, they argued, were the Vietnam War and racial hatred. In fact, some thought, the very idea of obscenity had to be rethought. "The dirtiest word in the English language is not 'fuck' or 'shit' in the mouth of a tragic shaman," one activist wrote, "but the word 'NIGGER' from the sneering lips of a Bull Conner."...

By the late sixties, then, countercultural politics might mesh with political radicalism. To be sure, the two movements never fit perfectly together. But there were connections. Even long hair could be a threatening statement laden with political overtones. One participant in the Columbia University uprising in 1968 welcomed the "bad vibrations" his long hair brought: "I say great. I want the cops to sneer and the old ladies [to] swear and the businessmen [to] worry. I want everyone to see me and say: "There goes an enemy of the state,' because that's where I'm at, as we say in the Revolution game."...

The debate in the late sixties was clouded by the polarization of the times. Hippies and violent political radicals were tailor-made for the mass media. But despite the preoccupation with the more extravagant behavior, the nation's manners were changing in more subtle ways. There was a large move toward the informalization of American society.

Informalization is a term invented by sociologists to describe periodic efforts to relax formal etiquette. These periods of informality are then followed by a more conservative "etiquette-prone" reaction. While Americans in the sixties pressed toward more informal social relations, the phenomenon was by no means unique to that period. A significant relaxation of manners took place in Jacksonian America, tied to both egalitarian sentiment and the desire for authenticity. Still another important stage was the 1920s. And as Barbara Ehrenreich has pointed out, sexual mores were becoming less rigid inside mainstream society in the 1950s, a prelude for the next decade.

The counterculture of the mid-1960s was only picking up on debates already under way in mainstream America. Disputes about long hair surfaced not in 1966 with the counterculture but in 1963 when the Beatles first became known in the United States. The *New York Times* first reported on the issue in December 1964, four months after the Beatles began their first full-length tour in the United States. In those early years, the debate over long hair had a very different feel than it would beginning in 1966. The discussion was *not* about basic rottenness of a civilization. Rather, for the boys involved, it was about fun and girls. The look, as it evolved in the United States, was a surfer look. The "mop top," as it was called, was simply a bang swooped over the forehead. The sides were closely and neatly cropped. It was moderate hair by 1966 standards....

Between 1963 and 1965, however, it was controversial. Adults who disliked the bangs claimed they blurred gender lines. Boys looked like girls, something both disquieting and disgusting. Nevertheless, the conservatives on this issue were like the "long hair" kids in not talking about the mop top as a frontal assault on civilization but in the more restricted terms of a threatening relaxation of order. It was only in 1966 that certain forms of male hair became associated with a wholesale attack on what was known as "the American way of life."

Something similar can be said about sexual mores. The urge to liberalize "official" sexual codes was certainly a prominent theme of the counterculture, but it was also a theme of Hugh Hefner's *Playboy,* first published in 1953. And a female variant, Helen Gurley Brown's *Sex and the Single Girl,* was a huge bestseller as early as 1962. By the mid-1960s there were a host of middle-class advocates for a more liberal sexuality, a trend culminating in the early 1970s in books like Alex Comfort's *The Joy of Sex.* The counterculture contributed, but it was neither the beginning nor the end of the change....

This shift at the center of American culture did not take place without opposition. There were plaints for the older norms. Nor did the changes take place independent of the law. In fact, they were sanctioned and encouraged through new attitudes toward decorum promulgated by the federal courts, principally the U.S. Supreme Court. A number of decisions, most coming between 1966 and

1973, changed the relationship of the "civilizing process" to the rule of law. This was the legal version of informalization.

In a number of instances, the Court refused to use arguments of bad taste or decorum to uphold a law. In one celebrated case, a young man opposed to the Vietnam War had been arrested in the corridor of the Los Angeles County Courthouse for wearing a jacket with the words "Fuck the Draft" prominently inscribed on it. The Court overturned the conviction noting that there was no sign of imminent violence at the courthouse and that while the phrase was crude and vulgar to many, the open debate the First Amendment guaranteed necessitated its protection. In a far-reaching departure from earlier decisions, the Court also raised doubts about the possibility of any evaluation of taste: "For, while the particular four-letter word being litigated here is perhaps more distasteful than others of its genre, it is nevertheless true that one man's vulgarity is another's lyric." Since government officials "cannot make principled decisions in this area," it was important to leave "matters of taste and style largely to the individual."

This was a far cry from *Chaplinsky v. New Hampshire* (1942), in which the Court simply asserted that some utterances were of "such slight social value" that the First Amendment did not protect them. In the Chaplinsky case, the defendant was convicted for calling someone a "damned racketeer" and a "damned Fascist." In the next few years, the Court would protect the use of "motherfucker" in public debate....

If the Court moved to open up public space to certain sorts of incivil behavior, there were limits. At no time did it accept the legitimacy of violence. The Supreme Court held fast to the notion that the state had a monopoly on the legitimate use of force. What the Court was doing was rewriting the line between behavior and violence, allowing far more space for aggressive words. Earlier laws had defended civil demeanor precisely because "incivil" behavior was thought to *lead* to discord. Now there was to be a toleration of more insulting behavior although it still had to stop short of violence....

Debate over institutional decorum also extended to discussion of hair and clothing. In 1975 the Court took up the case of a policeman who had broken the department's dress code by wearing his hair modestly over the collar. While he argued that the code infringed upon his civil rights, the Court's majority disagreed, arguing that the department's need for "discipline, esprit de corps, and uniformity" was sufficient reason for a dress code. Only Justice William O. Douglas dissented, asserting that the policemen should have the right to wear his hair "according to his own taste."...

All regimes wind up taking a stand on where decorum can be broken and where it has to be enforced. It is only where there is an abstract commitment to universal equal rights that decorum becomes legally problematic. But, to again repeat, there are different ways that such regimes can handle the issue. In the late 1960s there was a shift in American practice and law. The Supreme Court opened up all sorts of behavior in private life and in public. The Court would do nothing about people yelling "motherfucker" at school board meetings or in street protests. It declared unconstitutionally broad ordinances that outlawed incivil behavior because it "tended" to lead to a breach of the peace.... At the same time, however, the Court also carefully maintained the authority of institutions. The running of a school, a courtroom, or a workplace (for example, a police department) all demanded decorum. Here civil behavior, as defined by authorities, could be enforced by law....

Institutional decorum coupled with a relatively unregulated civic forum is one historic way liberal politics has handled the issue of order and freedom. This was the path chosen by U. S. courts in the late 1960s, a legal version of the informalization going on in American society at large. And for the time being, at least, it has remained the law of the land.

Incivility and Self-Destruction: The Real Sixties

GERARD J. DEGROOT

"If you remember the Sixties," quipped Robin Williams (and quite a few others), "you weren't there." He was referring, of course, to the haze created by all those mind-expanding drugs the beautiful people popped, mainlined, and smoked. In truth, however, time has proved an equally effective hallucinogen. As years go by, real events have given way to imagined constructs. The decade has been transformed into a morality play, an explanation of how the world went astray or, conversely, how hope was squandered. Problems of the present are blamed on myths of the past.

Memory acts like a filter, yielding a clearer image of the past. The impurities are removed, producing a distillation both logical and meaningful. We forget, for instance, that back then the music business made a lot of money from silly songs like "Yummy, Yummy, Yummy," or that Sergeant Barry Sadler's "Ballad of the Green Berets" outsold "Give Peace a Chance." We remember the Students for a Democratic Society but forget the Young Americans for Freedom....

The past is what happened—history the way we view it. For too long, the Sixties has been a sacred zone. The spotlight has been shone upon those people or events we would like to believe were important. But cast aside the rose-tinted spectacles and we see mindless mayhem, shallow commercialism, and unbridled cruelty....

Nostalgia for the Sixties is strong precisely because so much did not survive. The decade is important for reasons most people do not understand, or care to admit. Revolution was never on the cards. The door of idealism opened briefly and was then slammed shut, for fear of what might enter. Chauvinism and cynicism got the better of hope and tolerance. The Sixties was the time when the postwar consensus began to disintegrate, when society polarized and liberalism went into steep decline. Perhaps the most enduring bequest of the decade is the convenient gallery of scapegoats it provided. To this day, people have been eager to blame their problems—moral decay, crime, violence, and the plight of

Reprinted by permission of the publisher from Gerard J. De Groot, *The Sixties Unplugged: A Kaleidoscopic History of a Disorderly Decade*, p. 1–3, 243–250, 253–258, 369–375, 411–416, 449–450, Cambridge, Mass.: Harvard University Press. Copyright © 2008 by Gerard J. DeGroot.

the family—on a permissive generation of misfits, delinquents, and revolutionaries more powerful in myth than they ever were in life....

Sharon: Young Americans for Freedom

Students for a Democratic Society began, rather appropriately, at a United Auto Workers retreat in the working-class state of Michigan. Its alter ego, the right-wing Young Americans for Freedom, began, equally appropriately, at William F. Buckley's leafy estate in Sharon township, in the gentrified state of Connecticut. Because the staid YAF does not harmonize with the popular image of the 1960s, supposedly a decade of exuberant rebellion, it has often been ignored in studies of the period. Yet on many campuses conservative activism was more widespread and popular than the left-wing variety. YAF also had more identifiable long-term influence, given the direct line from its radicalism to the neoconservatism of today.

In 1961, Medford Stanton Evans, a disciple of Buckley, boasted that "the Conservative element on ... campus is now on the offensive; it is articulate, resourceful, aggressive. It represents the group which, in fifteen or twenty years, will be assuming the seat of power in the United States. That is why, in my estimation, it authentically represents the future of the country." This was not simply conservative hype; American news magazines confirmed that a tidal wave of conservatism was sweeping across college campuses, largely in reaction to Kennedy's election. US *News and World Report, Newsweek,* and *Time* all reported a right-wing revolt, pointing out that campus conservatives were not merely echoing the political prejudices of their parents. For many, in fact, turning right was rebellion. "My parents thought Franklin D. Roosevelt was one of the greatest heroes who ever lived." Robert Schuchman, chairman of YAF, remarked. "I'm rebelling from that concept." A young conservative at the University of Wisconsin chimed: "You walk around with your Goldwater button, and you feel the thrill of treason."

Buckley wanted YAF to act as a counterweight to the supposedly left-wing bias of universities, which seemed to threaten the American way of life. While at Yale in the late 1940s, he discovered "an extraordinarily irresponsible education attitude that, under the protective label 'academic freedom,' has produced one of the most extraordinary incongruities of our time: the institution that derives its moral and financial support from Christian individualists and then addresses itself to the task of persuading the sons of these supporters to be atheistic socialists."...

YAF's charter—"The Sharon Statement"—was drafted in Buckley's living room on September 11, 1960, by Evans. "In time of moral and political crises, it is the responsibility of the youth of America to affirm certain moral truths," the statement proclaimed. Foremost among these truths was free will. In the emphasis placed upon freedom, YAF and SDS had much in common, but while SDS also promoted equality, YAF never did. YAF maintained that "political freedom cannot long exist without economic freedom." The free market was endorsed as "the single economic system compatible with the requirements of personal freedom ... and ... the most productive supplier of human needs."...

"What is so striking in the students who met at Sharon is their appetite for power," Buckley later confessed. For them, politics was not a game but an intensely serious crusade. They equated conservatism with maturity and therefore saw themselves as "older" than their fellow leftist students, whose cultural rebellion seemed trivial. The generation gap hardly bothered them; materialism and conformity seemed worthy ideals. As a result, YAF did not waste its time on parochial issues relating to university life. Dissent was expressed in exclusively national and international terms. Nor did they court publicity, since publicity invited attack. In stark contrast to Hoffman and Rubin, YAF organized in secret and zealously preserved anonymity. "We never got the publicity and we weren't interested in that," one activist maintained. While the left sought immediate solutions to distinct social problems, the right concentrated on a gradual assumption of power which would eventually allow them to exercise authority in all realms. Some activists formulated five-year plans; others, more realistically thought in terms of a conservative millennium decades ahead....

At its inception, YAF espoused an instinctual conservatism, untainted by pragmatism. For this reason, members revered Barry Goldwater. His proclamation at the Republican convention in 1964 that "extremism in the defense of liberty is no vice" seemed written for YAF. Besotted with Goldwater's purity, they assumed that the rest of the nation would be equally smitten. For that reason, his landslide defeat left them heartbroken. Lessons were nevertheless learned. Most members concluded that fundamentalist crusades do not harmonize well with electoral politics. They also learned that an ideology, no matter how perfect, still needs an attractive voice. Goldwater's problem, they decided, was not so much his ideas but his personality.

The lessons of 1964 explain the enthusiasm with which YAF embraced Ronald Reagan, first in the 1966 California gubernatorial campaign and then, two years later, during the Republican presidential campaign. On the surface, Reagan was not a natural YAF standard bearer, since his populism contradicted the intellectual elitism of the movement. But while Reagan lacked ideological purity, he was indisputably a formidable candidate. YAF's enthusiasm demonstrates that, in contrast to students on the left, the group understood the importance of winning elections and was not irresistibly attracted to the purity of lost causes....

"The left battled for the campus; the right won politics," one YAF member reflected on his years of student activism. Despite its conservatism, YAF was not a collection of squares. They demonstrated that one could not automatically guess a person's belief by what he wore, the length of his hair, or the music and drugs he enjoyed. Many wore the uniform of the counterculture, tasted its pleasures, and shared its craving for freedom. What distinguished them was that they saw no need to indulge in left-wing politics in order to be part of the Sixties ethos and did not confuse the personal with the political. They accepted sex and drugs as simple pleasures, instead of investing them with profound political meaning. Ironically, they occupied a political position, as students, to which a good many of their campus adversaries would eventually gravitate, after their brief flirtation with socialism. As one activist who later served in the Reagan administration remarked: "My political views are no different than they [once were], but there has been a change [in] the mainstream—not that I went to the mainstream, but the mainstream came to where we were.... Before, I was on the outside; now I'm in the middle." As Evans rather perceptively remarked in 1961, "Historians may well record the decade of the 1960s as the era in which conservatism, as a viable political force, finally came into its own."

London: Love Is All You Need

At some point in 1967, a gang of drugged-up anarchists from the London Street Commune, backed by some really frightening Hell's Angels, raided the offices of *IT* (*International Times*), hallowed journal of the British Counterculture, intent upon seizing control. Chanting "Property is theft!" they ran amok for most of an afternoon. The invasion plunged the *IT* staff into a deep moral dilemma. Many believed that property was indeed theft, and had argued as much in their paper. After frenetic debate, staff members decided that the principle did not apply to one's own property. Unfortunately, they lacked the muscle to eject the invaders. An agonizing argument ensued over whether the police—hated agents of oppression—should be summoned. Eventually, principles gave way to pragmatism and the cops were called. Order was restored....

British hippies discussed "ideology," and occasionally quoted Marx, Sartre, or Camus, but the talk was like clouds of smoke from a well-rolled spliff, endlessly spiraling in the air. The one unanimous ideal was "a better quality of life," which did not involve gainful employment. "I think it was probably the first time the children went to college without any idea of getting a job at the end of it," said Sue Miles. "It had never occurred to me what I was going to do, never." The fellow traveler Richard Trench remembers wanting the world "to be sort of left-wing socialist, but I didn't want to work.... Everybody would work less, everybody would become middle-class like us, everybody would read poetry like us."...

Hippies espoused an alternative culture, but in reality created a parallel universe in which power, though differently distributed, was still crucially important. Labels changed but human nature did not. Middle-class values proved difficult to jettison. Thus, in common with the "straight" world, the counterculture had its own restaurants, bookshops, record stores, newspapers, art galleries, clothing stores, theaters, concert halls, cinemas, travel agencies, and people ripping each other off. Ambitious entrepreneurs did precisely what they might have done in the straight world, while convincing themselves they were rebelling. No surprise, then, that when the party ended, the elite had little difficulty rejoining reality.

Only the middle class could pretend to ignore money. "We weren't really living in Edge City," Jerome Burne thought. "We all had parents and backup systems, which the working-class people didn't have." Pretense was sometimes difficult, however, since pleasure carried a price. Hippies who eschewed government and politics happily lived off the welfare state, convincing themselves that accepting the dole was a bona fide act of rebellion against capitalism. When funds ran short, they resorted to shady practices to keep reality at bay. They stole, dealt drugs, and fleeced their fellow travelers....

San Francisco: It's Free Because it's Yours!

In 1966, thousands of young people went to San Francisco with flowers in their hair. The city could accommodate a small community of harmless nonconformists congregating around the intersection of Haight and Ashbury. It could not, however, adjust to hordes of wannabe hippies—penniless runaways armed only with their fantasies. The "invasion" occurred because of the publicity given to the hippie phenomenon in songs and in the media. Old-timers joked about "bead-wearing *Look* reporters interviewing bead-wearing *Life* reporters." "The media was publishing all these articles about the Haight," Peter Coyote recalled, "seducing and attracting young people to come out there.... The city was capitalizing on it and taking no responsibility for it; telling all these kids ... to get lost."

Coyote helped found the Diggers, self-appointed guardians of the hippie generation. "Our feeling was that they were our kids.... This was America.... We started feeding them and sheltering them and setting up medical clinics, just because it needed to be done." Charity was not the objective but the by-product; Diggers were trying to create a new society in which suffering would not occur. Like the [Dutch] Provos, they adhered to a philosophy centering on the concept of "free," which had two intertwined meanings. "Free" meant free of charge, but also free of restraint. That which was free cost nothing but was also liberated and therefore liberating. The word provided description and it implied obligation. The aim was to place the adjective before almost any aspect of human existence and then attempt to bring that imaginary construct into being.

The Digger philosophy was deeply rooted in liberal individualism—the American dream amplified through the prism of LSD. Diggers maintained that individuals should be free to be whatever they wanted to be. Nothing should be predetermined. Freedom could be discovered only through action—by "doing it"—"it" being whatever inspired the individual. Everything the Diggers did, from their free stores to their anarchic street happenings, was designed to expose the tension between freedom and conformity.

The Diggers emerged from the San Francisco Mime Troupe, a radical group of actors devoted to "guerrilla theater." The troupe's aim, according to the founder, R. G. Davis, was to present "moral plays and to confront hypocrisy in society." "This is our society," he argued. "If we don't like it, it's our duty to change it; if we can't change it, we must destroy it." Action-oriented radicalism appealed to Coyote, who had become disenchanted with traditional protest. "It came home to me indelibly that I was never going to change anything in America by walking around carrying a sign. It was great revelation. It saved me a lot of anxiety and a lot of wasted energy."...

During a 1967 SDS conference, a Digger staged an unusual protest when he suddenly stripped off his clothes. Asked to explain, he replied: "Somebody has to be naked around here." Ideologies, in other words, were protective clothing

which prevented the individual from emerging. Political labels violated autonomy and were therefore "bullshit." Communists were "creeps," Grogan felt,
while the New Left was "as full of puritanical shit as the country's right wing
was cowardly absurd." "From our perspective," Coyote wrote, "all ideological
solutions, left and right, all undervalued the individual, and were quick to sacrifice them to the expediencies of their particular mental empires." Instead of
allowing individuality to flourish, radicals clothed themselves in political "truths,"
while ritually attacking the intellectual garb of their opponents....

Diggers provided "alternatives to society's skimpy menu of life choices."
They opened "stores" that offered free food and clothing, set up a free medical
clinic, and ran a free bank. The bank consisted of a box full of cash from which
an individual could take what he needed. He could take, but he must not steal.
The oft-repeated slogan went: "It's free because it's yours." Every day, they provided Digger Stew and Digger Bread, sometimes feeding a thousand people.
Those who partook had first to pass through a huge wooden frame, brightly
painted yellow, called the "Free Frame of Reference." The frame was intended
as a doorway between the actual and the possible. By stepping through it, individuals would change the way they viewed their world....

Money to fund this great adventure often came from drug dealers who had
an interest in keeping the hippie community fed. The Haight Independent Proprietors (HIP) also contributed from profits made selling souvenirs to tourists.
Donations proved problematic, however, because, if everything was free, there
should technically be no charity. On occasion, when hip philanthropists tried to
donate cash, a Digger would burn the money in front of the startled benefactor.
When Allen Ginsberg, Gary Snyder, and other Beat writers organized a fund-
raiser at a North Beach bar, Diggers rejected the benevolence, explaining that
charity was simply a salve to the conscience and an escape from commitment.
In truth, however, moral standards were little more than self-righteous posturing.
Diggers could not have survived without help from friends. In order to satisfy
their own conscience, they convinced themselves that goods and cash donated
had in fact been "liberated." In some cases this was literally true, as stealing was
not unknown. But since property was not acknowledged, neither was theft.

The Diggers were products of affluence. The economic system they derided
was in fact their lifeblood. Great Society welfare programs cushioned the blows of
self-imposed poverty. Strictures against charity did not apply to welfare checks and
food stamps. More fundamentally, a buoyant economy provided a surplus which
could be redistributed as if it were free. "There's already enough stuff for everybody," Coyote maintained. "Money is a way of creating scarcity. There's machinery that can create a television set for every man and woman and child on the
planet.... The money is a valve that's been put between you and the TV."

At the heart of this philosophy was a rather traditional faith in American
technology as the Great Provider. Capitalist enterprise was usually seen as a monster, but sometimes as a savior, since it had the potential to provide for everyone,
while at the same time setting the masses free. "Give up jobs so computers can
do them," a Digger leaflet instructed. The group sincerely believed that within
ten years "machines and computers will do most of the work," giving the people

more time to pursue their dreams. Out of this belief grew the conviction that money would soon become obsolete. In one street pageant celebrating the "Death of Money," a giant coffin was carried through the streets, into which spectators threw bills and coins.

The attack upon conformity did not extend to a destruction of patriarchy.... Coyote admitted that "[women] were the real backbone of the whole deal," because they could use their charm to liberate supplies from local merchants and wholesalers. A skimpy blouse worn with no bra could buy a lot of free food. Digger women also had to deal with pregnancies and childrearing in what was a frontier existence. Coyote recalled fierce arguments between women who needed money for their babies, and men "who wanted truck parts or ... a bag of smack." A strict hierarchy existed in which the men were "creating mythologies, dreaming, scoring dope.... The guys held down a lot of the visionary, metaphysical end of things. You know, like in an orthodox Hebrew community. The men are studying Talmud and they're looking at heaven. The women are taking care of the household and paying the bills and cooking the food." Men's work was important because men did it, women's work trivial because women did it....

Mayfair: Casualties of the Cultural Revolution

In early January 1969, Jimi Hendrix entertained the reporter Don Short from the *Daily Mirror* at his new house in Mayfair [a suburb of London], next door to the former home of George Frideric Handel. "To tell you the God's honest truth, I haven't heard much of the fella's stuff," he confessed. "But I dig a bit of Bach now and again." In spite of himself, Short was charmed by Hendrix. Like so many others who first encountered the wild man of rock, he was surprised to find a polite, soft-spoken gentleman. Short asked him about his outrageous image. It wasn't an image, he insisted. "No, I'm just natural all the time. What others think or say doesn't worry me."

Hendrix embodied everything the counterculture held sacred—the exuberance, the excess, the fun, the music, the drugs. Yet those attributes competed with one another; they could not long coexist. Exuberance was difficult to maintain while consuming copious quantities of drugs. Perhaps more fundamentally, style threatened to smother substance. Hendrix made his reputation as a wild man, even though that image did not do justice to his complex sensitivity. Drugs masked his suffering: the more success he achieved, the more exploited he became, and the more he craved escape. His manager, the vile Michael Jeffrey, treated Hendrix like a mother lode to be stripped of ore as quickly as possible, until only a pile of poisonous slag remained. If Hendrix seemed destructive, it was perhaps because he was being destroyed....

"The 60s ended for me in 1970 when they announced on the radio that Jimi Hendrix was dead," John Marsh recalled. "My first reaction was I knew the 1970s were going to fuck it all. And by God they did." Marsh's reaction was not uncommon; quite a few people saw the death of Hendrix as the end of the party. The clues had long been there. "By 1969 it all broke apart and some went to money and others to total insanity," Spike Hawkins felt. "I saw the end coming with overdoses. It turned very nasty…. Deaths came left, right and centre…. The energy went."…

Among those who survived, the drug experience seemed in retrospect fun, colorful, and relatively harmless, something to be remembered nostalgically but (in most cases) to be stored securely in the past. "Sometimes being stoned helped you to perceive the things that were hidden from you by all the advertising," the actress Julie Christie reflected. "Perhaps getting stoned was the only way to over-throw the sort of mind-fucking that had been going on, this brainwashing. Al-though there were a lot of casualties, it wasn't such a bad thing—trying to get on another plane." Quite a few musicians convinced themselves that LSD improved their creativity, allowing them to discover harmonies otherwise elusive. "When you stop exploring with drugs, now that's a bad scene," Steve Winwood of Traffic argued. "I never want to stop exploring."

Explorers sometimes got swallowed by the jungle. Among the casualties, history remembers a few famous faces, immensely talented individuals like Hendrix, Janis Joplin, and Jim Morrison, who died far too young. Behind them rank thousands of faceless dead remembered only by their families. And then there are the living dead, those whose minds were ravaged by drugs but whose bodies somehow survived to torment those who knew them when….

People's Park: The Future in a Vacant Lot

Up until 1967, the San Francisco Bay Area neatly reflected the divisions in Six-ties rebellion. On one side of the bay was Haight-Ashbury, the epicenter of the lifestyle revolution. On the other side was Berkeley, a battleground in the polit-ical revolution. The two communities shared the paraphernalia of the counter-culture but were otherwise distinct and often mutually suspicious. Hippies thought the politicos a bad trip, while the New Left feared that the freaks would tarnish their image.

In 1967, the Human Be-In, billed as a "gathering of the tribes," attempted a synthesis of the two strands of rebellion. An even more significant blending, however, occurred when hippies began to put down roots in the shabby streets where Berkeley borders Oakland. The Haight had begun to crumble under the combined weight of curious tourists, unscrupulous drug dealers, repressive po-lice, and gouging landlords, causing hippies to flee to the cheap housing and tol-erance of Berkeley. The Haight's sordidness soon followed them. Berkeley's crime rate soared.

East Bay tolerance had limits. Conservative Republicans, always a force in the area, demanded that the university, which owned the slum housing where many hippies lived, take action. They were supported by William Knowland's *Oakland Tribune,* always proficient at firing up public wrath. Under immense pressure, the university decided in late 1967 to demolish an entire block border-ing Telegraph Avenue, thus forcing out the undesirables under the guise of ur-ban renewal and university expansion—two good liberal causes.

Berkeley radicals suspected a sinister design—namely, the goal, of "eliminat-ing the culture of protest by denying it its turf."…

In other words, the issue was not simply a matter of what to do with a plot of land. It became instead an argument over rights, a struggle for authority, and a battle for the soul of the Sixties....

Michael Delacour, boutique owner and hippie impresario, decided to seize the lot for "the people." The Berkeley left, always game to confront authority, rallied behind him.

The left saw the park as Shangri-La; the right, as Sodom and Gomorrah. Caught between these two views was the university chancellor, Roger Heyns, a thoroughly decent man despised by both sides because he kowtowed to neither. While the left rallied and the right fumed, Heyns desperately sought compromise, without success. On May 15, 1969, at the request of the Republican mayor, 250 police officers from various forces took over the park, evicted the squatters, and erected a fence. Word spread through the radical community, and within hours 4,000 demonstrators had mobilized. Neither side was in the mood for restraint. Demonstrators tossed bricks and rocks from the rooftops. The police, increasingly frustrated, used tear gas, then birdshot, then buckshot. As time passed, their aim grew more random, their range shorter. By the end of the day, more than a hundred demonstrators had been injured, thirteen of them requiring hospital treatment. A rioter named James Rector was killed when buckshot ripped open his stomach; another was blinded after being hit with birdshot. The police later claimed they had fired in self-defense, yet not a single police officer was seriously injured. "The indiscriminate use of shotguns [was] sheer insanity," Dr. Harry Brean, chief radiologist at Berkeley's Herrick Hospital later remarked.

That night, [Governor Ronald] Reagan sent in the National Guard. For the next seventeen days, Berkeley was a war zone. On one occasion, guardsmen threw tear gas canisters into a lecture hall for no apparent reason. On May 20, a National Guard helicopter sprayed tear gas on a bewildered crowd of staff and students. The outcry was tremendous, but Reagan remained unrepentant: "There was no alternative. Whether that was a tactical mistake or not, once the dogs of war are unleashed, you must expect that things will happen and that people, being human, will make mistakes on both sides."...

Altamont [San Francisco Bay Area]: The Day the Music Died

The Woodstock Festival of August 1969 was supposed to have been a beginning, the green shoots of the cooperative commonwealth in which everyone would be nice to one another and leaders would conform to the popular will. In fact it was the end—or, rather, a false dawn. Reality was revealed in gory Technicolor four months later at a dusty racetrack called Altamont....

Given the portents of doom, it is perhaps surprising that so many people thought Altamont was going to be like Woodstock, even though Woodstock was not really like Woodstock. As the rock journalist Michael Lydon found, the festival momentum was driven by the hippies' irrepressible ability to hope: "[Altamont] was the biggest gathering in California since the Human Be-In three years before, not only in numbers but in expectation.... It would, all believed, advance the trip, reveal some important lesson intrinsic to and yet beyond its physical fact. The 300,000, all in unspoken social contract, came not only to hear music, but to bear living testimony to their own lives." Altamont came at the end of a long and highly profitable Rolling Stones tour of America. It was, in essence, their way of saying thank you. In line with that sentiment, it was supposed to be a free concert and, as such, homage to a golden idea.

Agents representing the Stones met informally in San Francisco with some people from the Grateful Dead. The latter were experts at staging big, free outdoor events—or at least they claimed to be. Ambition, fueled by drugs, went unrestrained. The manager of the Sears Point raceway, in a generous mood, offered his grounds for free. Everything seemed to be going smoothly, but leaving organization to the Dead was like entrusting nutrition to Cap'n Crunch.

"An essential element of free concerts is simplicity," Lydon wrote. Unfortunately, nothing about the Stones could ever be simple. "Everybody wanted a piece of the action. Hustlers of every stripe swarmed to the new scene like piranhas to the scent of blood." After sleeping on it, that nice man at Sears Point started getting greedy. He asked for $6,000, plus another $5,000 deposit to cover possible damage. That was a hitch, but not an obstacle. In order to cover the steadily mounting costs, the Stones sold the film rights. It then turned out that the Filmways Corporation was the actual owner of Sears Point, and when their people got wind of a concert movie, they demanded distribution rights. The Stones told them to get lost, at which point the rent was raised to $100,000. This was on Thursday. The concert was scheduled for Saturday. Crowds were already gathering, and the stage was being built....

The presence of the Hell's Angels didn't help—they brought an air of menace to a gathering supposedly founded on love. The Stones had hired the Angels to provide unofficial security.... They were promised free beer, but the real attraction seems to have been the opportunity to run riot on such a large stage.

That opportunity did not go wasted. While Jefferson Airplane was in the middle of a furiously exuberant version of "Three-Fifths of a Mile in Ten Seconds," a fight broke out below the stage. Marty Balin, the lead singer, intervened, whereupon a Hell's Angel started beating him with a pool cue. The crowd, paralyzed in confusion and terror, could not decide whether this was a bad trip or, worse, reality....

The focus of the Angels' violence was Meredith Hunter, an eighteen-year-old from Oakland. The exact sequence of events remains a matter of dispute. Some claim that the Angels attacked first, perhaps because Hunter, a black man, had a white girlfriend. Others contend that, without provocation, Hunter pointed a gun at Jagger. No one disputes that he did brandish a gun, though whether he or the Angels were acting in self-defense remains unclear. Once that gun appeared, the result was inevitable. A witness later described an execution:

They hit him ... I couldn't tell whether it was a knife or not ... but on the side of the head. And then ... he came running towards me, and then fell down on his knees and the Hell's Angel ... grabbed onto both of his shoulders and started kicking him in the face about five times or so, and then be fell down on his face ... and then one of them kicked him off the side and rolled over and he muttered some words. He said, "I wasn't going to shoot you."

Rather bizarrely, given the circumstances, the Stones eventually resumed their set. By this stage, however, the spirit had evaporated. Most people wanted to go home. The Grateful Dead never did play. "Looking back, I don't think it was a good idea to have Hell's Angels there," Keith Richards admitted. "It was a complete mess and we were partly to blame," Jagger confessed in 1989. "You expected everyone in San Francisco—because they were so mellow, nice, and organized—that it was going to be all those things. But of course, it wasn't."...

After the decade died, it rose again as religion. For quite a few people, the Sixties is neither memory nor myth, but faith. Religions do not require a foundation of logic—indeed, they defy logic. So it is with the religion of the Sixties. Believers in the gospel cling faithfully to a dream that ignores the laws of economics, politics, and human nature. They imagine into existence a world where everyone is rendered peaceful by the power of love and where greed, ambition, and duplicity are banished. Reality itself is suspended.

The believers worship a few martyred gods (Che, Lennon, Kennedy, King, Lumumba) and seek truth in the teachings of an assortment of sometimes competing prophets (Malcolm X, Leary, Hoffman, Hendrix, Dylan, Dutschke, Muhammad Ali, et al.). Their reliquary includes the incense, hash pipes, beads, buttons, tie-dyed shirts, and Day-Glo posters still sold at sacred sites in Berkeley, Greenwich Village, Soho, and Amsterdam. Their gospel is peppered with stock slogans from the Heavenly Decade: "All you need is love," "Make love not war," "Power to the people," "Turn on, tune in, drop out."...

Those who bemoan the betrayal of the Sixties spirit are in effect arguing that the decade had no effect on our present, that it was a delightful interlude between the conformist Fifties and the self-indulgent Seventies. Yet this denies the law of historical continuity—the fact that everything develops from that which precedes it. No decade is unimportant; no period exists as anomaly. The Sixties was important, but not in ways that worshipers (or critics) of the myth like to admit. If the Sixties seems strange to us today, it is probably because we tend to look at the wrong things. By paying so much attention to what was happening on Maggie's Farm, we failed to notice the emergence of Maggie Thatcher.

The survival of the Sixties myth says something about the resilience of our spirit, if not about the reality of our world. The decade brought flowers, music, love, and good times. It also brought hatred, murder, greed, dangerous drugs, needless deaths, ethnic cleansing, neocolonialist exploitation, soundbite politics, sensationalism, a warped sense of equality, a bizarre notion of freedom, the decline of liberalism, and the end of innocence. Bearing all that in mind, the decade should seem neither unfamiliar nor all that special.

FURTHER READING

David Allyn, *Make Love, Not War: The Sexual Revolution, An Unfettered History* (2000).

John A. Andrew III, *The Other Side of the Sixties: Young Americans and the Rise of Conservative Politics* (1997).

Robert Cantwell, *When We Were Good: The Folk Revival* (1996).

Elizabeth Cobbs Hoffman, *All You Need is Love: The Peace Corps and the Spirit of the 1960s* (2000).

Alice Echols, *Scars of Sweet Paradise: The Life and Times of Janis Joplin* (1999).

Ignacio M. Garcia, *Chicanismo: The Forging of a Militant Ethos Among Mexican Americans* (2000).

Todd Gitlin, *The Sixties: Years of Hope, Days of Rage* (1987).

Richard N. Goodwin, *Remembering America: A Voice From the Sixties* (1988).

Van Gosse, *Where the Boys Are: Cuba, Cold War America, and the Making of a New Left* (1993).

Paul Lyons, *New Left, New Right, and the Legacy of the Sixties* (1996).

Mark S. Massa, *The American Catholic Revolution: How the Sixties Changed the Church Forever* (2010).

James Miller, *Democracy is in the Streets: From Port Huron to the Siege of Chicago (1994)*.

Douglas Rossinow, *The Politics of Authenticity: Liberalism, Christianity, and the New Left in America* (1998).

David Szatmary, *Rockin' in Time: A Social History of Rock-and-Roll* (1997).

Jon Wiener, *Come Together: John Lennon in His Time* (1991).

Tom Wolfe, *The Electric Kool-Aid Acid Test* (1968).

CHAPTER 14

Vietnam and the Downfall

of Presidents

The term cold war *is a misnomer. Although the conflict "froze" borders in Europe, the war burned brightly—indeed raged out of control—for the United States in Vietnam. In Vietnam, the United States experienced what some consider its greatest failure as a nation, as well as the most obvious conflict between its historic "Spirit of 1776" ideal of self-determination and its military practice as a superpower.*

The United States became involved in Vietnam when President Truman decided to back France's attempt to retain its mutinous colony in 1946, following World War II. The American president ignored letters from independence leader Ho Chi Minh, who sought to free his nation from colonialism. Minh asked for U.S. protection, but Truman decided to back his European Cold War ally instead. Retaining the goodwill of France seemed more vital at that time than cultivating the friendship of a fledgling, potentially communist nation in remote Southeast Asia. The French fought the Viet Minh (independence fighters under Ho Chi Minh) for eight bloody years, assisted financially by the United States. By the time France acknowledged defeat in 1954, U.S. leaders had become convinced that it was necessary to divide the small nation permanently to ensure that the popular but communist Ho Chi Minh did not end up ruling the whole country. Flouting the 1954 peace treaty signed at Geneva, which temporarily partitioned the country at the 17th parallel in anticipation of elections two years later, the United States opposed a vote that would reunify the nation democratically. What followed was a twenty-year military commitment to the Republic of South Vietnam, a government wracked by civil war, corruption, and the suppression of domestic critics, including the Buddhist clergy. Why the United States decided to continue the war into the 1970s—despite doubts within the government, the growing objections of our allies, and eventually the opposition of a majority of the American people—remains a subject for debate and national soul-searching.

The war boomeranged on the United States in a number of ways. It fueled a virulent protest movement, weakened the American economy, heightened racial and class conflicts, and brought home a generation of young men who were deeply disillusioned and in many respects damaged by the conflict. More than 58,000 Americans lost their lives. The

Vietnamese lost more than one million soldiers in combat, and approximately three million civilians. The war also contributed to the downfall of two American presidents. Lyndon Johnson was the first to be accused of a "credibility gap" because of his insistence that the United States was not entering into a full-fledged war, even though it was. When it became clear that his Vietnam policy had cost him the confidence of the American people, Johnson announced that he would not run for reelection in 1968. Public mistrust deepened considerably under Richard M. Nixon, who formed a "plumbers' unit" to stop news leaks related to the war and to punish domestic political opponents.

The Nixon administration eventually brought itself down when it attempted to cover up its "bugging" of the offices of the Democratic National Committee at the Watergate Hotel in Washington. Numerous administration members received jail terms or probation for their crimes, including Vice President Spiro Agnew, Attorney General John Mitchell, Chief of Staff H. R. Haldeman, and White House lawyers John Ehrlichman and John Dean. The bipartisan House Judiciary Committee voted to impeach President Nixon on three counts—obstruction of justice, abuse of power, and contempt of Congress. Before the full House could vote on the motion, Nixon resigned the Oval Office effective August 9, 1974. The president avoided indictment on criminal charges only because his successor Gerald Ford (who had not been elected to either the presidency or the vice presidency) issued him a blanket pardon one month later. The leadership of America was deeply compromised; the nation's people were sorely divided. Confidence in government was yet another casualty of the war.

QUESTIONS TO THINK ABOUT

Was the Vietnam War a tragic blunder, a noble cause, or one of the costs of American leadership of the so-called "Free World" or western alliance? What alternative choices might American leaders have made, considering the range of international problems they faced? How did the war affect the nation's people and government?

DOCUMENTS

The documents in this chapter reflect different aspects of the Vietnam War. In document 1, the U.S. ambassador reports the French president's threat that his nation might fall to communism if America is unable to show its worth as an ally by helping to restore France's strength (as an empire). Document 2 reveals the basic problem for the United States: did it want to support self-determination or colonialism? In this letter to President Harry Truman, Vietnamese independence leader Ho Chi Minh asks for the help of the United States, pointing to Roosevelt's "Four Freedoms" and the grant of independence to the Philippines. In document 3, President Eisenhower articulates the influential "domino" theory: if one country (like Vietnam) falls to communism, so will others. In document 4, a defense analyst in 1965 assigns percentage weights to U.S. war aims in Vietnam for Secretary of Defense Robert McNamara. The preponderant reason (70 percent) is to "avoid a humiliating U.S. defeat," and thus damage to its credibility on other fronts of the cold war—for example, its defense of the lines bisecting Korea and Germany. The least important reason (10 percent) is to help the South Vietnamese enjoy a "freer way of life." Presidential adviser George Ball advises Johnson in document 5 to compromise with the North Vietnamese. Foreign white troops will not be able to defeat guerrillas supported by the local population, Ball asserted just before the mass commitment of U.S. troops. The next two documents point to growing concerns about the war amongst American citizens, especially the young men called upon to fight. In document 6, a draftee relates his willingness to serve his own country without question, and the shock of returning home to find others questioning him. Document 7 contains the lyrics to a song by the San Francisco "psychedelic" band, Country Joe and the Fish. Folk and rock music played an important role in generating opposition to the war. This satirical "rag" became one anthem of the anti-war movement. Document 8 shows the escalating paranoia and vindictiveness of the Nixon administration toward its critics, especially those active in the antiwar opposition. In document 9, Senator Sam Ervin, head of the Watergate investigation for the Senate, lists the crimes of the corrupt administration. Both the Nixon administration and the U.S. war in Vietnam, concluded by the Paris Peace Treaty of January 1973, were over.

1. French Leader Charles de Gaulle Warns the United States, 1945

General [Charles] de Gaulle asked me to come to see him at 6. He spoke in very quiet, affable, friendly fashion, but this is what he said: "We have received word that our troops still fighting in Indochina have appealed for aid to your military authorities in China and the British military authorities in Burma. We have received word that they replied that under instructions no aid could be sent.["] They were given to understand that the British simply followed our lead.

He said also that several expeditionary forces for Indochina had been prepared: Some troops were in North Africa, some in southern France and some in Madagascar, and the British had promised to transport them but at the last minute they were given to understand that owing to American insistence they could not transport them. He observed: "This worries me a great deal for obvious reasons and it comes at a particularly inopportune time. As I told Mr. Hopkins when he was here, we do not understand your policy. What are you driving at? Do you want us to become, for example, one of the federated states under the Russian aegis? The Russians are advancing apace as you well know. When Germany falls they will be upon us. If the public here comes to realize that you are against us in Indochina there will be terrific disappointment and nobody knows to what that will lead. We do not want to become Communist; we do not want to fall into the Russian orbit, but I hope that you do not push us into it...."

Foreign Relations of the United States, 1945, v. VI, (Washington: GPO, 1969) p. 300.

2. Independence Leader Ho Chi Minh Pleads with Harry Truman for Support, 1946

I avail myself of this opportunity to thank you and the people of United States for the interest shown by your representatives at the United Nations Organization in favour of the dependent peoples.

Our VIETNAM people, as early as 1941, stood by the Allies' side and fought against the Japanese and their associates, the French colonialists.

From 1941 to 1945 we fought bitterly, sustained by the patriotism of our fellow-countrymen and by the promises made by the Allies at YALTA, SAN FRANCISCO AND POTSDAM.

When the Japanese were defeated in August 1945, the whole Vietnam territory was united under a Provisional Republican Government which immediately set out to work. In five months, peace and order were restored, a democratic republic was established on legal bases, and adequate help was given to the Allies in the carrying out of their disarmament mission.

But the French colonialists, who had betrayed in war-time both the Allies and the Vietnamese, have come back and are waging on us a murderous and pitiless war in order to reestablish their domination. Their invasion has extended to South Vietnam and is menacing us in North Vietnam. It would take volumes to give even an abbreviated report of the crimes and assassinations they are committing every day in the fighting area.

This aggression is contrary to all principles of international law and to the pledges made by the Allies during the World War. It is a challenge to the noble attitude shown before, during and after the war by the United States Government and People....

... [W]e request of the United States as guardians and champions of World Justice to take a decisive step in support of our independence.

What we ask has been graciously granted to the Philippines. Like the Philippines our goal is full independence and full cooperation with the UNITED STATES.

3. President Dwight Eisenhower Warns of Falling Dominoes, 1954

Q. Robert Richards, Copley Press: Mr. President, would you mind commenting on the strategic importance of Indochina to the free world? I think there has been, across the country, some lack of understanding on just what it means to us.

The President: You have, of course, both the specific and the general when you talk about such things.

Ho Chi Minh to Harry Truman, February 16, 1946, reprinted in *Vietnam: The Definitive Documentation of Human Decisions*, ed. Gareth Porter (Stanfordville, N.Y.: Earl M. Coleman Enterprises, 1979), vol. 1, p. 95.

Public Papers of the Presidents of the United States: Dwight D. Eisenhower, 1954 (Washington, D.C.: U.S. Government Printing Office, 1958), 381–390.

First of all, you have the specific value of a locality in its production of materials that the world needs.

Then you have the possibility that many human beings pass under a dictatorship that is inimical to the free world.

Finally, you have broader considerations that might follow what you would call the "falling domino" principle. You have a row of dominoes set up, you knock over the first one, and what will happen to the last one is the certainty that it will go over very quickly. So you could have a beginning of a disintegration that would have the most profound influences.

Now, with respect to the first one, two of the items from this particular area that the world uses are tin and tungsten. They are very important. There are others, of course, the rubber plantations and so on.

Then with respect to more people passing under this domination, Asia, after all, has already lost some 450 million of its peoples to the Communist dictatorship, and we simply can't afford greater losses.

But when we come to the possible sequence of events, the loss of Indochina, of Burma, of Thailand, of the Peninsula, and Indonesia following, now you begin to talk about areas that not only multiply the disadvantages that you would suffer through loss of materials, sources of materials, but now you are talking about millions and millions and millions of people.

Finally, the geographical position achieved thereby does many things. It turns the so-called island defensive chain of Japan, Formosa, of the Philippines and to the southward; it moves in to threaten Australia and New Zealand.

It takes away, in its economic aspects, that region that Japan must have as a trading area or Japan, in turn, will have only one place in the world to go—that is, toward the Communist areas in order to live.

So, the possible consequences of the loss are just incalculable to the free world.

4. Defense Analyst John McNaughton Advises Robert McNamara on War Aims, 1965

1. U.S. Aims:

70%—To avoid a humiliating U.S. defeat (to our reputation as a guarantor).

20%—To keep SVN [South Vietnam] (and the adjacent) territory from Chinese hands.

10%—To permit the people of SVN to enjoy a better, freer way of life.

ALSO—To emerge from crisis without unacceptable taint from methods used.

NOT—to "help a friend," although it would be hard to stay in if asked out.

"Annex—Plan for Action for South Vietnam," memorandum from John T. McNaughton, Assistant Secretary of Defense for International Security Affairs, for Secretary of Defense Robert S. McNamara, March 24, 1965; reprinted in *The Pentagon Papers: As Published by the New York Times* (New York: New York Times Co., 1971), 442.

5. Undersecretary of State George Ball
Urges Withdrawal from Vietnam, 1965

Morning Meeting of July 21

The President: Is there anyone here of the opinion we should not do what the [Joint Chiefs of Staff] memorandum says [increase U.S. troops in Vietnam by 100,000]? If so, I want to hear from him now, in detail.

Ball: Mr. President, I can foresee a perilous voyage, very dangerous. I have great and grave apprehensions that we can win under these conditions. But let me be clear. If the decision is to go ahead, I am committed.

The President: But, George, is there another course in the national interest, some course that is better than the one [Defense Secretary] McNamara proposes? We know it is dangerous and perilous, but the big question is, can it be avoided?

Ball: There is no course that will allow us to cut our losses. If we get bogged down, our cost might be substantially greater. The pressures to create a larger war would be inevitable. The qualifications I have are not due to the fact that I think we are in a bad moral position.

The President: Tell me then, what other road can I go?

Ball: Take what precautions we can, Mr. President. Take our losses, let their government fall apart, negotiate, discuss, knowing full well there will be a probable take-over by the Communists. This is disagreeable, I know.

The President: I can take disagreeable decisions. But I want to know can we make a case for your thoughts? Can you discuss it fully?

Ball: We have discussed it. I have had my day in court.

The President: I don't think we can have made any full commitment, George. You have pointed out the danger, but you haven't really proposed an alternative course. We haven't always been right. We have no mortgage on victory. Right now, I am concerned that we have very little alternatives to what we are doing. I want another meeting, more meetings, before we take any definitive action. We must look at all other courses of possibility carefully. Right now I feel it would be more dangerous to lose this now, than endanger a great number of troops. But I want this fully discussed.

Afternoon Meeting of July 21

Ball: We cannot win, Mr. President. The war will be long and protracted. The most we can hope for is a messy conclusion. There remains a great danger of intrusion by the Chinese. But the biggest problem is the problem of the long war. The Korean experience was a galling one. The correlation between Korean casualties and public opinion showed support stabilized at 50 percent. As

This document can be found in "Cabinet Room, Wednesday, July 21, 1965," Johnson Papers, Meeting Notes File, Box 2, Lyndon B. Johnson Presidential Library, Austin, Texas. Reprinted in Thomas G. Paterson & Dennis Merrill, *Major Problems in American Foreign Relations*, Vol II: Since 1914, Fifth Ed. (Lexington, Mass.: D.C. Heath & Company), 452–454.

casualties increase, the pressure to strike at the very jugular of North Vietnam will become very great. I am concerned about world opinion. If we could win in a year's time, and win decisively, world opinion would be alright. However, if the war is long and protracted, as I believe it will be, then we will suffer because the world's greatest power cannot defeat guerrillas. Then there is the problem of national politics. Every great captain in history was not afraid to make a tactical withdrawal if conditions were unfavorable to him. The enemy cannot even be seen in Vietnam. He is indigenous to the country. I truly have serious doubts that an army of Westerners can successfully fight Orientals in an Asian jungle.

The President: This is important. Can Westerners, in the absence of accurate intelligence, successfully fight Asians in jungle rice paddies? I want McNamara and General [Earle] Wheeler [chairman of the Joint Chiefs of Staff] to seriously ponder this question.

Ball: I think we all have underestimated the seriousness of this situation. It is like giving cobalt treatment to a terminal cancer case. I think a long, protracted war will disclose our weakness, not our strength. The least harmful way to cut losses in SVN [South Vietnam] is to let the government decide it doesn't want us to stay there. Therefore, we should put proposals to the GVN [government of Vietnam (South)] that they can't accept. Then, it would move to a neutralist position. I have no illusions that after we were asked to leave South Vietnam, that country would soon come under Hanoi control....

The President: But George, wouldn't all these countries say that Uncle Sam was a paper tiger, wouldn't we lose credibility breaking the word of three presidents, if we did as you have proposed? It would seem to be an irresponsible blow. But I gather you don't think so?

Ball: No sir. The worse blow would be that the mightiest power on earth is unable to defeat a handful of guerrillas.

6. Draftee Sebastian A. Ilacqua Recalls Coming Back to "The World," 1967 (1995)

The only thing on our minds was getting home. It was two days before Christmas and a long time since we had seen our family and friends. We stood in the milling crowd of the station, clothed in the dress green of our Army uniforms. It was the only clothing we had. Brought straight from the battlefield to a hospital in Japan, we had lost all our personal effects. Nonetheless we were proudly attired, though my buddy held a cane and I had a cast and a colostomy.

We chatted casually while we awaited the next train into Philadelphia. It would have been a routine scene to the casual observer, but to us it was nothing short of a miraculous ascension from hell. "The world" would never be the same. Trivial things like having floors in a house or refrigerators or running water took on a new and much appreciated meaning. It was good to be home. The shocking and terrible images of war were still fresh in our minds.

Reprinted courtesy of Sebastian A. Ilacqua.

The smell of Vietnamese mud was uniquely pungent; and there was plenty of mud—sometimes knee-deep. Living in the moisture-rich environment of South Vietnam had its drawbacks. Boots that never dry out, socks that rot and toenails that fall off, sleeping in water—that is, when you get a chance to sleep—and having to keep weapons and ammo clean and dry. Not to mention being the target of Vietnamese trying to kill you.

The danger and the objectionable conditions were not a source of regret, however. Being conscripted for military service was a tradition that, for two centuries, had maintained the most free and prosperous nation in the history of mankind. We were merely taking up the baton passed to us by generations of similarly dutiful patriots. This was our job and we accepted our fate without question.

The end of the journey had been rough, though. For me, it began on a gloomy, overcast morning with an unfamiliar feeling of impending doom. I could not shake this foreboding as I accompanied my platoon on a routine mission. I really did not want to be there, but you can't just get a pass from the teacher to go home early.

I struggled to keep my attention on task while walking through a potentially mined area. Stay off the paths and look for signs of any disturbance of the ground, I told myself. Without warning—an explosion! I turned my head to look back about fifty feet. A grey cloud speckled with black particles was expanding from the ground at the site of the explosion. For a long instant I was an intimate observer of the destruction of war, until knocked violently to the ground. Vague images followed: a helicopter evacuation and the surgical suite of a field hospital.

But now here we stood, on the next leg of the journey. I was almost home. Since there was time, we decided to have a bite to eat. We sat at the lunch counter at one end of the station. Waitresses were preparing food, cleaning up, and taking care of straggling breakfast customers. It was a little before lunchtime so we were almost the only ones at the counter. We sat there patiently waiting for service. And waiting. It did not come. The waitresses simply ignored us. My buddy and I finally looked at each other in disbelief. We were being intentionally shunned. We had come face to face with the politics of the Vietnam War.

It hit us that what we thought of as honorable service was actually reviled by some Americans. Our first experience with this animosity came before we even [had] a chance to recover from our wounds. The sudden reversal from "sacred duty" to "object of revulsion" was difficult to grasp. As we sat there at the counter trying to understand the complex socio-political history of the war as it related to our lunch, a waitress finally approached. She must have thought that we had been sufficiently punished or else realized that she had to serve whoever sat at the counter, despite what she thought of them. The juxtaposition of prejudice and condescension was a bit too much and we left.

It was dark by the time my bus arrived in the small New Jersey town. My traveling companion had gone his separate way from Philadelphia and, left alone with my thoughts during the final part of the trip, my enthusiasm returned at being home to surprise my family. The opportunity of walking into the house unannounced under my own power was too precious to pass up and I decided to splurge on a cab rather than call for a ride. The driver readily agreed to give me a lift in the cold December night. The brief trip ended at the curb of my familiar, dear home. I reached into my pocket to pay the friendly driver, but he told me to put my money away. It was tradition to honor returning veterans and the cab driver cheerfully wished me a very happy holiday. With a smile on my face, I approached the door that marked the end of my journey.

7. Rock Band Country Joe and the Fish Lampoons the Vietnam War, 1968

Well, come on all of you, big strong men,

Uncle Sam needs your help again.

He's got himself in a terrible jam

Way down yonder in Vietnam

So put down your books and pick up a gun,

We're gonna have a whole lotta fun.

And it's one, two, three,

What are we fighting for?

Don't ask me, I don't give a damn,

Next stop is Vietnam;

And it's five, six, seven,

Open up the pearly gates,

Well there ain't no time to wonder why,

Whoopee! We're all gonna die.

Come on Wall Street, don't be slow,

Why man, this is war au-go-go

There's plenty good money to be made

By supplying the Army with the tools of its trade,

Just hope and pray that if they drop the bomb,

They drop it on the Viet Cong.

And it's one, two, three,

What are we fighting for?

Don't ask me, I don't give a damn,

Next stop is Vietnam,

And it's five, six, seven,

Open up the pearly gates,

Well there ain't no time wonder why

Whoopee! We're all gonna die.

Well, come on generals, let's move fast;

Your big chance has come at last.

Now you can go out and get those reds

'Cause the only good commie is the one that's dead

And you know that peace can only be won

When we've blown 'em all to kingdom come....

Come on mothers throughout the land,

Pack your boys off to Vietnam.

Come on fathers, don't hesitate

Send 'em off before it's too late

Be the first ones on your block

To have your boy come home in a box....

8. White House Counsel John W. Dean III Presents the "Enemies List," 1971

[John W. Dean III to John D. Ehrlichman]   August 16, 1971
CONFIDENTIAL
MEMORANDUM
SUBJECT: *Dealing with our Political Enemies*

This memorandum addresses the matter of how we can maximize the fact of our incumbency in dealing with persons known to be active in their opposition to our Administration. Stated a bit more bluntly—how we can use the available federal machinery to screw our political enemies.

After reviewing this matter with a number of persons possessed of expertise in the field, I have concluded that we *do not* need an elaborate mechanism or game plan, rather we need a good project coordinator and full support for the project. In brief, the system would work as follows:

- Key members of the staff (e.g., [Charles] Colson, Dent Flannigan, [Patrick] Buchanan) should be requested to inform us as to who they feel we should be giving a hard time.
- The project coordinator should then determine what sorts of dealings these individuals have with the federal government and how we can best screw them (e.g., grant availability, federal contracts, litigation, prosecution, etc.).
- The project coordinator then should have access to and the full support of the top officials of the agency or department in proceeding to deal with the individual.

Memorandum reprinted in Senate Select Committee on Presidential Campaign Activities, *Hearings* (Washington, D.C.: U.S. Government Printing Office, 1973), vol. 4, pp. 1689–1690.

I have learned that there have been many efforts in the past to take such actions, but they have ultimately failed—in most cases—because of lack of support at the top. Of all those I have discussed this matter with, Lyn Nofziger appears the most knowledgeable and most interested. If Lyn had support he would enjoy undertaking this activity as the project coordinator. You are aware of some of Lyn's successes in the field, but he feels that he can only employ limited efforts because there is a lack of support.

As a next step, I would recommend that we develop a small list of names—not more than ten—as our targets for concentration. Request that Lyn "do a job" on them and if he finds he is getting cut off by a department or agency, that he inform us and we evaluate what is necessary to proceed. I feel it is important that we keep our targets limited for several reasons: (1) a low visibility of the project is imperative; (2) it will be easier to accomplish something real if we don't over expand our efforts; and (3) we can learn more about how to operate such an activity if we start small and build.

9. Senator Sam J. Ervin Explains the Watergate Crimes, 1974

Watergate was a conglomerate of various illegal and unethical activities in which various officers and employees of the Nixon reelection committees and various White House aides of President Nixon participated in varying ways and degrees to accomplish these successive objectives:

1. To destroy, insofar as the Presidential election of 1972 was concerned, the integrity of the process by which the President of the United States is nominated and elected.
2. To hide from law enforcement officers, prosecutors, grand jurors, courts, the news media, and the American people the identities and wrongdoing of those officers and employees of the Nixon reelection committees, and those White House aides who had undertaken to destroy the integrity of the process by which the President of the United States is nominated and elected.

To accomplish the first of these objectives, the participating officers and employees of the reelection committees and the participating White House aides of President Nixon engaged in one or more of these things:

1. They exacted enormous contributions—usually in cash—from corporate executives by impliedly implanting in their minds the impressions that the making of the contributions was necessary to insure that the corporations would receive governmental favors, or avoid governmental disfavors, while President Nixon remained in the White House. A substantial portion of the contributions were made out of corporate funds in violation of a law enacted by Congress a generation ago.

Senate Select Committee on Presidential Campaign Activities, *Final Report* (Washington, D.C.: U.S. Government Printing Office, 1974), 1098–1101.

2. They hid substantial parts of these contributions in cash in safes and secret deposits to conceal their sources and the identities of those who had made them.

3. They disbursed substantial portions of these hidden contributions in a surreptitious manner to finance the bugging and the burglary of the offices of the Democratic National Committee in the Watergate complex in Washington for the purpose of obtaining political intelligence; and to sabotage by dirty tricks, espionage, and scurrilous and false libels and slanders the campaigns and the reputations of honorable men, whose only offenses were that they sought the nomination of the Democratic Party for President and the opportunity to run against President Nixon for that office in the Presidential election of 1972.

4. They deemed the departments and agencies of the Federal Government to be the political playthings of the Nixon administration rather than impartial instruments for serving the people, and undertook to induce them to channel Federal contracts, grants, and loans to areas, groups, or individuals so as to promote the reelection of the President rather than to further the welfare of the people.

5. They branded as enemies of the President individuals and members of the news media who dissented from the President's policies and opposed his reelection, and conspired to urge the Department of Justice, the Federal Bureau of Investigation, the Internal Revenue Service, and the Federal Communications Commission to pervert the use of their legal powers to harass them for so doing.

6. They borrowed from the Central Intelligence Agency disguises which E. Howard Hunt used in political espionage operations, and photographic equipment which White House employees known as the "Plumbers" and their hired confederates used in connection with burglarizing the office of a psychiatrist which they believed contained information concerning Daniel Ellsberg which the White House was anxious to secure.

7. They assigned to E. Howard Hunt, who was at the time a White House consultant occupying an office in the Executive Office Building, the gruesome task of falsifying State Department documents which they contemplated using in their altered state to discredit the Democratic Party by defaming the memory of former President John Fitzgerald Kennedy, who as the hapless victim of an assassin's bullet had been sleeping in the tongueless silence of the dreamless dust for 9 years.

8. They used campaign funds to hire saboteurs to forge and disseminate false and scurrilous libels of honorable men running for the Democratic Presidential nomination in Democratic Party primaries....

One shudders to think that the Watergate conspiracies might have been effectively concealed and their most dramatic episode might have been dismissed as a "third-rate" burglary conceived and committed solely by the seven original

Watergate defendants had it not been for the courage and penetrating understanding of Judge Sirica, the thoroughness of the investigative reporting of Carl Bernstein, Bob Woodward, and other representatives of a free press, the labors of the Senate Select Committee and its excellent staff, and the dedication and diligence of Special Prosecutors Archibald Cox and Leon Jaworski and their associates.

ESSAYS

The Vietnam War remains a political issue in modern America. After all, many of the military officers, foot soldiers, widows, orphans, and witnesses are still alive. One of the most contentious problems remains the "necessity" of the conflict. There are at least three different arguments: that the conflict was important to winning the Cold War; that it was an unintentional detour from America's democratic mission in the world; and that it was an expression of covert American imperialism. The first essay, by Michael Lind of the New America Foundation (a non-partisan, public policy institute in Washington, D.C.), articulates the thesis that the war was both moral and necessary. Lind argues that Ho Chi Minh's communist principles were far more relevant than his defense of Vietnamese independence. He asserts that the U.S. involvement bolstered America's credibility as world leader and ultimately contributed to winning the Cold War, which liberated multiple countries trapped behind the iron curtain. In the second essay, Mark Atwood Lawrence, a professor from the University of Texas at Austin, asserts that the Vietnam War was a mistake. It brought unnecessary bloodshed to Southeast Asia, killed tens of thousands of Americans, and placed the United States on the wrong side of history and its own democratic, anti-colonial beliefs. Part of a new generation of historians who emphasize the global context of contemporary decision making, Lawrence bases his arguments on evidence found in British and French archives, as well as American. The United States didn't just "decide" to enter Vietnam, Lawrence suggests. To some extent at least, it was pushed.

Vietnam: A Necessary War

MICHAEL LIND

In the winter of 1950, Moscow was as cold as hell. On the evening of February 14, 1950, in a banquet hall in the Kremlin, three men whose plans would subject Indochina to a half century of warfare, tyranny, and economic stagnation, and inspire political turmoil in the United States and Europe, stood side by side: Joseph Stalin, Mao Zedong, and Ho Chi Minh.

Michael Lind, *Vietnam: The Necessary War* (New York: Free Press, 1999), p. 1, 4–5, 31–35, 38–41, 52, 54, 60–62, 64–65, 254, 256–257. Reprinted by permission.

In the 1960s, when the United States committed its own troops to battle in an effort to prevent clients of the Soviet Union and China from conquering Indochina, many opponents of the American intervention claimed that the North Vietnamese leader Ho Chi Minh's communism was superficial, compared to his nationalism. In reality, there *was* an international communist conspiracy, and Ho Chi Minh was a charter member of it. Beginning in the 1920s, Ho, a founding member of the French Communist party, had been an agent of the Communist International (Comintern), a global network of agents and spies controlled with iron discipline by the Soviet dictatorship. In the 1930s, Ho had lived in the USSR, slavishly approving every twist and turn of Stalin's policy; in the 1940s, he had been a member of the Chinese Communist party, then subordinated to Moscow. Ho Chin Minh owed not merely his prominence but his life to his career in the communist network outside of his homeland. Because he had been out of the country for so many years, he had survived when many other Vietnamese nationalists, noncommunist and communist alike, had been imprisoned or executed by the French or by the Japanese during World War II….

The Cold War was the third world war of the twentieth century. It was a contest for global military and diplomatic primacy between the United States and the Soviet Union, which had emerged as the two strongest military powers after World War II. Because the threat of nuclear escalation prevented all-out conventional war between the two superpowers, the Soviet-American contest was fought in the form of arms races, covert action, ideological campaigns, economic embargoes, and proxy wars in peripheral areas. In three of these—Korea, Indochina, and Afghanistan—one of the two superpowers sent hundreds of thousands of its own troops into battle against clients of the other side.

In the third world war, Indochina was the most fought over territory on earth. The region owed this undesirable honor not to its intrinsic importance but to the fact that in other places where the two superpowers confronted one another they were frozen in a stalemate that could not be broken without the risk of general war. The Soviet Union and the United States fought proxy wars in Indochina because they dared not engage in major tests of strength in Central Europe or Northeast Asia (after 1953) or even the Middle East. Indochina was strategic *because* it was peripheral.

Throughout the Cold War, the bloody military struggles in the Indochina theater were shaped indirectly by the tense but bloodless diplomatic struggles in the European theater. By going to war in Korea and simultaneously extending an American military protectorate over Taiwan and French Indochina, the Truman administration signaled its resolve to defend its European allies. American officials swallowed their misgivings about French colonialism and paid for France's effort in its on-going war in Indochina from 1950 until 1954, in the hope of winning French support for the rearmament of Germany. Khrushchev's humiliation of the United States in the Berlin crisis of 1961 persuaded the Kennedy administration that a show of American resolve on the Indochina front was all the more important. In 1968, concern by members of the U.S. foreign policy elite that further escalation in Indochina would endanger America's other commitments, particularly in the European theater, was one of the factors that led the Johnson administration to begin the process of disengagement from the Vietnam war. The Eastern European revolutions of 1989, which led to the collapse of the Soviet Union itself in 1991, deprived communist Vietnam of its superpower protector and ideological model....

The Vietnam War, like the Korean War, the Afghan War, the Greek Civil War, the Taiwan crises, and a number of other conflicts was at one and the same time a civil war and proxy battle in the Cold War. During the Cold War, Indochina mattered— and it mattered to the Soviet Union and China as well as to the United States.

Examining the Vietnam War in its Cold War context does not necessarily justify it. Indeed, some argue that while it was necessary for the United States to wage the Cold War, success in the Cold War did not require the United States to establish or defend a protectorate over most of Indochina. This is the claim that was made by a number of American "realists" at the time of the Vietnam conflict and in the succeeding decades. Realism, or realpolitik, is the theory of international relations that emphasizes the primacy and legitimacy of power struggles in world politics. Several of the most prominent American realist thinkers—diplomat George Kennan, journalist Walter Lippmann, and scholar Hans Morgenthau, among others—criticized the Vietnam War in particular and in some cases the Cold War as a whole, as an unnecessary or disproportionate response to the threats posed by Soviet expansionism and communist Chinese revolutionary radicalism. Within the U.S. government in the 1960s, Senator William Fulbright, chairman of the Senate Foreign Relations Committee, and Undersecretary of State George Ball, one of the Democratic party's most influential foreign policy experts, also used the language of realism to criticize what they considered to be an overly ambitious U.S. grand strategy.

The realist critique of the Vietnam War remains very popular today. It permits aging veterans of the sixties left, embarrassed by their former support for Ho Chi Minh's vicious dictatorship and their denunciations of American presidents as war criminals or their avoidance of the draft, to claim that they were right to oppose the war, even if their rationale was mistaken.... Finally, the fact that some of the policymakers who played a role in the war, like former Secretary of State Robert McNamara, have claimed that it was a mistake from the beginning has appeared to strengthen the realist critique (even though other policymakers, such as former national security adviser Walt Rostow, continue to argue that the war made sense in terms of U.S. strategy).

In light of all this, it is important to recall that there was, and is, a realist case in favor of the Vietnam War, as well as one against it. If some American realists such as Lippmann, Kennan, and Morgenthau doubted the importance of America's commitment to denying Indochina to the communist bloc, others, such as Walt and Eugene Rostow, Samuel P. Huntington, and John P. Roche, were convinced of the significance of that commitment. The fact that the United States was defeated in Vietnam does not necessarily discredit the strategic logic that inspired the U.S. commitment to South Vietnam, Laos, and Cambodia and their Southeast Asian neighbors. The failure of American policy in Indochina may have resulted from inappropriate military tactics, or the characteristics of the

North Vietnamese and South Vietnamese societies and governments, or the support provided Hanoi by the Soviet Union and China, or the peculiarities of American political culture—or some combinations of all of these factors. The case that Indochina was worth a limited American war of some kind, particularly in the circumstances of the Cold War in the 1960s, is compelling in light of what we now know about the pattern and result of the Cold War as a whole.

Contemporary critics of the Johnson administration spoke of its "credibility gap" in connection with the Vietnam War. In addition to having exaggerated the progress of the United States and its South Vietnamese allies in the war, Johnson and his aides were accused of a failure to clearly explain the goal of the war to the American public and the world. Typical of this line of criticism is a comment in 1968 by William R. Corson, a former marine colonel in Vietnam, in his critique of the war, *The Betrayal:* "The emergence of the credibility gap came from the ill-fated attempts of Secretary [of State Dean] Rusk to justify the war successively as, first, a defense of Vietnamese freedom, then a defense of our national interest, and finally the defense of the world from the yellow peril."

Indeed, Johnson and officials of his administration provided several rationales for the escalation of the U.S. effort in Vietnam. Johnson cited "the deepening shadow of China. The rulers in Hanoi are urged on by Peking." On another occasion he stressed the need to thwart guerrilla warfare as an instrument of communist expansion: "Our strength imposes on us an obligation to assure that this type of aggression does not succeed." Secretary of State Dean Rusk stressed the potential effects of a defeat of U.S. policy in Southeast Asia on America's global alliance system, including "our guarantees to Berlin."

From today's perspective, the Johnson administration does not appear to have been more inconsistent or disingenuous in describing the aims of U.S. foreign policy than other U.S. wartime administrations. During World War II, the Roosevelt administration sometimes justified the U.S. effort in terms of the security of the United States and at other times claimed that the defeat of the Axis powers would help promote a utopian world characterized by the "Four Freedoms." In the run–up to the Gulf War, the [first] Bush administration provided a number of rationales, including the atrocities committed by Saddam Hussein's regime (some of which were exaggerated) and the importance of Middle Eastern oil for American jobs. President Clinton and members of his administration explained the U.S.-led NATO war against Serbia in terms of a number of different rationales: the moral imperative of preventing or reversing the ethnic cleansing of Albanians in Kosovo by the Serbs, the need to demonstrate the military credibility of NATO and the United States, the economic importance of a stable Europe, and the danger that the conflict would expand and draw in Greece and Turkey. Government officials addressing different audiences on different occasions for different purposes may emphasize different goals of foreign policy. The apparent inconsistencies that result are not necessarily evidence of official duplicity or official confusion. Nor does the fact that some official goals were misguided or overemphasized mean that others were not sound.

What is more, the notion of the "credibility gap" ignores the possibility that in escalating the Vietnam War the Johnson administration had several purposes, not just one. By successfully defending South Vietnam against subversion from North Vietnam, a client of the Soviet Union and China, the United States could deter the Soviets, reassure its allies, discourage the adoption of the Chinese and Vietnamese model of revolutionary "people's war" by antiwestern insurgents in developing countries, and encourage the economic development and liberalization of South Vietnam as well as of South Korea and Taiwan, all at the same time.

While the U.S. intervention in Vietnam served a number of complementary purposes, there was a hierarchy among U.S. goals. The administrations of Kennedy, Johnson, and Nixon may not have made the hierarchy as clear as intellectuals would like. Nevertheless, in hindsight it is possible to identify the place assigned to different goals in the hierarchy of purposes by these three presidents and their aides. The chief purpose of the United States in Vietnam was to demonstrate America's credibility as a military power and a reliable ally to its enemies and its allies around the world. The danger was that if the United States were perceived to be lacking in military capacity, political resolve, or both, the Soviet Union and/or China and their proxies would act more aggressively, while U.S. allies, including important industrial democracies such as West Germany and Japan, would be inclined to appease the communist great powers. It was in this global geopolitical context that preventing "falling dominoes"—whether in Southeast Asia proper, or in Third World countries far from Vietnam—was important. Least important of all the U.S. purposes in intervening in Vietnam was promoting liberty, democracy, and prosperity in South Vietnam itself. The defeat of the attempted takeover of South Vietnam by North Vietnam was a necessary, but not sufficient, condition for the evolution of the authoritarian government of South Vietnam toward liberalism and democracy. But American's political goals in South Vietnam were appropriately incidental and subordinate to American's goals in Southeast Asian power politics, which, in turn, were incidental and subordinate to American's global strategy in the third world war....

Credibility, in power politics, is a country's reputation for military capability combined with the political resolve to use it in order to promote its goals. The concern of statesmen with the reputation of their states for military ability and resolve is as old as interstate politics....

The natural concern of U.S. leaders with credibility was heightened into something like an obsession by the peculiar dynamics of the Cold War—a world war fought by means of sieges and duels. Unlike World Wars I and II, the third global conflict of the twentieth century took the form of a half-century siege on the European front and duels or proxy wars in a number of other theaters. The forward deployment of U.S. troops in Central Europe, Japan, and South Korea following the Korean War, together with U.S. efforts to maintain conventional and nuclear superiority, made up the siege aspect of the Cold War. In the long run, the superior military-industrial capability of the United States and its affluent allies was bound to wear down the military-industrial base of the Soviet empire, as long as two conditions were met. The first condition for western success in the Cold War was alliance unity; the alliance of the United States, West Germany, Japan, Britain, French, and the other major democracies could not be split by a Soviet diplomatic strategy of divide-and-rule. Meeting this condition required periodic reaffirmations of alliance unity, like the development of the Euromissiles by NATO in the early 1980s in response to Soviet intimidation. In addition, the American bloc was required to match and surpass the Soviet imperium in the arms race. Because the goal was to spend the Soviet Union into bankruptcy, not merely to defend the western allies against an implausible threat of invasion, the American bloc could not accumulate a sufficiency of nuclear missiles and other weapons and then quit. The arms race was an auction that had to be continued until one side dropped out.

The military-industrial siege of the Soviet empire took far longer than early Cold War leaders such as Truman and Eisenhower and their advisers had expected. In the 1950s, Eisenhower hoped that U.S. troops might be withdrawn from Europe in the next decade. Instead, the siege lasted almost half a century. While manning the siegeworks in Europe and northeast Asia, the United States also had to demonstrate its determination by threatening war, or, if the threat failed, by waging limited war, with the Soviet Union and/or China and their proxies in regions on the periphery of the main theaters of Cold War competition. Sometimes the United States had to fight where it was challenged by its enemies, not where it would have preferred to fight. Because perceived power is power (except in times of war, when actual power is tested), the danger that a strategic retreat will be misinterpreted as evidence of a loss of will or capability is quite real. To refuse to duel is to lose the duel.

Thus defined, credibility became the central strategic concern of the United States in the Cold War. Henry Kissinger described the American interest in Indochina in terms of U.S. credibility in global power politics: "With respect to Indo-China, we are not equating the intrinsic importance of each part of the world, and we are not saying that every part of the world is strategically as important to the United States as any other part of the world.... [The question of aid to allies in Indochina] is a fundamental question of how we are viewed by all other people." John Foster Dulles made a similar point in calling on the United States to protect the anticommunist remnant of the Chinese Nationalist regime on Taiwan in spring 1950: "If we do not act, it will be everywhere interpreted that we are making another retreat because we dare not risk war."

Who was the intended audience for American displays of credibility? Makers and defenders of U.S. Cold War strategy reasoned that the United States had to deter its enemies and reassure its allies at the same time. In a speech at Johns Hopkins University on April 7, 1965, President Johnson invoked these two reasons for demonstrations of credibility in the context of the war in Indochina. First, he cited the need to reassure American's allies: "Around the globe, from Berlin to Thailand, are people whose well-being rests, in part, on the belief that they can count on us if they are attacked. To leave Vietnam to its fate would shake the confidence of all these people in the value of American's commitment, the value of America's word." Second, President Johnson sought to discourage America's enemies: "The central lesson of our time is that the appetite of aggression is never satisfied. To withdraw from one battlefield means only to prepare for the next. We must say in Southeast Asia, as we did in Europe, in the words of the Bible: 'Hitherto shalt thou come, but no further.'"

Using less orotund language, Johnson adviser John McNaughton, in a memo of March 25, 1965, emphasized American credibility in listing the aims of U.S. policy in Indochina:

70%:—To avoid a humiliating defeat (to our reputation as a guarantor)
20%:—To keep South Vietnam (and the adjacent territory) from Chinese hands
10%:—To permit the people of South Vietnam to enjoy a better, freer way of life....

In the mind of the western public, the idea of defeat in the Cold War was associated with nuclear armaggedon. But the defeat of the United States in the global struggle might have resulted from America's backing down in confrontations involving Berlin, or Korea, or Taiwan, or Indochina, or Cuba, or similar contested areas charged with significance by the superpower rivalry. After the first major defeat or retreat, or perhaps the second or third or fourth in a row, confidence in America's military capability, or its determination to use it, would have collapsed. At that point, something akin to a panic in the stock market would have ensued. In a remarkably short period of time—a few years, perhaps even a few months—the worldwide American alliance system would have unraveled, as European, Asian, Middle Eastern, African, and Latin American states hurriedly made deals with Moscow. Thanks to runaway bandwagoning, the United States would have found itself marginalized in a world now aligned around the Soviet Union (there having been no other military power with global reach and global ambitions at the time). The Soviets might not have had to fire a shot in anger. There need not have been any additional communist revolutions. The same elites might even have remained in power in the same capitals around the world. Indeed, America's alliances such as NATO and the U.S.-Japan alliance might have lasted formally for a few more years, though moribund. But Moscow would have displaced Washington at the apex of the global military hierarchy, and everybody would have known it.

The bandwagon effect is the reason why it was a mistake to argue that the Soviet empire was bound to collapse of overextension. Power in the international arena is relative, not absolute. If the Soviet Union had managed, by means of military intimidation, to divide the alliance of the United States, Western Europe, and Japan, or to frighten the United States into isolationism and appeasement, then it might have achieved and maintained a position as the world's leading military power in relative terms even while it reduced its expenditures on the military. In the same way, the abatement of the Soviet challenge permitted the United States to become relatively more powerful in world politics in the 1990s, even as it slashed its defense spending and overseas troop deployments....

The Cold War, then, was most likely to end with a rapid and more or less bloodless global diplomatic realignment in favor of the superpower that was perceived to be the most militarily powerful and the most politically deter-mined. We know that this is how the Cold War would have ended if the United States had lost, because this is how the Cold War ended when the Soviet Union lost....

It is possible to argue that even if the Soviet Union and China considered the fate of Indochina to be important, the United States could have ceded the region to one or both of the communist great powers with little or no damage to its foreign policy. During the cold war, minimal realists such as George Ball, George Kennan, and Walter Lippmann advocated a strategy of finite contain-ment limited to the North Atlantic and North Pacific as an alternative to the policy of global containment that the United States actually pursued. Ball wrote that U.S. strategy should focus on "the principal Atlantic nations." The only area of the non-European world of any importance, apart from Japan, was the Middle East, because of its oil reserves. The Vietnam War (and presumably the Korean War) was based on the mistaken equation of a commitment "in the jungles and rice paddies of a small country on the edge of nowhere with our most important treaty commitments to defend our Western allies in the heart of Europe—the centre of world power and hence the centre of danger." Like other minimal realists, Ball saw little reason for the United States to oppose Soviet imperial gains anywhere outside of an imaginary border that encircled North America, Westerns Europe, and the Middle East. Even the nearby nations of the Caribbean and Central America should be "free to create their own versions of chaos."...

... It might be argued that the "three fronts" of Korea, Taiwan, and Indo-china were not as important in Cold War power politics as American presidents from Truman to Nixon believed. The question of whether a given country or region is strategic or not can be approached by means of a simple question: Do the great powers of a given era consider it worth fighting for?...

... [B]etween 1946 and 1989, every major military power of the Cold War era—the United States, China, France, the Soviet Union, and the British Commonwealth—sent at least some troops into combat in Indochina or nearby countries in Southeast Asia. If Indochina was a peripheral region of no strategic importance in world politics, it is curious that this fact escaped the attention of policymakers in Washington, Moscow, Beijing, Paris, and London.

If Indochina *was* a key strategic region during the Cold War for which the two superpowers were willing to fight, directly or indirectly, why was it of stra-tegic importance? The answer has less to do with sea-lanes than with symbolism. The symbolic significance of Indochina in the global rivalry for world primacy between the American bloc and the communist bloc, and in the simultaneous competition within the communist bloc between the Soviet Union and China, arose from the fact that the Cold War was an ideological war as well as a power struggle....

Even the relatively moderate Soviet leader Nikita Khrushchev emphasized that Moscow's support for communist revolutionaries in Asia was inspired not by the "national interest" of "Russia" but by the Soviet regime's ideology. "No real Communist would have tried to dissuade Kim Il-Sung from his compelling desire to liberate South Korea from Syngman Rhee and from reactionary American influence. To have done so would have contradicted the Communist view of the world." The Soviet Union was not only a superpower but the headquarters of the global religion of Marxism-Leninism, with zealous adherents in dozens of countries who looked to Moscow not only for military and economic support but for ideological guidance. Mao and his colleagues also viewed support for foreign communists as a test of their commitment to Marxism-Leninism. Zhou Enlai told North Vietnamese leaders in 1971, "Not to support the revolution of the Vietnamese people is like betraying the revolution." This viewpoint can be compared instructively with a recent description of Shiite Iran's foreign policy: "Because Iran sometimes portrays itself as a guardian of Shiites worldwide, experts in the region said today that it may feel under pressure to respond with military force if it can be proven that the Shiites [in Afghanistan] were attacked for reasons of religious faith."

The global alliance that the United States led in the Cold War was far more diverse than the communist bloc; it included liberal democracies, military dictatorships, and Muslim theocracies that shared little more than a common fear of Soviet power and influence. To the disappointment of Americans who wanted the United States to crusade for a "global democratic revolution," U.S. policymakers properly limited the goal of American grand strategy to the negative one of preventing hostile great powers from winning military hegemony over Europe, Asia, or the Eurasian Supercontinent as a whole. The democratic wave of the 1990s was a byproduct of America's Cold War victory, not the goal of America's Cold War strategy. U.S. foreign policy had to be narrowly anticommunist because a pro-democratic foreign policy would have prevented the United States from having many allies outside of Western Europe, where most of the world's outnumbered democracies were found during the Cold War....

What conclusions are to be drawn about the morality of the methods used by the United States in the Vietnam War? Johnson administration adviser John McNaughton, in a 1964 memo about U.S. Vietnam policy, stressed how important it was that the United States "emerge from the crisis without unacceptable taint from methods used." A compelling case can be made that the United States was wrong for moral as well as for practical reasons to rely heavily on a strategy of attrition in South Vietnam between 1965 and 1968, when the war was a mixture of an insurgency and a conventional war. The attrition strategy was more defensible during the predominantly conventional stage of the Vietnam conflict from 1969–75.

The moral alternative to waging the Vietnam War by indiscriminate and disproportionate means, however, was waging it by more discriminate and proportionate means—not abandoning Indochina to Stalinism, to the detriment of both the peoples of Indochina and the U.S.-led alliance system. One can condemn many of the tactics used by the United States in Vietnam without condemning the war as a whole, just as one can condemn the terror bombing of civilians in Germany and Japan during World War II without arguing that the war against the Axis powers was unjust....

Once the Vietnam War is viewed in the context of the Cold War, it looks less like a tragic error than like a battle that could hardly be avoided. The Cold War was fought as a siege in Europe and as a series of duels elsewhere in the world—chiefly, in Korea and Indochina. Both the siege and the duels were necessary. Power in world politics is perceived power, and perceived power is a vector that results from perceived military capability and perceived political will. The U.S. forces stationed in West Germany and Japan demonstrated the capability of the United States to defend its most important allies. U.S. efforts on behalf of minor allies in peripheral regions such as South Korea and South Vietnam and Laos proved that the United States possessed the will to be a reliable ally. Had the United States repeatedly refused to take part in proxy-war duels with the Soviet Union, and with China during its anti-American phase, it seems likely that there would have been a dramatic pro-Soviet realignment in world politics, no matter how many missiles rusted in their silos in the American West and no matter how many U.S. troops remained stationed in West Germany.

Vietnam: A Mistake of the Western Alliance

MARK ATWOOD LAWRENCE

... Western policies during the Cold War have too often been described as uniquely American in origin, as if U.S. policymakers could sit safely behind impermeable national boundaries, survey the world, and pronounce their decisions. In fact, as this book demonstrates, the United States, in the Cold War era as much as in the period since the fall of the Berlin Wall, should be seen as one participant, albeit an inordinately powerful one, in an international web in which influence flowed in multiple directions. Other actors sometimes set the international agenda by advancing self-serving ideas, constraining choices, and practicing coercion. The ideas that underpinned Western policy for forty years during the Cold War were constructions crafted through constant interaction of decision makers from many nations....

The decision to throw American aid behind the French war marked the first definitive American step toward deep embroilment in Indochina affairs, the start of a long series of moves that would lead the administration of Lyndon Johnson to commit U.S. ground forces to Vietnam fifteen years later. But if 1950 signaled the beginning of that process, it marked the end of another. As U.S. officials began shipping weapons, aircraft, and other military supplies to Vietnam and as they set up the first U.S. military mission in Saigon, many had already embraced the set of fundamental assumptions about Vietnam that would guide American involvement over the following twenty-five years. They now believed that the fate of Vietnam carried heavy implications for the destiny of Asia. They saw Vietnamese insurgents as the agents of international communism and assumed that their success would serve the interests of Moscow and Beijing. And they embraced the idea that the United States, through the proper application of material aid and political guidance, could play a key role in establishing a new Vietnamese political order reconciling the nationalist aspirations of the local population with the requirements of Western security.

To be sure, U.S. thinking about Vietnam continued to evolve in significant ways in the 1950s and 1960s, and policymakers had opportunities to change course in those years. It would be going too far to argue that patterns of thinking established in the early Cold War years made a U.S.-Vietnamese war inevitable. Yet the pattern is unmistakable: basic ideas conceived in the late 1940s had remarkable staying power. To understand America's war in Vietnam, one must reckon seriously with the years before 1950, a period that figures only marginally in most Americans'—and even in many historians'—perceptions of the U.S. experience in Southeast Asia.

How did U.S. policymakers come to think of Vietnam as they did during those years? How did a faraway corner of the French empire acquire such significance that Americans saw fit to intervene with economic and military aid? Why were other roads not taken? Unsurprisingly, these questions, like so many connected to Vietnam, have drawn a good deal of interest from historians over the years. The resulting body of scholarship, although little accounted for in general histories of the war, is large, complex, and contentious. Fundamentally, historians have offered three explanations for American behavior—one stressing geostrategic calculations, another highlighting U.S. economic objectives, and a third focusing on the imperatives of domestic politics.

The first line of argument emphasizes that Vietnam acquired urgency in American minds in the late 1940s because the situation there increasingly seemed to conform to a global pattern of communist aggression against the West and its interests....

A second explanation for Vietnam's emergence as a major U.S concern stresses American calculations about the region's economic value. Few scholars, it is important to note, contend that Americans were guided by a belief that Vietnam's natural resources and markets were critical to U.S. prosperity.... Still, several historians have argued that economic considerations drove U.S. policy. Many U.S. officials, they argue, concluded by 1950 that Indochinese resources and markets mattered to the economic health of crucial U.S. allies, especially Britain and Japan. Vietnam's economic significance lay not in the territory's contribution to the American economy but in its potential contribution to industrialized nations that American policymakers regarded as crucial to the establishment of a new global order....

A third explanation for Vietnam's emergence as a major U.S. preoccupation emphasizes domestic politics. In this view the Truman administration fixed its attention on Southeast Asia and began pumping U.S. material assistance into the region to fend off critics at home. Central to this interpretation is the contention that Harry S. Truman's narrow reelection victory in 1948 left a frustrated Republican party searching for an issue it could use against the president. The administration's failure, despite years of effort and vast expenditures, to prevent a communist victory in China provided the cudgel the president's enemies sought. As Mao Zedong triumphed in 1949, Republicans assaulted Truman and the Democrats as weak willed and demanded vigorous action to prevent the further spread of communism in Asia. Truman, the argument runs, had little choice but to go along.

All three arguments hold merit, and none excludes the others. Taken together, this body of work leaves little doubt that several reciprocally reinforcing considerations helped propel the Truman administration toward supporting the French in Indochina. Nonetheless, this scholarship falls short of offering a satisfactory explanation of American behavior. Above all, it fails to reckon with the fact that Washington, as it crafted policy toward Vietnam, was merely one participant in a complicated, decidedly international dynamic in which other governments usually held the initiative and set the agenda....

Taking an approach that is both global and national, I argue that the transformation of American thinking about Vietnam occurred as part of a grand, transnational debate about Vietnam in particular and the fate of colonial territories in general following the Second World War. As the book's first half demonstrates, each capital [Washington, London, and Paris] became deeply divided over Vietnam during the war or in its early aftermath, torn between contradictory impulses to reestablish French colonial rule and to acknowledge the legitimacy of Vietnamese nationalism and permit at least a degree of self-determination. Although the precise dynamics of the debate differed among the three countries in question, the basic contours were the same. Each policymaking establishment wrestled with the same set of fundamental problems that faced Western nations as they confronted colonialism in the mid-twentieth century: Should they attach higher value to the stability of their own political and economic interests or to the desires and grievances of colonized peoples? Should they seek the near-term benefits of continued Western domination or the potential long-term advantages of harmonious relationships with Asian peoples?...

The solution to this conundrum, an awkward compromise that paid lip service to America's anticolonial principles while leaning toward the interests of France, established a pattern that would play out repeatedly in the Third World over the course of the Cold War. From Vietnam to Indonesia, Guatemala to the Dominican Republic, Ethiopia to South Africa, American policymakers would invoke dedication to liberal, democratic solutions and sometimes would take concrete steps in that direction by sponsoring elections, pushing the pace of reform, or attempting to build popular bases of power for the regimes that they preferred. Almost always, however, Americans set the highest priority on the protection of short-term U.S. economic and geostrategic interests and embraced policies geared to limit the scope of social reform and the expression of genuine nationalism if those developments seemed to threaten American objectives, as they often did. The United States, then, often invoked liberal principles and sometimes even insisted on concessions to those principles while carrying out illiberal policies. Vietnam provides a telling case study of the pressures that helped establish this pattern in the aftermath of the Second World War, a period of unique fluidity in the history of U.S foreign relations that might have yielded a different outcome.

This book also offers insight into the nature of the transatlantic partnership between the United States and Western European countries that came into existence over the five years following the Second World War. Above all, it demonstrates that European governments sometimes held the initiative in their relationship with the United States and dictated policies ultimately embraced in Washington. The Western economic and security system was, in other words, the work of government officials in multiple nations, not a unilateral imposition of U.S. preferences for remaking the world....

After carefully examining intragovernmental disputes over policy toward Vietnam, I argue that hawkish factions in each country—those who viewed the turmoil in Indochina as an expression of binary Cold War tensions—made common cause with one another to recast Vietnam, to assure the triumph of their policy preferences, and to marginalize those with different ideas. In each country, dissenters against the extension of Cold War thinking to the colonial world represented a serious threat to those who wished to pursue a vigorous anticommunist war in Vietnam. By working together and drawing strength from one another at critical moments of decision, factions in each country favoring a bold Cold War posture were able to have their way by 1950. The policy embraced by the three leading Western powers in that year represented not the triumph of democratic principles or processes but the victory of thinking that lacked subtlety and sensitivity to the peculiarities of Vietnamese history and society. This victory, achieved more through maneuvering and manipulation than democratic deliberation, marked a moment of great tragedy. Over the following twenty-five years, the Western powers would reap what they sowed in 1950.

Free France and the Recovery of Indochina

As Allied victory grew more certain in 1944, the Free French organization under General Charles de Gaulle became increasingly anxious about Indochina. To be sure, the matter ranked below the most pressing national concerns—the reestablishment of the French state, economic rehabilitation, and the war against Germany. Consumed by these challenges, ordinary citizens, the Free French media, and the renascent political parties showed little interest in the fate of a territory on the other side of the world. For the small leadership group concerned with recovering France's traditional role as a global power, however, the issue did not lag far behind the nation's top priorities. These men—bureaucrats, diplomats, politicians, and military officers—shared a conviction that their country's long-term prospects rested on its ability to preserve the empire, not least Indochina. François de Langlade, a one-time rubber planter who became one of de Gaulle's chief delegates for Indochinese affairs, succinctly stated the group's thinking in early 1945. "Without Indochina," he wrote, "France is no longer a world power."

While officials agreed on the need to recover Indochina, they differed over precisely how French rule should be reconstituted after the war....

To the conservatives, talk of "*le* self-government"—a phrase so alien that it was always rendered in English, as historian Martin Shipway has pointed out—flew in the face of the hallowed Jacobin principle of "France One and Indivisible." The conference's final declaration, though only an advisory document, left no doubt where the conservatives stood. The French "civilizing mission" in the colonies excluded "any idea of autonomy [and] all possibility of evolution outside the French bloc," the statement asserted. "Also excluded," it added, "is the eventual establishment of self-government in the colonies, even in a distant future."…

Of the two nations most likely to challenge French sovereignty in Indochina, China represented the lesser threat. French officials were keenly aware of long-standing Chinese designs on Indochinese territory and worried that any Chinese incursion into Tonkin might prove impossible to dislodge. They also feared that Chinese patronage of various Vietnamese political organizations during the war would lead to dangerous cross-border meddling in Indochinese politics after the fighting ended. Nevertheless, these dangers seemed manageable. Chinese Nationalist leader Chiang Kai-shek repeatedly assured Ambassador Pechkoff that his government had no territorial ambitions in Indochina and even suggested that he was willing to help restore French rule.…

The United States represented a much more serious threat. For years, both Vichy and Gaullist leaders had watched anxiously as Franklin Roosevelt had grown increasingly vocal about his desire to grant independence to colonial territories after the war. In August 1941 Roosevelt and British prime minister Winston Churchill had proclaimed the Atlantic Charter, whose third article, pledging to "respect the rights of all people to choose the form of government under which they will live," seemed to promise postwar independence to any nation seeking freedom from foreign rule.…

To make matters worse, Americans of all political persuasions appeared to share the president's agenda. "The colonial problem is one of the few issues on which American opinion is not divided," Foreign Ministry analysts wrote in a survey of U.S. attitudes in early 1945. "For different reasons, emancipation of European colonies is desired as much by Republicans as by Democrats, by conservative industrialists and radical intellectuals, by the *Chicago Tribune* as much as the *New Republic*." Both ideology and self-interest seemed to propel U.S. anticolonialism. French views on this matter echoed widely held stereotypes of Americans as simultaneously naive and materialistic. In its analysis of U.S. ideology the Foreign Ministry despaired of changing American minds. "The American people, born of an anticolonial revolution, are hostile to colonies by tradition," asserted the report, adding, with questionable historical insight, that the United States had always sought to avoid acquiring colonies of its own and had secured those it had merely "by accident." The American "penchant for crusades" compounded the problem. "Of the two wars that [the United States] fought before 1914, one was carried out to achieve its own emancipation, the other for that of black slaves," wrote the ministry, adding that in their latest war Americans naturally sought a new ideological aim to endow their sacrifices with ennobling purpose. Liberal internationalists, Europhobes, and Protestant moralizers, the study added, were filling the void by reviving Wilsonianism and promoting decolonization as the latest variation on the American commitment to self-determination for oppressed peoples.

Much as it decried such zealotry, the Foreign Ministry worried even more about a narrower segment of U.S. society allegedly motivated by avarice. The study contended that American businessmen, backed by a compliant political and military establishment, were cleverly exploiting anticolonialism in pursuit of less lofty objectives. "The people of the United States barely perceive these influences," the report stated. American businessmen seemed to support decolonization partly out of eagerness to exploit previously inaccessible raw materials. At the same time, the study asserted, American entrepreneurs were anxious to open new markets in the hope that new overseas customers for their goods would help maintain the pace of wartime production in the United States and minimize postwar unemployment. The overall aim seemed to be "an open door for merchandise as well as capital," contended the report, whose authors had no doubt as to who would win once colonial areas were opened to all comers: "The open door would favor powerful Americans over European competitors."...

French officials also suspected Washington of exploiting anticolonialism to mask its plans to extend U.S. military power around the globe. "It is possible that the American government favors independence in certain colonial territories only in order to gain possession of bases," asserted the Foreign Ministry's postwar planning committee. This theory rested on a widely held belief that U.S. leaders were determined, no matter what the objections of their own people or of foreign governments, to establish a new global order tailored to U.S. commercial and strategic interests. The postwar planning committee suspected that the U.S. military, bristling with power and convinced of its unique ability to keep the peace after the war, desired the means not only to defend the Western Hemisphere but also to project power into the Far East. Zealous assertions of anticolonial principle were, in this view, mere cover for illiberal designs on various Pacific islands and possibly even on the Asian mainland. The committee alleged that Washington policymakers suffered from a "guilty conscience" over these cynical plans and hoped to conceal them within idealistic language that would "satisfy the public's appetite for progress and new ideas."

All these anticolonial motives—ideological, economic, strategic—seemed to converge on Indochina. "The appetite for power that the dominant U.S. role in the war has excited in Washington, concern about security in the Pacific, the defense of American commercial interests in the Far East, and the Methodist ideology determined to liberate oppressed peoples have combined to create an attitude strongly unfavorable to the maintenance of our position in Indochina," [French] Ambassador Pechkoff wrote from Chungking....

For all this anxiety, however, some French officials detected cracks in the American anticolonial facade. The Foreign Ministry's office for Asian affairs, for example, judged that behind routine expressions of hostility to French rule the U.S. position on Indochina in fact remained "extremely fluid." Washington's policy seemed vague and contradictory. Exactly how would a trusteeship work? Who would take supervisory responsibility? Would China, the United States itself, perhaps even France take the leading role in preparing Indochina for independence? On these questions, French observers noted, U.S. policymakers appeared to have few answers. Imprecision in the U.S. position became especially obvious in February 1945, when Roosevelt, meeting with his Soviet and British counterparts at Yalta, seemed to backtrack on earlier pronouncements, agreeing that trusteeships would be established only with the consent of the imperial powers concerned.

Three further considerations inspired confidence that Washington would back down. First, as Foreign Ministry officials repeatedly emphasized in internal correspondence, U.S. diplomats had offered several assurances early in the war that the French empire would be fully restored following Germany's defeat. Ministry personnel acknowledged that those promises may have been desperate bids to maintain French fighting spirit, but they nevertheless expected that Washington would honor explicit commitments. Second, French officials speculated that Americans would ultimately back away from policies predicated on the inherent rights of colonized peoples—a principle that, if generally accepted in international affairs, might expose the United States to criticism for its treatment of its own minority populations. "Above all," asserted the Foreign Ministry's study of American anticolonialism, "the condition of blacks in the United States leaves the Americans open to easy counterarguments from their European interlocutors." Third, French officials doubted that Washington would push its anticolonial agenda at the risk of alienating France and Britain, countries whose cooperation the United States would obviously need in constructing a postwar order. "The American government," the ministry report insisted, "cannot ignore the resistance that [trusteeship] would encounter among European governments and public opinion."...

British observers also drew encouragement from increasingly apparent divisions within the U.S. bureaucracy. While Roosevelt and his supporters maintained their hostility to French colonialism, British diplomats watched with satisfaction as another body of opinion gathered strength. In Chungking, Ambassador Sir Horace Seymour found that Americans with practical experience dealing with colonial problems thought more realistically. "There is," Seymour reported, "among a considerable proportion of thinking Americans who have acquired some first-hand knowledge of dealing with 'dependent peoples,' a growing realization that the complexity of the problem of the 'Imperialist' Powers has not been fully appreciated at home." From Washington Ambassador Halifax similarly reported "a few encouraging signs." He wrote that "well-informed opinion" in the United States—a category that apparently did not include the president—was "moving towards a realization that ... problems of the treatment of dependent peoples cannot be disposed of by wholesale liberation or by a mere statement of liberal principles, but are complex and difficult of solution." Among the most encouraging trends seemed to be the growing realization among U.S. policymakers that China, in the throes of worsening internal chaos, would be unable to play a stabilizing role in Southeast Asia after the war. With China weak and unreliable, Americans seemed increasingly inclined to accept that European rule should be restored as the only way to preserve peace and stability to the region....

On one hand, some U.S. officials, most notably Franklin Roosevelt, advocated ending French colonialism in Indochina and setting the region on the road to independence. The president repeatedly expressed strong feelings on the subject during the course of the war. "Indochina should not be given back to the French Empire after the war," Roosevelt characteristically declared at a 1943 meeting of Allied war planners. "The French had been there for nearly one hundred years," the president growled, "and had done absolutely nothing with the place to improve the lot of the people." Early the following year, he spoke out even more strongly in favor of trusteeship, telling Ambassador Halifax that the French had "milked Indochina for a hundred years" and must not be allowed to return. Roosevelt's hostility probably sprang from numerous sources, including his dislike of de Gaulle, his contempt for the French performance in the face of Axis aggression, and his view of France as a decadent society that would require years to recover any international standing. France, he asserted in a relatively charitable moment, "would certainly not again become a first-class power for at least twenty years." If the French protested the Indochina trusteeship, he declared, "so what?"...

This set of ideas about Indochina might be called the "liberal" viewpoint. This term is not meant to imply anything especially praiseworthy or perceptive about officials who advanced these views. Indeed, liberal-minded officials held deeply paternalistic views of the Indochinese peoples and were driven by the perception of American self-interest far more than any sense of altruism. Nor is the term meant to imply that a fixed group of individuals held a static set of views. In fact, different elements of liberal thinking about Indochina ebbed and flowed at different moments, and different policymakers, depending on their particular decision-making roles, promoted different strands of the broader set of ideas. Those who advocated liberal opinions, in fact, constituted not so much a defined policymaking bloc as a loose collection of officials from different bureaucracies who followed different paths to the same basic conclusion—that the United States needed to promote Indochinese self-determination, at least in the medium term. Rather, the term *liberal* is apt because it captures two general characteristics of these individuals. First, they perceived of themselves as stewards of a new, Wilsonian world order based on free trade and self-determination, a complex of ideas that historians have sometimes dubbed "liberal internationalism." Second, these policymakers believed that the United States had to promote moderate change in the colonial world in order to head off a possibly dangerous explosion of revolutionary change later. In this way, *liberal* corresponds to the way American historians have often used that term—to denote political movements that seek to promote gradual change through existing political and economic structures....

Policymakers who advocated ending or loosening the bonds of colonialism also invoked a strategic rationale. Especially within the State Department, officials concerned with Asian affairs asserted that the Indochinese peninsula promised to be vital to the United States because of its position commanding shipping routes between the Far East, Australasia, and the Indian Ocean. A friendly Indochina fully integrated into a U.S.-oriented global security system seemed essential to preserving American access to the markets of East and South Asia. "Of all the dependent areas of the world, only the Caribbean is of greater importance to the

United States than … Southeast Asia," wrote Abbot Low Moffat, chief of the State Department's new Division of Philippine and Southeast Asian Affairs. The region's importance, Moffat added, was likely only to grow over the next "several decades at least" as American trade and investment expanded into regions acquiring their independence from Europe.

Moffat rated Indochina the most valuable of all Southeast Asian territories, explaining that "its geographical position on the southern flank of China, with its potential naval base at Camranh Bay, halfway between Hong Kong and Singapore and the same distance due west of Manila, gives Indochina great significance." Like Roosevelt, Moffat doubted whether the United States could rely on France to ensure stability in such a crucial area. "France, whose major interests are in Europe and North Africa, was never and can never be in a position to protect Indochina," wrote Moffat, who also doubted French willingness to participate in any new U.S.–organized security arrangements for the region. Simmering tensions between U.S. and Gaullist officials in New Caledonia, a French colony where Washington had established a major wartime military base, seemed to bode ill for future cooperation. "Even in those regions nominally Free French there has been not only serious lack of cooperation in the war effort, but even interference," Moffat complained.

While liberal officials fretted that restoration of French rule would place Indochina in unreliable hands, they worried too about the impact on the indigenous population. If Washington permitted recolonization, they charged, it would ensure decades of resentment against the West and lay the seeds of political turmoil that might prevent establishment of a stable Southeast Asia open to cooperation with the Unites States.…

But U.S. optimism also rested in part on a genuinely hopeful view among liberal policymakers of the capacity of the Indochinese people, above all the Vietnamese, for development. Policy papers advocating trusteeship or sharp curtailment of French control, while deeply patronizing in tone, gave the Vietnamese (called "Annamites" at the time) credit for significant levels of intelligence, cultural sophistication, and vigor. Kenneth P. Landon, assistant head of the State Department's Southeast Asian division and one of the few U.S. officials who had spent much time in Asia, went furthest in a June 1944 memo declaring that the Vietnamese had "a highly sophisticated, well-developed culture."…

Ranged against this cluster of liberal views stood a set of "conservative" ideas that favored allowing France to regain sovereignty over Indochina, As with *liberal,* the term *conservative* is not intended to imply the existence of a rigid or static set of views among a fixed group of decision makers. Rather, the term is useful because it aptly captures two important characteristics of the loose grouping of policymakers who favored restoring French control—principally State Department officials concerned with European affairs, but also War and Navy Department personnel and some OSS officials. In contrast to the liberals' vision of a Wilsonian order based on self-determination and free trade, conservatives believed, first, that the United States could best protect its interests through more traditional means of exerting power: close partnerships with like-minded industrial powers and the maintenance of geographical strong points from which power could be projected. Second, conservatives, in contrast to liberals' determination to channel revolutionary energies in moderate directions, detected no danger so great that it could not be managed by reestablished colonial regimes. Thus old forms of colonial control were still appropriate in the postwar international environment....

Many conservatives shared Roosevelt's antipathy toward de Gaulle and bitterness over the French performance against Nazi and Japanese aggression, but they disagreed with his assessment that France could not be a major power again for many years. On the contrary, those who backed French recovery of Indochina anticipated that the United States would depend heavily on French cooperation in the postwar period in rebuilding Europe and creating a new international system. Like their liberal counterparts, conservatives wished to sustain booming American productivity and protect U.S. economic interests over the long term. They differed, however, over the precise method to achieve this goal. Liberals sought to promote American prosperity by establishing a new free-trade regime that would break up exclusive colonial arrangements and permit equal access to resources and markets. Conservatives considered such a vision unrealistic, at least in the short term, and emphasized the necessity of preserving colonial arrangements in order to prevent economic chaos and the weakening of the powerful industrial economies of Europe that, once rebuilt from the war, could provide the United States with far more advantages than tiny, relatively undeveloped areas such as Indochina. For conservatives, French recovery trumped self-determination for Indochina as a U.S. policy objective, not only because of the value of France as an economic partner but also for the crucial role that Paris might play in the establishment of a new Western economic and security system that served U.S. interests around the world....

British defense planning for Europe also pointed to the need for dramatically increased assistance for the French war effort. The drain on French manpower and resources in Indochina threatened to weaken the French contribution to European defense at a time when the Attlee government [of Britain] urgently hoped to demonstrate to the United States the vigor of military cooperation among West European states. Washington had already given its blessing to the March 1948 Brussels Treaty, a mutual defense pact among Britain, France, Holland, Belgium, and Luxembourg, and promised to provide it with military assistance. But Foreign Secretary Bevin hoped for much more—nothing less than a North Atlantic Treaty carrying a guarantee from the United States to come to the defense of its West European allies in case of aggression against any of them. While the Truman administration generally backed that idea, reservations lingered through 1948 within the State Department and, more importantly, in Congress, where many wished to keep the United States free from such commitments. For London the key to allaying American concerns was to demonstrate a significant degree of European power and self-reliance—a task complicated by the French preoccupation with a draining war on the other side of the globe. Even after the signing of the North Atlantic Treaty in April 1949, British officials worried that the French commitment in Asia would prevent Paris from fulfilling its assigned role at the heart of the emerging Western security system. "Everything that France sends out to Indochina is, in a sense, at the expense of the Western Union," R. H. Scott, chief of the Foreign office's Southeast Asia department, complained in July....

Would the three powers be able to close the deal on a multilateral partnership? The worsening geopolitical situation clearly militated in favor of a positive answer. Mao's Chinese Communists achieved their final victory and declared the People's Republic of China in October [1949]. Four months later Moscow and Beijing announced a treaty of alliance, an ominous development that implied unity among world communist movements. There could now be little doubt in the minds of U.S. or British policymakers that a Viet Minh victory meant the further extension of the Sino-Soviet bloc. Longstanding connections between the Viet Minh leadership and international communism ruled out any other way of understanding the situation among officials disinclined to take risks and under increasing pressure to treat the communist menace with deadly seriousness....

In the second half of 1949, British officials saw mixed prospects of success in their bid to attract U.S. involvement. On the positive side, they recognized the rapid evolution of American attitudes toward Southeast Asia. Both public and official opinion in the United States seemed to be moving steadily in the direction of accepting a commitment to fight communism in Asia. Eventual American membership in a "Pacific Pact" or some other kind of organization involving both Asian and Western nations seemed to be possible. Above all, the Washington embassy reported, the Chinese Communists' looming victory was generating a strong sense within the Truman administration that the United States needed to "do something" about the spread of communism in Asia. Most promising of all, the Republican-controlled U.S. Congress was beginning to press the administration to spend $75 million previously allocated for the Chinese Nationalists on assistance for other Asian nations threatened by communism. In September the State Department issued a public declaration supporting the principle of Asian independence while warning against the dangers of communism and promising American aid for countries attempting to resist outside aggression. At last, a consensus seemed to be forming behind U.S. aid for Southeast Asia....

On the last day of June 1950, eight American C-47 transport aircraft carrying a cargo of spare parts and maintenance equipment lumbered to a halt at Saigon's Tan Son Nhut airfield. U.S. aid had at last arrived. French officials, still fearful that U.S. help would amount to too little, too late, complained throughout the summer about the slow pace of U.S. deliveries and maintained steady pressure on Washington for greater and faster assistance. But there was little reason for worry. The decision to support the French war effort marked a major turn in U.S. policy. By early summer the U.S. military had begun channeling not only planes but also naval vessels, vehicles, weapons, ammunition, spare parts, and communications equipment to Indochina, while plans went ahead to establish an elaborate aid disbursement and military training bureaucracy in Saigon, the U.S. Military Assistance Advisory Group. Meanwhile, U.S. specialists initiated public health, agricultural development, and other civilian programs.

The outbreak of the Korean War on June 25 produced a sharp intensification of American aid as U.S. officials sought to bolster Western defenses against the possibility of Chinese aggression in Southeast Asia. By the end of the year, the Truman administration had increased its near-term commitments to Indochina to about $133 million. The National Security Council approved a paper insisting that the United States must back the French war effort "by all means practicable short of the actual employment of United States military forces." Deliveries increased steadily. Washington sent about 11,000 tons of military equipment in 1950, 90,000 tons in 1951, 100,000 tons in 1952, and more than 170,000 tons in 1953. As fighting climaxed in Vietnam in the spring of 1954, the United States bore more than 80 percent of the war's material cost. In all, the United States paid nearly $3 billion over four years.

In the end, of course, French and American exertions failed to achieve their objective. Part of the problem was the Viet Minh's growing military prowess. The infusion of American aid provoked the Chinese government to dispatch substantial assistance to Ho Chi Minh's forces for the first time. Between April and September 1950 China sent the Viet Minh fourteen thousand rifles and pistols, seventeen hundred machine guns, and 150 mortars, as well as munitions, medicine, communications equipment, and a seventy-nine-man advisory team....

Nor did greater American involvement do much to alter the political situation that underpinned conflict in Vietnam. U.S. officials continued to apply pressure for new French concessions to the Bao Dai government, but American demands resulted in little more than French resentment and foot-dragging. Despite continued negotiations between Saigon and Paris between 1950 and 1954, the French government refused to concede self-rule in various key areas....

The Geneva Conference's decision to divide Vietnam at the seventeenth parallel also sharply altered the situation. Although the accords specified that the division had merely the short-term purpose of enabling former combatants to regroup and demobilize in separate zones, the existence of a noncommunist administrative entity in the south clearly suggested a chance to keep half the country—and the wealthier half, at that—out of the communist orbit....

By 1954 no American officials had any doubt—nor should they have—that Ho Chi Minh's movement served the interests of international communism. The link was real and obvious, even if Western policy was largely responsible for generating the outcome that Western policymakers most dreaded. Meanwhile, the wobbly French war effort encouraged American worries about the fate of the region as a whole in the event Vietnam fell under communist control. In 1954 President Eisenhower gave American fears their classic formulation, asserting that if Vietnam fell to communism, the rest of Southeast Asia would collapse like a row of dominos. Once the communists had their way in Indochina, he said, "you could have the beginning of a disintegration that would have the most profound influence." Unsurprisingly, as the final French defeat neared, the U.S. administration moved boldly to form an alliance of Asian and Western states, the Southeast Asian Treaty Organization, to resist communist expansion beyond Vietnam's northern half....

Between 1954 and 1965 the Eisenhower, Kennedy, and Johnson administrations took up this challenge, drawing the United States ever more deeply into

Vietnam as they sought to create a viable South Vietnamese state that would satisfy local nationalism while serving Western interests. This long and complex story has been well told elsewhere. For the purposes of this study, it is important to point out merely that the set of assumptions that drove American policy forward departed little from the ideas laid in place in 1950. In recent years historians writing about the American war have emphasized contingency; that is, they have stressed variations over time as different administrations with different needs, perceptions, and personalities reckoned with the Vietnam problem in their own ways. Thanks to this scholarship, we can now see that there was nothing wholly inevitable about the U.S. decisions for full-scale war in 1965. Above all, it seems, the Kennedy administration entertained grave doubts about America's Vietnam commitment and might have acted to scale back U.S. involvement if JFK had survived for a second term as president. Yet there is a danger in excessive attention to contingency. We can easily lose sight of the continuities that run through the entire American experience in Vietnam and of the possibility that these continuities may be the most important way to understand how the United States came to fight a war in Vietnam. The simple fact of the matter is that successive presidential administrations, however much latitude they enjoyed to change course in Vietnam, did not do so. In the end, patterns of thought laid in place in 1950 drove American policy uninterruptedly to 1965 and beyond. To understand the American war, then, it is vitally necessary to understand what transpired in the years leading up to 1950....

"The process of U.S. involvement in Vietnam began—seriously began—with the Truman administration and continued more or less uninterrupted through five presidents," argued Tran Quang Co, a long-time Vietnamese diplomat. The Kennedy and Johnson administrations, he added, merely followed the path of their predecessors "with readjustments made in accordance with the international context and the realities of the war at the time."...

Only when the hawks found a way to dampen misgivings about supporting colonialism and to reclassify Vietnam as a Cold War battleground could they have their way. Only, that is, when they redefined Vietnam a Cold War conflict, stemming from the same causes and requiring the same solutions as anticommunist fights elsewhere, could the three governments close ranks around a common policy. Dissenters still bridled against the drift of Western policy in 1949 and 1950. After the Communist victory in China, however, it became increasingly difficult to resist the notion that French policy served Western interests....

In this way American officials satisfied themselves that they were holding true to their country's anticolonial traditions, bolstered their self-perception as advocates of progress, and perhaps most important, insulated themselves from challenges from those who demanded fundamental reform. Often though, assertions of liberality masked an underlying agenda that sought to impose strict limits on the pace and scope of change. In Vietnam the conservatives' ambition to form a partnership among the Western powers in Indochina became feasible only after the Europeans offered them an apparently liberal political solution that enabled them to nullify or sidestep the hostility of their bureaucratic adversaries. Having mastered the rhetoric of liberalism, the conservatives achieved a total victory. One by one, progressive advocates of genuine change left government service or were forced out by Joseph McCarthy and his minions, who successfully silenced those Americans who viewed the decolonizing world with subtlety and sought to promote genuine change. The intimidation and in-civility faded over time, but the effect was lasting. Leaders with scant regard for anticolonial nationalism maintained their grip on U.S. decision making, all the while proclaiming their country—and themselves—the champion of liberalism. It is a peculiarly American formulation, and one that led to great agony in much of the world.

FURTHER READING

Stephen E. Ambrose, *Nixon*, 3 volumes (1987–1989).

Christian Appy, *Working-Class War: American Combat Soldiers and Vietnam* (1993).

Carl Bernstein and Bob Woodward, *All the President's Men* (1974).

Robert Buzzanco, *Vietnam and the Transformation of American Life* (1999).

George Herring, *LBJ and Vietnam* (1995).

Mary Hershberger, *Traveling to Vietnam: American Peace Activists and the War* (1998).

Andrew Johns, *Vietnam's Second Front: Domestic Politics, the Republican Party, and the War* (2010).

David Levy, *The Debate Over Vietnam* (1990).

Fredrik Logevall, *Choosing War: The Lost Chance for Peace and the Escalation of War in Vietnam* (1999).

Kathryn Statler, *Replacing France: The Origins of American Intervention in Vietnam* (2007).

Jonathan Shay, *Achilles in Vietnam: Combat Trauma and the Undoing of Character* (1994).

Melvin Small, *The Presidency of Richard Nixon* (1999).

Marilyn Young, *The Vietnam Wars, 1945–1990* (1991).

CHAPTER 15

The Rise of the New Right

Under the weight of the Vietnam War, the Great Society, and the social upheaval of the 1960s, the electoral coalition forged by Democrats during the New Deal cracked and then shattered. After dominating the presidency from 1932 to 1968, Democrats saw Republican nominees win nearly every presidential election between 1968 and 2004. Political initiative (and economic development) also moved south and west, away from the liberal, northeastern "Rustbelt." As Lyndon Johnson told his young speechwriter when he signed the Civil Rights Act of 1964: "I think we just delivered the South to the Republican Party for your lifetime." Historians debate why this happened, but the indisputable fact is that it did. And conservative southerners were not the only ones to leave the Democratic Party— so did blue-collar workers of the Northeast, and many middle- and upper-class voters in the far west. Indeed, this became the era of the "Sunbelt." Leading the charge against the New Deal/Great Society "welfare state" was a conservative reformer straight out of Hollywood, Ronald Reagan.

A former actor as well as governor of California, Reagan became the first man since Dwight D. Eisenhower to serve two full terms (1981–1989). He brought to Washington the charisma of a movie star, confidently proclaiming that America was destined to lead the free world and "stand tall" again. The Republican leader promised to fight the Cold War against the Soviet "evil empire" without compromise, diminish government interference in the economy, lower taxes, and restore "family values." Reagan expressed his personal admiration for Franklin D. Roosevelt while presiding over a trend towards dismantling regulations on business in place since the New Deal. He cut the income tax rate of the nation's wealthiest citizens from 70 percent to 28 percent. As federal income declined relative to expenditures—especially military expenditures to fight the Cold War—the budget deficit soared. In 1985, for the first time since 1914, the United States became a debtor nation. But the nation also recovered from a post-Vietnam recession that had sapped the popularity of Reagan's predecessor, President Jimmy Carter. Between 1982 and 2008 (despite two brief recessions in 1990 and 2000) the economy mostly grew—although the national debt burden did as well.

But the so-called Reagan Revolution was about more than the occupant of the Oval Office. Conservatives had railed against the New Deal state for several generations. Many believed that the Republican Party had taken its first wrong turn under Eisenhower by accepting too many New Deal reforms, including Social Security and Aid to Families with Dependent Children (welfare). Arizona Senator Barry Goldwater, who unsuccessfully ran for president in 1964, blazed the trail for Ronald Reagan. Goldwater and then Reagan protested that the federal government had grown too large and too intrusive in domestic affairs, while failing to be adequately aggressive in international affairs. Religious conservatives also gained prominence, riding a new wave of evangelical fervor. Mega-churches exhorted Americans to be "born again," and millions took their words to heart. Some urged parishioners to become politically active and speak out on social issues. The Southern Baptist Convention, for example, the nation's largest Protestant denomination, organized a boycott against Disney, a media company they said promoted "immoral ideologies such as homosexuality, infidelity, and adultery." The Baptists also condemned homosexuality as a willful sin.

Even environmental protection, a bipartisan cause under Johnson and Nixon, became politicized in the new, conservative climate. President Reagan claimed during his first campaign for office that "trees cause more pollution than automobiles," and subsequently cut back on enforcement of environmental protection laws. Religious conservatives, historically skeptical of modern science, also criticized environmentalism. In 2008, Louisiana became one of the first of several southern states to pass or consider new laws encouraging students to think more critically about such "scientific theories" as evolution and global warming.

And yet, as critics pointed out, Reagan himself was the first occupant of the presidency to have been divorced and remarried. More surprisingly, during the presidency of George W. Bush, a born again Christian, Vice President Richard Cheney greeted his sixth grandchild with open arms, despite the fact that the mother (his daughter) was in a lesbian partnership of fifteen years. A new tolerance of diversity in America made it difficult even for conservatives to punish individuals for what were increasingly seen as private choices. After all, didn't conservatives want government to be less intrusive?

QUESTIONS TO THINK ABOUT

Why did the New Right, as many called it, capture the imagination of the nation during this period? What social and economic concerns underlay the movement? Were its values truly traditional, and to what extent (or in what ways) did the movement change popular behavior?

DOCUMENTS

The documents in this chapter look at recent decades from a variety of perspectives. Document 1 is a cartoon that anticipates the election of 1960, when conservatives first alleged the Republican Party was headed the way of the wooly mammoth because of its increasingly liberal tendencies. The G.O.P. elephant needed to change directions, conservatives like Goldwater insisted. The next two documents highlight working-class sentiments in the

Sunbelt and the Rustbelt. In document 2, country-western singer Merle Haggard expresses his pride in America and scorn for liberals who "smoke marijuana" and try to evade military service. In document 3, the popular television character, Archie Bunker, expresses nostalgia for the good old days (like the Great Depression), when American industrial goods were tops and "men were men." In document 4, Republican activist Phyllis Schlafly scorns feminists who underappreciate the "power of the positive woman." Healthy women rejoice in the procreative power given to them by God, Schlafly says, and feminists only undermine women's status. Document 5 is an article on the California "tax revolt," when citizens voted to slash property taxes—and government budgets in consequence. In document 6, Reverend Jerry Falwell of Virginia explains why he founded Moral Majority, a political action group devoted to electing the most conservative Republicans, and lobbying Congress to defeat all "left-wing, social-welfare bills." President Ronald Reagan praises the American way in his second inaugural address, given on January 21, 1985. This speech, document 7, typifies the confidence that Reagan imparted to his fellow citizens. Document 8 reveals the illiberal side of the Reagan administration, challenged here by one of its more prominent members, Surgeon General Everett Koop. Koop found himself isolated within the administration when the AIDS crisis first emerged, due to what he later called "hatred of homosexuals." In time, however, values of charity and compassion asserted themselves, and scientific progress was made. Lastly, in document 9, the Sierra Club criticizes Reagan's record on the environment—while noting that its own membership rolls had swollen in reaction.

1. Liberal "Modern Republicanism" Seems to Doom the G.O.P., 1957

GOP Elephant cartoon

2. Country Singer Merle Haggard Is Proud to Be an "Okie From Muskogee," 1969

We don't smoke marijuana in Muskogee;

We don't take our trips on LSD

We don't burn our draft cards down on Main Street;

We like livin' right, and bein' free.

I'm proud to be an Okie from Muskogee,

A place where even squares can have a ball

We still wave Old Glory down at the courthouse,

And white lightnin's still the biggest thrill of all

We don't make a party out of lovin';

We like holdin' hands and pitchin' woo;

We don't let our hair grow long and shaggy,

Like the hippies out in San Francisco do.

And I'm proud to be an Okie from Muskogee,

A place where even squares can have a ball.

We still wave Old Glory down at the courthouse,

And white lightnin's still the biggest thrill of all.

Leather boots are still in style for manly footwear;

Beads and Roman sandals won't be seen.

Football's still the roughest thing on campus,

And the kids here still respect the college dean.

We still wave Old Glory down at the courthouse,

In Muskogee, Oklahoma, USA.

3. TV's Archie Bunker Sings "Those Were the Days," 1971

Boy the way Glen Miller played
Songs that made the hit parade.
Guys like us we had it made,
Those were the days.
And you knew who you were then,
Girls were girls and men were men,
Mister we could use a man

Like Herbert Hoover again.

Didn't need no welfare state,

Everybody pulled his weight.

Gee our old LaSalle ran great.

Those were the days.

4. Republican Activist Phyllis Schlafly Scorns Feminism, 1977

The first requirement for the acquisition of power by the Positive Woman is to understand the differences between men and women. Your outlook on life, your faith, your behavior, your potential for fulfillment, are all determined by the parameters of your original premise. The Positive Woman starts with the assumption that the world is her oyster. She rejoices in the creative capability within her body and the power potential of her mind and spirit. She understands that men and women are different, and that those very differences provide the key to her success as a person and fulfillment as a woman.

The women's liberationist, on the other hand, is imprisoned by her own negative view of herself and of her place in the world around her. This view of women was most succinctly expressed in an advertisement designed by the principal women's liberationist organization, the National Organization for Women (NOW), and run in many magazines and newspapers and as spot announcements on many television stations. The advertisement showed a darling curlyheaded girl with the caption: "The healthy, normal baby has a handicap. She was born female."

This is the self-articulated dog-in-the-manger, chip-on-the-shoulder, fundamental dogma of the women's liberation movement. Someone—it is not clear who, perhaps God, perhaps the "Establishment," perhaps a conspiracy of male chauvinist pigs—dealt women a foul blow by making them female....

This is why women's liberationists are compulsively involved in the drive to make abortion and child-care centers for all women, regardless of religion or income, both socially acceptable and government-financed. Former Congresswoman Bella Abzug has defined the goal: "to enforce the constitutional right of females to terminate pregnancies that they do not wish to continue."....

The Positive Woman will never travel that dead-end road. It is self-evident to the Positive Woman that the female body with its baby-producing organs was not designed by a conspiracy of men but the Divine Architect of the human race. Those who think it is unfair that women have babies, whereas men cannot, will have to take up their complaint with God because no other power is capable of changing that fundamental fact....

The new generation can brag all it wants about the new liberation or the new morality, but it is still the woman who is hurt the most. The new morality

Phyllis Schlafly, *The power of the Positive Woman* (New Rochelle, NY, Jove Publications, 1977), p. 11–19. Reprinted by permission of the author.

isn't just a "fad"—it is a cheat and a thief. It robs the woman of her virtue, her youth, her beauty, and her love—for nothing, just nothing. It has produced a generation of young women searching for their identity, bored with sexual freedom, and despondent from the loneliness of living a life without commit-ment. They have abandoned the old commandments, but they can't find any new rules that work. . . .

Men are philosophers, women are practical, and 'twas ever thus. Men may philosophize about how life began and where we are heading; women are concerned about feeding the kids today. No woman would ever, as Karl Marx did, spend years reading political philosophy in the British Museum while her child starved to death. Women don't take naturally to a search for the intangible and the abstract. The Positive Woman knows who she is and where she is going, and she will reach her goal because the longest journey starts with a very practical first step.

5. Californians Revolt Against Taxes—and Government, 1978

He raises his right fist high above his head like a heavyweight fighter who has just upset the champ. And the crowd roars.

It's Howard Jarvis and his traveling Proposition 13 road show which has made the feisty 75-year-old advocate of lower property taxes as well known as any of the candidates running for office in California's June primary.

Jarvis has caught the public fancy with a style reflecting the finesse of a pro-fessional football linebacker blitzing into the opponent's backfield.

His oratorical grace is at times reminiscent of the waterfront, complete with the usual four-letter words, and is supported by a booming voice that could seemingly be heard in several counties at once.

His issues revolve around the basic American right to own property and, he alleges, the attempts of a bunch of insensitive politicians to take away that right.

But for all of his earthiness and simplicity, Howard Jarvis appears to be, as the saw goes—the right man at the right place at the right time.

Although many Jarvis listeners are turned off by his know-it-all preachments and personal attacks on public figures, the basic appeal of dramatically lower property taxes is a strong one. . . .

The Jarvis initiative (cosponsored by Sacramento area resident Paul Gann) would cut all property taxes—commercial as well as residential—to about 1% of appraised value, or by about 57% off of current tax bills.

Home and other property appraisals would be rolled back to 1975–76 mar-ket values and could climb only 2% annually until the property was resold at which point it could be appraised to current market value. . . .

Jarvis' point is obvious. He feels he has touched a responsive chord among the electorate that goes beyond the property tax issue. The people, he firmly believes, are fed up with government that is insensitive to their needs.

From "Jarvis-Master of Crown Psychology," by Ronald D. Soble, *Los Angeles Times*, May 17, 1978. Reprinted by permission.

"This is the first time since the Boston Tea Party that we have a chance to vote for ourselves for once," he said in underscoring this concept a few days ago before a crowd in Santa Cruz Civic Auditorium.

Such polemics are well thought out by a man who has been a major Republican campaign worker for GOP White House candidates from Herbert Hoover to Richard M. Nixon. In short, Jarvis, for all of his casualness, is a master of crowd psychology and he is bringing all of his experience to bear on Proposition 13.

"I play on every emotion I can," said Jarvis in a candid interview.

One of those emotions, Jarvis said, is the use of the fear technique.

Ironically, one of Jarvis' most strident complaints about the tactics of his opponents is the use of the fear theme in arguments that allege that his initiative would curtail police and fire services.

"Mine is legitimate fear," he said. "The fear of losing property."

The fear ploy is brought home by Jarvis in statements such as he recently made to the California Mortgage Bankers Assn. in Palm Springs: "We should have the guts to let the elderly keep their homes," he said, declaring that more and more senior citizens on fixed incomes would be forced out of their homes if a lid was not put on rising property taxes.

The fear technique, he said, also is used to illustrate the difficulty middle-income groups have in meeting their property tax bills; and the negative impact soaring taxes have on the ability of younger people to purchase their first home.

Jarvis said his other basic psychological technique is to employ "the ambition to gain and keep property."

On that score, he recently told a group of business and civic leaders at a luncheon in the Redondo Beach Elks Club: "One human right above all other rights is the right to own property."

Another common Jarvis tactic is to hit the lawmakers in Sacramento.

"The general public doesn't believe a damn word of what any politician says," he told Town Hall, a Los Angeles group of primarily business people....

6. Reverend Jerry Falwell Calls America Back to the Bible, 1980

I believe that Americans want to see this country come back to basics, back to values, back to biblical morality, back to sensibility, and back to patriotism. Americans are looking for leadership and guidance. It is fair to ask the question, "If 84 per cent of the American people still believe in morality, why is America having such internal problems?" We must look for the answer to the highest places in every level of government. We have a lack of leadership in America. But Americans have been lax in voting in and out of office the right and the wrong people....

While sins of America are certainly many, let us summarize the five major problems that have political consequences, political implications that moral Americans need to be ready to face.

1. ABORTION—Nine men, by majority vote, said it was okay to kill unborn children. In 1973, two hundred million Americans and four hundred thousand pastors stood by and did little to stop it. Every year millions of babies are murdered in America, and most of us want to forget that it is happening….

2. HOMOSEXUALITY—In spite of the fact that the Bible clearly designates this sin as an act of a "reprobate mind" for which God "gave them up" (Rm.1:26–28), our government seems determined to legalize homosexuals as a legitimate "minority." The National Civil Rights Act of 1979 (popularly referred to as the Gay Rights Bill) would give homosexuals the same benefits as the 1964 Civil Rights Act, meaning they could not be discriminated against by any employing body because of "sexual preference."….

3. PORNOGRAPHY—The four-billion-dollar-per-year pornographic industry is probably the most devastating moral influence of all upon our young people. Sex magazines deliberately increase the problem of immoral lust and thus provoke increased adultery, prostitution, and sexual child abuse….

4. HUMANISM—The contemporary philosophy that glorifies man as man, apart from God, is the ultimate outgrowth of evolutionary science and secular education. In his new book *The Battle for the Mind*, Dr. Tim LaHaye argues that the full admission of humanism as the religion of secular education came after prayer and Bible reading were excluded from our public schools. Ultimately, humanism rests upon the philosophy of existentialism, which emphasizes that one's present existence is the true meaning and purpose of life. Existentialism has become the religion of the public schools. Applied to psychology, it postulates a kind of moral neutrality that is detrimental to Christian ethics. In popular terminology it explains, "Do your own thing," and "If it feels good, do it!" It is an approach to life that has no room for God and makes man the measure of all things.

5. THE FRACTURED FAMILY—With a skyrocketing divorce rate, the American family may well be on the verge of extinction in the next twenty years. Even the recent White House Conference on Families has called for an emphasis on diverse family forums (common-law, communal, homosexual, and transsexual "marriages"). The Bible pattern of the family has been virtually discarded by modern American society. Our movies and magazines have glorified the physical and emotional experience of sex without love to the point that most Americans do not even consider love to be important at all anymore. Bent on self-gratification, we have reinterpreted our moral values in light of our immoral life styles. Since the family is the basic unit of society, and since

the family is desperately in trouble today, we can conclude that our society itself is in danger of total collapse....

I am convinced that we need a spiritual and moral revival in America if America is to survive the twentieth century. The time for action is now; we dare not wait for someone else to take up the banner of righteousness in our generation. We have already waited too long....

The authority of Bible morality must once again be recognized as the legitimate guiding principle of our nation....

7. President Ronald Reagan Sees a Revitalized America, 1985

There are no words adequate to express my thanks for the great honor that you've bestowed on me. I'll do my utmost to be deserving of your trust.

This is as Senator Mathias told us, the 50th time we the people have celebrated this historic occasion. When the first President—George Washington—placed his hand upon the Bible, he stood less than a single day's journey by horseback from raw, untamed wilderness. There were 4 million Americans in a union of 13 States. Today, we are 60 times as many in a union of 50 States. We've lighted the world with our inventions, gone to the aid of mankind wherever in the world there was a cry for help, journeyed to the Moon and safely returned.

So much has changed. And yet, we stand together as we did two centuries ago. When I took this oath 4 years ago, I did so in a time of economic stress. Voices were raised saying that we had to look to our past for the greatness and glory. But we, the present–day Americans, are not given to looking backward. In this blessed land, there is always a better tomorrow.

Four years ago, I spoke to you of a new beginning, and we have accomplished that. But in another sense, our new beginning is a continuation of that beginning created two centuries ago, when, for the first time in history, government, the people said, was not our master, it is our servant; its only power that which we the people allow it to have.

That system has never failed us. But, for a time, we failed the system. We asked things of government that government was not equipped to give. We yielded authority to the national government that properly belonged to States or to local governments or to the people themselves. We allowed taxes and inflation to rob us of our earnings and savings and watched the great industrial machine that had made us the most productive people on Earth slow down and the number of unemployed increase.

By 1980 we knew it was time to renew our faith; to strive with all our strength toward the ultimate in individual freedom, consistent with an orderly society....

Public Papers of the Presidents of the United States: Ronald Reagan, 1985 (Washington, D.C.: U.S. Government Printing Office, 1988), Vol. 1, pp. 55–58.

At the heart of our efforts is one idea vindicated by 25 straight months of economic growth: Freedom and incentives unleash the drive and entrepreneurial genius that are a core of human progress. We have begun to increase the rewards for work, savings, and investment, reduce the increase in the cost and size of government and its interference in people's lives....

History is a ribbon, always unfurling; history is a journey. And as we continue our journey, we think of those who traveled before us....

A general falls to his knees in the hard snow of Valley Forge; a lonely President paces the darkened halls and ponders his struggle to preserve the union; the men of the Alamo call out encouragement to each other; a settler pushes west and sings a song, and the song echoes out forever and fills the unknowing air.

It is the American sound. It is hopeful, big-hearted, idealistic, daring, decent, and fair. That's our heritage, that's our song. We sing it still. For all our problems, our differences, we are together as of old. We raise our voices to the God who is the Author of this most tender music. And may He continue to hold us close as we fill the world with our sound—in unity, affection, and love. One people under God, dedicated to the dream of freedom that He has placed in the human heart, called upon now to pass that dream on to a waiting and a hopeful world. God bless you, and may God bless America.

8. Surgeon General Everett Koop Defends His Crusade on AIDS, 1987

WASHINGTON, April 5—The morning that Dr. C. Everett Koop went to Congress to testify in favor of condom advertising, his wife sent him off with these words: "Well, I'm glad your mother's dead." "And you know," the Surgeon General said, smiling behind his Captain Ahab beard, "I know what she meant."

His mother, a sheltered housewife from Brooklyn, would never have understood.

For that matter, many people in Washington do not understand Dr. Koop's extraordinary shift in image from someone who was regarded at the time of his appointment as a "right winger" and a fervent opponent of abortion to someone who is now so graphically outspoken on an issue like AIDS. A Hero or a Failure? Many of the liberals who once criticized Dr. Koop now praise him. Representative Henry Waxman, a California Democrat who heads the Health subcommittee of the Energy and Commerce Committee, used to find the Surgeon General "scary." Now he calls him "a man of heroic proportions."

On the other side, Howard Phillips, the chairman of the Conservative Caucus who pushed for Dr. Koop's confirmation six years ago, now says that he has "failed in moral courage."

Maureen Dowd, "Washington Talk: The Surgeon General; Dr. Koop Defends His Crusade on AIDS," *New York Times*, April 6, 1987.

While President Reagan and most of his top officials either avoid the issue of AIDS or speak brightly of the virtues of sexual abstinence, the 70-year-old Dr. Koop spreads the graphic gospel of AIDS prevention, in forums ranging from radio and television talk shows to college commencements.

"Advertising condoms in a tasteful way is a lot different than throwing them from a Mardi Gras float in New Orleans," he said, sitting in his office the other morning and wearing the gold-braided military-style uniform that has made him a familiar figure around town.

"Kids aren't dumb—they know about these things," he added, with exasperation. "If you go to a drugstore to get a pack of gum, you'll see a box of condoms next to it."

Acquired immune deficiency syndrome, a fatal viral disease that is spread through intercourse with an infected person or through exchanges of blood, as in shared hypodermic needles, has killed thousands of male homosexuals and intravenous drug users in this country....

Dr. Koop's vivid emphasis on science rather than values, and his defense of individual rights and confidentiality in opposing mandatory testing for the disease, have stunned and enraged many of his former supporters on the right. Nellie Gray, the chairman of the March for Life, last week rescinded an annual award her anti-abortion group had given Dr. Koop, notifying thousands of people on her mailing list that he was retroactively undeserving. The doctor has become a lightning rod for one of the most sensitive moral issues in the country: How do you talk about sex in a way that is explicit enough to give health information without seeming to condone certain practices? ...

Secretary of Education William J. Bennett has taken public issue with Dr. Koop, saying that schools should teach about sex only as part of marriage. And White House officials recently confirmed to NBC News that the President has never talked to his Surgeon General about AIDS nor read the report Dr. Koop sent him last October.

Dr. Koop is keenly aware of the irony of his situation. "The world has flip-flopped and it's bittersweet," he said. "Obviously, it's gratifying to have people like Senator Edward Kennedy and Henry Waxman saying I have integrity. But it's bitter to have people who liked me thinking that I've slipped the traces."...

But there are strong ironies. The man who was once labeled a right winger now talks about right wingers. "Some of these people seem more concerned with homosexual genocide, and with things like William Buckley's suggestion that AIDS victims be tattooed, than with the human tragedy," he said. When pressed, Dr. Koop concedes that it is impossible to be in the thick of a public health crisis like AIDS and not be personally touched.

"As you mature in any kind of situation, you become more understanding about it," he said. "I hate injustice of any kind and I don't like to see people excoriated in the midst of illness because there's some other part of their life style that people don't like."

---

9. Sierra Club Attacks the President's Policy, 1988

At half past four on election day, 1980, Sierra Club volunteers and staff gather around a borrowed television set at the Club's San Francisco headquarters to watch the returns....

Groans fill the room as soon as the television is turned on. Even though the polls will remain open for several hours in the far West, the networks are already proclaiming Reagan the winner.

Spirits slump further as the Senate and House results pour in. In state after state, senators who have fought for the environment are being upset by their opponents.... Frank Church of Idaho, one of the Senate's leading proponents of wilderness, is narrowly defeated by Steve Symms, a virulent advocate of public-land exploitation. By seven o'clock only a scattering of sorrowful Sierra Clubbers remain at the election-night party.

The next morning it is clear that very few pro-environment candidates have managed to claw their way to the top of the Reagan avalanche. Representative Morris Udall, chair of the House Interior Committee, is reelected, as are most of the other key environmental players in the House. Of the environmental leaders in the Senate facing strong 1980 challenges, only Alan Cranston of California wins a decisive victory. Senator Gary Hart of Colorado wins, but barely.

Reagan's coattails are so long that the Republicans finally wrest control of the Senate from the Democrats. The new chair of the Senate Energy Committee, with jurisdiction over the nation's public-land and energy resources, is Symms' ideological soulmate and fellow Idahoan, James McClure. The new head of the Senate Agriculture Committee is archconservative and wilderness foe Jesse Helms of North Carolina.

"The end of the environmental movement" is proclaimed by NBC News (along with the demise of feminism and civil rights). Mainstream Republicans who served on the staffs of environmental agencies under presidents Nixon and Ford, some of whom worked for Reagan when he was governor of California in the late 1960s and early '70s, are passed over for jobs. By Inauguration Day environmental policy is firmly in the hands of the "sagebrush rebels"—abrasive, conservative ideologues from the West. The rebels' antigovernment bias is strongly supported by Office of Management and Budget (OMB) Director David Stockman, a former Republican congressman from Michigan who only months earlier told Congress that toxic waste dumps are not a proper federal concern.

The Reagan Era has begun.

Today environmentalists are breathing slightly easier, and counting the few days left in Reagan's reign. The Sierra Club has moved to larger headquarters, a necessary response to a membership that soared from 180,000 during the Carter years to 480,000 in September of 1988. Ironically, Ronald Reagan has motivated

Carl Pope, "The Politics of Plunder," is reprinted from pp. 48–55 of the November/December 1988 issue of *Sierra* magazine, the magazine of the Sierra Club.

far more people to join the Club and other environmental organizations than all of his predecessors combined....

There can be no question that Reagan's appointees tried on numerous fronts to weaken America's commitment to the environment....

—A dentist from South Carolina, James Edwards, began dismantling conservation and renewable-energy programs soon after he was named Secretary of Energy....

—Reagan appointees rebuffed repeated pleas from Canada for a reduction of the acid rain that is destroying its forests, its economy, and life in its lakes. Instead of solutions, some Reaganites talked of "more studies" while Stockman made scornful references to "billion-dollar fish."

—Appointees at the EPA crippled the Superfund toxic-waste-cleanup program, and the program's key administrator, Rita Lavelle, went to jail.

—Morale at the EPA, the National Park Service, the Fish and Wildlife Service and the Bureau of Land Management collapsed in the Face of inadequate budgets, the administration's repeated refusals to enforce the laws, and its political interference in regulatory decisions....

But...we should not forget that on mountaintops and beaches, in small woodlands and majestic rainforests, in cities and playgrounds, in the oceans and the atmosphere itself, reminders of the Reagan Era will linger for decades....

Eight precious years have been lost. The patterns set by Reagan's policies could have irreversible consequences in ten, or twenty, or thirty years—very brief times to change the direction of cumbersome national and international economies and polities....

We now need a global environmental Reconstruction. We need to ask of ourselves and our leaders more self-discipline than ever before, in part to compensate for the callousness of the last eight years. We need greater fidelity to facts, in part because our most recent leader tried to wish them away. We need above all to remember that time matters, that events have consequences, and that the world is a wondrous and intermingled web that, when torn in one place, may unravel a thousand miles or a hundred years away.

ESSAYS

The following essays offer competing explanations for the rise of the New Right. Dan T. Carter, professor emeritus at the University of South Carolina, follows the line of thinking suggested by Lyndon Johnson: the Democratic coalition broke apart primarily over civil rights. By 1968, no politician dared use the "N-word" again, as Alabama Governor George Wallace had so freely. But Republicans—beginning with Richard Nixon—understood that if they wanted to woo the southern electoral block away from the party of Roosevelt, they were finally positioned to do so. They only had to find substitute phrases that nonetheless communicated a distinctly pro-white, anti-black message to receptive audiences. This was the so-called Southern Strategy. Bruce Schulman, professor at Boston University, says the battle was not over race, but over the role of government. From Georgia to California, citizens of the Sunbelt had reached the limit of what they wanted government to do, at least in terms of social welfare. They supported and benefitted from the expansion of federal military spending, including aerospace, but balked at "giveaways" they thought helped the undeserving (both blacks and the urban poor). The "Southernization" of American public life was not just political, but was reflected as well in the sudden fashionableness of country music, pick–up trucks, and a "redneck" lifestyle. Reagan epitomized "buoyant Sunbelt conservatism" and its deep suspicion of the Nanny state.

The Politics of Race and the Rise of the Right

DAN T. CARTER

After his hairbreadth loss to John Kennedy in 1960, Richard Nixon had played the role of the magnanimous loser, congratulating Kennedy and discouraging supporters who wanted to challenge questionable election returns from precincts in Mayor Daley's Chicago. Two years later, faced with another heartbreaking loss to California governor Pat Brown, his mask of control slipped; exhausted, hung over, and trembling with rage, he had stalked into the press room of his campaign headquarters and lashed out at assembled newsmen in rambling re-marks so incoherent that reporters—who are not noted for their empathy for wounded politicians—sat in silent embarrassment. For ten minutes (though it seemed like hours to his staff) the former vice president alternated between mawkish self-pity and bitter attacks on the press, which he blamed for his defeat. He closed with the line memorable for its unintended irony: "Well, you won't have Nixon to kick around anymore, because, gentlemen, this is my last press conference...." As stunned aides Herbert Klein and H. R. Haldeman pulled him from the room, the defeated candidate was unrepentant. "I finally told those bastards off, and every Goddamned thing I said was true."

By December 1967, memories of his losses had faded. With the determina-tion that had led his Duke Law School classmates to dub him Richard the Grind, Nixon fought his way back to political center stage....

If there was a turning point in the political recovery of Richard Nixon, it had come in 1964. Faced with the likelihood that his party would nominate conservative standard-bearer Barry Goldwater (and the certainty he would suffer a smashing defeat), the former vice president introduced the Arizona senator at the convention and then dutifully delivered more than one hundred and fifty speeches for Republican candidates in thirty-six states, always emphasizing his support for Goldwater even as he distanced himself from the nominee's more extreme positions. By the time the votes were counted in the Johnson landslide,

From Dan T. Carter, *The Politics of Rage: George Wallace, the Origins of the New Conservatism, and the Transformation of American Politics* (Baton Rouge: Louisiana State University Press, Revised edition, 2000), pp. 324–334, 337–338, 345, 347–349, 362–367, and 465–468. Reprinted with permission of the author.

Nixon had compiled a staggering number of chits from conservative and moderate Republicans. When he embarked on an equally aggressive speaking schedule for party candidates in the 1966 off-year elections, he became the odds-on favorite for the GOP nomination in 1968. And the long-coveted prize—the presidency—appeared within reach as the Democratic Party seemed to implode.

When Lyndon Johnson committed United States airpower and troops to support the tottering South Vietnamese government in 1964 and 1965, only a small minority of intellectuals and students challenged him. As the number of ground troops rose from fifty thousand in 1964 to nearly half a million in January of 1967, as casualties mounted, as the cost of the war doubled, tripled, then quadrupled, members of the antiwar movement, frustrated and impotent, escalated their tactics, from teach-ins to rallies to raucous street demonstrations. The war in Vietnam and the explosion of the antiwar movement, coupled with summer after summer of civil disorder, left the incumbent Democratic administration discredited and the nation deeply divided.

… Richard Nixon skillfully positioned himself to take advantage of the frustrations of middle-class and working-class Americans by holding out the chimerical promise that he could win the war by relying upon airpower rather than increasing the number of American ground troops.

But first he had to win the Republican nomination. And in that process, the South played a critical role.

To most political reporters, Richard Nixon's "Southern Strategy" was simply a continuation of Barry Goldwater's efforts to woo disgruntled whites in the old Confederacy, but Nixon adamantly rejected the notion that he had picked up where Goldwater left off.…

The Arizonan's huge majorities in the Deep South had made possible the election of dozens of Republican officeholders for the first time since the post-Civil War Reconstruction era, but his identification with hard-line segregationists weakened his party's appeal to moderates in the border states and in the North. The GOP, argued Nixon, should reach out to the South's emerging middle-class suburban constituency, more in tune with traditional Republican economic conservatism than with old-style racism.

If Nixon's analysis showed a shrewd grasp of the long-term weaknesses of the 1964 GOP campaign, it was disingenuous to pretend that his own manipulation of the politics of race bore no resemblance to that of Barry Goldwater. The political demands of the hour required him to walk a precarious ideological tightrope—to distance himself from Goldwater's explicit appeal to southern white racism while reaping the benefits of such a strategy.…

Nixon realized he couldn't be *too* moderate. Most southern GOP leaders were considerably to the right of the national political mainstream on economic, social, and racial issues. The majority of their mid-level and lower-level cadres had entered the party on the wave of the Goldwater campaign, and—while they were chastened by the Johnson landslide of 1964—they were not about to abandon their conservative and ultra-conservative views. To gain their allegiance required a deft political hand.

In the two years after the 1964 election, Nixon traveled 127,000 miles, visited forty states, and spoke to four hundred groups, nearly half of them in the South. On his southern swings, he was conservative, but not too conservative; a defender of civil rights, but always solicitous of white southerners' "concerns." He often prefaced his remarks with a reminder that he had supported the Supreme Court's decision in 1954 as well as the Civil Rights Acts of 1964 and the Voting Rights Act of 1965. His bona fides established, he would then launch into a stern lecture on the problem of "riots, violence in the streets and mob rule," or he would take a few swings at the "unconscionable boondoggles" in Johnson's poverty program or at the federal courts' excessive concern for the rights of criminals. The real culprits in the nation's racial conflicts were the "extremists of both races," he kept saying....

During one of those southern forays in the spring of 1966, Nixon traveled to Columbia, South Carolina, for a fund-raising dinner for the South Carolina GOP. Senator Strom Thurmond had easily assumed command of the state's fledgling Republican Party when he officially switched to the GOP during the Goldwater campaign. In the years after his 1948 presidential run, he modulated his rhetoric and shifted the focus of his grim maledictions to the "eternal menace of godless, atheistic Communism." He had even learned (when pressed) to pronounce the word "Negro" without eliciting grimaces from his northern fellow Republicans. But race remained his subtext; he continued to Red-bait every spokesman for civil rights from Whitney Young of the Urban League to Stokely Carmichael of the Black Panthers. For the traditional southern campaign chorus of "Nigger-nigger-nigger," he substituted the Cold War battle cry: "Commie-Commie-Commie." On the eve of Nixon's visit, Thurmond was still attacking the civil rights movement, still accusing the Supreme Court of fostering "crime in the streets" and of promoting "a free rein for communism, riots, agitation, collectivism and the breakdown of moral codes."

The senator assigned Harry Dent to act as the vice president's host. Despite Nixon's reputation as wooden and aloof, he charmed Thurmond's aide by bluntly acknowledging his presidential aspirations and soliciting advice. He had no illusions about the difficulties of getting the nomination and defeating Lyndon Johnson, he told Dent. But the man he feared most was George Wallace.

In his public statements, Nixon always professed to be unconcerned about the Alabama governor. As a third-party candidate, Wallace might hurt the GOP in the South, argued Nixon, but he would draw an equal number of votes from normally Democratic blue-collar voters in the North. "I don't think he'll get four million votes," said Nixon, who pointed to the dismal past experience of third-party candidates. Four million votes would translate into less than six percent of the expected turnout.

He was considerably more frank in his conversation with Dent.... If Wallace should "take most of the South," Nixon told Dent, as the Republican candidate he might be "unable to win enough votes in the rest of the country to gain a clear majority." Once the election went to the Democratic-controlled House of Representatives, the game was over.

Dent argued that Thurmond was the key to gaining the support of southern Republicans. Conservatives might privately deride the South Caroline senator as an egotistical fanatic, but his very estrangement from the traditional political process—his refusal to cooperate or compromise with fellow senators—made him the ideological measuring stick for southern GOP leaders baptized in the ideologically pure waters of Goldwater Republicanism.

At an afternoon press conference, Richard Nixon went out of his way to praise the former Dixiecrat. "Strom is no racist," he told reporters; "Strom is a man of courage and integrity." To Thurmond, laboring under the burden of his past as the "Dr. No" of American race relations, it was like being granted absolution from purgatory by the pope of American politics. Almost pathetically grateful, the senator seldom wavered in his support for Nixon in the years that followed.

Nixon's careful cultivation of southern white sensibilities and of power brokers like Thurmond paid off at the 1968 Republican convention....

Flanked by his impassioned sidekick, Strom Thurmond, Nixon summoned the southern delegations to his suite at the Hilton Plaza for a virtuoso performance. (The meeting was captured on tape by an enterprising *Miami Herald* reporter who persuaded a Florida delegate to carry a concealed recorder into Nixon's suite.) Nixon first reaffirmed his commitment to economic conservatism and a foreign policy resting upon equal parts of anticommunism and military jingoism. Still, the issue of race preoccupied the group. Once again, Nixon showed that he was the master of the wink, the nudge, the implied commitment. Without ever explicitly renouncing his own past support for desegregation, he managed to convey to his listeners the sense that, as President, he would do the absolute minimum required to carry out the mandates of the federal courts. In a Nixon administration, there would be no rush to "satisfy some professional civil-rights group, or something like that."

Although some members of his audience believed that George Wallace had the right solution ("take those bearded bureaucrats and throw them in the Potomac") or that the golden-tongued Reagan was the more authentic conservative, the bitter memories of the Goldwater debacle made them pause and listen to Thurmond. "We have no choice, if we want to win, except to vote for Nixon," he insisted. "We must quit using our hearts and start using our heads." Believe me, he said, "I love Reagan, but Nixon's the one."

After the convention, Texas Republican senator John Tower described Nixon's southern brigade as the "thin gray line which never broke." A more appropriate analogy might be found in Margaret Mitchell's *Gone With the Wind*. Like so many Scarlett O'Haras, Nixon's Dixie delegates reluctantly turned their backs on the dashing blockade-runner and resigned themselves to a marriage of convenience with the stodgy dry-goods merchant.

They received their first reward with Nixon's announcement that Spiro Agnew would be his running mate.

A few weeks before the convention, the candidate had accompanied his old law partner, John Mitchell, to an Annapolis restaurant to meet Maryland's governor. Afterward, Nixon told an aide: "That guy Agnew is really an impressive fellow. He's got guts. He's got a good attitude." Although he concealed his decision to the last to gain maximum leverage, it was a done deal....

The former Maryland governor seemed perfectly suited for the job....

... He had earned a reputation as a moderate in the Maryland gubernatorial contest when his opponent, a vociferous segregationist, promised to turn the clock back on civil rights. With his typical "on the one hand and on the other hand" rhetoric, Nixon insisted that he chose Agnew because he was a "progressive" border-state Republican who took a "forward-looking stance on civil rights, but... had firmly opposed those who had resorted to violence in promoting their cause."

What really sold Nixon, however, was the Maryland governor's performance during the five-day Baltimore race riot that followed Martin Luther King's assassination in April 1968. As the city returned to some degree of normality, Agnew summoned one hundred mainstream black city leaders—respected community organizers, middle-class preachers, lawyers, businessmen, and politicians—to a conference in Annapolis. Instead of holding a joint discussion, the governor lashed out at his audience's failure to condemn the "circuit-riding Hanoi-visiting ...caterwauling, riot-inciting, burn-American-down type of leader[s]" who, he said, had caused the rioting in the city. Pointing his finger for emphasis, he accused the moderates of "breaking and running" when faced with the taunts of "Uncle Tom" from black radicals like Stokely Carmichael and H. Rap Brown. Three fourths of his audience—many still exhausted from long days and nights on the street trying to calm the rioters—angrily walked out of the meeting. These were the "very people who were trying to end the riots," pointed out the executive director of the city's Community Relations Commission, but Baltimore's television stations reported a flood of telephone calls supporting the governor....

By the end of August, George Wallace held a commanding lead in the Deep South and trailed Nixon narrowly in much of the remainder of the region. In the long run, Nixon believed, Dixie's heartland—Mississippi, Alabama, Louisiana, and Georgia—would come home to the Republican Party because the national Democrats, sensitive to their black constituency, could not appeal to the region's racially conservative white voters. In the meantime, the GOP nominee abandoned his original goal of a southern sweep and adopted a modified Southern Strategy. Thurmond would give him South Carolina; he would work to carry the border South. His main weapon would be Spiro Agnew, who soon began sounding like a rather dignified clone of George Wallace....

A Chattanooga Baptist preacher heralded Wallace's reemergence on the campaign trail with an apocalyptic invocation: "Outside the visible return of Jesus Christ," shouted the Reverend John S. Lanham, "the only salvation of the country is the election of George Wallace." In the city's ramshackle municipal auditorium six thousand Tennessee farmers, factory employees and white-collar workers, small businessmen and retirees gave the Alabamian eleven standing ovations as he laid out his lambasted back-alley muggers, urban rioters, HEW bureaucrats, federal judges, and—most of all—the "out-of-touch politicians" who led the Democratic and Republican parties. "You could put them all in an Alabama cotton picker's sack, shake them up and dump them out; take the first one to slide out and put him right back into power and there would be no change." ...

More than eighty percent of the nine million dollars raised by the [Wallace] campaign came from small contributions of less than fifty dollars, solicited by the increasingly slick direct-mail fund-raising techniques of televangelists and, more important, by fund-raisers where Wallace was present to press the flesh. Instead of the discreet private "occasions" favored by leading Democratic and Republican candidates, at which donors were asked to contribute from five thousand dollars on up, the Wallace staff emphasized smaller contributions....

Wallace was not the first American political candidate to attract small donors through direct mailings and television appeals, but he broke new ground in the effectiveness of his campaign. In the early spring of 1968, an Alabama-based advertising agency, Luckey and Forney, threw together a half-hour television film, *The Wallace Story*. Little more than a crudely edited summary of the candidate's best applause lines delivered at rallies across America, the narrative was interrupted repeatedly with pleas for viewers to send in their dollars so that George Wallace could "stand up for America." When the agency marketed the film on small television stations in the South and in relatively inexpensive media markets in the Midwest and the Rocky Mountain states, even the Wallace people were stunned at the response. "The money is just coming in by the sackfuls," said an awed Jack House in April 1968. Most of it, he confided, was in small contributions from a dollar to a hundred dollars. "It's a gold mine."...

At least a dozen articles that appeared during the 1968 campaign compared Wallace to Louisiana's "Kingfish," Huey Long. Both were authoritarian, but the Kingfish rejected the politics of race. In speech after speech Wallace knit together the strands of racism with those of a deeply rooted xenophobic "plain folk" cultural outlook which equated social change with moral corruption. The creators of public policy—the elite—were out of touch with hardworking taxpayers who footed the bill for their visionary social engineering at home and weak-minded defense of American interests abroad. The apocalyptic rhetoric of anticommunism allowed Wallace to bridge the gap between theocratic and "moral" concerns and the secular issues of government economic policy, civil rights, and foreign policy....

The trick, for candidates who hoped to benefit from the "Wallace factor," was to exploit the grievances he had unleashed while disentangling themselves from the more tawdry trappings of his message. The Republican number-crunchers knew the figures by heart: eighty percent of southern Wallace voters preferred Nixon to [Democratic presidential candidate Hubert] Humphrey; by a much narrower margin, northern Wallace voters preferred Humphrey to Nixon. How could they drive the southern Wallace voters into the GOP without disturbing those in the North? That balancing act was proving more difficult than Nixon had imagined, particularly since he wanted to run a nondivisive campaign.

The counterattack against the Wallace threat to the Southern Strategy was executed by Strom Thurmond's assistant Harry Dent....

Dent repeatedly insisted that neither the Southern Strategy nor Nixon's generally conservative emphasis in 1968 was racist. And, in fact, he (like other members of the Nixon team) scrupulously avoided explicit references to race. The problem with the liberalism of the Democrats, Dent charged, was not that it was too problack, but that it had created an America in which the streets were "filled with radical dissenters, cities were literally burning down, crime seemed uncontrollable," and the vast social programs of the Democrats were creating an army of the permanently dependent even as they bankrupted the middle class. The rising tide of economic and social conservatism clearly complemented opposition to federal activism, north and south.

But the political driving force of Nixon's policies toward the South was *not* an abstract notion about the "preservation of individual freedom"; almost every aspect of the 1968 campaign was tightly interwoven with issues of race....

In much the same way, racial fears were linked to concerns over social disorder in American streets. The threat of crime was real; every index of criminality showed an increase in the number of crimes against property and in crimes of violence. Americans were still more likely to be maimed or killed by their friends and relatives than by strangers, but the growth of random, brutal urban violence— an escalation of black-on-white violence attracted the most attention—made law and orders an inevitable issue in the 1960s.

And Wallace simply erased the line between antiwar and civil rights protests, between heckling protesters and street muggers. By the fall, Nixon and even Humphrey were attempting to play catch-up with the crime issue, although both went to great lengths to insist that the issue was nonracial. (As the former vice president pointed out on several occasions, blacks were far more likely to be the victims of crime than whites were.) Occasionally, the façade slipped. Early in the campaign Nixon had taped a television commercial attacking the decline of "law and order" in American cities. As he reviewed it with his staff, he became expansive. That "hits it right on the nose," he said enthusiastically. "It's all about law and order and the damn Negro-Puerto Rican groups out there." Nixon did not have to make the racial connection any more than would Ronald Reagan when he began one of his famous discourses on welfare queens using food stamps to buy porterhouse steaks. His audience was already primed to make that connection.

For nearly a hundred years after the Civil War, politicians had manipulated the racial phobias of whites below the Mason-Dixon line to maintain a solidly Democratic South. To Nixon it seemed only poetic justice that the tables should be turned. The challenge lay in appealing to the fears of angry whites without appearing to become an extremist and driving away moderates....

... Ultimately, an enormous gender gap emerged: women—particularly non-southern women—proved far less willing than men to vote for the Alabama politician. In the eleven states of the old Confederacy, half of the men and forty percent of the women were ready to vote for Wallace in late September, at the high-water mark of his campaign. In the North, one-fifth of white males claimed he had their vote, but less than half that number of women supported him.

Cultural and regional differences undoubtedly played a role, but the reason women most often volunteered for opposing Wallace was that he was "dangerous." In his public performances—the speeches and rallies—Wallace often teetered along a razor's edge of violence. Where Nixon and Humphrey hated the hecklers and demonstrators, particularly the antiwar demonstrators, who appeared on the campaign trail, Wallace welcomed them, and had become a master at manipulating them....

... And in one rally after another, Wallace's angry rhetoric ignited fist-swinging, chair-throwing confrontations between these hardcore followers and antiwar and civil rights demonstrators, who on occasion pelted the candidate with various objects. Wallace was hit by rocks, eggs, tomatoes, pennies, a peace medallion, Tootsie Rolls, a sandal, and a miniature whiskey bottle. By October, television crews always set up two cameras: one to focus on the stage, the other to capture the mêlées and bloodied demonstrators in the audience.

Wallace's troubles gave Nixon the opening he needed....

During the last two weeks of the campaign, Nixon took to the air himself in advertisements specifically tailored to white southern voters: "There's been a lot of double-talk about the role of the South"—by which he meant the white people of the South—"in the campaign of nineteen sixty-eight, and I think it's time for some straight talk," he told his listeners. Without mentioning Wallace by name, Nixon warned that a "divided vote" would play into the hands of the Humphrey Democrats. "And so I say, don't play their game. Don't divide your vote. Vote for...the only team that can provide the new leadership that America needs, the Nixon-Agnew team. And I pledge to you we will restore law and order in this country...." ...

October 24, 1968, was overcast and drizzly, but unseasonably warm for New York City. More than a thousand police—a hundred of them on horseback—lined up on Seventh Avenue between West Thirty-first and West Thirty-third streets as the crowds began to pour into Madison Square Garden. Twenty thousand of the faithful packed the arena by eight p.m. for the largest political rally held in New York City since Franklin Roosevelt had denounced the forces of "organized money" from the same stage in 1936. At eight-twenty, George Wallace stepped out into the lights and the audience erupted. Although the campaign had another week to run, for Wallace, the evening was the emotional climax of his race for the presidency.

Across the street an astonishing collection of fringe groups gathered: a caravan of Ku Klux Klansmen from Louisiana who had driven all the way to New York; a delegation of followers of the "Minutemen of America," paramilitary ultra-rightists with neatly printed signs and armloads of brochures; a dozen jackbooted members of the American Nazi Party sporting swastika armbands and "I like Eich" buttons worn in memory of Adolf Eichmann, who had been sentenced to death by an Israeli court for his role in supervising the murder of millions of Jews during the Holocaust. New York police maintained an uneasy peace between the far-right contingent and the more than two hundred members of the Trotskyite Workers' World Party and several hundred members of the radical Students for a Democratic Society, bearing the black flag of Anarchy. Altogether, two thousand protesters—most in their early twenties—waved their picket signs and screamed their battle cries. Radical demonstrators mocked: *"Sieg heil! Sieg heil!"* The right wing countered: "Commie faggots! Commie faggots!"

Inside the Garden, while a brass band played a medley of patriotic songs, Wallace strode back and forth across the stage, saluting the crowd, which roared his name again and again in a chant that could be heard by the demonstrators half a block away. Soon he was joined by Curtis LeMay and his wife, Helen.

After more than fifteen minutes, Wallace finally brought his followers to order by having a country singer perform "God Bless America." Apparently overwhelmed by the fervor of the crowd, he began his speech awkwardly. In the southwest balcony of the Garden, a squarely built black man stood and held up a poster proclaiming "Law and Order—Wallace Style." Underneath the slogan was the outline of a Ku Klux Klansman holding a noose. Another demonstrator at his side suddenly turned on a portable bullhorn and began shouting: "Wallace talks about law and order! Ask him what state has the highest murder rate! The most rapes! The most armed robberies." The overwhelmingly pro-Wallace crowd exploded in rage, and police hurried to rescue three suddenly silent black demonstrators who were surrounded by a dozen Wallace followers shouting "Kill 'em, kill 'em, kill 'em."

The heckling seemed to ignite the Alabama governor: "Why do the leaders of the two national parties kowtow to these anarchists?" he demanded, gesturing toward the protesters in the balcony. "One of 'em laid down in front of President Johnson's limousine last year," said Wallace with a snarl. "I tell you when November comes, the first time they lie down in front of my limousine it'll be the last one they'll ever lay down in front of; their day is *over!*"

The crowd was on its feet for the first of more than a dozen standing ovations.

"We don't have a sick society, we have a sick Supreme Court," he continued, as he scornfully described "perverted" decisions that disallowed prayer in the classrooms even as they defended the right to distribute "obscene pornography."

Fifteen minutes into his talk, he shed his jacket as he weaved and bobbed across the stage, his right fist clenched, his left jabbing out and down as if he were in the midst of one of his youthful bantamweight Golden Gloves bouts. "We don't have riots in Alabama," shouted Wallace. "They start a riot down there, first one of 'em to pick up a brick gets a bullet in the brain, that's all. And then you walk over to the next one and say, 'All right, pick up a brick. We just want to see you pick up one of them bricks, now!'" …

Richard Nixon always saw the Alabama governor as the key to understanding the reshaping of American politics. Nearly twenty years after the former President left office in disgrace, historian Herbert Parmet interviewed him for a biography, *Richard Nixon and His America*. At the end of his fourth and last question-and-answer session, Parmet methodically outlined the conservative shifts Nixon had made after 1970 to placate the Wallace constituency.

"Your point is that we had to move to the right in order to cut Wallace off at the pass?" asked Nixon.

"Absolutely," replied Parmet.

"Foreign policy was my major concern. You start with that," said Nixon. "To the extent that we thought of it [the Wallace movement] at all—maybe subconsciously—anything that might weaken my base because of domestic policy reasons had to give way to the foreign policy priorities." There was "no question that all these things must have been there.... I think," he added, "it's a pretty clear-headed analysis." It was as close as the proud Nixon would ever come to admitting that, when George Wallace had played his fiddle, the President of the United States had danced Jim Crow.

In the decorous landscape of upscale malls, suburban neighborhoods, and prosperous megachurches that has become the heartland of the new conservatism, Ronald Reagan, not George Wallace, is the spiritual godfather of the nineties. During such moments of racial crisis as the spectre of cross-district busing, surburbanites occasionally turned to George Wallace in the 1960s and early 1970s to voice their protest, but he was always too unsettling, too vulgar, too overtly southern. With the exception of a few hard-line right-wingers like Patrick Buchanan, the former Alabama governor has been a prophet without honor, remembered (if at all) for his late-life renunciation of racism....

But two decades after his disappearance from national politics, the Alabama governor seems vindicated by history. If he did not create the conservative groundswell that transformed American politics in the 1980s, he anticipated most of its themes. It was Wallace who sensed and gave voice to a growing national white backlash in the mid-1960s; it was Wallace who warned of the danger to the American soul posed by the "intellectual snobs who don't know the difference between smut and great literature"; it was Wallace who railed against federal bureaucrats who not only wasted the tax dollars of hardworking Americans, but lacked the common sense to "park their bicycles straight." Not surprisingly, his rise to national prominence coincided with a growing loss of faith in the federal government. In 1964, nearly 80 percent of the American people told George Gallup's pollsters that they could trust Washington to "do what is right all or most of the time." Thirty years later, that number had declined to less than 20 percent.

If George Wallace did not create this mode of national skepticism, he anticipated and exploited the political transformation it precipitated. His attacks on the federal government have become the gospel of modern conservatism; his angry rhetoric, the foundation for the new ground rules of political warfare. In 1984, a young Republican Congressman from Georgia explained the facts of life to a group of young conservative activists. "The number one fact about the news media," said Newt Gingrich, "is they love fights. You have to give them confrontations." And they had to be confrontations in a bipolar political system of good and evil, right and wrong. The greatest hope for political victory was to replace the traditional give-and-take of American politics with a "battleground" between godly Republicans and the "secular anti-religious view of the left" embodied in the Democratic Party.

The notion of politics as a struggle between good and evil is as old as the Republic; that moral critique of American society lay at the very core of populism in the late nineteenth century. But angry reformers of an earlier generation had usually railed against the rich and powerful; Wallace turned the process on its head. He may have singled out "elitist" bureaucrats as symbols of some malevolent abstraction called "Washington," but everyone knew that his real enemies were the constituencies those federal officials represented: the marginal beneficiaries of the welfare state....

Much has changed in southern and American politics in the years since 1958 when George Wallace promised his friends that he would "never be out-niggered again." Middle- and upper-income suburbanites have fled the unruly public spaces of decaying central cities and created (or tried to create) a secure and controlled environment. Isolated from the expensive and frustrating demands of the growing urban underclass, suburbanites could control their own local government; they could buy good schools and safe streets—or at least better schools and safer streets than the inner city. "Big" government—the federal government—they complained, spent *their* hard-earned taxes for programs that were wasteful and inefficient and did nothing to help them....

George Wallace had recognized the political capital to be made in a society shaken by social upheaval and economic uncertainty. As the conservative revolution reached high tide, it was no accident that the groups singled out for relentless abuse and condemnation were welfare mothers and aliens, groups that are both powerless and, by virtue of color and nationality, outsiders. The politics of rage that George Wallace made his own had moved from the fringes of our society to center stage.

He was the most influential loser in twentieth-century American politics.

A Rejection of Government: Reagan and the Sunbelt

BRUCE J. SCHULMAN

A century after the last shot of the Civil War was fired, the South had at long last accepted defeat. In the wake of the civil rights revolution and the economic boom, the region no longer clung to a "southern way of life." But a hundred years later, after World War II, this "loser" reaped the spoils of victory. The Sunbelt South boomed in the 1970s while the old industrial heartland faced almost catastrophic decline. The *New York Times* devoted a four-part series to Dixie's resurgence: "All day and through the lonely night, the moving vans push southward, the 14-wheeled boxcars of the highway, changing the demographic face of America." As the United States approached its bicentennial, "a restless and historic movement" shifted people and power away from the northern states that had dominated American life since the nation's birth. Regional conflict once again captured national attention. *Business Week* even ran a cover story on "The Second War Between the States."

This battle was fought not over race but over government largesse....

In 1969, Kevin Phillips first diagnosed this sectional cleavage. Coining the term *Sunbelt,* Phillips identified a booming region stretching across the continental

Bruce Schulman, *The Seventies: The Great Shift in American Culture, Society, and Politics* (Da Capo, 2000), p. 106–109, 111–117, 219–220, 225–226, 228–232, 235–236, 240, 247, 251–252, 255–256. Reprinted by permission of Simon & Schuster Adult Publishing.

underbelly of the United States from Virginia and Florida to southern California. In *The Emerging Republican Majority,* Phillips portrayed the emerging South and West as the seedbed of a conservative majority in the United States, the foundation for a generation of Republican dominance in national politics....

A second controversial book, published in 1975, ratified and reiterated Phillips's argument concerning regional conflict. In *Power Shift,* Kirkpatrick Sale, a veteran of the 1960s radical left, reached similar conclusions. Sale, too, noted a "power shift" from the Northeast to the "southern rim," but he dreaded the new power of the Sunbelt as much as Phillips had anticipated it. According to Sale, the pillars of the southern rim, the bases for its spectacular growth and its waxing cultural power, were a handful of large industries: corporate agribusiness, defense, aerospace, oil, and leisure. Atop this economic foundation rested a conservative, reactionary, racist cowboy culture. From Orange County, North Carolina, to Orange County, California, the "3 Rs" defined the southern rim; not reading, 'riting, and 'rithmetic, but "racism, rightism, and repression."

So whether you cheered it like Kevin Phillips or feared it like Kirkpatrick Sale, few doubted in 1970s America that a resurgent conservative and potentially Republican Sunbelt was a force to be reckoned with. People of all sorts flocked South. The Sunbelt, after all, had hosted the religious revival of the 1970s. Into the region white Americans had fled the heterogeneity and the racial conflict of northeastern cities. There the elderly had built their own separate communities, and suburban shopping centers sprang up.

Sunbelt cities, the fastest-growing areas in the nation, reflected the privatism, the insularity, that was coming to dominate American life. These were cities without downtowns—vast sprawls where no one walked the streets and suburban malls served as the principal public meeting spaces....

The *San Diego Union* saw in the rise of the Sunbelt not just a new regional balance of power, but "America II emerging from the diminished promise of America I." The citizens of America II, the new majority of Americans living in the South and West, were innovators—sick of intrusive government and inhospitable communities. They were "building new kinds of cities less centralized and more livable than the congested urban centers of the North and East." ...

The dimensions of change alone proved staggering. A swarm of people headed South in the 1950s, 1960s, and 1970s. Retirees purchased condos in Florida or drove shiny new mobile homes across the southern rim. The armed forces ordered millions south for boot camp and active service, and eventually many decided to spend their retirements and pursue new careers in the Sunbelt. The defense and aerospace industries filled the suburbs surrounding Los Angeles, Houston, Dallas, Las Vegas, Atlanta, and North Carolina's Research Triangle Park. Between 1970 and 1990, the South's population exploded by 40 percent, twice the national rate....

These "citizens of America II" were many things, but they were not union members. And low labor costs for industry, especially low levels of union membership, was another major ingredient in the Sunbelt's favorable business climate. In 1976, one-quarter of the nation's nonagricultural workers carried union cards; these men and women had pulled themselves up from the assembly line into a solid middle-class existence. Working people built homes and communities with the help of the United Auto Workers in Flint, Michigan, the United Steelworkers in Pittsburgh, the Brewery Workers in Milwaukee, or the Longshoremen in Brooklyn. These unions and these communities had risen with the great industrial revolution in the heartland, and they were falling with it too. Union halls, once centers of social life, emptied as membership declined and factories closed down.

In the South, however, only 14 percent of nonfarmworkers belonged to unions in 1976. And as time passed, the nation more and more resembled the South. By the late 1980s, only 16 percent of American workers remained in unions; a big reason for the steady drop was the continuing movement of jobs from the union shop Frostbelt to the nonunion Sunbelt, from heavy manufacturing like steel and autos to Sunbelt industries like electronics and aerospace....

State governments also lured jobs and factories through aggressive promotion and special inducements. They offered generous subsidies to relocating businesses—free land and facilities, publicly financed training programs, and long-term tax abatements. Southern governors became famous for their "fishing expeditions"—ceaseless efforts to reel in businesses from other regions and from foreign nations. In 1970, half of annual foreign investment into the United States went below the Mason-Dixon line.

Still, as Hugh Carey's complaints and the broader Sunbelt-Frostbelt battle dramatized, the decisive factor in the rise of the Sunbelt was government action. Kirkpatrick Sale highlighted this irony—an antigovernment region so dependent on that which it claimed most to despise. The southern rim, Sale declared in *Power Shift*, was "an economy built on money from Washington.".…

The Republican party also harvested the fruits of southern economic development. The businessmen and professionals, managers and engineers who flooded the burgeoning cities and endless suburbs of the Sunbelt were a natural constituency for the GOP. Not only did Republican presidential candidates come to rely on southern votes, but for the first time since Reconstruction, the region began sending Republicans to the House and Senate and to the governors' mansions.

... The Sunbelt boom signaled the emergence of a new political force, a new kind of conservatism. For generations, American conservatism had been associated with the moneyed patricians of the Northeast, with Wall Street, Brooks Brothers, exclusive country clubs, and the "better sort" of prep school. Prudence, fiscal restraint, and noblesse oblige were its hallmarks. By 1970, however, American conservatism was emerging from a slow, painful transformation. As the geographic locus of conservative politics had moved south and west, its nature had changed; it became more populist, more middle class, more antiestablishment.

Along with the bonfire of political power, the Sunbelt boom ignited a cultural revival—the strongest reassertion of southern cultural identity and regional pride since the Civil War. By the early 1970s, embarrassment over segregation had faded away, and the South rejoined the national mainstream on questions of race relations. On the one hand, the worst excesses of southern racism had been outlawed, and African Americans began voting in southern elections. Atlanta sent black representatives to the mayor's office (Maynard Jackson), the state legislature (Julian Bond), and the U.S. House of Representatives (Andrew Young). A new generation of white politicians, led by Governors Rubin Askew of Florida and Jimmy Carter of Georgia, proved that a combination of racial moderation and economic boosterism could win elections in the South. The region no longer remained captive to the extremist politics of overt racial demagoguery....

More than that, they boasted a populist, conservative political philosophy. Without overt racial messages, they expressed subtle antiblack or anticity sentiments, usually directed against welfare and government programs. "There's folks who never work and they got plenty," Merle Haggard complained in "Big City." In another song, a slow, mournful ballad, Haggard asked over and over again, "Are the Good Times Really Over?" He longed for former and better days before welfare when "a man could still work and still would," before "microwave ovens, when a girl could still cook and still would," Is "the best of the free life behind us now, are the good times really over for good?" Haggard, of course, promised that they were not. Opposition to liberals, to bureaucrats, to trendy northerners became familiar motifs; in Muskogee, for instance, leather boots were "still in style for manly footwear."

The message and the music of country won increasing popularity throughout the 1970s and 1980s. Country radio outlets opened across the nation, record sales soared, and crossover hits—country songs that shot up the national pop music charts—became commonplace....

The old South had died, and few Americans—southerners included—would have wanted it back if they could only remember it as it truly was. Yet "redneck" culture, in a commercialized form, thrived and spread in the 1970s and 1980s. Country music, cowboy boots, pickup trucks, and even the Confederate flag became familiar badges of an influential American subculture. Millions of middle-class and upper-class Americans became "half a redneck." Along with boots and trucks, these demi-rednecks also brandished a set of shared political attitudes: they resented government interference, although they excluded military procurement from their hit list of despised government programs. They disliked bureaucrats, pointy-headed intellectuals, and "welfare Cadillacs."

Their beliefs and resentments created a potent political force. Sunbelt conservatives accomplished what Sixties radicals had only dreamed of: they captured a political party and won control of the White House. Demi-rednecks formed the foundation for conservative populism, the tax revolt, and the Reaganite assault on the welfare state....

Reagan's America had witnessed a profound transformation—a sea change in its public policy, national mood, and social and cultural profile. White House aide Martin Anderson proudly declared it a revolution. "What was happening in America," Anderson asserted, "was a revolution, not a violent, physical revolution driven by guns, but a revolution of political thought, a revolution of ideas." Reagan had unleashed an "earthquake that would shake the political establishment of the United States—and the world—for some time to come."

At the end of his presidency, Reagan defined his achievement in similar, if slightly more modest, terms. "They called it the Reagan Revolution," he conceded in his Farewell Address, "and I'll accept that, but for me it always seemed more like The Great Rediscovery: a rediscovery of our values and our common sense." The president pointed to "two great triumphs": the "economic recovery" and the "recovery of our morale."...

Reagan epitomized a buoyant Sunbelt conservatism—contemptuous of the Nanny state, unabashed in its red-blooded American patriotism, brimming with a cattle rustler's love for the hurly-burly of the marketplace. The early 1980s also represented the culmination of a decade-long ideological shift—a change in attitudes that sprang from but extended even further than the changes in latitudes. Reagan embodies a deep suspicion of the public sphere, finding the public purpose of old-style Rustbelt liberals both corrupt and counterproductive. At the same time, he possessed an exuberant faith in both the efficiency and the morality of the market....

When Reagan entered office, he [was] determined to reverse the direction of superpower relations in the 1970s. For over a decade, American foreign policy had drifted toward détente—peaceful coexistence and constructive engagement with the Soviet Union. Henry Kissinger had been the architect of détente, and Presidents Nixon, Ford, and Carter had pursued it. Détente featured trade and travel between the rival nations, cultural exchanges, and arms control agreements.

Reagan hated détente. He believed it immoral to negotiate with the Soviets and thought that trade agreements only propped up the communist regime. Rather than promote peace, he asserted, arms control left the United States vulnerable to attack and emboldened the Soviets to expand around the globe. Reagan decided to replace détente with confrontation. First and fore-most, he authorized a massive military buildup. In five years, from 1981 to 1986, the Pentagon budget more than doubled. The administration revived major weapons systems that Carter had iced and lavished resources on conventional forces, such as the building of 150 new naval ships....

President Reagan also mounted an unprecedented rhetorical attack on the Soviet Union. In spring 1983, appearing before the National Association of Evangelicals, Reagan labeled the Soviets an evil empire. They are, he declared, "the focus of evil in the world." The cold war was not "a giant misunderstanding," but a "struggle between right and wrong, good and evil."...

President Reagan's many-pronged strategy of confrontation backfired in August 1984. Speaking into a microphone that he did not know was recording, the president joked, "My fellow Americans, I'm pleased to tell you today that I've signed legislation that will outlaw Russia forever. We begin bombing in 5 minutes."

That unfortunate joke marked the crescendo of the confrontational approach. During the 1984 campaign, Reagan moved toward a new, much more flexible approach in U.S. relations with the Soviets....

When CIA reports informed the president that U.S. military exercises simulating the release of nuclear weapons had frightened the Soviets, Reagan was amazed. He confessed that he was surprised to learn that the Soviets genuinely feared an American attack.

Last but not least, the thaw in Soviet-American relations accelerated in 1985 when Konstantin Chernenko died. The decrepit Communist party general secretary had been the third Soviet leader to expire since Regan took office. This time the Politburo installed in the premiership fifty-four-year-old Mikhail Gorbachev—a healthy, energetic reformer. A former agriculture minister, Gorbachev understood the crippling weaknesses of the Soviet economy and the nation's pervasive social crises: rampant alcoholism, worker absenteeism, high infant mortality. The new general secretary moved immediately to scale down Soviet aid to revolutionary regimes in Third World, pull out of the quagmire of Afghanistan, and slow the arms race.

Gorbachev convinced many hard-line conservatives to take up the olive branches he proffered. Even that most hard-nosed of conservative leaders, the Iron Lady, British prime minister Margaret Thatcher, declared that "we can do business together with this man." Reagan initially resisted Gorbachev's blandishments, but finally agreed to a summit meeting and eventually met with the Soviet leader several times.

By the end of his presidency, the seemingly impossible had occurred. Ronald Reagan visited Moscow, embraced the Soviet leader in front of Lenin's tomb, and declared that the Soviets had changed. No longer were they the focus of evil in the modern world. The cold war was coming to an end. But ultimately, Reagan's rhetoric—his political commitments—redefined the cold war more decisively than his summit conferences or arms reductions. The Seventies vision of the Soviet Union—and of world politics—had changed so much that Americans could barely remember them.

"Government Is the Problem"

At home as well as abroad, Reagan wrestled with the legacies of the Seventies. For the president who succeeded Jimmy Carter, no other mission—not even the somber struggle with Soviet Union—mattered so much as nursing the United States itself back to health. But Reagan would pursue an unprecedented path to this objective, involving a direct assault on American government and public life, a culmination of Richard Nixon's fantasies that even he would have looked on with incredulity....

In practice, that "Second American Revolution" involved three great changes. First, Reagan demanded a dramatic reduction in taxes. The president proposed to reduce individual tax rates by 25 percent over three years. At the same time, he sharply cut the rates for the wealthiest taxpayers and indexed taxes to inflation, ending the bracket creep that had eroded Americans' few salary increases and made their tax burdens seem so heavy in the 1970s. Second, Reagan moved drastically to redefine the relationships—to shift the balance of power—among business, labor, and government. He accelerated deregulation, weakening the power of federal agencies to supervise industry's health, safety, and environmental performance. He struck hard at organized labor, removing the public backing that had armed unions in their struggle against business. And he devolved responsibility to the private sector, freeing entrepreneurs and giving business much more responsibility not just for economic but for social and cultural life as well.

Third, Reagan declared war on the federal government itself. He promised not only to end its interference in economic life, but to starve it of funds and shrink its bureaucracy. He targeted waste and inefficiency, but also attacked the welfare state he thought intrusive and counterproductive. He pledged to eliminate two cabinet departments....

Meanwhile, Reagan moved rapidly to free business from federal supervision. During the late 1970s, the Carter administration had begun easing the regulatory burden on American industry. In particular, Carter had dismantled the anticompetitive practices that had maintained artificially high prices in trucking, air travel, and telecommunications. Reagan accelerated and expanded the process of deregulation. The administration relaxed Depression-era controls on banks, brokerages, and savings and loan institutions. It decontrolled energy prices and permitted wider oil and gas exploration on federal land. It dropped restraints on offshore oil drilling, logging restrictions in national forests, and requirements for air bags and stronger automobile bumpers.

Reagan handed over the reins of the major oversight agencies to business leaders and opponents of federal regulation. As director of the Occupational Health and Safety Administration (OSHA), the president appointed a businessman who had once been cited for OSHA violations. The Antitrust Division of the Department of Justice announced a new policy of friendliness toward mergers, stimulating an unprecedented wave of corporate buyouts. The Consumer Product Safety Commission, the Federal Trade Commission, and the Federal Communications Commission also relaxed regulations in their bailiwicks....

Writing in the *Nation,* liberal critics Derek Shearer and Martin Carnoy called Reagan's program "the most significant income redistribution since the 1930s." Reaganomics, the liberal academics asserted, "does not really mean getting the government off people's backs; it means repealing the hard-won social gains of the last fifty years and using the government to transfer money to large corporations, high-income earners and military contractors."

Reagan certainly made no secret of his disdain for the welfare state. The president truly lacked sympathy for the downtrodden, accepting the canard that the poor deserved and even desired their own misery. Asked if he could have done more for the homeless, Reagan told his authorized biographer that his opponents had exaggerated the scope of the problem. There were few homeless people, he asserted, "and a lot of those are the type of people that have made that choice."...

Finally, Reagan shifted the terms of the welfare debate. For a generation, ever since President Lyndon B. Johnson had asked Americans to join in building what he called the Great Society, American social policy had aimed to eliminate poverty and redress the most blatant extremes of inequality. Johnson's successors lacked his commitment to total victory over poverty, but their welfare policies followed his lead. From Nixon's guaranteed income proposal to Carter's PBJI [Program for Better Jobs and Income], policymakers regarded poverty and inequality as economic and social defects and the welfare state as the medic.

Reagan turned the tables; welfare now became the problem, not the solution. Drawing on the work of conservative thinkers Charles Murray and George Gilder, Reagan's first economic report rejected "paternalism" in welfare policies, suggesting that antipoverty programs only aggravated the problems of the poor and trapped them in a cycle of poverty and dependence. Indeed, Reagan went so far as to argue that Great Society programs had actually harmed the impoverished—encouraging illegitimacy, welfare dependence, and hopelessness....

Taxation had always been unpopular, of course, but it had long remained a weapon of class warfare—a way ordinary Americans could limit the power and influence of the nation's wealthiest citizens. After all, it was not Ronald Reagan, but Franklin D. Roosevelt's adviser Harry Hopkins who coined the term tax-and-spend Democrat. But for Hopkins, that had been a recipe for success: "tax and spend and elect, tax and spend and elect." Reagan transformed taxation; it ceased to be an issue of equity, and it became a matter of tyranny or freedom. Instead of dividing rich and poor, business and labor, the tax issue united them against big government and elitist bureaucrats. Reagan did not begin the tax revolt, but he guided it to victory....

Not surprisingly, as the public sector did less, businesses and the well-to-do began to take some of government's basic functions into their own hands. In policing, for example, suburban communities and downtown business districts began relying more and more heavily on the burgeoning private security industry. The nation, the *New York Times* reported, "is putting less emphasis on controlling crime for everyone—the job of publicly employed police officers—and more emphasis on private police officers who carve out secure zones for those who pay for such protection." As one security expert concluded at the end of the decade, "We are securing more and more private space and putting less effort into securing public space."

A legion of "faux police" (privately hired neighborhood patrols) developed across the nation. In Sun City, Arizona, outside Phoenix, public safety became the responsibility of the 183-man Sun City Posse. The uniformed "posse," outfitted with handcuffs, mace, and specially equipped cars with flashing lights and stars painted on the door, closely resembled a real police force. Recognizing that the posse possessed superior manpower and better equipment, Maricopa Country authorities happily allowed these private guards to arrogate much of the police work in the area. These security forces aggrandized police power without public control or democratic accountability....

The drift to starboard continued through the 1980s. Despite his strong ties to organized labor, the party's 1984 standard-bearer, Walter Mondale, relied heavily on business Democrats for funds and policy advice. With his acceptance speech promise to raise taxes, Mondale made fiscal rectitude the centerpiece of his campaign—a program that reassured the Democratic Business Council and disappointed labor supporters who hoped Mondale would campaign for an ambitious jobs program. Mondale's principal Democratic opponent in 1984, Colorado senator Gary Hart, exalted entrepreneurship and the free market even more forcefully. Hart's brand of yuppie "neoliberalism" trumpeted tax relief for business, spurs to investment, and support for high-tech industry.

Over the 1980s, the party apparatus and Democratic politicians adopted the prevailing views that markets work better than government, that the public sector should free business to "grow the economy" rather than protect the market's victims from unregulated free enterprise. Since the 1930s the Democratic party had recognized that markets frequently produced bad outcomes—that the state should regulate business and redress the worst abuses of capitalism. The party abrogated that historic commitment during the mid-1980s. Democratic support for regulation, social programs, progressive taxation, and labor organization abated. The domestic agenda of Richard Nixon, even the "Modern Republicanism" of Dwight D. Eisenhower, would have made those men too liberal for the Democrats by the late 1980s....

During the Seventies, national power shifted south and west. Throughout his Senate career, Lyndon Johnson had assumed that a southerner could never become president. The North, he believed, wielded all the economic might and political muscle in American life; Yankees would never countenance a southerner in the White House. Even after LBJ won the presidency in his own right and imposed racial integration on a reluctant Dixie, Johnson felt the scorn and condescension of a still-dominant northern cultural elite. But during the Seventies, the tides of American politics turned. Drawing strength from its burgeoning population and booming economy, the South and Southwest wrested control of national politics. Since the late Sixties, Sunbelt candidates have won every presidential election, sending to the White House residents of Georgia, California, Texas, and Arkansas. In fact, since Gerald Ford's close race against Jimmy Carter in 1976, no northerner has seriously contended for the nation's highest office.

Sunbelt power has extended far beyond the White House. For most of the Clinton years, the president and vice president, House Speaker and Senate majority leader hailed from states of the Old Confederacy. The South's historic policy prescriptions—low taxes and scant public services, military preparedness and a preference for state and local government over federal supremacy—came to define the national agenda during the Seventies and have remained the motive forces in American public policy ever since. In the Seventies, the torch passed from politicians like Connecticut senator Prescott Bush in the 1950s, an avatar of New England moderate Republicanism and WASP noblesse oblige, to men like his son, the preppie reborn as a Texas oil man, an advocate of state's rights, free enterprise, and voluntarism. It has since passed on to the generation of George W. Bush, a man truly at home among the good ol' boys and the faux Bubbas, comfortable with the wide-open style and deeply religious sensibilities of the Sunbelt.

Indeed, the United States experienced more than a regional power shift in the 1970s; it witnessed a thoroughgoing southernization of American life. Religion, especially the frank expression of personal spirituality, assumed a public and powerful role in American life. Public figures—politicians, actors, and artists—openly avow their religious feelings....

Beyond religion, country music and stock car racing developed huge national followings, as popular in Boston and Denver as in Daytona and Nashville.

Garth Brooks has sold more albums than any other solo performer, and musicians from all over the world have recorded in Nashville. More important, a kind of wide-open, libertarian boosterism, once distinctively southern, has come to permeate American life.

This "southernization" complemented and reinforced a second enduring legacy of the Seventies. Over the past two decades, entrepreneurship has replaced social and political activism as the source of dynamic cultural and political change in the United States. The political realm emptied out; in the era from Nixon to Reagan, Americans relied less on the instruments of democratic governments, almost forgetting what it is that politics does, what only the public sphere can accomplish....

FURTHER READING

Paul Boyer, ed., *Reagan as President: Contemporary Views of the Man, His Politics, and His Policies* (1990).

Douglas Brinkley, *The Unfinished Presidency: Jimmy Carter's Journey Beyond the White House* (1998).

Joseph Crespino, *In Search of Another Country: Mississippi and the Conservative Counterrevolution* (2007).

Donald T. Critchlow, *Phyllis Schlafly and Grassroots Conservatism: A Woman's Crusade* (2005).

Sean Cunningham, *Cowboy Conservatism: Texas and the Rise of the Modern Right* (2010).

Darren Dochuk and Michelle Nickerson, eds., *Sunbelt Rising: The Politics of Space, Place, and Region in the American South and Southwest* (2011).

Matthew D. Lassiter, *The Silent Majority: Suburban Politics in the Sunbelt South* (2006).

Joseph E. Lowndes, *From the New Deal to the New Right: Race and the Southern Origins of Modern Conservatism* (2008).

Lisa McGirr, *Suburban Warriors: The Origins of the New American Right* (2001).

Bethany Moreton, *To Serve God and Wal-Mart: The Making of Christian Free Enterprise* (2009).

Kim Phillips-Fein, *Invisible Hands: The Making of the Conservative Movement from the New Deal to Reagan* (2009).

Gil Troy, *Morning in America: How Ronald Reagan Invented the 1980s* (2005).

Daniel Williams, *God's Own Party: The Making of the Christian Right* (2010).

CHAPTER 16

End of the Cold War,

Terrorism, and Globalization

This book is titled Major Problems in American History. *As we approach the present, however, we near the point where history meets journalism. It is not yet clear what future scholars will assess as being, in the long run, the most "major" of the issues that faced the nation at the turn of the century and in the new millennium.*

Three developments appear to be the most likely candidates: the emergence of the United States as the sole military super-power at the end of the cold war; the involvement of the United States in attempts to repress terrorism and reshape governments in the Middle East following 9/11; and, an increasing sense of economic vulnerability as the result of intensifying global production and trade.

After four decades, the cold war unexpectedly came to an end in 1989. Despite a spike in tensions when Ronald Reagan took office, the United States and the U.S.S.R. entered into a series of fruitful talks in the 1980s that gradually decreased enmity between the super-powers. Some of this was due to new, more youthful leadership in the Soviet Union itself. Most importantly, when Soviet President Mikhail Gorbachev refused to stop popular movements from overthrowing communist governments in Eastern Europe, local dictators found they could not hold back reform without Russian help. The Berlin Wall came down on November 9, 1989. President George H. W. Bush (1989–1993) proclaimed the cold war over.

Arkansas Governor Bill Clinton won the presidency (1993–2001) on a platform of fiscal prudence, economic reinvestment, welfare reduction, and post–cold war cuts in defense. The economy boomed, but the "peace dividend" was short-lived. Months after George W. Bush (the son of the first President Bush) took the oath of office (2001–2009), the lull in international tension ended with the terrorist bombings of the Pentagon and the World Trade Towers on the sunny morning of September 11, 2001. Also at an end was the relative insulation from international conflict on its own soil that had nurtured American growth and tranquility for more than 200 years. On the command of Osama bin Laden, a Saudi Arabian terrorist based in Afghanistan, 2,986 American civilians perished in the space of minutes.

The following years saw an upswing in patriotism, as well as sharp debates over the wisest methods of combating terrorism. Spending on national defense soared once again and the federal deficit grew apace. On October 7, 2001, the United States and Great Britain initiated war against the Taliban, the theocratic government of Afghanistan, for refusing to give up bin Laden or punish his organization, known as Al Qaeda. Then, on March 20, 2003, the United States began a second war against the dictatorial regime of Saddam Hussein in Iraq, supported by a coalition of forty nations, including the United Kingdom, Italy, Poland, and Spain. But war on two fronts sparked intense criticism from domestic opponents, as well as from many post–World War II allies, including France and Germany.

In these same years, Americans became ever more aware of seismic shifts in the global economy, many of which the nation had encouraged. Communist China, for example, rejoined the world trading system in the late 1970s, adopting the very open-door policy that the United States had articulated and promoted one hundred years earlier. Chinese imports flooded world markets, including the United States. The nations of Europe, after having fought two world wars against one another in the twentieth century, joined together in a peaceful, prosperous Union whose single currency, the euro, outperformed the dollar by the year 2010. Nation-states weren't the only major players on the scene. New technologies sparked a level of world integration never before possible. The "dot.com" revolution that began in the 1980s—and the proliferation of personal computers, web sites, satellite transmissions, and international cell phones—exposed Americans to an exhilarating and frightening world of global interdependence. Corporations seemed less and less identifiable as national entities, and more and more like conglomerates of multinational elites. Many worried that such companies were committed only to their own enrichment. As a consequence of globalization, Americans had trouble deciding whether they were "on top of the world" at the start of the new millennium, or slipping fast. When the so-called Great Recession hit in 2008, many feared that the latter description was the more accurate.

Complicating domestic problems was increasing partisanship in national government. Although Democrats and Republicans acted together to quell the recession that began under President Bush, cooperation faltered quickly. When Congress voted on a bill to create a national health care system to cover uninsured Americans, not a single Republican crossed the aisle to endorse the proposal by the nation's first African-American president, Barack Obama of Hawaii.

The twenty-first century began with a bang—a terrifying one. Americans showed resiliency in responding to a series of catastrophes, but they struggled to make sense of where the greatest threats to their future security and prosperity lay: in world policing, terrorism, or globalization.

QUESTIONS TO THINK ABOUT

Is globalization stoppable? What effects have terrorism and war in the Middle East had on American society? How did social values change in this era?

DOCUMENTS

The documents in this chapter look at recent decades from a variety of perspectives. In document 1, a union organizer expresses concern about the growing "export" of American jobs with the advent of new technologies. Document 2 reflects the political and economic optimism that initially accompanied the end of the cold war. In this selection, President George H. W. Bush foresees a more peaceful, prosperous world, free of the arms race with the Soviet Union. Document 3 is one of dozens of posters from a mass demonstration against globalization that occurred in Seattle, Washington, in 1999, at a meeting of the World Trade Organization (WTO). The WTO was first envisioned at the end of World War II, but its birth was delayed by the onset of the cold war and it did not officially commence until 1995. Document 4 describes the inferno inside the World Trade Towers on September 11, 2001, as well as the deep gratitude felt by all Americans toward the common heroes who came to the rescue. Document 5 shows the political opposition engendered by President Bush's decision to go to war in Iraq. Speaking on the floor of Congress, Democratic Senator Robert Byrd of West Virginia claimed that Bush had worsened terrorism and damaged the nation's foreign alliances. In document 6, the president addresses an audience in Riga, Latvia, where he defends his decision. He criticizes the United States (and Franklin Roosevelt, by implication) for excessive caution at the start of the cold war, when more might conceivably have been done to counter the Soviet Union. Bush pledges not to repeat what he calls the mistake of "sacrificing freedom in the vain pursuit of stability," and to continue intervening in the Middle East as long as necessary to bring democracy to the troubled region. In document 7, the American Civil Liberties Union warns that the price of these efforts might be the subversion of freedom in the United States. Document 8 is perhaps the most remarkable one in this collection. Almost 400 years after the first slave landed in Jamestown, the citizens of the United State elected their first African-American president. Glory, hallelujah, the abolitionists of yore might have said. In this selection, Henry Louis Gates, Jr., describes the victory on his web site. The last document of this book concerns the Great Recession. The roles of men and women had changed dramatically in the preceding century, but fathers still worried about how to keep roofs over the heads of their families. Document 9 shows that the recession that began in 2008 affected the body as well as the mind.

1. A Unionist Blasts the Export of Jobs, 1987

For the past 15 years, we have been occupied with the very real problem of jobs leaving this country. In most cases, these are jobs like the making of a wrench, or making apparel, steel, autos. We have tried to deal with this problem through

Speech in possession of Eileen Boris. This document can be found in Eileen Boris and Nelson Lichtenstein, *Major Problems in the History of American Workers* (Boston: Houghton Mifflin, 1991), pp. 646–647.

legislation as well as in collective bargaining. However, with the advent of new technology, such as satellite communications and computers, it is easier than ever for employers to move new technology and capital across borders.

One example of this is American Airlines, which historically used keypunch operators earning between $8 and $10 an hour to process the previous day's used tickets and handle the billing and record-keeping. This is now done in Barbados for $2 an hour!

Each day an American Airlines aircraft flies to Barbados and deposits the tickets which are keypunched at one-fourth or one-fifth the U.S. wage level, and then transmitted back to the United States via satellite in finished form.

2. President George H. W. Bush Declares the Cold War Over, 1990

Tonight I come not to speak about the state of the Government, not to detail every new initiative we plan for the coming year nor to describe every line in the budget. I'm here to speak to you and to the American people about the state of the Union, about our world—the changes we've seen, the challenges we face—and what that means for America.

There are singular moments in history, dates that divide all that goes before from all that comes after. And many of us in this Chamber have lived much of our lives in a world whose fundamental features were defined in 1945; and the events of that year decreed the shape of nations, the pace of progress, freedom or oppression for millions of people around the world.

Nineteen forty-five provided the common frame of reference, the compass points of the postwar era we've relied upon to understand ourselves. And that was our world, until now. The events of the year just ended, the Revolution of '89, have been a chain reaction, changes so striking that it marks the beginning of a new era in the world's affairs.

Think back—think back just 12 short months ago to the world we knew as 1989 began....

A year ago in Poland, Lech Walesa declared that he was ready to open a dialog with the Communist rulers of that country; and today, with the future of a free Poland in their own hands, members of Solidarity lead the Polish Government.

A year ago, freedom's playwright, Václav Havel, languished as a prisoner in Prague. And today it's Václav Havel, President of Czechoslovakia.

And 1 year ago, Erich Honecker of East Germany claimed history as his guide, and he predicted the Berlin Wall would last another hundred years. And today, less than 1 year later, it's the Wall that's history.

From "Address before a Joint Session of the Congress on the State of the Union," 31 January 1990, *Public Papers of the Presidents, George Bush 1990* (Washington, D.C.: Government Printing Office, 1991), Book I, pp. 129–134.

Remarkable events—events that fulfill the long-held hopes of the American people; events that validate the longstanding goals of American policy, a policy based on a single, shining principle: the cause of freedom....

At a workers' rally, in a place called Branik on the outskirts of Prague, the idea called America is alive. A worker, dressed in grimy overalls, rises to speak at the factory gates. He begins his speech to his fellow citizens with these words, words of a distant revolution: "We hold these truths to be self-evident, that all men are created equal, that they are endowed by their Creator with certain unalienable Rights, and that among these are Life, Liberty and the pursuit of Happiness."...

For more than 40 years, America and its allies held communism in check and ensured that democracy would continue to exist. And today, with communism crumbling, our aim must be to ensure democracy's advance, to take the lead in forging peace and freedom's best hope: a great and growing commonwealth of free nations. And to the Congress and to all Americans, I say it is time to acclaim a new consensus at home and abroad, a common vision of the peaceful world we want to see.

3. Poster: "No Globalization Without Representation," 1999

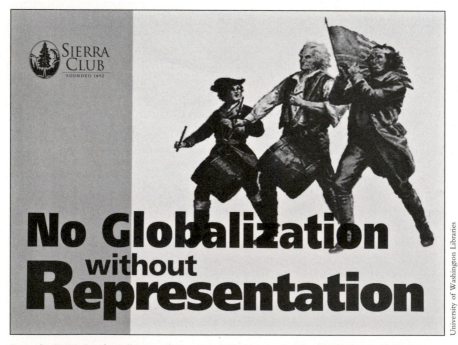

From the WTO Seattle Collection, University of Washington Archives WTO Seattle Collection, #5177-3, Box 13, Folder 4.

4. Two Workers Flee the Inferno
in the Twin Towers, 2001

[Mike]

Being blind since birth and having grown up not far from the San Andreas Fault in California, I've had my share of obstacles to deal with in life. But I've also had my triumphs. When the plane struck our tower, I knew the drill. I'd been through the emergency training sessions. We did fire drills every six months. Avoid the elevators. Use the nearest staircase. Don't panic. Follow the fire wardens' instructions. And in my case, keep Roselle at my side. She is a yellow Labrador retriever from Guide Dogs for the Blind. We have a team relationship.

When the building started to vibrate so violently, Roselle got up right away. She'd been napping under my desk. Normally, she wouldn't stir when the wind shook the tower, but this time she was looking around, knowing something needed to happen. I went and stood in a doorway, something you learn to do when you've lived in earthquake country. Roselle was eager for my commands and carefully steered me through the debris in the office and hallway. She remained focused, even with things falling on top of her. I directed her toward the stairs, and with David in front of us, we headed down.

Some people wanted to go faster, so we let them go around us. I was not going to run down the stairs. I stayed to the right and let the dog set the pace. I have had a dog from Guide Dogs for the Blind since I was fourteen. The mantra has always been the same: Follow your dog. So I did. The way down was very organized. Every so often, there were people telling us which way to go. There was an order enforced by all of us in the stairwell. That helped me remain composed and helped Roselle guide better. I never felt a sense of panic. Intellectually, I was looking for that, but it never happened.

I am a physicist by training, so I always intellectualize things. When it got slippery on the stairs, I thought to be careful. I didn't want to become a problem by falling and hurting myself. But instead of getting really worked up about the difficult footwork, I started to think of ways to improve it for next time. When this is over, I thought, I am going to suggest that they install anti-skid strips on the stairs.

[David]

Someone had a radio and turned it on. A plane had hit our building. Then it was two planes. That explained the smell of jet fuel. We certainly had inhaled a lot of it. Around the 40s, we heard voices from above, yelling, "Move right! Burn victims coming down!" I caught my first glimpse of her on the staircase above me. She was in her twenties or early thirties. She turned the corner toward us. Two

---

or three people behind her. She walked like a zombie. Eyes straight ahead, expressionless. Clothes burned off of half her body. Third-degree burns. Skin flapping and falling off her arms, neck and face. Her blond hair caked in gray slime. Fully ambulatory. Totally in shock. I had never seen anything like that. About fifteen minutes later, a second woman followed. It was bizarre. She looked almost the same age, height and weight. She had the same hair color, burns and emotionless expression. She didn't say a thing. I don't think she even touched the hand railing.

As we got into the low 40s, the jet fuel fumes got much more intense to the point where I thought I might pass out. People were clearly suffering and others were beginning to panic. Roselle was not doing well, panting heavily. We all needed water. Some people began passing small Poland Spring water bottles up to us from the floor below. This was a real relief. We gave some to the dog, and she loved it. It cut some of the fuel taste burning our throats and it eased our sense of dehydration and smoke inhalation....

It was somewhere after that, maybe in the high 30s, we ran into our first real hero. A New York City firefighter. He was coming up. Walking from the lobby on his way to the top. He was clothed in a firefighter's hat, a fire-retardant jacket, pants and heavy gloves. He had yellow glow strips around the biceps, thighs and hat. More were behind him. They were carrying an unbelievable array of equipment. Axes, picks, shovels, fire hoses and oxygen tanks. Each guy must have been saddled with 75 pounds, by the time you added in the clothing. They were perspiring profusely and looked exhausted. Some of them were leaning heavily on the railings. And they had to go all the way to the 90s, straight into hell. This was not lost on the crowd. We all broke into applause at one point. It was a wonderful moment. Mike and I patted many of them on the back with a, "God bless you." They were extremely polite and solicitous. "Are you alright?" they'd ask Mike. "I'm fine, thank you," Mike would reply. "Are you with this guy?" they'd ask me. "Yes, I'm with Mike. We are okay, thank you," I'd assure them. We had that conversation with 35 or 40 of them. In a little while, we would be out of the building and they would be inside. And then the building would be gone and they would all be lost. I can't praise their spirit enough.

When we got down to the very last landing in the stairwell, there was water everywhere. It was around 9:35 or 9:40. We proceeded carefully and exited into the lobby, it was a war zone. I know this is an overused phrase, but it really fits. There were pieces of debris—wall material, ceiling tiles, paper and garbage—all in a lake of water that was about ankle deep. Ahead of us, there was a torrential rainfall occurring over the exit turnstiles. I warned Mike that he was about to get soaked but that there was no apparent danger. As we went through the turnstiles, police and security personnel kept yelling and gesturing, "Keep moving!" We went into the underground shopping mall that connects the two towers. More water and lots of noise. We went left and headed north. "Keep moving!" The lights were on. Up some stairs. Down a dark narrow corridor with more light at the end. The sky. We were out. It was about 9:45 or 9:50....

We thought we were clear. As I looked over my shoulder, I saw what I thought was the most monstrous sight of my life. Both towers ringed by fire.

Flames sharp and lapping at steel. A huge plume from the North Tower joined up with one from the South Tower, creating a stream of gray and black smoke against a perfectly blue sky. My God, this was no accident. We had to keep moving....

Then we heard a very distinctive and unforgettable sound. The South Tower was coming down. The sound was like a freight train combined with metal poles snapping. The chorus of screams was shrill and terrifying. I was ripped from head to toe with sheer panic, too afraid to even scream. A 300-foot-tall debris cloud came at us at a high speed. We ran for our lives.

5. Senator Robert Byrd Condemns Post–9/11 Foreign Policy, 2003

To contemplate war is to think about the most horrible of human experiences. On this February day, as this nation stands at the brink of battle [against Saddam Hussein], every American on some level must be contemplating the horrors of war.

Yet, this Chamber is, for the most part, silent—ominously, dreadfully silent. There is no debate, no discussion, no attempt to lay out for the nation the pros and cons of this particular war. There is nothing.

We stand passively mute in the United States Senate, paralyzed by our own uncertainty, seemingly stunned by the sheer turmoil of events. Only on the editorial pages of our newspapers is there much substantive discussion of the prudence or imprudence of engaging in this particular war.

And this is no small conflagration we contemplate. This is no simple attempt to defang a villain. No. This coming battle, if it materializes, represents a turning point in U.S. foreign policy and possibly a turning point in the recent history of the world.

This nation is about to embark upon the first test of a revolutionary doctrine applied in an extraordinary way at an unfortunate time. The doctrine of preemption— the idea that the United States or any other nation can legitimately attack a nation that is not imminently threatening but may be threatening in the future—is a radical new twist on the traditional idea of self defense. It appears to be in contravention of international law and the UN Charter....

This Administration, now in power for a little over two years, must be judged on its record. I believe that that record is dismal....

In foreign policy, this Administration has failed to find Osama bin Laden. In fact, just yesterday we heard from him again marshaling his forces and urging them to kill. This Administration has split traditional alliances, possibly crippling, for all time, international order-keeping entities like the United Nations and NATO. This Administration has called into question the traditional world-wide perception of the United States as well-intentioned peacekeeper. This

Senator Robert Byrd, "Reckless Administration May Reap Disastrous Consequences," a speech on the Senate floor, Feb. 12, 2003. Obtained at: http://www.commondreams.org/views03/0212-07.htm

Administration has turned the patient art of diplomacy into threats, labeling, and name calling of the sort that reflects quite poorly on the intelligence and sensitivity of our leaders, and which will have consequences for years to come.

Calling heads of state pygmies, labeling whole countries as evil, denigrating powerful European allies as irrelevant—these types of crude insensitivities can do our great nation no good. We may have massive military might, but we cannot fight a global war on terrorism alone. We need the cooperation and friendship of our time-honored allies as well as the newer found friends whom we can attract with our wealth....

The war in Afghanistan has cost us $37 billion so far, yet there is evidence that terrorism may already be starting to regain its hold in that region. We have not found bin Laden, and unless we secure the peace in Afghanistan, the dark dens of terrorism may yet again flourish in that remote and devastated land....

One can understand the anger and shock of any President after the savage attacks of September 11. One can appreciate the frustration of having only a shadow to chase and an amorphous, fleeting enemy on which it is nearly impossible to exact retribution.

But to turn one's frustration and anger into the kind of extremely destabilizing and dangerous foreign policy debacle that the world is currently witnessing is inexcusable from any Administration charged with the awesome power and responsibility of guiding the destiny of the greatest superpower on the planet. Frankly many of the pronouncements made by this Administration are outrageous. There is no other word.

6. President George W. Bush Ranks Freedom Above Stability, 2005

This week, nations on both sides of the Atlantic observe the 60th anniversary of Hitler's defeat. The evil that seized power in Germany brought war to all of Europe, and waged war against morality, itself. What began as a movement of thugs became a government without conscience, and then an empire of bottomless cruelty. The Third Reich exalted the strong over the weak, overran and humiliated peaceful countries, undertook a mad quest for racial purity, coldly planned and carried out the murder of millions, and defined evil for the ages. Brave men and women of many countries faced that evil, and fought through dark and desperate years for their families and their homelands. In the end, a dictator who worshiped power was confined to four walls of a bunker, and the fall of his squalid tyranny is a day to remember and to celebrate....

...For much of Germany, defeat led to freedom. For much of Eastern and Central Europe, victory brought the iron rule of another empire. V-E Day marked the end of fascism, but it did not end oppression. The agreement at Yalta followed in the unjust tradition of Munich and the Molotov-Ribbentrop Pact.

"President Discusses Freedom and Democracy in Latvia," Speech at Riga, Latvia, May 2005. Accessed at: http://presidentialrhetoric.com/speeches/05.07.05.html

Once again, when powerful governments negotiated, the freedom of small nations was somehow expendable. Yet this attempt to sacrifice freedom for the sake of stability left a continent divided and unstable. The captivity of millions in Central and Eastern Europe will be remembered as one of the greatest wrongs of history.

The end of World War II raised unavoidable questions for my country: Had we fought and sacrificed only to achieve the permanent division of Europe into armed camps? Or did the cause of freedom and the rights of nations require more of us? Eventually, America and our strong allies made a decision: We would not be content with the liberation of half of Europe—and we would not forget our friends behind an Iron Curtain. We defended the freedom of Greece and Turkey, and airlifted supplies to Berlin, and broadcast the message of liberty by radio. We spoke up for dissenters, and challenged an empire to tear down a hated wall. Eventually, communism began to collapse under external pressure, and under the weight of its own contradictions. And we set the vision of a Europe whole, free, and at peace—so dictators could no longer rise up and feed ancient grievances, and conflict would not be repeated again and again....

For all the problems that remain, it is a miracle of history that this young century finds us speaking about the consolidation of freedom throughout Europe. And the stunning democratic gains of the last several decades are only the beginning. Freedom is not tired. The ideal of human dignity is not weary. And the next stage of the world democratic movement is already unfolding in the broader Middle East.

We seek democracy in that region for the same reasons we spent decades working for democracy in Europe—because freedom is the only reliable path to peace. If the Middle East continues to simmer in anger and resentment and hopelessness, caught in a cycle of repression and radicalism, it will produce terrorism of even greater audacity and destructive power. But if the peoples of that region gain the right of self-government, and find hopes to replace their hatreds, then the security of all free nations will be strengthened. We will not repeat the mistakes of other generations, appeasing or excusing tyranny, and sacrificing freedom in the vain pursuit of stability. We have learned our lesson; no one's liberty is expendable. In the long run, our security and true stability depend on the freedom of others. And so, with confidence and resolve, we will stand for freedom across the broader Middle East.

7. ACLU Warns against the "Patriot Act," 2002

If one can talk of good news amidst such tragedy, these actions would be the topic. And there is more good news in the form of statements by President Bush and many public officials, who urge Americans to respect the rights of others and warn that attacks on Arabs and Muslims "will not stand." Although that is exactly what a US President should be saying, the fact is that has not

---

Anthony D. Romero, "In Defense of Liberty," *Vital Speeches of the day* 68 (1 January 2002): 169–172.

always been the case. We know from our history that in times of national emergencies government officials have targeted particular groups for harassment or outright discrimination....

The terrorists apparently took insidious advantage of this tolerance, living in our communities and enjoying our freedoms. Does that mean that those freedoms are somehow at fault? Or that respecting the rights of others is wrong? The answer is an emphatic "No." These fundamental values, established in our Constitution, are the bedrock of our country. They are what truly distinguish us; they are the source of our unique strength; they are our legacy to the world.

I also think there is another reason for the greater measure of tolerance and respect we have witnessed so far. That is, that our message—and by "our," I refer to the ACLU and other civil liberties groups—has actually gotten through. We may be the favorite whipping post of conservative editors and the best laugh-line for the late-night talk show hosts, but our efforts have not been in vain....

I would list the following five proposals of the patriot Act as among the most offensive:

1. The overly broad definition of "terrorism"—A definition that could easily be used against many forms of civil disobedience, including legitimate and peaceful protest. The language is so ambiguous that it is possible that if an organized group of peace demonstrators spray painted a peace sign outside of the State Department, they could be charged as terrorists for their actions.

2. Indefinite detention of immigrants based on the Attorney General's certification of a danger to national security—A harmful provision with language so vague that even the existence of judicial review would provide no meaningful safeguard against abuse.

3. Expanded wiretap authority—The new legislation minimized judicial supervision of law enforcement wiretap authority by permitting law enforcement to obtain the equivalent of blank warrants in the physical world; authorizing intelligence wiretaps that need not specify the phone to be tapped or require that only the target's conversations be eavesdropped on. And the new law extends lower surveillance standards to the Internet....

4. The use of "sneak and peek" searches to circumvent the Fourth Amendment—Under this segment of the legislation, law enforcement officials could enter your home, office or other private place and conduct a search, take photographs and download your computer files without notifying you until after the fact. This delayed notice provision undercuts the spirit of the Fourth Amendment and the need to provide information to citizens when their privacy is invaded by law enforcement authorities.

5. Eviscerating the wall between foreign surveillance and domestic criminal investigation—The new legislation gives the Director of the Central Intelligence the power to manage the gathering of intelligence in America and mandate the disclosure of information obtained by the FBI about terrorism in general—even if it is about law abiding American citizens—to the CIA....

Terror, by its very nature, is intended not only to destroy, but also to intimidate a people; forcing them to take actions that are not in their best interest.

That's why defending liberty during a time of national crisis is the ultimate act of defiance. It is the ultimate act of patriotism. For, if we are intimidated to the point of restricting our freedoms, the terrorists have won....

8. Harvard Professor, Henry Louis Gates, Jr., Marvels at Obama, 2008

We have all heard stories about those few magical transformative moments in African-American history, extraordinary ritual occasions through which the geographically and socially diverse black community—a nation within a nation, really—molds itself into one united body, determined to achieve one great social purpose and to bear witness to the process by which this grand achievement occurs....

But we have never seen anything like this. Nothing could have prepared any of us for the eruption (and, yes, that is the word) of spontaneous celebration that manifested itself in black homes, gathering places and the streets of our communities when Sen. Barack Obama was declared President-elect Obama. From Harlem to Harvard, from Maine to Hawaii—and even Alaska—from "the prodigious hilltops of New Hampshire...[to] Stone Mountain of Georgia," as Dr. King put it, each of us will always remember this moment, as will our children, whom we woke up to watch history being made.

My colleagues and I laughed and shouted, whooped and hollered, hugged each other and cried. My father waited 95 years to see this day happen, and when he called as results came in, I silently thanked God for allowing him to live long enough to cast his vote for the first black man to become president. And even he still can't quite believe it!

How many of our ancestors have given their lives—how many millions of slaves toiled in the fields in endlessly thankless and mindless labor—before this generation could live to see a black person become president? "How long, Lord?" the spiritual goes; "not long!" is the resounding response. What would Frederick Douglass and W.E.B. Du Bois say if they could know what our people had at long last achieved? What would Sojourner Truth and Harriet Tubman say? What would Dr. King himself say? Would they say that all those lost hours of brutalizing toil and labor leading to spent, half-fulfilled lives, all those humiliations that our ancestors had to suffer through each and every day, all those slights and rebuffs and recriminations, all those rapes and murders, lynchings and assassinations, all those Jim Crow laws and protest marches, those snarling dogs and bone-breaking water hoses, all of those beatings and all of those killings, all of those black collective dreams deferred—that the unbearable pain of all of those tragedies had, in the end, been assuaged at least somewhat through Barack Obama's election?...

I think they would, resoundingly and with one voice proclaim, "Yes! Yes! And yes, again!" I believe they would tell us that it had been worth the price that we, collectively, have had to pay—the price of President-elect Obama's ticket....

The award for prescience, however, goes to Jacob K. Javits, the liberal Republican senator from New York who, incredibly, just a year after the integration of Central High School in Little Rock, predicted that the first black president would be elected in the year 2000. In an essay titled "Integration from the Top Down" printed in *Esquire* magazine in 1958, he wrote:

> *What manner of man will this be, this possible Negro Presidential candidate of 2000? Undoubtedly, he will be well-educated. He will be well-traveled and have a keen grasp of his country's role in the world and its relationships. He will be a dedicated internationalist with working comprehension of the intricacies of foreign aid, technical assistance and reciprocal trade.... Assuredly, though, despite his other characteristics, he will have developed the fortitude to withstand the vicious smear attacks that came his way as he fought to the top in government and politics those in the vanguard may expect to be the targets for scurrilous attacks, as the hate mongers, in the last ditch efforts, spew their verbal and written poison....*

I wish we could say that Barack Obama's election will magically reduce the numbers of teenage pregnancies or the level of drug addiction in the black community. I wish we could say that what happened last night will suddenly make black children learn to read and write as if their lives depended on it, and that their high school completion rates will become the best in the country. I wish we could say that these things are about to happen, but I doubt that they will.

But there is one thing we can proclaim today, without question: that the election of Barack Obama as president of the United States of America means that "The Ultimate Color Line," as the subtitle of Javits' *Esquire* essay put it, has, at long last, been crossed. It has been crossed by our very first postmodern Race Man, a man who embraces his African cultural and genetic heritage so securely that he can transcend it, becoming the candidate of choice to tens of millions of Americans who do not look like him.

How does that make me feel? Like I've always imagined my father and his friends felt back in 1938, on the day that black heavyweight boxer Joe Louis knocked out Max Schmeling. But ten thousand times better than that. All I can say is "Amazing Grace! How sweet the sound."

9. The Great Recession Has Men Grinding Their Teeth, 2010

A few weeks ago, Tom Lelievre, 46, who owns a home renovation business in Westford, Mass., noticed that he'd "chipped" a back tooth and so he visited his dentist, Dr. Thomas Connelly.

Michael Winerip, "Dealing with the Nightly Grind," *New York Times*, Feb. 12, 2010. Copyright © 2010 by the New York Times Co. All rights reserved. Reprinted by permission.

Dr. Connelly examined him and saw a sight all too common in the mouths of his middle-aged male patients during this Great Recession. "His molar was smashed, and his front teeth flattened," Dr. Connelly recalled.

"Tom, you under a lot of stress?" he asked.

A lot of stress? Mr. Lelievre used to do the finish work on a dozen homes a year; in the last year he's done two. He used to employ three men; now he hires subs as needed. He used to have a waiting list of eight months of work. "Now they call me a week before I'm scheduled to start, 'Sorry, I lost my job, I can't go forward.' And I'm thinking, What do I do for the next month?"

"I'm not sleeping well," Mr. Lelievre continued. "I wake at 1:30 and think, How will we pay the bills and keep the kids warm?"

In the market downturn, he and his wife lost much of the money that they'd saved for their three children's college educations. "That thought keeps coming up," he said.

And now his dentist was explaining that the stress was leading him to grind his teeth—and that was just half of it. "I'm grinding at night," Mr. Lelievre said, "and clenching during the day."

Stress?

Alan Beck, 63, who owns a New Jersey-based cosmetics company named Beauty Bridge, knows it well. "Yes, lots of stress," he told Dr. Irwin Smigel of Manhattan.

Until the recession, Mr. Beck's company had a staff of 33 and 100 independent contractors nationwide. Before that, he was the president of the United States subsidiary of Jean Patou, the perfume company. Now he works as a solo consultant.

"Last year was a disaster, just a disaster," he said. "People wouldn't commit. Lots of talk, lots of proposals, and no one wants to sign on the dotted line."

Nine months ago, he started having toothaches but did not go to the dentist. "I used to provide dental insurance for 33 people—now I don't have it myself," he said....

This is the longest recession in modern history, and when people say that they're worn down, their dentists say it's literally true....

Traditionally, grinding damage manifests in middle age, as teeth weaken over time, and those who seek treatment are predominantly women. Researchers don't know if this is due to differences in estrogen levels (studies are inconclusive) or if, as Dr. Smigel believes, women are simply more concerned about the appearance of their teeth.

But most striking has been the recent increase of grinding among men. Dr. Messina, the dental association representative, has seen a 25 percent jump in the number of male patients he's treated for grinding in the last year. Dr. Smigel said that, while female grinders still predominate in his practice, their male counterparts have doubled to 40 percent of his caseload....

Remediation costs vary widely. Mr. Beck, the New Jersey cosmetics consultant, spent $1,200 for a night guard and minor work on his teeth. A patient who needs a rebuilt mouth of 28 crowns could face a $100,000 bill, Dr. Connelly said. Little of that, if any, would be covered by insurance....

Mr. Lelievre, the Massachusetts home renovator, asked his wife if she'd noticed the grinding at night. "She said: 'Yeah, pretty bad. And clenching.'" Dr. Connelly fitted him with a night guard, but Mr. Lelievre has put off more corrective work until the economy improves. "My wife bought me gum—so I don't clench, I chew all day," he said. "I can't afford to clench my teeth."

ESSAYS

The following essays show where the meeting of history and journalism can provide insight (and may be unavoidable) when considering contemporary times. Both essays examine globalization and its implications for national security and America's economic well-being. In the first essay, Walter LaFeber, professor emeritus at Cornell University, examines the spectacular career of Michael Jordan, a basketball star who parleyed his athletic fame into a global athletic-shoe empire. LaFeber argues that enterprises of this type allowed American companies—and even some African Americans—to dominate the world economy by the start of the new millennium. LaFeber points out that their success sometimes provoked hostility, and asserts that terrorism is one consequence of economic globalization benefiting Americans disproportionately. In the second essay, Thomas L. Friedman, a *New York Times* columnist who has written extensively about the Middle East, argues almost the opposite: that Americans may be falling behind rather than sprinting ahead of the competition. The world became "flat" when new technologies and the end of the Cold War democratized the "global competitive playing field." Economic events might produce far more change in the Middle East than governmental attempts to promote democracy, Friedman contends. And meanwhile, the United States itself is going to have to struggle to keep pace with its rivals in a world economy that is changing as rapidly as a computer screen linked to high-speed Internet.

Michael Jordan and the New Capitalism: America on Top of Its Game

WALTER LAFEBER

At the end of the twentieth century, Americans, their economy, and their culture seemed to dominate many parts of the globe. A basketball player who lived in Chicago, Michael Jordan, was arguably the most recognized and revered of those Americans to billions of people worldwide. In China, schoolchildren ranked him with Zhou Enlai as the two greatest figures in twentieth-century history. The children knew Zhou because he helped create their Communist Revolution. They knew Jordan because he miraculously floated through the air as both an athlete and as a pitchman for American-produced advertisements for

Walter LaFeber, *Michael Jordan and the New Global Capitalism* (Norton, 2002), p. 27–28, 54–58, 71, 155–156, 159–162, 163–164. Copyright © 1999 by Walter LeFeber. Reprinted by permission of W.W. Norton & Company, Inc.

Nike shoes, which the children avidly followed on television. His coach in Chicago, Phil Jackson, believed that Jordan "had somehow been transformed in the public mind from a great athlete to a sports deity"—especially when an amazed Jackson saw people kneeling before the statue of Jordan that stands in front of the United Center, home of the Chicago Bulls....

To...many others, Jordan personified not only the imaginative, individual skills that Americans dream of displaying in a society that adores graceful and successful individualism, but the all-out competitive spirit and discipline that Americans like to think drove their nation to the peak of world power. Coach Jackson phrased it directly: "Michael is a little bit of a shark. He's competitive to the extent that he'd like to beat you for your last cent and send you home without your clothes."

Such skills quickly translated into money and power in the world of the late twentieth century. But Jordan was not just an athlete, he was an African-American athlete who earned $30 million a year for playing with the Bulls and twice that amount from his endorsements and personal businesses. Within his own lifetime, African-American athletes had been victimized and exploited—not made multimillionaires. They were also often condemned for choosing merely to dunk basketballs or catch footballs, rather than acting as role models for future doctors, lawyers, or business leaders. That Jordan became a hero for the many races in American society was thus somewhat surprising. That he could transform this role into becoming the most successful advertising figure in the world was historic....

By the 1990s, teenagers shot and sometimes murdered each other to steal Nike's Air Jordan sneakers and other athletic clothing. The shoes, which cost well under fifty dollars to make in Southeast Asian factories paying some of the lowest manufacturing wages in the world, cost up to three times that in stores. Customers of all ages willingly paid the huge profit to Nike because of Jordan's name, the highly advertised technology that went into the shoe, and the almost supernatural aura that seemed to surround Nike's world-famous Swoosh symbol and motto, "Just Do It"—which, critics claimed, was exactly the advice gun-toting teenagers followed to obtain their Nikes.

After Jordan had become the world's most glamorous athlete in the mid-1990s, Nike was a $9 billion company with about half its sales overseas. It spent nearly $50 million in research and development and more than a half-billion dollars on advertising and marketing worldwide, a figure that dwarfed the spending of such competitors as Reebok, Fila, and Adidas. Nike churned out profits not only by dominating its markets. The Beaverton, Oregon, company exemplified something new and most significant in American history: a corporation that made nearly all its products abroad and sold half or more of those goods in foreign markets. In other words, although known as an American corporation, most of its laborers and its sales were abroad.

Multinational corporations are not new. In the late nineteenth century, such U.S. firms were rising from the ashes of the Civil War to dominate markets. These included Standard Oil in petroleum products, Eastman Kodak in film, Singer in sewing machines, and McCormick in farm harvesters. But these companies differed from their late-twentieth-century descendants in at least five respects.

First, the 1890s firms largely employed Americans to produce their product; in the 1990s, the firms extensively employed foreign labor and made the overwhelming bulk of their goods abroad. By 1980, a stunning 80 percent of these U.S. corporations' revenues came from overseas production, and less than 20 percent arose from exporting American-made goods to foreign markets.

Second, while the late-nineteenth-century firms largely traded in natural resources (oil, iron) or industrial goods (steel, paint), the late-twentieth-century firms traded in designs, technical knowledge, management techniques, and organizational innovations. The key to success was not so much the goods, as it was knowledge: the quickly formulated and transferred engineering and marketing information, the control of advanced rapidly changing technology (such as how to make computer software—or Air Jordans).

A third revolutionary characteristic of transnationals, such as Nike or Coca-Cola, was their increasing dependence on world markets—not solely U.S.—for profits. For the corporations that drove the U.S. economy, and on which nearly all Americans depended directly or indirectly for their economic survival, relied in turn on global markets. In 1996 for example, the Atlanta, Georgia-based Coca-Cola Company, that most American of all firms, stopped dividing its markets between "domestic" and "international." Instead, it organized sales along the lines of specific regions and, in this regard, "North America" was not substantially different from, say, "Southeast Asia." This new policy was logical: in 1996 four of every five bottles of Coke were sold outside the United States.

A fourth difference followed: as the Nike budget demonstrated, transnationals of the late twentieth century depended on massive advertising campaigns to make people want their products. The advertising too was revolutionary in that by the late 1980s it could be instantaneously seen on as many as thirty to five hundred television channels in many countries through the new technology of communication satellites and fiber-optic cable. Such advertising often sold not merely a product (as sneakers), but a lifestyle ("Just Do It") that in most instances was based on American culture....

Finally, because the old multinationals were not only headquartered, but produced and/or sold much of their product, in the United States, they could usually be made accountable to the government in Washington. Even the richest of all Americans, John D. Rockefeller, learned this hard lesson when the government broke up his Standard Oil monopoly into a number of smaller companies in 1911. The new transnational, however, became so global by the 1980s that a single government had power over only a part of the firm's total operation. The size of many transnationals, moreover, dwarfed the size of many governments. Of the hundred largest economic units in the world of the 1980s, only half were nations. The other half were individual corporations....

Nike exhibited all five of the new corporate characteristics in varying degrees. It also shared another trait with this new breed of company, for it, like many other modern transnationals, enjoyed its greatest growth—its take off into immense profitability—in the 1970s to 1990s. These are the years that, in reality, began the twenty-first century, for they produced the forces that will shape at least the early part of that century. During these decades, such new global technologies as computers, communication satellites, and fiber optics transformed the globe's economy. It should be pointed out that this new era in world history began not with the collapse of the Soviet Union and the end of the Cold War in 1989–1991, but with the appearance of the post-industrial technology nearly a generation earlier. For this technology changed the lives of peoples around the world and, in so doing, brought down the Communist system, which could not adjust to this revolution....

Whenever innovative technology appears, swashbuckling entrepreneurs quickly materialize to exploit it. In the 1880s and 1890s, it had been the robber barons (Rockefeller, steelmaker Andrew Carnegie, banker J. P. Morgan), whose understanding of industrial technology's potential made them very rich. In the 1980s and 1990s, those made very rich by satellite and cable included Michael Jordan and Phil Knight, but also such media barons as American Ted Turner and Australian Rupert Murdoch. For it was the few, led by Turner and Murdoch, who created the satellite-cable networks on which Jordan and Knight sold the NBA and Nike shoes to the many around the world....

The post-1970s commercial success of Jordan, Nike, the NBA, and Turner-Murdoch media raised other fundamental questions. Observers debated, for example, whether U.S.-based sports, media, and transnational corporations were parts of a new post-1960s imperialism that threatened to change (some would say corrupt) other cultures. After all, in 1998 all of Spain's ten most popular movies were American; in Great Britain, Germany, and Italy nine came from Hollywood; and even in France seven were U.S.-made. The U.S. dominance in film and television meant huge profits: in 1993, Americans made $4 billion more from Europeans than European film television, and video sales earned from the Americans....

Some analysts, such as former State Department official Joseph Nye, thought the United States would indeed wield its cultural power, and that everyone would benefit.

The soft power of the American media and popular culture would bestow on the world's peoples "its liberalism and egalitarian currents" by dominating "film, television and electronic communications." Soft power would make the twenty-first century "the period of America's greatest preeminence." Some examples of this "preeminence" were stunning. McDonald's, blaring Michael Jordan's endorsement, operated in 103 nations and fed one percent of the world's population each day. "Within the East Asian urban environment," one historian of the firm notes, "McDonald's fills a niche once occupied by the teahouse, the neighborhood shop, the street-side stall, and the park bench."

Is such soft power a new information-age disguise for age-old imperialism? The reality is more complex, and interesting. *Webster's* defines imperialism as "the policy of extending the rule or authority of an empire or nation over foreign countries, or of acquiring and holding colonies and dependencies." Such a definition bears little relationship to the extension of transnational power since the 1970s. Certainly there was no interest in holding "colonies and dependencies" in the traditional political sense. And Europeans and Asians and Latin Americans did not have Nikes and Big Macs imposed on them against their will. Of special importance, the extension of that new power was not in the hands of states, but of corporations and individual capitalists such as Knight and Murdoch....

"Soft power," it seems, can become a mere cover for "tough power"—that is, the tough creation of important new classes, and the tough politics of transnational-government relations. The larger question is whether this combination of soft and tough power will, in Nye's words, make the twenty-first century "the period of America's greatest preeminence."

One important dissent from Nye's thesis came from Samuel Huntington, whose *Clash of Civilizations and the Remaking of World Order* (1996) was widely debated. Huntington suggested that cultures, especially religious based cultures, such as Islam, Hinduism, and Confucianism as well as Christianity, would conflict, and that this conflict would to a great degree shape twenty-first century global affairs. Huntington argued that some of these cultures already viewed U.S. culture as a dangerous, corrupting influence that had to be stopped, if necessary, by force.

Huntington's thesis seemed to turn into reality in mid-1998 when bombs blew up U.S. diplomatic embassies in Kenya and Tanzania and later the World Trade Towers in New York. Twelve Americans and more than 250 Africans died. The U.S. government blamed the blasts on Osama Bin Laden, an Islamic fundamentalist. Bin Laden hated the United States for, in his view, corrupting his native Saudi Arabia through the stationing of U.S. troops and the growing influence of American culture in that country. The United States struck back with missile attacks on bin Laden's supposed supply bases in Afghanistan and Sudan. U.S. officials declared what they termed a "new war" —the "war of the future" — against terrorists such as bin Laden.

Clearly, the expansion of transnationals and American culture was not universally hailed. But equally clearly, the opposition—contrary to Huntington— did not run only along the lines of different "civilizations," as he termed them. When French leaders, German newspapers, and Canadian observers condemned the inroads of American influence, the condemnation came from within the "civilization" that included the United States. Indeed, some analysts suggested that most critical splits in our new information age would occur between moderates and political radicals (or religious fundamentalists) *within* each "civilization." In the United States, the worst terrorist attacks of the 1990s (such as the bombing of the Oklahoma City Federal Building that killed 168 people), were the work of few U.S. citizens who saw the U.S. government as engaged in a vast conspiracy against individuals' freedom. Bin Laden himself had been thrown out of Saudi Arabia by Saudi conservatives.

In the post–1970s information age, neither the "clash of civilizations" nor the clash of capital with a culture could be easily and simply described. But some tried. Two authors who celebrated American triumphialism in the aftermath of the Cold War wrote in 1997 that "the end of the Cold War also saw the triumph of a set of ideas long championed by the United States: those of the free market economy and to some extent [sic] liberal democracy.... This cleared the way," they believed, "for the creation of a truly global economy.... Everybody on the planet [is] in the same economy." But as people as different as the French Cultural Minister and Osama bin Laden illustrated, not "everybody" wanted to be in that "same economy" if American principles and images were to dominate it. By late 1998, moreover, that "truly global economy" was in deep trouble. Many nations, led by Malaysia, Russia, and the new Chinese territory of Hong Kong (once a rabid free-market bastion), began to rebel against the U.S. "free-market economy and...liberal democracy." They did so for two reasons: First, they had developed doubts about that economy and democracy. And second, they turned against U.S. leadership after concluding that the power of transnationals, especially banks, had become dangerous to their economic survival, and even corrupt.

These recent crises highlighted an interesting and explosive paradox noted by Huntington. Millions of Americans now make their living in the world economy, either at home or abroad. These Americans, however, remain alien to—even quite ignorant of—the cultures that pay their bills. Consequently when other peoples react, sometimes with violence, against U.S. influence, Americans tend to turn inward, or respond unilaterally and angrily. Both of those responses—turning inward or responding unilaterally (and sometimes with force)—are deeply rooted in the American character. The roots go back, indeed, several centuries and are accurately called "isolationism." These two responses in our time are deeply problematic, for in the integrated electronic global village, turning inward is impossible and unilaterally using force in such a village can be suicidal....

In the late 1990s, some nations began to discuss how to control that struggle to prevent U.S. influences and the disruption those influences have generated. As noted above, a few nations, led by Malaysia and Hong Kong, placed some controls on foreign capital. A mid-1998 conference called by the Canadian government convened nineteen nations, but did not include the United States. The conference discussed how to keep U.S. cultural influences out while nurturing ordinary commerce. The United Nations sponsored a similar meeting in Sweden. European officials met in England to discuss "the Digital Age," but as the *Economist* noted, the real subject was "How Can We Keep the Americans, Especially Rupert Murdoch, Out?" Murdoch actually appeared at the conference. His message was direct: "eliminate barriers to the free flow of capital, labor, and talent." The other conference delegates held a different view. To them, since labor did not move easily, and since capital could control talent, the real problem was capital—such as Murdoch's....

In the new tightly wired world, Americans cannot escape these questions. They can only begin to deal with them by understanding the history of how we all became part of a global market economy and market society.

Running to Keep Up: The Perils of Globalization

THOMAS L. FRIEDMAN

As an American who has always believed in the merits of free trade, I had an important question to answer after my India trip: Should I still believe in free trade in a flat world? Here was an issue that needed sorting out immediately—not only because it was becoming a hot issue in the presidential campaign of 2004 but also because my whole view of the flat world would depend on my view of free trade. I know that free trade won't necessarily benefit every American, and that our society will have to help those who are harmed by it. But for me the key question was: Will free trade benefit America *as a whole* when the world becomes so flat and so many more people can collaborate, and compete, with my kids? It seems that so many jobs are going to be up for grabs. Wouldn't individual Americans be better off if our government erected some walls and banned some outsourcing and offshoring?

I first wrestled with this issue while filming the Discovery Times documentary in Bangalore. One day we went to the Infosys campus around five p.m.—just when the Infosys call-center workers were flooding into the grounds for the overnight shift on foot, minibus, and motor scooter, while many of the more advanced engineers were leaving at the end of the day shift. The crew and I were standing at the gate observing this river of educated young people flowing in and out, many in animated conversation. They all looked as if they had scored 1,600 on their SATs, and I felt a real mind-eye split overtaking me.

My mind just kept telling me, "Ricardo is right, Ricardo is right, Ricardo is right." David Ricardo (1772–1823) was the English economist who developed the free-trade theory of comparative advantage, which stipulates that if each nation specializes in the production of goods in which it has a comparative cost advantage and then trades with other nations for the goods in which they specialize, there will be an overall gain in trade, and overall income levels should rise in each trading country.

So if all these Indian techies were doing what was their comparative advantage and then turning around and using their income to buy all the products from America that are our comparative advantage—from Corning Glass to Microsoft Windows—both our countries would benefit, even if some individual Indians or Americans might have to shift jobs in the transition, And one can see evidence of this mutual benefit in the sharp increase in exports and imports between the United States and India in recent years.

But my eye kept looking at all these Indian zippies and telling me something else: "Oh, my God, there are so many of them, and they all look so serious, so eager for work. And they just keep coming, wave after wave. How in the world can it possibly be good for my daughters and millions of other young Americans that these Indians can do the same jobs as they can for a fraction of the wages?"

When Ricardo was writing, goods were tradable, but for the most part knowledge work and services were not. There was no undersea fiberoptic cable to make knowledge jobs tradable between America and India back then. Just as I was getting worked up with worry, the Infosys spokeswoman accompanying me casually mentioned that last year Infosys India received "one million applications" from young Indians for nine thousand tech jobs.

Have a nice day.

I struggled over what to make of this scene. I don't want to see any American lose his or her job to foreign competition or to technological innovation. I sure wouldn't want to lose mine. When you lose your job, the unemployment rate is not 5.2 percent; it's 100 percent. No book about the flat world would be honest if it did not acknowledge such concerns, or acknowledge that there is some debate among economists about whether Ricardo is still right.

Having listened to the arguments on both sides, though, I come down where the great majority of economists come down—that Ricardo is still right and that more American individuals will be better off if we don't erect barriers to outsourcing, supply-chaining, and offshoring than if we do. The simple message of this chapter is that even as the world gets flat, America as a whole will benefit more by sticking to the basic principles of free trade, as it always has, than by trying to erect walls.

The main argument of the anti-outsourcing school is that in a flat world, not only are goods tradable, but many services have become tradable as well. Because of this change, America and other developed countries could be headed for an absolute decline, not just a relative one, in their economic power and living standards unless they move to formally protect certain jobs from foreign competition. So many new players cannot enter the global economy—in service and knowledge fields now dominated by Americans, Europeans, and Japanese—without wages settling at a newer, lower equilibrium, this school argues.

The main counterargument from free-trade/outsourcing advocates is that while there may be a transition phase in certain fields, during which wages are dampened, there is no reason to believe that this dip will be permanent or across the board, as long as the global pie keeps growing. To suggest that it will be is to invoke the so-called lump of labor theory—the notion that there is a fixed lump of labor in the world and that once that lump is gobbled up, by either Americans or Indians or Japanese, there won't be any more jobs to go around. If we have the biggest lump of labor now, and then Indians offer to do this same work for less, they will get a bigger piece of the lump, and we will have less, or so this argument goes.

The main reason the lump of labor theory is wrong is that it is based on the assumption that everything that is going to be invented has been invented, and that therefore economic competition is a zero-sum game, a fight over a fixed lump. This assumption misses the fact that although jobs are often lost in bulk—to outsourcing or offshoring—by big individual companies, and this loss tends to make headlines, new jobs are also being created in fives, tens, and twenties by small companies that you can't see. It often takes a leap of faith to believe that it is happening. *But it is happening.* If it were not, America's unemployment rate would be much higher today than 5 percent. The reason it is happening is that as lower-end service and manufacturing jobs move out of Europe, America, and Japan to India, China, and the former Soviet Empire, the global pie not only grows larger—because more people have more income to spend—it also grows more complex, as more new jobs, and new specialties, are created.

Let me illustrate this with a simple example. Imagine that there are only two countries in the world—America and China. And imagine that the American economy has only 100 people. Of those 100 people, 80 are well-educated knowledge workers and 20 are less-educated low-skilled workers. Now imagine that the world goes flat and America enters into a free-trade agreement with China, which has 1,000 people but is a less developed country. So today China too has only 80 well-educated knowledge workers out of that 1,000, and it has 920 low-skilled workers. Before America entered into its free-trade agreement with China, there were only 80 knowledge workers in its world. Now there are 160 in our two-country world. The American knowledge workers feel like they have more competition, and they do. But if you look at the prize they are going after, it is now a much expanded and more complex market. It went from a market of 100 people to a market of 1,100 people, with many more needs and wants. So it should be win–win for both the American and Chinese knowledge workers.

Sure, some of the knowledge workers in America may have to move *horizontally* into new knowledge jobs, because of the competition from China. But with a market that big and complex, you can be sure that new knowledge jobs will open up at decent wages for anyone who keeps up his or her skills. So do not worry about our knowledge workers or the Chinese knowledge workers. They will both do fine with this bigger market.

"What do you mean, don't worry?" you ask. "How do we deal with the fact that those eighty knowledge workers from China will be willing to work for so much less than the eighty knowledge workers from America? How will this difference get resolved?"

It won't happen overnight, so some American knowledge workers may be affected in the transition, but the effects will not be permanent. Here, argues Stanford new economy specialist Paul Romer, is what you need to understand: The wages for the Chinese knowledge workers were so low because, although their skills were marketable globally like those of their American counterparts, they were trapped inside a stifled economy. Imagine how little a North Korean computer expert or brain surgeon is paid inside that huge prison of a nation! But as the Chinese economy opens up to the world and reforms, the wages of Chinese knowledge workers will rise up to American/world levels. Ours will not go down to the level of a stifled, walled-in economy. You can already see this happening in Bangalore, where competition for Indian software writers is rapidly pushing up their wages toward American/European levels—after decades of languishing while the Indian economy was closed. It is why Americans should be doing all they can to promote more and faster economic reform in India and China.

Do worry, though, about the 20 low-skilled Americans, who now have to complete more directly with the 920 low-skilled Chinese. One reason the 20 low-skilled Americans were paid a decent wage before was that, relative to the 80 skilled Americans, there were not that many of them. Every economy needs some low-skilled manual labor. But now that China and America have signed their free-trade pact, there are a total of 940 low-skilled workers and 160 knowledge workers in our two-country world. Those American low-skilled workers doing fungible jobs—jobs that can easily be moved to China—will have a problem. There is no denying this. Their wages are certain to be depressed. In order to maintain or improve their living standards, they will have to move *vertically*, not horizontally. They will have to upgrade their education and upgrade their knowledge skills so that they can occupy one of the new jobs sure to be created in the much expanded United States—China market....

As Romer notes, we know from the history of our own country that an increase in knowledge workers does not necessarily lead to a decrease in their pay the way it does with low-skilled workers. From the 1960s to the 1980s, the supply of college-educated workers grew dramatically, and yet their wages grew even faster. Because as the pie grew in size and complexity, so too did people's wants, and this increased the demand for people able to do complex work and specialized tasks.

Romer explains this in part by the fact that "there is a difference between idea-based goods and physical goods." If you are a knowledge worker making and selling some kind of idea-based product—consulting or financial services or music or software or marketing or design or new drugs—the bigger the market is, the more people there are out there to whom you can sell your product. And the bigger the market, the more new specialties and niches it will create. If you come up with the next Windows or Viagra, you can potentially sell one to everyone in the world. So idea-based workers do well in globalization, and fortunately America as a whole has more idea-driven workers than any country in the world.

But if you are selling manual labor—or a piece of lumber or a slab of steel—the value of what you have to sell does not necessarily increase when the market expands, and it may decrease, argues Romer. There are only so many factories that will buy your manual labor, and there are many more people selling it. What the manual laborer has to sell can be bought by only one factory or one consumer at a time, explains Romer, while what the software writer or drug inventor has to sell—idea-based products—can be sold to everyone in the global market at once.

That is why America, as a whole, will do fine in a flat world with free trade—provided it continues to churn out knowledge workers who are able to produce idea-based goods that can be sold globally and who are able to fill the knowledge jobs that will be created as we not only expand the global economy but connect all the knowledge pools in the world. There may be a limit to the number of good factory jobs in the world, *but there is no limit to the number of idea-generated jobs in the world.*

If we go from a world in which there were fifteen drug companies and fifteen software companies in America (thirty in all) and two drug companies and two software companies in China (four in all) to a world in which there are thirty drug and software companies in America and thirty drug and software companies in China, it is going to mean more innovation, more cures, more new products, more niches to specialize in, and many more people with higher incomes to buy those products.

"The pie keeps growing because things that look like wants today are needs tomorrow," argued Marc Andreessen, the Netscape cofounder, who helped to ignite a whole new industry, e-commerce, that now employs millions of specialists around the world, specialists whose jobs weren't even imagined when Bill Clinton became president. I like going to coffee shops occasionally, but now that Starbucks is here, I *need* my coffee, and that new need has spawned a whole new industry. I always wanted to be able to search for things, but once Google was created, I *must* have my search engine. So a whole new industry has been built up around search, and Google is hiring math Ph.D.'s by the bushel—before Yahoo! or Microsoft hires them. People are always assuming that everything that is going to be invented must have been invented already. *But it hasn't.*

"If you believe human wants and needs are infinite," said Andreeseen, "then there are infinite industries to be created, infinite businesses to be started, and infinite jobs to be done, and the only limiting factor is human imagination. The world is flattening and rising at the same time. And I think the evidence is overwhelmingly clear: If you look over the sweep of history, every time we had more trade, more communications, we had a big upswing in economic activity and standard of living."

America integrated a broken Europe and Japan into the global economy after World War II, with both Europe and Japan every year upgrading their manufacturing, knowledge, and service skills, often importing and sometimes stealing ideas and equipment from the United States, just as America did from Britain in the late 1770s. Yet in the sixty years since World War II, our standard of living has increased every decade, and our unemployment rate—even with all the outcry about outsourcing—stands at only a little above 5 percent, roughly half that of the most developed countries in Western Europe....

As a person who grew up during the Cold War, I'll always remember driving along down the highway and listening to the radio, when suddenly the music would stop and a grim-voiced announcer would come on the air and say, "This is a test of the emergency broadcast system," and then there would be a thirty-second high-pitched siren sound. Fortunately, we never had to live through a moment in the Cold War where the announcer came on and said, "This is not a test" That, however, is exactly what I want to say here: *This is not a test.*

The long-term opportunities and challenges that the flattening of the world puts before the United States are profound. Therefore, our ability to get by doing things the way we've been doing them—which is to say, not always tending to our secret sauce and enriching it—will not suffice anymore. "For a country as wealthy as we are, it is amazing how little we are doing to enhance our natural competitiveness," said Dinakar Singh, the Indian-American hedge fund manager. "We are in a world that has a system that now allows convergence among many billions of people, and we had better step back and figure out what it means. It would be a nice coincidence if all the things that were true before are still true now—but there are quite a few things you actually need to do differently... You need to have a much more thoughtful national discussion." The flat world, Singh argued, is now the elephant in the room, and the question is, What is it going to do to us, and what are we going to do to it?

If this moment has any parallel in American history, it is the height of the Cold War, around 1957, when the Soviet Union leaped ahead of America in the space race by putting up the Sputnik satellite. Yes, there are many differences between that age and our own. The main challenge then came from those who wanted to put up walls; the main challenge to America today comes from the fact that all the walls are being taken down, and other countries can now compete with us much more directly. The main challenge in that world was from those practicing extreme communism, namely, Russia, China, and North Korea. The main challenge to America today is from those practicing extreme capitalism, namely, China, India, and South Korea. The main objective in that era was building a strong state; the main objective in this era is building strong individuals.

What this era has in common with the Cold War era, though, is that to meet the challenges of flatism requires as comprehensive, energetic, and focused a response as did meeting the challenge of communism. It requires our own version of the New Frontier and Great Society adapted to the age of flatness. It requires a president who can summon the nation to get smarter and study harder in science, math, and engineering in order to reach the new frontiers of knowledge that the flat world is rapidly opening up and pushing out. And it requires a Great Society that commits our government to building the infrastructure, safely nets, and institutions that will help every American become more employable in an age when no one can be guaranteed lifetime employment. I call my own version of this approach *compassionate flatism*.

Getting Americans to rally around compassionate flatism is much more difficult than getting them to rally around anticommunism. "National peril is a lot easier to convey than individual peril," noted Johns Hopkins University foreign policy expert Michael Mandelbaum. Economics, as noted, is not like war, because economics can always be a win–win game. But sometimes I wish economics were more like war. In the Cold War, we actually got to see the Soviets parade their missiles in Red Square. We all got to be scared together, from one end of the country to the other, and all our politicians had to be focused and serious about marshaling the resources and educational programs to make sure Americans could keep pace with the Soviet Union.

But today, alas, there is no missile threat coming from India, The "hot line," which used to connect the Kremlin with the White House, has been replaced by the "help line," which connects everyone in America to call centers in Bangalore. While the other end of the hotline might have had Leonid Brezhnev threatening nuclear war, the other end of the help line just has a soft voice eager to help you sort out your AOL bill or collaborate with you on a new piece of software. No, that voice has none of the menace of Nikita Khrushchev pounding a shoe on the table at the UN, and it has none of the sinister snarl of the bad guys in *From Russia with Love*. There is no Boris or Natasha saying "We will bury you" in a thick Russian accent. No, that voice on the help line just has a friendly Indian lilt that masks any sense of threat or challenge. It simply says: "Hello, my name is Rajiv. Can I help you?"

No, Rajiv, actually, you can't.

When it comes to responding to the challenges of the flat world, there is no help line we can call. We have to dig into ourselves. We in America have all the tools to do that…. But…. we have not been tending to those tools as we should. Hence, our quiet crisis. The assumption that because America's economy has dominated the world for more than a century, it will and must always be that way is as dangerous an illusion today as the illusion that America would always dominate in science and technology was back in 1950. But this is not going to be easy. Getting our society up to speed for a flat world is going to be extremely painstaking. We are going to have to start doing a lot of things differently. It is going to take the sort of focus and national will that President John F. Kennedy called for in his famous May 25, 1961, speech to Congress on "urgent national needs." At that time, America was recovering from the twin shocks of Sputnik and the Soviet space launch of a cosmonaut, Yuri Gagarin, less than two months before Kennedy's speech. Kennedy knew that while America had enormous human and institutional assets—far more than the Soviet Union—they were not being fully utilized.

"I believe we possess all the resources and talents necessary," said President Kennedy. "But the facts of the matter are that we have never made the national decisions or marshaled the national resources required for such leadership. We have never specified long-range goals on an urgent time schedule, or managed our resources and our time so as to ensure their fulfillment." After then laying out his whole program for putting a man on the moon within ten years, President Kennedy added, "Let it be clear that I am asking the Congress and the country to accept a firm commitment to a new course of action, a course which will last for many years and carry very heavy costs… This decision demands a major national commitment of scientific and technical manpower, materiel and facilities, and the possibility of their diversion from other important activities where they are already thinly spread. It means a degree of dedication, organization and discipline which have not always characterized our research and development efforts."

In that speech, Kennedy made a vow that has amazing resonance today: "I am therefore transmitting to the Congress a new Manpower Development and Training program, to train or retrain several hundred thousand workers, particularly in those areas where we have seen chronic unemployment as a result of technological factors, in new occupational skills over a four-year period—in order to replace those skills made obsolete by automation and industrial change with the new skills which the new processes demand."

Amen. We too have to do things differently. We are going to have to sort out what to keep, what to discard, what to adapt, what to adopt, where to re-double our efforts, and where to intensify our focus. That is what this chapter is about. This is just an intuition, but the flattening of the world is going to be hugely disruptive to both traditional and developed societies. The weak will fall farther behind faster. The traditional will feel the force of modernization much more profoundly. The new will get turned into old quicker. The developed will be challenged by the underdeveloped much more profoundly. I worry, because so much political stability is built on economic stability, and economic stability is not going to be a feature of the flat world. Add it all up and you can see that the disruptions are going to come faster and faster. Think about Microsoft trying to figure out how to deal with a global army of people writing software for free! We are entering an era of creative destruction on steroids. Even if your country has a comprehensive strategy for dealing with flatism, it is going to be a challenge of a whole new dimension. But if you don't have a strategy at all...well, you've been warned.

This is not a test.

FURTHER READING

Alison Brysk, *Globalization and Human Rights* (2002).

Beth Fischer, *The Reagan Reversal: Foreign Policy and the End of the Cold War* (1997).

Raymond Garthoff, *The Great Transition: American-Soviet Relations and the End of the Cold War* (1994).

Samuel P. Huntington, *The Clash of Civilizations and the Remaking of World Order* (1996).

Burton Kaufman, *The United States and the Arab Middle East* (1995).

John Lanchester, *I.O.U.: Why Everyone Owes Everyone and No One Can Pay* (2010).

Joanne Meyerowitz, *History and September 11* (2003).

Joseph S. Nye, *The Powers to Lead* (2008).

Kevin Phillips, *American Dynasty: Aristocracy, Fortune, and the Politics of Deceit in the House of Bush* (2004).

Ronald Powaski, *Return to Armageddon: The United States and the Nuclear Arms Race, 1981–1999* (2003).

Samantha Power, *A Problem From Hell: America and the Age of Genocide* (2002).

Garry Wills, *Bomb Power: The Modern Presidency and the National Security State* (2010).

Bob Woodward, *Bush at War* (2002).